CONTROVERSIES IN
VOTING BEHAVIOR

CONTROVERSIES IN VOTING BEHAVIOR

Fourth Edition

Edited by

RICHARD G. NIEMI
University of Rochester

HERBERT F. WEISBERG
The Ohio State University

A Division of Congressional Quarterly Inc.
Washington, D.C.

CQ Press
A Division of Congressional Quarterly Inc.
1414 22nd St. N.W.
Washington, DC 20037
(202) 822–1475; (800) 638–1710

www.cqpress.com

∞ The paper used in this publication meets the minimum requirements of the American National Standard for Information Sciences–Permanence of Paper for Printed Library Materials, ANSI Z39.48-1992.

Printed in the United States of America

05 04 03 02 01   5 4 3 2 1

Library of Congress Cataloging-in-Publication Data

Controversies in voting behavior / edited by Richard G. Niemi, Herbert F. Weisberg— 4th ed.
    p.   cm.
  Includes bibliographical references and index.
  ISBN 1-56802-334-0 (paper)
    1. Elections. 2. Voting. I. Niemi, Richard G. II. Weisberg, Herbert F.

JF1001.C575 2001
324.9—dc21   00-67454

Contents

Preface   vii

Introduction

1. The Study of Voting and Elections   1

Part I Political Participation

2. Why Is Voter Turnout Low (And Why Is It Declining)?   22

3. Tuning in, Tuning out: The Strange Disappearance of
   Social Capital in America   38
   Robert D. Putnam

4. Solving the Puzzle of Participation in Electoral Politics   69
   Steven J. Rosenstone and John Mark Hansen

5. Electoral Participation   83
   Mark N. Franklin

Part II Political Information

6. Does Lack of Political Information Matter?   100

7. Information Effects in Collective Preferences   114
   Scott L. Althaus

8. Voting Correctly   139
   Richard R. Lau and David P. Redlawsk

9. Rational Public Opinion   164
   Benjamin I. Page and Robert Y. Shapiro

Part III Vote Determinants

10. What Determines the Vote?   180

11. National Economic Voting in U.S. Presidential Elections   200
    Richard Nadeau and Michael S. Lewis-Beck

12. Multiple-Stage Explanation of Political Preferences   221
    Warren E. Miller and J. Merrill Shanks

13. The Responsive Voter: Campaign Information and the
    Dynamics of Candidate Evaluation   240
    Milton Lodge and Marco R. Steenbergen, with Shawn Brau

Part IV Divided Government

14. Do Voters Prefer Divided Government?   271

15. Balancing Explanations of Divided Government   291
    Morris Fiorina

16. A New Approach to the Study of Ticket Splitting   301
    Barry C. Burden and David C. Kimball

Part V Party Identification

17. How Much Does Politics Affect Party Identification?   322

18. Generational Changes and Party Identification   338
    Warren E. Miller

19. Partisan Stability: Evidence from Aggregate Data   356
    Donald P. Green, Bradley L. Palmquist, and Eric Schickler

20. Macropartisanship: The Permanent Memory of
    Partisan Evaluation   364
    Robert S. Erikson, Michael B. MacKuen, and James A. Stimson

Part VI Party System Change

21. Is the Party System Changing?   371

22. Party Coalitions in Transition: Partisanship and Group Support,
    1952–1996   387
    Harold W. Stanley and Richard G. Niemi

23. The Sixth American Party System: Electoral Change,
    1952–1992   405
    John H. Aldrich and Richard G. Niemi

References   427
Name Index   477
Subject Index   487

Preface

In this new edition of *Controversies in Voting Behavior*, we have again selected what we regard as the best research in contemporary voting behavior. Like its subject matter, the study of voting remains lively, full of controversy, and yet often enlightening. These new readings nicely capture all these elements, collectively describing the current state of the field as well as suggesting the new directions in which research is headed.

In response to new elections, as well as to ever changing theoretical and methodological developments, scholarly articles on voting behavior retain their freshness for perhaps a half-dozen years. By then, a few have achieved classic status; others have faded into the background. With this in mind, we have focused this new edition on very recent work, although a few articles from the early 1990s are included. As in the previous editions, we have written introductions in which we provide the background and context that will allow students to understand as fully as possible the research described in the readings.

When we prepared the original reader on controversies in voting behavior in the mid-1970s, we saw a need to pull together the debates in the field so that people would see the disputes more clearly and solve them. The field looked so neat and tidy in the mid-1960s, when scholars at the University of Michigan published their main research, but by the mid-1970s the most scientific field in the study of political behavior was coming apart under the weight of disagreements in the literature. We assumed the differences would soon be resolved, as research would move to a new plateau. We now realize that controversies never go away in an academic field; progress occurs fitfully, by resolving some aspects of a controversy while new aspects arise. Thus, as will be explained more in Chapter 1, the controversies reviewed in this book are based on those considered in the previous three editions, but they often take new directions as the field evolves. Still, we are surprised that a book about fundamental ways of viewing the electorate is now in a fourth edition; we take this as testimony to the enduring ability of researchers to view the world in multiple and conflicting ways and of our determination to make sense of it all (at least for the moment).

We continue our past practice of reprinting unabridged readings, whenever possible, so that students can see the full arguments along with all the details of the methods employed. In the case of material from books, this means including whole chapters. In three instances, however, essential readings were spread across multiple book chapters, making it necessary either to exclude them altogether or to reprint selected pages, as we have done. In the selection from Page and Shapiro (Chapter 9), the information comes from two chapters, one explaining the theoretical outlook and another describing some of the major findings. Although the book contains other important material, our selection presents the essence of Page and Shapiro's argument and gives evidence about the nature of aggregate, as opposed to individual-level, public opinion. Miller and Shanks's book presented us with a much bigger challenge. Their methodology is explained in one chapter, with important parts of the analysis spread over several more. We believe that our selection (Chapter 12) gives as quick an overview as possible, although the original work contains additional important findings. Chapter 15 includes part of a chapter from the first edition of Fiorina's book as well as his update to that section in the second edition.

We would like to thank the many people who helped us put this edition together. We are especially grateful to two groups of authors—Bob Erikson, Mike MacKuen, and Jim Stimson and Don Green, Brad Palmquist, and Eric Schickler—for writing brief, original summaries of their now very extensive and methodologically complicated work on party identification. The specialist will want to work through the original material; for others, these summaries provide an excellent overview of the arguments involved and the evidence supporting each side.

We would like to thank the many people who helped us put this edition together. At CQ we are especially grateful to Brenda Carter for her continuing support of this project. Gwenda Larsen was very helpful throughout the editorial process. Kerry Kern handled the difficult job of copy editing with skill and fortitude. Jim Campbell provided us with astute comments on all our introductory essays. And we are grateful to Alan Abramowitz, Rory Austin, Brad Lockerbie, Steve Mockabee, and Zoe Oxley for useful reactions to individual chapters. We would also like to thank Kelly Corbett for her frequent assistance in preparing the manuscript and Allyson Marino and Jennifer McLernon for their considerable help on the index. For help in entering and endlessly editing references, we thank Kelly Corbett and Mildred Li.

R.G.N.
H.F.W.

CONTROVERSIES IN VOTING BEHAVIOR

INTRODUCTION

1. The Study of Voting and Elections

Aside from the lengthy drama involved in counting the votes, the 2000 election in the United States was not especially exciting. Indeed, the public was bored by politics generally and the presidential candidates in particular. Although some looked forward to the election as a solution for their problems, and others were captivated by the changes it would bring in public policy, most realized all too soon that it was likely to change little.

At some point the public wonders, why all this excitement about elections? One answer has been vividly provided by the movement toward democracy in the 1980s and 1990s in Eastern Europe, Latin America, and Asia. The peoples of those countries have frequently embraced democracy, even if they felt some letdown when they realized that a change in regime was not a cure-all for economic woes. Still, they recognized the essential truth of Winston Churchill's comment that "democracy is the worst form of government except all those other forms that have been tried from time to time." Democracy and free elections might not solve all problems, but their absence can be even more serious a problem. This leads us to contemplate what the functions of elections are in a democracy.

According to one textbook image, elections serve several functions. They allow citizens to choose the government, and they also restrain political leaders who behave in a way that maximizes their chances of reelection. Elections are thus one means of linking public attitudes with governmental policy. In addition, electing a government is a way of legitimizing its authority. Elections provide a peaceful means for political change, while permitting individuals and groups to resolve their conflicting needs peacefully. Along with this view of elections is a corresponding view of voters as choosing intelligently among the candidates. Although no one would argue that all voters are well informed, the view from this perspective is that voters as a whole make careful and informed choices.

An opposite view holds that elections are just symbolic in character. According to this position, elections are a secular ritual of democracy, and voting makes citizens consider themselves participants in the nation's governance. Voters feel they have fulfilled their civic duty by voting, even if the chance that a single vote affects the election outcome is nearly nil and even if the election outcome is not really going to alter the future of public policy. Correspondingly, according to this view voters do not necessarily make intelligent, informed decisions. Few know

1

anything about the candidates, and what they do know is often irrelevant to governance. Consequently, election results are uninterpretable. This view of elections emphasizes that voting does more to make citizens feel good than to alter political outcomes.

Those who view elections as symbolic usually emphasize the limited effectiveness of elections as effective instruments of popular control. One reason is that institutional structures are sometimes created to limit majority rule, often with the purpose of protecting minority rights. For example, bicameral legislatures slow down the passage of bills, and the filibuster in the U.S. Senate can frustrate majority rule. Second, centrist establishment political parties do not offer voters a full range of choices. Additionally, policy making in some areas is "depoliticized," as when the Federal Reserve Board makes decisions on monetary policy, government bureaucrats make de facto policy in many areas, and the judiciary's rulings control policy on such issues as abortion and civil rights. As a result, elections do not necessarily affect the course of government policies.

The controversy as to the role of voting and elections turns to a considerable extent on the actual effects of elections. Do elections matter? In the United States, do Democratic and Republican administrations pursue different polices? In other nations, is public policy different under left-wing and right-wing governments? To some extent, these are subjective questions. A Libertarian would perceive little difference between Democratic and Republican polices in the United States. A Marxist in Europe might regard polices of left-wing and right-wing governments with equal disdain.

Fortunately, whether elections matter is also partly an empirical question. Government policy outputs under Democratic and Republican administrations can be compared, as can those under left-wing and right-wing governments. There is, in fact, an increasing body of such studies, and they nearly always find policy differences between governments. A variety of research, for example, shows a relationship between party leadership of government and spending on social welfare (see Hicks and Swank 1992, and the references cited therein). Increasingly, researchers are trying to relate policy decisions directly to public opinion, usually finding a close connection between the two (Bartels 1991; Stimson 1991; Glynn, Herbst, O'Keefe, and Shapiro 1999).

It does not always require scholarly studies to reveal the consequences of elections. In 1964 Barry Goldwater ran for president of the United States as a conservative candidate offering "a choice and not an echo," and when he lost in a landslide President Lyndon B. Johnson instituted liberal Great Society programs, such as the War on Poverty. In 1980 Ronald Reagan ran on virtually an antigovernment platform, and he turned his large victory margin over President Jimmy Carter into a mandate for conservative action by restraining the growth of the government's domestic programs and lowering taxes. George Bush's 1988 election over Michael Dukakis was just as clearly a choice in favor of continued restraint on social welfare programs, while Bill Clinton's 1992 victory over Bush was a choice in favor of changed economic management. Margaret Thatcher's

1979 victory over James Callaghan in Britain led to the denationalization of some industries that previous Labour governments had nationalized, and the reelection of Conservative governments in 1983, 1987, and 1992 reinforced that decision, whereas Tony Blair's election in 1997 resulted in careful movements toward increased cooperation with the European Union. These are policy consequences of elections that voters will notice. The election of black mayors in a number of U.S. cities in the 1980s—though not a policy shift as such—suggests another important kind of change; the extensive voting along racial lines in many of those mayoral elections is prima facie evidence of voter awareness of at least this difference in candidates, and it shows as well a presumption that who gets elected makes a difference.

Mart A more difficult question is whether even these consequences make a difference in the long run. Does it really matter if there is a war on poverty, restrained growth of federal programs, or denationalization of industry? Problems seem to remain in any case. From the early 1980s through the early 1990s the United States seemed to be on an economic roller coaster, going from severe inflation to harsh unemployment and then back again to inflation. In the later 1990s and into the new century there was unprecedented economic well-being, along with budget surpluses, leading to discussion of a "New Economy" fueled by technological advances in the information age. Yet there remained concern over whether the New Economy was truly inflation-proof or unemployment-proof and whether it served primarily those who were better off to begin with. Moreover, there was continued skepticism about government in general and about many government-run programs. The result was that voters did not line up enthusiastically behind a continuation of Democratic rule in the 2000 election despite the economic prosperity.

Significantly, the electorate has had a reaction if not an answer to these possibly unanswerable questions. There seems to be a trend toward voting on the basis of perceived candidate competence or other candidate traits. Carter's defeat in 1980 was less a mandate for Reagan's conservative polices than a rejection of Carter's inability to handle inflation, the American hostage situation in Teheran, and other such problems (Miller and Wattenberg 1981). Thatcher's reelection in 1983 reflected public satisfaction with her successful victory against Argentina in the Falkland Islands war as well as simultaneous dismay over Labour's extreme and sometimes incoherent disarmament policy. Despite the success of the U.S.-led coalition forces in the Persian Gulf War, President Bush was in trouble with the U.S. electorate in 1992 because he was not perceived as able to translate his foreign policy successes into domestic economic solutions. Many Americans became interested in a possible independent candidacy by Ross Perot in 1992, partly because of his demonstrated successes in the business realm. Clinton's reelection in 1996 signaled a desire to stay with successful economic solutions. On the state level, the election of Jesse Ventura as governor of Minnesota was a vote in favor of a new personality who was decidedly not a traditional politician. In the end, it may be that there are no solutions that work, but the public knows enough to reject leaders who cannot deliver and keep those who achieve some success. The public does not always reward politicians if times are good, but it punishes them if times are not good enough, which keeps politicians on their toes, even if they are not always responsible for prevailing conditions.

Whether in terms of policy consequences or leadership choices, elections retain their importance in democracies. They make a difference, at least in the short run. And voters to some degree make choices on the basis of this difference. At the same time, it must be admitted that we do not yet fully understand voting and elections. Our understanding of these topics has changed a great deal in the past few decades, paralleling changes in our ways of studying them. Yet to our frequent dismay, many of the major questions in the field are not yet settled, despite the considerable attention that has been paid to them. Nevertheless, we are getting closer to answering some of these questions.

How to Study Voting

Methodology

Modern voting studies rely heavily on survey research. There are certainly other ways of studying elections, but the most direct and often the most valid way of understanding why people vote as they do is to ask them. Of course, not all surveys provide reliable results. Indeed, one might wonder why one should accept any results based on surveys of perhaps 1,500 voters out of an electorate of millions. A complete explanation would require a lengthy statistical explanation (see, for example, Weisberg, Krosnick, and Bowen 1996), but some brief points can be made, especially to underscore the point that reliable polls are not conducted haphazardly but according to scientific principles. Most important in conducting a survey is the way in which the sample is selected. Surveys that interview a few "typical" voters or that interview people at a single street corner should not be taken seriously, for there is no reason to believe that the people interviewed are typical of the electorate. By contrast, the best scientific sampling procedures give everyone in the population an equal (or at least a known) probability of being part of the sample. Probability theory can then be used to estimate how close results for the sample are to those for the population of interest. For example, using conventional sampling techniques, a sample of about 1,500 people will give results that are generally (95 percent of the time) within 3 percent of the true result. Thus a survey finding that 65 percent of the electorate supports a particular party can be interpreted as meaning that its level of support in the population as a whole is (almost certainly) between 62 and 68 percent.

There is inevitable error, of course, in attempting to describe a population with just a sample, but such error is generally tolerable. For example, it does not matter for predicting election outcomes if a party's support really is 62 percent or 68 percent. Moreover, the 3 percent error margin could be reduced, though that would generally not be cost effective, since cutting the error to, say, 1.5 percent would require the expense of about 4,500 interviews. Only when trying to predict a very close election might greater accuracy be necessary, but no reasonable size sample could predict an election as close as the 2000 Bush-Gore nationwide contest (which last-minute polls recognized was "too close to call"). Note, by the way, that the size of the sample is what matters for most purposes, not the size of the population. Thus one would want about 1,500 interviews for a national sample or for a sample of the California electorate.

Aside from these sampling issues, the validity of a survey depends on the wording of the questions that are asked, and for this task mathematical principles are of less help. Different question wordings obtain different results, often only marginally different but occasionally very much so. At best, researchers "pretest" a question wording to make sure it is valid before using it in an actual survey. Sometimes, though, researchers gradually realize that a standard wording that has been used for years is not ideal and then change that wording, which can lead to problems in over-time comparisons. In any case, there is no perfect wording for survey questions, so dependence on wording is always important to acknowledge.

While we emphasize the importance of surveys, experiments are increasingly being used in voting studies. Researchers as different in their orientations as political psychologists and formal theorists now use experiments to test their theories of voter decision making. These studies often use small numbers of participants and often rely on student participants. As examples, political psychologists have shown participants campaign brochures and ads and have used their recollection of topics in those materials as tests between different theories of the process of candidate evaluation (Lodge, McGraw, and Stroh 1989) and to determine the effects of campaign material in general (Lodge, Steenbergen, and Brau 1995) and negative TV ads in particular (Ansolabehere, Iyengar, Simon, and Valentino 1994). Formal theorists have used experiments to test whether participants who are given particular utility functions end up in predicted equilibrium solutions (McKelvey and Ordeshook 1985), as well as how people deal with limited party and candidate information (Lupia and McCubbins 1998).

Surveys and experiments each have advantages and disadvantages. Surveys excel in their representativeness, which allows ready generalization from samples to the mass public. They are also the most direct way to get at people's motivations, although many political psychologists give more credence to statistical analyses of motivations than to respondents' self-reports of their reasons for voting for one candidate rather than another (Nisbett and Wilson 1977; Rahn, Krosnick, and Bruening 1994; Kessel and Weisberg 1999). They can provide information about almost any topic, including some—such as how people voted—that are impossible to know on an individual level without asking people. At the same time, many individuals think about politics only casually, causing problems of response instability, sensitivity to question wording, and various kinds of "response effects" (Zaller 1992, chap. 2). Surveys can also mismeasure political reality, as when the National Election Studies (NES) postelection surveys find exaggerated turnout rates (Silver, Anderson, and Abramson 1986) and overstated votes for winning candidates (Wright 1993). Surveys may misrepresent attitudes on sensitive issues because individuals choose "don't know" rather than revealing a politically incorrect response (Berinsky 1999).[1] Finally, it is also difficult to assess causation in surveys, since all variables are measured simultaneously.

Experiments are better able to establish causation, as the researcher manipulates the experimental variable and controls (or randomizes) for the effects of extraneous variables. However, experiments are often based on limited groups of participants who are not representative of the entire population, especially experiments using student participants. The choice of participants may not matter for some topics, but using college students limits results to people who are used to dealing with abstract concepts. Because of this, it is also becoming common to perform experiments as part of telephone or Internet surveys, for example by giving different "lead-ins" to issue questions to random halves of a sample so as to assess the effect of issue "framing" on responses (Nelson and Kinder 1996; Nelson, Oxley, and Clawson 1997). All in all, experiments are a useful addition to the toolbox of voting researchers, as should be clear when reading the Lodge, Steenbergen, and Brau contribution (Chapter 13), although we expect political surveys to remain the dominant mode of studying elections because they are able to employ representative samples in a real world setting.

In addition to surveys and experiments, voting studies make use of several other types of data. Aggregate election data have been analyzed from the earliest voting studies. Logical difficulties in making statements about individual-level behavior on the basis of aggregate data have limited the usefulness of this approach — although Burden and Kimball in Chapter 16 demonstrate the usefulness of new statistical procedures for dealing with the "ecological fallacy." Shaw (1999a, 348) also notes some advantages to the use of aggregate data to study campaign effects. State legislative research has also relied heavily on aggregate data because of the sheer number of races involved and the variability of institutional settings, which is absent in congressional elections.[2] Even in congressional studies, however, aggregate data are used frequently — as, for example, when developing measures of candidate quality on the basis of candidates' past elective offices or when studying the effects of campaign spending. Aggregate economic data are often used as well; when combined with aggregate election data or data on presidential or prime ministerial approval, they provide useful insight into the influence of economic conditions on voting and leadership evaluation. Those studies often are historical, covering lengthy time periods, sometimes including the period before surveys were widely taken.

Yet another important type of data is written and electronic material, including party platforms, campaign information, newspaper articles on campaigns, and television ads. Methods of content analysis help digest these large volumes of material. For example, Dalton, Beck, and Huckfeldt (1998) use a content analysis to summarize material in major daily newspapers read by people in a nationally representative set of forty U.S. counties (and a sample of people living in those counties). Mondak (1995) developed measures of incumbent integrity and competence by using descriptions of House members from Barone and Ujifusa's *Almanac of American Politics*. Geer (1998, and Finkel and Geer 1998) has content analyzed ads, and Freedman and Goldstein (1999) use what may now be a standard source of data on when ads are shown. The study of campaign effects often utilizes events data (Holbrook 1996; Shaw 1999b). The availability of newspaper archives on the Internet through LEXIS/NEXIS is particularly important in facilitating the use of these materials in studying elections (Nadeau, Niemi, Fan, and Amato 1999). We expect this increased use of aggregate data and written and electronic documents to continue, even while political surveys remain the dominant mode of studying elections.

The Data Base

The articles in this book are generally based on special surveys rather than on commercial polls, such as the Gallup Poll. Why is this the case? The main reason involves what each is studying. The Gallup organization must forecast election results for their newspaper customers. Newspapers want to publish interesting stories, and predictions of election outcomes are certainly that. Gallup does very well in this prediction game. However, political scientists are typically studying the last election rather than the next. This is because they do not want to predict *who* will win a particular election so much as to understand *why* someone won. Explaining election outcomes requires asking people many more questions than the commercial pollsters do. Voters cannot just be asked for whom they will vote. They must be asked their feelings about each candidate, each party, each issue, how they obtained information on the election, how they voted in the past, and so on. This requires separate polls.

Some academic political polls were reported in the 1920s, but the first important voting surveys were not conducted until the 1940s (see Table 1-1). Continuous national political surveys began with the formation of the University of Michigan's well-known Institute for Social Research. The Survey Research Center (and more recently the Center for Political Studies) section of the institute has continued surveying up to the present day. The Michigan surveys are now administered by the NES under a continuing grant from the National Science Foundation, with researchers from universities across the country able to participate in preparing questions for the surveys and in analyzing the results. Special surveys have sometimes been conducted to study particular topics, but the Michigan surveys—with their hundreds of questions about the parties, the candidates, and the issues—have become the standard data base for the study of U.S. elections. Many of the studies reported in this book are based on NES surveys.

The usual pattern for the NES surveys in presidential election years has been to interview the same people before and after the election. A desire to focus on electoral change, however, has led to some other study designs. An important

Table 1-1   Major Columbia and Michigan NES Surveys and Major Reports
              on Them

Year	Study	Report
1940	Columbia University, Bureau of Applied Social Research, sample of Erie County, Ohio	P. Lazarsfeld, B. Berelson, and H. Gaudet, *The People's Choice* (New York: Duell, Sloan & Pearce, 1944).
1944	National Opinion Research Center	
1948	Columbia University, Bureau of Applied Social Research, sample of Elmira, N.Y.	B. Berelson, P. Lazarsfeld, and W. McPhee, *Voting* (Chicago: University of Chicago Press, 1954).
1948	University of Michigan SRC	A. Campbell and R. Kahn, *The People Elect a President* (Ann Arbor: SRC, University of Michigan, 1952).
1950	Columbia University, Bureau of Applied Social Research, four state samples	W. McPhee and W. Glaser, *Public Opinion and the Congressional Elections* (New York: Free Press, 1962).
1952	University of Michigan SRC	A. Campbell, G. Gurin, and W. Miller, *The Voter Decides* (New York: Row, Peterson, 1954); *see also* 1956 listing.
1954	University of Michigan SRC, preelection only	A. Campbell and H. Cooper, *Group Differences in Attitudes and Votes* (Ann Arbor: SRC, University of Michigan, 1956).
1956	University of Michigan SRC	A. Campbell, P. Converse, W. Miller, and D. Stokes, *The American Voter* (New York: Wiley, 1960).
1958	University of Michigan SRC, representation study	D. Stokes and W. Miller, "Party Government and the Saliency of Congress," *POQ* (Winter 1962); W. Miller and D. Stokes, "Constituency Influence in Congress," *APSR* (March 1963); A. Campbell, "Surge and Decline," *POQ* (Fall 1960).
1960	University of Michigan SRC	P. Converse, A. Campbell, W. Miller, and D. Stokes, "Stability and Change in 1960: A Reinstating Election," *APSR* (June 1961). *See also* A. Campbell, P. Converse, W. Miller, and D. Stokes, *Elections and the Political Order* (New York: Wiley, 1966).
1956– 1958– 1960	University of Michigan SRC, panel study	P. Converse, "The Nature of Belief Systems in Mass Publics," in *Ideology and Discontent,* ed. D. Apter (New York: Free Press, 1964).
1962	University of Michigan SRC	

Table 1-1 *continued*

Year	Study	Report
1964	University of Michigan SRC	P. Converse, A. Clausen, and W. Miller, "Electoral Myth and Reality: The 1964 Election," *APSR* (June 1965).
1966	University of Michigan SRC	
1968	University of Michigan SRC	P. Converse, W. Miller. J. Rusk, and A. Wolfe, "Continuity and Change in American Politics: Parties and Issues in the 1968 Election," *APSR* (December 1969).
1970	University of Michigan CPS	
1972	University of Michigan CPS	A. Miller, W. Miller, A. Raine, and T. Brown, "A Majority Party in Disarray," *APSR* (September 1976).
1974	University of Michigan CPS	
1976	University of Michigan CPS	A. Miller, "Partisanship Reinstated," *BJPS* (April 1978).
1972– 1974– 1976	University of Michigan CPS, panel study	P. Converse and G. Markus, "Plus ça Change: The New CPS Election Study Panel," *APSR* (March 1979).
1978	University of Michigan NES	L. Maisel and J. Cooper, eds., *Congressional Elections* (Beverly Hills, Calif.: Sage, 1981).
1980	University of Michigan NES, panel study	W. Miller and J. M. Shanks, "Policy Directions and Presidential Leadership," *BJPS* (July 1982); G. Markus, "Political Attitudes During an Election Year: A Report on the 1980 Panel Study," *APSR* (September 1982).
1982	University of Michigan NES	
1984	University of Michigan NES, continuous monitoring	L. Bartels, *Presidential Primaries* (Princeton: Princeton University Press, 1988).
1984	University of Michigan NES	J. M. Shanks and W. Miller, "Policy Direction and Performance Evaluation," *BJPS* (April 1990).
1986	University of Michigan NES	
1988	University of Michigan NES	J. M. Shanks and W. Miller, "Partisanship, Policy and Performance," *BJPS* (April 1991).
1988	University of Michigan NES, sixteen states with "Super Tuesday" primaries	P. Abramson, J. Aldrich, P. Paolino, and D. Rohde, " 'Sophisticated' Voting in the 1988 Presidential Primaries," *APSR* (March 1992).

table continues

Table 1-1 *continued*

Year	Study	Report
1988– 1990– 1992	University of Michigan NES, pooled Senate study	*Legislative Studies Quarterly* (November 1990).
1990	University of Michigan NES	
1992	University of Michigan NES	W. Miller and J. M. Shanks, *The New American Voter* (Cambridge: Harvard, 1996); H. Weisberg, *Democracy's Feast* (Chatham, N.J.: Chatham House, 1995).
1990– 1991– 1992	University of Michigan NES, panel study	
1994	University of Michigan NES	
1996	University of Michigan NES	P. Abramson, J. Aldrich, and D. Rohde, *Change and Continuity in the 1996 Elections* (Washington, D.C.: CQ Press, 1999); H. Weisberg and J. Box-Steffensmeier, *Reelection 1996* (Chatham, N.J.: Chatham House, 1999).
1998	University of Michigan NES	
2000	University of Michigan NES	

Note: All the above studies involve postelection interviews, except for the 1954 preelection study. The presidential-year studies (except for 1944 and 1948) also involve one or more preelection interviews. All are national samples unless otherwise stated. *APSR* = *American Political Science Review, BJPS* = *British Journal of Political Science,* CPS = Center for Political Studies, NES = National Election Studies, *POQ* = *Public Opinion Quarterly,* SRC = Survey Research Center.

variation is repeated pre-election interviews with the same person to analyze changes in vote intentions, as was done in the 1940 and 1948 Columbia studies and the 1980 NES study. Another important variant is interviewing the same people across election years so that voting change between elections can be examined, as was done in the 1956–1958–1960, 1972–1974–1976, and 1990–1991–1992 Michigan "panel" studies. A final variation for presidential elections is weekly interviewing of different people throughout the election year, as was done in the 1984 NES "rolling thunder" (continuous monitoring) study. The above studies all focus on the presidential election itself, although in 1988 NES conducted a major study of presidential primary voting on "Super Tuesday."

A simpler study design has been used for NES studies in congressional election years, with interviews conducted only after the election has taken place. The first Michigan study of a congressional election was a major study in 1958, which included interviews with the congressional candidates in those districts where voters had been interviewed. There were minor Michigan studies of the 1962, 1966, 1970, and 1974 congressional elections. By 1978 congressional scholars were doubting many of the findings from the 1958 study and were developing new theories of congressional voting. The 1978 survey became a major study of congressional voting and resulted in a vast explosion of work on the topic. Similarly, a specially designed study in 1988–1992 focused attention on elections to the U.S. Senate.[3] Data from all the NES surveys are also freely downloadable from their website (http://www.umich.edu/~nes/).

The most significant trend, started in the 1980s, is an expansion of the number and variety of large-scale data sets and therefore in the subject matter covered. There are several explanations for these developments. For one, the shift from door-to-door interviews to telephone interviews has made it easier to conduct national surveys from a single site, without the difficulty of training separate teams of interviewers in multiple communities. As a result, the national news media, political parties, and academic political scientists are able to conduct more frequent national surveys. Another reason for the growth of available studies is greater cooperation between academic and commercial organizations; studies that once might have sat unused in the electronic equivalent of file drawers are now easily available to researchers through the Inter-university Consortium for Political and Social Research and other data archives.

Additionally, as indicated in Table 1-2, there are important political surveys conducted outside the NES aegis. For example, a National Black Election Study was conducted in 1984, 1988, and 1996, and a Latino National Political Survey was taken in 1989–1990. The National Opinion Research Center's General Social Survey (GSS) often contains questions on political issues. The Voter News Service (and previously various other news organizations) conducts "exit polls" after presidential primaries and presidential and off-year general elections. These polls focus most on how people just voted, but they include a few additional questions that are increasingly used in academic studies. Wright, Erikson, and McIver (1985), for example, used the CBS News/*New York Times* exit polls to establish rankings of the states in terms of their Republican-Democrat balance and their liberal-conservative balance, and Norrander (1989a) used these data to rank the states according to their proportions of political independents.

The monthly polling by some of these organizations (especially Gallup) has led to extensive time series on political indicators; these time series have shown that some political attitudes are more variable than was previously thought to be the case (see Chapter 17 for a discussion of such change in party identification). The political parties have also sponsored some polls of these types, although, unfortunately, their data are generally less accessible to academics. Some political scientists have also been able to secure funding for separate election surveys to study particular topics, as in a national survey by scholars at the University of Minnesota to test a political psychology model of the vote (Rahn, Aldrich, Borgida, and Sullivan 1990) and in a study by scholars at Ohio State University of split-ticket voting in Ohio (Beck, Baum, Clausen, and Smith 1992).

Table 1-2   Other Major Election Surveys and Major Reports on Them

Year	Study	Report
1961	University of North Carolina, sample of South	D. Matthews and J. Prothro, *Negroes and the New Southern Politics* (New York: Harcourt, 1966).
1967	NORC, University of Chicago, national sample	S. Verba and N. Nie, *Participation in America* (New York: Harper & Row, 1972).
1968	Opinion Research Corp., national sample	B. Page and R. Brody, "Policy Voting and the Electoral Process," *APSR* (September 1972).
1968	University of North Carolina, thirteen state samples	D. Kovenock, J. Prothro, and Associates, *Explaining the Vote* (Durham: Institute for Research in Social Science, University of North Carolina, 1973).
1972	Syracuse University, Onondaga County, N.Y.	T. Patterson and R. McClure, *The Unseeing Eye* (New York: Putnam, 1976).
1976	Syracuse University, Erie County, Pennsylvania, and Los Angeles	T. Patterson, *The Mass Media Election* (New York: Praeger, 1980).
1978	CBS/*New York Times*, national and congressional candidate sample	G. Bishop and K. Frankovic, "Ideological Consensus and Constraint among Party Leaders and Followers in the 1978 Election," *Micropolitics* (no. 2, 1981).
1984	University of Michigan, NBES, national sample	K. Tate, R. Brown, S. Hatchett, and J. Jackson, *The 1984 National Black Election Study: A Sourcebook* (Ann Arbor: Institute for Social Research, 1988).
1984	Decision/Making/Information, national sample, continuous monitoring	D. Allsop and H. Weisberg, "Measuring Change in Party Identification in an Election Campaign," *AJPS* (November 1988).
1984	Aldrich, Sullivan, Borgida national (Gallup) sample	W. Rahn, J. Aldrich, E. Borgida, and J. Sullivan, "A Social-Cognitive Model of Candidate Appraisal," in *Information and Democratic Processes,* ed. J. Ferejohn and J. Kuklinski (Urbana: University of Illinois Press, 1990).
1968–1989	State legislative elections (aggregate data)	*Legislative Studies Quarterly* (February 1991).
1988	University of Michigan, NBES national sample	K. Tate, "Black Political Participation in the 1984 and 1988 Presidential Elections," *APSR* (December 1991).
1989	Civic Participation Study, national sample, oversample of blacks, Latinos, and political activists	S. Verba, K. Schlozman, and H. Brady, *Voice and Equality* (Cambridge: Harvard, 1995).

Table 1-2   *continued*

Year	Study	Report
1989– 1990	Latino National Political Survey	R. de la Garza et al., *Latino Voices* (Boulder, Colo.: Westview, 1992).
1996	NBES national sample	C. Gay and K. Tate, "Doubly Bound: The Impact of Gender and Race on the Politics of Black Women," *Political Psychology* (May 1998).
ongoing	Gallup Poll; CBS/*New York Times*; ABC/*Washington Post*; Voter News Service: national surveys, exit polls, and special surveys	

Note: AJPS = American Journal of Political Science; APSR = American Political Science Review; NBES = National Black Election Study; NORC = National Opinion Research Center.

There also has been an increasing use of sophisticated analysis methods in election studies, such as the use of techniques to study the stability of attitudes over time, as in Chapters 20 and 21. Additionally, there is more attention to proper modeling of the political process being studied, as in Timpone's (1998) separating the causes of registration and voter turnout and Lacy and Burden's (1999) treatment of abstention along with vote direction in studying the effect of the Perot candidacy in 1992. What is surprising is that this greater method-ological sophistication is not necessarily leading to greater consensus on the leading controversies in the field. Instead, the more sophisticated techniques fre-quently require arbitrary decisions and untestable assumptions. As a result, the debates become more methodologically advanced without leading to incon-testable conclusions.

Surveys about elections are also used extensively outside the United States. In countries where the election date is not fixed (such as Canada, Britain, and a number of others), prime ministers and party leaders now consult these polls before deciding on the timing of the election. The media poll extensively during the campaigns, so much so that there are almost daily reports of new polls in countries (again such as Britain) that have short election campaigns. In some sit-uations, especially when multiple parties are competing, polls have also been important in suggesting to people how to maximize the impact of their vote.[4]

Some of the early cross-national academic polls represented attempts to replicate the Michigan surveys in other countries, often by collaboration between some of the original Michigan researchers and investigators from the country in question (for example, Butler and Stokes 1969; Converse and Pierce 1986). These early studies frequently found that the concepts and questions developed in the American surveys were not applicable in other countries, as will be brought out in the discussion of party identification (Chapter 17). As a result, later election studies have been conducted by native researchers based on their understanding of their countries; see Mochmann, Oedegaard, and Mauer (1998) for an extensive listing of non-U.S. academic surveys and published reports on those surveys.

There are also important initiatives for taking comparable election surveys across countries. In the early 1990s the Comparative National Elections Project (CNEP) used similar surveys across five countries — Great Britain, Germany, Japan, Spain, and the United States — to study the role of intermediaries in voting, especially personal discussants, mass media, and organizations such as parties. In the late 1990s the Comparative Study of Electoral Systems (CSES) initiative developed a set of sixteen questions to be added to surveys by any national survey organization willing to join the project, resulting in fairly comparable data for about twenty countries. Both of these projects have subsequently been expanded with more nations joining in the efforts.

How to Understand Voting

The Theories

There are countless ways to understand voting. Two potential paradigms were explored by a research team at Columbia University, but neither had a lasting impact. The 1940 Columbia study was based on a consumer preference model, in which each party was seen as presenting a product to the public, the campaign was seen as an advertising campaign during which the competing products were weighed by the public, and the voters were seen as recording their final choices when they stepped into the booth on election day. The problem with this model was that most people knew how they would vote even before the national conventions were held, particularly since President Franklin D. Roosevelt was running for a third term in office in 1940. People knew whether they were going to vote for him without listening attentively to the campaign.[5] In the end, the Columbia researchers explained the 1940 election with a sociological model, relating voters' socioeconomic status (education, income, and class), religion, and place of residence (urban or rural) to their votes. These social group factors accounted for most of the observed differences in voting in this study of a single county, but the model did not explain why those social group differences appeared; nor did it hold when applied by the Michigan scholars to their national sample in 1948. More complex consumer preference and sociological models might have been useful (and indeed have received attention in recent years), but the time had come for a sharp break with these early models.

The Michigan researchers analyzed the 1952 election using a *social-psychological model*, which developed into one of the dominant paradigms in the field. The major emphasis was on three attitudes: the person's attachment to a party, the person's orientation toward the issues, and the person's orientation toward the candidates. The emphasis on parties, candidates, and issues explicitly incorporated political variables into the voting model. A theory mapping how these three factors interrelate in their effects on the vote came in the landmark Michigan report on the presidential elections of the 1950s, *The American Voter* (Campbell, Converse, Miller, and Stokes 1960). A person's identification with a party became the core of the model. It in turn affected the person's attitude toward candidates and issues. The authors describe this in terms of a "funnel of causality." The phenomenon to be explained—voting—is at the tip of the funnel, but it is preceded by, and dependent on, a variety of factors. The funnel's axis is time. Events follow one another, converging in a series of causal chains and moving from the mouth of the funnel to its tip. Thus a multitude of causes narrows into the voting act. At the mouth of the funnel are sociological background characteristics (ethnicity, race, region, religion, and the like), social status characteristics (education, occupation, class), and parental characteristics (class, partisanship). All affect the person's choice of party identification, which is the next item in the funnel. Party identification in turn influences the person's evaluation of the candidates and the issues, which again takes us further into the funnel. The next part of the funnel features incidents from the campaign itself, as these events are reported by the media. Even closer to the tip are conversations the voter has with family and friends about the election. Finally comes the vote itself. While each of the prior factors affects the vote, the Michigan group concentrated on parties, candidates, and issues, rather than on the early social characteristics or the later communications network.

This remains the basic Michigan model (Beck 1986), with a more explicit division today between what are designated long-term and short-term factors. Party identification is an important long-term factor affecting the vote. Issues and especially candidates are short-term factors specific to the election. (Even if the issues and candidates are carry-overs from previous elections, they are interpreted by voters in a new context in the given election.) This social-psychological model of the vote has affected virtually all later research, serving as the prime paradigm of the vote decision through most of the post-1950 period. And it continues to affect research in other countries, even though it was eventually decided that party identification itself might not be applicable everywhere.

Another model of voting became popular by the 1970s: the *rational voter model*. According to this model, voters decide whether to vote and which candidate to vote for on some rational basis, usually which action gives them greater expected benefits. They vote only if they perceive greater gain from voting than the cost (mainly in time) of voting. In the usual formulation, they vote for the candidate closest to them on the issues. A major contribution of this approach is that it provides a more explicit and precise theoretical basis for voting decisions and for their analysis than do other approaches. If voters are rational in the sense indicated, then we can expect certain types of behavior in specific circumstances. In addition, the rational voter model lends itself more than others to predicting what effects changes in external conditions will have. The early work was more mathematical than empirical, but increasingly surveys became a mechanism for testing some of the conclusions of the rational voter model. Substantively, the major contribution of the rational voter approach has been to emphasize the role of issues, which were submerged in most readings of the early findings of the Michigan researchers (see, for example, Fiorina 1981). The early antagonism between the social-psychological and rational voter approaches has long since declined, and several studies have bridged the differences. Increasingly, rational voter models are tested with the same empirical data used to test social-psychological models, and this has lessened the barriers between the two.

A third approach has formed around what might be termed *modern political psychology*. Social psychology has developed considerably since the 1950s when *The American Voter* was written. In particular, that field has experienced what is often referred to as a "cognitive revolution," as psychologists have achieved better understandings of the basis of human thoughts. Simultaneously, the field has given greater attention to human emotions and their effects on behaviors. These developments have been applied widely across the social sciences, with one result being a new field of political psychology. Given the basis of this approach in psychology, many of the studies following this approach use experimental methods. The political psychology perspective has been particularly powerful in dealing with the problem of decision making under limited information, which is one way of conceptualizing the voting task. Rational choice and political psychology perspectives were originally seen as at odds with one another, but it is now more common to view them as complementary, with political psychology dealing with the origin of preferences and rational choice with strategic behavior once individual preferences are chosen. Political psychology perspectives on voting behavior are represented at several places in this book, especially Chapters 6 and 10.

All in all, the articles reprinted in this book reflect a variety of theories about voting. They are based largely on the social-psychological approach, sometimes modifying and adapting the Michigan model of the 1950s to accommodate later elections and new interpretations of voting. Several of the pieces, however, are strongly influenced by the rational voter perspective or the political psychology approach. While there has been some convergence between these different overarching theories of voting behavior, several areas of substantive controversies remain in the field, reflected, for example, in Lodge, Steenbergen, and Brau's discussion in Chapter 13 of alternative ways of interpreting the influence of campaign events.

The Controversies

This book is organized around a series of substantive controversies in the voting behavior literature. We begin with voter turnout and political participation more generally, looking at why these are low and have been declining. We concentrate on three types of explanation: those focusing on individual, societal, and institutional factors. The form of argument is academic, but the implications of this debate for our democratic system are important, as widespread participation is considered by many to be vital for the survival of democracy.

The second controversy has to do with the electorate's ability to deal with matters political. In previous editions of this book, this section focused on the public's level of ideological thinking and their level of politically sophistication, but in this edition we instead emphasize a more fundamental matter: the public's ability to process political information, taking for granted their relatively low level of knowledge. This controversy has important ramifications throughout the voting behavior field. One of the most important findings of the early voting studies was that the electorate had limited information about the issues of the day. V. O. Key Jr. (1966) felt compelled to respond to that view, mustering evidence to demonstrate that "voters are not fools," but this evidence did not challenge the limited information level of voters. The rational choice perspective has been useful in showing that voters can make rational decisions even with limited information, as by judging past performance of the parties rather than having to pay attention to their promises for the future. However, the political psychology approach has tackled the matter more head on, showing that there are ways that people make good decisions with limited information. For example, most people do not know a lot of facts and figures about comparative automobile performance, but they are still able to make sensible decisions about car purchases. Similarly, voters have ways to make decisions they consider reasonable and appropriate without listening to every speech given by the presidential nominees. This discussion is most relevant to Part 2 of the book, where we look at the debate over how much the lack of political information matters or whether people make good decisions despite low levels of knowledge, but the nature of the electorate is an underlying issue that affects views of most of the topics covered here.

The third part of this book deals directly with vote determinants. Given the early view of voters as having limited capacities to deal with political matters, the initial edition of this book considered a controversy as to whether issue voting occurs. By the second edition the debate had turned to what kind of issues affect voting, and the third edition contrasted issue voting with voting on the basis of candidates. In this edition, we turn to the more basic question of whether election outcomes should be seen as largely predetermined or as affected by issues, candidates, and the media in election campaigns. People generally assume that campaigns matter, but it is possible to predict many election outcomes fairly well even before the campaign begins, so it is important to take a close look at the extent to which campaigns do matter.

The fourth section of this book turns to legislative elections. The early literature saw these as basically partisan, and we organized the section of our first edition around whether this characterization was correct. Soon it became clear that these elections cannot be seen as exclusively partisan, so the next two editions examined whether these elections should be seen as primarily national or local. That debate may still not be totally answered, but another concern has dominated the literature in recent years: the causes of why different parties have controlled the executive and legislative branches so often. Is divided government intentional on the part of voters, or does it just reflect a shift to more candidate-centered politics?

One of the most important variables in our modern understanding of voting is party identification, but there has been continuing debate about its stability. In the fifth section of this book, we look at how much politics affects partisanship. If partisanship is fairly immune to politics, then party identification is a force for stability in voting. However, if partisanship is strongly affected by other political and even economic variables, then the political system can change more easily.

The final part of this book focuses on party system change. The previous editions of this book have looked at controversies as to whether the party system is realigning or dealigning. In addition to these distinct possibilities, in this edition we review important new work that suggests that partisanship is being reinvigorated rather than simply being realigned or wearing away. This debate is over the shape of recent political change, but it has broader implications in terms of how to analyze party system change more generally.

The controversies examined in this book thus play off controversies reviewed in previous editions, but often with some new twist in how the debate is now framed. At times this is virtually stylistic, as when the old controversy as to how ideological the public is turned into a debate over the public's use of its limited stock of information. More often the controversy is now phrased in more complex terms. For example, instead of just arguing whether party identification is stable, the question now is how much contemporary politics affects partisanship. The largest change has to do with our treatment of subnational elections, focusing for the first time on the causes of divided government, one of the most important developments since the voting studies began.

While there remain controversies in the field, it is also important to acknowledge that we have learned much about voting behavior over the years. Voter turnout at elections in the United States is low despite rising education levels. Information levels among the public are also remain low. Many citizens decide how to vote before the campaign really begins. Divided government cannot be treated as a rare event. Party identification is not fully stable. The party system of today is not the same as the system that developed out of the New Deal era of the 1930s. Voting behavior is much more complex than it was believed to be when *The American Voter* was written.

The persistence of controversies in this field is in itself important. One might expect that the combination of sophisticated methodology, high-quality data, and effective theories would yield a commonly accepted understanding of voting and elections. This has not been the case. Controversy remains over the reasons for low turnout, the implications of limited citizen information, the importance of campaigns, the causes of divided government, the impact of day-to-day politics on partisan attachments, and the nature of recent changes in the party system. Controversy remains, but what could be more appropriate in the elections field? Elections are about controversy, and the study of elections will always evoke controversy.

Notes

1. Lodge et al. also argue that surveys give biased results about the significance of recall of campaign events and that experiments are a better method for determining this. See especially Chapter 13 in this book.
2. Recently, however, surveys—both of state legislators themselves and of citizens about their legislators—have become more common. See, for example, some of the chapters in Thomas and Wilcox (1998), as well as Carey, Niemi, and Powell (2000) and Powell and Niemi (2000).
3. In addition to these studies, NES has conducted several research and development "pilot studies" that are designed to test new survey questions. Complete information on these studies is available at the NES website.
4. See Crewe and Harrop (1989) on the role of polls and the media in advertising "tactical voting" in the British general election of 1987.
5. Since 1952 an average of 63 percent of voters in presidential elections said they made their vote decision before or during the nominating conventions (Campbell 2000, 8).

Further Readings

The Role of Elections

Grofman, Bernard, and Chandler Davidson, eds., *Controversies in Minority Voting: The Voting Rights Act in Twenty-Five Year Perspective* (Washington, D.C.: Brookings, 1992). Electoral success of minorities and other results of the Voting Rights Act.

Hicks, Alexander M., and Duane H. Swank, "Politics, Institutions, and Welfare Spending in Industrialized Democracies, 1960–1982," *American Political Science Review* 86 (1992): 658–674. Effect of partisanship of governing coalition, electoral competition, and turnout on social welfare expenditures in eighteen countries.

Public Opinion and Public Policy

Page, Benjamin I., and Robert Y. Shapiro, *The Rational Public: Fifty Years of Trends in American's Policy Preferences* (Chicago: University of Chicago Press, 1992). Assessment of public opinion and its sources, with some discussion of its effects on policy.

Stimson, James A., *Public Opinion in America* (Boulder, Colo.: Westview, 1991). The interpretability of the public's "mood" and its electoral connections.

CNN/IFES Election Watch: www.cnn.com/world/election.watch

Comparative Study of Electoral Systems (CSES): http://www.umich.edu/~nes/cses/cses.htm

Lijphart Elections Archive (election results around the world): http://dodgson.ucsd.edu/lij/

International Foundation for Electoral Systems (IFES): http://www.aceproject.
org; http://www.electionstoday.org; http://www.electionguide.org
Inter-university Consortium for Political and Social Research (ICPSR):
http://www.icpsr.umich.edu/cgi/subject.prl?path=ICPSR&query=XIV_
U.S. National Election Studies (NES): http://www.umich.edu/~nes/. See especially the NES Guide to Public Opinion and Electoral Behavior.

Books Studying Voting across a Series of U.S. Elections

Abramson, Paul R., John H. Aldrich, and David W. Rohde, *Change and Continuity in the 1996 and 1998 Elections* (Washington, D.C.: CQ Press, 1999).
Factors affecting voting in the 1996 and 1998 elections.

Flanigan, William H., and Nancy H. Zingale, *Political Behavior of the American
Electorate,* 9th ed. (Washington, D.C.: CQ Press, 1998). Textbook treatment
of issues, candidates, and elections.

Niemi, Richard G., and Herbert F. Weisberg, eds., *Classics in Voting Behavior*
(Washington, D.C.: CQ Press, 1993). Reprints of numerous classic voting
studies along with summary introductions.

Books on Recent Elections

Miller, Warren, and J. Merrill Shanks, *The New American Voter* (Cambridge:
Harvard University Press, 1996). Analysis of voting change in the 1980–1992
presidential elections, with emphasis on 1992.

Weisberg, Herbert F., ed., *Democracy's Feast* (Chatham, N.J.: Chatham House,
1995). Analysis of NES data on 1992 U.S. presidential election.

Weisberg, Herbert F., and Janet M. Box-Steffensmeier, ed., *Reelection 1996*
(New York: Chatham House, 1999). Analysis of NES data on 1996 U.S. presidential election.

Books Emphasizing the Political Psychology Approach

Sniderman, Paul M., Richard A. Brody, and Phillip E. Tetlock, *Reasoning and
Choice* (New York: Cambridge University Press, 1991). Redirects attention to
reasoning processes, particularly the use of heuristics, in citizen choices on
political matters.

English Language Books on Public Opinion and Voting Behavior in Other
Countries

Anderson, Christopher, *Blaming the Government: Citizens and the Economy in
Five European Democracies* (Armonk, N.Y.: M.E. Sharpe, 1995).

Anderson, Christopher, and Carsten Zelle, eds. *Stability and Change in German
Elections* (Westport, Conn.: Praeger, 1998).

Bartolini, Stefano, and Peter Mair, *Identity, Competition and Electoral Availability: The Stabilization of European Electorates, 1885–1985* (Cambridge: Cambridge University Press, 1990).

Dalton, Russell J., *Citizen Politics in Western Democracies*, 2d ed. (Chatham, N.J.:
Chatham House, 1996). Political attitudes, behavior, and party systems in
France, Great Britain, Germany, and the United States.

Evans, Geoffrey, and Pippa Norris, eds., *Critical Elections: British Parties and Voters in Long Term Perspective* (Thousand Oaks, Calif.: Sage, 1999).

Flanagan, Scott, Bradley Richardson, Joji Watanuki, Ichiro Miyake, and Shinsaku Kohei, *The Japanese Voter* (New Haven: Yale University Press, 1991).

Franklin, Mark, Tom Mackie, Henry Valen, et al., *Electoral Change: Responses to Evolving Social and Attitudinal Structures in Western Countries* (Cambridge: Cambridge University Press, 1992).

Inglehart, Ronald, *Modernization and Postmodernization: Cultural, Economic, and Political Change in 43 Societies* (Princeton, N.J.: Princeton University Press, 1997).

LeDuc, Larry, Richard G. Niemi, and Pippa Norris, eds. *Comparing Democracies 2: Elections and Voting in Global Perspective* (London: Sage, forthcoming).

Lewis-Beck, Michael, ed., *How France Votes* (Chatham, N.J.: Chatham House, 1999).

Mochmann, Ekkehard, Ingvill C. Oedegaard, and Reiner Mauer, *Inventory of National Election Studies in Europe 1945–1995* (Bergisch: Edwin Ferger Verlag, 1998). Contains an extensive bibliography of books and articles (often in the native language).

Reif, Karlheinz, and Ronald Inglehart, eds., *Eurobarometer: The Dynamics of European Public Opinion* (New York: St. Martin's, 1991).

White, Stephen, Richard Rose, and Ian McAllister, *How Russia Votes* (Chatham, N.J.: Chatham House, 1996).

PART I
POLITICAL PARTICIPATION

2. Why Is Voter Turnout Low (and Why Is It Declining)?

Ten to twenty years ago one could view declining turnout as a fascinating intellectual puzzle (Brody 1978; Miller 1992b): despite an array of factors that should have stimulated turnout—a dramatic increase in education levels, the effective enfranchisement of southern blacks and ensuing increase in competition throughout the South, the entrance of large numbers of women into the workplace, and the loosening of registration laws—the number of voters going to the polls had declined significantly from its high point in 1960 (Table 2-1). Today, instead of an intellectual puzzle, one is likely to read of a near-crisis situation (National Commission on Civic Renewal 1998; NASS 1999).

In addition to the perception of a continued slide in turnout, the near-crisis tone comes from at least four factors. First, the absolute level of turnout in 1996 dropped below half of the eligible electorate (at least in early accounts). Second, there have been parallel declines in participation in many civic organizations, which some see as a foundation stone of American democracy. Third, political engagement, in the sense of interest in politics and a willingness to follow (if not participate in) what is happening in government, has also fallen. Fourth, observed declines are concentrated especially among the young, making the prospects of further declines likely and of a quick recovery implausible.

In response to low voter turnout and other forms of political involvement and the crisis tone of recent rhetoric, there has been a renewed interest in participation and its causes and consequences among both the academic and policymaking communities. Likewise, new organizational efforts have sprung up to combat disengagement and encourage involvement. There have also been a number of recent arguments over the basic facts of the matter, including detailed calculations of the "true" level of voter turnout and over the possible replacement of voting with other (unconventional) forms of political behavior. In this chapter we summarize this literature under three broad categories of explanatory variables—individual factors, societal factors, and institutional factors.

Declining Turnout Is Due to Individual Factors

The most useful framework for thinking about political participation generally and voting turnout in particular is the cost-benefits logic developed by

Table 2-1 Voter Turnout Rates, United States, 1960–1998

	Presidential Elections				Nonpresidential Elections		
Year	United States	Nonsouth	South	Year	United States	Nonsouth	South
1960	65.4	72.8	43.2	1962	47.5	54.8	24.2
1964	63.3	68.6	46.4	1966	46.6	52.1	29.4
1968	62.3	65.7	51.8	1970	46.1	50.2	33.2
1972	57.0	61.1	45.1	1974	38.1	42.5	25.4
1976	55.2	57.9	47.5	1978	37.1	40.8	27.1
1980	54.3	56.0	48.1	1982	40.3	43.8	31.1
1984	54.9	56.9	49.5	1986	36.1	38.0	31.5
1988	52.2	54.5	46.6	1990	35.4	37.5	30.1
1992	56.8	58.9	51.7	1994	38.5	40.0	33.2
1996	50.8	52.4	47.1	1998	36.0	38.8	28.3

Source: Stanley and Niemi (2000, 12–13).

Note: These figures represent, insofar as possible, the percentage of the eligible electorate that cast votes. In the time shown, this has been the citizen voting-age population (not reduced for felons who have been disfranchised). See source for details.

Downs (1957) and amplified by Tullock (1967) and Riker and Ordeshook (1968). On the one hand, there is a cost (C) associated with the participatory act, whether the time cost involved in participation or the cost of becoming informed enough to participate. A rational person participates if and only if the benefits expected from participation exceed those costs. The benefits side of the equation for voting turnout is the product of the extent to which the citizen feels that one candidate will produce greater benefit (B) for him or her than the other candidate times the probability (P) that the citizen's act of voting will affect the election outcome, plus any psychological gratification (for example, expressive benefits or feeling of solidarity) the citizen receives from voting (usually labeled D, as it originally referred to "citizen duty"). Thus it is considered rational to vote only if PB + D > C. (Niemi and Weisberg 1993a, chap. 2 provides a more complete discussion of this model.) Citizens do not, of course, explicitly measure these terms and perform these mathematical calculations, but they may implicitly compare the gains they might expect from participation against the inevitable costs thereof. The implication of this logic is that low participation and turnout are due to either high costs or low expected benefits, and correspondingly that declining participation and turnout are due to either increasing costs or decreasing expected benefits. Virtually all accounts of participation can be considered within this framework, but it is particularly useful for emphasizing the way in which individuals think about voting.

Given the emphasis of the cost-benefit logic on individual decision making, one of the standard approaches to the study of political participation is to study the individual correlates of involvement. Thus it is natural to try to account for *declines* in involvement by looking for changes in these same factors. As noted, however, two of the usual factors—education and legal restrictions—have moved in the "wrong" direction. Education has increased dramatically over the past half century, and since greater education has routinely been associated with higher levels of participation (Milbrath 1965; Wolfinger and Rosenstone 1980, chap. 2; Rosenstone and Hansen 1993, 130; Nie, Junn, and Stehlik-Barry 1996, 35), it cannot explain declining involvement. Likewise, legal restrictions (particularly on voting) have been reduced or removed, which should have resulted in higher, not lower, rates of participation.

Researchers have responded to this "puzzle" by looking for *different* individual factors that could explain the observed declines. Much of this work has focused on the act of voting itself (though increasingly, the same models are used to study all manner of participation). It was noted, for example, that strong partisanship was associated with higher turnout, and to some extent with other forms of involvement (for example, Campbell et al. 1960, 97–101; Teixeira 1987; Rosenstone and Hansen 1993, 130–131), and identification with political parties declined after the mid-1960s (see Chapter 21). Similarly, young people have traditionally gone to the polls at lower rates than older voters (Wolfinger and Rosenstone 1980), so the adoption in 1969 of the 26th Amendment, which lowered the voting age from twenty-one to eighteen, surely accounted for some of the post-1960 drop in turnout.

These and other factors were first brought together in a comprehensive model by Teixeira (1987). He concluded that demographic changes (a lower voting age, increased mobility, more single people) accounted for close to 40 percent of the socioeconomic status-adjusted decline, while changes in sociopolitical characteristics (declining partisanship, newspaper reading, and political efficacy) accounted for the other 60 percent. Rosenstone and Hansen (1993, 211–219), in the reading included here as Chapter 4, use the same basic approach but come to a strikingly different conclusion. They find that demographic changes (a lower voting age) and individual-level sociopolitical characteristics (less social involvement, weaker partisanship, lower efficacy, and less satisfaction with candidate choices) *together* account for only about 45 percent of the decline in turnout over roughly the same period. The other 55 percent of the decline is due to mobilization—"the intensity of efforts by candidates, parties, campaigns, interest groups, and social movements to mobilize people to take part." They find a similar role for mobilization on voting turnout of African Americans and for various kinds of conventional political behavior other than voting.[1]

Rosenstone and Hansen also remind us that turnout since 1960 has been affected by the civil rights movement. For one thing, it quickly eliminated barriers to voting by African Americans. Turnout among blacks, at one time very low, rose quickly and has been "only" 5–10 percentage points below white turnout in the past twenty years. In a slightly longer time frame, it led to greater political competition in the South, where previously the only competition was in Democratic primaries. Overall, turnout in the South—once 30–40 percent below the rest of the country—grew quickly in the 1960s and was little changed between 1972 and 1996. (For percentage turnout by race and region, see Stanley and Niemi 2000, Table 1-1.)

Another, innovative approach to explaining low turnout has been to reexamine the connection between education and participation, reopening the question of whether higher education should be expected to translate into higher turnout and other forms of political involvement. Nie et al. (1996) argue that "political engagement can be seen as more of a zero-sum game, bounded by finite resources and conflict, where one's gain will necessarily be another's loss" (101). There is an upper bound to the capacity of government to respond to citizen activities, and individual payoffs are constrained by the number of individuals who are competing for those rewards. Given this reality, they argue, what is important is *relative* education. No matter that the overall level of education in society has increased; some are still more advantaged by being more educated than others. Thus "the impact of education . . . [on participation] must be estimated by a *relative* measure of educational attainment that takes into account the context of educational competition" (105).

Applying their theory to National Election Studies data on political involvement between 1972 and 1994, Nie et al. find supportive evidence. In a multivariate model including a variety of other variables, years of education and what the authors call the educational environment (mean years of education of adults aged 25–50 at the time a given individual reached age 25) virtually canceled each other; the overall effects of increasing education were therefore near zero (141–142). Also as predicted, years of education and educational environment are cumulative for an important political attitude—tolerance of unpopular political opinions—which they argue is free of the limits imposed by greater numbers of individuals.

As impressive as these results are, a question remains about the application to turnout. It is unclear why voting should be subject to the same competitive pressures as other forms of involvement. Individuals with "only" a high school education may be somewhat disadvantaged presently in their ability to argue a point at a town meeting, but they are no more or less able to vote because their education puts them in the middle of the pack or below. Moreover, it hardly seems likely that voter turnout in the 60 percent range seriously taxed government capacity to respond in the 1950s and 1960s. If the authors' reasoning applies to voter turnout, it must be that those with relatively less education feel less able to understand politics or more often believe that they cannot influence political matters, and that this spills over into a feeling that their vote is of little consequence.[2] It would be good to have confirmation of this mechanism.[3]

Another take on the question of education comes from analyses by Verba, Schlozman, and Brady (1995, 358–361) and Brady, Verba, and Schlozman (1995). They argue that turnout is driven by political interest, which arises from sources other than education alone; increases in education levels do not necessarily lead to greater interest and therefore greater turnout. Earlier work, they feel, "has not treated political interest as a possibly unreliable and endogenous measure, . . . [and that] it has substantially underestimated the impact of interest and overestimated the direct impact of education" (Brady et al. 1995, 283). Indeed, we will see below that political interest has, by many accounts, declined sharply in recent decades. Thus, while Verba et al. do not directly address the decline in turnout, their (partial) decoupling of turnout and education, combined with others' observations about declining interest, provide a ready explanation.[4]

One other point that is important to keep in mind when examining declining turnout is that the decline may not be real—it may just be caused by problems in measuring who is eligible to vote. McDonald and Popkin (1999), in particular, argue that turnout in presidential years since 1972 has been largely flat (other than the obvious spike in 1992 associated with the Perot candidacy) once one properly takes into account the growing number of aliens in the population (who are ineligible to vote) and the vastly increased number of disfranchised felons. Yet these calculations are open to dispute: neither the number of aliens (for obvious reasons) nor the number of disfranchised felons (because of varying state laws about eligibility) is simple to count, and one can raise questions about McDonald and Popkin's numbers (especially the large drop they report from 1992 to 1994 in the number of noncitizens). Yet, if nothing else, this work reminds us of the importance of careful measurement and of the need to pay attention to exactly what it is we are trying to explain.

Other studies address individual factors that influence turnout but do not specifically address the question of change. Timpone (1998) uses a "selection bias" technique that separates the effects of independent variables on registration and turnout (using pooled data for 1980–1988). He finds that many of the "usual" variables, including many of those in Rosenstone and Hansen's model, explain registration differences more than turnout differences among the registered. In particular, long-term predispositions, especially external efficacy and strength of partisanship, have a major impact on registration but relatively little effect on turnout. Age and education likewise influence registration much more than turnout among the registered. Conversely, Timpone finds that a few variables thought to no longer be of much consequence, such as race and gender, affect turnout once one removes the effects of differential registration.

It is important to recognize that Timpone's analysis does not mean that voting rates would soar were we to drop registration requirements. If individuals who failed to register were suddenly eligible to vote, the relationship between efficacy, education, and so on, and turnout per se would very likely increase sharply. Simply being registered, or not having to register at all, does not automatically turn likely nonvoters into voters (see the discussion below about election-day registration). Viewed this way, the most important part of Timpone's separate estimations may be to highlight the way that a number of specific factors—especially race, gender, and marital status—affect voting.

The most comprehensive study of the individual factors leading to political participation in the United States is Verba, Schlozman, and Brady's (1995) survey of 15,053 respondents in late 1989 for their civic participation study. They defined voluntary political participation broadly to include noncompensatory activity that seeks to influence government action either directly or indirectly. The most theoretically rich aspect of their analysis is their emphasis on the resources for political activity, including time, money, and civic skills (as measured by their familiarity with the English language, a vocabulary test designed to assess verbal ability, and the extent to which they have attended decision meetings, planned meetings, written letters, or given speeches). Regression analysis shows that political interest and information affect overall political participation, with civic skills, education, family income, and free time also having significant effects, but they also find differences between different types of political activity. For example, family income, political interest, and partisan strength are the only significant predictors of political contributions. Civic skills affect several political activities (which they term *time-based acts*), but not voting. They do not find education significant in predicting turnout, although vocabulary skills are significant. The participation process favors those with early advantages from highly educated parents or from parents who are politically involved, although there is an alternative path through attachment to the community, particularly church involvement. Verba, Schlozman, and Brady do not directly address declining levels of participation, but by implication they direct our attention to causal factors that may have declined, which suggests the possibility that society has changed in such a way as to diminish the opportunities for the development of civic skills conducive to participation.

Declining Turnout Is Due to Societal Factors

Rosenstone and Hansen's model (and Teixeira's earlier model) account statistically for the full decline in turnout over the past forty years, and Nie, Junn, and Stehlik-Barry's analysis helps explain why rising education levels do not automatically lead to greater involvement. One might quibble with the precise specification and operationalization of their models, but altogether they do a remarkably good job of explaining what groups participate less now than then and what the motivations are that caused people to withdraw from the active electorate. Yet their explanations fail in a major way to identify what has happened. In particular, they fail to note that the decline in participation has a strong generational component. Not everyone has become less interested in politics, lost their feelings of efficacy, and adopted a more independent political posture. Rather, citizens who have come of age since the 1960s account for the lion's share of the decline in turnout and other forms of participation. Thus, in searching for the causes of the decline, one needs to look for changes that are "societal" in the sense that their effect is widespread and yet targeted in the sense that their effect is greatest in specific cohorts.[5]

With respect to turnout per se, Miller and Shanks (1996, chaps. 3–6; see also Miller 1992b) are vehement in arguing that declines observed in recent decades are generational in origin. They note, in particular, that an older cohort of individuals—the New Deal cohort, defined as those first eligible to vote between 1932 and 1964—never wavered from its high propensity to go to the polls. Thus the weakened partisanship and other sociopolitical changes noted by Rosenstone and Hansen had no apparent net effect on this generation's behavior. At the same time, the finding that turnout among the older generation was unchanged between the 1960s and 1980s means that the younger generation had to be very different from previous ones to account for the overall decline. Matching generations by age (and education) shows this to be the case. Thus, for example, among high school graduates, turnout by the New Deal generation ranged from 67 percent (when they were 21–24 years old) to 90 percent (when they were 41–44 years old). Comparable figures for the post-New Deal generation were 41 percent and 69 percent, respectively (Miller and Shanks 1996, 66).

As Miller and Shanks indicate, this transforms but does not solve the original puzzle. Turnout declined because the post-New Deal generation voted in much smaller numbers than their predecessors; evidently they, but not older citizens, were affected by something about politics in the 1960s and after. As to what that is, they have no direct evidence "beyond our surmise that [it was] four decades of discouraging news about our political system" (112). Their inability to explain the decline is not for lack of trying. They examine the same sorts of factors studied by Rosenstone and Hansen and others, concluding that while social connectedness, partisanship, and interest in elections were relevant to the explanation (that is, generational differences in turnout were smaller and larger, respectively, among those who were high and low on social connectedness, strength of partisanship, and interest in elections), while efficacy, sense of governmental responsiveness, and sense of civic obligation were not, none of these factors accounted for intergenerational differences in turnout (111).

The theme of generational change is an important component in Putnam's (1995a, 2000) extensive discussion of the decline of community in the second half of the twentieth century. His description of that decline and his search for explanations of it are reprinted here as Chapter 3. As portrayed by Putnam, the decline in turnout is only a small part of a much broader change in the American political and civic landscape. There have been major declines in all sorts of political activities, including working for a political party, attending town and school meetings, running for office, signing petitions, writing letters to newspapers, and so on (Putnam 2000, 37–47). But these changes, too, are only a part of the picture, as Americans at the end of the twentieth century participated less in clubs, churches, unions, and social visits than they had twenty to forty years earlier. Even such mundane activities as card playing and, as suggested by the title of his book, bowling together in leagues, declined sharply.[6]

As with voting turnout, the decline in many sorts of activities is largely generational in origin. For example, when Putnam compares individuals in various age groups during the early 1970s with same-aged individuals during the 1990s (Chapter 3; see also 2000, chap. 14), he finds that the greatest dropoff in all sorts of civic acts is concentrated in younger cohorts. Similarly, interest in politics and attitudes such as feeling that most people can be trusted fell off sharply among younger generations (even when controlling for education), while materialism climbed sharply (Chapter 3; Putnam 2000, 252–253, 260, 273). Moreover, Putnam argues that among Gen Xers (those born between 1965 and 1980) "all forms of civic engagement . . . continued to plummet. . . , accelerat[ing] the tendencies to individualism found among boomers" (2000, 259).[7]

While it is clear that generations differ, sometimes dramatically, Putnam, like Miller and Shanks, cannot say with certainty what caused the change. He notes in Chapter 3 of this text that "it is as though the post-war [World War II] generations were exposed to some mysterious X-ray that permanently and increasingly rendered them less likely to connect with the community" and that "*it*. . . accounts for most of the civic disengagement that lies at the core of our mystery." What this X-ray consisted of is much harder to say, and Putnam can only speculate that World War II and television may be at the root of it—the former having heightened civic involvement among the older generation and the latter having lowered civic engagement among more recent generations.

Putnam's work has inevitably led to further analysis of the concepts of social capital and social connectedness. In particular, Brehm and Rahn (1997) have moved the analysis down to the individual level, using General Social Survey (GSS) data from 1972 through 1994 to look at the causal network involving social capital. They find a reciprocal relationship between civic engagement and interpersonal trust, but with civic participation leading to trust more than vice versa. Confidence in federal institutions has a strong effect on trust. Civic engagement is affected not only by education, income, and partisanship, but also by television usage—television is a drain from civic participation, confirming Putnam's speculation. A recent controversial study by Nie and Erbring (2000) finds that Internet use also detracts from social interactions and, by implication, from social connectedness.

It is worth noting that a decline in voter turnout is widespread in contemporary democracies, suggesting that more is at work than simply changes in U.S. society. Dalton (1996a, 45) reports turnout figures for twenty-four countries by decade from the 1950s to the 1990s. Turnout declined almost everywhere, with average levels going from 82 percent in the first two decades to 81, 79, and 76 percent, respectively, in the last three. Wattenberg's (1998a, 17; also Lijphart 1997, 6) figures, comparing turnout in the first two elections in the 1950s with the two most recent elections (at the time of his compilation), show even bigger drops, with many nations experiencing declines of 7 to 19 percentage points (and only Denmark and Sweden showing increases). Partisanship has also been declining in many countries besides the United States (Inglehart 1990, 357–358; Dalton 2001), which may explain some of the decline in turnout (see also Wattenberg 1998a, 17–19). The important point is that a decline in so many countries over the same time frame suggests that the roots of this phenomenon lie in changes that are occurring throughout society and, indeed, throughout the world.

Others argue that changes have occurred in turnout because perceptions about appropriate and meaningful venues for political participation have changed. According to this argument, interest in politics has not flagged. Rather, political discussions have increased and, most significantly, participation in "unconventional" or "protest" politics has increased at the same time that voter turnout has declined. Inglehart (1990, chap. 10; 1997, chap. 10) provides extensive support for this argument that noninstitutional "elite-challenging" forms of participation have increased. Relying chiefly on data from twenty-one countries taking part in the 1981 and 1990 World Values Surveys, he finds increases in most countries in political interest, discussions of politics with friends, signing petitions (Putnam 2000, 43–44, 229 on the United States), and saying that they have taken part in or might take part in boycotts, demonstrations, unofficial strikes, and occupying buildings. These changes in type of behavior are linked to strong generational changes in people's values. Specifically, Inglehart has shown that people he labels "post-materialists" (who care more about noneconomic goals) are more often found among recent generations and that they are more likely to participate in unconventional ways (1990, chap. 9; 1997, chap. 5). Thus it would be useful if Putnam's analysis were expanded to include unconventional participation to see if earlier forms of mass participation have been replaced by organized movements.

One other societal factor that has recently been cited in connection with low turnout is televised negative political advertisements. However, evidence on this potential cause is decidedly mixed. The early finding by Ansolabehere and Iyengar (1995) was that negative ads depressed turnout. Some other studies have found supportive results. But a recent meta-analysis does not support such a claim (Lau, Sigelman, Heldman, and Babbitt 1999), and the absence of impact is consistent with the failure to find a connection between negative evaluations of government and voter turnout (Rosenstone and Hansen 1993, 146–150). Especially insightful in this debate is Kahn and Kenney's (1999) distinction between the provision of negative but appropriate information and "mudslinging." Their finding that the former stimulated turnout while the latter depressed it may be an important key to understanding such variable results.[8]

Low Turnout Is Due to Institutional Factors

A different perspective on low turnout is given when one takes a comparative or historical view. Turnout in the United States, both currently and at its modern high point in 1960, is considerably lower than in most other countries (see Tables 2-1 and 5-1). It is also well below turnout levels in the U.S. during the second half of the nineteenth century. There is something anomalous in this, because with respect to other kinds of participation, both conventional and unconventional, the U.S. is more typical, close to the top on some activities (signing petitions) and below average on others (Inglehart 1997, chap. 10), but never so extreme as in the case of voting.

There is widespread agreement that low turnout in the United States is explained, in part, by the legal and institutional environment in the U.S. compared to that in other countries. Powell (1986), for example, cites two factors as accounting for a 14 percentage point difference between U.S. turnout and average turnout in some twenty other developed democracies. The first factor is the lack of competitiveness of U.S. elections (accounting for more than 10 points). The use of single-member districts for Congress and of the electoral college for the presidency means that some constituencies are likely to be written off as hopeless, with less mobilization by the parties and less incentive for voters to go to the polls. In contrast, in nations that rely on proportional representation throughout the country or in large districts, there is incentive for parties to mobilize and for voters to cast ballots everywhere. The second factor is the weakness of linkages between parties and groups of citizens in the U.S. compared to elsewhere (accounting for more than three points). Powell notes, for example, that in some countries knowing one's occupation or religion quite reliably allows one to identify his or her voting preferences. This is much less true in the United States, and the weaker linkages make it more difficult for parties to mobilize voters. Several observers also associate the lower turnout in the U.S. and the fall in turnout with the decoupling of presidential and state elections, which in many states weakens the incentives for political parties to mobilize their supporters.

In the reading included here as Chapter 5, Franklin also finds that the proportionality of the electoral system contributes substantially to turnout differences. In contrast to Powell, who defined proportionality in terms of the type of electoral system in a country, Franklin uses a direct measure of the proportionality between seats and votes (which is, of course, heavily dependent on the type of electoral system).[9] His results attribute a large fraction of the differences across countries—12 percentage points—to this one factor. Franklin also includes in his model a broad set of legal factors—including compulsory voting, postal voting, and Sunday voting—that collectively account for a good deal of intercountry variation.

The single factor most often cited as responsible for low turnout in the U.S. is yet another legal consideration—voter registration. Unlike in the U.S., registration in most countries is automatic (that is, voter rolls are kept by the state); no separate action is required on the part of the voter to be sure he or she qualifies to vote on election day. Powell estimates that another 14 percentage point difference between turnout in the U.S. and elsewhere can be attributed to this factor.[10] Studies within the U.S. that have relied on comparisons of citizens in states with differing registration requirements support this finding, although at somewhat lower levels. In their study of the 1972 elections, Wolfinger and Rosenstone (1980) concluded that liberalized registration laws would lead to about a 9 percentage point increase in turnout. In a update, using results of four elections, Mitchell and Wlezien (1995) estimate that substantial liberalization would lead to a 7.6 percent increase. Highton and Wolfinger (1998, 79, 94) recently estimated that elimination of a separate step to register would increase turnout between 4.7 and 8.7 percentage points, and elimination of purging of election rolls would lead to an increase of about 2 points (for a combined effect of as much as 10 percentage points).

A look at turnout in the United States throughout its history strongly supports the argument that registration laws and the legal and institutional environment more generally are at the root of most changes in turnout levels. In the second half of the nineteenth century, when the party system was highly competitive and registration was not required, turnout outside the South was on the order of 75–80 percent.[11] The decline in the strength of the parties and the introduction of registration systems in the 1890s and early 1900s—and the enactment of Jim Crow laws in the South—led to large, rapid declines. The adoption of the 19th Amendment in 1920 reduced turnout yet again, as women were slow to exercise their new right to vote. And, as noted earlier, the legal changes brought about by the civil rights movement, along with greater party competition, resulted in sharply increased turnout among African Americans and in the South generally.[12]

Recently, concern over declining numbers of voters has led to a number of national and state efforts designed to stimulate turnout. Most prominent is the National Voter Registration Act of 1993, most often known as the "motor voter" law. The provision that allows for registration when applying for a driver's license reduces time and effort so sufficiently that Highton and Wolfinger (1998) regard it as effectively the same as election-day registration (with results noted above). A problem has been that few states have fully implemented provisions of this law (except perhaps mail registration, which had a small but surprising negative effect on turnout), leading to a small overall effect (Highton and Wolfinger 1998).

Other recent efforts to stimulate turnout include allowing voters to cast an absentee ballot by mail for any reason, all-mail voting, and early voting in person (Stein 1998, 57). These practices are relatively new and have been implemented in only a handful of states, making it impossible to draw firm conclusions yet about their effects. It appears as if early voting has only a marginal impact on turnout (Stein and Garcia-Moner 1997; Richardson and Neeley 1996). On the other hand, in a study of all-mail voting (in Oregon) that controlled for a variety of confounding factors, the authors found a 10 percentage point increase in turnout (Southwell and Burchett 2000). The similarity of this figure to those reported in studies of liberalized registration is striking. A related finding is that aversion to jury duty—sometimes cited as a cause of low registration because, it is claimed, people avoid registering to vote because registration lists are used to select potential jury members—accounts for less than a 1 percentage point drop in turnout (Oliver and Wolfinger 1999).

While legal and institutional factors go a long way toward explaining low turnout in the United States, it is not clear that they in any way account for the decline in turnout over the past forty years. In fact, as Wattenberg (1997) has noted, states with no registration (North Dakota) or election-day registration (Wisconsin and Minnesota) have experienced declines just as other states have—although election-day registration permits turnout spikes if the election proves exciting at the last minute, as happened when ex-professional wrestler Jesse Ventura won the Minnesota governorship in 1998. And many of the states with motor voter registration systems in the 1970s and 1980s showed declines in turnout after their introduction (Highton and Wolfinger 1998, 82).

Conclusion

Turnout in U.S. elections—never as high as that in most other established democracies—has declined significantly since 1960. In the 1996 presidential election turnout dropped to just over 50 percent of the eligible electorate, and even the parties' best get-out-the-vote drive in the 2000 presidential election boosted turnout only to 51 percent (based on initial estimates). Reacting to the steady decline in the numbers of adults going to the polls, governments have begun to respond with concerted efforts to reverse the downward slope. After years of delay, the national government passed the National Voter Registration Act of 1993. As mentioned above, states have begun experimenting with easier registration requirements (see Highton and Wolfinger 1998), mail voting, early in-person voting, and so on. To date, none of these reforms has had a noteworthy impact; if they have worked at all, they have only slowed the pace of decline.

Will federal and state governments introduce still more reforms and better implement existing ones? Possibly, but the record of implementation of the motor voter law is not encouraging (see Highton and Wolfinger 1998). Moreover, as various studies have made clear, lowering the cost of voting is not likely to boost turnout greatly. Major reforms (eliminating all registration requirements, making election day a holiday, freely allowing advance voting) might do the job, but even that is not certain.

In any case, reforms of this magnitude are unlikely because political leaders evidently remain persuaded that increased turnout would have significant partisan consequences—namely, that greater turnout would come primarily from those who are less educated, have low incomes, and are predominantly minority and is therefore likely to be strongly pro-Democratic. The various U.S. studies cited above (Wolfinger and Rosenstone 1980; Teixeira 1992; Mitchell and Wlezien 1995; Highton and Wolfinger 1998; see also Erikson 1995, Nagel and McNulty 1996) are unanimous in concluding that the impact of eliminating registration on the partisan division of the vote would be negligible. As Highton and Wolfinger (1998, 95) explain, "The largest categories of nonvoters are not individuals who can be assumed to like Democratic candidates but the residentially mobile and young people: neither group has identifiable partisan inclinations." Yet as long as the perception of significant partisan consequences remains, the chances of bipartisan cooperation to encourage greater turnout are severely limited.

Will citizens, in the absence of systematic changes that make voting far easier, conclude that democracy itself is at stake and respond by going to the polls in greater numbers? Possibly, especially if major educational efforts are made both among current young adults and those who will become adults in the next few elections. Yet we think it unlikely that such efforts will have either large or immediate effects. What might increase turnout is a new, major issue on which the parties take opposing stands and which greatly increases the perceived meaningfulness of one's vote. That, however, is hardly something that can be effectively planned.

Two other factors that could spark greater turnout are more competitive elections and more attractive candidates. As with the other possible changes, however, these are unlikely to occur in the immediate future because they are, at least in part, tied to the advantages that incumbents hold through their greater ability to attract resources, provide services to constituents, and construct politically favorable districts—advantages that incumbents are not likely to give up easily.

Until one or more of these admittedly unlikely changes occur, the United States will continue to occupy a place near the bottom of lists of voter turnout in established democracies, and political scientists will continue their analysis of low U.S. voting rates.

Notes

1. As Cassel and Luskin (1988) emphasize, the validity of such attempts to account for 100 percent of the decline in turnout depends on whether the underlying model is fully specified in terms of inclusion of all relevant causal factors; we have included a sample of Rosenstone and Hansen's appendix tables so that readers can judge for themselves the adequacy of the model underlying these calculations.
2. Empirically, the results are similar when several different forms of participation (including voting only) are used as the dependent variable. What is unclear is why it should work for voting.
3. Another possible explanation of the education effect is that the value of given amounts of education have changed over the years. Going to college was a high level of educational attainment in 1950, for example, but is more routine today. Furthermore, the nature of higher education has changed, with less overall emphasis on liberal arts and greater specialization today.
4. As this discussion of interest and education makes clear, it is somewhat misleading and perhaps impossible to distinguish fully between explanations based on individual and societal factors. If changes in individual factors account for the decline in turnout, one is naturally led to ask what caused those changes. In the case of variables such as mobilization or political interest, it seems natural to conclude that changes have come about because of large-scale forces at work in society. We distinguish the two kinds of explanations here simply because some studies have emphasized the individual correlates of turnout and are especially concerned with their relative strengths, while others have emphasized the extent to which societywide changes are taking place (often in those same characteristics).
5. Actually, variables such as political efficacy, strength of partisanship, and extent of mobilization begin to get at these kinds of factors. But they are usually modeled as if they affect all adults, rather than given cohorts, and there is little emphasis on what lies behind changes in their distributions.
6. Ladd (1999) challenges Putnam's thesis by suggesting, among other things, that new kinds of groups have taken up the slack caused by obvious declines in other groups.

Putnam responds by noting that while certain kinds of memberships have increased (for example, in environmental organizations), it is often participation only in the sense of writing out a check (2000, 157ff.).

7. Not all changes are generational in origin. Some, such as the decline in card playing and bowling in leagues, are due to societywide declines or to a combination of societywide changes and generational replacement (2000, 265-266). Overall, Putnam suggests that about half of the decline in civic engagement can be attributed to generational replacement.

8. As one might also note that while Rosenstone and Hansen's approach and many of the factors they cite are individual-level, the importance of mobilization might properly be attributed to societal influences. In brief, if the rise of candidate-centered elections (see Chapter 21) has weakened the ability of political parties to mobilize voters, then the decline in turnout is ultimately societal in nature.

9. Cox (1999) discusses the way in which electoral rules relate to parties' incentives to mobilize and therefore to voting turnout, introducing still more legal and institutional factors and reviewing a large U.S. and comparative literature.

10. Franklin, surprisingly, finds no effect of the type of registration system once other variables are controlled. Although he disputes the notion, it may be that his definition of the "saliency" variable for the United States and Switzerland underlies this result. That is not to say, however, that the saliency variable is ill-founded. Jackman and Miller (1995, 482-483) argue, as does Franklin, that the high frequency of elections in the United States and Switzerland explain their exceptionally low turnout. See also Cox (1999, 415, n. 16).

11. These developments—and the debate about the role of party decline versus legal changes—are reviewed in Niemi and Weisberg (1993a). A recent study of the effects of introducing the Australian ballot is Heckelman (2000).

12. Franklin and Hirczy de Miño (1998) provide suggestive evidence that another institutional characteristic—divided government—has also dampened turnout in the United States.

Further Readings

Individual Factors

Brady, Henry E., Sidney Verba, and Kay Lehman Schlozman, "Beyond SES: A Resource Model of Political Participation," *American Political Science Review* 89 (1995): 271–294. Political interest, skills, and income explain turnout, acts taking time, and donations, respectively.

Teixeira, Ruy, *Why Americans Don't Vote: Turnout Decline in the United States 1960–1984* (New York: Greenwood Press, 1987). Declines in partisan strength, political efficacy, and newspaper reading, along with a younger electorate, help explain turnout declines.

Timpone, Richard J., "Structure, Behavior, and Voter Turnout in the United States," *American Political Science Review* 92 (1998): 145–158. Estimates separate effects of independent variables on registration and turnout, finding many explain registration more than turnout.

Verba, Sidney, Kay Lehman Schlozman, and Henry E. Brady, *Voice and Equality: Civic Voluntarism in American Politics* (Cambridge: Harvard University Press, 1995). Major study of voluntary political participation emphasizes resources of time, money, and civic skills.

Societal Factors

Lau, Richard R., Lee Sigelman, Caroline Heldman, and Paul Babbitt, "The Effects of Negative Political Advertisements: A Meta-Analytic Assessment," *American Political Science Review* 93 (1999): 851–875. Negative political ads are widely disliked but no more effective than positive ads and do not decrease turnout.

Nie, Norman H., Jane Junn, and Kenneth Stehlik-Barry, *Education and Democratic Citizenship in America* (Chicago: University of Chicago Press 1996). Relative education has varying relationships to participation and to commitment to democratic values.

Putnam, Robert, *Bowling Alone: The Collapse and Revival of American Community* (New York: Simon & Schuster, 2000). Data-rich argument describes declining participation in political and civic life.

Legal/Institutional Factors

Highton, Benjamin, and Raymond E. Wolfinger, "Estimating the Effects of the National Voter Registration Act of 1993," *Political Behavior* 20 (1998): 79–104. Intention and implementation of National Voter Registration Act and the estimated effects of "motor voter" law and nonpurging of rolls.

Jackman, Robert W., and Ross A. Miller, "Voter Turnout in the Industrial Democracies during the 1980s," *Comparative Political Studies* 27 (1995): 467–492. Institutional factors such as disproportionality and unicameralism are more important than cultural factors.

Mitchell, Glenn E., and Christopher Wlezien, "The Impact of Legal Constraints on Voter Registration, Turnout, and the Composition of the American Electorate," *Political Behavior* 17 (1995): 179–202. Liberalized registration laws would lead to a 7.6 percentage point increase in turnout but would have little effect on partisan composition of voters.

Powell, G. Bingham, "American Voter Turnout in Comparative Perspective," *American Political Science Review* 80 (1986): 17–43. Individual factors push U.S. turnout up; institutional factors, including registration, party linkages, and competition, keep it down.

Skocpol, Theda, and Morris P. Fiorina, eds., *Civic Engagement in American Democracy* (Washington, D.C.: Brookings, 1999). Alternative views, especially of a historical and institutional perspective, on civic engagement in the United States.

Gender Differences in Participation

Schlozman, Kay, Nancy Burns, and Sidney Verba, "Gender and the Pathways to Participation," *Journal of Politics* 56 (1994): 963–990. Women are less active in politics beyond the electoral arena due to their resource disadvantage.

Schlozman, Kay, Nancy Burns, and Sidney Verba, " 'What Happened at Work Today?': A Multistage Model of Gender, Employment, and Political Participation," *Journal of Politics* 61 (1999): 29–53. The gender gap in political activity can largely be explained by gender differences in the workplace.

Racial Differences in Participation

Calhoun-Brown, Allison, "African American Churches and Political Mobilization," *Journal of Politics* 58 (1996): 935–953. Attendance at a "political" church is an influential indicator of political involvement for African Americans.

Harris, Frederick C., *Something Within: Religion in African-American Political Activism* (New York : Oxford University Press, 1999). Church participation influences the political participation of African Americans, especially African American women.

Participation around the World

Inglehart, Ronald, *Materialism and Postmaterialism: Cultural, Economic, and Political Change in 43 Societies* (Princeton: Princeton University Press 1997), chap. 10. Analysis of participation in conventional and unconventional activities in some twenty countries in 1981 and 1990.

Turnout Studies/Reports Web Sites

International Institute for Democracy and Electoral Assistance (IDEA): http://www.idea.int/voter_turnout/index.html. Global report on turnout since 1945. Reports figures for individual countries and analyzes probable causes of turnout differences.

3. Tuning in, Tuning out: The Strange Disappearance of Social Capital in America

Robert D. Putnam

. . . I have been wrestling with a difficult mystery. It is, if I am right, a puzzle of some importance to the future of American democracy. It is a classic brain-teaser, with a corpus delicti, a crime scene strewn with clues, and many potential suspects. As in all good detective stories, however, some plausible miscreants turn out to have impeccable alibis, and some important clues hint at portentous developments that occurred long before the curtain rose. Moreover, like Agatha Christie's *Murder on the Orient Express*, this crime may have had more than one perpetrator, so that we shall need to sort out ringleaders from accomplices. Finally, I need to make clear at the outset that I am not yet sure that I have solved the mystery. In that sense, this chapter represents work-in-progress. I have a prime suspect that I am prepared to indict, but the evidence is not yet strong enough to convict. . . .

Theories and Measures of Social Capital

Allow me to set the scene by saying a word or two about my own recent work.[1] Several years ago I conducted research on the arcane topic of local government in Italy (Putnam 1993). That study concluded that the performance of government and other social institutions is powerfully influenced by citizen engagement in community affairs, or what (following Coleman 1990) I termed *social capital.* I am now seeking to apply that set of ideas and insights to the urgent problems of contemporary American public life.

By "social capital," I mean features of social life — networks, norms, and trust — that enable participants to act together more effectively to pursue shared objectives. Whether or not their shared goals are praiseworthy is, of course, entirely another matter. To the extent that the norms, networks, and trust link substantial sectors of the community and span underlying social

Source: PS: Political Science & Politics, vol. 38, no. 4 (December 1995).

Editors' Note: This chapter provides an excellent overview of many of Putnam's findings about declining social capital and its causes. A much fuller description, with many additional findings and some amendments and extensions of the argument, can be found in Robert Putnam, *Bowling Alone: The Collapse and Revival of American Community* (New York: Simon & Schuster, 2000).

cleavages—to the extent that the social capital is of a "bridging" sort—then the enhanced cooperation is likely to serve broader interests and to be widely welcomed. On the other hand, groups like the Michigan militia or youth gangs also embody a kind of social capital, for these networks and norms, too, enable members to cooperate more effectively, albeit to the detriment of the wider community.

Social capital, in short, refers to social connections and the attendant norms and trust. Who benefits from these connections, norms, and trust—the individual, the wider community, or some faction within the community—must be determined empirically, not definitionally.[2] Sorting out the multiple effects of different forms of social capital is clearly a crucial task, although it is not one that I can address here. For present purposes, I am concerned with forms of social capital that, generally speaking, serve civic ends.

Social capital in this sense is closely related to political participation in the conventional sense, but these terms are not synonymous. Political participation refers to our relations with political institutions. Social capital refers to our relations with one another. Sending a check to a PAC is an act of political participation, but it does not embody or create social capital. Bowling in a league or having coffee with a friend embodies and creates social capital, though these are not acts of political participation. (A grassroots political movement or a traditional urban machine is a social capital-intensive form of political participation.) I use the term "civic engagement" to refer to people's connections with the life of their communities, not merely with politics. Civic engagement is correlated with political participation in a narrower sense, but whether they move in lock-step is an empirical question, not a logical certitude Some forms of individualized political participation, such as check-writing, for example, might be rising at the same time that social connectedness was on the wane. Similarly, although social trust—trust in other people—and political trust—trust in political authorities—might be empirically related, they are logically quite distinct. I might well trust my neighbors without trusting city hall, or vice versa.

The theory of social capital presumes that, generally speaking, the more we connect with other people, the more we trust them, and vice versa. At least in the contexts I have so far explored, this presumption generally turns out to be true: social trust and civic engagement are strongly correlated. That is, with or without controls for education, age, income, race, gender, and so on, people who join are people who trust.[3] Moreover, this is true across different countries and across different states in the United States, as well as across individuals, and it is true of all sorts of groups.[4] Sorting out which way causation flows— whether joining causes trusting or trusting causes joining—is complicated both theoretically and methodologically, although John Brehm and Wendy Rahn (1995) report evidence that the causation flows mainly from joining to trusting. Be that as it may, civic connections and social trust move together. Which way are they moving?

Bowling Alone: Trends in Civic Engagement

Evidence from a number of independent sources strongly suggests that America's stock of social capital has been shrinking for more than a quarter century.

- Membership records of such diverse organizations as the PTA, the Elks club, the League of Women Voters, the Red Cross, labor unions, and even bowling leagues show that participation in many conventional voluntary associations has declined by roughly 25 percent to 50 percent over the last two to three decades (Putnam 1995b, 1996).
- Surveys of the time budgets of average Americans in 1965, 1975, and 1985, in which national samples of men and women recorded every single activity undertaken during the course of a day, imply that the time we spend on informal socializing and visiting is down (perhaps by one quarter) since 1965, and that the time we devote to clubs and organizations is down even more sharply (probably by roughly half) over this period.[5]
- While Americans' interest in politics has been stable or even growing over the last three decades, and some forms of participation that require moving a pen, such as signing petitions and writing checks, have increased significantly, many measures of collective participation have fallen sharply (Rosenstone and Hansen 1993; Putnam 1996), including attending a rally or speech (off 36 percent between 1973 and 1993), attending a meeting on town or school affairs (off 39 percent), or working for a political party (off 56 percent).
- Evidence from the General Social Survey demonstrates, at all levels of education and among both men and women, a drop of roughly one-quarter in group membership since 1974 and a drop of roughly one-third in social trust since 1972.[6] Moreover, as Figure 3-1 illustrates, slumping membership has afflicted all sorts of groups, from sports clubs and professional associations to literary discussion groups and labor unions.[7] Only nationality groups, hobby and garden clubs, and the catch-all category of "other" seem to have resisted the ebbing tide. Furthermore, Gallup polls report that church attendance fell by roughly 15 percent during the 1960s and has remained at that lower level ever since, while data from the National Opinion Research Center suggest that the decline continued during the 1970s and 1980s and by now amounts to roughly 30 percent (Putnam 1996).

Each of these approaches to the problem of measuring trends in civic engagement has advantages and drawbacks. Membership records offer long-term coverage and reasonable precision, but they may underrepresent newer, more vibrant organizations. Time budgets capture real investments of time and energy in both formal and informal settings, not merely nominal membership, but the available data are episodic and drawn from relatively small samples that are not entirely comparable across time. Surveys are more comprehensive in their

Figure 3-1   Membership Trends (1974–1994) by Type of Group
(Education Controlled)

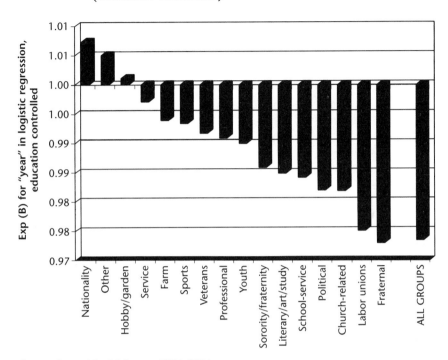

Source: General Social Survey, 1974–1994.

coverage of various types of groups, but (apart from church attendance) comparable trend data are available only since the mid-1970s, a decade or more after the putative downturn began, so they may understate the full decline. No single source is perfect for testing the hypothesized decline in social connectedness, although the consistency across different measuring rods is striking.

A fuller audit of American social capital would need to account for apparent counter-trends.[8] Some observers believe, for example, that support groups and neighborhood watch groups are proliferating, and few deny that the last several decades have witnessed explosive growth in interest groups represented in Washington. The growth of "mailing list" organizations, like the American Association of Retired People or the Sierra Club, although highly significant in political (and commercial) terms, is not really a counter-example to the supposed decline in social connectedness, however, since these are not really associations in which members meet one another. Their members' ties are to common symbols and ideologies, but not to each other. These organizations are sufficiently different from classical "secondary" associations as to deserve a new rubric—perhaps "tertiary" associations. Similarly, although most secondary associations are not-for-profit, most prominent nonprofits (from Harvard University to the Metropolitan Opera) are bureaucracies, not secondary associations, so the growth of the "Third Sector" is not tantamount to a growth in social connectedness. With due regard to various kinds of counter-evidence, I believe that the weight of the available evidence confirms that Americans today are significantly less engaged with their communities than was true a generation ago.

Of course, lots of civic activity is still visible in our communities. American civil society is not moribund. Indeed, evidence suggests that America still outranks many other countries in the degree of our community involvement and social trust (Putnam 1996). But if we compare ourselves, not with other countries but with our parents, the best available evidence suggests that we are less connected with one another.

This prologue poses a number of important questions that merit further debate:

- Is it true that America's stock of social capital has diminished?
- Does it matter?
- What can we do about it?

The answer to the first two questions is, I believe, "yes," but I cannot address them further in this setting. Answering the third question—which ultimately concerns me most—depends, at least in part, on first understanding the *causes* of the strange malady afflicting American civic life. This is the mystery I seek to unravel here: Why, beginning in the 1960s and accelerating in the 1970s and 1980s, did the fabric of American community life begin to fray? Why are more Americans bowling alone?

Explaining the Erosion of Social Capital

Many possible answers have been suggested for this puzzle:

- Busyness and time pressure
- Economic hard times (or, according to alternative theories, material affluence)
- Residential mobility
- Suburbanization
- The movement of women into the paid labor force and the stresses of two-career families
- Disruption of marriage and family ties
- Changes in the structure of the American economy, such as the rise of chain stores, branch firms, and the service sector
- The Sixties (most of which actually happened in the Seventies), including
  —Vietnam, Watergate, and disillusion with public life
  —The cultural revolt against authority (sex, drugs, and so on)

- Growth of the welfare state
- The civil rights revolution
- Television, the electronic revolution, and other technological changes

Most respectable mystery writers would hesitate to tally up this many plausible suspects, no matter how energetic the fictional detective. I am not yet in a position to address all these theories—certainly not in any definitive form—but we must begin to winnow the list. To be sure, a social trend as pervasive as the one we are investigating probably has multiple causes, so our task is to assess the relative importance of such factors as these.

A solution, even a partial one, to our mystery must pass several tests.

Is the proposed explanatory factor correlated with trust and civic engagement? If not, it is difficult to see why that factor should even be placed in the lineup. For example, many women have entered the paid labor force during the period in question, but if working women turned out to be more engaged in community life than housewives, it would be harder to attribute the downturn in community organizations to the rise of two-career families.

Is the correlation spurious? If parents, for example, were more likely to be joiners than childless people, that might be an important clue. However, if the correlation between parental status and civic engagement turned out to be entirely spurious, due to the effects of (say) age, we would have to remove the declining birth rate from our list of suspects.

Is the proposed explanatory factor changing in the relevant way? Suppose, for instance, that people who often move have shallower community roots. That could be an important part of the answer to our mystery *only if* residential mobility itself had risen during this period.

Is the proposed explanatory factor vulnerable to the claim that it might be the result of civic disengagement, not the cause? For example, even if newspaper readership were closely correlated with civic engagement across individuals and across time, we would need to weigh the possibility that reduced newspaper circulation is the result (not the cause) of disengagement.

Against that set of benchmarks, let us consider various potential influences on social capital formation.

Education

Human capital and social capital are closely related, for education has a very powerful effect on trust and associational membership, as well as many other forms of social and political participation. Education is by far the strongest correlate that I have discovered of civic engagement in all its forms,

Figure 3-2   Social Trust and Group Membership by Years of Education

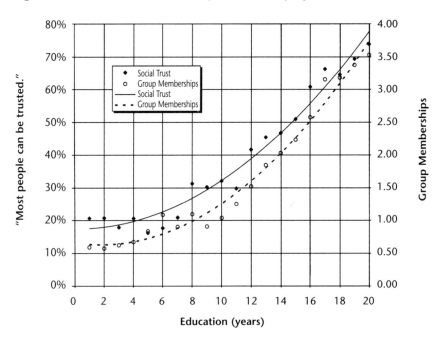

Source: General Social Survey, 1972–1994.

including social trust and membership in many different types of groups.[9] In fact, as Figure 3-2 illustrates, the relationship between education and civic engagement is a curvilinear one of increasing returns. The last two years of college make twice as much difference to trust and group membership as the first two years of high school. The four years of education between 14 and 18 total years have *ten times more impact* on trust and membership than the first four years of formal education. The same basic pattern applies to both men and women, and to all races and generations. Education, in short, is an extremely powerful predictor of civic engagement.

Sorting out just why education has such a massive effect on social connectedness would require a book, not a mere chapter.[10] Education is in part a proxy for social class and economic differences, but when income, social status, and education are used together to predict trust and group membership, education continues to be the primary influence. (Income and satisfaction with one's personal financial situation both have a significant independent effect.) In short, highly educated people are much more likely to be joiners and trusters, partly because they are better off economically, but mostly because of the skills, resources, and inclinations that were imparted to them at home and in school.

It is widely recognized that Americans today are better educated than our parents and grandparents. It is less often appreciated how massively and rapidly this trend has transformed the educational composition of the adult population during just the last two decades. Since 1972, the proportion of all adults with fewer than 12 years of education has been cut in half, falling from 40 percent to 18 percent, while the proportion with more than 12 years has nearly doubled, rising from 28 percent to 50 percent, as the generation of Americans educated around the turn of this century (most of whom did not finish high school) passed from the scene and were replaced by the baby boomers and their successors (most of whom attended college).

Thus, education boosts civic engagement sharply, and educational levels have risen massively. Unfortunately, these two undeniable facts only deepen our central mystery. By itself, the rise in educational levels should have *increased* social capital during the last 20 years by 15–20 percent, even assuming that the effects of education were merely linear. (Taking account of the curvilinear effect in Figure 3-2, the rise in trusting and joining should have been even greater, as Americans moved up the accelerating curve.) By contrast, however, the actual GSS figures show a net *decline* since the early 1970s of roughly the same magnitude (trust by about 20–25 percent, memberships by about 15–20 percent). The relative declines in social capital are similar *within* each educational category—roughly 25 percent in group memberships and roughly 30 percent in social trust since the early 1970s, and probably even more since the early 1960s.

Thus, this first investigative foray leaves us more mystified than before. We may nevertheless draw two useful conclusions from these findings, one methodological and one substantive:

1. Since education has such a powerful effect on civic engagement and social trust, we need to take account of educational differences in our exploration of other possible factors, in order to be sure that we do not confuse the consequences of education with the possible effects of other variables.[11]

2. Whatever forces lie behind the slump in civic engagement and social trust, those forces have affected all levels in American society.[12] Social capital has eroded among the one in every twelve Americans who have enjoyed the advantages (material and intellectual) of graduate study; it has eroded among the one in every eight Americans who did not even make it into high school; and it has eroded among all the strata in between. The mysterious disengagement of the last quarter century seems to have afflicted all echelons of our society.

Pressures of Time and Money

Americans certainly *feel* busier now than a generation ago: the proportion of us who report feeling "always rushed" jumped by half between the mid-1960s and the mid-1990s (Robinson and Godbey 1995). Probably the most obvious suspect behind our tendency to drop out of community affairs is pervasive busyness. And lurking nearby in the shadows are those endemic economic pressures so much discussed nowadays—job insecurity and declining real wages, especially among the lower two-thirds of the income distribution.

Yet, however culpable busyness and economic insecurity may appear at first glance, it is hard to find any incriminating evidence. In fact, the balance of the evidence argues that pressures of time and money are apparently *not* important contributors to the puzzle we seek to solve.

In the first place, time budget studies do *not* confirm the thesis that Americans are, on average, working longer than a generation ago. On the contrary, Robinson and Godbey (1995) report a five-hour per week *gain* in free time for the average American between 1965 and 1985, due partly to reduced time spent on housework and partly to earlier retirement. Their claim that Americans have more leisure time now than several decades ago is, to be sure, contested by other observers. Schor (1991), for example, reports evidence that our work hours are lengthening, especially for women. Whatever the resolution of that controversy, however, the thesis that attributes civic disengagement to longer workdays is rendered much less plausible by looking at the correlation between work hours, on the one hand, and social trust and group membership, on the other.

The available evidence strongly suggests that, in fact, long hours on the job are *not* associated with lessened involvement in civic life or reduced social trust. Quite the reverse: results from the General Social Survey show that employed people belong to somewhat *more* groups than those outside the paid labor force. Even more striking is the fact that among workers, longer hours are linked to *more* civic engagement, not less.[13] This surprising discovery is fully consistent with evidence from the time budget studies. Robinson (1990a) reports that, unsurprisingly, people who spend more time at work do feel more rushed, and these harried souls do spend less time eating, sleeping, reading books, engaging in hobbies, and just doing nothing. Compared to the rest of the population, they also spend a lot less time watching television—almost 30 percent less. However, they do *not* spend less time on organizational activity. In short, those who work longer forego "Nightline," but not the Kiwanis club; "ER," but not the Red Cross.

I do not conclude from the positive correlation between group membership and work hours that working longer actually *causes* greater civic involvement—there are too many uncontrolled variables here for that—but merely that hard work does not *prevent* civic engagement. Moreover, the nationwide falloff in joining and trusting is perfectly mirrored among full-time workers, among part-time workers, and among those outside the paid labor force. So if people are dropping out of community life, long hours do not seem to be the reason.

If time pressure is not the culprit we seek, how about financial pressures? It is true that people with lower incomes and those who feel financially strapped are less engaged in community life and less trusting than those who are better off, even holding education constant. On the other hand, the downtrends in social trust and civic engagement are entirely visible at all levels in the income hierarchy, with no sign whatever that they are concentrated among those who have borne the brunt of the economic distress of the last two decades. Quite the contrary, the declines in engagement and trust are actually somewhat greater among the more affluent segments of the American public than among the poor and middle-income wage-earners. Furthermore, controlling for both real income and financial satisfaction does little to attenuate the fall in civic engagement and social trust. In short, neither objective nor subjective economic well-being has inoculated Americans against the virus of civic disengagement; if anything, affluence has slightly exacerbated the problem.

I cannot absolutely rule out the possibility that some part of the erosion of social capital in recent years might be linked to a more generalized sense of economic insecurity that may have affected all Americans, nor do I argue that economic distress *never* causes disengagement. Studies of the unemployed during and after the Great Depression (Jahoda, Lazarsfeld, and Zeisel 1933; Ginzberg 1943; Wilcock and Franke 1963) have described a tendency for them to disengage from community life. However, the basic patterns in the contemporary evidence are inconsistent with any simple economic explanation for our central puzzle. Pressures of time and money may be a part of the backdrop, but neither can be a principal culprit.[14]

Mobility and Suburbanization

Many studies have found that residential stability and such related phenomena as homeownership are associated with greater civic engagement. At an earlier stage in this investigation (Putnam 1995b, 30), I observed that "mobility, like frequent repotting of plants, tends to disrupt root systems, and it takes time for an uprooted individual to put down new roots." I must now report, however, that further inquiry fully exonerates residential mobility from any responsibility for our fading civic engagement. Data from the U.S. Bureau of the Census 1995 (and earlier years) show that rates of residential mobility have been remarkably constant over the last half century. In fact, to the extent that there has been any change at all, both long-distance and short-distance mobility have *declined* over the last five decades. During the 1950s, 20 percent of Americans changed residence each year and 6.9 percent annually moved across county borders; during the 1990s, the comparable figures are 17 percent and 6.6 percent. Americans, in short, are today slightly *more* rooted residentially than a generation ago. If the verdict on the economic distress interpretation had to be nuanced, the verdict on mobility is unequivocal. This theory is simply wrong.

But if moving itself has not eroded our social capital, what about the possibility that we have moved to places—especially the suburbs—that are less congenial to social connectedness? To test this theory, we must first examine the correlation between place of residence and social capital. In fact, social connectedness does differ by community type, but the differences turn out to be modest and in directions that are inconsistent with the theory.

Controlling for such demographic characteristics as education, age, income, work status, and race, citizens of the nation's 12 largest metropolitan areas (particularly their central cities, but also their suburbs) are roughly 10 percent less trusting and report 10–20 percent fewer group memberships than residents of other cities and towns (and their suburbs). Meanwhile, residents of very small towns and rural areas are (in accord with some hoary stereotypes) slightly more trusting and civically engaged than other Americans. Unsurprisingly, the prominence of different *types* of groups does vary significantly by location: major cities have more political and nationality clubs; smaller cities more fraternal, service, hobby, veterans, and church groups; and rural areas more agricultural organizations. But overall rates of associational memberships are not very different.

Moreover, this pallid pattern cannot account for our central puzzle. In the first place, there is virtually no correlation between gains in population and losses in social capital, either across states or across localities of different sizes. Even taking into account the educational and social backgrounds of those who have moved there, the suburbs have faintly higher levels of trust and civic engagement than their respective central cities, a fact that *ceteris paribus* should have produced growth, not decay, in social capital over the last generation. The central point, however, is that the downtrends in trusting and joining are virtually identically everywhere — in cities, big and small, in suburbs, in small towns, and in the countryside.

There are, of course, suburbs and suburbs. Evanston is not Levittown is not Sun City. The evidence available does not allow us to determine whether different types of suburban living have different effects on civic connections and social trust. However, these data do rule out the thesis that suburbanization per se has caused the erosion of America's social capital. In this respect, size of place is like mobility — a cross-sectional correlate that cannot explain our trend. Both where we live and how long we've lived there matter for social capital, but neither explains why it is eroding everywhere.

The Changing Role of Women

Most of our mothers were housewives, and most of them invested heavily in social capital formation — a jargony way of referring to untold, unpaid hours in church suppers, PTA meetings, neighborhood coffee klatches, and visits to friends and relatives. The movement of women out of the home and into the paid labor force is probably the most portentous social change of the last half century. However welcome and overdue the feminist revolution may be, it is hard to believe that it has had no impact on social connectedness. Could this be the primary reason for the decline of social capital over the last generation?

Some patterns in the available survey evidence seem to support this claim. All things considered, women belong to somewhat fewer voluntary associations than men (Edwards, Edwards, and Watts 1984 and the sources cited there; more recent GSS data confirm this finding). On the other hand, time budget studies suggest that women spend more time on those groups and more time in informal social connecting than men (Robinson and Godbey 1995). Although the absolute declines in joining and trusting are approximately equivalent among men and women, the relative declines are somewhat greater among women. Controlling for education, memberships among men have declined at a rate of about 10–15 percent a decade, compared to about 20–25 percent a decade for women. The time budget data, too, strongly suggest that the decline in organizational involvement in recent years is concentrated among women. These sorts of facts, coupled with the obvious transformation in the professional role of women over this same period, led me in previous work to suppose that the emergence of two-career families might be the most important single factor in the erosion of social capital.

As we saw earlier, however, work status itself seems to have little net impact on group membership or on trust. Housewives belong to different types of groups than do working women (more PTAs, for example, and fewer professional associations), but in the aggregate working women are actually members of slightly more voluntary associations.[15] Moreover, the overall declines in civic engagement are somewhat greater among housewives than among employed women. Comparison of time budget data between 1965 and 1985 (Robinson and Godbey 1995) seems to show that employed women as a group are actually spending more time on organizations than before, while nonemployed women are spending less. This same study suggests that the major decline in informal socializing since 1965 has also been concentrated among nonemployed women. The central fact, of course, is that the overall trends are down for all categories of women (and for men, too—even bachelors), but the figures suggest that women who work full-time actually may have been more resistant to the slump than those who do not.

Thus, although women appear to have borne a disproportionate share of the decline in civic engagement over the last two decades, it is not easy to find any micro-level data that tie that fact directly to their entry into the labor force. It is hard to control for selection bias in these data, of course, because women who have chosen to enter the workforce doubtless differ in many respects from women who have chosen to stay home. Perhaps one reason that community involvement appears to be rising among working women and declining among housewives is that precisely the sort of women who, in an earlier era, were most involved with their communities have been disproportionately likely to enter the workforce, thus simultaneously lowering the average level of civic engagement among the remaining homemakers and raising the average among women in the workplace. Obviously, we have not been running a great national controlled experiment on the effects of work on women's civic engagement, and in any event the patterns in the data are not entirely clear. Contrary to my own earlier speculations, however, I can find little evidence to support the hypothesis that the movement of women into the workplace over the last generation has played a major role in the reduction of social connectedness and civic engagement. On the other hand, I have no clear alternative explanation for the fact that the relative declines are greater among women than among men. Since this evidence is at best circumstantial, perhaps the best interim judgment here is the famous Scots verdict: not proven.

Marriage and Family

Another widely discussed social trend that more or less coincides with the downturn in civic engagement is the breakdown of the traditional family unit—mom, dad, and kids. Since the family itself is, by some accounts, a key form of social capital, perhaps its eclipse is part of the explanation for the reduction in joining and trusting in the wider community. What does the evidence show?

First of all, evidence of the loosening of family bonds is unequivocal. In addition to the century-long increase in divorce rates (which accelerated in the mid-1960s to the mid-1970s and then leveled off), and the more recent increase in single-parent families, the incidence of one-person households has more than doubled since 1950, in part because of the rising number of widows living alone (Caplow, Bahr, Modell, and Chadwick 1991, 47, 106, 113). The net effect of all these changes, as reflected in the General Social Survey, is that the proportion of all American adults who are currently unmarried climbed from 28 percent in 1974 to 48 percent in 1994.

Second, married men and women do rank somewhat higher on both our measures of social capital. That is, controlling for education, age, race, and so on, single people—both men and women, divorced, separated, and never-married—are significantly less trusting and less engaged civically than married people.[16] Roughly speaking, married men and women are about a third more trusting and belong to about 15–25 percent more groups than comparable single men and women. (Widows and widowers are more like married people than single people in this comparison.)

In short, successful marriage (especially if the family unit includes children) is statistically associated with greater social trust and civic engagement. Thus, some part of the decline in both trust and membership is tied to the decline in marriage. To be sure, the direction of causality behind this correlation may be complicated, since it is conceivable that loners and paranoids are harder to live with. If so, divorce may in some degree be the consequence, not the cause, of lower social capital. Probably the most reasonable summary of these arrays of data, however, is that the decline in successful marriage is a significant, though modest part of the reason for declining trust and lower group membership. On the other hand, changes in family structure cannot be a major part of our story, since the overall declines in joining and trusting are substantial even among the happily married. My own verdict (based in part on additional evidence to be introduced later) is that the disintegration of marriage is probably an accessory to the crime, but not the major villain of the piece.

The Rise of the Welfare State

Circumstantial evidence, particularly the timing of the downturn in social connectedness, has suggested to some observers (for example, Fukuyama 1995, 313–314) that an important cause—perhaps even *the* cause—of civic disengagement is big government and the growth of the welfare state. By "crowding out" private initiative, it is argued, state intervention has subverted civil society. This is a much larger topic than I can address in detail here, but a word or two may be appropriate.

On the one hand, some government policies have almost certainly had the effect of destroying social capital. For example, the so-called "slum clearance" policies of the 1950s and 1960s replaced physical capital, but destroyed social capital, by disrupting existing community ties. It is also conceivable that certain social expenditures and tax policies may have created disincentives for civic-minded philanthropy. On the other hand, it is much harder to see which government policies might be responsible for the decline in bowling leagues and literary clubs.

One empirical approach to this issue is to examine differences in civic engagement and public policy across different political jurisdictions to see whether swollen government leads to shriveled social capital. Among the U.S. states, however, differences in social capital appear essentially uncorrelated with various measures of welfare spending or government size.[17] Citizens in free-spending states are no less trusting or engaged than citizens in frugal ones. Cross-national comparison can also shed light on this question. Among 19 OECD countries for which data on social trust and group membership are available from the 1990–1991 World Values Survey, these indicators of social capital are, if anything, *positively* correlated with the size of the state.[18] This simple bivariate analysis, of course, cannot tell us whether social connectedness encourages welfare spending, whether the welfare state fosters civic engagement, or whether both are the result of some other unmeasured factor(s). Sorting out the underlying causal connections would require much more thorough analysis. However, even this simple finding is not easily reconciled with the notion that big government undermines social capital.

Race and the Civil Rights Revolution

Race is such an absolutely fundamental feature of American social history that nearly every other feature of our society is connected to it in some way. Thus, it seems intuitively plausible that race might somehow have played a role in the erosion of social capital over the last generation. In fact, some observers (both black and white) have noted that the decline in social connectedness and social trust began just after the greatest successes of the civil rights revolution of the 1960s. To some, that coincidence has suggested the possibility of a kind of sociological "white flight," as legal desegregation of civic life led whites to withdraw from community associations.

Like the theory about the welfare state, this racial interpretation of the destruction of social capital is highly controversial and can hardly be settled within the compass of these brief remarks. Nevertheless, the basic facts are these.

First, racial differences in associational membership are not large. At least until the 1980s, controlling for educational and income differences, blacks actually belonged to more associations on average than whites, essentially because they were more likely than comparably situated whites to belong to religious and ethnic organizations and no less likely to belong to any other type of group.[19] On the other hand, racial differences in social trust are very large indeed, even taking into account differences in education, income, and so on. On average, during the 1972–1994 period, controlling for educational differences, about 17 percent of blacks endorsed the view that "most people can be trusted," as compared to about 45 percent of whites, and about 27 percent of respondents of other races.[20] These racial differences in social trust, of course, reflect not collective paranoia, but real experiences over many generations.

Second, the erosion of social capital has affected all races. In fact, during the 1980s the downturns in both joining and trusting were even greater among blacks (and other racial minorities) than among the white majority. This fact is inconsistent with the thesis that "white flight" is a significant cause of civic disengagement, since black Americans have been dropping out of religious and civic organizations at least as rapidly as white Americans. Even more important, the pace of disengagement among whites has been uncorrelated with racial intolerance or support for segregation. Avowedly racist or segregationist whites have been no quicker to drop out of community organizations during this period than more tolerant whites. Figure 3-3 presents illustrative evidence, its three parallel slopes showing that the decline in group membership is essentially identical among whites who favor segregation, whites who oppose it, and blacks.[21]

This evidence is far from conclusive, of course, but it does shift the burden of proof onto those who believe that racism is a primary explanation for growing civic disengagement over the last quarter century, however virulent racism continues to be in American society.[22] This evidence also suggests that reversing the civil rights gains of the last 30 years would do nothing to reverse the social capital losses.

Generational Effects

Our efforts thus far to localize the sources of civic disengagement have been singularly unfruitful. The downtrends are uniform across the major categories of American society—among men and among women; in central cities, in suburbs, and in small towns; among the wealthy, the poor, and the middle class; among blacks, whites, and other ethnic groups; in the North, in the South, on both coasts and in the heartland. One notable exception to this uniformity, however, involves age. In all our statistical analyses, age is second only to education as a predictor of all forms of civic engagement and trust. Older people belong to more organizations than young people, and they are less misanthropic. Older Ameri-

Figure 3-3   Group Membership by Race and Racism, 1974–1994
(Education Controlled)

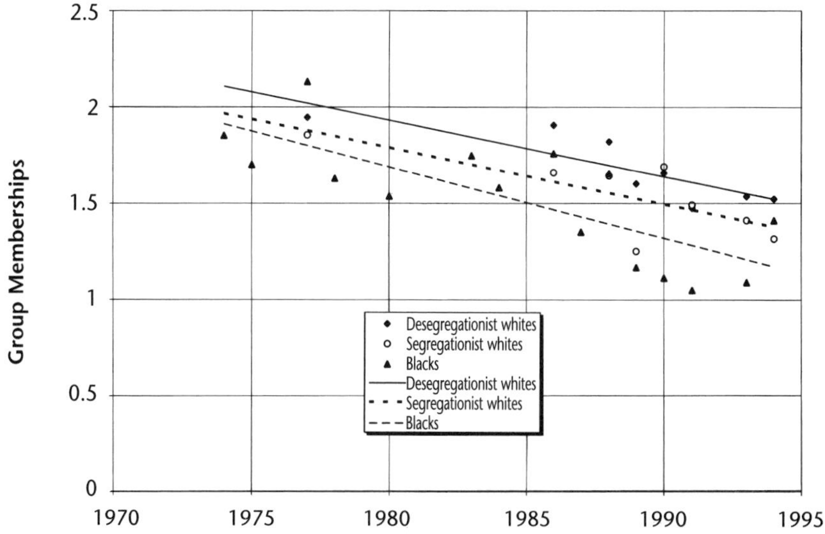

Source: General Social Survey, 1974–1994.

Note: Equal weighting of three educational categories. White segregationism measured by support for racial segregation in social club.

cans also vote more often and read newspapers more frequently, two other forms of civic engagement closely correlated with joining and trusting.

Figure 3-4 shows the basic pattern—civic involvement appears to rise more or less steadily from early adulthood toward a plateau in middle age, from which it declines only late in life. This humpback pattern, familiar from many analyses of social participation, including time-budget studies (Robinson and Godbey 1995), seems naturally to represent the arc of life's engagements. Most observers have interpreted this pattern as a life cycle phenomenon, and so, at first, did I.

Evidence from the General Social Survey (GSS) enables us to follow individual cohorts as they age. If the rising lines in Figure 3-4 represent deepening civic engagement with age, then we should be able to track this same deepening engagement as we follow, for example, the first of the baby boomers—born in 1947—as they aged from 25 in 1972 (the first year of the GSS) to 47 in 1994 (the latest year available). Startlingly, however, such an analysis, repeated for successive birth cohorts, produces virtually no evidence of such life cycle changes in civic engagement. In fact, as various generations moved through the period between 1972 and 1994, their levels of trust and membership more often fell than rose, reflecting a more or less simultaneous decline in civic engagement

Figure 3-4   Civic Engagement by Age (Education Controlled)

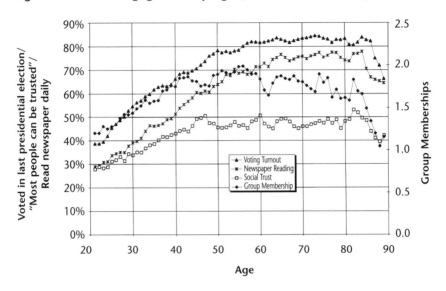

Source: General Social Survey, 1972–1994.

Note: Respondents aged 21–89. Three-year moving averages. Equal weighting of three educational categories.

among young and old alike, particularly during the second half of the 1980s. But that downtrend obviously cannot explain why, throughout the period, older Americans were always more trusting and engaged. In fact, the only reliable life cycle effect visible in these data is a withdrawal from civic engagement very late in life, as we move through our 80s.

The central paradox posed by these patterns is this: Older people are consistently more engaged and trusting than younger people, yet we do not become more engaged and trusting as we age. What's going on here?

Time and age are notoriously ambiguous in their effects on social behavior. Social scientists have learned to distinguish three contrasting phenomena:

1. *Life-cycle effects* represent differences attributable to stage of life. In this case individuals change as they age, but since the effects of aging are, in the aggregate, neatly balanced by the "demographic metabolism" of births and deaths, life cycle effects produce no aggregate change. Everyone's close focus eyesight worsens as we age, but the aggregate demand for reading glasses changes little.
2. *Period effects* affect all people who live through a given era, regardless of their age.[23] Period effects can produce both individual and aggregate change, often quickly and enduringly, without any age-related differ-

ences. The sharp drop in trust in government between 1965 and 1975, for example, was almost entirely this sort of period effect, as Americans of all ages changed their minds about their leaders' trustworthiness. Similarly, as just noted, a modest portion of the decline in social capital during the 1980s appears to be a period effect.

3. *Generational effects,* as described in Karl Mannheim's classic essay on "The Problem of Generations," represent the fact that "[i]ndividuals who belong to the same generation, who share the same year of birth, are endowed, to that extent, with a common location in the historical dimension of the social process" (Mannheim 1952, 290). Like life cycle effects (and unlike typical period effects), generational effects show up as disparities among age groups at a single point in time, but like period effects (and unlike life cycle effects) generational effects produce real social change, as successive generations, enduringly "imprinted" with divergent outlooks, enter and leave the population. In pure generational effects, no individual ever changes, but society does.

At least since the landmark essay by Converse (1976), social scientists have recognized that to sort out life cycle, period, and generational effects requires sensitivity to a priori plausibility, "side knowledge," and parsimony, not merely good data and sophisticated math. In effect, cohort analysis inevitably involves more unknowns than equations. With some common sense, some knowledge of history, and some use of Ockham's razor, however, it is possible to exclude some alternatives and focus on more plausible interpretations.

Returning to our conundrum, how could older people today be more engaged and trusting, if they did not become more engaged and trusting as they aged? The key to this paradox, as David Butler and Donald Stokes (1974) observed in another context, is to ask, not *how old people are,* but *when they were young.* Figure 3-5 addresses this reformulated question, displaying various measures of civic engagement according to the respondents' year of birth.[24] Figure 3-5 includes data on voting from the National Election Studies (NES), since Miller 1992b and Miller and Shanks 1996 have drawn on that data to demonstrate powerful generational effects on turnout, and it is instructive to see how parallel are the patterns that they discovered for voting turnout and the patterns for civic engagement that concern us here.[25] The figure also includes data on social trust from the National Election Studies, which will prove useful in parsing generational, life cycle, and period interpretations.

The Long Civic Generation

In effect, Figure 3-5 lines up Americans from left to right according to their date of birth, beginning with those born in the last third of the nineteenth century and continuing across to the generation of their great-grandchildren, born in the last third of the twentieth century. As we begin moving along this queue

Figure 3-5 Social Capital and Civic Engagement by Generation (Education Controlled)

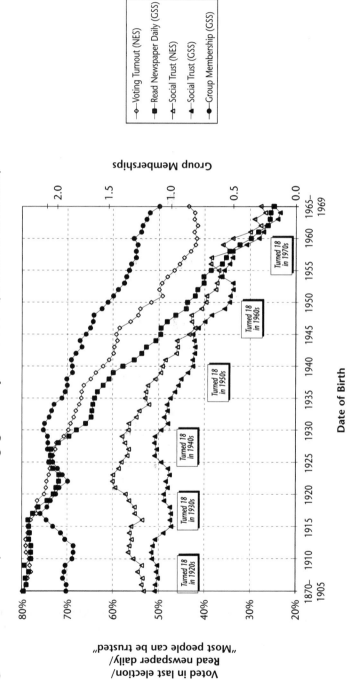

Source: General Social Survey (GSS), 1972–1974, and National Election Studies (NES), 1952–1992.

Note: Respondents aged 25–80. Five-year moving averages. Equal weighting of three educational categories.

from left to right—from those raised around the turn of the century to those raised during the Roaring Twenties, and so on—we find relatively high and unevenly rising levels of civic engagement and social trust. Then rather abruptly however, we encounter signs of reduced community involvement, starting with men and women born in the early 1930s. Remarkably, this downward trend in joining, trusting, voting, and newspaper reading continues almost uninterruptedly for nearly 40 years. The trajectories for the various different indicators of civic engagement are strikingly parallel: each shows a high, sometimes rising plateau for people born and raised during the first third of the century; each shows a turning point in the cohorts born around 1930; and each then shows a more or less constant decline down to the cohorts born during the 1960s.[26]

By any standard, these intergenerational differences are extraordinary. Compare, for example, the generation born in the early 1920s with the generation of their grandchildren born in the late 1960s. Controlling for educational disparities, members of the generation born in the 1920s belong to almost twice as many civic associations as those born in the late 1960s (roughly 1.9 memberships per capita, compared to roughly 1.1 memberships per capita). The grandparents are more than twice as likely to trust other people (50−60 percent compared, compared with 25 percent for the grandchildren). They vote at nearly double the rate of the most recent cohorts (roughly 75 percent compared with 40−45 percent) and they read newspapers almost three times as often (70−80 percent read a paper daily compared with 25−30 percent). And bear in mind that we have found no evidence that the youngest generation will come to match their grandparent's higher levels of civic engagement as they grow older.

Thus, read not as life cycle effects, but rather as generational effects, the age-related patterns in our data suggest a radically different interpretation of our basic puzzle. Deciphered with this key, Figure 3-5 depicts a long "civic" generation, born roughly between 1910 and 1940, a broad group of people substantially more engaged in community affairs and substantially more trusting than those younger than they.[27] The culminating point of this civic generation is the cohort born in 1925−1930, who attended grade school during the Great Depression, spent World War II in high school (or on the battle field), first voted in 1948 or 1952, set up housekeeping in the 1950s, and watched their first television when they were in the late twenties. Since national surveying began, this cohort has been exceptionally civic: voting more, joining more, reading newspapers more, trusting more. As the distinguished sociologist Charles Tilly (born in 1928) said in commenting on an early version of this essay, "we are the last suckers."

To help in interpreting the historical contexts within which these successive generations of Americans matured, Figure 3-5 also indicates the decade within which each cohort came of age. Thus, we can see that each generation who reached adulthood since the 1940s has been less engaged in community affairs than its immediate predecessor.

Further confirmation of this *generational* interpretation comes from a comparison of the two parallel lines that chart responses to an identical question about social trust, posed first in the National Election Studies (mainly between 1964 and 1976) and then in the General Social Survey between 1972 and 1994.[28] If the greater trust expressed by Americans born earlier in the century represented a *life cycle* effect, then the graph from the GSS surveys (conducted when these cohorts were, on average, 10 years older) should have been some distance *above* the NES line. In fact, the GSS line lies about 5–10 percent *below* the NES line. That downward shift almost surely represents a *period* effect that depressed social trust among all cohorts during the 1980s.[29] That downward period effect, however, is substantially more modest than the large generational differences already noted.

In short, the most parsimonious interpretation of the age-related differences in civic engagement is that they represent a powerful reduction in civic engagement among Americans who came of age in the decades after World War II, as well as some modest additional disengagement that affected all cohorts during the 1980s. These patterns hint that being raised after World War II was a quite different experience from being raised before that watershed. It is as though the post-war generations were exposed to some mysterious X-ray that permanently and increasingly rendered them less likely to connect with the community. Whatever that force might have been, *it*—rather than anything that happened during the 1970s and 1980s—accounts for most of the civic disengagement that lies at the core of our mystery.

But if this reinterpretation of our puzzle is correct, why did it take so long for the effects of that mysterious X-ray to become manifest? If the underlying causes of civic disengagement can be traced to the 1940s and 1950s, why did the effects become conspicuous in PTA meetings and Masonic lodges, in the volunteer lists of the Red Cross and the Boy Scouts, and in polling stations and church pews and bowling alleys across the land only during the 1960s, 1970s, and 1980s?

The visible effects of this generational disengagement were delayed for several decades by two important factors:

1. The postwar boom in college enrollments boosted massive numbers of Americans up the sloping curve of civic engagement traced in Figure 3-2. Miller and Shanks (1996) observe that the postwar expansion of educational opportunities "forestalled a cataclysmic drop" in voting turnout, and it had a similar delaying effect on civic disengagement more generally.

2. The full effects of generational developments generally appear several decades after their onset, because it takes that long for a given generation to become numerically dominant in the adult population. Only after the mid-1960s did significant numbers of the "post-civic generation" reach adulthood, supplanting older, more civic cohorts. Figure 3-6 illustrates this generational accounting. The long civic generation (born between 1910 and 1940) reached its zenith in 1960, when it comprised 62 percent of those who chose between John Kennedy and Richard Nixon. By the time that Bill Clinton was elected president in 1992, that cohort's

Figure 3-6   The Rise and Decline of a "Civic" Generation

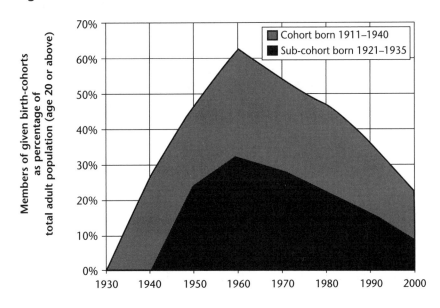

Source: Calculated from U.S. Census Bureau, Current Population Reports.

share in the electorate had been cut precisely in half. Conversely, over the last two decades (from 1974 to 1994) boomers and X-ers (that is, Americans born after 1946) have grown as a fraction of the adult population from 24 percent to 60 percent.

In short, the very decades that have seen a national deterioration in social capital are the same decades during which the numerical dominance of a trusting and civic generation has been replaced by the dominion of "post-civic" cohorts. Moreover, although the long civic generation has enjoyed unprecedented life expectancy, allowing its members to contribute more than their share to American social capital in recent decades, they are now passing from the scene. Even the youngest members of that generation will reach retirement age within the next few years. Thus, a generational analysis leads almost inevitably to the conclusion that the national slump in trust and engagement is likely to continue, regardless of whether the more modest "period effect" depression of the 1980s continues.

More than two decades ago, just as the first signs of disengagement were beginning to appear in American politics, Ithiel de Sola Pool (1973, 818–821) observed that the central issue would be—it was then too soon to judge, as he rightly noted—whether the development represented a temporary change in the weather or a more enduring change in the climate. It now appears that much of the change whose initial signs he spotted did in fact reflect a climatic shift. Moreover, just as the erosion of the ozone layer was detected only many years after the proliferation of the chlorofluorocarbons that caused it, so too the erosion of America's social capital became visible only several decades after the underlying process had begun. Like Minerva's owl that flies at dusk, we come to appreciate how important the long civic generation has been to American community life just as its members are retiring. Unless America experiences a dramatic upward boost in civic engagement (a favorable "period effect") in the next few years, Americans in 2010 will join, trust, and vote even less than we do today.

The Puzzle Reformulated

To say that civic disengagement in contemporary America is in large measure generational merely reformulates our central puzzle. We now know that much of the cause of our lonely bowling probably dates to the 1940s and 1950s, rather than to the 1960s and 1970s. What could have been the mysterious anti-civic "X-ray" that affected Americans who came of age after World War II and whose effects progressively deepened at least into the 1970s?[30]

A number of superficially plausible candidates fail to fit the timing required by this new formulation of our mystery.

- Family instability seems to have an ironclad alibi for what we have now identified as the critical period, for the generational decline in civic engagement began with the children of the maritally stable 1940s and 1950s.[31] The divorce rate in America actually fell after 1945, and the sharpest jump in the divorce rate did not occur until the 1970s, long after the cohorts who show the sharpest declines in civic engagement and social trust had left home. Similarly, working mothers are exonerated by this respecification of our problem, for the plunge in civicness among children of the 1940s, 1950s, and 1960s happened while mom was still at home.
- Our new formulation of the puzzle opens the possibility that the *Zeitgeist* of national unity and patriotism that culminated in 1945 might have reinforced civic-mindedness. On the other hand, it is hard to assign any consistent role to the Cold War and the Bomb, since the anti-civic trend appears to have deepened steadily from the 1940s to the 1970s, in no obvious harmony with the rhythms of world affairs. Nor is it easy to construct an interpretation of Figure 3-5 in which the cultural vicissitudes of "the Sixties" could play a significant role.
- Neither economic adversity nor affluence can easily be tied to the generational decline in civic engagement, since the slump seems to have affected in equal measure those who came of age in the placid Fifties, the booming Sixties, and the busted Seventies.

I have discovered only one prominent suspect against whom circumstantial evidence can be mounted, and in this case, it turns out, some directly incriminating evidence has also turned up. This is not the occasion to lay out the full case for the prosecution, nor to review rebuttal evidence for the defense. However, I want to illustrate the sort of evidence that justifies indictment. The culprit is television.

First, the timing fits. The long civic generation was the last cohort of Americans to grow up without television, for television flashed into American society like lightning in the 1950s. In 1950 barely 10 percent of American homes had television sets, but by 1959 90 percent did, probably the fastest diffusion of a technological innovation ever recorded. The reverberations from this lightning bolt continued for decades, as viewing hours per capita grew by 17–20 percent during the 1960s and by an additional 7–8 percent during the 1970s. In the early years, TV watching was concentrated among the less educated sectors of the population, but during the 1970s the viewing time of the more educated sectors of the population began to converge upward. Television viewing increases with age, particularly upon retirement, but each generation since the introduction of television has begun its life cycle at a higher starting point. By 1995, viewing per TV household was more than 50 percent higher than it had been in the 1950s.[32]

Most studies estimate that the average American now watches roughly four hours per day.[33] Robinson (1990b), using the more conservative time-budget technique for determining how people allocate their time, offers an estimate closer to three hours per day, but concludes that as a primary activity television absorbs 40 percent of the average American's free time, an increase of about one-third since 1965. Moreover, multiple sets have proliferated: by the late 1980s, three quarters of all U.S. homes had more than one set (Comstock 1989), and these numbers too are rising steadily, allowing ever more private viewing. In short, as Robinson and Godbey 1995 conclude, "television is the 800-pound gorilla of leisure time." This massive change in the way Americans spend our days and nights occurred precisely during the years of generational civic disengagement.

Evidence of a link between the arrival of television and the erosion of social connections is, however, not merely circumstantial. The links between civic engagement and television viewing can instructively be compared with the links between civic engagement and newspaper reading. The basic contrast is straightforward: newspaper reading is associated with high social capital, TV viewing with low social capital.

Controlling for education, income, age, race, place of residence, work status, and gender, TV viewing is strongly and negatively related to social trust and group membership, whereas the same correlations with newspaper reading are positive. Figure 3-7 shows that within every educational category, heavy readers are avid joiners, whereas Figure 3-8 shows that heavy viewers are more likely to be loners.[34] Viewing and reading are themselves uncorrelated—some people do lots of both, some do little of either—but Figure 3-9 shows that (controlling for education, as always) "pure readers" (that is, people who watch less TV than aver-

Figure 3-7   Group Membership by Newspaper Readership and Education

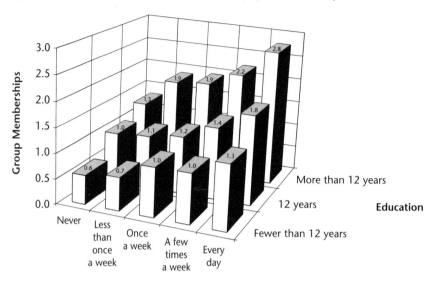

Source: General Social Survey, 1974–1994.

age and read more newspapers than average) belong to 76 percent more civic organizations than "pure viewers." Precisely the same pattern applies to other indicators of civic engagement, including social trust and voting turnout. "Pure readers," for example, are 55 percent more trusting than "pure viewers."[35]

In other words, each hour spent viewing television is associated with less social trust and less group membership, while each hour reading a newspaper is associated with more. An increase in television viewing of the magnitude that the United States has experienced in the last four decades might directly account for as much as one-quarter to one-half of the total drop in social capital, even without taking into account, for example, the indirect effects of television viewing on newspaper readership or the cumulative effects of "life-time" viewing hours.[36]

How might television destroy social capital?

- *Time displacement.* Even though there are only 24 hours in everyone's day, most forms of social and media participation are positively correlated. People who listen to lots of classical music are more likely, not less likely, than others to attend Cubs games. Television is the principal exception to this generalization—the only leisure activity that seems to inhibit participation outside the home. TV watching comes at expense of nearly every

Figure 3-8   Group Membership by Television Viewing and Education

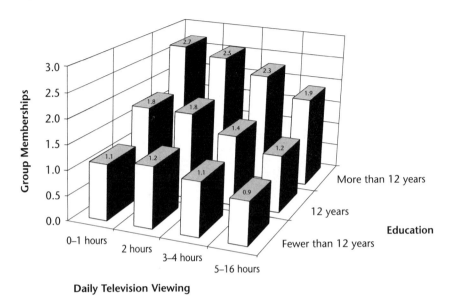

Source: General Social Survey, 1974–1994.

social activity outside the home, especially social gatherings and informal conversations (Comstock et al. 1978; Comstock 1989; Bower 1985; and Robinson and Godbey 1995). TV viewers are homebodies.

Most studies that report a negative correlation between television watching and community involvement (including my Figure 3-8) are ambiguous with respect to causality, because they merely compare different individuals at a single time. However, one important quasi-experimental study of the introduction of television in three Canadian towns (Williams 1986) found the same pattern at the aggregate level across time: a major effect of television's arrival was the reduction in participation in social, recreational, and community activities among people of all ages. In short, television is privatizing our leisure time.

- *Effects on the outlooks of viewers.* An impressive body of literature, gathered under the rubric of the "mean world effect," suggests that heavy watchers of TV are unusually skeptical about the benevolence of other people— overestimating crime rates, for example. This body of literature has generated much debate about the underlying causal patterns, with skeptics suggesting that misanthropy may foster couch-potato behavior rather than the reverse. While awaiting better experimental evidence, however, a

Figure 3-9 Group Membership by Media Usage (Education Controlled)

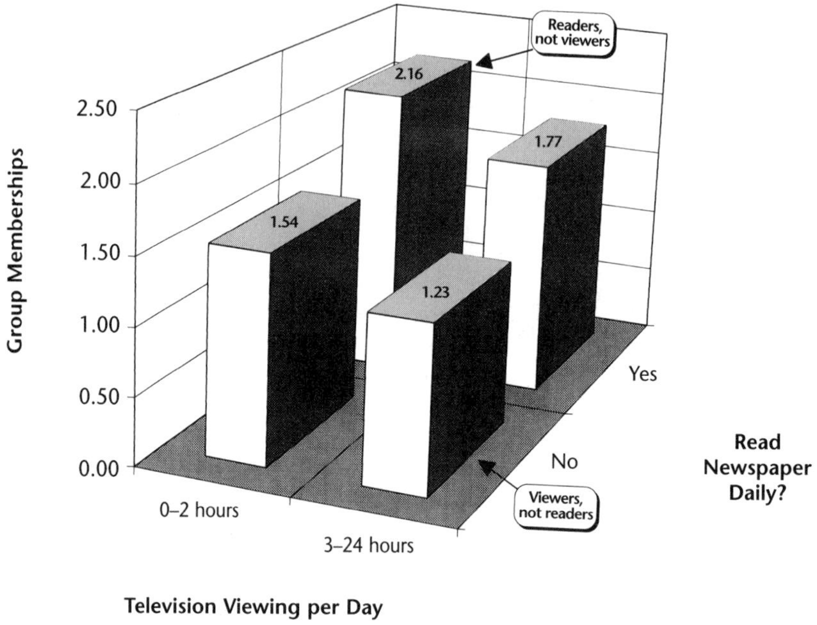

Source: General Social Survey, 1974–1994.

Note: Entries based on three equally weighted educational categories.

reasonable interim judgment is that heavy television watching may well increase pessimism about human nature (Gerbner et al. 1980; Dobb and MacDonald 1979; Hirsch 1980; Hughes 1980; and Comstock 1989, 265–269). Perhaps, too, as social critics have long argued, both the medium and the message have more basic effects on our ways of interacting with the world and with one another. Television may induce passivity, as Postman (1985) has claimed, and it may even change our fundamental physical and social perceptions, as Meyrowitz (1985) has suggested.

- *Effects on children.* TV occupies an extraordinary part of children's lives — consuming about 40 hours per week on average. Viewing is especially high among preadolescents, but it remains high among younger adolescents: time-budget studies (Carnegie Council on Adolescent Development 1993, 5, citing Timmer, Eccles, and O'Brien 1985) suggest that among youngsters aged 9–14 television consumes as much time as *all other discretionary activities combined,* including playing, hobbies, clubs, outdoor activities, informal visiting, and just hanging out. The effects of television on childhood socialization have, of course, been hotly debated

for more than three decades. The most reasonable conclusion from a wel-
ter of sometimes conflicting results appears to be that heavy television
watching probably increases aggressiveness (although perhaps not actual
violence), that it probably reduces school achievement, and that it is statistically associated with "psychosocial malfunctioning," although how
much of this effect is self-selection and how much causal remains much
debated (Condry 1993). The evidence is, as I have said, not yet enough to
convict, but the defense has a lot of explaining to do.

Notes

1. This chapter was presented as the Ithiel de Sola Pool lecture. Introductory and concluding material relating to Pool have been deleted.
2. In this respect I deviate slightly from James Coleman's "functional" definition of
   social capital. See Coleman (1990, 300–321).
3. The results reported in this paragraph and throughout the paper, unless otherwise
   indicated, are derived from the General Social Survey. These exceptionally useful data
   derive from a series of scientific surveys of the adult American population, conducted
   nearly every year since 1972 by the National Opinion Research Center, under the
   direction of James A. Davis and Tom W. Smith. The cumulative sample size is
   approximately 32,000, although the questions on trust and group membership that
   are at the focus of our inquiry have not been asked of all respondents in all years. Our
   measure of trust derives from this question: "Generally speaking, would you say that
   most people can be trusted, or that you can't be too careful in dealing with people";
   for this question, $N = 22,390$. For evidence confirming the power of this simple measure of social trust, see Uslaner (1995). Our measure of group membership derives
   from this question: "Now we would like to know something about the groups or organizations to which individuals belong. Here is a list of various organizations. Could
   you tell me whether or not you are a member of each type?" The list includes fraternal groups, service clubs, veterans' groups, political clubs, labor unions, sports groups,
   youth groups, school service groups, hobby or garden clubs, social fraternities or
   sororities, nationality groups, farm organizations, literary, arts, discussion or study
   groups, professional or academic societies, church-affiliated groups, and any other
   groups. For this question, $N = 19,326$. Neither of these questions, of course, is a perfect measure of social capital. In particular, our measure of multiple memberships
   refers not to total groups, but to total *types* of groups. On the other hand, "noise" in
   data generally depresses observed correlations below the "true" value, so our findings
   are more likely to understate than to exaggerate patterns in the "real world."
4. Across the 35 countries for which data are available from the World Values Survey
   (1990–1991), the correlation between the average number of associational memberships and endorsement of the view that "most people can be trusted" is r = .65. Across
   the 42 states for which adequate samples are available in the General Social Survey
   (1972–1994), the comparable correlation is r = .71. Across individuals in the General
   Social Survey (1972–1994), controlling for education, race, and age, social trust is significantly and separately correlated with membership in political clubs, literary
   groups, sports clubs, hobby and garden clubs, youth groups, school service groups, and
   other associations. The correlation with social trust is insignificant only for veterans
   groups, labor unions, and nationality groups.
5. The 1965 sample, which was limited to nonretired residents of cities between 30,000
   and 280,000 population, was not precisely equivalent to the later national samples, so

appropriate adjustments need to be made to ensure comparability. For the 1965–1975 comparison, see Robinson (1981, 125). For the 1975–1985 comparison (but apparently without adjustment for the 1965 sampling peculiarities), see Cutler (1990). Somewhat smaller declines are reported in Robinson and Godbey (1995), although it is unclear whether they correct for the sampling differences. Additional work to refine these cross-time comparisons is required and is currently underway.

6. Trust in political authorities — and indeed in many social institutions — has also declined sharply over the last three decades, but that is conceptually a distinct trend. As we shall see later, the etiology of the slump in social trust is quite different from the etiology of the decline in political trust.

7. For reasons explained below, Figure 3-1 reports trends for membership in various types of groups, *controlling for* the respondent's education level.

8. Some commentaries on "Bowling Alone" have been careless, however, in reporting apparent membership growth. *The Economist* (1995, 22), for example, celebrated a recent rebound in total membership in parent-teacher organizations, without acknowledging that this rebound is almost entirely attributable to the growing member of children. The fraction of parents who belong to PTAs has regained virtually none of the 50 percent fall that this metric registered between 1960 and 1975. Despite talk about the growth of "support groups," another oft-cited counter-example, I know of no statistical substantiation for this claim. One might even ask whether the vaunted rise in neighborhood watch groups might not represent only a partial, artificial replacement for the vanished social capital of traditional neighborhoods — a kind of sociological Astroturf, suitable only where you can't grow the real thing. See also Glenn (1987, S124) for survey evidence of "an increased tendency for individuals to withdraw allegiance from . . . anything outside of themselves."

9. The only exceptions are farm groups, labor unions, and veterans' organizations, whose members have slightly less formal education than the average American. Interestingly, sports clubs are *not* an exception; college graduates are nearly three times more likely to belong to a sports group than are high school dropouts. Education is uncorrelated with church attendance, but positively correlated with membership in church-related groups.

10. For a thorough recent investigation of the role of education in accounting for differences in political participation, see Verba, Schlozman, and Brady (1995).

11. As a practical matter, all subsequent statistical presentations here implement this precept by equally weighing respondents from three broad educational categories — those with fewer than 12 years formal schooling, those with exactly 12 years, and those with more than 12 years. Conveniently, this categorization happens to slice the 1972–1994 GSS sample into nearly equal thirds. The use of more sophisticated mathematical techniques to control for educational differences would alter none of the central conclusions of this chapter.

12. The downturns in both joining and trusting seem to be somewhat greater among Americans on the middle rungs of the educational ladder — high school graduates and college dropouts — than among those at the very top and bottom of the educational hierarchy, but the differences are not great, and the trends are statistically significant at all levels.

13. This is true with or without controls for education and year of survey. The patterns among men and women on this score are not identical, for women who work part-time appear to be somewhat more civically engaged and socially trusting than either those who work full-time or those who do not work outside the home at all. Whatever we make of this intriguing anomaly, which apparently does not appear in the time budget data (Robinson and Godbey 1995) and which has no counterpart in the male half of the population, it cannot account for our basic puzzle, since female part-

time workers constitute a relatively small fraction of the American population, and the fraction is growing, not declining. Between the first half of the 1970s and the first half of the 1990s, according to the GSS data, the fraction of the total adult population constituted by female part-time workers rose from about 8 percent to about 10 percent.

14. Evidence on generational differences presented below reinforces this conclusion.

15. Robinson and Godbey (1995), however, report that nonemployed women still spend more time on activity in voluntary associations than their employed counterparts.

16. Multivariate analysis hints that one major reason why divorce lowers connectedness is that it lowers family income, which in turn reduces civic engagement.

17. I have set aside this issue for fuller treatment in later work. However, I note for the record that (1) state-level differences in social trust and group membership are substantial, closely intercorrelated and reasonably stable, at least over the period from the 1970s to the 1990s, and (2) those differences are surprisingly closely correlated (R^2 = .52) with the measure of "state political culture" invented by Elazar (1966), and refined by Sharkansky (1969), based on descriptive accounts of state politics during the 1950s and traceable in turn to patterns of immigration during the nineteenth century and before.

18. Public expenditure as a percentage of GDP in 1989 is correlated r = $-$.29 with 1990–1991 trust and r = $-$.48 with 1990–1991 associational memberships.

19. For broadly similar conclusions, see Verba, Schlozman, and Brady (1995, 241–247) and the sources cited there.

20. As elsewhere in this essay, "controlling for educational differences" here means averaging the average scores for respondents with fewer than 12 years of schooling, with exactly 12 years, and with more than 12 years, respectively.

21. White support for segregation in Figure 3-3 is measured by responses to this question in the General Social Survey: "If you and your friends belonged to a social club that would not let Blacks join, would you try to change the rules so that Blacks could join?" Essentially identical results obtain if we measure white racism instead by support for antimiscegenation laws or for residential segregation.

22. As we shall see in a moment, much civic disengagement actually appears to be generational, affecting people born after 1930, but not those born before. If this phenomenon represented white flight from integrated community life after the civil rights revolution, it is difficult to see why the trend should be so much more marked among those who came of age in the more tolerant 1960s and 1970s, and hardly visible at all among those who came of age in the first half of the century, when American society was objectively more segregated and subjectively more racist.

23. Period effects that affect only people of a specific age shade into generational effects, which is why Converse (1976), when summarizing these age-related effects, refers to "two-and-a-half" types, rather than the conventional three types.

24. To exclude the life cycle effects in the last years of life, Figure 3-5 excludes respondents over 80. To avoid well-known problems in reliably sampling young adults, as discussed by Converse (1976), Figure 3-5 also excludes respondents aged under 25. To offset the relatively small year-by-year samples and to control for educational differences, Figure 3-5 charts five-year moving averages across the three educational categories used in this essay.

25. I learned of the Miller/Shanks argument only after discovering generational differences in civic engagement in the General Social Survey data, but their findings and mine are strikingly consistent.

26. Too few respondents born in the late nineteenth century appear in surveys conducted in the 1970s and 1980s for us to discern differences among successive birth cohorts with great reliability. However, those scant data (not broken out in Figure 3-5) sug-

gest that the turn of the century might have been an era of rising civic engagement. Similarly, too few respondents born after 1970 have yet appeared in national surveys for us to be confident about their distinctive generational profile, although the slender results so far seem to suggest that the 40-year generational plunge in civic engagement might be bottoming out. however, even if this turns out to be true, it will be several decades before that development could arrest the aggregate drop in civic engagement, for reasons subsequently explained in the text.

27. Members of the 1910–1940 generation also seem more civic than their elders, at least to judge by the outlooks of the relatively few men and women born in the late nineteenth century who appeared in our samples.

28. The question on social trust appeared biennially in the NES from 1964 to 1976 and then reappeared in 1992. I have included the 1992 NES interviews in the analysis in order to obtain estimates for cohorts too young to have appeared in the earlier surveys.

29. Additional analysis of indicators of civic engagement in the GSS, not reported in detail here, confirms this downward shift during the 1980s.

30. I record here one theory attributed variously to Robert Salisbury (1985), Gerald Gamm, and Simon and Garfunkel. Devotees of our national pastime will recall that Joe DiMaggio signed with the Yankees in 1936, just as the last of the long civic generation was beginning to follow the game, and he turned center field over to Mickey Mantle in 1951, just as the last of "the suckers" reached legal maturity. Almost simultaneously, the Braves, the Athletics, the Browns, the Senators, the Dodgers, and the Giants deserted cities that had been their homes since the late nineteenth century. By the time Mantle in turn left the Yankees in 1968, much of the damage to civic loyalty had been done. This interpretation explains why Mrs. Robinson's plaintive query that year about Joltin' Joe's whereabouts evoked such widespread emotion. A deconstructionist analysis of social capital's decline would highlight the final haunting lamentation, "our nation turns its *lonely* eyes to you" [emphasis added].

31. This exoneration applies to the possible effects of divorce on children, not to its effects on the couple themselves, as discussed earlier in this essay.

32. For introductions to the massive literature on the sociology of television, see Bower (1985), Comstock et al. (1978), Comstock (1989), and Graber (1993). The figures on viewing hours in the text are from Bower (1985, 33) and *Public Perspective* (1995, 47). Cohort differences are reported in Bower (1985, 46).

33. This figure excludes periods in which television is merely playing in the background. Comstock (1989, 17) reports that "on any fall day in the late 1980s, the set in the average television owning household was on for about eight hours."

34. In fact, multiple regression analysis, predicting civic engagement from television viewing and education, suggests that heavy TV watching is one important reason *why* less educated people are less engaged in the life of their communities. Controlling for differential TV exposure significantly reduces the correlation between education and engagement.

35. Controlling for education, 45 percent of respondents who watch TV two hours or less a day and read newspapers daily say that "most people can be trusted," as compared to 29 percent of respondents who watch TV three hours or more a day and do not read a newspaper daily.

36. Newspaper circulation (per household) has dropped by more than half since its peak in 1947. To be sure, it is not clear which way the tie between newspaper reading and civic involvement works, since disengagement might itself dampen one's interest in community news. But the two trends are clearly linked.

4. Solving the Puzzle of Participation in Electoral Politics

Steven J. Rosenstone and John Mark Hansen

Americans participate in electoral politics for a mixture of personal and political reasons. An abundance of political resources allows some citizens to bear the costs of involvement, and a lack of resources prevents others. Powerful interests and identities motivate some citizens to seek the benefits of participation, and weaker interests and identities fail to stir others. Finally, candidates, parties, campaigns, interest groups, and social movements mobilize some citizens and neglect others, step up their efforts at some times and scale them back at others. Their labors, when they occur, promote political participation, offsetting the costs and augmenting the social benefits of citizens' political activism.

In this brief chapter, we compare the contributions of the personal and the political to the solution of one of the puzzles with which we began this book: the puzzle of declining participation in American elections (Brody 1978). In the 1960s, we noted in Chapter 3 [of Rosenstone and Hansen, 1993], about 62 percent of eligible Americans turned out to vote in presidential elections, but in the 1980s, barely half did. In the 1960s, 10.4 percent of the electorate contributed money to a party or candidate, but in the 1980s, just 8.2 percent did. In the 1960s, 5.5 percent of adult Americans worked for a party or candidate, but in the 1980s, only 3.7 percent did. Put differently, the ranks of participants in electoral politics have dwindled by between a sixth and a quarter over the last three decades. Why is that? Why has participation in American elections declined during the last thirty years?

In Chapters 5 and 6 [of Rosenstone and Hansen] we showed some of the proposed solutions to the puzzle to be right, some to be wrong, and all to be importantly incomplete.[1] The decline of turnout we have shown, occurred despite the stimulating effect of increased education and the liberating effect of reduced legal barriers (as Richard Brody in fact noted in his original framing of the puzzle). The causes of the decline, as recent analysts have asserted and as we have shown, include political efficacy, partisan identification, and satisfaction with the choices offered, all of which themselves have recently declined. The causes of the decline do not include, as several other analysts have suggested, dis-

Source: "Solving the Puzzle of Participation in Electoral Politics," pp. 211–227; Table D-1, "Causes of Voter Turnout, 1956–1988 Presidential Election Years," pp. 273–275, from *Mobilization, Participation, and Democracy in America,* by Steven J. Rosenstone and John Mark Hansen. Copyright © 1993 by Macmillan Publishing Company. Reprinted by permission of Addison-Wesley Educational Publishers, Inc.

avowals of responsibility, distrust toward government, or generalized alienation from the political system: As we have shown, these attitudes had no effect on the probability that citizens took part. Finally, the causes of the decline include elements that almost every other analysis has overlooked: the intensity of efforts by candidates, parties, campaigns, interest groups, and social movements to mobilize people to take part. As we have shown, party contacts, electoral competition, and active social movements muster ordinary citizens into electoral politics.

We have yet to assess, however, the relative *magnitudes* of the effects of resources, interests, and strategic mobilization on participation in electoral politics. In this chapter we do just that. Drawing on the theory of participation we outlined in Chapter 2 [of Rosenstone and Hansen], and working from the empirical results we presented in Chapters 5 and 6 [of Rosenstone and Hansen], we decompose the trends of electoral participation into their underlying causes. We calculate how much of the decline in citizen participation can be attributed to changing resources, how much can be blamed on changing evaluations of the parties and their candidates, how much can be laid to changing degrees of involvement in communities, and how much results from changing patterns of electoral mobilization.

To aid in the assessment, we "transformed" the citizens of the 1960s into the citizens of the 1980s. One variable at a time, we gave each of the respondents to the 1960, 1964, and 1968 National Election Studies the characteristics of their counterparts in the 1980s: their more advanced educations, more fragile sense of political efficacy, more diffident attachments to political parties, more skeptical assessments of the candidates, more tenuous integration into communities, less frequent exposure to the mobilization efforts of parties, campaigns and social movements, and greater freedom from the burdens of discriminatory voter registration and election laws.[2] For each variable, then, we computed how much more or less likely members of the 1960s electorate would have been to participate in elections had they been like the members of the 1980s electorate.

The results, to foreshadow, are dramatic. In every case the changing pattern of mobilization by parties, campaigns, and social movements accounts for at least half of the decline in electoral participation since the 1960s. Explanations of political involvement that have focused exclusively on the personal attributes of individual citizens — their demographic characteristics and political beliefs — have missed at least half the story.

The Decline of Voter Turnout Since the 1960s

The most interesting, most important, and most conjectured puzzle of recent American electoral history is the 11-percentage-point decline in reported voter turnout since the 1960s.

As we already noted, the decline in voter turnout is all the more problematic, of course, because it runs counter to two important demographic and structural changes that should have fostered voter participation but did not.

Table 4-1   Decomposition of the Decline in Voter Turnout in Presidential
Election Years Between the 1960s and 1980s

Change	Effect on Percentage Change in Turnout Between 1960s and 1980s	Percentage of Decline in Turnout Explained
An easing of voter registration laws	+1.8	
Increased formal education	+2.8	
A younger electorate	−2.7	17
Weakened social involvement	−1.4	9
Declining feelings of efficacy	−1.4	9
Weakened attachment to and evaluations of the political parties and their candidates	−1.7	11
A decline in mobilization	−8.7	54
		100
Net change in voter turnout:	−11.3	

Source: Appendix.

First, the educational attainment of the American public has increased markedly during the last thirty years. In 1960, only four out of ten American adults had earned a high school diploma, and only one out of thirteen had taken a college degree. In 1988, in contrast, three out of four adults had completed high school, and one out of five had finished college. The knowledge and skills that facilitate political involvement have never been more broadly distributed.

Second, the legislated barriers to voter participation have diminished significantly during the last thirty years. Constitutional amendments, federal statutes, and federal court decisions have abolished the poll tax and literacy tests and all but ended periodic voter registration. In addition, court rulings and state laws have made it easier for people to register to vote closer to election day. The legal obstacles to citizen involvement in elections have not been lower in this century.

As our simulation indicates, voter turnout would indeed have increased had education and legal requirements been the only elements of the electoral landscape to have changed over the last three decades (see Table 4-1). Had the stimulative effects of better education and the emancipating effects of liberalized election laws not occurred, the decline of voter turnout would have been even more severe—nearly 16 percentage points. Instead, more widespread access to education raised voter turnout 2.8 percentage points above what it would have been had Americans been no better educated than they were in the 1960s. Removal of impediments to the exercise of the franchise advanced voter turnout by 1.8 percentage points. Other changes, however more than canceled the gains.

Where better education augmented the electorate's resources, other developments reduced them. Between the 1960s and the 1980s, the voting-age population grew substantially younger. When the Twenty-sixth Amendment lowered the voting age to eighteen in 1972, the size of the voter group least likely to participate increased by 40 percent overnight, accounting for the substantial drop in voter participation in that one year. Throughout the 1960s and 1970s, moreover, the enormous postwar "baby boom" generation moved into the electorate — in Raymond Wolfinger's vivid analogy, "like a pig through a boa constrictor." Where only 27 percent of the 1960 electorate was under the age of thirty-five, 40 percent of the 1984 electorate belonged to the youngest age group. This simple demographic change reduced aggregate rates of voter turnout. As our estimates indicate, the younger and less experienced electorate accounted for about a sixth of the decline in voter participation, 2.7 percentage points, between the 1960s and the 1980s. All by itself, in fact, the electorate's youthful inexperience erased nearly all of the positive effects of its more extensive education.

The electorate of the 1980s was not only less able to draw upon the resources of experience, it also faced the electoral arena with a diminished sense of the efficacy of its actions. Between the 1960s and the 1980s, more and more citizens came to believe that politics and government were so complicated that ordinary people could not understand them; internal efficacy fell. Likewise, more and more citizens came to doubt that public officials cared about the views of the people and came to wonder whether they had any say in what the government did; external efficacy fell. Declining efficacy accounted for about a tenth of the total decline in voter participation, or 1.4 percentage points. It was not, however, by any means a primary or even a substantial cause of declining voter turnout, as some have argued.[3]

On the benefit side of the ledger, voter participation declined because people saw fewer benefits from involvement. First, Americans were far less satisfied with the choices the 1980s offered them — Jimmy Carter, Ronald Reagan, Walter Mondale, George Bush, Michael Dukakis — than with the choices the 1960s offered them — John Kennedy, Richard Nixon, Lyndon Johnson, Barry Goldwater, Hubert Humphrey, George Wallace. They cared far less about who actually won the White House. They had many fewer good things to say even about their favorite political parties and candidates. In addition, Americans had much weaker partisan loyalties in the 1980s than they had in the 1960s. The percentage of strong partisans in the electorate fell from 35 percent in the 1960s to only 29 percent in the 1980s. Weakening identification with the Democrats and the Republicans undermined the rewards of helping the "right side" to win. Taken together, the electorate's diminished sense that anything was at stake in elections and its weakening ties to political parties accounted for about a tenth of the decline in voter turnout — 1.7 percentage points (Abramson and Aldrich 1982, 509–510).

Finally, Americans were much less integrated into the social life of their communities in the 1980s than they had been in the 1960s. Fewer people lived near where they were born, and fewer people attended religious services regularly. Their shallower social attachments also accounted for about a tenth of the drop in voter participation since the 1960s, about 1.4 percent. Fewer people had ties of long standing to the friends and associates who expect them to participate and reward them when they do.

Between the 1960s and the 1980s, in sum, Americans withdrew from voting because they had fewer resources to devote to politics and less to gain from taking part. Although they had more of the knowledge and skills that derive from education, they had less of the knowledge and fewer of the skills that arise from experience and less of the self-confidence that comes from a sense of personal efficacy. They were less closely involved in social life, less closely identified with political parties, and less deeply invested in the outcomes of elections. Altogether, our estimates indicate, the electorate's depreciated resources and diminished involvements, identifications, and stakes account for 7.2 percent of the 15.9 percent "real" decline in reported voter turnout since the 1960s.

To consider the conclusion differently, however, the usual suspects in research on voter participation fall well short of explaining the most important puzzles of recent American politics. The personal attributes of Americans — their resources, involvement in communities, identifications with political parties, and opinions of the candidates — leave over half of the decline in voter turnout still missing and unaccounted for, but we know now just exactly where to find the remainder. Half of the decline of voter turnout since the 1960s occurred because electoral mobilization declined.

First, partisan mobilization declined. Political parties and campaign organizations increased their efforts to contact people in the 1960s, never failing to mobilize less than a quarter of the American electorate directly. As campaigns abandoned the labor-intensive canvassing methods of the 1960s for the money-intensive media strategies of the 1980s, they contacted fewer and fewer Americans.

Second, electoral competition declined. Kennedy defeated Nixon in 1960 and Nixon defeated Humphrey in 1968 by less than 1 percent of the votes cast; Reagan beat Carter in 1980 and Bush beat Dukakis in 1988 by margins of 9 and 8 percentage points, respectively. The average margin of victory for incumbents in House races increased from 63 percent in the 1960s to 67 percent in the 1980s. Between 1968 and 1980, seventeen states moved gubernatorial elections and their campaign activities out of presidential election years and into midterm years. Fewer competitive campaigns for the White House, the Congress, and the governor's mansion meant fewer occasions for voter mobilization.

Third, demands on campaign resources intensified. The number of contested presidential primaries nearly doubled between 1968 and 1980. By increasing the number of separate occasions on which voters were called to the polls, the proliferation of presidential primaries spread the resources of both citizens and campaigns thinner and thinner.

Finally, social movement activity declined. The civil rights protests, marches, boycotts, and voter registration drives of the 1960s tapered off in the 1980s. The movement's ebb removed a powerful stimulus to participation for both blacks and whites.

The decline of electoral mobilization from the 1960s to the 1980s, our simulation indicates, produced 8.7 percent of the 15.9 "real" decline in voter turnout over the same three decades. Had candidates, parties, campaigns, interest groups, and social movements been as active in mobilizing voters in the 1980s as they were in the 1960s, even leaving the legal structure and the condition of individual voters unchanged, reported voter participation would have fallen only 2.6 percent, rather than the 11.3 percent that it did.

The resolution of the puzzle of voter turnout, then, is clear. The attributes of individual citizens alone are not sufficient to account for declining public involvement in American elections. People vote because they have the resources to bear the costs and because they have the interests and identities to appreciate the benefits. But people also turn out to vote substantially because somebody helps them or asks them to participate. The actions of parties, campaigns, and social movements mobilize public involvement in American elections. The "blame" for declining voter turnout, accordingly, rests as much on political leaders as on citizens themselves.

The Rise and Decline of Black Voter Turnout

The puzzles of citizen participation in American elections do not begin and end with the decline of national voter turnout. . . . [T]he postwar trends of voter participation among African-Americans differed significantly from the trends of the rest of the population. In the 1952 and 1956 presidential elections, barely one-third of the black population reported voting. Over the next decade and a half, however, African-American turnout expanded, and in the 1968 and 1972 elections, nearly two-thirds of the black population participated in the selection of the president. From there, black turnout declined, in parallel with the decline in voter participation nationally.

. . . [W]e can also account for the rise and decline of African-American voter turnout. As before, we decompose the changes in black turnout from one era to another by transforming the black electorate from one decade into the black electorate in another decade, characteristic by characteristic. We analyze the increase of black voter turnout in the 1950s and 1960s and the decrease of black voter turnout in the 1970s and 1980s separately. Table 4-2 summarizes the source of the rise in black turnout between the 1950s and the late 1960s.

Unsurprisingly, the relaxation of discriminatory voter registration laws made the largest single contribution, by far, to the rise in black turnout in the 1950s and 1960s. The prohibition of the poll tax and literacy tests, the move to permanent (instead of periodic) systems of registration, the shortening of the closing date, and the implementation of the Voting Rights Act (VRA) of 1965 opened doors to black voters. Taken together, the elimination of legal barriers that had been used to shut blacks out of the political process increased African-American turnout by 15.8 percentage points, accounting for almost half the gains of the 1950s and 1960s.[4]

Table 4-2   Decomposition of the Increase in Black Voter Turnout in
Presidential Election Years Between the 1950s and 1968–1972

Change	Effect on Percentage Change in Turnout Between 1950s and 1968–1972	Percentage of Rise in Black Turnout Explained
Weakened social involvement	−1.3	
An increase in personal resources	+18.6	24
Increasing feelings of efficacy	+11.3	1
Strengthened attachment to and evaluations of the political parties and their candidates	+4.8	13
An increase in mobilization	+6.6	18
An easing of voter registration laws	+15.8	44
		100
Net change in black voter turnout:	+34.8	

Source: Appendix.

There was more to encourage black voters to participate, however, than simply permitting them to vote. Throughout the 1950s and 1960s the civil rights movement grew and spread, reaching its peak around the campaign for voting rights during the Johnson administration. Throughout the 1950s and 1960s, moreover, the political parties paid increasing attention to newly enfranchised African-American voters — Southern blacks were 15 percent more likely to be contacted by political parties after 1964 than before. More intensive civil rights movement activities and more extensive contacts with political parties mobilized black voters, increasing black turnout by 6.6 percentage points.

In addition to the political innovations, black turnout increased because of changes in the political outlooks and personal characteristics of black Americans. On the benefits side, as the national Democratic Party became the champion of civil rights, the differences between the parties widened and blacks perceived more benefits from political participation. In the 1964 presidential election, President Lyndon B. Johnson, the sponsor of the 1964 Civil Rights Act, confronted Senator Barry Goldwater, who had voted against it. In the 1968 presidential election, Vice President Hubert H. Humphrey, a veteran crusader for civil rights and the author of the first civil rights plank to appear in a party platform since Reconstruction, battled former Vice President Richard M. Nixon and segregationist Alabama governor George C. Wallace, both of whom pursued deliberate "Southern strategies" of appeals to Southern whites. In response, African-Americans developed stronger partisan loyalties to the Democratic Party and reached more positive evaluations of Democratic presidential nominees. Their growing attachment to the Democrats increased their turnout by 4.8 percentage points.

On the resource side, African-Americans' fortunes increased. The experiences of the civil rights era fostered greater political efficacy, which contributed 0.3 percentage points to the increase in black turnout. More important, the policy achievements of the civil rights movement, especially the 1964 Civil Rights Act and the programs of the Great Society, significantly increased opportunities for African-Americans and gave them access to better educations and jobs. In the space of fifteen years, the proportion of black Americans who had completed high school rose 20 percentage points to 61 percent. In the space of fifteen years, the proportion of black Americans who earned incomes that placed them in the lowest third of American families declined 15 percentage points to 56 percent. Better educations, better incomes, and a slight aging of the black population extended the money, skills, and experience of the black community and increased black voter turnout by 8.6 percentage points, accounting for about a quarter of the gains between the 1950s and the 1960s.

Although increasing mobility and declining church attendance loosened blacks' connections to their communities and slightly depressed black turnout, on the whole the rise in black turnout was dramatic: an increase of almost 35 percentage points in the course of only fifteen years. The largest part of the increase stemmed from the demolition of the legal barriers that excluded black Americans from voting, of course, but deeper attachments to political parties, more abundant resources, and increasing encouragement and mobilization by political parties and social movements all played important parts.

These same forces that were so instrumental in raising black turnout to its peak in the 1968 and 1972 presidential elections also produced the decline in participation in the two decades after. As shown in Table 4-3, the years of schooling of black Americans continued to grow throughout the 1970s and 1980s and raised African-American turnout by 2.6 percentage points. Likewise, the legal obstacles to voter participation continued to drop throughout the 1970s and 1980s and lifted African-American turnout by 2.6 percentage points. As with all Americans, the decline in voter turnout among African-Americans would have been far worse had not education continued to rise and barriers continued to fall.

All in all, though, personal and political causes of black voter turnout moved in directions that depressed political involvement. By the end of the 1980s, African-Americans as a group had fewer political resources. During the 1970s and 1980s, the black population grew considerably younger and less experienced, cutting voting rates by 3.2 percent, more than offsetting the gains from better education. By the end of the 1980s, African-Americans were less well integrated into supportive communities. Mobility increased, home ownership fell, and church attendance waned, reducing turnout rates by 0.8 percentage points. By the end of the 1980s, finally, African-Americans as a group perceived fewer benefits from participation. As the Democratic Party's commitment to social welfare programs faded, blacks' identification with the party slipped. As the Democratic Party's nominees turned more centrist, most distinctly in the case of the only

Table 4-3   Decomposition of the Decrease in Black Voter Turnout in
Presidential Election Years Between 1968–1972 and the 1980s

Change	Effect on Percentage Change in Turnout Between 1968–1972 and 1980s	Percentage of Decline in Black Turnout Explained
An easing of voter registration laws	+2.6	
Increased formal education	+2.6	
A younger electorate	−3.2	18
Weakened social involvement	−0.8	4
Declining feelings of efficacy	0.0	0
Weakened attachment to and evaluations of the political parties and their candidates	−2.6	14
A decline in mobilization	−6.2	34
A decline of voter registration efforts around the Voting Rights Act	−5.2	29
		99
Net change in voter turnout	−12.8	

Source: Appendix.

winner, Jimmy Carter, blacks' enthusiasm for the ticket flagged. Rising disaffection from the Democratic Party and its candidates reduced African-American voter turnout by 2.6 percentage points.

By far the most important drag on African-American voter turnout, however, was the atrophy of instruments of mobilization. In the 1970s and 1980s, efforts to register black voters slowed considerably, as the inspiration of the 1965 VRA faded into history. In the 1970s and 1980s, the civil rights movement slowed, as white resistance and internal disputes sapped its energy in the 1970s and 1980s, political parties lagged in their efforts to contact black voters as they did in their efforts to contact all Americans. In the 1970s and 1980s, gubernatorial campaigns disappeared, as states moved gubernatorial elections out of presidential years. In the 1970s and 1980s, finally, contested presidential primaries — which twice featured an African-American, Jesse Jackson — diverted campaigns' and voters' efforts into the primaries and out of the November elections. As political parties, campaigns, and social movements subsidized fewer costs and created fewer benefits, black voter turnout declined by 11.4 percentage points. Curtailed mobilization accounts for nearly two-thirds of the drop in African-American voter participation since 1968.

The forces that brought African-Americans into electoral politics, in sum, were the same forces that brought other Americans into electoral politics, although in different proportions. Abundant resources, attractive benefits, and active mobilization sustained black voter turnout, but mobilization mattered most of all. The historic deprivation of the African-American community makes

Table 4-4 Decomposition of the Decline in Working for a Political Party or Candidate in Presidential Election Years Between the 1960s and 1980s

Change	Effect on Percentage Change in Working for a Party or Candidate Between 1960s and 1980s	Percentage of Decline in Working for a Party or Candidate Explained
Increased formal education	+.4	
A younger electorate	−.2	9
Weakened social involvement	−.1	4
Declining feelings of efficacy	−.3	13
Weakened attachment to and evaluations of the political parties and their candidates	−.5	22
A decline in mobilization	−1.2	52
		100
Net change in working for a political party or candidate:	−1.9	

Source: Appendix.

the mobilizing activities of outside forces like political parties and indigenous forces like the civil rights movement all the more important.

The Decline of Work for Parties and Contributions to Campaigns

The puzzles of citizen participation in American elections extend beyond the decline of voter turnout to a more general decline of involvement in campaign activities of all sorts. From the 1960s to the 1980s, the percentage of Americans who volunteered to work for political parties or candidates dropped 1.9 percentage points, and the percentage of Americans who contributed money to a campaign fell 2.6 points. By this point in the chapter, the reasons for the decline are so familiar that we will try to avoid belaboring them.

Involvement in electoral politics declined, first of all, because resources diminished. As shown in Tables 4-4 and 4-5, the electorate's increasing youth and inexperience and its declining sense of efficacy reduced campaign work and contributions by small amounts, with gains in education offsetting the losses in both cases.

Involvement in campaigns declined, second of all, because interests and identities weakened. Looser attachments to the political parties and less-favorable evaluations of their candidates accounted for about one-fifth of the decline in both campaign work and contributions across the 1970s and the 1980s.

Table 4-5 Decomposition of the Decline in Contributing Money to a Political Party or Candidate in Presidential Election Years Between the 1960s and 1980s

Change	Effect on Percentage Change in Contributing Money Between 1960s and 1980s	Percentage of Decline in Contributing Money Explained
Increased formal education	+1.4	
A younger electorate	−.2	5
Weakened social involvement	.0	0
Declining feelings of efficacy	−.5	13
Weakened attachment to and evaluations of the political parties and their candidates	−.8	20
A decline in mobilization	−2.5	62
		100
Net change in contributing money to a political party or candidate	−2.6	

Source: Appendix.

Involvement in electoral politics declined, most of all, because the efforts of parties, campaigns, and social movements abated. Less vigorous attempts to involve people in politics reduced volunteer activity in campaigns by 1.2 percentage points. Less vigorous attempts to involve people in politics reduced financial contributions to campaigns by 2.5 percentage points. The failure of political leaders and institutions to solicit, support, and encourage political participation accounted for over half the decline in work for political parties and almost two-thirds of the decline in contributions to political campaigns.

Conclusion

Thus, for all three kinds of citizen involvement in elections, not only for voting but also for campaign work and contributions, changes in the personal characteristics and political outlooks of the individuals in the electorate explain at best only half of the three-decade decline in political participation. Political parties, campaign organizations, and social movements presented voters with fewer chances to take part in elections, fewer opportunities to share the burdens of political involvement, and fewer occasions to gain the rewards and satisfactions of political activity. Citizens did not fail the political system; if anything, the political system failed them.

Our theory of political participation not only explains *who* participates in electoral politics, it also explains *when* people participate in electoral politics.

Part of the solution to the puzzle of electoral participation lies in the ways in which the American people have changed: changes in their resources, social ties, and evaluations of the political parties and candidates. An equally large part of the solution to the puzzle lies in the changes that have taken place in the political world that people confront: changes in the actions of political parties, the nature of political campaigns, and the actions of social movements. The level of electoral participation in the United States waxes and wanes in response to political mobilization. People participate in electoral politics in all of its forms when they are mobilized to do so. When political mobilization falls, so does the propensity of people to take part.

APPENDIX

Participation in Electoral Politics: Estimated Equations

Table 4A-1   Causes of Voter Turnout, 1956–1988 Presidential Election Years (Probit Estimates)

Variable	Coefficient	Standard Error	Effect on Probability of Voting (in Percent)
Resources			
Income	.550	.059	15.8
Education	.584	.053	16.6
Unemployed	−.095	.063	−2.7
Age	.054	.005	29.0
Age squared (× .01)	−.040	.005	
Internal efficacy	.102	.033	2.9
External efficacy	.360	.035	10.6
Evaluation of Parties and Candidates			
Strength of party identification	.364	.046	10.6
Affect for a party	.423	.079	11.4
Care which party wins presidential election	.219	.030	6.4
Affect for presidential candidate	.201	.065	5.6
Social Involvement			
Years in community, natural logarithm*	.096	.016	10.7
Church attendance	.518	.037	15.1
Homeowners*	.265	.029	7.5
Currently working	.075	.033	2.1
Mobilization by Parties			
Contacted by a party	.283	.033	7.8

Table 4A-1 *continued*

Variable	Coefficient	Standard Error	Effect on Probability of Voting (in Percent)
Mobilization by Campaigns			
Close presidential election	.384	.147	3.0
Perceived closeness of election	.057	.032	1.6
Gubernatorial election	.179	.033	5.0
Presidential primary election	−.131	.030	−3.7
Mobilization by Social Movements			
Civil rights movement actions	.041	.008	7.3
Legal Organization of Elections			
Literacy tests × blacks	−.500	.188	−16.0
Poll tax × blacks	−.319	.238	−10.2
Periodic registration × blacks	−.387	.146	−11.6
1965 Voting Rights Act × blacks	.582	.211	26.4
1965 Voting Rights Act × whites	.332	.110	19.5
Voter registration closing date	−.003	.001	−5.6
Other Demographic Variables			
Live in Southern state	−.542	.034	−16.3
Live in border state	−.217	.051	−6.1
Blacks	−.150	.051	−4.4
Mexican-Americans and Puerto Ricans	−.194	.103	−5.7
(Constant)	−2.417	.111	

Source: Appendix B [of Rosenstone and Hansen].

Note: Likelihood Ratio Index = .23. Percent of cases correctly predicted = 75.7 (null model = 68.4). Chi-square = 3,245.5 with 31 degrees of freedom (probability < .001). Number of cases = 11,310.

*Coefficient reported for equation reestimated for 1968–1988 presidential election years only.

Notes

1. For a sampling of some of the other solutions proposed for Brody's puzzle, see Shaffer (1981), Abramson and Aldrich (1982), Cassel and Luskin (1988), Teixeira (1987).
2. We use the probit equations [illustrated] in the Appendix to estimate the magnitude of the effect each of the political and social changes that occurred between the 1960s and 1980s had on the decline in electoral participation. In the first step, we used the equations to generate the predicted probabilities of participation for each respondent to the 1960, 1964, and 1968 National Election Studies. We then altered the scoring of the independent variable of interest to reflect the change in that variable between the 1960s and the 1980s. (For example, to estimate the impact of rising levels of education, we raised each respondent's level of education to reflect the increased level of formal education that prevailed in the 1980s.) Finally, we calculated the probability of partic-

ipation under this simulated condition. The difference between the actual probability of taking part in the 1960s and the simulated probability of taking part under the conditions of the 1980s, averaged across the respondents, yielded an estimate of the marginal effect on participation of that particular change. We repeated this procedure for each variable to calculate its contribution to the decline in electoral participation since the 1960s.

3. Gans (1978a, b); Shaffer (1981); Abramson and Aldrich (1982).

4. This estimate is remarkably parallel to estimates of the negative impact of the initial adoption of poll taxes and literacy tests on voter turnout in the South. See Rusk (1974).

5. Electoral Participation

Mark N. Franklin

Participation is the lifeblood of democracy, involving different numbers of people in different activities at different times. Maintaining viable party organizations requires the commitment of a few people over a considerable period. Campaigning, lobbying, or protesting require a rather greater commitment by rather more people, but over a shorter period. Voting requires a minimum commitment for a brief period, but involves the greatest number of people. In a book about elections, it seems natural to focus on voting. Indeed, the health of a democracy is often seen in terms of its level of turnout, and this will be our primary concern. However, low turnout may, as we shall see, be associated with the widespread use of alternative avenues for participatory activities; so those alternatives are not irrelevant even when we take a perspective that is primarily electoral.

This chapter starts by examining variations in voting turnout by country and by various social characteristics. In seeking to explain these variations, we consider three theories that have dominated research in this area ever since the start of behavioral political studies—one based on individual resources, one based on political mobilization, and the third based on instrumental motivation. The central argument in this chapter is that *instrumental motivation*, largely determined by the context in which elections are held, has been unduly neglected yet plays a critical role in driving electoral turnout. The salience of elections, the use of compulsory voting, a highly proportional electoral system, postal voting, and weekend polling provide the most plausible explanations of cross-national differences in voting turnout because these influence the costs and benefits of casting a ballot. The last section of the chapter considers cross-national variations in other types of political participation and the implications of these variations for democracy and democratization.

Turnout in Democracies

We can start by comparing turnout in 37 democracies.[1] Table 5-1 shows average turnout at free elections for the lower house in these countries, conducted between 1960 and 1995, along with the number of elections on which each aver-

Source: Lawrence LeDuc, Richard G. Niemi, and Pippa Norris, eds., *Comparing Democracies: Elections and Voting in Comparative Perspective,* pp. 216–235, copyright ©1996 by Sage Publications. Reprinted by permission of Sage Publications, Inc.

Table 5-1   Average Turnout in Free Elections to the Lower House in 37
Countries, 1960–1995 (in percentages)

Australia[a] (14)	95	Norway[a] (9)	81
Malta[a] (6)	94	Bulgaria[b] (2)	80
Austria[a] (9)	92	Israel[a] (9)	80
Belgium[a, b] (12)	91	Portugal[a, b] (9)	79
Italy[a, b] (9)	90	Finland[a] (10)	78
Luxembourg[a, b] (7)	90	Canada[a] (11)	76
Iceland[a, b] (10)	89	France[a, b] (9)	76
New Zealand[a] (12)	88	United Kingdom[a, b] (9)	75
Denmark[a, b] (14)	87	Ireland[a, b] (11)	74
Germany[a, b] (9)	86	Spain[a, b] (6)	73
Sweden[a] (14)	86	Japan[a] (12)	71
Greece[a, b] (10)	86	Estonia[b] (2)	69
Lithuania[b] (1)	86	Hungary[b] (2)	66
Latvia[b] (1)	86	Russia[b] (2)	61
Venezuela[a] (7)	85	India[a] (6)	58
Czech Republic[b] (2)	85	United States[a, b] (9)	54
Brazil[a] (3)	83	Switzerland[a] (8)	54
Netherlands[a,b] (7)	83	Poland[b] (2)	51
Costa Rica[a] (8)	81		

Source: Mackie and Rose (1991), Katz (1997), and *Electoral Studies* (vols. 5–14).

Note: Numbers in parentheses are the number of elections included in each average. For the United States, only "on year" congressional elections are included (i.e., elections held in conjunction with presidential elections). U.S. midterm elections do not respond to the same forces as elections elsewhere, because executive power is not at stake. For the Netherlands, the series starts in 1968, after the abolition of compulsory voting there.

[a]Included in country-level analysis (29 countries).

[b]Included in individual-level analysis. Romania (86 percent turnout) is included in these analyses (for a total of 22 countries), but it does not qualify as a democracy according to the criteria established in LeDuc, Niemi, and Norris (1996, chap. 1)—i.e., a Gastil Political Rights Score of 3 or less (Karatnycky 1995, 15–16) and a population of more than 3 million.

age is based.[2] Countries marked with an [a] in this table are countries for which systemic characteristics have been compiled by Katz (1997). These countries are used in the country-level analyses reported later in this chapter.[3] Countries flagged with a [b] in this table are countries for which we have obtained survey data from the early 1990s. These countries are used in the individual-level analyses reported later in this chapter.[4] These overlapping data sets provide a snapshot of electoral participation across a wide variety of political systems, including those with emerging and established democratic institutions, parliamentary and presidential systems, and very different electoral and party systems.

When we turn to other types of participation, these are compared on the basis of studies conducted in seven countries by Verba et al. (1978), in five countries by Barnes et al. (1979), in Western Europe by Fuchs and Klingemann

Table 5-2   Turnout for Different Groups of Individuals in 22 Countries (in percentages)

	Turnout in Group With		Variance Explained by	
Variable	Lowest	Highest	Individual Effects	Country Effects
Age	58.8	88.9	6.3	9.9
Strength of party identification	70.1	89.2	1.6	9.9
Political discussion	69.7	83.1	2.1	9.9
Education	73.8	86.1	0.6	9.9
Religious participation	76.3	83.0	0.7	9.9
Union membership	76.8	81.6	0.3	9.9
Income	75.4	89.2	0.3	9.9
N	21,601	21,601	21,601	21,601

Source: Based on Eurobarometer 41a; U.S. National Election Study, 1988; East European Barometer 2.

Note: Number of categories—age (5); strength of party identification (4); political discussion (2); education (2); religious participation (3); union member (2); income (5). The 22 countries are those marked [b] in Table 5-1 (see Table 5-1, note b).

(1995), and in the United States by Rosenstone and Hansen (1993) and by Verba, Schlozman, and Brady (1995).

Who Participates?

Tables 5-1 and 5-2 show turnout variations between countries and across the social characteristics of individuals. The most striking message is that turnout varies much more from country to country than it does between different types of individuals. It matters whether one is rich or poor, educated or uneducated, interested in politics or not, but none of these things matter nearly as much as whether one is an Australian or an American. Five countries show turnout averaging over 90 percent (one shows turnout of 95 percent), whereas four show turnout averaging under 60 percent (one shows turnout of 51 percent)—an average difference across these nine countries of nearly 40 percent. No difference in turnout levels across categories of individuals averages more than two-thirds that. The strongest individual-level effect that might be subject to manipulation—political discussion—averages only 13 percent (83.1 less 69.7 in Table 5-2). Individual-level differences are very similar across Eastern and Western Europe, although rather greater in the United States where education accounts for a 41 percent difference in turnout levels, whereas age, income, and political discussion have effects that exceed 30 percent. But only the first of these differences even comes close to matching the difference between the United States and the high-turnout countries.

To make it clear that within-country effects never approach between-country effects, the final columns of Table 5-2 compare the variance explained by individual variables with that explained by country differences in a two-way analysis of variance. Only three variables have more than a tenth of the explanatory power of country differences, and only one has more than a fifth (that one being age, a variable hardly subject to manipulation).

This suggests that if one wants to increase electoral participation in a low-turnout country, the answer lies not in increasing levels of education or political interest of the citizens of that country—the only individual-level characteristics that appear amenable to manipulation. Even if everyone in the United States were college educated, for example, this would not bring turnout there even to levels found in medium-turnout countries such as Britain.[5] Of course, the effect of education might be additive with effects of political interest, party identification, and other variables so as to cumulatively raise turnout considerably, or the effects of those other variables might be largely subsumed by education. This question can only be evaluated by means of multivariate analysis (see below). In the meantime, our preliminary findings clearly imply that to increase the level of turnout in the United States, India, or Switzerland, we need to establish what factors make people more likely to participate in some countries than in others, and then see whether these factors can be imported by the low-turnout countries (cf. Powell 1986).

Why Participate?

Although a great many theories have been proposed to explain variations in political participation, these essentially boil down to explanations involving three different features that distinguish people from one another: *resources, mobilization,* and the desire to affect the course of public policy (what we shall call "*instrumental motivation*"). Resources are what people individually bring to the democratic process: knowledge, wealth, and time. Mobilization is the heightened awareness of their role that can be inculcated in people through the operations of the media, parties, and groups. Instrumental motivation is the sense that individuals may have that their actions (at least taken in concert with the actions of other individuals who share the same concerns) might affect an election outcome.[6]

Of these, the resource theory of political participation has been most widely studied. According to this theory, people participate who have the time and money to do so. The classic formulation of this approach was by Verba and Nie (1972), who proposed what they called a "baseline model" of political participation that generated an expected level of participation from education, income, and occupational variables.[7] This baseline produced expectations that might be modified by other individual characteristics, but generally not by much. The trouble with this approach is that it cannot explain the large differences in turnout that exist between countries. We have already seen that differences in turnout by levels of education and income are less than differences in turnout by country. Moreover, high-turnout countries do not have richer or more educated people than low-turnout countries. Indeed, two of the richest and most highly educated countries (Switzerland and the United States) are among the lowest in terms of turnout.

Taking account of the activities of groups and organizations (especially political parties) has recently gained prominence in studies of political participation (Rosenstone and Hansen 1993; Verba et al. 1995).[8] However, variations in mobilizing activities do not go far toward remedying the problems of the resource approach. According to Rosenstone and Hansen (1993), citizens (even those with most resources) are more likely to participate if encouraged to do so, and one source of encouragement comes from efforts made to "get out the vote." Yet in countries for which we have measured these effects (in the context of the European elections of 1989), country differences in mobilizing activities are smaller even than country differences in education or political interest.[9]

Both the resource and the mobilization theories indirectly address the instrumental motivations of citizens to affect the course of public policy. Those whose education and experience lead them to feel politically efficacious will vote because they are motivated to do so, and those who are mobilized to vote are evidently motivated as a consequence of involvement and persuasion (Verba et al. 1995). The role of the election *contest* as a source of instrumental motivation, however, has often been neglected by scholars who focus on the behavior of individuals. Among scholars who study differences between countries, on the other hand, the importance of institutional and contextual differences in affecting turnout has been a major theme in the literature of political participation since the earliest studies (Tingsten 1937; Crewe 1981; Powell 1980, 1986; Jackman 1987; Jackman and Miller 1995), and a link can be made between institutions and motivations if we consider differences between elections in how much is at stake (van der Eijk, Franklin, et al. 1996, chap. 19; van der Eijk, Franklin, and Marsh 1996). An election that does not decide the disposition of executive power (e.g., an election for the European Parliament or a U.S. midterm election) can be expected to prove less important (and therefore less likely to motivate voter turnout) than a national election in Europe or an American presidential election. If executive power is at stake, then we would expect that more people will turn out—especially if the election is a close one, the outcome seems likely to determine the course of public policy, and there are large perceived differences between policy alternatives. For example, the unprecedentedly high turnout in the 1992 Louisiana gubernatorial primary contested by the ex-Ku Klux Klan member David Duke shows the possible consequences in terms of turnout of an election whose outcome is expected to be close and whose protagonists arouse strong feelings.

This also means that an electoral system that ensures no votes are wasted will presumably motivate more people to vote and that a country like Switzerland, where the outcome of parliamentary elections has no discernible policy implications (because the same coalition will take office whatever the outcome and all important policies are in any case subject to referendum), will probably see lower turnout than a country like Malta, where every important political decision is going to be affected by the outcome of a single electoral contest (Hirczy 1995). Of course, the mobilization approach can also to some extent take account of differing electoral contexts because important elections will stimulate more electoral activity by parties and candidates, but the instrumental approach subsumes such activities. An electoral contest that stimulates voters to turn out in large numbers will evidently also stimulate parties and candidates to redouble their efforts to obtain the participation of those who might still stay at home.

In brief, the instrumental approach to understanding political participation is superior to the other two common approaches because it subsumes them both while explaining additional aspects of political participation that neither of the other approaches can address. Indeed, this approach is the only one that makes sense when we focus on the importance of the electoral context in conditioning people's motivations, and only differences in context show promise of explaining country differences in turnout.

Nevertheless, the fact that instrumental motivation has mainly to do with the benefits of voting should not blind us to the fact that voting also involves costs. Countries may differ not only in how important elections seem to voters but also in how difficult it is to vote. Later, we will describe some relevant ways in which countries differ from each other in these respects, but first we need to validate what so far has been merely suggested: that what matters in explaining turnout are differences between countries not differences between individuals.

Effects on Individual - Level Electoral Participation

We saw earlier that the differences between types of individual in terms of turnout were generally much less than differences between countries. The implication of that finding was that individual - level differences have less effect than country - level differences. This implication can be more formally confirmed if we conduct a multivariate analysis that attempts to explain individual - level electoral participation on the basis of demographic and other characteristics of individuals, and contrast the effects with those that can be seen when the country contexts in which individuals find themselves are taken into account. Such an analysis can assess the cumulative effects of many attributes at once, in contrast to our earlier descriptive approach.

A great many variables have been suggested as determining the resources that individuals bring to the participatory context and the success of parties in mobilizing these voters to turn out. In the data available to us for 22 countries (those of Western and Eastern Europe, together with the United States), relatively few variables are available that are relevant to electoral mobilization—only strength of party identification might be construed as a variable that would make voters responsive to mobilizing efforts. However, other analyses of specifically West European data (van der Eijk, Franklin, et al. 1996) has shown that cam-

Table 5-3   Effects on Individual-Level Electoral Participation in
22 Countries

Variable	Individual Level Only		With National Effects Considered		With Missing Data Indicators	
	b	SE	b	SE	b	SE
Constant	.636	.017*	.065	.022	.069	.022
Age	.064	.002*	.063	.002*	.062	.002*
Strength of party identification	.010	.004	.040	.004*	.039	.004*
Political discussion	.097	.006*	.091	.006*	.093	.006*
Education	.005	.003	.025	.003*	.025	.003*
Religious participation	.008	.004	.024	.005*	.030	.004*
Union membership	−.081	.006*	−.023	.006*	−.024	.006*
Income	.001	.001	.004	.009*	.004	.001*
Average country effect			.478	.017*	.489	.017*
Missing religious participation					−.041	.009*
Adjusted R^2	.055		.195		.195	
N	21,601		21,601		21,601	

Source: See Table 5-2.

Note: For number of categories, see Table 5-2.

*p < .001.

paign mobilization contributed less than one eighth of total individual-level effects on electoral participation, and the resource variables at our disposal do include virtually all those ever suggested in past research (cf. van der Eijk, Franklin, et al. 1996; Oppenhuis 1995).

Table 5-3 shows the effects of variables found to have statistically significant (at the .001 level) influences on individual-level electoral participation in three separate models: the first, where only individual-level influences are considered;[10] the second, where these effects are considered within their national contexts;[11] and the third, where missing data indicators are taken into account.[12] As can be seen, individual-level characteristics explain only 5.5 percent of variance in electoral participation. Taking account of national context (in the central column of the table) multiplies this variance explained virtually fourfold. Taking account of missing data adds trivially (but significantly) to variance explained.[13] Effects (b) of the various variables included in the table are readily interpretable. The important finding is the extent to which national context exceeds in importance the effects of individual-level variables.[14] This is shown not only in terms of variance explained but also in the magnitude of the average country effect. Explicating these country differences is the purpose of the next section.

Country Differences in the Costs and Benefits of Voting

We have already suggested that the extent to which policy outputs are expected to depend on an election outcome will be important in determining both the costs of failing to vote and the benefits of voting. Our example was Switzerland—a country where election results for the lower house are hardly linked to the political complexion of the executive. Another country with tenuous linkage between legislative election outcomes and government complexion is the United States. In these two countries, public policy outputs evidently rest on many imponderables apart from the outcome of legislative elections (cf. Hirczy, 1992), reducing the stakes of such elections (and hence the benefits of voting) compared to what they would be in systems where the linkage was tighter. A second feature of the electoral context that we have suggested will differentiate low-turnout countries from others is the number of electoral contests that are held. A country with federal as well as state elections, and frequent referenda (or propositions), is likely to see lower turnout than other countries. This feature will be hard for us to separate in practice from poor legislative-executive linkage, because the two countries in our data with least evident linkage between legislative electoral outcomes and government complexion are the same two countries (the United States and Switzerland) that have the largest number by far of electoral contests.[15] Because of the coincidence that these two countries are the only ones with both these reasons for low turnout, we cannot readily disentangle the two influences, and in the analyses conducted in this chapter we thus take both effects together, indicating their presence by means of dummy variable (which we refer to as "electoral salience" in the tables that follow) that picks out these two countries in contradistinction to all others.[16]

Another variable already mentioned as contributing to the benefits of voting is the proportionality of the electoral system. A country with single-member districts and a winner-takes-all electoral system will be one in which a large number of electoral contests have foregone conclusions because one candidate is known to be virtually certain of winning. People are less likely to vote in such contests, so overall turnout will be lower than in countries where a proportional electoral system ensures that fewer votes are wasted. In this research, we measure proportionality according to the votes/seats ratio (calculated over all parties in each country) observed in the last election held in each country during the 1980s (data from Mackie and Rose 1991).

Several potentially important variables have not yet been mentioned. Whether voter registration is automatic (as in most countries) or voluntary (as in the United States and some Latin American countries) will make a difference in the number of people registered to vote and hence able to respond to a late awareness of an election's importance. Voluntary voter registration is the reason customarily given for low turnout in U.S. elections (Piven and Cloward 1977; Wolfinger and Rosenstone 1980; Crewe 1981).[17] Whether the election occurs on a weekend or workday will evidently affect the ease with which working people can vote (Crewe 1981). In many countries, compulsory voting provides an incen-

Table 5-4 Three Models Explaining Turnout in 29 Countries

Variable	Mackie-Rose		29 Countries		Switzerland and U.S. Deleted	
	b	SE	b	SE	b	SE
Constant	21.94	14.78	26.46	13.53*	26.26	13.82*
Proportionality	0.62	0.15*	0.59	0.15*	0.60	0.15*
Compulsory voting	7.29	2.12*	7.30	1.74*	7.34	1.78*
Postal voting	4.06	1.99*	4.43	1.74*	4.42	1.78*
Sunday voting	5.29	1.20*	6.48	1.74*	6.32	1.84*
Number of polling days	−1.86	2.43	−5.02	1.02*	−5.04	1.05*
Electoral salience	−28.19	3.24*	−26.93	3.02*		
Adjusted R^2	0.866		0.881		0.797	
N	25		29		27	

Source: Analysis of data from Mackie and Rose (1991) and Katz (1997, Table 13.3).

Note: Number of categories—proportionality (numerical, range is from 79 to 99); compulsory voting (2); postal voting (2); Sunday voting (2); number of polling days (numerical, 1–5); electoral salience (2). The 29 countries are those marked [a] in Table 5-1.

*$p < .05$.

tive to vote (even if the penalties for not voting are nominal), and in some countries advance voting or postal voting will make it easier to obtain the participation of those away from their homes due to employment and other reasons. Finally, the number of days the polls are open might be thought to increase the opportunity to vote—except that it is also possible that having the polls open for more than a day will only happen in countries where there is some reason to suppose that the population will find it hard to get to the polls.[18] In that case, it is an empirical question whether the additional days the polls are open actually compensate for the additional difficulties of voting in such countries.

Effects of Country Differences on Turnout

Across the 29 countries for which we have adequate data (this analysis excludes East European countries because of a lack of sufficient electoral contests), the country characteristics we have posited as being important prove somewhat sensitive to precisely which countries are included.[19] This can be seen in Table 5-4, which displays the findings from three different analyses. The first focuses on the 25 countries included in Mackie and Rose's *International Almanac of Electoral History* (1991), the only countries for which we have complete data on all the variables. The second adds another four countries for which we have most (but not all) of the relevant data. The third repeats this analysis with Switzerland and the United States omitted.[20]

The first two models explain a highly respectable 88 percent of variance in turnout, but the number of polling days only proves significant in the second of these two models. Five other variables are significant in both models. Of these, by far the most potent is electoral salience. Salient elections give rise to some 27 percent greater turnout than nonsalient elections. Because of the nature of this variable, our findings are driven by the low turnout in Switzerland and the United States, together with a plausible but unproven supposition about the reason for the anomalous turnout in these countries. These countries are omitted from the third model, with the consequence that salience plays no role in explaining turnout there, but the remaining coefficients are little changed; variance explained remains high at 80 percent. In the next section, we will report the results of an independent test of the importance of electoral salience in determining turnout, but first we should list the other variables that help to distinguish one country from another.

Compulsory voting, postal voting, and the proportionality of the electoral system between them can have an effect approaching that of electoral salience. Compulsory voting apparently increases turnout by about 7 percent in countries that make voting obligatory. Postal voting is worth about 4 percent. Proportionality is worth about six tenths of a percentage point in turnout for every percent by which the distribution of seats in the legislature approaches proportionality with the distribution of votes. Because countries vary in terms of the proportionality of their electoral systems from a low of 79 in Britain to a high of 99 in Germany, that is a 20-point difference, which (multiplied by 0.6) translates into a difference of about 12 percent in turnout. Sunday voting is worth 5–6 percent, and the effect of keeping polls open, in the second and third models, is actually negative—suggesting that countries where people have difficulty getting to the polls (such as India, Norway, and Finland) do not adequately compensate by means of additional polling days for the difficulties that lead such countries to extend their elections in this way.[21] In India, which keeps its polls open 4 days more than normal, this corresponds to a turnout that is 20 percent lower than in countries with only a single day of polling.[22] On the basis of these findings, we can assert (as we have in other work; see van der Eijk, Franklin, et al. 1996) that there are different routes to high turnout. Electoral salience is most important, but even in a country with low-salience elections, the use of compulsory voting, a highly proportional electoral system, postal voting, and weekend polling could apparently still raise turnout to 80 percent or more.

One proposed variable did not yield significant effects in any of the three analyses. Voluntary voter registration does not appear to reduce turnout when other effects are controlled.[23] This finding will come as something of a surprise to those who have assumed that low turnout in the United States can be largely attributed to this factor. Yet it is not possible that the factor has simply been included within the effects of low salience. Not only does Switzerland not have voluntary voter registration, but several other countries do have this attribute. So the research design we have adopted should have succeeded in detecting any general effect of voluntary voter registration. It failed to do so, reinforcing suggestions made elsewhere that the effects of this variable, even in the United States, may be less than had been supposed (see note 17).

Effects of the Nature of the Electoral Contest on Turnout

We have pointed out that the most powerful influence reported in Table 5-4 has not been unambiguously identified. Switzerland and the United States may indeed be low-turnout countries because of low electoral salience. But there might be other reasons for the poor turnout in those countries.[24] One way to validate our assumption about the centrality of electoral salience is to establish its operation in a different context. Although there might be some question as to whether elections in Switzerland and the United States are of lower salience than elsewhere, there is little dispute among scholars that elections to the European Parliament are of lower salience than national elections in European countries. The difference between the two types of election is supposedly due to the fact that national executive power is not at stake in elections to the European Parliament (Reif and Schmitt 1980; Reif 1985; van der Eijk, Franklin, et al. 1996) any more than it is in Swiss or U.S. legislative elections. But European Parliament elections have an additional feature that makes them particularly suited to investigating the importance of electoral salience: They occur at different times in relation to elections in which national political power is at stake.

Careful analysis of votes cast in European elections held at different points in the national election cycle has validated the assumption that time until the next national election can be employed as a surrogate for electoral salience (van der Eijk, Franklin, et al. 1996, 301–302). The validation did not involve a study of turnout variations. Instead, it looked at the parties voters chose to support. The theory was that in elections of lowest salience — those occurring immediately after national elections — voters would have no reason to vote other than for their most-favored party. Such elections have no role as barometers of opinion, because better indicators of the standing of political parties already exist in the results of the recent national elections. However, as those most recent elections fade into the past, commentators and politicians become interested in the outcome even of elections that do not decide the allocation of political power — simply as markers of what might happen in real elections. The additional salience of these elections in such circumstances is attested to by the increasing tendency of voters to vote other than for their preferred party: indeed, to vote tactically in such a way as to signal their displeasure (if any) with the performance of the party they really prefer, or to signal their approval of parties they would never support in real elections (cf. Franklin, Niemi, and Whitten 1994).

In other words, even European elections become useful as vehicles for transmitting information from voters to leaders as they occur later in the electoral cycle. At such times, turnout should be higher because the elections have greater salience. Table 5-5 shows that in European elections held at the start of the elec-

Table 5-5   Regression of Electoral Participation on Systemic Characteristics
(European Union Elections, 1989)

Independent Variable	Aggregate Level b	Individual Level b
Systemic		
Compulsory voting	26.08	0.264
Sunday voting	9.35	0.093
Proportionality of electoral system	0.46	0.005
Political		
Electoral salience[a]	−0.30	−0.003
Constant	17.77	0.180
R^2	0.918	0.142
N^b	14	10,500

Source: Adapted from van der Eijk, Franklin et al. (1996, 318). The source does not give standard errors.

[a] Time until next national election in months, coded 0 in the case of concurrent national elections.

[b] In 1989, the EC had 12 members; however, the analysis was run separately for Britain and Northern Ireland and for Flanders and Wallonia.

toral cycle (as much as 5 years before the next national elections in some countries) turnout will be 18 percent lower (30 percent of 60 months) than turnout in European elections held on the same day as national elections (such a conjunction occurred in three countries in 1989). This finding does not prove that electoral salience is the variable that chiefly accounts for low turnout in the United States and Switzerland, but it does confirm the importance of electoral salience — a necessary condition for our assumption to hold. So it adds plausibility to our assumption about the distinctiveness of Switzerland and the United States, without definitively ruling out possible alternative explanations.[25]

Other Types of Political Participation

When it comes to forms of political participation other than voting, differences between countries are again generally found to be greater than differences between social categories of voters, although the disparity is not as notable as in the case of voting (Verba et al. 1978, 57–62; Barnes et al. 1979, 541–542).[26] Moreover, the same studies show that the United States, in contrast to its relative position as lowest in voting turnout, is highest of all countries investigated in these volumes in terms of other forms of conventional political participation — particularly being active in community problem-solving organizations, and contacting officials about community and other social problems (Verba et al. 1978, 58).

Another marked difference between voting and other forms of participation is that (except in the United States) whether people vote is hardly at all affected by their socioeconomic status (SES) and hence the resources they bring to the political world. By contrast, other forms of participation are strongly affected by socioeconomic resources in all countries—some to an even greater extent than in the United States (Verba et al. 1978, 419–431). With our new perspective on the importance of contextual factors in turnout, we can shed light both on the different role of SES in the United States than elsewhere and on the different role of SES for different modes of participation.

Where turnout is virtually perfect, there is little room for individual-level factors to play a part (and it is notable that in the Verba et al. 1978 tables, SES plays the least part in explaining turnout in Austria and the Netherlands—the two countries with highest turnout of the seven they investigate). By contrast, where turnout is low there is space for other factors to play a role, as resources do in determining turnout in the United States (Verba et al. 1978, 122–123). The point about other forms of participation is that in no country does everyone work for a party or everyone contact government officials. These and other nonvoting activities are unevenly spread across the population, so there is room for individual characteristics to play a role in determining who participates and who does not. In such circumstances, differences in resources and the mobilizing efforts of parties and other political players can play a role unattenuated by systemic effects (cf. Verba et al. 1978, 6–7; Verba et al. 1995, 358).

The fact that Americans participate more than people in other nations in nonvoting activities has an additional implication. Evidently, Americans are not apathetic when it comes to politics. When we consider acts that citizens of other countries find difficult or unrewarding, Americans perform those acts in large numbers. In general, among countries for which we have relevant data, there appears to be a slight but significant inverse relationship between electoral and other forms of political participation, with low-turnout democratic countries showing greater participation of other types than high-turnout countries. Unfortunately, we do not have data for Switzerland on political participation other than voting—data that would provide a critical test of this tendency. For the moment, the hypothesis rests largely on contrasting one idiosyncratic country (the United States) with all others. Nevertheless, even in terms of an untested hypothesis, the relationship still is worth elaborating on. One reason for such an apparent inverse relationship between turnout and other kinds of political participation might be the fact that people who have exhausted themselves in other participatory acts do not have energy left for voting, but this seems unlikely—particularly because Verba and Nie (1972) showed that those who participate in other ways are likely also to be voters.

A much more likely reason for the relationship would provide indirect confirmation of our assumption that low turnout in the United States is partly due to the perceived lack of connection in that country between election outcomes and public policy. People who wish to determine the course of public policy may find the electoral route particularly unrewarding in the United States and Switzerland and hence be more inclined than in other countries to employ supplementary measures.

Conclusions

In this chapter, we have shown that going to the polls is an activity motivated primarily by the desire to affect the course of public policy. It is true that the stick of compulsory voting and the carrots of weekend polling and postal votes do lead more people to vote than otherwise would do so, but the major factors determining turnout—the importance of the electoral contest (what we have called electoral salience) and the likelihood that one's vote will not be wasted (encapsulated by the proportionality of the electoral system)—could only operate if people were motivated to use their votes to achieve a political goal.

A country with low-salience elections and an electoral system that was not very proportional could easily show turnout levels 40 percent below a country with high-salience elections and a highly proportional electoral system. Such differences arise purely from differences in the institutional context within which elections are conducted—differences affecting the extent to which a political system will be responsive to the electoral choices made by voters.[27] Voters are not fools, and an unresponsive system will motivate many fewer of them to vote.

The fact that voters are not fools is also suggested by the extent to which they bypass electoral routes where those routes prove unresponsive. The United States suffers much from the unresponsive nature of its institutional character,[28] but the United States is the country (among those for which we have relevant data) in which citizens most frequently turn to nonelectoral modes of political participation. This concomitant of low turnout is no more than hypothesized on the basis of analyses reported in this chapter, but the hypothesis is highly consonant with the instrumental basis of political action that seems so clear in our findings.

Notes

1. These are the only countries for which adequate information could readily be obtained for use in the analyses conducted in this chapter—see notes to Table 5-1.
2. This number may be less than the total number of elections actually conducted in certain countries, due to missing data. Countries of Eastern Europe did not have free elections before 1989, so for them the table contains average turnout for elections held during the 1990s.
3. Because the systemic characteristics are available only for the period 1960–1985, turnout in the country-level analyses is also restricted to this period (see Katz 1997, Table 13.3).
4. See notes to Table 5-1. In addition, Romania is included even though it is not a democracy.
5. The 41 percent increment mentioned above would only apply to those who would not otherwise have completed high school (11 percent of the sample). For 37 percent of the sample, there would be no gain, because they already have a college-level education. The remaining half of the population might find its turnout increased by about 30 percent if everyone were college educated—an overall gain in turnout of 16 percent. Add the 4 percent (one tenth of 40) from those who now do not even have a

high school education, and turnout in the United States might be raised 20 percent by this stratagem, bringing it to 74 percent—still 4 percent lower than in Britain and 20 percent below the level found in high-turnout countries.

6. Essentially, the instrumental approach views voters as social beings who see their vote not individually but as one of many. No individual vote, of course, has much chance of affecting the course of political events, but voters can take satisfaction in affirming their solidarity with others who feel the same way, knowing that together they might be able to affect the course of events (cf. Hirczy 1992).

7. Variations on this approach characterize much of the work on political participation. See, in particular, Milbrath and Goel (1977); Verba et al. (1978); Barnes et al. (1979); Wolfinger and Rosenstone (1980); Parry, Moiser, and Day (1990); Teixeira (1992); Rosenstone and Hansen (1993); and Verba et al. (1995).

8. This approach does, however, have a long pedigree. For earlier examples, see Huck-feldt (1979, 1986), Giles and Dantico (1982), Leighley (1990), and Kenny (1992).

9. Powell (1986) found significant effects from a variable he termed "group-party link-ages," but his data came from the 1960s. By the 1970s, such linkages had declined in many countries (Franklin, et al. 1992), and analysis of turnout in the late 1980s found no remaining trace of this effect (van der Eijk, Franklin, et al. 1996, chap. 19). Other work has shown that the declining importance of group-party linkages can explain some part of the decline in turnout in European countries since the 1960s (Franklin, van der Eijk, and Oppenhuis 1995; but see Topf 1995 for evidence that this decline was from a historically high point in electoral turnout). In the analyses conducted for Table 5-4 (in which turnout is averaged for the period 1960 to 1985), we do find (barely) significant effects (not shown) of group-party linkage across those countries for which the extent of this linkage can be measured—the countries of the (then) European Community. Fuchs and Klingemann (1995) also find significant effect from a similar variable (which they call "political linkage") over the same countries in a slightly later period. However, the extent of missing data costs the relationship sig-nificance even in the smallest subset of countries employed in Table 5-4.

10. Because the dependent variable in this analysis is a dichotomy (voted or not) many scholars consider regression analysis to be an inappropriate statistical method. In other work with identical variables (but whose case base was restricted to West Euro-pean countries), logistic regression effects were calculated along with the ordinary least squares (OLS) regression effects shown here (van der Eijk, Franklin, et al. 1996, chap. 19). That analysis did not indicate any way in which researchers would have been misled by relying on OLS regression, which, because of the interpretability of its results, is the method employed here.

11. To measure the maximum possible effect of national context, 21 dummy variables were included in the analysis whose results are reported in the second column of Table 5-3, one for each country less one for the base country (the United States in this instance). These variables will encapsulate differences between countries that go beyond anything that can specifically be measured at the national level, but we will see that in practice we can account for some 90 percent of the variance explained by these variables. By employing country dummies at this point in our investigations, we avoid the need to specify the variables we will use to explain country differences, which are introduced in the next section. We are also able to employ all the countries for which we have individual-level data, regardless of the fact that for some of them we do not have corresponding country-level data (see below).

12. In the analyses reported in this chapter, data missing on any variable have been replaced by mean values of that variable. Dummy variables were then defined that indicated the presence or absence of missing data for the corresponding substantive variable, as recommended by Cohen and Cohen (1983, 275–300). In all analyses,

these dummy variables were included along with the corresponding substantive variables. However, this is the only analysis where any such missing data indicators proved significant.

13. Respondents who fail to disclose their extent of religious participation are 4 percent less likely to vote than those who are willing to disclose this information. The same was found over Western European countries taken alone. See van der Eijk, Franklin, et al. (1996, chap. 19) for a discussion of this point.

14. Note that "national context," as used in this chapter, excludes social context variables. If education, for example, had proved to have large individual-level effects, some of these effects might properly have been attributed to the country level if people were more educated in some countries than in others. In this chapter, we ascribe all such effects to the individual level to give that level the greatest chance of showing its importance. Other research (van der Eijk, Franklin, et al. 1996) has shown that social context has no discernible effects, at least in countries of the European Union. More highly educated populations or wealthier populations, for example, are not more likely to show high turnout.

15. The Swiss are called to the polls on average seven times a year, mainly to render referendum verdicts (see LeDuc, Niemi, and Norris 1996, Table 1.2). Americans face federal, state, or local elections more than twice a year on average (Boyd 1981, 45), less often than the Swiss, but many times more often than anyone else.

16. Finding that this variable has significant effects will not, of course, validate our assumption about its substantive meaning. That requires other analyses (see below).

17. But see Ayres (1995) and Mitchell and Wlezien (1995) for suggestions that the effects of this variable might have been overstated even in the United States. Hirczy (1992) suggests that its effects might actually be nil, based on comparison of North Dakota (which has no registration requirement) and adjacent states (cf. Erikson 1989).

18. For example, this occurs in large countries with widely separated polling places. In fact, not all large countries have multiple days of voting, but it is not implausible to assume that even large countries vary in the difficulty found in getting to the polls. The suggestion here is that multiple polling days may serve as an indicator of otherwise unmeasured difficulties in achieving adequate turnout, whatever the reason for those difficulties.

19. Including East European countries would greatly increase this sensitivity because of the noise introduced by idiosyncratic factors that cannot be averaged out over a short sequence of elections.

20. Missing data indicators were included in the analyses but did not prove significant. See note 12.

21. The number of polling days has to meet a more stringent requirement for significance than other variables because we were prepared to accept either a positive or a negative relationship in the case of this variable. Thus, the appropriate test is two tailed, unlike the tests for other variables in the table.

22. The finding regarding polling days is essentially driven by India. Excluding it (or including a dummy variable that picks out that one country) leaves polling days insignificant, as in the first model. Substantively it makes no difference which course is taken, because we do not know why Indians find it harder than others to go to the polls. If India is omitted from the analysis, we explain 89.5 percent of variance in turnout, with all effects but that of polling days retaining virtually the same values and remaining highly significant. Indeed, if we had sufficient contextual information we might be able to code India as a "low electoral salience" country, along with Switzerland and the United States—removing the need for special treatment. Doing so leaves all coefficients except for polling days virtually the same as in the second model in Table 5-4, with variance explained of 90.5 percent.

23. Countries without automatic voter registration that did have compulsory voting were coded as though registration was automatic. If this was not done, the effect of the variable proved significant *and negative*. That is, countries with automatic voter registration saw *lower* turnout than countries with voluntary registration if voluntarism was not deemed to be vitiated by a legal requirement to vote.

24. It can be argued that our use of legislative elections treats U.S. turnout unfairly, because congressional elections are, of course, less salient than presidential elections there. However, even in presidential elections turnout in the United States averages less than 58 percent. So, even had we employed presidential voting, the United States would still have been one of the three countries in our data with lowest turnout. Another problem with treating U.S. elections as low-salience elections arises from the fact that in the 19th century turnout was much higher—yet presumably elections had no greater salience then. In fact, even in the 19th century turnout was no higher than the level found today in medium-turnout countries, leaving plenty of room for low salience to have played a role—especially because one reason generally given for the higher turnout prior to wide-ranging reforms, conducted around the turn of the century, was the prevalence of electoral fraud (Converse 1974; Rusk 1974; but see Burnham 1965).

25. The effect of electoral salience on turnout in countries of the European Union appears to be less (at 18 percent) than the 27 percent measured in a wider universe. The effect of compulsory voting is also greater than in that wider universe. The differences are partly attributable to the different countries employed in the two analyses and partly to the fact that Table 5-4 contains a more fully specified model than Table 5-5. Note that in Table 5-5, an analysis conducted at the individual level yields findings that are identical (to within rounding error) with those found in an analysis conducted at the aggregate level. Moreover, the variance explained at the individual level is very similar to the additional variance explained by country differences in Table 5-3. See van der Eijk, Franklin, et al. (1996, chap. 19) for further discussion of these points.

26. Barnes et al. (1979) studied political participation in Austria, Britain, Germany, the Netherlands, and the United States. Verba et al. (1978) focused on Austria, India, Japan, the Netherlands, Nigeria, the United States, and Yugoslavia.

27. Again, it must be stressed that our attribution of responsiveness (or lack thereof) to Switzerland and the United States drives over half of this effect. Effects of electoral salience are lower in countries of the European Union, where they can be measured without the need for heroic assumptions. But even if we take the estimate generated from Table 5-5, of effects reaching 18 percent from electoral salience (when added to the maximum effect of proportionality), we still get total effects of some 35 percent attributable to institutional variations that affect government responsiveness to electoral behavior.

28. To say it "suffers" from its institutions is to look at things purely from the perspective of electoral turnout. The founding fathers, of course, designed a system that would be unresponsive to the popular will, and their system works pretty much as intended. Our findings suggest that low turnout is an inevitable concomitant.

PART II
POLITICAL INFORMATION

6. Does Lack of Political Information Matter?

W hich amendment to the U.S. Constitution established the direct election of senators? In what year did it take effect? Put these questions to a representative cross-section sample of American adults, and many—if they answered honestly—would not only be unable to answer the questions, they would be surprised to learn that senators were not always directly elected. If this seems too trivial a detail, since we have directly elected senators since the 17th Amendment was adopted in 1913, ask whether the Republican or the Democratic Party is more conservative; what was the stand on any given issue taken by any of the presidential candidates in the last election; or any of countless other questions about historical or contemporary, structural, or procedural matters relating to American politics. Many—sometimes most—American adults would not be able to answer correctly. Such is the knowledge of politics in the general public.

That the political knowledge of most adults is very low is no longer in doubt. "Study after study documents the breadth and depth of citizen ignorance" (Lupia and McCubbins 1998, 1). "The public's lack of information was so well established [after early surveys] that scholars lost interest in studying the subject" (E. Smith 1989, 159). "The results of these surveys [about voter information levels] have usually been interpreted as somewhere between disappointing and disastrous" (Niemi and Junn 1998, 5). "Large numbers of citizens plainly lack elementary pieces of political information . . . [and] are woefully ill-informed about major issues, including issues frequently and visibly in the news" (Sniderman, Brody, and Tetlock 1991, 15).[1]

What is not fully resolved is what to make of this lack of knowledge. As we ask in the title of this chapter: Does lack of political information matter? Do people make reasonable decisions despite their ignorance? Would they make different or better decisions if they were more fully informed? Does the (mal)distribution of political information matter? And, ultimately, does a healthy democracy depend on a well-informed electorate? Having agreed that citizen ignorance is rampant, the controversy has moved to these second-order questions.

People Have Too Little Knowledge

The question of whether ordinary citizens have the capacity to govern goes back at least to Plato. But it is scientific sample surveys of the past half-century that have given political scientists their best look into the knowledge of "the average citizen." These surveys have repeatedly shown a high level of ignorance of facts and figures about politics and government. But the findings go well beyond that simple point. In the 1960s, for example, it was found that citizens knew little about individual public policy issues and, moreover, that many were unable to conceptualize political arguments in any meaningful sense (such as by understanding the liberal-conservative distinction that is the coin of the realm for elite discussions). Similarly, voters were found to be ill-informed about fundamental principles of democracy, and, as a consequence, they frequently expressed politically intolerant views.

The notion of an unsophisticated electorate formed the basis of a long debate between 1965 and 1990. Against this perspective, researchers argued that: (a) the 1950s (which were the basis for many of the initial findings) were unusual in being relatively issueless, and voters showed their inherent capacity for ideological thinking in the 1960s and beyond; (b) voters were issue specialists, knowing about issues of concern to them if not about all issues; (c) citizens *recognized and understood* candidate names and ideological arguments even if they failed to use them spontaneously; (d) the casual atmosphere of a survey and the nature of survey questions greatly underestimate the stability and coherence of opinions; and (e) the observed level of sophistication depends on the environment in which voters find themselves (which helped account for the evidently greater ideological sophistication of European electorates). In addition, it was pointed out that voting decisions are partially based on *candidate* evaluations, and that many of those evaluations are about politically relevant characteristics, such as perceived competence. Similar arguments were made with respect to political tolerance. For example, it was said that intolerance of the 1950s declined rapidly by the 1970s, proving that prejudice was not endemic to the general population.[2]

While many of these arguments carried some weight, in the end the evidence of ignorance was overwhelming. Nuances aside, the general public is ill-informed and ideologically impoverished. Indeed, our contemporary understanding of public opinion reflects this. We now believe that the public responds to surveys with top-of-the-head responses stimulated by the specific questions asked, and that individual responses often betray characteristics such as instability and internal inconsistencies (Zaller 1992).

Yet it must be conceded that many democracies function reasonably well—at least in the sense that they move along with few revolutions, military takeovers, or even major disruptions. So what does it mean to say that people have too little knowledge? One major argument concerns how responsive governments are to their citizens, especially to those who are less well informed.

This argument begins by noting that there is a connection between political knowledge and the ability to form meaningful opinions and to act in accordance with them. There is, first of all, a modest connection between being more informed and holding any opinion at all (for example, Krosnick and Milburn 1990). But it is the quality of opinions that really varies by knowledge levels.

Response stability, for example, is much greater among the well informed (Feldman 1989; Delli Carpini 1996, 232–233). So is the consistency of opinions, whether one means internal consistency (for example, consistent conservatism) on a set of issues (Converse and Markus 1979; Zaller 1992, 113–114), the correlation between self-stated liberalism/conservatism or party identification and issue positions (Zaller 1992, 109–111; Delli Carpini 1996, 253), or the extent to which attitudes are structured in a simple—usually unidimensional—fashion (Stimson 1975; Delli Carpini and Keeter 1996, 236–237). Thus, even though most citizens express opinions quite readily, there is some concern about how meaningful those opinions are among the poorly informed. Indeed, in extreme cases, they might fit Converse's (1964) description of "nonatttitudes."

Poor quality opinions, in any of these senses, might not matter if people sincerely believe them and act in accordance with them. Recent studies, however, have suggested that uninformed individuals may not know their own best interests. This is a difficult proposition to establish; yet recent work is surprisingly convincing.[3] One approach considers whether informed and uninformed people with otherwise similar characteristics have the same preferences. Delli Carpini and Keeter (1996, 238–254), for example, use a regression model involving respondents' knowledge levels and twenty-two other characteristics (such as race, sex, age, and income) to predict their attitudes on a variety of issues. Having controlled for this large number of alternative characteristics that might explain attitudinal differences, they then ask whether uninformed and informed individuals have different opinions. Thus, for example, they compare the attitudes of financially secure and financially distressed individuals toward governmental social welfare problems; they do this separately for those who are extremely uninformed and for those who are extremely well informed. In the uninformed group the difference is quite small, with those who are distressed just slightly more in favor of welfare. In the well-informed group the difference is larger, with those who are distressed considerably more in favor of welfare. Clearly, information has made a difference in attitudes. It is but a short inferential leap to the conclusion that the views of those who are well informed are somehow more "correct," or at least that well-informed individuals hold attitudes that are more consistent with their group interests.[4]

Delli Carpini and Keeter go a step further and connect people's opinions with their partisanship, their evaluations of the president, and their votes. Among other things, they conclude that "each additional increment of knowledge tightens the connection between attitudes and the vote" (256), and that "for the substantial portion of citizens who are poorly informed, . . . voting was poorly connected to their views on issue[s]" (258).[5]

Bartels (1996) takes still another step in this vein by asking whether individuals, if "fully informed," would cast the same ballots as they in fact did. His approach is similar to Delli Carpini and Keeter's in that he estimates the effects of knowledge after controlling for social and demographic characteristics. For presidential elections from 1972 to 1992, he finds that the average deviation (across some 20 groups) from fully informed voting ranges from 7 to 12 percentage points. He interprets these results as indicating that individuals make candidate choices "significantly better than they would by chance, but significantly less well than they would with complete information" (217). Two other findings add to the significance of the results. First, the deviation from the overall vote (that is, taking into account that some individual "mistakes" cancel out) is often several percentage points, which is large enough for Bartels to conclude that the electorate as a whole is not acting as if it is fully informed. Second, there is a significant bias among the uninformed votes toward incumbents and Democrats; the bias toward incumbents is especially disturbing because it may be "simply a kind of natural default option for voters too uninformed to compare the candidates on their merits" (220).[6]

Althaus (1998), in the reading included here as Chapter 7, extends this analysis in yet another direction. Using a similar approach, in which opinions are regressed on numerous social and demographic characteristics in addition to political knowledge, he finds that the uneven distribution of knowledge leads to a bias in survey results compared to what they would be in a fully informed electorate. The results are often small, but they are persistent and tend to be unidirectional (with a "fully-informed" citizenry tending to be more liberal, in our reading of the results). While Althaus shies away from an interpretation of what the "true" interests of the public are, he notes that his findings "demonstrat[e] that survey results sometimes look the way they do because so many people are ill-informed about politics and because certain people tend to be better informed than others." Thus, to the extent that representatives rely on opinion polls, "information effects can impair the responsiveness of governments to their citizens."

The analyses by Delli Carpini and Keeter, Bartels, and Althaus show significant effects from lack of political knowledge. However, these effects might well be misestimated. Their estimation methodology requires assuming that people who are not fully informed would be similar to their demographic twins if they were fully informed. Yet it is not at all clear that highly informed individuals with similar demographics will or should have identical opinions or come to the same judgment about competing candidates. For example, is it in the best interest of the poor to vote for a candidate who promises to expand the welfare state or for a candidate who promises to cut taxes and stimulate job and income growth? A good case can be made either way, and we need to be careful about labeling different views as not being in a person's best interest. In addition, the assumption of common interests does not take into account why some people are willing to get along with less information than others do. There are reasons why some people have less interest in politics than other people with the identical demographic characteristics, and these reasons might affect their opinions.[7]

There are at least three other concerns that stem from the low levels of knowledge among ordinary citizens. One is that an uninformed populace can be manipulated. Manipulation may be by the media, by experts, by bureaucrats, and it may even be self-imposed by people's prejudices. In one of the more interesting, if narrow, demonstrations of this effect, Kuklinski and Hurley (1994) used an experiment to demonstrate how people's reactions to hypothetical statements about racial subjects were greatly affected by who was thought to have made them. More broadly, discussions by Zaller (1992, chap. 12) and Page and Shapiro (1992, chap. 9) offer equally insightful if sharply contrasting views of the likelihood of such manipulation. Zaller is relatively optimistic, believing that policy experts who are independent of government and of organized interests routinely provide information that allows even an uninformed electorate to put a check on political leaders and, on occasion, to remove them. Page and Shapiro are more pessimistic, emphasizing the possibilities of control of information by governments and international corporations, an argument they illustrate with various cases of presumed misinformation. Regardless of the relative balance, these discussions each raise the specter that under certain conditions a lack of knowledge in the mass public allows it to be misled about important policy matters.[8]

The second concern about the public's ignorance is that lack of information is closely associated with antidemocratic views. It has been demonstrated repeatedly that more education is associated with greater support for democratic norms, especially the willingness to allow the free expression of ideas — including ideas one is personally opposed to (Stouffer 1954; Prothro and Grigg 1960; Nunn, Crockett, and Williams 1978; Sullivan, Piereson, and Marcus 1982; McClosky and Brill 1983; McClosky and Zaller 1984; Gibson and Bingham 1985; Sniderman et al. 1991; Nie, Junn, and Stehlik-Barry 1996). Education involves more than absorption of political knowledge, of course, and there are several reasons for the connection between amount of schooling and political tolerance. Nevertheless, knowledge appears to play a crucial role. When, for example, Delli Carpini and Keeter (1996, 221–223) control for both education levels and knowledge of the Supreme Court and civil liberties, it is education that loses its predictive power. Perhaps more to the point, *absolute* levels of support for democratic norms are sometimes shockingly low among the less well educated; our most cherished freedoms are sometimes endangered because of lack of popular support associated with political ignorance.[9]

The third concern about public ignorance is that lack of information contributes to low levels of political participation. As with tolerance, the connection between education and participation is thoroughly documented (for example, Rosenstone and Hansen 1993; Verba, Schlozman, and Brady 1995; Nie et al. 1996), and there is some evidence that knowledge per se plays an important part in making that connection (Delli Carpini and Keeter 1996, 224–227; National Association of Secretaries of State 1999, 36–38).

Overall, then, many citizens are saddled with low-quality or nonexistent opinions, a questionable ability even to articulate or act on their own interests, opinions that may be manipulated by others and influenced by their own prejudices, a relative absence of support for democratic norms, and a lack of political participation — all attributable to some degree to low levels of political knowledge. Often these characteristics are benign. But not always. Moreover, there is concern that, despite rising education levels, low political knowledge and its correlates are only becoming worse. Indeed, young people today are sometimes described as disinterested, disengaged, and distrustful (Astin et al. 1997, 28, 45, 57; Bennett and Rademacher 1997; Putnam 2000). Levels of turnout and other forms of political participation are so low among the young as to cause concern over the future of American democracy (National Association of Secretaries of State 1999; Putnam 1995a, 2000), and they have led to calls for a reinvigoration of civic education and other remedial actions (Task Force on Civic Education 1997; National Commission on Civic Renewal 1998). Whether these concerns are exaggerated, and whether the proposed remediation efforts will work, the existence of concern among so many individuals and groups powerfully illustrates the argument that low levels of knowledge create political risks. Cues and shortcuts (described below) often enable people to make sound political decisions, but they contain fewer guarantees than are inherent in a more knowledgeable electorate.

People (at Least Collectively) Make Reasonable Decisions

As early as 1966, V. O. Key Jr. (1966, 7) made what he called the "perverse and unorthodox argument . . . that voters are not fools." And, as noted earlier, there were assaults on the "unsophisticated electorate" viewpoint throughout the next two and a half decades. Yet, in the end, these efforts failed because they could not refute the evidence that citizens are ill-informed about politics. In the last decade, however, this same mass public has been rehabilitated. Voters are now seen as anything but fools. Rather, they are seen as individuals who are able to reason effectively about complex matters, to arrive at good decisions about candidates, and, in general, to act as if they were well informed. And even if there are deficiencies among individual voters, the public as a whole is seen as reaching reasonable decisions.

A dramatic change in thinking has come about because researchers changed the focus of investigation. They began, rather than ended, with the finding that voters have little political interest and information. Having accepted what Sniderman et al. (1991, chap. 2) refer to as the "minimalist" view of voter information and ideology, they then ask how voters can make decisions that are, to some degree at least, quite sensible. Voters do not choose among candidates randomly; public opinion does not fluctuate wildly, as if choices were made willy-nilly. How is it, then, that citizens decide for whom to vote? How do they form their opinions about political issues? How is it that collective decisions often seem so sensible? The answer comes in two parts, one referring to the way in which individuals use "shortcuts" to overcome information deficits and the other to the way in which statistical aggregation overcomes individual shortcomings. Each of these arguments will be treated in turn, and we have reprinted a reading about each of them.

According to the first argument, individuals do not need full information to make sensible decisions. Indeed, it is noted that in most areas of life, such as purchasing an automobile, people make decisions without being fully informed. Yet these decisions are, by and large, good ones. This perspective is sometimes labeled that of "low information" or "limited information" rationality (Popkin 1994, chap. 1; Lupia and McCubbins 1998, chap. 1).[10] Researchers note that instead of gathering vast amounts of data—which would almost certainly be irrational given the cost (of time) involved—voters rely on all sorts of mechanisms that give them information that is sufficient for their tasks. These mechanisms are variously referred to as shortcuts, heuristics, cues, and information aids (see especially Sniderman, Brody, and Tetlock 1991 for the first major statement of the importance of heuristics in voter decision making).[11]

There are a number of strands to this argument. One prominent feature is the extent to which voters obtain and use information from various "experts." Experts may be technical gurus who understand the intricacies of taxation, agriculture, natural resources, the Internet, or whatever. They may be political experts who follow and interpret the daily activities and pronouncements of candidates and public officials. Their views sometimes come to us directly through the media—television and newspapers, of course, but also an incredible number and variety of electronic media, general purpose and specialized magazines, newsletters, flyers, and so on. But expert views also come to us through a two-step flow, in which ideas and opinions expressed in the media are passed along from one person to another. Thus voters who themselves pay little day-to-day attention to policies and politics nonetheless act on information that originates with experts.[12]

Another feature of the argument is that citizens in fact obtain a good deal of relevant information in their daily lives. Popkin (1994) notes that people make many mundane economic decisions all the time—buying gas, filing income tax forms, looking for jobs, deciding on insurance, and so on. Thus "one need not be an economist to see which way the economy is going" (23). Similarly, information about government programs forces itself on many voters—through entitlement programs, for example. Moreover, he reminds us of the existence of issue publics—groups of people who for one reason or another follow particular issues quite closely—and that most citizens may be part of an issue public on some issue, albeit different issue publics for different citizens. All the while there are news junkies who will "sound the alarm"[13] when there is something that large numbers of people should pay attention to.[14]

No matter where and when we get our information, an essential part of the limited rationality argument is that it often takes only a little information to permit reasonable decisions. Lupia and McCubbins (1998, 30–36) explain this in terms of a concept drawn from cognitive science called "connectionism." People make all sorts of connections between and among concepts that allow them to make good decisions with a remarkably small amount of information. One of the most obvious connections related to voting is between a candidate's partisanship and his or her issue positions; although there are sizable numbers of voters who do not know the parties' positions, those who do have quite distinct perceptions of where they stand on most issues, and these perceptions are used to estimate candidate issue placements (Conover and Feldman 1989). Another widely used connection is the nature of group support for candidates; if one knows only that blacks (or the religious right, gays, or some other group) support a candidate, that alone may be sufficient reason to believe that the candidate's issue positions are similar to—or different from—one's own views.[15] Occasionally these kinds of connections will mislead us, and sometimes they have to be adjusted (as when a restaurant chain that we have long associated with good food experiences a significant decline in the quality of its meals). But most of the time, they lead to good decisions.

Models of limited rationality thus show how it is possible for citizens to make good decisions with little information.[16] Yet, as Bartels (1996, 198) noted, "it is easier to assume than to demonstrate that cues and shortcuts do, in fact, allow relatively uninformed voters to behave as *if* they were fully informed." Lau and Redlawsk (1997), in the reading included here as Chapter 8, turn directly to this task, asking whether people "vote correctly." In an experiment in which they provide subjects with relatively complete information *after* they have made their vote decisions, Lau and Redlawsk find that 70 percent would not have changed their vote, suggesting that they voted correctly (that is, in accordance with their fully informed interests) This may overstate the amount of voting correctly, however, since some people may not want to be appear inconsistent by changing their vote (see their footnote 4). Using national election survey data from 1972 to 1988, they estimate that a slightly higher proportion, about 75 percent, voted correctly. Interpreting these results cautiously, they conclude that "this high a level of 'correct' voting certainly validates the efficiency of heuristic-based information processing that underlies our notion of human nature" (594).[17]

Moving to the macro-level and supposing that individual decisions are correct "most of the time," the second argument about the decision-making quality of the electorate suggests that this is good enough, in that statistical aggregation will overcome individual shortcomings. As Page and Shapiro (1992, 26) explain in the reading included here as Chapter 9, "if individuals have even a modest tendency to be correct, a collective decision by those individuals can have a very high likelihood of being right." The basic, but powerful, idea is that random "errors" will cancel out. One individual will vote Republican when his own best interests would be served by the Democrats, but another individual will vote Democratic when her best interests would be served by the Republicans.

Page and Shapiro demonstrate the power of the aggregation argument in another context—that is, by countering what they refer to as "the myth of capricious change" in public opinion. Despite evidence that individual opinions are often unstable (for example, Converse 1964; Feldman 1989), Page and Shapiro show that at the aggregate level opinions are most often highly stable over long periods. There are exceptions, but the authors find these to be rare but certainly not nonexistent (see their Table 9-3). When large changes *are* observed, they typically come about "very gradually, as part of glacial movements in Americans' beliefs and life circumstances [and] certainly do not constitute evidence of capricious changes in public opinion" (51). Moreover, "virtually all cases of abrupt opinion change have been related to significant events that rational citizens would take into account" (56). Altogether, whatever shortcomings exist among individual citizens are submerged when one looks at public opinion as a whole.

As to the other concerns about the possible effects of limited knowledge — manipulability, intolerance, and nonparticipation — a frequent argument is that they are grossly exaggerated. While no one has devised a test, analogous to those for voting correctly, for how a fully informed versus an uninformed electorate would respond to attempts at manipulation, it is hard to make a case that the population is routinely deceived. Indeed, Mueller (1999, 148–150) argues that tyrants have found it necessary to abandon democracy precisely because people will not be fooled for long. While there may be some persistent, strong biases in the information that Americans receive (Page and Shapiro 1992, chap. 9) — such as procapitalist and nationalistic biases — it is unclear, as they recognize, that one would want to altogether eliminate them.

Regarding antidemocratic views, there is no doubt that people — especially those with limited education — express intolerance. Yet it does not automatically follow that we have an intolerant society. For one thing, it has long been known that people often display tolerance in practice even while speaking intolerance.[18] As for joint efforts, Mueller wryly notes (1999) that it is hard to get individuals to express their intolerance collectively; "after all, that would require a certain amount of work" (151). Moreover, as Weissberg (1998, chap. 7) observes, society has devised ways of exercising tolerance in practice despite the absence of "hearts and minds tolerance." He notes, for example, that compulsory tolerance (for example, in the armed forces), communal separatism (for example, the Amish), and self-imposed "invisibility" have been used both historically and in the contemporary United States to avoid confrontations and discrimination.

Finally, some would argue that low participation levels might not be an entirely bad thing. For one thing, not voting might be a "correct vote" for some citizens who are cross-pressured. If a person cares only about two issues and passionately takes the Republican position on one (say, affirmative action) and equally strongly takes the Democratic position on the other (say, abortion), would it not be "rational" for that person to abstain? Additionally, although it is presently not fashionable to say so, apathy may serve a purpose. We have already noted that with respect to tolerance. But others have observed that indifference and noninvolvement contribute to the smooth operation of a democracy. Berelson made the point nearly fifty years ago when he noted that we have a variety of conflicting expectations. For example, we expect individuals to care deeply about elections, but afterwards we expect reconciliation. With that in mind, he asked rhetorically, "How could a mass democracy work if all the people were deeply involved in politics?" (Berelson et al. 1954, 314).[19] What we may, in fact, want is for all individuals to have the opportunity to participate when they feel sufficiently strongly about an issue but that most of the time, most individuals will not feel much need to get involved (at least beyond voting).

Conclusion

In a previous edition of this volume, we noted that controversies are rarely resolved, only changed or redirected. Here is one instance in which we seem genuinely to have resolved a controversy. The knowledge level of the American electorate — indeed, of mass electorates everywhere — is very low. Of course, there is a distribution of knowledgeability, with some individuals being highly informed; nearly everyone pays attention to politics some times and under some conditions; and levels of knowledge and sophistication vary with circumstances. But overall, there is no longer any real dispute with the proposition that citizens are, on average, not sophisticated political consumers.

Having resolved one question, we have raised another closely related one. Does the admittedly low level of information matter? About this, there is still plenty of uncertainty. Researchers have made a convincing case that citizens make reasonable vote choices and other political decisions on the basis of extremely limited information. Yet, while "reasonable," are these really good decisions? Would better decisions be made if individuals were more knowledgeable? And in what sense are they good? Is the appropriate standard whether individuals vote in the way that best promotes their own interests?

Consider that one implication of full information is that "group interests would be more clearly articulated" (Delli Carpini and Keeter 1996, 251). Would society be better off if this were to occur? Or would group conflict be more intense, with society unable to rely on what Mueller (1999, 152) refers to as "minority rule with majority acquiescence"? Would individuals who felt more intensely about issues, and who were better able to understand the consequences of policy decisions, be more, or less willing to compromise?

Perhaps the most difficult question of all is whether, and how, we can increase information levels if we ultimately adopt that as a goal. Can we, in fact, do a better job of civic education? Recent work lends hope, in the sense that secondary school civics and government course work is related to greater political knowledge (Niemi and Junn 1998) and enrollments in such courses, after dipping sharply in the 1960s and 1970s, appear to be on the increase (Niemi and Smith 2001). Moreover, heightened concern over the state of civic knowledge, participation, and education is likely to focus even more attention on such efforts (see, for example, National Commission on Civic Renewal 1998). Yet the fact that rising education levels over the past half-century have been accompanied by flat knowledge curves (Delli Carpini and Keeter 1996) and declining participation (Chapter 2) suggest that there are severe limits to what can be attained.

In the end, perhaps what is needed are better theories about and more empirical work on the real — not supposed — consequences of lack of knowledge. Having settled the question of what citizens know, and having recently been convinced that citizens can operate quite effectively with limited knowledge and considerable uncertainty even about their own opinions, it will prove useful to

understand more clearly whether, and in what ways, democracy and citizen information and attitudes are related.

Notes

1. As one of us wrote elsewhere, "demonstrating the ignorance of the public has become
   something of a cottage industry, with one researcher after another trying to find a
   more absurd example of what Americans do not know about politics and government
   or a more apt metaphor to express their collective ignorance" (Niemi and Junn 1998,
   5). Two of our favorites: Zaller (1992, 16) suggests that citizens can name more members on the starting line-up of their home-town major league baseball team than jus-
   tices on the U.S. Supreme Court; novelist James Michener writes that while research-
   ing the U.S. electoral system, he was told by one person that "every boy and girl
   should go to college and if they can't afford Yale or Harvard, why, Electoral is just as
   good, if you work" (1969, 43).
2. The arguments with respect to the unsophisticated electorate are reviewed, and some
   of the seminal readings are reproduced, in Niemi and Weisberg (1993a, Part II;
   1993b, Part II). These sources include a discussion of the evidence about levels of ideological thinking in European electorates.
3. At one level, such a proposition is obvious. For example, even well-informed individuals may not know which of two proposed tax bills is in their best interest because
   the consequences of particular provisions may not be obvious. But it is quite another
   matter to suggest that uninformed individuals somehow have "inappropriate" opinions on issues such as gay rights, abortion, or the death penalty, and these are the
   issues researchers are concerned about.
4. Nonetheless, we should note the difficulty of making this kind of argument. Consider, for example, who should be more "pro-choice," women or men. The obvious
   argument is that women should be more supportive because it is their bodies that are
   affected. Yet if men are more supportive of choice, is this because women (or the men,
   for that matter) are uninformed about their own best interests?
5. A related finding is that the political reasoning used by less educated (and presumably less well-informed) individuals is driven more by affect, while that of more educated individuals is driven more by ideology (Sniderman et al. 1991, 79–88).
6. Bartels speculates that bias toward the Democrats may be the result of a Democratic
   advantage in partisanship "inherited" from parents (220). If the effect on election outcomes does not seem all that large, one might think about what it must be in congressional elections, where the effect of incumbency voting is quite large (see Chapter 14 of this text).
7. For example, consider the effect of issue publics on the logic in these pieces. Althaus
   gives people without opinions on an issue the same position as those with informed
   preferences who have the same demographic features and who gave opinions. The
   people without an opinion on an issue are clearly not part of the issue public on that
   issue, while some of the people with an opinion might care intensely about that issue
   because of variables not included in the model. To take a specific case, women who
   have had abortions are likely to have intense opinions on that topic, so giving people
   more political information would not necessarily give people without opinions on
   that issue the same views as those who already have intense opinions.
8. Expert opinions and their influence on decision making by the general public have been
   the subject of considerable study in the area of "economic voting" (see Chapter 10 of
   this text). MacKuen, Erikson, and Stimson (1992a) argue that mass opinion is positively

influenced by the opinions of economic experts, allowing the electorate to act as if it were highly informed. Others have emphasized systematic biases in experts' views and in media reporting of economic news, along with the relative absence of elite views in the public's decision making (see Sanders, Marsh, and Ward 1993; Blood and Philips 1995; Nadeau, Niemi, Fan, and Amato 1999; Nadeau, Niemi, and Amato 2000).

9. Hibbing and Theiss-Morse (1995, chap. 4) contribute a valuable point in their discussion of the roots of cynicism about Congress. They emphasize that what the public needs is not so much information about specific features, such as the size of the congressional staff. Rather, the public needs more information about the nature of democratic processes such as the role of "public disagreements, debates, compromises, competing interests, conflicting information, and slowness" (82).

10. As Popkin (1994, 9–12) points out, voting is not precisely analogous to buying a television set. He prefers the analogy of investing money because of the uncertainty involved and the extent to which rewards depend on the actions of others. Lupia and McCubbins (1998, 30–36) speak of a "cognitive stock market," but they are referring to the way in which people process information rather than to the subject matter of the decisions they make.

11. Heuristic processing is the use of simple decision rules, such as trust in experts' statements or acceptance of consensus judgments, instead of systematically processing all available information in reaching judgments (Chaiken 1980). It is based on Tversky and Kahneman's (1974) study of inference in which they describe specific psychological shortcuts employed in inference situations, such as the availability heuristic used when people estimate frequencies of occurrence of events by how easily they can remember examples of the event. The usage of these terms in the political science literature is much looser, often being applied to any shortcut procedure regardless of its psychological basis.

12. A related argument is that voters' values may matter more than their issue positions and knowledge. Voters may not know each candidate's position on all the issues, but they may instead see which candidate they agree with on underlying values, even if they are not especially self-conscious of those values.

13. Popkin credits this apt analogy to W. Russell Neuman in the *New York Times*, May 29, 1989, p. 31.

14. Of course, not all information that comes to us is equally credible or equally persuasive. Much of Lupia and McCubbins' (1998) work is devoted to uncovering the conditions under which people trust others and accept their advice and how democratic institutions can be more or less effective in promoting "enlightenment and reasoned choice" in the electorate and in legislative bodies.

15. Related to this sort of inference is what Brady and Sniderman (1985) call the *likeability heuristic*, which says that voters quite accurately estimate the issue positions of major groups by combining their own beliefs with how much they like or dislike the group.

16. One other recent argument is that people in fact use more information than they are given credit for. The on-line model of information processing suggests that people incorporate new information as they receive it, update their views of the subject accordingly, and then quickly forget the input, although retaining their updated views. Thus, when people are asked for what they know about a subject, they may "know" very little, even of what has gone into their current view. We discuss this argument in more detail in Part III.

17. Of course, others might interpret these figures as low, showing that 25–30 percent of decisions are not correct. Additionally, one can reasonably take issue with their definition of correct voting. For example, if people vote on the basis of perceived national interests rather than narrow personal interests, is this voting correctly? Indeed, a point similar to this is raised in the so-called economic voting literature, in which it is often

noted that individuals vote on the basis of perceived national economic conditions rather than on the state of their own finances. See Chapter 10.

18. See LaPiere's (1934) well-known field experiment in the 1930s, in which hotel and restaurant owners expressed an unwillingness to host Chinese and yet provided a Chinese couple with service when they appeared.

19. Not surprisingly, this argument has not gone unchallenged all these years. It was labeled an elitist view and generated a lively debate. See especially Walker (1966). Moreover, even those who would concede that apathy can be useful may feel that current levels of noninvolvement in the United States are too high.

Further Readings

Individual Political Opinions

Zaller, John R., *The Nature and Origins of Mass Opinion* (Cambridge: Cambridge University Press, 1992). Classic account of the nature of individual opinions, how people form them, and how individuals answer survey questions.

Aggregate Public Opinion

Page, Benjamin I., and Robert Y. Shapiro, *The Rational Public: Fifty Years of Trends in Americans' Policy Preferences* (Chicago: University of Chicago Press, 1992). Effects of aggregation on individual opinions; public opinion is generally stable and changes sensibly.

Information Limits

Bartels, Larry M., "Uninformed Votes: Information Effects in Presidential Elections," *American Journal of Political Science* 40 (1996): 194–230. The effects of greater political information on presidential voting and the vote outcome are shown through simulated results.

Delli Carpini, Michael X, and Scott Keeter, *What Americans Know about Politics and Why It Matters* (New Haven: Yale University Press, 1996). Wide-ranging analysis of knowledge levels of Americans and the difference it makes in political attitudes and behavior.

Hibbing, John R., and Elizabeth Theiss-Morse, *Congress as Public Enemy: Public Attitudes toward American Political Institutions* (New York: Cambridge University Press, 1995). Discussion of ignorance and cynicism about Congress and politics.

Kuklinski, James H., and Norman H. Hurley, "On Hearing and Interpreting Political Messages: A Cautionary Tale of Citizen Cue-Taking," *Journal of Politics* 58 (1994):729–751. Individuals form opinions based on supposed endorsements.

Kuklinski, James H., and Paul J. Quirk, "Reconsidering the Rational Public: Cognition, Heuristics, and Mass Opinion," in *Elements of Reason: Understanding and Expanding the Limits of Political Rationality,* ed. Arthur Lupia, Mathew D. McCubbins, and Samuel L. Popkin (New York: Cambridge University Press, 2000). Effective use of political heuristics might be overstated. Citizens may often function suboptimally in a political environment strategically created by elites.

Kuklinski, James H., Paul J. Quirk, Jennifer Jerit, David Schwieder, and Robert F. Rich, "Misinformation and the Currency of Citizenship," *Journal of Politics* 62 (2000): 790–816. Confidently held, mistaken beliefs influence people's issue preferences; given correct information, people change these beliefs only under demanding circumstances.

Informational Shortcuts

Lupia, Arthur, "Shortcuts Versus Encyclopedias: Information and Voting Behavior in California Insurance Reform Elections," *American Political Science Review* 88 (1994): 63–76. Use of group endorsements and other shortcuts in referendum voting.

Lupia, Arthur, and Mathew D. McCubbins, *The Democratic Dilemma: Can Citizens Learn What They Need to Know?* (New York: Cambridge University Press, 1998). Discussion of conditions for trusting others and accepting their advice and how democratic institutions help or hurt.

Mueller, John, *Capitalism, Democracy, and Ralph's Pretty Good Grocery* (Princeton: Princeton University Press, 1999). Thought-provoking argument that democracy should not be idealized with respect to equality, civic knowledge, and participation.

Popkin, Samuel L., *The Reasoning Voter: Communication and Persuasion in Presidential Campaigns* (Chicago: University of Chicago Press, 1994). Readable account of how voters gather information simply and use gut reasoning to make decisions.

Sniderman, Paul M., Richard A. Brody, and Philip E. Tetlock, *Reasoning and Choice: Explorations in Political Psychology* (New York: Cambridge University Press, 1991). People make reasonable decisions through the use of heuristics, affect-driven reasoning.

7. Information Effects in Collective Preferences

Scott L. Althaus

A number of path-breaking studies in recent years have suggested that the mass public's inattention to politics may have less bearing on the quality of its collective opinions than previously thought (e.g., Converse 1990; Page and Shapiro 1992; Sniderman, Brody, and Tetlock 1991; Wittman 1995). These studies emphasize that while most individuals tend to be ill informed about the political world, the availability of heuristic shortcuts and the filtering process of statistical aggregation may help compensate for this lack of knowledge in measures of collective opinion, such as election results or opinion surveys. If this line of thinking is correct, then we can conclude with Page and Shapiro (1992, 385) that opinion surveys provide a "good deal of coherent guidance about policy." If the mass public is unable to compensate effectively for its lack of political knowledge, then the use of surveys and other measures of collective opinion as inputs to the political process may be rightly questioned.

In this article I extend recent work by Delli Carpini and Keeter (1996) and Bartels (1996) on the measurement of information effects in collective preferences. Contrary to much of the literature on collective opinion, this study finds that the low levels and uneven social distribution of political knowledge in the mass public often cause opinion surveys to misrepresent the mix of voices in a society. Correcting for information asymmetries reveals that many collective policy preferences would look quite different if all citizens were equally well informed about politics.

Because knowledgeable respondents are better able to form opinions consistent with their political predispositions (Bennett 1995; Converse 1964; Delli Carpini and Keeter 1996; Lockerbie 1991; Stimson 1975; Zaller 1992), and because they tend to give opinions more frequently than other people (Althaus 1996a; Delli Carpini and Keeter 1996, 230–231; Krosnick and Milburn 1990), the demographic characteristics of well-informed people — who tend to be more affluent, older, white, and male compared to the ill informed — can cause collective preferences to reflect disproportionately the opinions of some groups more than others. These two dynamics can create information effects in measures of public opinion. By *information effect* I mean a bias in the shape of collective opinion caused by the low levels and uneven social distribution of political knowledge in a population. While others have examined the individual-level effects of political knowledge on response stability (e.g., Delli Carpini and Keeter 1996,

Source: American Political Science Review 92, 3 (September 1998): 545–558.

231–234; Feldman 1989, following Converse 1964) and the role of political knowledge as a link between political predispositions and policy or voting preferences (e.g., Bennett 1995; Delli Carpini and Keeter 1996, chap. 6; Zaller 1992), the focus here is more narrowly on the macrolevel impact of these effects on measures of collective opinion.

Building on the simulation approach developed independently by Delli Carpini and Keeter (1996) and Bartels (1996), this article examines the substantive impact of information effects in policy preference data from the American National Election Studies (NES). Simulating "fully informed" collective preferences from actual survey data shows that group differences in knowledge, along with the public's rather modest average level of political information, can cause significant distortions in measures of collective opinion. More important, the direction and magnitude of these distortions fall into predictable patterns. The uneven social distribution of political knowledge causes the mass public consistently to appear more progressive on some issues and more conservative on others than might be the case if all citizens were equally well informed about politics. To the extent that opinion polls influence democratic politics, this finding suggests that information effects may impair the responsiveness of governments to their citizens.

How Political Knowledge Affects Collective Opinion

Survey after survey has shown that citizens are often at a loss to relate basic facts about the players, issues, and rules of the game that structure American political life (Delli Carpini and Keeter 1996). The extent of this ignorance led several early and influential studies to suggest that the public's political opinions are often fickle and not to be trusted (Almond 1950; Berelson, Lazarsfeld, and McPhee 1954; Converse 1964, 1970). Yet, in recent years this pessimistic view of public opinion has been challenged on several fronts. The first challenge stems from work in cognitive psychology showing that people who are ill informed about public affairs can nonetheless form opinions consistent with their political predispositions. They can do this by taking cues from trusted political elites about which policies they should prefer and by harnessing a variety of heuristic strategies to deduce their political preferences, thus avoiding the need to infer preferences from factual bits of knowledge stored in long-term memory (e.g., Ferejohn and Kuklinski 1990; Lupia 1994; Mondak 1994; Popkin 1991; Smith and Squire 1990; Sniderman, Brody, and Tetlock 1991; Zaller 1992). From this perspective, the public's low levels of information may not be a significant problem because many people apparently can compensate for their lack of knowledge with information shortcuts.

The second challenge comes from a line of work suggesting that aggregate opinion may be able to reflect the public's interests even when the opinions of most individuals are ill informed, ambivalent, indifferent, or inconsistent (e.g., Converse 1990; Ferejohn and Kuklinski 1990; Page and Shapiro 1992). This view suggests that the process of aggregating opinions should tend to cancel out the more or less random opinions given by ill-informed respondents. To the extent that this occurs, measures of collective opinion should reflect the nonrandom opinions of knowledgeable respondents. A related argument stemming from Condorcet's jury theorem suggests a similar conclusion. Based entirely on statistical probabilities, the theorem shows that, under certain conditions, groups tend to provide more informed decisions than individuals (Condorcet [1785] 1972; Grofman and Owen 1986; Ladha 1992; Miller 1986; but see Austen-Smith and Banks 1996). From this perspective, it is the aggregation process itself which generates meaningful collective opinions.

Further support for "revisionist" challenges comes from experimental studies suggesting that the common methods used to measure information about politics may actually test recall ability rather than knowledge-in-use. Known as the "on-line" or "impression-driven" model of information processing (Lodge, McGraw, and Stroh 1989; Lodge, Steenbergen, and Brau 1995), this view suggests that many people process information at the time they are exposed to it, update their opinion accordingly, and then quickly forget the information itself while retaining the updated summary judgment. Thus, people may express informed preferences even though they may be unable to recall the factual information used to shape those preferences. From this perspective, the public's apparently low levels of political knowledge may be a red herring. Its judgments may be more informed than they seem in light of the apparently poor performance of those citizens on knowledge tests.

Despite the note of optimism sounded by these revisionist arguments, empirical evidence in support of their claims is quite modest. A number of studies have detailed how people *can* use on-line processing and various information shortcuts to make up for a lack of factual knowledge, but there is surprisingly little evidence that large numbers of people *do* use these strategies effectively, regularly, and across a wide range of situations and issues. More glaring still is the lack of support for the collective rationality hypothesis. I am aware of only two attempts to test this idea empirically. One study (Bartels 1996) found that aggregation helped voters act as if they were somewhat better informed than they actually were, but not as if they were fully informed. The other (Althaus 1995) found that statistical aggregation had quite limited information-pooling qualities.

Revisionist perspectives also tend to overlook an important fact: Low information levels are only half the problem. Just as important is the observation that some kinds of people tend to be better informed than others. Knowledge of politics is concentrated among those who are politically and socially advantaged. College graduates and relatively affluent people tend to be consistently well informed, while high school dropouts and relatively poor people tend to be consistently ill informed (Delli Carpini and Keeter 1996; Neuman 1986; Sigelman and Yanarella 1986). Political knowledge also is distributed unevenly among groups with distinctive and potentially competing political interests. For instance, whites tend to be more informed than blacks, men more than women, and older people more than younger people (Bennett 1988; Delli Carpini and Keeter 1996; Neuman 1986; Sigelman and Yanarella 1986).

There are two ways that information asymmetries among groups can undermine representation in opinion surveys. The first is by affecting the demographic correspondence between a survey sample and the group of people who give substantive responses. Those who are poorly informed about politics tend to give "don't know" and "no opinion" responses at much higher rates than more knowledgeable people (Althaus 1996a; Delli Carpini and Keeter 1996, 230–231; Krosnick and Milburn 1990). This tendency leaves the group of opinion givers disproportionately well educated, affluent, male, white, and middle aged relative to the population they are supposed to represent (Althaus 1996b). Because these voices tend to be overrepresented in the ranks of opinion givers, the particular needs, wants, and values expressed by some groups may come to be represented disproportionately in collective preferences.

The second way that information asymmetries affect representation is by influencing the quality of opinions that respondents provide. Our ability to form preferences consistent with our political predispositions is often mediated by the quality and quantity of political information we can bring to bear on an issue. The importance of knowledge to the formation of policy preferences comes from the way that values are connected to attitudes through beliefs: beliefs about the state of the world, cause-and-effect processes, what government is currently doing, and the likely outcomes of government actions (Delli Carpini and Keeter 1996, chap. 6; Downs 1957, 79–80). Some ill-informed people may believe a policy is the "correct" solution without knowing whether it is consistent with their predispositions or whether it is the best way to achieve a given end. Others may believe a policy serves their interests while someone with more perfect or complete information can see that the policy is diametrically opposed to them. Because the well informed are likely to have more accurate beliefs than the ill informed, they are more likely to express policy preferences consistent with their political predispositions (Converse 1964; Lockerbie 1991; Stimson 1975; Zaller 1992). As a result, the interests of respondents who are relatively well informed may come to be more accurately reflected in measures of collective opinion. In other words, such measures may reflect the needs, wants, and values of whites better than those of blacks, men better than women, and the rich better than the poor.

It would seem that the low levels and uneven social distribution of political knowledge may indeed have an important bearing on the quality of surveyed public opinion. The problem is how best to measure any potential distortion in collective preferences brought about by information asymmetries. One must find a way to estimate how the opinions people express in surveys might change if respondents were more completely informed about the issues.

Measuring Information Effects in Collective Preferences

Ever since Marx suggested that "false consciousness" distracts workers from their material interests, students of politics have grappled unsuccessfully with how to determine whether people's interests are at odds with their opinions.

Some, like Marx and Edmund Burke before him, argue that political interests are objective and can be identified for any group of people without regard to their stated preferences. Some, like Jeremy Bentham and John Stuart Mill, claim that interests are subjective and thus inseparable from the expressed wishes of individuals speaking for themselves. But in light of inherent problems with each of these definitions, more recent work has focused instead on interests as "fully informed" or "enlightened" preferences (Bartels 1990; Connolly 1972; Dahl 1989, 180–181; Delli Carpini and Keeter 1996; Lippmann 1955, 42; Mansbridge 1983, 24–26). In this perspective, as Jane Mansbridge (1983, 25) puts it, interests are revealed in "the preferences that people would have if their information were perfect, including the knowledge they would have in retrospect if they had a chance to live out the consequences of each choice before actually making a decision." By equating interests with hypothetical fully informed preferences, this perspective provides a useful approach for determining when the preferences expressed by individuals may be at odds with their "fully informed" needs, wants, and values.

The difficulty lies in sorting out the best among several possible ways of operationalizing this definition of interests. Two traditional approaches have been used to explore what collective opinion might look like if opinion givers were relatively better informed than the general public. The first is to purge ill-informed respondents from among the ranks of opinion givers through the use of filtering questions. While this is a particularly blunt method—it ignores completely how individual opinions might change with more political knowledge—it is nevertheless widely used by survey organizations to isolate "informed" public opinion.

The second approach manipulates the amount and quality of information available to people who express preferences of various kinds. Experimental methods for assessing the role of information in preference formation have been used extensively in social and cognitive psychology. These methods have also been used to explore what fully informed collective policy preferences might look like. To date, the most ambitious use of such methods has been by James Fishkin (1991, 1995) in experiments with deliberative opinion polls, which bring a random sample of ordinary citizens to a central location where they are provided with detailed policy information and an environment in which to discuss issues. In this way, argues Fishkin (1995, 171), "the deliberative poll can be thought of as an actual sample from a hypothetical society—the deliberative and engaged society we do not have."

Yet, even experimentation provides an unsatisfactory measure of fully informed collective preferences. It is possible in an experimental setting to provide people who are normally oblivious of the political world with information that they can use to formulate preferences, but ill-informed subjects cannot be equipped with other important traits normally associated with being well informed: the cognitive styles and information processing strategies characteristic of politically knowledgeable people (Fiske, Lau, and Smith 1990; Krosnick and Milburn 1990; McGraw and Pinney 1990; Sniderman, Brody, and Tetlock 1991), the knowledge stored in long-term memory that affects how new information is perceived and used to update attitudes (Delli Carpini and Keeter 1996; Krosnick and Milburn 1990; Zaller 1992), and the confidence, developed through experience, that one is able to understand complicated political issues and events (Krosnick and Milburn 1990). Moreover, typical experimental settings also fail to duplicate the social contexts in which political information is acquired and used to form preferences (Huckfeldt and Sprague 1995). It would seem that while experimental methods are especially useful in differentiating informed from ignorant people, they are less suited to predicting the sorts of policies a fully informed public might prefer.

Where filter questions and experimental methods fall short, a third way of simulating fully informed preferences offers promise. Independently pioneered in work by Delli Carpini and Keeter (1996, chap. 6) and Bartels (1996), this approach uses multivariate regression to simulate how individual opinions might change if opinion givers were better informed about politics. Unlike filter questions and experimental methods, this approach is explicitly premised on the concept of "enlightened preferences" and on the social construction of political interests. Estimates of fully informed opinions are generated by assigning the preferences of the most highly informed members of a given demographic group to all members of that group, simultaneously taking into account the influence of a wide range of demographic variables. For instance, if policy preferences of well-informed respondents from union families differ from those of ill-informed respondents from union families, then this approach assigns the mix of fully informed preferences to all respondents from union families. But instead of considering only the bivariate relationship between union membership and policy preferences, this method looks at union respondents who are women, from a certain income level, who live in eastern states, are married, own homes, of a certain age, and so on. If the most informed people sharing all these characteristics have different preferences from the least informed people, then their mix of fully informed preferences is assigned to everyone who shares their demographic characteristics.

The present study extends this basic approach in several ways. First, I use logistic regression to avoid the restrictive assumption that political information must have a linear relationship with preferences.[1] Second, I estimate fully informed preferences for people who give "don't know" and "no opinion" responses in the actual data, following the assumption that as information levels rise, the proportion of people who give opinions or turn out to vote should also rise. Third, while Bartels examined vote choices in presidential elections and Delli Carpini and Keeter analyzed five scales representing different policy domains, I conduct simulations on individual policy questions representing a broad range of political issues. Although the individual questions analyzed here may be less reliable measures of attitudes than scales composed of multiple questions, analyzing the marginals of specific questions has two distinct advantages.

It can reveal the influence of question wording on information effects and, since marginal percentages seem to be the lingua franca of opinion surveys in the political sphere, how the surveyed opinion that "counts" politically may be skewed by the social distribution of political knowledge.

The logit model I use for simulating fully informed opinions is structured as follows:

$$\text{prob } (Y_i = 1)$$
$$= \alpha + \beta_1 I_i + \Sigma \, \beta_k D_{ik} + \Sigma \, \delta_k (I_i * D_{ik}) + e_i,$$

where Y_i is respondent i's dichotomous policy preference (e.g., 1 = "favor," 0 = "oppose"); I_i is respondent i's score on a scale of political information; D_{ik} is respondent i's score on the kth demographic characteristic; $I_i * D_{ik}$ is the product of respondent i's information score multiplied by respondent i's score on the kth demographic characteristic; and e_i is the error term for the ith observation. In this equation, β_1 is the coefficient for the information variable, β_k is the coefficient for the kth demographic characteristic, δ_k is the coefficient for the kth interaction term.

The measures of political information are scales developed for NES data by Delli Carpini and Keeter (1993, 1996). These scales, which are detailed in Appendix A, are built primarily from direct measures of factual knowledge, in contrast to the exclusive reliance by Bartels on subjective ratings of interviewers.[2] The political information scale for the 1992 NES has a maximum value of 23, with a mean of 12.7 and a standard deviation of 5.8; the scale for the 1988 NES has a maximum value of 20, mean of 10.3, and standard deviation of 5.0. These scales have respective alpha reliabilities of .893 and .876.

The D_{ik} terms account for the effects of *Education, Income, Age, Partisanship, Race, Gender, Marital Status, Occupation, Religious Affiliation, Union Membership, Homeowner Status, Parental Status, Financial Status, Region,* and *Type of Community* (see Appendix A for coding details). For the 1992 data I also included *Receiving Welfare Benefits* and *Receiving Other Benefits.*[3] These characteristics represent all the available demographic variables that tend to be relatively stable features of a respondent's makeup and that may be expected to have some bearing on policy preference. Excluded from the analysis were attitudinal variables that may be determined by or confounded with levels of political information. The resulting mix of demographic variables is quite similar to that used by Bartels (1996) and by Delli Carpini and Keeter (1996), with one significant exception. I include party identification because it is a relatively stable trait, which puts it on par with the other demographic variables; more important, partisanship is a widely used cueing mechanism and information shortcut for issue positions (Campbell et al. 1960; Page 1978; Rahn 1993; Rahn and Cramer 1996). To the extent that party identification serves as a heuristic shortcut, excluding it from analysis could exaggerate the apparent importance of factual information to policy preferences (cf. Dimock and Popkin 1995).

This model was applied to a set of policy questions asked in the 1988 and 1992 NES. Since a logistic regression (logit) model was used to estimate coefficients, the data set consists of all policy questions from these studies with binary response options and any other policy questions that can be collapsed straightforwardly into dichotomous distributions. This made for a total of 45 usable questions out of the approximately 100 available.

The simulation proceeds in four steps. First, policy preferences are regressed on the full set of information, demographic, and interaction variables. This step estimates the relationships among these variables and provides a set of coefficients for simulating fully informed opinions. Second, each respondent's score on the political information scale is changed to the highest possible value. In the 1992 NES, for instance, that value was 23 points, so all respondents in the 1992 study were assigned a score of 23. Third, each respondent's fully informed opinion is calculated by plugging the coefficient values obtained from step one into each respondent's actual demographic characteristics, substituting only the new values of the altered information variable and interaction terms. Fully informed opinions are also estimated in this step for respondents who gave "don't know" or "no opinion" responses in the actual survey. Thus, respondents counted as "missing" in the actual data were assigned the same mix of fully informed preferences as the people who share their demographic characteristics and who actually gave opinions. In essence, this is a sophisticated way of weighting the preferences of opinion givers who have a certain combination of demographic characteristics by the number of respondents who share those characteristics. Fourth, all the individual fully informed opinions, including those of people who originally responded "don't know" and "no opinion," are aggregated into a fully informed collective preference. I use the mean of the Y_i probabilities to construct fully informed marginal percentages that can be compared directly to actual marginal percentages. Using marginals to gauge the substantive influence of information effects provides what is probably the most easily interpretable test statistic that can be generated with logistic regression methods.

It is important to note that the marginals resulting from this simulation process can be compared directly to the actual marginals only because they are operationalized as the mean of the individual probabilities that $Y_i = 1$ instead of the sum of the predicted values of Y_i. For instance, if 60 percent of all respondents sharing a certain demographic profile favor a certain policy, each respondent has a probability of .6 for favoring the policy. The mean of these probabilities recovers the actual percentage in favor (.6 = 60 percent), but since the predicted value of Y_i for each respondent is 1 (because .6 > .5), estimates from predicted values would mistakenly show a group that is 100 percent in favor of the policy. The upshot is that most ordinary least squares applications (including the simulation method used in Delli Carpini and Keeter 1996) are less suited for estimating information effects than maximum likelihood applications because they introduce large amounts of error into such estimates.

The end results of this four-step transformation are uniformly high information levels across demographic groups and substantive opinions for all respondents. Using only the observed differences between well- and ill-informed respondents, this method imputes to all respondents the information processing strategies and cognitive styles employed by well-informed people. It also allows political information to interact with demographic characteristics in ways that may move preferences in one direction for some groups and in the opposite direction for other groups. This flexibility allows the model to reflect accurately the social diversity of needs, wants, and values. Of course, increasing levels of information may lead instead to greater consensus of opinion across groups, and the simulation method leaves that possibility open as well. Most important, this method is not predisposed to finding any information effects at all: If well- and ill-informed respondents give essentially the same mix of preferences, then the shape of the resulting fully informed preference should be about the same as the actual one (Bartels 1996, 208–209).

Information Effects in Collective Preferences

The appropriate test for the significance of information effects in the model used here is the likelihood ratio test (Bartels 1996, 209).[4] This test was found to be significant at the $p < .01$ level in 84.4 percent of the 45 questions and at the $p < .05$ level in 88.9 percent. In other words, the unrestricted model, which takes information effects into account, tends to provide a substantially better fit to the data than does the restricted model, which assumes no information effects. Information effects in policy questions appear to be the norm rather than the exception.

Information Effects in Attitudes toward Spousal Notification Laws

Before discussing the general findings from these simulations, it will be helpful to take a close look at an example of how information asymmetries can bias collective preferences. A question from the 1992 NES asked: "Would you favor or oppose a law in your state that would require a married woman to notify her husband before she can have an abortion?" To illustrate how the fully informed collective preferences discussed later were obtained, the logit coefficients for this question are displayed in Table 7-1. Although this equation correctly predicts responses for nearly three-quarters of opinion givers and represents a statistically significant improvement over the restricted model,[5] the relative paucity of significant coefficients is notable. A similar pattern was found in the Bartels simulation of information effects in vote choices: Only between 14 percent and 24 percent of coefficients achieved conventional levels of significance (Bartels 1996, calculated from Tables 1 and 4 through 8). The reason for this pattern appears to be a multicolinearity problem stemming from the abundance of interaction terms correlated with political information scores as well as with the

Table 7-1 Logit Coefficients for Opposition to Spousal Notification Laws (1 = Oppose)

Independent Variables	Main Effects		Interaction Effects (× Information)	
Information (1–23)	−.027	(.089)	—	—
Education (years)	−.043	(.072)	.013**	(.005)
Income (percentile)	.011	(.008)	−.000	(.001)
Age (years)	.009	(.014)	−.001	(.001)
Republican	.568	(.443)	−.075*	(.033)
Democrat	−.149	(.408)	.015	(.031)
Black	.663	(.447)	−.057	(.034)
Female	.062	(.358)	.053*	(.024)
Married	.783*	(.367)	−.072**	(.026)
Union family	−.353	(.460)	.028	(.031)
Homeowner	−.948**	(.358)	.048	(.025)
Parent w/child at home	.069	(.352)	−.003	(.024)
Receive welfare benefits	.045	(.472)	.020	(.034)
Receive other benefits	.397	(.428)	−.046	(.034)
Financially worse off	.178	(.321)	−.015	(.022)
Protestant	.186	(.473)	−.041	(.032)
Catholic	.188	(.518)	−.063	(.035)
Other religion	−.353	(.587)	−.006	(.040)
East	−.328	(.524)	.004	(.034)
Midwest	−.683	(.479)	.024	(.031)
South	−.645	(.456)	.030	(.030)
Urban	−.194	(.352)	.021	(.023)
Rural	−.575	(.398)	.026	(.028)
Retired	−.021	(.670)	−.018	(.047)
Homemaker	−.058	(.499)	−.004	(.038)
Executive/Professional	−.244	(.573)	.020	(.036)
Clerical	.606	(.531)	−.036	(.039)
Technical/Sales	.873	(.585)	−.050	(.039)
Constant	−1.808	(1.262)		

Note: Standard errors of parameter estimates are in parentheses. Beginning log likelihood = −1221.9; ending log likelihood = −1031.8. Beginning correct classifications = 65.4%; ending correct classifications = 73.1%. N = 1,894.

*p < .05.

**p < .01.

demographic variables.[6] Examining the restricted form of this equation confirms that, absent the information and interaction terms, almost half the coefficients attain conventional levels of significance (data not shown). Rerunning the regression using only the significant variable clusters identified in Table 7-1 produces no unexpected changes in the size or direction of coefficients. These findings suggest that the relatively large standard errors of many of the coefficients in the unrestricted equation should have little or no effect on the unbiasedness of the coefficients themselves.

A more substantial concern with the data shown in Table 7-1 is the potential for specification error that comes from excluding attitudinal variables. Given the need to exclude such obviously relevant measures as attitudes toward abortion and women's rights, in the analyses that follow I avoid any suggestion that the model used here can *explain* individual-level opinions. Instead, I focus on what the model is intended to capture: differences in opinion between groups as well as the relationship between information and policy preferences within groups.

Figure 7-1 provides a detailed comparison of the actual marginal percentages for this question and those simulated for a public with uniformly high levels of political knowledge. In the actual marginals, nearly two-thirds of respondents said they favored a spousal notification law. Yet, in contrast to this apparently strong majority opinion, the fully informed collective preference is almost evenly divided on the issue. The only difference between these two measures is that the latter controls for the uneven social distribution of political knowledge.

As a precaution, I also tested whether the presence of insignificant coefficients in Table 7-1 affected the simulated marginal percentages. A second measure of fully informed collective opinion was estimated using a regression containing only the significant variable clusters shown in Table 7-1 (information, education, partisanship, gender, marital status, and home ownership). The result of this alternative simulation was a fully informed collective preference that was 52 percent opposed and 48 percent in favor of spousal notification laws. Deviating only about three percentage points from the simulated marginals of the full equation, this result confirms the accuracy of the model shown in Table 7-1, despite the frequency of insignificant coefficients.[7]

Even more interesting than the substantive shift in the collective preference are the underlying dynamics of change among male and female respondents. Figure 7-1 shows that the direction of change from actual to simulated opinion is identical for both genders: Controlling for information asymmetries led to decreased support among both men and women for spousal notification laws. But the magnitude of this change was much smaller for men than for women. Opinion among male respondents shifted only eight percentage points, compared to twenty points among females. This smaller change among males was primarily due to a ceiling effect from their higher average information scores and to the weaker relationship for males between political information levels and opposition to notification laws (data not shown).

After assigning all respondents equally high information levels, the group preference of fully informed men (i.e., support for notification laws) remained unchanged from that of actual opinion. Thus, the fifteen-point swing in collective opinion came mostly from changes in the opinions of female respondents. As shown in Figure 7-1, group opinion among women shifted twenty percentage points in a pro-choice direction once information levels were raised and

Figure 7-1 Actual and Fully Informed Opinion on Spousal Notification Laws

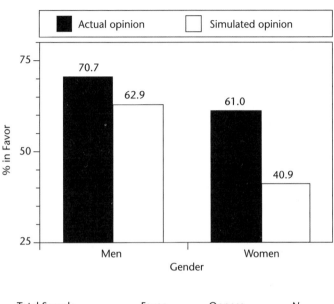

Total Sample	Favor	Oppose	N
Actual marginals	65.5%	34.5%	100% (1894)
Simulated marginals	51.2%	48.8%	100% (1969)

standardized. This resulted in an almost perfect reversal of majority opinion among female respondents: Whereas 61 percent of women said they favored a spousal notification law in the actual data, 59 percent said they opposed it in the simulated data.

These findings suggest that the information imbalances between men and women suppress the magnitude of pro-choice opinion revealed in opinion surveys. The fully informed majority preference of women on the issue of spousal notification laws is diametrically opposed to that of men, while their actual majority preference is the same as that of men.

General Patterns of Information Effects in Collective Preferences

With this insight into the effects of information disparities on collective preferences, we now turn to the general findings from the simulation data. Table 7-2 displays these overall results for each of four issue categories and for all questions together (Appendix B contains results for individual questions). Foreign policy covers the use of military force abroad, economic sanctions, arms agreements, and whether the United States should become more involved in solving problems around the world. The fiscal category addresses levels of government spending and taxation. Operative issues deal with the size and scope of the federal government, the election of legislators, and government regulation of the economy. Social policy covers such topics as abortion, gay rights, the death penalty, and affirmative action.

The first column shows the mean percentage point change between actual and fully informed opinion for all questions in each category. A score of five, for example, indicates a five-point shift in the marginals of one of the response options, as when collective opinion changes from 50 percent to 55 percent in favor. Table 7-2 shows that the average difference between actual and fully informed opinion was about seven percentage points. Questions dealing with fiscal issues had the largest average point change, while social policy questions had the smallest average difference between actual and simulated opinion measures.

These averages give a somewhat misleading picture, however, as the distribution of point differences is skewed toward the low end of the scale. Twenty of the 45 questions (44 percent) had a difference of between zero and five points, 13 (29 percent) differed between six and ten points, nine questions (20 percent) had differences of between eleven and fifteen points, and three (7 percent) differed by more than fifteen points. In the more than half of observations in which nontrivial changes were observed—that is, changes on a magnitude greater than five percentage points—the differences between actual and fully informed opinion averaged 10.8 points. When collective opinion changed by more than a few points, it tended to shift quite dramatically.

Earlier it was suggested that the point differences between actual and simulated opinion might be exaggerated if party identification variables were omitted from the simulation equations. This expectation turned out to be incorrect. Rerunning the simulations without party identification variables (data not shown) produced estimates of information effects that were essentially identical to the simulation results reported here.[8]

While Table 7-2 shows that correcting for information asymmetries can lead to substantial shifts in collective opinion, changes of equal size may not be equally meaningful. A change from 80 percent to 90 percent in favor of a policy is in some ways less important than a change from 45 percent to 55 percent support; the former merely reinforces the majority opinion, while the latter indicates a substantive shift in majority opinion. The relative importance of the differences between actual and fully informed opinion can thus be clarified by noting when they cause collective policy preferences to change.

The middle column of Table 7-2 shows the number of questions in each category for which the preference order of fully informed opinion differed from that of actual opinion. Three possible collective preferences were considered: a majority in favor, a majority opposed, or a tie between options.[9] Any case in

Table 7-2 Differences between Actual and Fully Informed Collective
Preferences

Category	Average Point Change	N with Different Preference Order	Fully Informed Opinion Relative to Actual Opinion
Foreign policy issues (N = 8)	6.13 (3.80)	1 of 8	More dovish and interventionist
Fiscal issues (N = 6)	11.61 (7.28)	3 of 6	More willing to pay for more services and deficit reduction, less willing to maintain high defense spending
Operative issues (N = 8)	9.22 (6.41)	2 of 8	More opposed to government control of economy, more in favor of free market approaches
Social policy issues (N = 23)	5.49 (4.16)	3 of 23	More progressive in general, but slightly less progressive on some racial issues
All issues	7.08 (5.35)	9 of 45	

Source: Pooled data from 1988 and 1992 National Election Studies.

Note: Standard deviations are in parentheses.

which the collective preference in actual opinion differed from that in the simulated marginals was coded as a change in preference order.

The frequency with which preference shifts occurred is a significant finding. After controlling for information effects, collective preferences changed in fully one-fifth of policy questions. Change was most frequent in the fiscal category and least frequent in the area of foreign policy, although the small number of questions makes it difficult to draw any firm conclusions about differences between issue categories. The important point is that controlling for the effects of information on individual responses often results in new collective preferences. This contrasts somewhat with the findings of Bartels (1996), who studied information effects in presidential election outcomes. Although Bartels found information effects in vote choices that are comparable to the patterns examined here, in every election he studied, correcting the popular vote totals for the presence of information effects would have resulted in the same outcome as was historically the case.[10] In contrast, the collective ordering of policy preferences seems to be much more sensitive than aggregate vote choices to information effects.

My interpretation of what fully informed opinion looks like relative to actual opinion is given in the third column of Table 7-2. Fully informed opinion on foreign policy issues is relatively more dovish and interventionist than actual opinion. For example, while 29 percent of respondents in 1988 agreed that the United States should stay out of problems in other parts of the world, the level of agreement dropped to just 18 percent of fully informed responses. An example of dovishness in fully informed foreign policy preferences comes from another question from the 1988 NES: "Do you favor or oppose using American military forces in the Middle East to protect oil shipments?" While 64 percent of actual responses favored military deployment, support dropped to 58 percent of fully informed responses.

Simulated opinion on fiscal issues is more favorable toward paying for deficit reduction and for a larger number of governmental services than is actual opinion. The proportion of respondents willing to pay higher taxes in order to reduce the deficit rose from 31 percent in the actual data to an impressive 53 percent in the simulated data. And while 35 percent of actual respondents agreed that "the government ought to cut taxes even if it means putting off some important things that need to be done," agreement dropped to 22 percent when controlling for information effects. Likewise, only 30 percent of actual respondents in the 1992 NES said that they would be willing "to pay more in taxes so that the government could spend more on the services you favor," but support rose to 47 percent among fully informed respondents. There were only two exceptions to the tendency for fully informed opinion to favor increased federal spending. While 68 percent of actual respondents felt that the United States should maintain high levels of defense spending, support dropped to 64 percent for fully informed respondents, and in terms of satisfaction with current levels of Social Security, 40 percent of actual respondents said benefits were about right or too high, compared to 48 percent of fully informed respondents.

With regard to operative issues, fully informed opinion is relatively more opposed than actual opinion to the idea of "big government." While 63 percent of actual opinion givers in 1988 agreed that "the government is getting too powerful," the level of agreement rose to 71 percent among fully informed respondents. Likewise, in 1992, 65 percent of actual respondents felt "there are more things that government should be doing," compared to only 50 percent of fully informed respondents. In simulated opinion, this option tied with "the less government the better."

In the area of social policy, fully informed opinion is more progressive than actual opinion on most issues. Simulated opinion is consistently more pro-choice than actual opinion (39 percent versus 25 percent opposed to parental notification laws) and more supportive of gay rights (40 percent versus 29 percent favored allowing gay couples to adopt children). A similar direction of change was observed for most social policy issues, the one exception being specific programs aimed at giving preferential treatment to African Americans. On matters such as affirmative action and school integration, fully informed opinion tends to be slightly less supportive than actual opinion. At the same time, simulated opinion is slightly more progressive than actual opinion on the general need for government to guarantee equal opportunity and fair treatment to blacks (see Appendix B).

The general pattern emerging from the simulations is for fully informed opinion to be more dovish and interventionist on foreign policy, more progressive on social and fiscal issues, and more conservative on operative issues. It is interesting that the same general trends were found when the simulations were reestimated using years of education in place of the factual knowledge scales and using only statistically significant variable clusters (data not shown). Furthermore, these general patterns of differences between actual and fully informed opinion are consistent with results from other simulation methods (Althaus 1996a; Delli Carpini and Keeter 1996, chap. 6), with the broad patterns of opinion change among participants in the National Issues Convention held in January 1996 (Public Broadcasting Corporation 1996), and with the results of question filter experiments (Bishop, Oldendick, and Tuchfarber 1983). They are also consistent with previous studies comparing differences between well- and ill-informed survey respondents on a variety of policy issues (e.g., Althaus 1996a; Dimock and Popkin 1995; Key 1961, 331–341; Neuman 1986, chap. 3; Popkin and Dimock 1995).

Conclusion

Correcting for the low levels and uneven social distribution of political knowledge can change our understanding of collective preferences in significant ways. This study found that the effects of information asymmetries on collective opinion are both larger and more common than suggested by previous work. Controlling for information effects produces an average change of seven percentage points in question marginals and reveals that one in five policy questions might have a different collective preference if everyone were equally well informed about politics.

Obviously, these findings only suggest what collective opinion might look like in a hypothetical world of politically attentive citizens. While it is tempting to suppose that simulations of fully informed opinion somehow reflect the underlying political interests of the mass public, I draw no such conclusion from these data. The key contribution of this study lies not with speculating about the public's true interests but with demonstrating that survey results sometimes look the way they do because so many people are ill-informed about politics and because certain people tend to be better informed than others.

Interpreting the findings presented here in light of the existing literature on public opinion is a surpassingly difficult task, for the results of this study seem to both challenge and support the idea that the mass public's command of political knowledge is related to the quality of its collective preferences. On the one hand, the results can be seen as validating the hypothesis that on-line processing, heuristic shortcuts, and statistical aggregation help the mass public compensate for its lack of political knowledge. After all, the optimist might say, nearly half the question marginals shifted less than six points after correcting for information effects, and the ordering of collective preferences remained unchanged for eight in ten questions. On the other hand, the findings can be seen as challenging the view that heuristics, on-line processing, and statistical aggregation help an ill-informed public express policy preferences similar to those it might give if it were more knowledgeable about politics. After all, the pessimist might say, more than half the question marginals shifted at least five percentage points, and one-quarter shifted more than ten points after correcting for information effects. Moreover, the pessimist might add, the ordering of collective preferences changed for one out of five questions when information effects were controlled.

Choosing between these competing interpretations requires a standard for determining when information effects are a problem. Earlier I made use of three such standards for evaluating individual questions: when likelihood ratio tests for the presence of information effects attain statistical significance, when differences between actual and fully informed collective opinions exceed five percentage points (which corresponds roughly to exceeding the 95 percent confidence interval for point estimates made from 1988 and 1992 NES data), and when correcting for information effects results in different preference orderings for collective opinions. Yet, such standards are of little help when moving beyond individual questions to evaluate more general patterns in groups of questions. Here the issues of interest are how often preference orderings must change for information effects to be called frequent, and how sizable mean point changes must be for information effects to be called large. As the answers to these questions vary with the vantage point and expectations of the individual observer, I submit my own assessment of the relative importance of information effects, recognizing that it is one among several valid interpretations of these results.

Given the frequency of shifts in collective preferences and the sizable point changes that occurred with some regularity when controlling for information asymmetries, I am inclined to see these results as challenging more than supporting the revisionist arguments that collective preferences are "rational" and reliable guides for public policy. Yet, the familiar warnings about the public's civic incompetence that have been made since the early 1950s are similarly challenged by this analysis. It would seem that a middle position fits best with the results presented here: Sometimes collective policy preferences are significantly influenced by the public's modest level of knowledge about politics, and sometimes they are not. Most of the time, at least in NES data, the aggregate effect of information asymmetries seems likely to be palpable but not decisive.

APPENDIX A: Variables and Coding

Demographics

Income is measured as income percentiles, *Education* is measured as years of formal schooling, and *Age* is measured in years. *Republican* and *Democrat* are coded 1 for the appropriate partisan identification (including Independent "leaners") and 0 for all others. *Black* is coded 1 for African Americans and 0 for all others, *Female* is coded 1 for women and 0 for men, *Union Family* is coded 1 if any member of the respondent's household belongs to a union. *Homeowner* is coded

1 for people who own their own home and 0 for all others, and *Parent with a Child at Home* is coded 1 for respondents whose minor children reside with them and 0 for all others. *Receiving Welfare Benefits* is coded 1 for people living in a household where they or family members receive food stamps, Medicaid, unemployment, and/or AFDC and is coded 0 for all others. *Receiving Other Benefits* is coded 1 for people living in a household where they or family members receive payments from Medicare and/or Social Security. *Financially Worse Off* is coded 1 for respondents who reported being worse off financially compared to one year before and 0 for all others. *Protestant, Catholic,* and *Other Religion* are each coded 1 for the appropriate religious affiliation and 0 for all others, with atheists, agnostics, and those with no religious affiliation comprising the reference category for this set. *East, Midwest,* and *South* are coded 1 for respondents living in the respective census region and 0 for all others, with those from western states as the reference category for this set. *Urban* and *Rural* are coded 1 for those from the appropriate census-defined place of residence and 0 for all others, with suburban as the reference category for this set. *Retired, Homemaker, Executive/Professional, Clerical,* and *Technical/Sales* are coded 1 for the respective occupational status and 0 for all others.

Political Information

The information measures used in this study were originally constructed and tested by Delli Carpini and Keeter (1993, 1996). These scales are primarily additive measures of correct answers to factual knowledge questions (correct = 1; incorrect or no answer = 0). They also incorporate a subjective assessment of respondent knowledge level made by the interviewer at the conclusion of each interview. Three kinds of factual knowledge items were used to construct these scales: relative location tests, in which correct answers are constructed by comparing responses to two different questions; open-ended questions asking respondents to identify the job or political office held by a public figure; and closed-ended questions testing knowledge of constitutional powers, which party held majority status in both houses of Congress, and which party was more conservative than the other. An example of a correct answer to a relative location test is placing the Republican Party as relatively more conservative than the Democratic Party on a seven-point ideology scale, regardless of where on the ideology scale a respondent actually places the two parties.

Besides the interviewer rating score (v555, reverse coded), the questions for the 1988 NES information scale included identifying the offices held by Ted Kennedy (v871), George Shultz (v872), Margaret Thatcher (v875), Yasser Arafat (v876), William Rehnquist (v873), Michail Gorbachev (v874), and Jim Wright (v877); naming the majority party in the House (v878) and Senate (v879); identifying the relative ideological locations of Bush and Dukakis (v231, v232), identifying the relative ideological locations of the Republican and Democratic parties (v234, v235), and locating the relative positions of the Republican and

Democratic parties on national health insurance (v321, v322), government services (v307, v308), defense spending (v315, v316), and job assurances (v328, v329).

Aside from the interviewer rating score (v4205, reverse coded), the questions for the 1992 NES information scale included identifying the offices held by Dan Quayle (v5916) William Rehnquist (v5917), Boris Yeltsin (v5918), and Thomas Foley (v5919); identifying which branch of the federal government was responsible for deciding the constitutionality of laws (v5920) and for nominating federal judges (v5921); naming the majority party in the House (v5951) and Senate (v5952); identifying which was the more conservative party (v5915); identifying the relative ideological locations of Republicans and Democrats (v3517, v3518), Bush and Clinton (v3514, v3515); and identifying the relative position of the parties on government services (v3704, v3705), Bush and Clinton on government services (v3702, v3703), the parties on defense spending (v3710, v3711), Bush and Clinton on defense spending (v3708, v3709), the parties on job assurance (v3721, v3722), Bush and Clinton on job assurance (v3719, v3720), and Bush and Clinton on abortion (v3733, v3734).

APPENDIX B: Simulation Results for Individual Questions

Table 7A-1   Levels of Actual Opinion and Simulated Estimates of Fully Informed Opinion, by Question

Question	Type	Year (Var. #)	Actual Opinion	Simulated Opinion
"I am going to read you a statement about U.S. foreign policy and I would like you to tell me whether you agree or disagree: 'This country would be better off if we just stayed home and did not concern ourselves with problems in other parts of the world.' " (percent disagreeing)	Foreign	1988 (v254)	71.1	81.6
		1992 (v3604)	73.7	85.8
"The United States and the Soviet Union have recently reached agreements to reduce the number of nuclear arms. Do you approve or disapprove of these agreements?" (percent disapproving)	Foreign	1988 (v364)	12.6	8.7
"Do you favor or oppose using American military forces in the Middle East to protect oil shipments?" (percent opposed)	Foreign	1988 (v366)	35.7	42.6
"Some people think that the U.S. should increase the pressure on the South African government to change its racial laws. Others think the U.S. should not do this. What do you think—should the U.S. apply more pressure or not?" (percent opposed to more pressure)	Foreign	1988 (v861)	41.3	34.5

Table 7A-1 *continued*

Question	Type	Year (Var. #)	Actual Opinion	Simulated Opinion
"The U.S. should maintain its position as the world's most powerful nation even if it means going to the brink of war." (percent disagreeing)	Foreign	1988 (v972)	42.9	48.2
"Do you think we did the right thing in sending U.S. military forces to the Persian Gulf or should we have stayed out?" (percent saying should have stayed out)	Foreign	1992 (v3608)	21.0	18.4
"Some people think that the U.S. and its allies should have continued to fight Iraq until Saddam Hussein was driven from power. Others think that the U.S. was right to stop fighting after Kuwait was liberated. What do you think? Should the war have continued or should it have stopped?" (percent saying should have stopped)	Foreign	1992 (v3630)	36.7	35.4
"In order to reduce the size of the federal budget deficit are you willing or not willing to pay more in federal taxes?" (percent unwilling)	Fiscal	1988 (v249)	68.9	46.3
"The government ought to cut taxes even if it means putting off some important things that need to be done." (percent disagreeing)	Fiscal	1988 (v944)	64.5	78.0
"Some people say the U.S. should maintain its position as the world's strongest military power even if it means continuing high defense spending." (percent disagreeing)	Fiscal	1992 (v3603)	31.9	35.6
"Would you personally be willing to pay more in taxes so that the government could spend more on the services you favor or would you rather keep your taxes the same even if this meant the government couldn't increase its spending as you would like?" (percent saying keep taxes the same)	Fiscal	1992 (v5922)	70.0	52.9
"In your opinion, are Social Security retirement benefits too low, about the right amount, or too high?" (percent saying about right/too high)	Fiscal	1992 (v6132)	40.1	48.7
"Do you favor or oppose taxes on Social Security benefits?" (percent opposed)	Fiscal	1992 (v6134)	87.0	81.0

table continues

Table 7A-1 *continued*

Question	Type	Year (Var. #)	Actual Opinion	Simulated Opinion
"Some people have suggested placing new limits on foreign imports in order to protect American jobs. Others say that such limits would raise consumer prices and hurt American exports. Do you favor or oppose placing new limits on imports, or haven't you thought much about this?" (percent opposed)	Operative	1988 (v376)	23.7	39.7
		1992 (v3802)	33.1	38.5
"What is your feeling, do you think the government is getting too powerful or do you think the government is not getting too strong?" (percent saying government not getting too strong)	Operative	1988 (v848)	36.7	29.2
		1992 (v6016)	29.9	31.1
"Over the past year would you say that the economic policies of the federal government have made the nation's economy better, worse, or haven't they made much difference either way?" (percent saying worse)	Operative	1992 (v3541)	43.2	60.0
"A law has been proposed that would limit members of Congress to no more than 12 years of service in that office. Do you favor or oppose such a law?" (percent opposed)	Operative	1992 (v3747)	18.5	19.8
"Choose which of two statements I read comes closer to your own opinion . . . One, the less the government the better; or two, there are more things that government should be doing?" (percent saying there are more things government should do)	Operative	1992 (v5729)	64.9	50.3
"Choose which of two statements I read comes closer to your own opinion . . . One, we need a strong government to handle today's complex economic problems; or two, the free market can handle these problems without government being involved?" (percent favoring free market)	Operative	1992 (v5730)	26.5	41.5
"Do you favor or oppose laws to protect homosexuals against job discrimination?" (percent opposed)	Social	1988 (v852)	45.8	41.8
		1992 (v5923)	39.9	34.5
"Do you favor or oppose the death penalty for persons convicted of murder?" (percent opposed)	Social	1988 (v854)	19.9	24.8
		1992 (v5933)	20.6	24.0

Table 7A-1 *continued*

Question	Type	Year (Var. #)	Actual Opinion	Simulated Opinion
"Some people say that because of past discrimination, blacks should be given preference in hiring and promotion. Others say that such preference in hiring and promotion of blacks is wrong because it gives blacks advantages they haven't earned. What about your opinion—are you for or against preferential hiring and promotion of blacks?" (percent against)	Social	1988 (v856)	79.9	83.1
		1992 (v5935)	79.9	84.0
"Should the government in Washington see to it that black people get fair treatment in jobs or is this not the federal government's business?" (percent saying this is not the government's business)	Social	1988 (v865)	42.7	39.7
		1992 (v5938)	42.7	42.9
"Some people say that because of past discrimination it is sometimes necessary for colleges and universities to reserve openings for black students. Others oppose quotas because they say quotas give blacks advantages they haven't earned. What about your opinion— are you for or against quotas to admit black students?" (percent against)	Social	1988 (v869)	63.7	65.8
		1992 (v5947)	67.4	68.4
"Equal opportunity for blacks and whites is very important but it's not really the government's job to guarantee it." (percent disagreeing)	Social	1988 (v965)	43.2	49.0
"Do you think the government should require companies to allow up to six months unpaid leave for parents to spend time with their newborn or newly adopted children, or is this something that should be left up to the individual employer?" (percent favoring decision left to employers)	Social	1992 (v3717)	68.8	63.0
"Would you favor or oppose a law in your state that would require parental consent before a teenager under 18 can have an abortion?" (percent opposed)	Social	1992 (v3735)	24.5	39.2

table continues

Table 7A-1 *continued*

Question	Type	Year (Var. #)	Actual Opinion	Simulated Opinion
"Would you favor or oppose a law in your state that would allow the use of government funds to help pay for the costs of abortion for women who cannot afford them?" (percent opposed)	Social	1992 (v3737)	49.1	46.9
"Would you favor or oppose a law in your state that would require a married woman to notify her husband before she can have an abortion?" (percent opposed)	Social	1992 (v3739)	34.5	48.8
"Do you think government should provide child care assistance to low and middle income working parents, or isn't it the government's responsibility?" (percent saying government is not responsible)	Social	1992 (v3745)	38.8	40.3
"Do you think homosexuals should be allowed to serve in the United States Armed Forces or don't you think so?" (percent saying gays should not be allowed to serve)	Social	1992 (v5925)	41.4	37.2
"Do you think gay or lesbian couples, in other words, homosexual couples, should be legally permitted to adopt children?" (percent opposed)	Social	1992 (v5927)	72.3	59.0
"Do you think the government in Washington should see to it that white and black children go to the same schools, [or that it should] stay out of this area as it is not the government's business?" (percent saying government should stay out)	Social	1992 (v5932)	50.8	59.5
"Some people feel that we should use government funds only to support children who go to public schools, others feel that we should use government funds to support children's schooling regardless of whether their parents choose to send them to a public, private, or parochial school. How do you feel, or haven't you thought much about it?" (percent in favor of funding all schooling)	Social	1992 (v6023)	42.9	33.5
"Do you favor or oppose expanding Medicare to pay for nursing home care and long hospital stays for the elderly?" (percent opposed)	Social	1992 (v6136)	12.0	21.5

Table 7A-1 *continued*

Question	Type	Year (Var. #)	Actual Opinion	Simulated Opinion
"Do you favor a law making English the official language of the United States, meaning government business would be conducted in English only, or do you oppose such a law?" (percent opposed)	Social	1992 (v6233)	30.6	28.7
"Do you think that immigrants who come to the U.S. should be eligible as soon as they come here for government services such as Medicaid, Food Stamps, Welfare, or should they have to be here a year or more?" (percent saying immigrants should wait a year or more)	Social	1992 (v6242)	78.9	70.8

Notes

1. Delli Carpini and Keeter (1996) use ordinary least squares to estimate parameters in their simulation; Bartels (1996) uses a probit model to estimate parameters, which are then transformed in a way that assumes linearity of information effects.
2. Interviewer ratings of respondent knowledge levels discriminate well relative to factual knowledge scales (Zaller 1985), but correlations between these measures run between .57 and .68, which demonstrates that the two are not synonymous (Delli Carpini and Keeter 1992, 1993; see also Luskin 1987). While interviewer ratings are frequently used as components of political knowledge scales (Delli Carpini and Keeter 1996; Zaller 1985), these findings suggest that they may be poor stand-alone substitutes for direct measures of political knowledge.
3. These two variables were not available in the 1988 data. Including the constants and interaction terms, there were 52 parameters estimated in the 1988 data and 56 parameters in the 1992 data. While the number of parameters is substantial, the large sample size of the NES studies (1,775 completed interviews in 1988; 2,255 in 1992) should ensure the asymptotic properties of efficiency, lack of bias, and normality (Aldrich and Nelson 1984, 53; also see King 1989, 74–80).
4. Similar to the F-test used to compare improvement of fit in OLS equations, the likelihood ratio test compares the log likelihoods of an unrestricted logit model, which includes all the variables, and a restricted logit model, which lacks the information and interaction terms, to determine the significance of the differences between them. For example, the -2 log likelihood of the unrestricted equation in Table 7-1 is 2063.7, while that of the restricted equation without interaction terms (not shown) is 2159.0. The result is a χ^2 value of 95.3, with $m = 28$ degrees of freedom, where m is equal to the number of parameters in the restricted model. This value is significant at the $p < .00001$ level, so the null hypothesis of no information effects can be safely rejected.
5. See footnote 4.
6. Most of this multicolinearity comes from the nature of the demographic variable clusters. For instance, in the 1992 NES, Republican partisanship is correlated with Democratic partisanship at $-.78$. Likewise, living in a suburban area is correlated at

−.57 with living in an urban area and −.42 with living in a rural area. The rest is due to associations between different variables. For example, the scale of political information is correlated at .56 with education and .42 with income. Being married is correlated at .42 with income and .33 with being a homeowner. All of this is complicated by the set of interaction terms, which are linearly but imperfectly related to both the information scale and the set of demographic terms. Despite these associations, the theoretical approach to information effects adopted here dictates that all these variables be included in the logit model. The result is a large number of insignificant coefficients, but the coefficients themselves should nonetheless be valid for the purposes to which they are put.

7. In this particular case, a shift on the magnitude of three points nevertheless signals a reversal in the collective preference simulated for a fully informed public. Although a shift of this magnitude does not count as a change in preference ordering for this study (it would still be counted as a tie: see footnote 9 below), it demonstrates the importance of examining the size of point changes in conjunction with any changes in preference ordering.

8. Of the simulations controlling for party identification, 57.8 percent ($n = 26$) produced smaller estimates of information effects than the simulations that omitted party identification variables, hardly an improvement over chance. Moreover, the mean difference between simulations that omitted party identification and the measures of fully informed opinion listed in Appendix B was only two-thirds of a percentage point. Contrary to expectations, controlling for party identification seems to have little influence on the size or direction of information effects in these data.

9. A tie was defined as any marginals falling within plus or minus 3 percentage points of the 50 percent mark. These boundaries approximate the 95 percent confidence interval for point estimates from these data. It follows that a majority is defined as at least 53.5 percent of responses.

10. Calculated from Table 2 of Bartels (1996) and popular vote totals from the *Statistical Abstract of the United States*. Correcting actual popular vote totals with the estimated aggregate deviations from fully informed voting reported in Table 2 of Bartels (1996) has the following results: Nixon wins by 59.0 percent instead of 60.7 percent in 1972, Carter by 51.5 percent instead of 50.1 percent in 1976, Reagan by 56.3 percent instead of 50.7 percent in 1980 and by 53.9 percent instead of 58.8 percent in 1984, Bush by 56.4 percent instead of 53.4 percent in 1988, and Clinton by 45.2 percent instead of 43.0 percent in 1992.

8. Voting Correctly

Richard R. Lau and David P. Redlawsk

The classic texts of democratic theory (such as J. S. Mill and Rousseau) assume that for a democracy to function properly the average citizen should be interested in, pay attention to, discuss, and actively participate in politics. The attention and discussion provide information about political affairs, which allows citizens to make political decisions (e.g., a vote) based on rationally considered principles reflecting their own self-interest and the common good. All citizens may not be able to live up to these standards — some may be too disinterested, or lack sufficient information or the skills to understand politics, and as a consequence they vote by habit or narrow prejudices, or do not vote at all. But as long as a clear majority lives up to these standards, the collective wisdom of the people will prevail.

Five decades of behavioral research in political science have left no doubt, however, that only a tiny minority of the citizens in any democracy actually live up to these ideals. Interest in politics is generally weak, discussion is rare, political knowledge on the average is pitifully low, and few people actively participate in politics beyond voting (e.g., Berelson, Lazarsfeld, and McPhee 1954; Campbell, Converse, Miller, and Stokes 1960; Converse 1964; Delli Carpini and Keeter 1996). And what good is even voting if for so many it is based on so little information?

The wide divergence between classic normative theory and political reality has led to two widely divergent responses. On the one hand are those who accept both the normative theory and the empirical data and who conclude as a consequence that governments calling themselves "democracies" are not truly democratic. An apathetic public cannot possibly constrain government officials, this line of argument goes; instead, some capitalist power elite, military-industrial complex, and/or giant media conglomerate uses democratic institutions and a complacent citizenry to manipulate government policy toward its own ends (e.g., Bennett 1988, 1992; Burnham 1965, 1974; Fishman 1980; Gans 1979; Mills 1971).

On the other hand are those who accept the empirical evidence but revise downward the requirements of normative theory so that modern governments can still be considered mostly "democratic." For instance, Page and Shapiro (1992) show how aggregate public opinion can be fairly stable and "rational" — and even, perhaps, guide public policy — while based on mostly ill-formed

Source: American Political Science Review 91, 3 (September 1997): 585–598.

"nonattitudes" among individual citizens. Fiorina (1981) shows the advantages of basing vote decisions on retrospective judgments of the party's past performance rather than spending the time to learn about the candidates' future policy proposals. Others argue that the widespread ignorance of and indifference toward politics typically seen in Western democracies is in fact a good thing, for it reduces social conflict and contributes to greater system stability (Berelson, Lazarsfeld, and McPhee 1954; McClosky 1964; Mueller 1992; Prothro and Grigg 1960). In other words, democracy still "works," and in fact may even work better, if only some *minority* of the population is attentive to politics, ideological in its thinking, and so on (see also Dahl 1961, 1989; Huntington 1968; Lindblom 1965; Schattschneider 1960).

Although we are somewhat in sympathy with each of these divergent responses, we take issue with the very point on which they both agree: Do the empirical data in fact require so drastic a revision of classic democratic theory? True, if modern citizens paid the type of attention to public affairs that Rousseau prescribed several centuries ago, they would do nothing else but follow politics. Such standards are unrealistically high and, we argue, not necessary for the average citizen. Classic democratic theory prescribes active attention to and close scrutiny of government policy because, logically, it seems the only way that citizens can make "correct" decisions. If A (an active, attentive public) is necessary for B (democracy), and A is not true, then logically B cannot be true.

This syllogism holds only if we accept the premise that close attention to politics and the actions of government officials and the promises of competing candidates are *necessary* for correct voting decisions. But what if they are not? What if people can make reasonably good decisions, most of the time, without all the motivation and attention and knowledge required by classic theory?

Modern cognitive psychology teaches us that humans are limited information processors (Fiske and Taylor 1991, Lau and Sears 1986). People process only a small fraction of the information to which they are exposed. The human mind, although effectively unlimited in its long-term storage capacity, is severely limited in how much information can be kept in short-term or active memory at any given time (Simon 1979). As a consequence, both perception and storage of incoming information, as well as subsequent recall of that information from memory, are structured (and thus biased) by prior expectations or cognitive "schemata" that help determine what information is noticed, where it is stored, and how likely it is to be retrieved from memory. Thus, citizens do not have all the information about politics that is required of them by classic democratic theory, and they do not process that information in as logical a way as those theorists hoped, in large part because of strict cognitive limitations. It is not so much that we do a particularly bad job of processing political information; rather, we do an equally bad job of processing any type of complex information. If the same standards that classic democratic theory holds up for citizens were to be applied to any other area of human life, such as finding mates or buying cars or choosing colleges, then people would be found to be just as inept in those areas as well.

Most people nonetheless seem to make an adequate marriage, get a decent education, and make reasonably good automobile purchases. How is this possible, if people behave and make decisions in ways that are so far from the dictates of normative theory? Quite simply, human beings have adaptively developed a large series of cognitive heuristics or shortcuts that allow them to make "pretty good" judgments most of the time (Kahneman, Slovic, and Tversky 1982; Nisbett and Ross 1980; Tversky and Kahneman 1974). These heuristics "do sometimes lead people astray when they are overextended or misapplied . . . [but] people's intuitive inferential strategies are probably used appropriately and effectively in the great majority of cases" (Nisbett and Ross 1980, 255).

As a consequence, if we are going to make judgments about the "democratic" nature of different forms of government, we should do so at least initially on the basis of the quality or "correctness" of the political decisions citizens make within that system of government rather than on the basis of the ways in which those decisions are reached. Democracy is not a simple form of government, and judgments about the nature of different governments that claim to be democratic should not be made in a simplistic, either-or manner. Certainly, "degrees" of democracy are possible; and we argue that a crucial criterion is the proportion of citizens voting correctly at any particular time, rather than the manner in which those vote decisions are reached. That is, if most people, most of the time, vote "correctly," then we should not be too concerned if those vote decisions are reached on the basis of something less than full information about the different policies espoused by different candidates, much less information about how government actually carries out policy decisions or who the important players are.

What Is a "Correct" Vote Decision?

Determining the "correctness" of a vote decision is not an easy task. Who is to decide what is "correct"? We are reluctant to define what is "good" for everyone; even if we were not, we doubt that many people would be willing to accept our judgments. Instead, we begin by defining "correctness" *based on the values and beliefs of the individual voter,* not on any particular ideology that presumes the values and preferences which *ought* to be held by members of different social classes, for instance, and not on any larger social goods or universal values. Given the limitations of human cognitive abilities discussed above, however, we are equally reluctant to accept as "correct" any individual vote just because it is freely chosen by that individual, as Downs (1957) and his followers might. Instead, we adopt a theoretical middle ground by defining "correctness" based on the "fully informed" interests of individual voters. As Dahl (1989, 180–181) writes, "a person's interest or good is whatever that person would choose with fullest attainable understanding of the experiences resulting from that choice and its most relevant alternatives." (See also Bartels 1990; Connolly 1972; Delli Carpini and Keeter 1995; Lippmann 1955; Mansbridge 1983.) Thus, we define a "correct" vote decision as one that is the same as the choice which would have been made under conditions of full information. Ideally, this determination can best be made subjectively, by the voter, on an individual basis.

This chapter has several purposes. First, we describe experimental work that attempts to operationalize this ideal of fully informed voters determining for themselves what is the correct vote decision. Second, we use this operationalization as a means of validating an easily obtainable measure of correct voting. In so doing, we move from a completely subjective, individually determined definition to a more objective, expert-determined judgment of which candidate best matches the voter's own stated preferences. The experimental data are crucial for justifying and validating an objective, externally determined measure. Third, having obtained it, we briefly illustrate the use of such measures with the 1972–1988 American National Election Studies (NES). These latter results provide important predictive validity for this measure. Finally, we return to the question of what ought to be required of citizens by democratic theory, once we have a better idea of just how well our disinterested, apathetic, uninformed citizens actually do in making their vote decisions.

A Dynamic, Process Tracing Method for Studying the Vote Choice

We have designed an interactive experimental paradigm to study voter decision making that captures the crucial features of modern political campaigns: They are media-based; they provide an overwhelming amount of relevant information, some of which voters choose to expose themselves to, some of which comes to voters without any conscious decision to learn it, and much of which is simply missed; and they are dynamic, in the sense that information available today may be gone tomorrow (see Lau 1995 and Lau and Redlawsk 1992 and 2001 for more details). Our experiments involve a primary election with from two to four candidates in the Democratic and Republican primaries, followed by a general election campaign involving one candidate from each party.

In our experiment, brief descriptions of information available about candidates in the election (e.g., "Fisher's Stand on Welfare," "Martin's Family Background") scroll down a computer screen, and subjects (voters) must actively "access" the information in which they are interested by clicking on it with a mouse. This conscious search reveals the type of information which might be learned about a candidate from an opening paragraph in a newspaper or magazine article. Six of these descriptive labels appear on the screen at any given time, but only one item may be accessed at a time. Moreover, when an item is accessed the scrolling continues, hidden in the background, while subjects read the information they have chosen. Thus, an entirely new set of options faces a subject when he or she has finished reading the particulars of the item he or she chose and returns to the campaign. The information available at any point in a campaign is determined by a stochastic process within certain constraints meant largely to replicate the type of information available during American presidential campaigns.[1] At certain points, the computer screen is "taken over" by 20-second political advertisements for one of the candidates running in the election. Voters can close their eyes and ears when the ads come on, but they cannot do anything else relevant to the campaign until the commercial is over.

Our goal in designing this mock election simulation was to overwhelm people with information to force them to be selective in what they learn. The experiment that provided the data used here involved 212 distinct items which could be accessed during the primary campaign, including 26 individual policy stands, background information, and personality descriptions about each of six different candidates in the two parties' primary elections; endorsements by 11 different groups for candidates in each primary; the results of 24 different surveys conducted at various points during the campaign; and the results of five earlier primaries in each party. Eight to ten "televised" political advertisements also appeared during the course of the primary campaign. Thus, the simulation provided far more information than could possibly be handled by anyone, even under ideal conditions.

Method

Subjects

Subjects were recruited from the central New Jersey area during fall 1994. The only two provisos were that they be American citizens at least 18 years old (i.e., eligible voters) and not currently going to college. Subjects were recruited by ads in local newspapers and by approaching charitable organizations (such as churches, PTA chapters, the American Legion) that could provide experimental subjects in return for the subject payment fee of $20. Subjects who responded directly to our advertisements were paid the $20 upon completion of the experiment.

We recruited 303 subjects for the experiment; the analyses reported below rely on data from 293 of them.[2] We make no claims that this is a representative sample of central New Jersey voters, much less the nation as a whole. We were successful in recruiting a broad range of people, but our subjects were slightly more likely to be female, college educated, and retired than is true of the area from which we recruited (according to the 1990 Census).

Procedure

All subjects participated in the experiment individually and in a reasonably private setting where there would be no interruptions. The complete experimental procedure is sketched in some detail in Figure 8-1. For current purposes, the crucial features are these. (1) Subjects initially completed a fairly standard political attitudes questionnaire in which their political preferences, knowledge, and so on, were determined. (2) After the nature of a mock 1996 presidential election was described and subjects were given practice using the computer, (3) subjects

Figure 8-1 Outline of Experimental Procedure

1. Political Attitudes Questionnaire
      Questions to measure subjects'
      • political preferences;
      • political interest, participation, knowledge,
        and media usage;
      • importance of different types of political information
        for 1992 vote choice;
      • background/demographic information   (about 30–40 minutes)
2. Mock Election Campaign
      a. Practice session accessing information with the
         mouse about 1988 presidential election   (about 8 minutes)
      b. Explicit instructions and 1996 campaign scenario;
         random assignment to different experimental
         conditions (hidden from subjects)   (about 5 minutes)
      c. Primary election campaign involving six candidates   (about 22 minutes)
      d. Vote in party's primary election; evaluate all six
         candidates; manipulation check on difficulty of choice   (about 3 minutes) *
      e. Break for party conventions; general election
         candidates selected   (about 2 minutes)
      f. General election campaign involving two candidates   (about 12 minutes)
      g. Vote in party's primary election; evaluate all six
         candidates; manipulation check on difficulty of choice   (about 3 minutes)
3. Unexpected Memory Task
      Subjects were asked to remember as much as they
      could about two general election candidates.   (about 10 minutes)
4. Correct Voting Determination
      Subjects were presented with complete information about
      two candidates from the primary (the one for whom they
      voted and, of the remaining candidates in that same party,
      the candidate closest to the subject on the issues) and
      asked to decide the one for whom they would have voted
      if they had obtained all this information when they actually
      had to make their choice.   (about 10–15 minutes)
5. Debriefing
      Subjects' general impressions of the experiment were
      gathered; any remaining questions were answered;
      and so forth.   (about 5 minutes)

*Experiment II subjects completed the unexpected memory task (step 3) at this point for candidates in their party's primary. They then completed a detailed guided protocol analysis, to explain why they had selected the items they chose to examine during the primary, before determining their correct vote choice (step 4).

registered to vote in either the Democratic or Republican primary. They then experienced a primary campaign involving six candidates (two from one party and four from the other) and much more information than can possibly be processed. (4) After the primary campaign, subjects voted for one of the candidates in their party's primary. Finally, after several activities of no concern here,[3] (5) subjects determined if their vote was "correct."

Determining "Correct" Vote Choices

After the mock election campaign was over, subjects were questioned about their impressions of the experiment and were asked to complete one final task. The experimenter commiserated with each subject about how difficult the election had been but explained it was very important to know whether the subject thought he or she had voted "correctly." The pictures of two candidates from the primary election were shown on the computer screen, the one for whom the subject voted and another from that same party. If only two candidates from the party ran in the primary, then those two were shown. For the four-candidate primary there was some discretion, however, and to make this choice as difficult as possible, the computer was programmed to select the candidate (from the three available) who was closest to the subject on the issues.

The experimenter brought out a notebook in which all the information about these two candidates was laid out side-by-side, so that it was very easy to compare. Explaining that it was not possible to learn everything about any candidate during the experiment, the experimenter asked the subject to examine the material carefully and decide if he or she still would have voted the same way if he or she had known all the available information about these two candidates. These instructions were designed to get subjects to take this final task seriously and to set up a context in which they would feel free to change their mind about their initial vote choice in the primary without feeling defensive or foolish about that choice.

After the subjects carefully considered all the information about the two candidates, if they decided they still would have voted as they did, then we classified them as voting "correctly." If they would have *changed* their initial vote, then we classified them as voting "incorrectly." This is our first, and probably most defensible, measure of correct voting.[4]

A Second Measure of Correct Voting

None of us can learn everything there is to know about the candidates in a real election, and few people are motivated to learn even what is readily available. Nonetheless, almost everyone *tries* to vote correctly, given what they have learned about the candidates (and parties) by election day. We now attempt to model how people could "naively" or "intuitively" go about making these decisions.

From the preelection questionnaire, we knew subjects' political preferences and policy stands. We also knew the candidates' stands, and those can be expressed on the same scales employed by subjects through the use of expert judges.[5] Most important, we knew exactly the information to which a voter was exposed about the different candidates. We did not know precisely how that information was evaluated by each individual, but we could make very informed guesses based on our knowledge of the voter's preferences. Thus, we were in an excellent position to try to model the vote decisions that people actually made in our experimental elections.

In fact, assuming that people try to vote correctly, this is essentially a second measure of correct voting—a *normative* measure of naive vote preferences. It is based on the voter's own values, to be sure, but ultimately is determined by the authors rather than the voter. We consciously juxtapose the terms "normative" and "naive" in the description of what we are trying to model. This variable is "naive" or "intuitive" in that it is based on the voter's actual information-gathering strategies rather than any ideal, logical, or expert-determined process; but it is "normative" in that it is based on an objective evaluation of that information. Thus, an objective determination can be made of the candidate for whom the subjects *should* have voted, given their own political preferences and the differential candidate information to which they were exposed.

Unfortunately, there is an almost infinite number of ways in which voters can combine information about the candidates with their own values and policy preferences to form candidate evaluations. After examining in some detail various methods that span the range of possibilities (but provide results very similar to those presented below), we provide data from one of the simplest procedures. We assume that voters average together the favorableness of all information they have learned about a candidate, weighting some parts of it more heavily than others. After comparing the summary evaluation of each candidate, voters should choose the candidate with the highest evaluation. This is essentially the method assumed by many popular models of the vote decision (e.g., Fiorina 1981; Kelley and Mirer 1974; Lau 1986, 1989; Lodge, McGraw, and Stroh 1989; Lodge, Steenbergen, and Brau 1995; Markus and Converse 1979).

Three types of information went into each candidate evaluation in our experiment. First, the favorableness of a candidate's issue stands was calculated by the directional method (Rabinowitz and Macdonald 1989), with the mean rating of our seven experts providing the stands (refer to footnote 5). Whenever a voter learned a candidate's position on an issue, and if the voter had expressed an opinion about it in our initial questionnaire, agreement or disagreement on that issue (rescaled to range from -1 to $+1$) was added into the candidate's total evaluation. Second, group endorsements learned by a subject were scored $+1$ if the subject liked the group (i.e., rated it above the mean of all groups evaluated and above the midpoint of the scale), -1 if the subject disliked the group, and 0 if the subject was indifferent toward the group. Third, the favorableness of personality descriptions learned about candidates and the attractiveness of their picture used in campaign ads were based on the ratings of 67 independent pretest subjects, again rescaled such that $+1$ was the highest possible evaluation and -1 was the lowest possible.[6]

Each bit of information was weighted according to subjects' judgments (from the preexperiment questionnaire) about how important different broad types of information were to their vote in the last presidential election. The weights ranged between 0 ("Not at All Important") to 1 ("Most Important"). Because every individual evaluation was scaled to range between -1 and $+1$, and the total evaluation was divided by the number of items upon which it was based, the summary evaluation itself ranges between -1 and $+1$. A detailed example of our method of calculating candidate preference is given in the Appendix [to this chapter].

Results

Candidate Choice

The first analytic task is to see how well this simple method of determining differential candidate preference predicts the actual vote choice of our subjects. This question is not as interesting in the context of a mock election campaign as it would be in a real election, but it is the question in which most studies of voting behavior are primarily interested, and it will demonstrate that our simple normative method of determining naive candidate preference is reasonable. We specified a logistic regression in which vote choice in the primary election is regressed on the difference between the candidate evaluation measures calculated for the two candidates offered to subjects for closer inspection after completing the main experiment. This single variable (which, of course, incorporates issue voting, group endorsements, and candidate appearance and personality) was highly significant ($p < .001$), correctly predicting more than 60 percent of the actual vote choices against a baseline of 50 percent—about as good as can be expected in a primary election campaign in which party cannot be used as a voting cue.

Predicting "Correct" Voting

Survey designs of actual elections are far better vehicles for learning why one particular candidate wins, of course, or for building methods to predict the direction of the vote choice. In contrast, we are primarily interested in understanding whether people voted correctly according to their fully informed interests. Since 70 percent of the subjects (206 out of 293) would not have changed their vote after learning everything there was to learn about the two candidates, by our definition they voted correctly. The remainder, by their own determination, voted "incorrectly."[7] This is our first important finding, although it is impossible to say how generalizable this proportion is, given that it is based on a mock election, albeit one designed to simulate the crucial aspects of real campaigns.

The first major question we pose is how well our normative measure of naive or intuitive candidate preference predicts fully informed correct voting. If the prediction is good, then we are justified in referring to it as a "normative" measure, and we are justified in using it as a second measure of correct voting, a surrogate for the more complete, but much more difficult to obtain, fully informed correct vote determination.

Thus, we specified a second logistic regression in which the subject's fully informed determination of the correct candidate was regressed on the normative candidate differential variable described above. This single variable is again highly significant ($p < .001$) and correctly predicts almost 66 percent of the correct vote choices—better than this same variable predicts the actual vote choice! This is strong validation of our normative candidate differential variable as another measure of correct voting. Just as important, *our normative method of determining candidate preferences does almost as well in determining "correct" voting decisions as did voters themselves* (who voted for the "correct" candidate 70 percent of the time).

This finding is the crux of our argument, and we want to put it in clear perspective. We have good, but certainly incomplete, knowledge of voters' preferences; based on this knowledge, we can make reasonable (but again far from perfect) inferences about how subjects evaluated the information they learned about the candidates. Knowing nothing about how voters actually combine these evaluations into a vote choice but by modeling a plausible alternative, *we can do almost as well in determining correct vote decisions as do voters themselves,* who have *perfect* knowledge of their own preferences and perfect knowledge of how favorably they responded to the candidate information to which they were exposed.

The reason our normative measure of naive candidate preference predicts a fully informed vote choice better than an actual vote choice is that voters, under normal information processing circumstances, cannot possibly achieve the care and objectivity that would be possible if they were given more time and the opportunity to become fully informed about two opposing candidates. With the aid of a powerful computer to help keep track of what has been learned about the multiple candidates, we can reasonably approximate that care and objectivity. In other words, under normal circumstances the vote decision is an intuitive, global judgment, and people with limited cognitive resources have a very hard time combining complex sets of information to make such judgments. Only when given the time and presented with the information in a very focused (only two candidates, not all six) and easily comparable format (similar information about the two candidates presented side by side) can people approach the objectivity of our simple averaging algorithm.[8]

Our results suggest that (1) voters in our experiment confronted with the same type of time constraints and information overload faced by voters in actual elections, nevertheless do a pretty good job of selecting the candidate for whom they would have voted had there been no constraints on their information-gathering capabilities (i.e., if they have full information); but (2) they could clearly do better than they do under current circumstances, given more time or presented with information in a more easily "digestible" manner; and (3) we as researchers or external observers can determine fairly accurately who individual voters, given full information, would want to pick as their best choice.

Further Validation of the Normative Measure

We can provide additional evidence that our normative candidate differential measure is a reasonable approximation of a fully informed correct vote decision and is, in fact, what voters were trying to achieve during the correct vote

Table 8-1 Willingness to Change Original Vote as a Function of the "Quality" of the Original Choice

	Would Not Change	Would Change	Total	(N)
Worst candidate chosen	56%	44%	100%	(82)
Intermediate candidate	62%	38%	100%	(58)
Best candidate chosen	83%	17%	100%	(148)
	Tau $c = .26$, $p<.001$			

determination stage of our experiment. First, we can ask if the *additional* information subjects learn about the candidates during the final correct voting determination task can predict whether they will want to change their initial choice. If we cannot understand how additional information may *change* decisions, then we probably do not have a very good grasp of how those decisions are reached in the first place.

To explore this question, we put subjects' actual vote choices into three categories according to our normative measure of candidate preference: Had subjects voted for the best possible alternative, the worst possible alternative, or (in the four-candidate condition) a candidate who fell between these two extremes? If our measure reasonably captures voters' fully informed preferences, then we should observe a much higher percentage of voters who want to change their vote among those who (according to our measure) originally voted for the worst possible candidate than among those who voted for the best possible candidate. The data, shown in Table 8-1, reflect just this pattern: Almost 44 percent of those who we thought picked the worst alternative were willing to admit a mistake after examining more information about the candidates, while less than 17 percent of those who we believed picked the best possible candidate wanted to change their mind.

As a final check that our normative measure of differential candidate preference is a good approximation of how voters would try to process information and decide who is their best choice if they had the opportunity, we can use the same procedures to model the *additional* information subjects gained about the candidates during the final task—that is, information not available to them when they made their actual vote choice. If our method is a good one, then this new variable, which incorporates all the new information presumably gained only after the campaign was over, should predict which of the two candidates was selected by subjects as their correct choice, after controlling for the actual vote choice.

To address this issue we (1) recoded the dependent variable to represent whether Candidate A or Candidate B (an arbitrary distinction) was determined by the subject to be the correct choice, (2) used as predictors whether subjects had originally voted for Candidate A or Candidate B, and (3) added a new variable reflecting an evaluation of the information learned about the two candidates after

Table 8-2   Effect of New Information on Decision to Change Vote

	B	Wald	Significance
Direction of actual vote	1.76	41.86	.000
	(.27)		
Effect of new information	.28	5.35	.010
	(.12)		
Constant	−1.32	42.12	.000
	(.20)		

Note: The B coefficients come from a logistic regression analysis; standard errors are in parentheses. For this analysis, −2 times the log likelihood was 323.93, while the model chi-square with 2 degrees of freedom was 5.03 ($p<.000$). Classification was correct for 71.2 percent of the cases. $N = 288$.

the original vote. The original vote reflects the intuitive or naive candidate choice. Whatever information was learned about the candidates during the primary election (plus whatever inferences people were willing to make) is reflected in this vote choice. We already know this will be a highly significant predictor; after being presented with more information, 70 percent of subjects reported they had voted correctly—a substantial improvement over a chance level of 50 percent.

The more interesting variable is the second in the equation, that is, the effect of the additional information gained from the fully informed correct voting task. If we as outside observers, knowing only the voters' preferences and the stands of the candidates, can predict fully informed choices better than can voters with their own intuitive methods (that is, if we do indeed have a good idea of what voters will believe is their best choice), then our information-gain variable should add significantly to the predictive power of the equation. As shown in Table 8-2, that is the case. Therefore, we are now even more confident that we understand how voters are determining their "correct" vote choice because we can predict how additional information about the alternatives influences that decision. Thus, we feel reasonably confident in offering our "normative" method for determining candidate preference as an alternative criterion for correct voting.

An Application to American Presidential Elections

The results from our experiment are quite impressive. Confronted by an information environment in some ways even more difficult than an actual campaign, our subjects nevertheless voted correctly 70 percent of the time. Some skepticism may remain, however, about generalizing to an actual election. Any experimental study of the vote choice, no matter how realistic it attempts to be, is a far cry from a real campaign. In this section we illustrate how our method can be applied to NES data.[9]

It is certainly possible to construct a measure analogous to our normative method of determining naive or intuitive candidate preference using the information in the typical NES survey. There is no analog to our importance weights, but in analyses not reported here, an equal-weights version of our normative measure performed almost as well as the weighted version. Likewise, we have no direct measure of the candidate information to which a voter has been exposed, but we can use willingness to answer NES questions about the candidates (e.g., to attribute an issue stand to a candidate) as a reasonable indirect measure. Using this analog, we can determine (with a great many qualifications, of course) the percentage of "correct" voting in different American presidential elections.

We pose three simple macro-level hypotheses about differences across elections in the percentage of voters who should have voted "correctly." To the extent these hypotheses are supported, they provide important predictive validity for our surrogate measure of correct voting as it can be operationalized from survey data.

HYPOTHESIS 1. *Given limited cognitive resources, voters are more likely to make correct decision when there are fewer candidates than when there are more alternatives in the choice set. This suggests that voters were more likely to make correct choices in 1972, 1976, 1984, and 1988 than in 1980, when there was a reasonably successful third-party candidate running in the general election.*[10]

HYPOTHESIS 2. *If the number of candidates is held constant, then voters will be more likely to make correct decisions when the candidates are easy to distinguish than when they are difficult to distinguish. This suggests rates of correct voting were higher in 1972, 1984, and 1988, when more ideologically extreme candidates captured the two parties' nominations, than in 1976, when more centrist candidates opposed each other.*

HYPOTHESIS 3. *All else equal, voters will be more likely to make correct decisions when campaign resources are reasonably balanced, giving all candidates an equal opportunity to get their case across than when resources are imbalanced. Phrased more cynically, this suggests that candidates whose campaign resources are greater than those of opponents can attract more support than should have been the case if everyone had voted "correctly."*

Table 8-3 presents the results of a preliminary test of these hypotheses. Without going into all the details (which are left for the Appendix), we have replicated as closely as possible with NES data an equal-weights version of our normative measure of naive candidate preference. In addition to party identification, every policy issue and candidate-group linkage that could be objectively estimated was included in the analysis. Taking this measure as our criterion of "correct" voting, we can determine the proportion of correct voters in recent American presidential elections.

Table 8-3 is broken into five sections, one for each presidential election between 1972 and 1988. The top row of each section displays the proportion of voters for each candidate (and the overall proportion) who, by our determination,

Table 8-3   Correct Voting in American Presidential Elections, 1972–1988

Presidential Candidate	% Supporters Voting Correctly	% Reported Vote	% Predicted Correct Vote	Deviation, Reported–Predicted	% General Election Spending	Deviation of Spending from Proportional Share	Overall Accuracy
1972							79%
McGovern	74.5	35.7	38.5	−2.8	33.7	−16.3	
Nixon	81.5	64.3	61.5	2.8	66.3	16.3	
1976							75.5%
Carter	72.2	51.1	47.1	4.0	52.4	2.4	
Ford	78.9	48.9	52.8	−3.9	47.6	−2.4	
1980							67.8%
Carter	64.0	40.0	34.6	5.4	40.0	6.7	
Reagan	73.7	51.6	46.5	5.1	47.7	14.3	
Anderson	50.6	8.5	19.0	−10.5	12.3	−21.0	
1984							76.8%
Mondale	89.0	41.8	55.7	−13.9	40.5	−9.5	
Reagan	68.0	58.2	44.2	14.0	59.5[a]	9.5	
1988							77.1%
Dukakis	78.2	47.1	49.4	−2.3	53.0	3.0	
Bush	76.1	52.9	50.5	2.4	47.0	−3.0	

Note: Data are from the 1972, 1976, 1980, 1984, 1988 NES.

[a]Includes spending during primaries because Reagan was essentially unchallenged, and his campaign manager is quoted as saying that all spending during the primaries was aimed at the general election campaign.

voted correctly. These numbers range between a low of 51 percent for John Anderson in 1980 to a high of 89 percent for Walter Mondale in 1984. Overall accuracy of voting across these five elections ranges from just under 68 percent up to 79 percent, with a mean of 75 percent.

Consistent with hypothesis 1, the mean number of correct votes in years with two major candidates, 77.1 percent, is significantly higher than the mean of 67.8 percent ($z = 5.81, p < .001$) for 1980, when there was an important third-party candidate.[11] Consistent with hypothesis 2, the mean number of correct votes in the three two-candidate elections with ideologically distinct candidates, 77.7 percent, is greater than in the one year with two centrist candidates, 75.5 percent ($z = 1.83, p < .04$, one-tailed).

The data necessary for testing hypothesis 3 are less straightforward. Each section of Table 8-3 provides NES data on the percentage of voters who reported voting for each of the major presidential candidates that year; the percentage each candidate would have received if all voters, by our calculations, had voted correctly; and the difference between the two (a positive difference indicates the candidate received more than he "should" have, while a negative difference means he received fewer votes than he should have); the percentage of all money spent by each candidate (or on his behalf) during the general election campaign;[12] and the difference between that percentage and a proportional share of all spending (i.e., 100 percent divided by the number of candidates).

The crucial data for hypothesis 3 are in the two rows of deviation or difference scores. If hypothesis 3 is correct, then candidates with a disproportionately larger share of campaign resources (i.e., a positive difference in the bottom row of each section of the table) should be able to win more votes than they correctly "should" have (i.e., a positive difference in the fourth row of each section of the table), while candidates with a disproportionately smaller share should, all else equal, receive fewer votes than they should have. The Spearman rank-order correlation between two difference scores is .77, $p < .01$, providing strong confirmation of the third hypothesis.

Discussion

Any political philosophy presumes a view, a psychological theory, of human nature (Lau 1985). Classic democratic theory sets unrealistic standards for ideal citizens at least in part because it holds unrealistic expectations about the very nature of human cognition. Beginning with a more circumscribed human psychology, we can set more realistic goals for democratic citizens — and still judge how readily those goals are met.

We offer a very simple standard: Irrespective of how the vote decision is reached, how frequently do voters vote correctly? To ask this question implies that one has an answer, or at least a method for obtaining the answer. Relying on notions of "fully informed" interests, we have suggested one such method. Our analyses of both experimental and survey data show that our method does a reasonably good job of measuring correct voting. Had we relied only on the experimental data and its rather artificial full-information determination of correct voting, our findings would have been of more limited value. But the second measure of correct voting, available in both experiments and surveys, should prove to be much more useful because it is much more widely applicable. Moreover, that we have found corroborating evidence from two very different research designs lends more credence to our overall findings than either set of results alone.

We do not want to suggest that our method is the only way, or even the best way, of determining "correct" voting. Recently, Bartels (1996) and Delli Carpini and Keeter (1995) have presented research that, although aimed at a very different purpose, could be construed as alternative approaches to correct voting. Bartels (1996) seeks to find the political consequences of an electorate which, as a whole, is notoriously low in political knowledge. He addresses this question by estimating a logistic analysis which includes the vote decision regressed on 20 variables representing various demographic characteristics and the interaction between each of them and a measure of political knowledge. Based on significant interaction terms, Bartels concludes that the informed and uninformed portions of the electorate do vote differently and, moreover, that the results of close elections could change if uninformed voters voted as if they had full information. Although Bartels does not use the term "correct" to describe the votes of the fully informed, it is easy to make that interpretation and to call the votes of the less well informed, to the extent they differ, incorrect. His approach is drastically different from ours in that it completely avoids the "political values and preferences" that form the basis of our determination of what is correct, presumably because if the vote decisions of the less informed could be wrong, then so, too, could the political preferences upon which those decisions are based.

Delli Carpini and Keeter (1995) have the same aim as Bartels, to demonstrate the political consequences of low political information. They begin with two plausible assumptions: (1) Material interests differ across various gender, class, race, and age divisions in society, and (2) the more politically informed will be better able to discern their interests. The latter assumption clearly allows us to label the opinions of the most politically informed as "correct" and the opinions of the less politically informed, if they differ, as "incorrect," although Delli Carpini and Keeter are not this explicit. Their finding that the well-informed hold political opinions different from those of the poorly informed shows that information matters and, in general, tends to increase group differences on political issues. Delli Carpini and Keeter go on to show that the amount of political information affects the extent of issue voting. They note that the most politically informed women had a strong vote preference for Bill Clinton in 1992, but women in the lowest quartile of information preferred George Bush. Delli Carpini and Keeter do not take the step that for our purposes would be most relevant—tracing the extent to which holding "incorrect" opinions led the least politically informed to vote "incorrectly"—although we could imagine how one could perform this analysis.

Thus, we can point to three quite different methods of determining a "correct" vote. Each has its merits and problems, and we are not suggesting that our method is superior to the others. But we do suggest that the issue of "correct voting" is a very important one, and we hope that we have illustrated at least one way in which it can be addressed empirically.

Taking our results at face value, we can return to the question with which we began: Is 75 percent of voters voting correctly in a typical presidential election "good enough" for a system of government to be considered truly democratic? We are pleasantly surprised by these results: This high a level of "correct" voting certainly validates the efficiency of heuristic-based information processing that underlies our view of human nature (but see Bartels 1996). Moreover, it challenges those critics who hold that democracies' problems stem primarily from people not having the motivation to gather sufficient information to figure out what is in their best interest. Most people, most of the time, can make this calculation, at least in presidential elections.

But is this level high enough for us to consider that (at least) the American version of democracy "works" at some minimal level? It is certainly too soon to draw any firm conclusions about this question in any case, and we should mention several very important caveats.

First, if 75 percent of voters are voting correctly in the typical presidential election, then 25 percent are voting incorrectly. If this group were distributed randomly, then it would not be much of a problem, but our test of hypothesis 3 demonstrates otherwise. Candidates with more money have an advantage. Here is yet one more argument for serious campaign reform of American elections.

Second, the analyses in Table 8-3 only consider voters, but barely half of eligible Americans vote. The interests of nonvoters are beyond the scope of this chapter but certainly not beyond the scope of theoretical concern.

Third, we have only examined presidential elections, but our federal system ensures that much of what is important in politics happens at lower levels of government. At those levels, we would expect even less correct voting—or at least for elections with less media attention than presidential campaigns, which is to say all others. If 75 percent of voters were to vote correctly for president and 65 percent were to vote correctly for mayor, we would be quite happy. If 75 percent were to vote correctly for president and 25 percent were to vote correctly for mayor, we would not.

Political science as a field has only begun to map out the "correct voting" landscape. A great deal more research must be conducted before empirical political science can be of much help to normative theorists struggling with this question.

Whatever may ultimately prove to be the answer to the question of the extent to which any system of government can be considered truly democratic, no one would argue that things cannot be improved. Given a metric of "correct" voting, we can turn to the equally important issue of what leads people to make more or less optimal decisions. This can be addressed at both the individual and institutional level. For example, we could ask if particular information search tactics or different decision or choice strategies lead some individuals to make better decisions than others. Bartels's (1996) recent findings warn us not to assume that all voters use heuristics and other information shortcuts equally effectively. We could ask whether different practices the media have developed for covering campaigns encourages or discourages the more effective information-processing strategies. We could ask whether institutional arrangements that favor two-party systems or that separate the fates of executives and legislators change the probability of correct voting. And we could study whether certain campaign tactics are particularly effective in distorting the "correct" outcome of an election and, if so, consider means of discouraging those tactics. All these questions—which a "relevant" political science ought to be asking—can only be addressed with a defensible measure of correct voting.

APPENDIX

Calculating "Naive" Candidate Evaluations in the Experiments

We assume that voters consider four general types of information in forming evaluations of candidates: party affiliation, issue stands, group endorsements, and a candidate's personality/appearance. For the first three categories the voter's own values or preferences are important (i.e., their party identification, issue stands, and their evaluation of the groups doing the endorsing), along with "objective" standards of where the candidates stand on the issues and the facts about the party each candidate belongs to and which candidate a group endorses. Because we are looking only at choice during a primary election, party affiliation becomes irrelevant as a means of choosing between candidates and, for present purposes, was ignored.

Issue Stands. Every issue for which a subject (1) expressed a stand on the pre-experiment questionnaire, and (2) learned a candidate's position (generally by choosing to "access" that information during the campaign, but also by exposure to a campaign advertisement) contributed one item toward that candidate's summary evaluation. We employed Rabinowitz and Macdonald's (1989) "directional theory" of issue voting, which argues that being on the same "side" of an issue is the most important consideration in issue voting. For computation, Rabinowitz and Macdonald suggest subtracting the midpoint of the scale from the voter's own opinion and from some determination of the candidate's position before multiplying the two together. With 7-point scales, the resulting product can range in theory from -9 to $+9$, but in practice depends on the range of opinions expressed by voters and the actual stand taken by the candidate. Each item was rescaled to range between -1 and $+1$. The candidate's positions were determined objectively by a panel of experts who carefully read each position taken by a candidate and placed it on the same scale subjects were using to express their political opinions (see footnote 5).

Group Endorsements. Eleven groups endorsed a candidate in each party's primary. Subjects had previously evaluated those groups (e.g., the American Civil Liberties Union) on 100-point feeling thermometers. Voters were considered to "like" groups they evaluated above the midpoint of the scale (50) and (to control for individual differences in use of the feeling thermometer) above the mean of all groups evaluated; they were considered to "dislike" groups rated below 50 and below their personal mean of all groups evaluated. Then any time a voter learned (through accessing that item) that a group endorsed a particular candidate, the endorsement (scored $+1$ if the group was liked and -1 if the group was disliked) counted one additional item toward that candidate's evaluation.

Candidate Personality/Appearance. Four different brief personality descriptions were available about each candidate, and one picture. (The picture could be accessed as a separate item, but it also appeared for the last five seconds of every campaign commercial.) All these items were rated for their "attractiveness" by 67 pretest subjects. The mean ratings of the 67 pretest subjects, rescaled to range between -1 and $+1$, were treated as the "objective" value of that information. Every personality description accessed by a subject contributed one additional item toward that candidate's evaluation. Because all subjects saw every candidate's picture at least once (during a campaign advertisement sponsored by the candidate), the mean rating of the picture contributed one last item to each candidate's total.

Importance Weights. Early in the preelection questionnaire subjects were asked to think back to the 1992 presidential election and to explain briefly, in their own words, why they had voted for (or preferred, if they had not voted in 1992) one of the candidates over the others. After this recollection, subjects were asked to look at ten reasons people sometime give for voting for one candidate over another, and to pick the *one* that was the most important factor they used in deciding how to vote in 1992. The ten factors listed for consideration were "Appearance/I Just Liked Him Best," "Candidates' Party Affiliations," "Groups/Persons Supporting Him," "Couldn't Stand the Other Two Candidates," "Just Time for a Change," "Most Trustworthy Candidate," "Foreign/Defense Policies," "Economic Policies," "Social Policies," "Most Competent/Qualified Person." After subjects had chosen the one most important factor, they were asked to consider the remaining ones and select those that were "very important" in their vote decision. Subjects were allowed to select any number of reasons as very important. Finally subjects were asked to consider any remaining factors and select those that were "not at all important" in their vote decisions. Again, any number of factors could be chosen. The most important factor was given a weight of 1; "Very Important" reasons were given a weight of .67; "Not at All Important" reasons were given a weight of 0; and any remaining reasons were considered to be "Somewhat Important" and given a weight of .33.

The information available about the mock candidates was then matched up with one of these ten reasons (all but "Couldn't Stand the Other Two Candidates" and "Just Time for a Change"), and the weight assigned to that reason was used as the "importance weight" of that particular type of information.

Summary Evaluations. Each item was multiplied by its weight before the mean was calculated. Then "naive differential candidate evaluations" were computed by subtracting the mean rating of the candidate a subject did not vote for from the summary evaluation of the candidate a subject did vote for. This difference score is positive if the subjects voted for the candidate we calculated they should like the most, and negative if they voted for the other candidate. The greater the difference in evaluation of these two candidates, the stronger the presumed preference.

As an example, suppose a subject voted for "Chris Rodgers" during the primary election and, at the conclusion of the experiment, was asked to consider carefully all information about Rodgers and "Pat Thomas," another candidate in the same primary. During the campaign this subject learned Rodgers's stand on affirmative action (objectively determined to be 6), abortion (7), and defense spending (5), and Thomas's stand on abortion (4) and crime (6). To make life easy, let us assume this subject took conservative stands (i.e., 6) on all of these issues herself. During the course of the campaign two group endorsements were learned: the National Taxpayers Association preferred Rodgers, as did the National Rifle Association. This subject had previously rated "groups that try to limit taxes" 85 on a feeling thermometer, well above her personal mean of all groups rated (63); but disliked the National Rifle Association (thermometer rating of only 25). Two personality descriptions were learned about Rodgers, a family friend's description (rated .75 by the 67 pretest subjects) and an anecdote from the candidate's mother (rated .20); and two personality descriptions were learned about Thomas, a staff member's description (.67) and a political opponent's description (−.50). Pictures of both Rodgers (.10) and Thomas (.25) were seen during political advertisements. During the pre-election questionnaire this subject had selected "Social Policies" as the most important reason for her 1992 presidential vote choice (given a weight of 1), "Foreign/Defense Policies" and "Groups/Persons Supporting Him" as very important reasons (weights of .67), "Most Trustworthy Candidate" and "Most Competent/Qualified Person" as somewhat important (weights of .33), and "Appearance/I Just Liked Him Best" as not at all important (weight of 0).

Table 8A-1 summarizes this information, and the way each bit of it was presumed to be evaluated. Rabinowitz and Macdonald's "directional" calculations (shown in the table only for Rodgers) are straightforward. These values are the numerator for the "rescaling." The denominator varies across issues; it is based on the presumption that subjects will use the entire 1 through 7 range of the attitude scale (and hence the first multiplicand is −3 or +3 at its extreme). The second multiplicand is constant across subjects, however, always equaling the objective rating of the candidate's position minus 4. The difference in the potential range of values across Rodgers's stand on abortion, affirmative action, and defense spending is reflected in the denominator used for the rescaling of those three issues (9, 6, and 3, respectively). The National Taxpayers Association endorsement counts +1 for Rodgers (because that group is liked), but the NRA endorsement counts −1, as that group is disliked. Ratings of the personality descriptions and appearance of the candidates have already been rescaled in the figures listed in the table. The mean candidate evaluation is simply calculated by summing the evaluation of every individual bit of information learned about a candidate, multiplied by its importance weight, and dividing by the total number of such bits of information. We would predict that this subject, "naively" calculating differential candidate evaluations, should decide to vote for Rodgers, because in this example he was the more highly evaluated candidate.

Calculating "Correct Voting" in the NES Surveys

Our goal in establishing criteria for determining the candidate a respondent should have voted for was to include as many of the criteria for candidate evaluation that have been identified by prior research as possible, allowing respondents to determine their own preferences while relying primarily on "objective" criteria

Table 8A-1 Hypothetical Ratings of Two Candidates in Experiment

	Hypothetical Voter's Stand	Rodgers's Stand	Rabinowitz Directional Calculation	Rescaled	Importance Weights	Thomas's Stand	Rescaled	Importance Weights
Issue stands								
Abortion	6	7	(6 − 4) × (7 − 4) = 6	6/9 = .67	× 1.00	4	0	× 1.00
Affirmative action	6	6	(6 − 4) × (6 − 4) = 4	4/6 = .67	× 1.00			
Crime	6					6	4/6 = .67	× 1.00
Defense spending	6	5	(6 − 4) × (5 − 4) = 2	2/3 = .67	× .67			
Group endorsements								
Nat'l Taxpayers Assoc.		(liked group)		1.00	× .67			
Nat'l Rifle Assoc.		(disliked group)		−1.00	× .67			
Personality descriptions								
from family friend		.75			× .33			
from staff member						.67		× .33
from political opponent						−.50		× .33
anecdote from mother		.20			× .33			
Candidate's appearance		.10			× 0	.25		× 0
Weighted sum					Σ = 2.08			Σ = .72
Mean candidate evaluation					.30			.18

for rating the candidates. We included four categories of predictors: party affiliation, agreement with a candidate's policy stands, candidate-social group linkages, and (for incumbents running for reelection) performance evaluations. Emotional responses and trait ascriptions were not included because we could think
of no defensible way to get an objective measure of them. The bulk of the items
on which we rely were not introduced into the NES surveys until 1972, and thus
we go back only that far. We do not include 1992 in the analysis because there is
a dramatic difference in the number of items available to evaluate Perot relative
to Clinton and Bush. In general (although the survey analysis included a few
more "types" of information), the "correct voting determination in these surveys
was calculated in exactly the same way as the "naive" candidate evaluations in the
experiments, with one major exception: All weights were either 0 or 1. In all cases
we rescaled the individual items to range between -1 and $+1$, with -1 representing the most negative evaluation and $+1$ representing the most positive evaluation. Summary evaluations of each candidate were determined by the simple
mean of all nonmissing evaluative items; the "correct" candidate that should have
been voted for is the one with the highest summary evaluation.

Party Identification. The 7 points of the standard party identification scale
were recoded to equidistant values between -1 and $+1$, with "Strong Democrat"
at -1 and "Strong Republican" at $+1$. The resulting item was included in this
form in the summary evaluation of Republican candidates; it was multiplied by -1
before being included in the summary evaluation of Democratic candidates. As an
example of how this variable worked, all weak Democrats received a $+.67$ toward
their summary evaluation of McGovern in 1972, and a $-.67$ toward their summary evaluation of Nixon. Because Anderson ran in the general election as an independent in 1980, party identification was not relevant to his summary evaluation.

Agreement with Candidates' Policy Stands. All political attitudes on which
respondents were asked for their own opinions and for their perceptions of the
candidates' positions were considered. We established "objective" criteria for
where each candidate stood on those issues by first creating a scale of political
knowledge (from responses to all questions that clearly had a correct answer), and
then taking the mean perceptions of where the candidates stand on the issues of
all respondents above the median on the resulting political knowledge scale.
Tables 8A-1 and 8A-2 list the particular items that were used to gather the
respondent's opinion of these issues, and the resulting objective placements of
each candidate on those same issues. As in the experiments, agreement scales
were computed via the "directional" method suggested by Rabinowitz and Macdonald (1989). Thus, each political attitude on which a respondent expressed an
opinion contributed one additional item to the evaluation of each candidate.

Candidate-Social Group Linkages. Beginning in 1972 the NES surveys ask
respondents which of a list of social groups they feel "close to." We then calcu-

Table 8A-2   Correct Voting, 1972 NES

Issue Stands	Respondent's Position	Political Experts' Mean Determination	
		Nixon's Stand	McGovern's Stand
Guaranteed jobs	v172	4.7	2.3
Tax rates	v178	4.5	2.8
Vietnam withdrawal	v184	4.8	1.6
Fighting inflation	v190	3.4	3.1
Legalizing marijuana	v196	5.5	3.3
School busing	v202	5.3	3.1
National health insurance	v208	4.8	2.4
Pollution	v214	3.3	2.5
Women's role	v232	3.5	2.7
Treatment of criminals	v621	4.3	2.8
Minority aid	v629	4.3	2.4
Liberalism-conservatism	v652	5.1	2.2
Solving urban unrest	v670	4.3	2.5
Student demonstrations	v678	5.1	2.8
Job performance evaluation	v46	3.9	
Groups with close links to Nixon: Businessmen, southerners, conservatives			
Groups with close links to McGovern: Liberals, poor people, blacks			
Party identification	v140		

Note: Data come from the 1972 NES.

lated a simple crosstab between each "closeness" item and the reported vote. Whenever this crosstab resulted in a significant relationship between feeling close to a group and preference for one of the candidates, a candidate-group linkage item was created, scored 0 for respondents who did not feel close to the group and 1 for respondents who did feel close to the group, and added to the summary evaluation of that candidate. As an example, in 1972 respondents who felt close to liberals, poor people, and blacks all showed a significant vote preference for McGovern; while respondents who felt close to businessmen, southerners, and conservatives showed a significant vote preference for Nixon.

Incumbent's Job Performance. In every election year where a sitting president was running for reelection, survey respondents were asked for their perceptions of the incumbent's job performance, both an overall perception and more specific (e.g., economic policy; foreign policy) perceptions. We recoded each such performance evaluation to run from +1 (Strongly Approve) to −1 (Strongly Disapprove), and added them to the summary evaluation of the incumbent candidate.

Table 8A-2 lists the specific items that were used in the correct voting determination for the 1972 NES, along with the objective criteria that were used in this determination. Similar tables for the 1976–1988 NES are available from the authors upon request.

Notes

1. To make these probabilities realistic, we first conducted an elaborate study of the prevalence of different types of information in newspapers during the 1988 presidential campaign (Lau 1992). We then modeled the probabilities after the actual prevalence of those types of information during the 1988 campaign.
2. Of the 303 recruits, three were eliminated when they could not complete the study for time reasons (some subjects took more than 2½ hours to complete the experiment), two were eliminated because of computer errors, and another five were dropped because the experimenter, after running a subject, believed he or she had not taken the experiment at all seriously. Of the remaining 293 subjects, 60 percent were female; 84 percent were non-Hispanic whites; 22 percent had a high school education or less, while 52 percent were college educated; and 22 percent had family income under $25,000, while 25 percent had family income over $75,000. The median age was 52; half were currently employed, and one-third were retired; 30 percent were Catholic, 29 percent Protestant, 18 percent Jewish, with the remainder expressing some other or "no" religious preference. Forty percent were Democrats, 25 percent Republicans, and the remainder Independents.
3. We actually ran two different experiments that diverged after the vote in the primary election, but in this chapter we only use information from the primary election campaign, which was essentially identical across the two experiments. The experiments also involved several other random manipulations, but only the two-versus four-candidate manipulation affected the probability of a correct vote, and for present purposes the other manipulations are ignored. For simplicity we have collapsed together subjects from the two experiments.
4. Besides random error, there are at least three plausible reasons subjects may not be completely accurate in their own assessment of the correctness of their initial vote choice. One is self-presentation: Despite our efforts to make it acceptable to revise one's decision—and we were careful to avoid such words as "mistake" and "incorrect"—some subjects still may have been reluctant to do so. A closely related reason is avoiding postdecision dissonance, or any unpleasant internal state resulting from learning that one has made a bad decision. A third reason is fatigue. This final task was presented after an average 126 minutes of prior effort (the range was 93 to 160, with a standard deviation of about 13 minutes), and the material about the two candidates was almost twelve pages long, single spaced. Nonetheless we stressed the importance of this "final task," and most subjects made a very serious effort.
5. Seven "experts" (the two authors, four graduate students in political science at Rutgers, and one local elected official) read all issue positions taken by eight different candidates and rated them on seven-point scales, in keeping with the items and scales on the political attitudes questionnaire given to subjects. We used the mean rating of these seven judges, rounded to the nearest whole number, as the objective stand of each candidate on that issue.
6. Thus, most information learned about a candidate figured into the evaluation. We have no way of knowing how subjects evaluated some of the available information, however, particularly about candidates' personal background. Although we have no reason to suspect systematic biases, it is quite possible that some subjects preferred senators over governors, people from Florida over people from California, lawyers over former newsmen, 45-year-olds rather than 65-year-olds, and so on. It is important to note that our knowledge of subjects' preferences is incomplete.
7. Since fully 30 percent of the subjects were willing to say they would change their vote, implicitly admitting that they had voted "incorrectly," self-presentation concerns were probably not a major issue to most subjects (refer to footnote 4).

8. The finding that fairly simple but objective algorithms for combining multiple criteria for judgment outperform naive (or expert) decision makers who rely on a global judgment is fairly common in the decision-making literature. Perhaps the classic example is Meehl's (1954) summary of 20 different studies comparing what he called "clinical" judgment to a statistical summary of objective information available to the decision maker. In no case was the global judgment found to be superior to the statistical summary. Dawes (1988) reviews many subsequent studies, all of which reach the same conclusion.

9. The data used in the following analyses were made available by the Inter-university Consortium for Political and Social Research.

10. The sporadic Ross Perot candidacy in 1992 appeared unlikely when the NES staff made the final decisions about their preelection survey. This resulted in a dearth of questions about Perot in the survey and precludes that election from this analysis.

11. If we consider only Carter and Reagan voters as the most appropriate comparison group (and ignore Anderson voters), then the 1980 proportion increases to 69.4 percent voting correctly but the hypothesis is still strongly supported ($z = 4.53$, $p < .001$).

    One reviewer suggested this hypothesis could be confounded by "strategic" vote considerations (e.g., Abramson, Aldrich, Paolino, and Rohde 1992), for example, voters realizing that Anderson was their "best" choice but that he could not win and thus voting for their "second best," who had a much better chance. Such considerations should not affect the relative rankings of the three candidates on feeling thermometer evaluations, however. We repeated this analysis, substituting the relative ranking measure for the actual vote choice. With this alternative criterion the overall proportion of correct votes (or rankings) actually falls to 66.9 percent. If we limit the analysis to voters who evaluated Carter or Reagan highest, the proportion correct remains at 69.4 percent. In neither case would it appear that strategic voting considerations provide an alternative explanation for these results.

12. These spending figures are reported in great detail in Alexander (1975, 1979, 1983), Alexander and Bauer (1991), and Alexander and Haggerty (1987).

9. Rational Public Opinion

Benjamin I. Page and Robert Y. Shapiro

. . . It is undeniable that most Americans are, at best, fuzzy about the details of government structure and policy. They do not know with any precision how much money is being spent on the military, foreign aid, education, or food stamps. They have only a dim idea of what is going on in foreign countries or (in many cases) even where those countries are. They do not know much about monetary policy or economic regulation or labor relations or civil rights. Thus it would be unrealistic to expect the average American to hold well-worked-out, firmly based preferences about a wide range of public policies. Surely this is one reason that responses to survey questions often change from one interview to the next. And surely Lippmann (1955) was right to deride the myth of the omnicompetent citizen.

We take little comfort from the fact that this political ignorance is generally "rational" in the economist's sense of that term. As Anthony Downs (1957, chaps. 11–13) long ago pointed out, rational decision making (i.e., decision making that tries to maximize happiness or utility) leads ordinary citizens *not* to gather a great deal of political information. People have other things to do and to think about: work, family, friends, recreation. To gather and analyze political information is costly in time and foregone opportunities. It requires energy and thought and sometimes money. The benefits are not great; usually they are not worth much investment except by those who happen to enjoy watching the political fray. A single individual cannot hope to wield any appreciable influence through his or her vote, so there is not much point to studying hard in order to vote right. Widespread political ignorance, therefore, and attention only to whatever bits of information come easily to hand, follows from rational self-interested behavior.

Our own argument, however, does not stop with this rather weak assertion about individual rationality, which makes public ignorance seem natural and inevitable. Our claim is a very different one. While we grant the rational ignorance of most individuals, and the possibility that their policy preferences are shallow and unstable, we maintain that public opinion as a *collective* phenomenon is nonetheless stable (though not immovable), meaningful, and indeed rational in a higher, if somewhat looser, sense: it is able to make distinctions; it is organized

Source: The Rational Public: Fifty Years of Trends in Americans' Policy Preferences, Benjamin I. Page and Robert Y. Shapiro, published by the University of Chicago. © 1992 by The University of Chicago.

in coherent patterns; it is reasonable, based on the best available information; and it is adaptive to new information or changed circumstances, responding in similar ways to similar stimuli. Moreover, while we grant that recorded responses of individuals to survey questions vary from one interview to another, we maintain that surveys accurately measure this stable, meaningful, and reasonable collective public opinion.

How is this possible? By what magic can it occur? The answer has to do with the statistical aggregation process, in which the expressed opinions of many individuals are summed or combined into a collective whole, and with social processes in which many people receive communications and think and talk with each other. These processes give collective public opinion and collective survey responses certain properties ("emergent" properties) that are not shared by the individual opinions and responses that make them up (see Schelling 1978). The simple process of adding together or averaging many individuals' survey responses, for example, tends to cancel out the distorting effects of random errors in the measurement of individuals' opinions. Similarly, statistical aggregation tends to eliminate the effects of real but effectively random (i.e., offsetting) opinion changes by individuals. And social processes involving division of labor and collective deliberation mean that collective opinion responds—more fully and attentively than most individuals can hope to do—to new events and new information and arguments.

In order to see how this can occur, it is necessary to examine the nature of individual and collective policy preferences and the relationship between them.

From Individual Ignorance to Collective Wisdom

A typical individual's policy preferences, it seems fair to assume, are neither perfectly informed and fixed nor totally uninformed and random. Instead, they are based on some fundamental needs and values that are relatively enduring (see Feldman 1988); on some uncertain beliefs concerning how public policies relate to those needs and values; and on some incomplete fragments of information that tend on the whole—though not, perhaps, with total consistency—to support those beliefs.

If this is so—if citizens' preferences are dependent upon uncertain beliefs, bolstered by incomplete bits of information—then new information or arguments that bear upon beliefs about policy alternatives can change people's policy preferences. (Mass media stories bearing on who is responsible for a problem, for example, may affect citizens' attributions of responsibility, thereby altering their preferences: see Iyengar 1991; Entman 1989; Krosnick and Kinder 1990.)

Thus pieces of new information, some enduring but some transient and quickly contradicted, may push an individual's preferences back and forth in a seemingly random fashion, so that he or she may give fluctuating survey responses of the sort that have been interpreted as revealing "nonattitudes." Similar fluctuations in expressed opinions can result if an individual is ambivalent about a given policy and entertains a set of conflicting considerations (Hochschild 1981), perhaps randomly choosing one, in "top of the head" fashion, under the pressure of the interview situation (Zaller and Feldman 1992). Shifting responses can also result from various sources of measurement error.

Yet it is also consistent with this picture that at any given moment an individual has real policy preferences, based on underlying needs and values and on the beliefs held at that moment. Furthermore, over a period of time, each individual has a central tendency of opinion, which might be called a "true" or *long-term preference*, and which can be ascertained by averaging the opinions expressed by the *same individual* at several different times. If the individual's opinions fluctuate randomly around the same central tendency for a sustained period of time, his or her true long-term preferences will be stable and ascertainable, despite observed momentary fluctuations in opinion.

If this picture of individuals' opinions is correct, then at any given moment the public as a whole also has real *collective* policy preferences, as defined by any of various aggregation rules: majority-preferred policy choices (if such exist), or average positions on attitude scales, or proportions of the public choosing particular policy alternatives over others. (We will be particularly concerned with what proportion of the public favors one policy or another.)

Moreover—and this is the key point—at any given moment, the random deviations of individuals from their long-term opinions may well cancel out over a large sample, so that a poll or survey can accurately measure collective preferences as defined in terms of the true or long-term preferences of many individual citizens. As a result, the measurement of collective public opinion is largely free of the random error associated with individual attitudes. Further, if the true (long-term) opinions of individuals remain fairly stable over a lengthy period of time—or if they change in offsetting ways—collective public opinion as measured by surveys will be stable, quite unlike the fluctuating individual opinions and responses that make it up.

More generally, if individuals' real opinions, or measurements of those opinions, are subject to *any* sort of random variation—whether from transient scraps of information that temporarily change beliefs and preferences, or from question ambiguity or interviewing mistakes or key-punch errors, or from "top of the head" sampling of conflicting considerations, or from mood swings, or any other factor that is independent from one citizen to another—then simple statistical reasoning indicates that those errors will tend to cancel each other out when the opinions of individuals are aggregated. Collective measurements—averages (means or medians), majority or plurality choices, marginal frequencies of responses—will tend accurately to reflect the "true" underlying or long-term opinions of the individuals.

That is to say, even if individual opinions or survey responses are ill-informed, shallow, and fluctuating, collective opinion can be real, highly stable, and, as we will see, based on all the available information; and it can be measured with considerable accuracy by standard survey techniques. *If* the available information is accurate and helpful (which depends upon the nature of a society's information system), collective opinion can even be wise.

These assertions about the stability and meaningfulness and measurability of collective public opinion are very general; they do not depend upon any particular theory of exactly how individuals form and change opinions, process information, or give survey responses. They are consistent with a wide variety of psychological and measurement theories.

Similarly, there are many ways in which individual (and collective) opinion could respond to new, policy-relevant information, which we see as a central aspect of collective rationality. It is possible—though we doubt it often happens—that individuals make elaborate cost-benefit calculations on their own each time new information is available. More likely, responsiveness to new information results from individuals using cognitive shortcuts or rules of thumb, such as reliance upon trusted delegates or reference figures (friends, interest groups, experts, political leaders) to do political reasoning for them and to provide guidance. If such cue givers are available and reliable, people may be able to form or adjust their opinions sensibly without elaborate instrumental calculations. . . .

The Myth of Capricious Change

It is widely believed that the American public's policy preferences shift frequently, rapidly, and arbitrarily. This supposed capriciousness is sometimes invoked as an argument against unrestrained democracy: as a reason to limit the working of the popular will and to leave decision making to the wise and able.

Such antidemocratic views have an impressive pedigree. In the debate over ratification of the U.S. Constitution, for example, Federalist Paper no. 63 argued that a "select and stable" U.S. Senate would serve, like senates elsewhere, as "an anchor against popular fluctuations" and as a defense to the people against their own "temporary errors and delusions." Even the extensive American states, it said, were not immune to infection from "violent passions" (Hamilton, Madison, and Jay 1961, 382, 384–385). James Madison objected, in Federalist Paper no. 49, to Jefferson's proposal that Virginia should allow for popular conventions to alter its constitution or correct breaches in it. Madison alluded to the "danger of disturbing the public tranquility by interesting too strongly the public passions" (315).

Similarly, Hamilton in Federalist Paper no. 68 advocated indirect election of the president on the grounds that it would permit judicious deliberation, and not afford opportunity for "tumult and disorder" or "convulse the community with any extraordinary or violent movements." Separate assembly of the electors in the states where they were chosen would expose them much less to "heats and ferments" (412). Hamilton also—in Federalist Paper no. 71, arguing for an energetic and independent executive—declared that the republican principle does not require an unqualified complaisance to every "sudden breeze of passion" or to every "transient impulse" of the public. The people sometimes err; it is the duty of the guardians of their interests to withstand any "temporary delusion" in order to give them time for more cool and sedate reflection (432).

Thus one important element in the Founders' suspicion of public opinion was a belief that it was subject to rapid and extreme change. This notion has retained currency up to the present day, particularly with respect to foreign policy. . . .

The only safe way to identify opinion change is to compare answers to *identical survey questions*. . . .

A . . . source of confusion about opinion volatility is a failure to distinguish between policy preferences and other kinds of public opinion. Most of the credible evidence of rapidly changing public opinion does not involve policy preferences at all. Rather it concerns beliefs or attitudes about objects that themselves change, or about which information alters rapidly. . . .

Fluctuations in what Americans see as the "most important problem" or in the popularity of candidates or presidents, then, do not necessarily tell us anything, one way or the other, about the stability or instability of policy preferences.

Not much direct evidence has been produced concerning the stability of policy preferences themselves. Over the years, in fact, a number of students of public opinion have expressed skepticism about claims of capricious change and have observed that collective public opinion about policy is ordinarily quite stable (e.g., Key 1961; Erikson and Luttbeg 1973; Monroe 1975; Ladd 1983; Erikson, Luttbeg, and Tedin 1988; Sussman 1988). Even de Tocqueville (1945 [1835, 1840]) and Lippmann (1955), while criticizing public opinion on other grounds, characterized it as stable — as perhaps all too slow to change. According to Lippmann (23), the public tends to say simply "No" to any change in course on momentous matters of war and peace, vetoing the judgments of informed and responsible officials. De Tocqueville (1945 [1835, 1840]) declared, "When once an opinion has spread over the country and struck root there, it would seem that no power on earth is strong enough to eradicate it" (2: 271). But such judgments have been based on general impressions and distillations of experience rather than systematic data analysis, so that we cannot be sure whether or not they are correct.

There do exist some good collections and reports of trend data using identical survey questions: Cantril with Strunk (1951); Davis and Smith (1990); Smith and Rich (1980); Miller, Miller, and Schneider (1980); Miller and Traugott (1989); Niemi, Mueller, and Smith (1989); "Poll Trends"—formerly "The Polls" and, much earlier, "The Quarterly Polls"—articles in *Public Opinion Quarterly; The Gallup Poll Monthly* (formerly *The Gallup Report* and the *Gallup Opinion Index*); the poll sections of *Public Opinion* magazine (no longer in publication—similar sections appear in *The American Enterprise* and in the Roper Center for Public Opinion Research's *The Public Perspective*); and various private and proprietary reports (e.g., the original sources for Cambridge Reports, Inc., 1985). But these are, individually, limited in scope—often to a single topic or a single survey organization—and they have not, to date, been fully used to assess the general extent of stability and change in policy preferences. (Important exceptions are Simon 1974; Mayer 1992; and, using mainly NORC-GSS data, J. Davis 1980, T. Smith and Rich 1980, and T. Smith 1982, 1989.) Accordingly, we assembled our own comprehensive collection of data.

Our Data

Over the course of ten years we have systematically gathered aggregate data ("marginal frequencies" of responses: i.e., the percentages of respondents giving various answers to survey questions) from many national surveys—in fact, from *all* published or otherwise available surveys of the American public's policy preferences that we could find, beginning with the first Gallup and Roper polls of 1935 and continuing into 1990.

This collection includes data from many thousands of questions asked in many hundreds (into the thousands) of surveys conducted by prominent organizations like the American Institute of Public Opinion (AIPO or Gallup, founded by George Gallup); Louis Harris and Associates; the Survey Research Center/Center for Political Studies (SRC/CPS) at the University of Michigan, which conducts the American National Election Studies (NES), and which we will usually refer to as SRC/CPS; NORC (formerly the National Opinion Research Center) at the University of Chicago, which conducts the General Social Survey (NORC-GSS); Hadley Cantril's old Office of Public Opinion Research (OPOR) at Princeton; the Roper Organization, founded by Elmo Roper; the television networks and major newspapers (CBS News/*The New York Times*, ABC News/*The Washington Post*, NBC News/Associated Press, and the *Los Angeles Times, LAT*); TRENDEX, Inc. (for the General Electric Quarterly Index of Company Relations: see J. Black 1983); Yankelovich, Skelly, and White; Penn + Schoen Associates; Cambridge Reports, Inc. (CRI); and the Opinion Research Corporation (ORC). In addition, with help from a mail questionnaire sent to a broad list of survey organizations, market research firms, and members of the American Association for Public Opinion Research (AAPOR), we uncovered many polls done by smaller market research or political consultant firms (see Shapiro and Dempsey 1982).

We cannot hope to have found everything, but we believe we have gathered the largest and most comprehensive set of information about Americans' policy preferences ever assembled.

Given our interest in opinion stability and change, it was essential to find questions that were asked more than once with identical wording. . . . [W]e sorted through more than 10,000 policy preference questions, seeking those that were repeated in identical form. For the period of more than fifty years we found well over one thousand such questions, covering a broad range of policies. Somewhat more than half concern domestic policy and somewhat less than half concern foreign policy. They deal with government spending, taxes, laws, regulations, court decisions, and officials' actions. They concern executive, legislative, and judicial policies at all levels of government—particularly policy at the national level, but also including many state and local issues. They touch upon all sorts of policy areas, ranging from nuclear weapons and military alliances and foreign aid for various countries, to spending on education and health and highways, to the rights of the accused, school desegregation, and abortion.

While these repeated questions do not represent a random sample of all policy issues or of all hypothetically possible survey questions—one can hardly imagine how such a sample could be drawn—they are extraordinarily diverse and are, in a broad sense, representative. And, of course, they constitute very nearly the universe of actual repeated questions. The data from these repeated survey questions (supplemented, upon occasion, by particularly illuminating one-shot surveys and by questions asked with slight and carefully noted wording variations) provide the main data for this book, much of which concerns the instances of statistically significant change in public opinion.

The present chapter draws upon a large subset of these data, for which we have been able to calculate precise measures of opinion stability and change: namely, data from 1,128 survey questions that were asked with identical wording at two or more time points by five survey organizations—NORC, Gallup, SRC/CPS, Harris, or OPOR. The 1,128 were assembled by sorting through more than 6,000 survey questions. They constitute a vast and fully representative majority of the repeated items in our entire collection to date. They, too, are quite diverse, addressing all types of policy activity by all levels and branches of government, covering a wide variety of foreign (38 percent) and domestic (62 percent) policy issues. They provide an exceptionally good opportunity to examine whether American public opinion about policy has in fact behaved in a volatile or capricious manner.

Using this set of 1,128 repeated survey questions, we made several calculations. First, for each question we ascertained whether or not any statistically significant change in opinion occurred, taking a movement of six percentage points (excluding "don't know," "no opinion," or "not sure" responses) to constitute a significant change. In most of our surveys, a 6 percent change is statistically significant at better than the .05 level. That is to say, there is less than one chance in twenty that the observed change in responses could have resulted from random sampling error when there was no real opinion change in the population. Thus a change from 61 percent to 67 percent of the public supporting federal aid to education would be counted as significant, but a change from 61 percent to 66 percent would not.

Next, whenever significant changes occurred—whether only once, or more than once if a single question was repeated several times—we classified each as a separate *instance* of change, to be used as a unit of analysis for investigating the magnitude and rapidity of opinion changes that did occur.

Finally, for a limited subset of 173 questions that were repeated often enough, we calculated whether or not opinion fluctuated: that is, whether or not it changed significantly back and forth within a short time.

Table 9-1   Frequency of Significant Changes in Collective Opinion on Repeated Policy Questions

	No Change		Change		Total Questions	
	%	(N)	%	(N)	%	(N)
All issues	58	(655)	42	(473)	100	(1,128)
Domestic policy	63	(440)	37	(263)	62	(703)
Foreign and defense policy	51	(215)	49	(210)	38	(425)

Note: Entries refer to the proportion of repeated survey questions upon which collective public opinion changed significantly (by 6 percentage points or more). Gamma = Yule's $q = -.24$; $p < .05$.

The Stability of Collective Public Opinion

Our data reveal a remarkable degree of stability in Americans' collective policy preferences, clearly contradicting any claim of frequent changes or wild fluctuations in public opinion.

The most striking finding is that more than half—58 percent—of the 1,128 repeated policy questions showed no significant opinion change at all: that is, no change of 6 percent or more. Domestic policy opinions (63 percent of them having no significant changes) were somewhat more stable than foreign policy opinions (51 percent), but it is interesting that even in the realm of foreign policy, the home of the "mood theory," half our repeated questions showed no significant opinion change (see Table 9-1). That is to say, on many issues, both domestic and foreign, Americans' collective opinions remained very nearly the same on survey questions that were repeated a number of months or years after they were first asked.

To be sure, this does not prove that opinion about those policies did not change while no surveys were in the field. But data on frequently repeated survey questions, discussed below, cast doubt on the likelihood of unobserved changes. And pollsters and scholars have incentives to find opinion changes so that they can write interesting columns and articles; hence available poll data are more likely to overstate than to understate the frequency of change.

Moreover, even most of the significant changes we found were not very large. When we examined all 556 significant changes in collective preferences (which occurred in response to the 473 questions with one or more opinion changes), it became clear that many of these were rather modest. Nearly half of them (242, or 44 percent) were less than ten percentage points. Most of those involved changes of 6 percent or 7 percent—statistically significant but hardly startling (see Table 9-2).

Contrary to what one might expect, foreign and defense opinion changes were not appreciably larger than domestic. There were, however, some variations among specific types of foreign and domestic issues, as shown in the first column of Table 9-3. Certain issues on which there have been sweeping, long-term

Table 9-2 Magnitude of Significant Changes in Collective Policy Preferences

	6–7%		8–9%		10–14%		15–19%		20–29%		30%+		Total	
	%	(N)	%	(N)	%	(N)	%	(N)	%	(N)	%	(N)	%	(N)
All issues	22	(125)	21	(117)	29	(162)	14	(79)	10	(53)	4	(20)	100	(556)
Foreign and domestic policy	21	(54)	22	(55)	28	(71)	15	(38)	12	(30)	3	(7)	46	(255)
Domestic policy	24	(71)	21	(62)	30	(91)	14	(41)	8	(23)	4	(13)	54	(301)

Note: Gamma = $-.05$ (n.s.).

Table 9-3   Magnitudes and Rates of Opinion Change for Different Types
of Issues

	Average Magnitudes of Opinion Change (Percentage Points)	Percentage of Opinion Changes 10 Percentage Points or More per Year	(N)
All issues	12.5	41	(556)
Foreign/defense policies:[a]	12.6	58	(255)
World War II	12.0	100	(24)
Korean War	11.5	88	(8)
Vietnam War	10.0	79	(28)
Middle East	13.6	68	(18)
Foreign aid	11.3	65	(26)
National defense	14.0	61	(23)
Soviet Union	12.2	44	(27)
International organization	10.4	41	(22)
Draft	10.2	40	(5)
China	17.2	37	(19)
Fight communism	15.5	32	(22)
Other foreign	12.1	48	(23)
Other foreign - domestic, mixed[a]	9.9	33	(21)
Domestic policies:[a]	12.4	27	(301)
Nixon/Watergate	16.6	100	(10)
Economic issues	11.8	65	(43)
Labor	11.9	44	(18)
Civil rights	12.5	28	(25)
Social welfare	9.6	20	(15)
Big government	10.8	15	(20)
Political reform	12.3	13	(23)
Abortion	18.2	8	(13)
Crime	15.1	6	(16)
Social - style issues	12.6	4	(27)
Gun control	9.8	0	(9)
Education	10.5	0	(6)
Civil liberties	18.0	0	(24)
Other domestic	10.0	32	(41)

[a]The other foreign/domestic, mixed items were reclassified as foreign or domestic, depending upon their substantive content, in calculating the total foreign vs. domestic magnitudes of opinion change and rates of change (as a result the N's for specific policies do not sum directly to 255 for foreign and defense, and 301 for domestic, but they do so when the 21 foreign - domestic cases are reclassified).

opinion trends (China, communism, civil liberties, abortion, crime) or big events (Nixon and Watergate) naturally involved instances of change that were, on the average, larger.

Thus when we analyzed the public's responses to more than 1,000 policy preference questions, each repeated over fairly long time intervals, we found, for most of them, little or no change in public opinion. Often a question produced

Figure 9-1 Opinion Stability: Foreign Policy Activism, 1942–1956

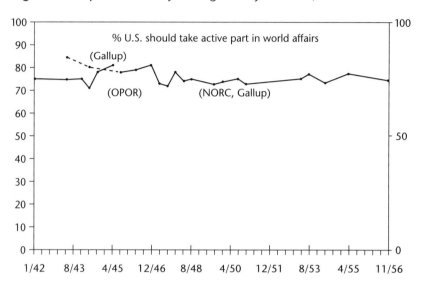

about the same answers when it was first asked as when it was asked again a year or two, or even several years, later.

It is worth repeating that foreign policy items did not differ much from domestic ones in this respect. As Tables 9-1 and 9-2 make clear, significant opinion changes were only moderately more frequent on foreign than domestic policy, and the magnitude of those changes was not noticeably greater. The public's "moods," as reflected in policy preferences, apparently do not change on foreign policy much more frequently or by any greater amount than on domestic policy.

In order to illustrate the stability of collective public opinion (and to introduce the kind of graph that will be prominent), we display in Figure 9-1 the trend in responses to a survey question about whether or not the United States should take an "active part" in world affairs. This is the same general foreign policy issue examined in Caspary (1970), but we have included identical items from both Gallup and NORC and have excluded "don't know" and "no opinion" responses from the calculation of percentages. Every one of the eighteen times this question was asked between 1945 and 1956—during the tumultuous early years of the Cold War—about 70–80 percent of Americans with opinions said they wanted the United States to take an "active part" in world affairs. Such flat trend lines are not universal, but they are not uncommon, either. . . .

Further examples of opinion stability, concerning both domestic and foreign policy spending issues, are given in Figure 9-2. In many surveys throughout the 1970s and 1980s, Roper and the NORC General Social Survey repeatedly found that about 65 percent to 75 percent of Americans with opinions thought that we were spending "too little" on "halting the rising crime rate"; only

Figure 9-2 Stable Spending Preferences, 1971–1990

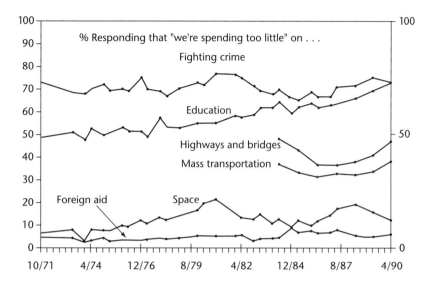

4–8 percent said "too much," and the rest "about right." Similarly, a fairly steady (though slowly growing) 50–70 percent the public said we were spending "too little" on improving the nation's education system, while a small and declining 12–3 percent said "too much." An equally stable but far lower 5 percent or so said "too little" was being spent on foreign aid, with a steady 70–80 percent saying "too much."

Similar decades-long stability or gradual change of collective opinion is characteristic of most other Roper/NORC-GSS spending items with the very striking exception of the 1979–1980 jump and 1980–1981 reversal in desires for increased military spending. . . . Throughout the 1970s and 1980s, about 60–70 percent said "too little" was being spent on "dealing with drug addiction"; 50–70 percent said "too little" was spent on "improving and protecting the environment" (. . . the figure dipped to the bottom of that range in 1980 and then recovered reaching 75 percent in 1990); and 55–70 percent on improving and protecting the nation's health. By contrast, only 8–20 percent said "too little" was being spent on space exploration (more said so in the 1980s than the 1970s), with fully 40–60 percent saying "too much."

The persistently high levels of support for a wide range of social spending programs are especially noteworthy given the supposed "right turn" in public opinion in the late 1970s and early 1980s. They suggest that Reagan administration policy moved more in a conservative direction than ordinary Americans' opinions did (see . . . Ferguson and Rogers 1986).

In addition, the sharp differentiation of the public's reactions to different programs that is apparent in Figure 9-2 and related data—the very high support for spending on crime and drugs, for example, and nearly as high on education, the environment, and health, but very low support for space exploration and even lower for foreign aid—supports a central argument of the following chapters [of Page and Shapiro]: that collective public opinion makes meaningful distinctions. It is hard to see how such big differences could be artifacts of the question format (which was kept identical across issues) or could result from purely random, equiprobable "doorstep opinions." The data indicate that people have genuinely different opinions about different government programs.

The finding of collective opinion stability is an important piece of evidence about the rationality of public opinion; it provides a fundamental background for the rest of our research. But stability is dull. Once this basic tendency has been established, there isn't a lot more to say about stability per se, except to provide periodic examples and reminders of it. Moreover, stability forms only one element in our overall conception of opinion rationality.

Much of our attention from here on, therefore, will be devoted to the more interesting topic of opinion change: when, how, and why, over a fifty-year period, Americans' policy preferences have altered, and how those changes fit our argument about the rational public.

Large Opinion Changes

To return to Table 9-2 once again, our data indicate that very large opinion changes, of twenty percentage points or more, are quite uncommon. They constitute only 13 percent of our 556 instances of significant change. Changes of thirty percentage points or more constitute only a tiny 4 percent. Or, to put it another way, in the 1,128 cases of repeated items we examined—many of which were repeated several times over long periods, so that there were plenty of chances to detect opinion change—we found a total of only seventy-three cases in which opinion changed by more than twenty percentage points. In only twenty cases did opinion change by more than thirty percentage points. It is very hard to reconcile this with the notion that public opinion is labile or volatile or moves violently.

At the same time, however, the large opinion changes—while few in number—have had great political importance. Some of them signaled extraordinary transformations of American politics. For that reason, even though they are atypical, they deserve close attention in later chapters and a brief mention here.

In domestic affairs, for example, there were large increases from the 1950s to the 1970s in support of civil liberties for Communists, Socialists, and atheists. Opinion also became much more favorable toward abortion, interracial marriage, desegregation of housing, and desegregation of schools. It moved against—and later for—capital punishment. After the 1960s, large numbers of Americans turned toward favoring greater strictness by the criminal courts, and during the unraveling of the Watergate scandal there was a strong swing toward favoring the impeachment of President Nixon. Less familiar large changes include a twenty-eight percentage point drop between 1942 and 1977 in support for the idea of national identification cards, and a steep (32 percent) increase between 1949 and 1974 in approval for employing epileptics.

One of the most impressive opinion changes we have encountered (though it is not included in any of our tabulations because it does not explicitly concern public policy) is the remarkable forty-eight percentage point increase that Gallup found between 1938 and 1975 (NORC-GSS tracked further changes) in public approval "of a married woman earning money in business or industry if she has a husband capable of supporting her."

Most of these large opinion changes came very gradually, as part of glacial movements in Americans' beliefs and life circumstances. They certainly do not constitute evidence of capricious changes in public opinion.

With respect to foreign policy, there have been substantial changes in preferences concerning defense spending, size of the army and navy, stationing troops abroad, and giving military aid. Feelings about postwar policy toward Germany became markedly more harsh in the course of World War II. Attitudes toward China and the Soviet Union mellowed considerably during and after the 1950s. There were greatly increased desires for de-escalation as the wars in Korea and Vietnam dragged on. Support for the SALT II treaty dropped markedly during the ratification debate. Support for increased military spending jumped up temporarily at the close of the 1970s and fell again in the early 1980s. One of the largest changes in foreign policy preferences was a drop of thirty-seven percentage points, between 1935 and 1973, in support for the idea of requiring a popular referendum before declaring war. . . .

Abrupt Changes in Preferences

Many critics of public opinion have implied that public opinion changes quickly. Madison and Hamilton did so when they wrote of "sudden breeze(s)" of passion, or "impulse(s)," or "violent passions" among the public. Almond's (1960) "mood theory," too, refers to sudden, as well as frequent and large, opinion changes. Our computation of rates of change for each instance of significant opinion change, with a rate of ten percentage points or more per year defined as "abrupt," permits us to judge just how frequently U.S. public opinion has undergone rapid change.

Despite the general prevalence of stability or gradual change, abrupt opinion changes are in fact rather frequent. Fully 229, or 41 percent, of our 556 significant change cases (from the 473 questions showing at least one change) met the criterion of abruptness. This is not an enormous number relative to the 1,128 repeated questions we examined, nor relative to the much larger number of pairs of time points—over 4,000—we compared. (Many questions were repeated several times.) Still, the rapidity of change in a number of cases was quite striking, especially with respect to foreign policy.

We calculated the annual rate of opinion change for each of our instances of significant change simply by dividing the number of percentage points of observed change by the number of years (or fraction of a year) within which the change took place. There is a strong contrast in rates between foreign and domestic issues. The average (mean) rate of change for all our foreign policy instances of change was thirty-one percentage points per year, compared to only twelve percentage points for domestic cases. (The medians were twelve and four percentage points, respectively.) That is, foreign policy opinion changes were nearly three times as rapid as domestic, on the average, presumably because circumstances tend to change more quickly in international affairs.

A similar contrast appears when comparing the frequency of abrupt changes on foreign and domestic issues. The second column of Table 9-3 indicates the proportion of our significant change cases, within various policy areas, that occurred at a rate of ten percentage points per year or faster. Only 27 percent of the domestic policy cases, but 58 percent of the foreign policy cases, were abrupt according to this criterion. Opinions on many foreign policy issues related to World War II, the Korean War, the Vietnam War, foreign aid, defense policy, and the Middle East changed at rapid rates. In the domestic realm, comparable frequencies of abrupt change occurred only on issues related to the economy and to Nixon and Watergate. In all cases, sudden changes in events and circumstances led to correspondingly quick changes in public opinion, but such changes are more common in the realm of foreign policy.

One complication in interpreting the foreign/domestic contrast is that survey organizations have tended to repeat foreign policy questions at much shorter time intervals than domestic. (Based on the 473 questions showing change in Table 9-1, an average of seventy-six days elapsed between surveys for foreign policy questions as opposed to 145 days for domestic.) Abrupt changes are more likely to be detected when questions are asked frequently, so our data may overstate the rapidity of foreign as opposed to domestic changes. Comparing foreign and domestic policy questions that were asked equally often, however, we still found more rapid changes in responses to the former. Survey organizations no doubt choose to repeat foreign affairs questions at shorter intervals precisely because they expect to find—and do find—quicker opinion changes.

On the face of it, the substantial number of abrupt opinion changes, especially on foreign policy, must seem to confirm the "mood theory." But three considerations work against this conclusion. First, collective opinion on most of our repeated opinion questions (including foreign policy issues) did not undergo any significant changes at all, and when it did the changes were not usually very large; even the cases we have classified as "abrupt" were mostly quick but relatively small (six or seven percentage points, for example, within seven or eight months). There is little evidence of violent movement in opinion. Second, as we will see below [in Page and Shapiro], when preferences about foreign policy change rapidly in response to events they seldom "snap back"—fluctuations are rare.

Third, just as collective opinion stability is not sufficient evidence of rationality, rapidity of opinion change is not enough in itself to constitute evidence of capriciousness. One must go on to inquire into the patterns and the causes of change. We will do so in later chapters, finding sensible reasons for most abrupt opinion changes. Virtually all cases of abrupt opinion change have been related to significant events that rational citizens would take into account. In particular, most abrupt foreign policy opinion changes have followed wars, confrontations, or crises, in which major changes in the actions of the United States or other nations have understandably affected calculations about the costs and benefits of alternative policies. . . .

PART III
VOTE DETERMINANTS

10. What Determines the Vote?

Most fundamentally, the study of voting behavior is about what determines the vote. Are people's votes primarily based on issues, with voters choosing between candidates on the basis of the great issues of the day—or, for that matter, the minor issues of the moment? Or are votes primarily based on reactions to the candidates—whether characteristics such as their leadership ability or attributes such as their personal appearance? Is voting heavily party-based, with issue and candidate preferences strongly shaped by a standing identification with a party? Or is voting based on age-old social cleavages, such as social class, religion, or ethnic divisions? And to the extent that issues are important, which issues? Do they vary unpredictably from one election to another, or are certain kinds of issues important over multiple elections? These questions have been debated since empirical studies of voting began in the 1940s.

One of the first discoveries of scientific election surveys was the surprising extent to which individuals have strong opinions about parties even before the candidates for a particular election are chosen and about candidates at the start of an election campaign. In fact, analyses of the first national voting studies in the United States (especially Campbell, Converse, Miller, and Stokes 1960) were (mis)interpreted by some as saying that voting decisions are based on parties and candidates, but not on issues. Later work, especially in the 1960s and 1970s, therefore emphasized the importance of issues. Key (1966) made a major contribution by noting that voters often rely on retrospective images, which are often infused with views about issues and their relationship to candidates and parties. RePass (1971) made an important methodological point by noting that when voters were asked about what they liked and disliked about parties and candidates (as at the beginning of the Michigan interviews), their attention was being directed away from issues. Converse (1964) pointed out that there were issue publics—sets of individuals intensely concerned with specific issues, even if unconcerned about issues in general. Pomper (1972), Nie, Verba, and Petrocik (1976), and others used longitudinal work to argue that issues became more important in the 1960s than they had been in the first elections that were scientifically studied. (For a summary of these and other works, see Niemi and Weisberg 1993b, chap. 9).

Nevertheless, the exact role of parties, candidates, and issues continued to be debated. At one point in the 1970s it appeared as if the right survey design and analytical model might allow a final statistical determination of their relative importance in determining the vote (especially with inclusive models such as in Markus and Converse 1979 and Page and Jones 1979). But such models proved controversial in their own right, as it became clear that conclusions about the relative importance of parties, candidates, and issues depend to some degree on the assumptions made. For example, Page and Jones (1979) found that issues dominated in 1976 voting, while Markus and Converse (1979) found that candidate characteristics had the greatest effect, and these differences are directly due to their differing models. With controversy about which assumptions are appropriate, we now know that consensus is unlikely.

In the 1980s there was further evidence about the importance of issues; for example, it was shown that foreign policy issues—often believed to be too remote for most individuals to care about—were understood and used by voters (Aldrich, Sullivan, and Borgida 1989). In addition, candidate evaluations came to be viewed as more meaningful than had been thought. That is, it was found that voters often responded to characteristics such a candidate's competence and integrity and not simply to the candidate's physical appearance (Markus 1982; Kinder 1986; Funk 1996). Coincidentally, the perceived importance of party loyalties waned—at least as a primal cause of political perceptions and judgments—as the number of Independents rose and as partisanship came to be viewed as less immutable and more often influenced by political events and figures (see Chapter 17).

Most recently, the question of what determines the vote has reemerged. Though there is now a consensus that, in one way or another, issues are important, there is still reason to ask just how significant their role is. The considerable success of forecasting models, for example, suggests that campaigns in general have limited effects on the vote. Among the variety of such models (see Campbell and Garand 2000 and the *International Journal of Forecasting*, March 1999), some use only variables determined well before the campaign begins—for example, the state of the economy in the second quarter of the election year and whether there is an incumbent president. Yet they have generally done a remarkable job of predicting the vote in November, except in the 2000 presidential election when they were unanimous—and wrong—in predicting an easy Gore victory, an expectation that did not prove true. So the question arises as to how the campaign can be significant if the outcome can be predicted so well before it begins.[1] Then there is the question of the media. Modern political campaigns are carried out very heavily via television and newspapers. At least until recently, however, media studies emphasized the surprising weakness of the media's power to persuade. Yet if the media carry little influence, it is hard to see how campaigns can be a major factor in election results.

So, the question now posed is whether election outcomes are largely "predetermined"—based on prior political forces and on factors external to the campaign—or whether they are dependent on the current campaign. Does it even make a difference who the candidates are or what issues they discuss? And what is the role of the media? The question "What determines the vote?" now takes on these and a host of related questions.

There are two major ways in which researchers have addressed this question. The direct way has been to look for the effects of factors that first arise or are most relevant during the campaign season. These include specific issues, candidate characteristics and performance, the media, and campaign events. While some studies test directly for such effects, much of the work has been indirect. The indirect approach examines whether factors that exist before the campaign begins determine the election outcome. These include factors such as partisanship, group attachments, and the state of the economy. The underlying logic of the indirect approach is that factors that arise during the campaign must not matter much if these prior factors largely determine the outcome. We look at both direct and indirect evidence in the sections that follow, but we start with indirect effects in each case because most studies have followed that route.

The Election Outcome Is Largely
Determined before the Campaign Begins

In 1960, when *The American Voter* (Campbell et al. 1960) was published, the concept of party identification was introduced as a way of conceptualizing the feelings that voters brought with them to each election campaign. That is, many voters were found to have judgments about the two parties that were long-standing—based on issues, events, and personalities from past elections. These views were often strong, especially among individuals who had been voting for many years or who had parents with strong views. The discovery of this "long-term" factor led to the (exaggerated) conclusion that only party mattered or, in a less exaggerated form, that only parties and candidates mattered. Such extreme arguments have not survived subsequent research. Yet the view that election outcomes are largely predetermined has proved remarkably resilient.

After being under attack for decades, the view that partisanship is a major determinant of the vote received a significant boost recently in work by Bartels (2000). Bartels argues that "partisan voting"—the relationship between self-reported partisanship and vote choice—declined in the 1970s but underwent a strong revival in presidential elections in the 1980s and 1990s. Thus, while there might be turbulent times, such as in the 1960s and 1970s, in which the partisan division of the electorate is less important and the predictability of elections is reduced, they are the exception and party identification remains a potent variable for explaining individual voting decisions and election outcomes.

Likewise, group attachments remain an important factor explaining voting behavior. As with partisanship, early, extreme views have been rejected. The notion that social characteristics are direct causes of the vote, implied in such studies as Lazarsfeld, Berelson, and Gaudet (1948) and Berelson, Lazarsfeld, and McPhee (1954), has been rejected in favor of the view that social attributes are connected to the vote through a variety of attitudinal correlates. Gender, for example, is not inherently (genetically) relevant to candidate choice; it is important only if some political force (such as a focus on abortion or family issues) makes it relevant. Even so, group attachments remain an excellent guide to how people will vote, and whatever the precise causal mechanisms, they are formed well in advance of any given election campaign and are subject to little change over the short run—both because the characteristics themselves and the issues related to them change only gradually, if at all.

There is, of course, a recognition that the significance of particular social characteristics changes over time, as when scholars worldwide noted the decline of social class as a predictor of voting (Dalton 1996b, 322–325; Nieuwbeerta 1995) or when U.S. scholars declared the demise of the group basis of the New Deal coalition of southern whites, Catholics, blacks, Jews, and union members (Stanley and Niemi 1995). Nevertheless, a variety of social attributes are currently thought to be important in guiding individual voting decisions, including race (Tate 1994), gender (Manza and Brooks 1999; Norrander 1999), religion (Leege and Kellstedt 1993; Miller and Shanks 1996, chaps. 9–10; Layman 1997), and marital status (Weisberg 1987; Miller and Shanks 1996, 262–267).

Yet another in the list of predetermined factors—incumbency—has been used chiefly to explain results in legislative elections. As long as twenty years ago, Charles Jones (1981, 458) entertained the profession with the line, "I am convinced that one more article demonstrating that House incumbents tend to win reelection will induce a spontaneous primal scream among all congressional scholars across the nation." Not that it helped. Nine years later, Jacobson (1990c, 25) noted that congressional scholars had continued with "blithe disregard" of Jones's admonishment to turn out papers on the incumbency advantage. Moreover, in the ensuing nine years, they were joined in force by those studying state legislative elections.

There remain numerous debates and side issues about the incumbency advantage. One measurement problem was solved with Gelman and King's (1990) introduction of a measure that avoided the downward bias inherent in using the vote share of a winning candidate as an initial baseline, as previous models had done. However, other questions remain—about the extent to which greater vote margins increase incumbent safety (Jacobson 1987; Bauer and Hibbing 1989; Garand 1991; Ansolabehere, Brady, and Fiorina 1992) and the related question of whether to measure the incumbency advantage using vote-denominated models (which measure vote shares of winning candidates) or outcome-denominated models (which directly measure the likelihood of winning or losing elections) (see Chapter 14, note 11). Similarly, though there is considerable agreement that incumbents' vote shares have risen in recent decades, there is uncertainty about the causes of that growth (for a recent discussion, see Ansolabehere, Snyder, and Stewart 2000; see also Carey, Niemi, and Powell 2000; Berry, Berkman, and Schneiderman 2000). But the larger point should not be lost: incumbency is a potent factor in legislative elections, and, like many others, it is determined prior to the start of an election campaign.[2]

Even some research that recognizes the role of issues effectively downplays the significance of the campaign. This is most apparent in what is now a vast literature on "economic voting." Much of the contemporary issue voting literature focuses on the role of economics in elections, and almost all of it assumes, often implicitly, that economic factors operate to the exclusion of other factors apart from partisanship, group attachments, and political events. We give major attention to the economic argument in this section because the idea that election outcomes are largely predetermined by the health of the economy has gained considerable currency in both the academic literature and pundits' analyses of elections.

Evidence for the impact of economic conditions on voting behavior is not new, dating back almost three decades to Kramer's (1971) analysis of the congressional vote outcome.[3] Recently, studies of this topic have been extended both "outward" and "downward." The outward extension refers to studies of the impact of economic conditions on voting in the developing democracies of Eastern Europe and elsewhere, where it was found that economic factors influenced voters early in the process of reform (Pacek 1994; Pacek and Radcliff 1995; Gibson and Cielecka 1995; Powers and Cox 1997). The downward extension refers to U.S. and British studies of the effects of economic conditions at the regional (Johnston et al. 2000), state (Books and Prysby 1999; Atkeson and Partin 1995; Niemi, Stanley, and Vogel 1995; Stein 1990), and even the neighborhood levels (Mondak, Mutz, and Huckfeldt 1996).[4]

Many of these studies rely exclusively on aggregate data—that is, aggregate economic measures such as rates of unemployment, inflation, interest, and personal income, and aggregate measures of the vote (such as the percentage voting for the incumbent party) or other aggregate indicators of support for the government or for particular political leaders. The models are often statistically complex because they need to take into account changing administrations, single-party governments and coalitions, majority and minority governments, exogenous shocks (economic shocks such as the oil crisis of the early 1970s or political shocks such as assassinations), and so on, and deal with questions such as whether voters react to levels of economic variables (is unemployment high or low) or to changes in economic conditions (has unemployment gone up or down). Yet for all their complexity, economic voting models tend to rely exclusively on economic variables, along with such long-term factors as partisanship or group identification.

Work by Nadeau and Lewis-Beck, reprinted here as Chapter 11, illustrates a number of these points. Following up on Markus's (1988, 1992) use of a combination of survey data and "hard" economic statistics, they first estimate an equation that includes two economic variables—the perceived state of the respondent's personal finances and the change in real per capita disposable income. They then replace the hard statistic with one derived from survey reports, but they use an aggregated form (the percentage "better" minus percentage "worse"). Ultimately, they incorporate yet another aggregated survey variable. In doing so, they cite MacKuen, Erikson, and Stimson's (1992a, 599) argument that individual judgments may be too noisy (that is, contain too much error) to be useful at the individual level but that their noise cancels out in an aggregated measure (see also Kramer 1983). In addition to the economic variables, Nadeau and Lewis-Beck include only partisanship, race, and incumbency—all variables that are completely or largely determined prior to the start of any given election campaign.

There is considerable debate about the precise way in which economic conditions affect voting behavior. The sharpest debate is over retrospective versus prospective evaluations, a matter that is central to the question of whether the election outcome is largely determined prior to the campaign. One perspective, originating with Key (1966) and later Fiorina (1981), is that the electorate views parties and leaders retrospectively. That is, voters rely largely on their sense of how well the economy has been in the preelection period. As a result of a lag in people's perceptions, the most important period is often considered to be three to twelve months prior to the election. The notion that economic voting is retrospective has been most forcefully supported by Norpoth (1996b, c); Nadeau and Lewis-Beck (2001, reprinted here as Chapter 11) argue that retrospective voting is especially likely when there is an incumbent running, and Lacy and Grant (1999) suggest that retrospective voting hurts incumbents in bad economic times by depressing the turnout of their partisans. Others (notably Jacobson and Kernell 1983 and Erikson 1990a, 379) have pointed out that the preelection economy is important for another reason as well. Potential candidates make their entry decisions well before the campaign begins, which means that the opposition party is likely to field weaker candidates when the economy is strong a year or so before the election.[5]

What should not be lost while reviewing these debates is that they are all about the precise way in which economic variables influence voters, not about whether they do. Indeed, as noted earlier, many economic voting models include little else in the way of candidate and noneconomic issue factors, as if they were of little importance. When other variables, such as candidate evaluations, are included, it is sometimes pointed out that those "control" variables are themselves influenced by economic factors.[6]

Not all studies have been so exclusionary. When a variety of issue positions have been incorporated along with perceptions of the economy, the conclusion, at least for recent elections, is that the economy is a major, if not preeminent explanation for the election outcome. Alvarez and Nagler (1998, 1362), for example, concluded that a number of issues were significant in 1996, but, "simply put, again [as in 1992] it was the economy. . . ." Likewise, Weisberg and Mockabee (1999, 67) note that economic views, along with candidate characteristics, were significant in a multivariate model, whereas voters' positions on other issues were correlated with the vote but became insignificant when all were brought together in a single model.

Miller and Shanks's *The New American Voter* (1996, partially reprinted as Chapter 12) provides the most elaborate effort to sort out the importance of various explanatory variables, in what becomes a lengthy, complicated, and controversial picture. It also lends support to the notion that some of the most important "themes" that explain the vote are determined prior to any given election campaign. The authors classify potential explanations of the vote into eight general themes and then arrange them temporally "based on a causal order of six stages in which we believe voters acquire their positions on different types of variables" (191). Given this presumed causal order, they were able to determine the statistical importance of the various themes for the elections of 1988 and 1992. As with other large-scale modeling efforts, the method is controversial because of the assumptions built into the analysis. Assuming, for example, that party identification is causally prior to prospective evaluations of the candidates and parties almost guarantees that partisanship will be more important in Miller and Shanks's analysis than in analyses not beginning with that assumption. At the same time, the inability to bring stable social and economic characteristics (for example, race, gender) into their "importance" analysis (their Chapter 17) may well bias upward the stated importance of issues as well as all other attitudinal characteristics. Perhaps tellingly, subsequent election analysts, such as Alvarez and Nagler (1995, 1998) and Lacy and Burden (1999), have chosen to use single-equation models (with allowance for the vote variable being multi-category rather than binary) rather than following the bloc-recursive approach of Miller and Shanks.[7]

In any event, in partitioning importance, Miller and Shanks distinguish between explanations of the aggregate election result and differences between individual voters (their Chapter 17; see esp. Table 17.9). With respect to the latter, the two most statistically important of their eight themes—party identification and policy-related predispositions—are described as "already 'in place' before the current campaign began" and as "generally not changed by short-term forces based on campaign issues or candidates personality" (192). These themes are also of considerable importance to the aggregate election result. Moreover, two additional themes—current policy preferences and perceptions of current conditions—appear to be at least partly predetermined.[8] Indeed, one of the major components of "current conditions" is the state of the economy, which is surely based on much more than campaign activities. Altogether, the authors conclude that factors determined prior to the start of the campaign are major contributors to both individual decisions and the election outcome.

The research cited so far, as extensive as it is, is indirect. It tries to demonstrate the unimportance of the campaign by establishing the importance of predetermined factors. Not content with this indirect approach, some analysts have tried to estimate directly the magnitude of campaign effects. At least until recently (see the next section), such studies have largely supported the "minimal effects" model of presidential campaigns.

Finkel (1993), for example, concluded that for presidential elections in the 1980s, "the effect of the general election campaign in shifting the aggregate vote distribution was small, and the maximum overall net impact of the campaign was about 3%" (14). Markus (1988), on the basis of a longer series of elections, also cited three percentage points as the "mean prediction error" of a model that excludes "information about the candidates, their issue positions, the unfolding of the campaign, and a host of other seemingly relevant factors" (151). Likewise, Bartels (1992) found little change during campaign periods apart from predictable patterns, such as an underdog effect. Also lending support to the minimal effects argument is a recent finding about negative advertising. Negative ads are sometimes thought to be particularly effective in influencing voters, even if they are universally disliked. Yet a "meta-analysis" of numerous studies concludes that *"there is simply no evidence in the research literature that negative political advertisements are any more effective than positive political ads"* (Lau, Sigelman, Heldman, and Babbitt 1999, 857). In short, the major effect of political campaigns may be to activate people's existing predispositions or "enlighten" the preferences of voters so as to bring their votes into alignment with their social and economic interests (Gelman and King 1993).

Collectively, the indirect and direct evidence that we have reviewed makes a strong case for the predictability of elections and the derivative argument that campaigns are of only minor consequence. There is considerable contradictory evidence, however, and we now turn to that side of the argument.

The Importance of Issues, Candidates, Media, and Election Campaigns

Since the introduction of party identification into the vocabulary of political scientists, no one has doubted that long-term factors play an important role in voting decisions and election campaigns. Yet the thrust of much recent work has been that predetermined factors have been overrated and that the more immediate factors—issues, candidates, the media, and election campaigns— have been underrated, sometimes to the point of ignoring them altogether. As with the earlier argument, however, researchers have asked two kinds of questions—first asking whether long-term factors really determine the election outcome and only then asking whether there is direct evidence of campaign effects. As above, we begin with a brief review of the indirect evidence before turning to the direct support.

Start with party identification. While clearly an important factor, there is now recognition that there was a weakening of partisanship after 1964 in the United States (Nie, Verba, and Petrocik 1979; Stanley and Niemi 2000, 113–114) and in the 1970s and later in other countries (Dalton, Flanagan, and Beck 1984; Crewe and Denver 1985; Schmitt and Holmberg 1995). Despite increases in partisan voting in U.S. presidential elections (Bartels 2000), weakened party loyalties are still much in evidence in a large number of democratic polities (Dalton 2001). Similarly, there was a decline in the salience of party ties, as indicated by fewer citations of party factors in candidate evaluations (Wattenberg 1991, 27), higher levels of split-ticket voting (Stanley and Niemi 2000,

133), and so on. The changes have been sufficiently noteworthy that many have dubbed the period since the 1960s as one of candidate-centered politics (see Chapter 21).[9]

Even more significant, however, is how researchers now conceive of partisanship. In its original formulation, party identification was thought of as extremely resistant to change—so much so that it often remained unchanged throughout a person's lifetime, responding only to major social upheavals. Now, many believe that partisanship is updated more or less constantly, changing in response to day-to-day events (see Chapter 17 for a review of this controversy). If this view is correct, it means that issues and candidates are important not only through their direct impact on election outcomes, but also indirectly through their influence on partisanship. Indeed, everything that partisanship influences is indirectly touched by issues and candidates.

Group attachments are similarly weakening as explanations of voting behavior. The decline of so-called cleavage-based politics is most evident outside the United States, as social class, religion, region, and urban-rural divisions lose their grip over voters. Dalton (1996b, 329), citing his own and others' research—especially that by Franklin, Mackie, and Valen et al. (1992)— concludes that it is now "conventional wisdom" in comparative electoral research that social cleavages have weakened in the past half-century. In the U.S. it is more difficult to write off group attachments because of the strength of the religious right in recent elections, along with the well-publicized rise of the gender gap. Yet here, too, major divisions have declined in significance. Most notable is the disappearance of the one-party South, but social class and Catholic/non-Catholic differences have also weakened considerably, and newer divisions have yet to develop the size and strength of the earlier cleavages (Dalton 1996b; Stanley and Niemi 1999, reprinted here as Chapter 21; Manza and Brooks 1999). In their stead, candidate and issue factors have taken on greater importance.

As with partisanship, researchers now think of group attachments in different terms than a generation ago. There is a presumption that social group characteristics, while perhaps meaningful themselves, serve at least in part as proxies for other variables. Marital status, for example, may be a proxy for the higher incomes of two-earner families. Gender may be a proxy for the lower incomes of women. Assuming that there is nothing genetic about voting, the argument is that variables such as these only become relevant if some political force makes them relevant, as when candidates or parties raise relevant issues (such as family issues, tax policy). With other group attachments, the issue basis is even more evident. Religious affiliation, for example, is tied to major differences between candidates and parties on such issues as abortion and school prayer.

As for incumbency, it would be foolish to deny that it is important in congressional (and other) voting, but it would be equally foolish to deny the importance of challenger quality, constituency service, scandals and various special conditions, presidential popularity, economic conditions, and campaign expenditures—all of which are the subject of numerous studies (see Chapter 14). Each of these factors is subject to some degree of controversy, and most have at least an element of predetermination (for example, challenger quality is fixed once the election campaign begins). Collectively, however, they indicate that a variety of factors influence subpresidential voting and that many of them involve characteristics of candidates and campaigns.[10]

With respect to economic voting, the final entry on the list of supposedly predetermined factors, the results are in fact quite ambiguous. In sharp contrast to Norpoth's strong support of retrospective voting (which emphasizes past events and decisions), MacKuen et al. (1992b, 1996) in the United States and Sanders and his colleagues in Britain (Sanders 1991, 1993; Marsh, Ward, and Sanders 1991) have made strong claims that voters are forward- rather than backward-looking. Others (especially Lewis-Beck 1988, 157; Clarke and Stewart 1994) argue that both perspectives are significant. As noted, Nadeau and Lewis-Beck (see Chapter 11) suggest that retrospective voting is prevalent in elections when there is an incumbent and prospective voting when there is not. Even the matter of a lengthy lag in perceptions is questionable, at least at times like the early 1980s when prices were spiraling or in the summer of 2000 when consumers could not help noticing very high prices for gasoline.

Nor is it true that economic factors are invariably more important than other issues or, indeed, important at all. If one believes voters' open-ended candidate evaluations, for example, the economy was not much of a concern in the United States in the 1950s (Wattenberg 1991, 27). In addition, comparative studies have shown that the importance of the economy varies widely across time and space as a result of institutional factors (such as single-party versus coalition governments) and temporal factors (such as the size of the largest government party) that affect clarity of responsibility for public policy (Paldam 1991; Powell and Whitten 1993; Anderson 1995, 2000; Whitten and Palmer 1999; Nadeau, Niemi, and Yoshinaka 2001).[11]

These arguments "against" predetermined factors, like those against campaign effects, are arguments by indirection. Until recently, what little direct evidence there was supported the minimal effects interpretation, but that has now changed. There is new direct evidence that issues and candidates as well as media and campaign events all matter.

First, the economy is not the only issue that matters in elections. Many studies have found that specific issues raised in the election campaign affected particular races. For example, Miller and Shanks (1996) found that attitudes on homosexuals in the military affected the 1992 presidential vote, even with everything else in their model controlled. Likewise, Smith, Radcliffe, and Kessel (1999) showed that social benefits helped Clinton in 1996, again with controls on other variables. The abortion issue has been found to be significant in several multivariate analyses of the 1992 and 1996 votes (Abramowitz 1995; Alvarez and Nagler 1995, 1998; Lacy and Burden 1999; cf. Miller and Shanks 1996).

The growing research on candidate factors in voting implicitly argues that the campaign matters since candidates are election-specific. Some of this research uses open-ended comments about the candidates, while other work employs the National Election Studies questions that ask for ratings of the candidates on a series of traits (for example, intelligent, moral, cares about people like me). These comments and traits are often combined under more general rubrics, such as candidate competence, leadership, integrity, and empathy (Kinder 1986; Miller, Wattenberg, and Malanchuk 1986; Funk 1999). As an example of the effects of the candidate factor in a specific election, Smith, Radcliffe, and Kessel's (1999) analysis of open-ended comments about the candidates and parties found that Clinton lost considerable support in the 1996 election because of the trust dimension. However, Weisberg and Mockabee's (1999) analysis of the trait items found that competence, leadership, integrity, and empathy all affected the 1996 presidential vote, even with party identification, ideology, economic evaluations, and demographics controlled, with Clinton's advantage over Dole on empathy overcoming his deficit on trust. The contrast between these two sets of results shows that conclusions inevitably depend on which research questions are analyzed (Kessel and Weisberg 1999), but the larger point is that both agree that evaluations of the candidates—mostly formed during the election year—do affect the vote.

Candidates matter more directly, too. Take, for example, Ross Perot's third-party candidacy in the elections of the 1990s. Did Perot's candidacy help Clinton win, or did Perot steal votes away from him? After all, it would be hard to argue that election results are predetermined if the entry of a third-party candidate affected the outcome of the election. Of course, it would be too much to expect analysts to agree on the effects of the Perot candidacy. Alvarez and Nagler's (1995) multinomial probit analysis of the vote found that Perot voters in 1992 were slightly more pro-Bush than non-Perot voters, so that Perot's presence increased Clinton's winning margin. Lacy and Burden (1999) include nonvoting as a fourth possibility, finding that Clinton's winning margin was reduced by 7 percent with Perot in the race because Perot drew to the polls many people who rated Bush second over Clinton but would not have voted due to their dissatisfaction with Bush's handling of the economy. These two sets of analysts thus disagree on the direction of the effect (while agreeing that Clinton would still have won had Perot not been in the race). But the relevant point here is that they are in accord that Perot's candidacy affected the results.

The recent evidence of media effects on elections is especially important. Early media studies, including the classic election studies by Lazarsfeld et al. (1948) and Berelson et al. (1954) replaced notions of an all-powerful media with a "minimal effects" model in which the media did little other than possibly reinforce existing public opinion. This model, which extended to television as well as newspapers (Patterson and McClure 1976), was so dominant that few media studies of elections were even conducted. In the 1970s a new role was found for the media when the notion of "agenda setting"—the idea that the media play a major role in determining what people talk about—took hold. This notion was enlarged later to include "priming"—the idea that the media not only determine what people think about but how they think about it (for example, the standards by which they evaluate political leaders) (Iyengar and Kinder 1987). Even when expanded in these ways, however, media were still given a limited role in that they were thought not to change people's opinions.

Authors recently have begun to suggest that even this view is too limiting. The evidence is still slim, but an increasing number of both experimental and survey studies show that the media have considerable power to persuade. Perhaps the most compelling demonstrations of media effects are those by Zaller (1992, 1996). What makes them compelling is his effort to model the way in which various news flows influence the electorate, or portions thereof. He notes, for example, that media effects are often curvilinear; in congressional elections, defection to the incumbent is most likely among people who are in the middle on a scale of habitual news reception because they are the most likely to hear the incumbent's message but not the challenger's (1996, 21–36).[12] In circumstances where messages are one-sided, the effects are more straightforward, although even then there is a need to consider such factors as individuals' partisan and ideological predispositions (1996, 42–59).

Bartels's (1993) demonstration of media effects also hinges on careful modeling, in this case the use of regression models that correct for measurement error. Bartels cautions that his improved modeling is a double-edged sword; allowing for measurement error leads to a finding of much more stable opinions over the course of an election campaign. Nevertheless, to the extent that opinions change, movement can be attributed more confidently to newspaper and television exposure. The magnitude of the change is small yet "especially impressive" when one takes into account the amount of media exposure of the average citizen (270–271).

Studies of political advertising also suggest direct persuasion by the media. The exact nature of that influence is subject to considerable debate, with much of the argument over the possible effects of negative ads on voting turnout (see Chapter 2) and over the relative strength of negative versus positive ads (as noted in the previous section). In any event, studies of candidate choice sometimes report greater support for the sponsor of the ads, sometimes note a backlash against the sponsor (Ansolabehere and Iyengar 1996; Lau et al. 1999), and sometimes find no effect at all. Overall, however, the evidence lends additional weight to the argument that the media directly persuade voters.[13]

Moreover, the so-called predetermined factors are not free of media influence. Economic conditions, for example, are often observed indirectly through media reports. While the media are to some extent neutral reporters of uninterpreted statistics or simply the mechanism by which experts' opinions are transmitted to the general population (MacKuen et al. 1992a; Zaller 1992, chap. 12), they also inject their own perspective into the news. Clearly, this is to be expected where media are more partisan than in the United States (Sanders, Marsh, and Ward 1993; Nadeau and Niemi 1999; Nadeau et al. 2000), but it is characteristic of U.S. media as well (Nadeau et al. 1999).

In short, it may be too early to revive the notion of massive media influence, as Zaller (1996, 17–19) would have us do. If nothing else, *net* influence of the media is sometimes small because competing messages are mutually canceling, a result that is especially likely when the stakes are high, as in presidential elections. Yet it is clear that the media have more than minimal influence on voters and elections. Precisely when and how that influence is exercised will be the subject of a continuous stream of future research.

New research has also found direct support for the importance of campaign events. Especially significant is a view of the candidate evaluation process that fundamentally alters the way in which we interpret and measure campaign effects. In the past, we have typically assumed that events influenced respondents only if they were able to recall them. The problem is that most individuals can recall only a few such events, and when they do, they often remember them only vaguely. Thus was born the minimal effects model of political campaigns, but such a model may not represent what actually happens. A strikingly new model was introduced by Lodge, McGraw, and Stroh (1989). In their "impression-driven model" of candidate evaluation, voters immediately integrate information about candidates into a "running tally" or "on-line" evaluation (identical to the running tally often used to describe party identification; see Chapter 17). The specific ingredients (campaign events, candidate information) are most often quickly forgotten, but voter evaluations reflect the integration that has occurred. In the article reprinted here as Chapter 13, Lodge, Steenbergen, and Brau (1995) reiterate this view and support it with an impressive set of experiments.

Petrocik's (1996) work on "issue ownership" also suggests that we need to reconceptualize what it means for a campaign to have an effect. Petrocik assumes that each party "owns" certain issues (for example, the Republicans were perceived as better able to handle most foreign policy issues in the late 1980s). A major goal of the campaign, therefore, is to get voters to think of the election as all about "its" issues. Theoretically, the underlying process is identical to priming by the mass media. Candidates, in this view, need not persuade voters directly about their policies, but only need to "prime" voters to think about the election in a certain way; if they are successful, the campaign has had an effect, and the candidate will "automatically" win support.[14]

Researchers have also begun to use new data and methods in searching for campaign effects. The availability of frequent trial heats, especially since 1984, have made it possible to examine changes over the course of the campaign in presidential preferences (Campbell 2000; Wlezien and Erikson 2000) and even to relate changes in preferences to campaign speeches, televisions ads, candidate appearances, nominating conventions, debates, blunders, and so on.[15] Although some campaign events are easily identified (for example, debates), it is often necessary to compile special lists. For ad hoc events, Holbrook (1996, chap. 6) and Shaw (1999b) scoured a variety of sources, such as *Facts on File* and a chronology of political events compiled by the Gallup Poll. For more regularly scheduled events, Shaw (1999a) compiled a detailed list of candidate appearances and a measure of the volume of television advertising in each state. Content analyses of campaign coverage in the *New York Times* were used by Petrocik (1996), looking for issue content, and by Holbrook (1996a, 59, 80–81, 83), examining the volume, partisan direction, and tone of coverage.

When all these factors are related to presidential preferences, researchers find a mixture of minimal, transitory, and substantial effects. Overall, however, the results paint a new and different picture of campaign effects from that portrayed previously, one that acknowledges that many individual events pass by with little impact but that, collectively, they make a significant contribution to voters' decisions and to the election outcome itself.[16] While there is no single way to assess their overall impact, Holbrook (1996a, 148–149) finds that the results in each of three campaigns he analyzes could have turned out quite differently under scenarios drawn from the other two campaigns, including a change in which party won the election. Campbell (2000, chap. 3) assesses the impact of campaigns somewhat differently, but he also finds that the net effect of the campaign is sometimes large enough to have changed the outcome. This pair of analyses also raises important questions about how to assess campaign effects. Holbrook views the campaign as a series of discrete events that operate in an environment established by the precampaign political and economic climate. Campbell, in contrast, views national factors as being played out through the campaign, allowing him to distinguish between systematic and unsystematic campaign effects.

The final point to make is that campaigns can have crucial effects even if predetermined factors are important. Political parties view campaigns as ways to activate their supporters as much as ways of drawing in Independents and other nonsupporters. In other words, the campaign is necessary in order to translate the long-term forces, such as partisanship, into relevant considerations affecting the vote. Thus polls taken early in the election year show many people planning to vote against their party; but most are later reminded by the campaign of why they usually support the same party and then end up voting for their party's candidate.

Conclusion

As we noted at the outset, a final statistical determination of the relative importance of issues, candidates, and party was never made, as determining relative causal importance turned out to be much harder than had been thought. That abortive attempt was revealing, however, and few researchers now believe that we can decide, in some ultimate sense, whether predetermined factors or campaign-related factors are the more important.[17] Nonetheless, we have learned much from past and present research.

Clearly, each election is not fought from scratch. Socioeconomic backgrounds, partisanship, and policy predispositions all play a role in how individuals will vote. So, too, do one's personal well-being and the state of the macroeconomy. And, with congressional incumbency reelection rates of 90 percent or better, it would be foolhardy to dismiss the importance of prior service.

Yet issues and candidates are also important. While in some sense we have always known that, the early studies of voting behavior deemphasized them and focused attention on the newly discovered long-term factors. Even after the roles of issues and candidates were recognized, media and campaign events were still nearly dismissed outright, as inadequate theories and insufficient data made it impossible to detect their contributions. Recent studies have restored the balance, providing convincing evidence of their contribution to voting decisions and election outcomes. Thus, while we are left with no final ranking of importance, we have accomplished a good deal.

Notes

1. These models did not perform well in 2000, unanimously predicting an easy victory for Vice President Al Gore, with between 53 and 57 percent of the nationwide vote. Gore did obtain a slight majority in the popular vote, regardless of how the disputed ballots in Florida are counted, but the models clearly overpredicted Gore's vote total.
2. Indeed, it is likely that incumbency is a direct contributor to the irrelevance of campaigns insofar as it discourages quality candidates from running (Jacobson and Kernell 1983; Krasno 1994; Cox and Katz 1996; Levitt and Wolfram 1997).
3. For a brief review of the first round of studies, see Niemi and Weisberg (1984); a recent review is Norpoth (1996d). Good cross-national studies include Lewis-Beck (1988); Norpoth, Lewis-Beck, and Lafay (1991); Anderson (1995); and Lewis-Beck and Paldam (2000).
4. Amidst this expansion of our understanding of the apparent influence of economic conditions on voting behavior, it is ironic that the one area in which researchers have seriously questioned their impact is on the congressional vote. A number of studies have indicated, minimally, that congressional voting is less sensitive to economic conditions than is presidential voting (Alesina, Londregan, and Rosenthal 1993; Chappell and Suzuki 1990). However, the matter is still controversial, and results depend on the model used (cf. Erikson 1990a; Jacobson 1990b; Grier and McGarrity 1998). In addition, it may be that the economy has a considerable indirect influence through approval of the president, even if it has little direct influence on the vote (Campbell 1993, chap. 6).
5. There is also debate about whether voters rely more on national ("sociotropic") economic perspectives or on concerns about their individual pocketbooks. In the United States, there is widespread agreement that national conditions are more important (Kinder and Kiewiet 1981, chap. 11), though Palmer (1999, 22) has recently argued that, when properly modeled, "pocketbook concerns matter more than sociotropic concerns."
6. See, for example, Markus's (1988, 147) remark that Tufte (1978) underestimated the effects of the economy because he included comparative evaluations of the candidates, which are partly influenced by the economy. See also Durr (1993), who argues that liberal/conservative policy sentiment is, in part, a reflection of the health of the economy. On the other hand, see Freeman, Houser, Kellstedt, and Williams's (1998, 1318–1321) analysis suggesting that, contrary to the conclusion of MacKuen et al. (1992a), presidential approval drives economic expectations rather than the other way around.
7. A single-equation model includes all potential influences in a model at once; the model is agnostic about how independent variables influence each other and gives each variable an equal opportunity to influence the dependent variable. A bloc-recur-

sive model assumes that certain variables are causally prior to other variables. Thus, in many of their models (that is, many of the numbered rows of their tables), they show coefficients for equations with a limited number of variables controlled, only those that are considered causally prior. This runs the risk of a form of misspecification error known as *excluded variable bias*, as well as simultaneity bias that arises from running single-equation models rather than simultaneous equation models. A simultaneous-equation model could make allowance for the possibility of reciprocal causation, such as the possibility that party identification and ideology each cause the other, and could also model psychological processes by which voters' distances from candidates on issues are affected by which candidate they prefer on other grounds. These models are often challenged, though, because their solution requires finding "exogenous" variables that affect only some of the "endogenous" variables (such as claiming that gender affects evaluations of candidates but not issue positions).

8. They note of these two themes that "none of these opinions and perceptions are expressed in terms of evaluations of the parties or candidates" (193). Moreover, at least one of their current policy preferences (those concerning the military) "could be classified as somewhere in between a general predisposition and a current policy preference" (329). On the other hand, see the interpretations cited in the next section of our overview.

9. Whether there has been a reversal of this trend in recent years is one of the subjects taken up in Chapter 21.

10. Admittedly, even the most recent congressional research focuses heavily on characteristics that are external to particular races and very little on individual candidates and campaigns. This is, in part, a function of the difficulty (and frustration) of studying multiple races, most of which are of little salience to voters. When individual campaigns are studied, it is readily apparent that there is variability in candidate awareness, positive and negative feelings, perceived ideology, and so on, and that not all these differences can be traced to external factors (see, for example, Mann 1978). For a review of what determines the congressional vote, focusing on whether national or "local" factors are more significant, see Niemi and Weisberg (1993b, chap. 13).

11. A methodological point also needs to be made. While it is true that economic voting models typically exclude other issues, the reason has as much to do with data availability as with theory. Economic data, including perceptual data, have been collected for many years, with largely invariant methods (including survey questions). Including them in time series models is straightforward. Other issues vary widely over time in their importance and therefore in whether they are even asked about in surveys. Moreover, methods of asking issue questions—not to mention exact question wordings—have varied considerably over the years. Thus even though theory (such as spatial modeling) as well as everyday observations about electoral campaigns suggest that voting models should contain policy issues, it is difficult to do so in models covering lengthy time periods. When economic conditions *are* evaluated alongside other policy issues, the results are mixed (see, for example, the contrasting results for "current policy preferences" and "perceptions of current conditions" in 1988 and 1992 in Miller and Shanks 1996, 490; see also the brief summary in Lewis-Beck 1991, 2).

12. Dalton, Beck, and Huckfeldt (1998) also find a curvilinear pattern in the effect of newspaper editorials on candidate preferences, with the effect being significant only among people giving moderate attention to the campaign.

13. In addition, the distinction between priming and direct persuasion, while theoretically clear, is often faint in practice. That is, if the media change the basis on which people make their judgments, it is likely that they also change the judgments themselves. A clear example of this dual effect is Miller and Krosnick's (1996) work on priming and presidential approval.

14. There is another analogy with media studies. In high stakes races, the *net* effect may be small because of mutually canceling events. Nonetheless, in Petrocik's reformulation (as in that by Lodge et al.), campaign events affect the electorate on a more or less continuous basis, and the overall effect on voters is probably quite large.

15. Presidential preferences are typically tracked with small daily polls. The results from several days are aggregated for greater reliability; a moving average is created by dropping off one day and adding a new day as one moves through the campaign period.

16. As when evaluating media impact, the question of net versus total effects is relevant. Most recent research on campaign effects implicitly assumes total effects. (For a cogent discussion of the difference, with an argument in favor of total effects, see Zaller 1996, 37–38.) In any event, the net effect is not necessarily trivial. In presidential preferences since 1948, net changes have often been four to five percentage points (and sometimes double that or more) between the first poll after the nominating conventions and the election. See Bartels (1992, 266), Stanley and Niemi (2000, 123), and Campbell (2000, 76).

17. Some of the difficulties of sorting out relative causal importance are nicely illustrated in recent work. We have already noted the distinction between effects on individual voting decisions and on the election outcome, and that what is important for one (in a given year) may not be important for the other. We have also noted the distinction between net effects and total effects. With respect to the media, specifically, there is the question of whether "information effects" represent independent influence of the media or the effect of the campaign as transmitted by the media (for a good, brief discussion, see Dalton, Beck, and Huckfeldt 1998, 124). Finally, one campaign effect may be to activate predetermined factors, and, as Miller and Shanks (1996, 387) note, it may be impossible ever to assign proper credit for the proximate cause and the activated factor.

Further Readings

Economic Factors (U.S.)

Clarke, Harold D., and Marianne C. Stewart, "Prospections, Retrospections, and Rationality: The 'Bankers' Model of Presidential Approval Reconsidered," *American Journal of Political Science* 38 (1994): 1104–1123. Error correction model suggests that voters react both retrospectively and prospectively to the economy.

MacKuen, Michael B., Robert S. Erikson, and James A. Stimson, "Peasants or Bankers? The American Electorate and the U.S. Economy," *American Political Science Review* 86 (1992): 597–611. Voters react prospectively to the economy.

Markus, Gregory B., "The Impact of Personal and National Economic Conditions on the Presidential Vote: A Pooled Cross-Sectional Analysis," *American Journal of Political Science* 32 (1988): 137–154; follow-up: *American Journal of Political Science* 36 (1992): 829–834. Personal financial situations influence individual voting decisions; the national economy influences voting and election outcomes.

Nadeau, Richard, Richard G. Niemi, David P. Fan, and Timothy Amato, "Elite Economic Forecasts, Economic News, Mass Economic Judgments, and Presidential Approval," *Journal of Politics* 61 (1999): 109–135. Events and objective economy influence news reports and mass expectations. Media transmit but also interpret experts' views.

Norpoth, Helmut, "Presidents and the Prospective Voter," *Journal of Politics* 58 (1996): 776–792. Voters react retrospectively to the economy.

Economic Factors (comparative, non-U.S.)

Anderson, Christopher, *Blaming the Government: Citizens and the Economy in Five European Democracies* (Armonk, N.Y.: M. E. Sharpe, 1995).

Clarke, Harold D., Marianne C. Stewart, and Paul F. Whiteley, "New Models for New Labour: The Political Economy of Labour Party Support, January 1992–April 1997," *American Political Science Review* 92 (1998): 559–575. Economic evaluations affect party support and best prime minister perceptions, which in turn influence vote intentions.

Lewis-Beck, Michael S., *Economics and Elections: The Major Western Democracies* (Ann Arbor: University of Michigan Press, 1988). Uses Eurobarometers for individual-level analysis of economic voting in five countries.

Lewis-Beck, Michael S., and Martin Paldam, eds., "Economics and Elections," *Electoral Studies* 20 (June/September 2000, special issue). More than a dozen articles on economic voting, covering many countries and numerous specific topics.

Nadeau, Richard, Richard G. Niemi, and Timothy Amato, "Elite Economic Forecasts, Economic News, Mass Economic Expectations, and Voting Intentions in Great Britain," *European Journal of Political Research* 38 (2000): 135–170. Challenges the view that mass expectations and voting are linked by dissemination of elite forecasts to the public.

Nadeau, Richard, Richard G. Niemi, and Antoine Yoshinaka, "A Cross-National Analysis of Economic Voting: Taking Account of the Political Context across Time and Nations," *Electoral Studies* 20 (2001): forthcoming. Refines the idea of clarity of responsibility for economic performance to incorporate variations across time as well as between countries.

Whitten, Guy D., and Harvey D. Palmer, "Cross-National Analyses of Economic Voting," *Electoral Studies* 18 (1999): 49–67. Refines Powell and Whitten's path-breaking paper on how clarity of responsibility helps determine the importance of the economy.

Causal Models

Miller, Warren E., and J. Merrill Shanks, *The New American Voter* (Cambridge: Harvard University Press, 1996), parts IV–V. A major effort to sort out determinants of the vote, relying on debatable assumptions about causal priorities.

Media Effects

Bartels, Larry, "Messages Received: The Political Impact of Media Exposure," *American Political Science Review* 87 (1993): 267–285. Media are influential after correcting for measurement error.

Dalton, Russell J., Paul A. Beck, and Robert Huckfeldt, "Partisan Cues and the Media: Information Flows in the 1992 Presidential Election," *American Political Science Review* 92 (1998): 111–126. Newspapers influence candidate preferences even though perception of information is shaped by individuals' partisan views.

Mondak, Jeffery J., *Nothing to Read: Newspapers and Elections in a Social Experiment* (Ann Arbor: University of Michigan Press, 1995). A study of media effects based on comparing a city where the local newspaper is on strike with a comparable city with normal news coverage.

Zaller, John R., "The Myth of Massive Media Impact Revisited: New Support for a Discredited Idea," in *Political Persuasion and Attitude Change,* ed. Diana C. Mutz, Paul M. Sniderman, and Richard A. Brody (Ann Arbor: University of Michigan Press, 1996). Sophisticated modeling reveals significant media impacts.

Campaign Effects

Campbell, James E., *The American Campaign: U.S. Presidential Elections and the National Vote* (College Station: Texas A&M University Press, 2000). Estimates net campaign effects and systematic and ad hoc elements. Competition narrows front-runners' leads.

Holbrook, Thomas M., *Do Campaigns Matter?* (Thousand Oaks, Calif.: Sage, 1996). Conventions, debates, campaign events, and momentum explain how candidate support varies from an equilibrium value, which is determined by national political and economic conditions.

Petrocik, John R., "Issue Ownership in Presidential Elections, with a 1980 Case Study," *American Journal of Political Science* 40 (1996): 825–850. Each party "owns" certain issues. Voters are influenced when candidates shift the emphasis to a favorable issue.

Shaw, Daron R., "The Effect of TV Ads and Candidate Appearances on Statewide Presidential Votes, 1988–96," *American Political Science Review* 93 (1999a): 345–362. Campaigning (personal appearances and TV advertising) has strong, direct effects on voter preferences.

_____, "A Study of Presidential Campaign Event Effects from 1952 to 1992," *Journal of Politics* 61 (1999b): 387–422. Campaign events have variable effects; some cause significant and relatively durable changes in voters' preferences.

Candidate Evaluations

Funk, Carolyn, "Bringing the Candidate into Models of Candidate Evaluation," *Journal of Politics* 61 (1999): 700–720. Trait dimensions vary in their effects on evaluations of candidates across candidates and campaigns.

Lodge, Milton, Kathleen M. McGraw, and Patrick Stroh, "An Impression-Driven Model of Candidate Evaluation," *American Political Science Review* 83 (1989): 399–419. Explains the on-line model and tests it with an experiment involving the evaluation of a hypothetical member of Congress.

Negative Advertising

Ansolabehere, Stephen, and Shanto Iyengar, *Going Negative: How Political Advertising Shrinks and Polarizes the Electorate* (New York: Free Press, 1995). High volume campaigns more often use negative ads. Negative ads reduce voter turnout.

Lau, Richard R., Lee Sigelman, Caroline Heldman, and Paul Babbitt, "The Effects of Negative Political Advertisements: A Meta-Analytic Assessment," *American Political Science Review* 93 (1999): 851–876. Negative ads generally are no more effective than positive ads and do not have detrimental effects on the political system.

Election Studies/Reports Websites
See Further Readings in Chapter 1. Several of these websites provide immediate access to tables, graphs, and data on public opinion, electoral behavior, and choice in U.S. and non-U.S. elections.

11. National Economic Voting in U.S. Presidential Elections

Richard Nadeau and Michael S. Lewis-Beck

National economic conditions regularly influence outcomes in U.S. presidential elections. Voluminous research has secured certain propositions about this link between economics and elections. In aggregate-level time series models, a macroeconomic indicator has an almost obligatory presence as a central variable (Abramowitz 1988; Campbell and Wink 1990; Erikson 1989a; Fair 1988, 1996; Hibbs 1982c; Lewis-Beck and Rice 1992; Tufte 1978). Most recently, such models were applied to forecast accurately the outcome of the 1996 election (Abramowitz 1996; Campbell 1996; Holbrook 1996b; Lewis-Beck and Tien 1996; Norpoth 1996a; Wlezien and Erikson 1996).

Individual-level survey work on presidential contests in the post-World War II period consistently demonstrates the presence of collective, or sociotropic, economic voting. (Classic studies are Fiorina 1981 and Kiewiet 1983. Follow-up papers are numerous. See the compilations of Eulau and Lewis-Beck 1985 and Norpoth, Lewis-Beck, and Lafay 1991. More recent efforts are cited below.) Voters who perceive an improvement in national economic conditions are clearly more likely to support the incumbent candidate. But little is known about which indicators they generally look at—gross national product (GNP), income, unemployment, etc.—let alone the weights given those indicators. Further, the relative importance of the retrospective versus prospective economic evaluations remains unsettled. While initial work assumed that voters only judged past performance, that limit on the time horizon has come under increasing challenge. Finally, the literature stands virtually silent about the institutional context of each presidential race and how it might change the impact of economics.

We focus on these areas of uncertainty, organizing the chapter into four substantive sections: voter measures of national economic conditions; national economic voting in a survey design; the conditioning effects of electoral institutions; and the time horizon of economic voting. Analysis is carried out on the American National Election Studies (NES), 1956–1996, to which are grafted other data incorporating national-level economic variables.[1]

Source: Journal of Politics, 63, 1 (January 2001): 159–181. Copyright © 2001 Southern Political Science Association. Reprinted by permission of Blackwell Publishers.

Voter Measures of the National Economy

A central question is how the national economy and the individual voter are joined. On the one hand, aggregate studies demonstrate that macroeconomic indicators are linked to overall election outcomes. On the other hand, survey studies demonstrate that collective economic evaluations are linked to personal vote choice. An assumption is that the aggregate result arises from some combination of the individual perceptions and preferences. It might work this way. Voters are asked about "business conditions" over the past year. Their responses record the changes they have observed (from direct experiences or the media) in the economy. When averaged, these responses amount to an estimate of the change in, say, the annual GNP. Strong economic growth, revealed in high positive change in GNP, would be mirrored in the assessments of individual voters, who go on to reward the incumbent.

Such a scenario provides a neat micro-underpinning for the macro-models of elections that employ change in GNP (or gross domestic product, GDP) as the principal economic predictor (Abramowitz 1996; Campbell 1996; Fair 1988; Lewis-Beck and Tien 1996; Norpoth 1996b). However, the scenario is flawed. It is unlikely that voters, when they assess the national economy, look only at GNP. Different aggregate studies of economic voting have used other macroeconomic indicators—disposable income, inflation, unemployment, leading indicators—to good effect. (See the review in Lewis-Beck and Rice 1992, chap. 6.) A plausible assumption is that a voter looks at more than one indicator, and places different weights on them. Respondent Jane Smith, in arriving at an overall assessment of business conditions, may evaluate economic growth and the unemployment rate, giving the former more importance than the latter. In contrast, respondent Betty Brown, when asked about business conditions, may weigh unemployment, inflation, and the trade deficit, giving unemployment the most weight.

Granting a micro-foundation of this sort, the aggregation problem cannot be solved by using a single macroeconomic variable, such as GNP, or even by some overall combination of macroeconomic variables. As Lewis-Beck (1991, 5) observed, "Only models with carefully built general economic indicators can hope to capture the shifting weighting scheme utilized in the political economic calculus of the democratic voter." What is needed, then, is a national measure that represents a sum of the individual accounting on the different indicators. We make a simple proposal: sum the responses to a "business conditions" survey item and use that value as a global indicator of economic performance. The Survey of Consumer Attitudes and Behavior, University of Michigan, regularly asks, "Would you say that at the present time business conditions are better or worse than a year ago?" To create a National Business Index, first assign a score of $+1$ for "better," -1 for "worse," and 0 for "same." Then calculate the percentage in each response category, and subtract the percentage "worse" from the percentage "better." For example, for the last quarter of 1996, this yields a total of 28 (i.e.,

54.5 percent − 26.5 percent = 28.0 percent). During this period, economic optimism clearly exceeded economic pessimism, apparently providing President Bill Clinton with many votes. For 1992, in contrast, this National Business Index equaled −21, underlining the economic difficulties President George Bush faced in his reelection campaign.

In Table 11-1, column 2, this National Business Index (NBI) is reported for presidential election years, 1956–1996. For comparison, the annual change in Real Disposable Personal Income Per Capita (RDI) is given in column 3. The comparison seems especially apt, given the pioneering role the income variable has played in the macro-studies, beginning with Tufte (1978) and extending to Erikson (1989a), Hibbs (1982), Rosenstone (1983), Wlezien and Erikson (1996). The business index generally tracks the income index. For instance, when the RDI is above average (> 2.5 in 1956, 1964, 1968, 1972, 1976, 1984, 1988), so is the NBI (>10.8). However, the latter is by no means determined by the former. When the NBI is regressed on the RDI, the adjusted R^2 = .77. This supports our expectation that other macroeconomic forces, weighted subjectively by the voters, also shape the NBI. The results for 1992 and 1996 are telling. For the former the RDI = 1.7, for the latter RDI = 2.0, similar below average numbers suggesting serious economic vote losses for Presidents Bush and Clinton. However, the NBI for the two years is quite different: 1992 = −21; 1996 = 28. These estimates imply a heavy economic vote loss for President Bush but a big economic vote gain for President Clinton.

Before NBI is utilized as a global economic indicator, the question of the subjective evaluation of its objective components must be further reconsidered. We have rejected a "strict constructionist" position, that the voter responds to one and only one macroeconomic measure, thereby making any variation in response mere error (Kramer 1983). Voters look at different economic indicators, and their assessments may honestly and accurately differ. As Kiewiet and Rivers (1985, 223–224) noted, "variation in perceptions of national trends arises from many sources. . . . For example, in depressed areas voters may perceive national conditions to be worse than do voters in booming areas." As an amalgam of economic perceptions, the NBI plays a unique measurement role. The value of that role depends, of course, on its performance under rigorous theoretical and statistical testing, to which we now turn.[2]

National Economic Voting and Survey Research Design

We hypothesize that as national economic conditions change, voters tend to change their presidential preference. For example, in election years where the NBI is above average, we expect individual voters will increase their support of the incumbent party. To test directly this dynamic hypothesis requires moving beyond a single cross-section, to a pool of repeated election surveys. The methodology of Markus (1988, 1992) provides our starting point.[3] To assess the impact of economic conditions, he pooled the 1956–1984 (and later the

Table 11-1   A National Business Index and Disposable Personal Income Change, Presidential Election Years 1956–1996

Year	National Business Index	Real Disposable Per Capita Personal Income Change
1956	15	2.9
1960	−16	0.1
1964	32	5.5
1968	26	2.9
1972	29	3.2
1976	14	2.6
1980	−48	−1.1
1984	40	4.9
1988	20	2.9
1992	−21	1.7
1996	28	2.0
Mean	10.8	2.5
S.D.	27.3	1.9

Data Sources: The NBI was constructed from the Surveys of Consumer Attitudes and Behavior, University of Michigan, for the last quarter of every presidential year. (November was the target month. Earlier in the series there were more missing months than later. For 1956–1976, the November survey was used; for 1980–1996, the November survey could be averaged with October and December readings. If the November survey is used exclusively across the series, the results are virtually unchanged.) The RDI data come from the National Bureau of Economic Research.

1956–1988) NES studies and estimated a model of the following general specification (see Markus 1988, 146).[4]

$$\text{Vote} = a + \text{Personal Finances} + \text{Real Disposable Income}$$
$$+ \text{Incumbent Party} + (\text{Party ID} \times \text{Incumbent Party})$$
$$+ (\text{Race} \times \text{Incumbent Party}) \tag{1}$$

In Table 11-2, measures of these variables are described and the model estimated with the important addition of the 1992 and 1996 elections. These results support and extend the earlier conclusions of Markus (1988, 146; 1992, 831). The overall model fit as indicated by the adjusted R^2 is about the same, and the political variables of Party Identification, Incumbent Party, and Race continue to be statistically significant and substantively important. With regard to economic conditions, a small effect from Personal Finances persists.[5] Voters who see their own pocketbook as improved are slightly more likely to stay with the incumbent. And, more to our concerns, there remains the larger national effect from RDI. For the total effect (that is, the direct plus the indirect effects) of RDI, Markus estimates the reduced form of the equation, with RDI considered exogenous and Personal Finances excluded (Markus 1992, 831). This reduced-form equation, calculated on the updated series, appears in column 2 of Table 11-2. The estimate,

Table 11-2 Comparing Two National Economic Conditions Measures in a
Presidential Voting Model, OLS Estimates, 1956–1996

Variable	(1)	(2)	(3)	(4)	(5)
RDI	.0023**	.0026**	−.0017	−.0036	
	(.002)	(.002)	(.004)	(.004)	
NBI			.0019**	.0015**	.0020**
			(.000)	(.000)	(.000)
Personal Finances	.0041**			.0040**	
	(.004)			(.004)	
Incumbent Party	−.053**	−.059**	−.060**	−.055**	−.060**
	(.004)	(.004)	(.004)	(.004)	(.004)
Party ID × Incumbent Party	.139**	.138**	.139**	.140 **	.139**
	(.001)	(.001)	(.001)	(.001)	(.001)
Race × Incumbent Party	.165**	.178**	.178**	.178**	.178**
	(.010)	(.010)	(.010)	(.010)	(.010)
Constant	.460**	.462**	.502**	.493**	.505**
	(.006)	(.006)	(.008)	(.008)	(.004)
Adj. R^2	.50	.48	.49	.51	.49
N	11,969	12,991	12,991	11,969	12,991

Data and Measures: The survey data are pooled from the American National Election Studies, which bears no responsibility for the analysis or interpretations given herein. The dependent variable is a presidential vote dichotomy (1 = incumbent party candidate, 0 = candidate of the other major party). The other variables are coded as follows: Incumbent Party (+1 = Democratic president, −1 = Republican president); Party ID (Strong Republicans = −3, Weak and Leaning Republicans = −2, Independents = 0, Weak and Leaning Democrats = +2, Strong Democrats = +3); Race (1 = nonwhite, 0 = white); Personal Finances (+1 = see their own situation is "better," 0 = "the same," −1 = "worse."). Measures and data sources for the national economic variables, RDI, and NBI appear in Table 11-1. ** = statistically significant at .001 or better.

which suggests that a 1 percentage point increase in RDI will lead to a 2.6 percentage point increase overall in incumbent support, is virtually identical to his earlier estimate (of 2.5).

So far, RDI seems sufficient as a measure of national economic conditions. However, it or GNP—or any other single macroeconomic indicator—photographs only part of the economic picture. We have argued that NBI is a more theoretically useful and empirically comprehensive measure. To test this proposition, we include NBI in the model specification, alongside RDI (Table 11-2, column 3). One observes that the RDI coefficient falls far short of statistical significance, not even reaching one-half of a standard error in magnitude despite a sample size of almost 13,000. In contrast, the NBI coefficient is highly significant and appears substantively important. This conclusion is reinforced by the respecifications in columns 4 and 5. The former includes the Personal Finances variable, the latter excludes Personal Finances and RDI for a reduced form equation (to parallel that of column 2).

How to interpret the NBI coefficient? Note that it is rather stable across specifications. We focus on the coefficient (b = .0020) in the reduced form equation, which allows an assessment of its total effects. First postulate a small change in the NBI of ten points (suppose, say, that 5.0 percent more voters saw a "better" economy, and 5.0 percent fewer saw it as "worse"). Then, the expectation is that the incumbent vote share would rise by 2.0 percent, other things being equal. Now postulate a mid-range change, say of one standard deviation (S.D. = 27.3). (As Table 11-1 shows, across six election pairs—1956–1960, 1960–1964, 1976–1980, 1980–1984, 1988–1992, 1992–1996—the change in the NBI actually exceeded one standard deviation). Then, the incumbent party could expect an impressive increase of 5.5 percent. Changes in national economic conditions, as measured by the NBI, appear to have a strong impact on incumbent fortune. Further, to the extent a comparison can be made, this standard deviation impact is somewhat stronger than that estimated from the RDI. For example, a one standard deviation increase in RDI (S.D. = 1.9) would be expected to generate a 4.9 percentage point increase in incumbent support, according to the RDI coefficient in column 2 (i.e., $1.9 \times 2.6 = 4.9$). The use of the RDI, and by implication other single macroeconomic measures, may lead to an underestimation of the impact of national economic conditions on presidential vote.[6] (We develop this point further in more elaborate specifications below, and do find that national economic effects are clearly greater than the RDI model suggests.)

We utilize this new, theoretically and empirically more pleasing, measure of national economic conditions to explore enduring and emerging controversies in the economic voting literature. But before doing so, some methodological points are in order. A few questions may well have occurred to the reader. First, "Why not just employ the NES sociotropic item, which has essentially the same phrasing, to construct this National Business Index?" The answer is because the item was not introduced into the election survey until 1968. Its employment would mean we would lose the first three elections in our series—1956, 1960, 1964—years of important political and economic change. Without that variance, a key part of the story is missing. Second, "Why not run it all with another technique, such as probit or logistic regression?" We did this for the equations reported here and found, as did Markus (1992, 830), that it made "little practical difference." (For direct evidence, see the accompanying logistic regression equations in the tables, beginning with Table 11-2A). Further, we wanted to preserve the interpretive advantages the linear probability model of OLS provides—particularly, its ability to predict a change in the election outcome from aggregate economic data.

Table 11-2A   Comparing Two National Economic Conditions Measures in
a Presidential Voting Model, Logistic Regression Estimates,
1956–1996

Variable	(1)	(2)	(3)	(4)	(5)
RDI	.189**	.206**	−.022	.041	
	(.015)	(.015)	(.030)	(.032)	
NBI			.014**	.012**	.016**
			(.002)	(.002)	(.001)
Personal	.337**			.329**	
Finances	(.034)			(.034)	
Incumbent	−.411**	−.434**	−.444**	−.423**	−.446**
Party	(.030)	(.029)	(.029)	(.030)	(.029)
Party ID ×					
Incumbent	.791**	.777**	.782**	.795**	.782**
Party	(.013)	(.012)	(.013)	(.013)	(.013)
Race ×					
Incumbent	1.65**	1.69**	1.68**	1.64**	1.68**
Party	(.109)	(.103)	(.102)	(.109)	(.103)
Constant	−.312**	−.288**	.018	−.060	−.061
	(.048)	(.047)	(.063)	(.068)	(.030)
Percent					
Predicted	83.8	83.2	82.9	83.8	82.9
N	11,969	12,991	12,991	11,969	12,991

Data and Measures: The variables are measured the same as for Table 11-2. ** = statistically significant at .001 or better; * = statistically significant at .01 or better.

Third, "What about simultaneous equation bias from the NBI measure?"
Since NBI is based on perceptions, those perceptions may be distorted by subjective bias. For example, Republicans may tend to vote for a Republican incumbent and (because they are Republican) perceive that the economy is doing better than it actually is. (See the recent discussion of this problem in Nannestad and
Paldam 1997, 123–124.) Such a link between partisanship and economic perception would bias upward the NBI coefficient, and the bias might not be completely removed by the party identification control on the right-hand side in our
single-equation model (e.g., there might be an errors-in-variables problem). To

explore this threat, we ran several tests. Using an instrumental variables strategy, we constructed a proxy variable, NBI-hat, exogenous to the system. This proxy variable was then substituted for the original NBI variable, and the basic model reestimated. All of the conducted tests fail to uncover any simultaneous equation bias from use of original NBI.[7]

We are emboldened to argue that this aggregate perceptual measure, NBI, is preferred to the usual macroeconomic indicators, which are not sacrosanct. Speaking of national objective measures like Real Disposable Personal Income and Gross Domestic Product, Norpoth (1996a, 13) observed they are "crude ones, rough approximations, at best, of how the economy affects individual voters."

The aggregation of individual perceptions can produce measures with "emergent properties," properties not observable at the micro-level (Lewis-Beck and Skalaban 1989, 151). An individual judgment of how the economy is doing, taken by itself, may appear a random shot. But, when many of these judgments are aggregated, the noisiness subsides. MacKuen, Erikson, and Stimson (1992a, 599, 607) call this the "powers of aggregation," where the "idiosyncratic sources of variation in economic judgment cancel out . . . to leave only a signal surviving." The NBI is precisely that—a signal surviving.

National Economic Voting and Electoral Institutions

In any mature democratic system, the basic psychology of economic voting may seem simple enough. (See the lasting essay on this subject by Peffley 1984.) Responsibility is attributed to the political economic manager. When the economy is doing well, the manager is rewarded with support; when the economy is doing badly, that support goes elsewhere. However, the institutional dynamics of the U.S. case can make this attribution uncertain. Congress, the Federal Reserve, and the president are all political economic actors, at various times and for varying terms. The standard assumption is that economic voters blame the president. But the president may be a weak economic leader, or at least perceived to be so, in the face of a partisan rivalry with Congress. During the 1996 campaign, the claim was made that President Clinton had not been able to link himself in the public mind with national economic success. As presidential scholar Charles O. Jones observed, "You never have a feeling that this is the guy who's in charge. If he is not projecting an image of being in control, then why should people give him any credit or blame?" (*New York Times*, April 1, 1996).

The foregoing suggests the first institutional hypothesis: presidential economic voting is influenced by divided government. During the elections under study, partisan division between the president and Congress has varied. At one extreme, there may be partisan unity, with the presidential party controlling both houses of Congress during the entire four year mandate. For example, in 1980 Democrat Jimmy Carter was president, and he had presided over Democratic majorities in both houses of Congress throughout his term. At the other extreme, the presidential party may have a total lack of partisan congressional control. For example, in 1992 Republican president Bush had never commanded a majority in either house. Of course, there is variation between these two extremes. Our expectation is that as partisan unity of government increases, economic voting will increase. Voters, to the extent they observe the president has partisan control, are less hesitant to attribute to him or her responsibility for economic management. They reason that he has the power to get programs through Congress, and so reward or punish subsequent economic performance heavily at the ballot box.

But even under the assumption that government is unified and the president is the exclusive locus of public economic management, other institutional constraints, in the form of constitutional rules, may cloud the attribution of responsibility. Foremost among them is term rules. A president has a fixed amount of time to accomplish his or her economic goals and may extend that time through reelection no more than once. Necessarily, then, there were elections where the president could not run, and the target of economic voting had to shift from him or her to the party itself. The classic V.O. Key economic voter then compares an in-party to an out-party, rather than an in-candidate to an out-candidate (since both candidates are "out"). For example, in 1988, President Ronald Reagan was barred by the 22nd Amendment from running again. Thus, both major party candidates, Bush and Michael Dukakis, were from "outside" the presidential office. The 1988 economic voter was forced to compare the incumbent Republican *Party* and the Democratic *Party* opposition. Attribution of economic responsibility to the incumbent party, rather than to the incumbent as a person, is a more ambiguous task. A president running for reelection is the economic manager personified. Voters can look at his or her economic record in office and cast a ballot accordingly. In contrast, a party running for reelection is more abstract, especially when considered as an economic manager. Voters may think about the party candidate — Bush in 1988 — who is someone different from the president (Reagan), and conclude they really do not know much about his economic program.

While the term limit is the firmest barrier against a president's remaining in office, it is not the only constitutional constraint. Fear of impeachment led President Richard Nixon to resign in 1974, which meant Vice President Gerald Ford succeeded to the presidency. Thus Ford found himself in office half-way through the term, nominal overseer of an economic program he had inherited, rather than campaigned for and developed from an electoral mandate. It would hardly seem surprising if 1976 voters attributed to him relatively little responsibility for the state of the economy. Under the same article, Vice President Lyndon Johnson was also brought to the presidency, in the aftermath of the Kennedy assassination in November 1963. Going into the 1964 contest Johnson was an appointed, not an elected, president, in the White House less than one year. He was caretaker for Kennedy's economic program rather than his own. It would be more than a small wonder if the electorate made strong attributions to him as manager of the nation's economy.

These above rules of presidential service and succession, as spelled out by the Constitution, have meant that in several contests across the period under study no elected president was in the competition.[8] All told, five presidential contests had no elected president running: 1960, 1964, 1968, 1976, and 1988. The remaining six—1956, 1972, 1980, 1984, 1992, and 1996—had an elected president running for a second term. These incumbency differences suggest our second institutional hypothesis: When an elected president is not running, economic voting will be weaker. As a shorthand, we refer to this as the elected incumbent hypothesis.

Our institutional hypotheses argue that the effect of economic voting is conditioned by two independent variables: Divided Government and Elected Incumbent Candidacy. In principle, the impact of the national economy on presidential vote should be stronger if there is no partisan division between the White House and Congress, or if a popularly elected president is campaigning. To test our hypotheses, we respecify the basic economic equation (Table 11-2, column 5) to include the institutional variables with interaction terms. Let us first consider the divided government hypothesis. To maximize the possibility of its effect, we initially treat the Divided Government variable as a simple dichotomy. Under the condition of a totally unified government (the presidential party has had a majority in both houses for four years), the economic vote effect should be most clearly enhanced. According to these expectations, the coefficient of the NBI variable interacted with the Divided Government variable (coded 1 = not divided at all, 0 = divided) will be positive and significant. One observes, from the results in Table 11-3, column 1, that this is not the case. The other coefficients of the basic model are stable, and the main effect of NBI remains virtually unchanged, at .0022. However, the coefficient of the interaction variable (Not Divided × NBI) is not close to statistical significance. And it is negative implying that, if anything, unified government might diminish economic voting.

Importantly, this null—not to say counterintuitive—finding persists with more refined measures of divided government. In particular, it persists if number of houses controlled (one or two), and length of time of the control (two years versus four years) are taken into account. (See the discussion of these alternative measures of divided government in the footnote.)[9]

In sum, we find no support for the divided government hypothesis. Economic voters focus solely on the president, giving him or her leadership responsibility, regardless of whether Congress is an ally. The president appears to shoulder alone the public praise or blame for the political management of the national economy.

The results are more encouraging for the second institutional hypothesis. In Table 11-3, column 2, one observes that, when no elected incumbent is running, economic effects are much weakened. The coefficient of the interaction term (No Incumbent × NBI) is highly significant and negative, as expected. The total impact of economic voting, under the no incumbent running condition is

Table 11-3 National Economic Voting and Electoral Institutions

	OLS		Logit	
Variable	(1)	(2)	(1a)	(2a)
NBI	.0022**	.0024**	.017**	.019**
	(.000)	(.000)	(.002)	(.001)
Not Divided × NBI	−.0005		−.004	
	(.000)		(.002)	
Not Divided	−.023		−.188	
	(.014)		(.115)	
No Incumbent Running × NBI		−.0014**		−.013**
		(.000)		(.004)
No Incumbent Running		−.022*		−.148
		(.009)		(.067)
Incumbent Party	−.050**	−.049**	−.368**	−.358**
	(.006)	(.005)	(.050)	(.034)
Party ID × Incumbent Party	.139**	.139**	.784**	.791**
	(.001)	(.001)	(.013)	(.013)
Race × Incumbent Party	.179**	.178**	1.67**	1.68**
	(.010)	(.010)	(.103)	(.104)
Constant	.512**	.524**	.123	.206*
	(.007)	(.005)	(.058)	(.037)
Adj. R^2	.49	.49		
Percent predicted			82.9	82.8
N	12,991	12,991	12,991	12,991

Data and Measures: NBI, Incumbent Party, Party ID × Incumbent Party, Race × Incumbent Party are measured as described in Table 11-2. No Incumbent Running = a dichotomy scored 0 if a president was standing for reelection, and 1 otherwise; No Incumbent Running × NBI = an interaction term, with the retrospective economic variable NBI multiplied by the No Incumbent Running variable. ** = statistically significant at .001 or better; * = statistically significant at .01 or better. OLS = ordinary least squares.

reduced to .0010 (i.e., the main effect + the interaction effect = .0024 − .0014 = .0010).[10] The strictures of the U.S. Constitution on service and succession, operating directly and indirectly, largely shape whether a popularly elected president will be able to make another run. If they can, they will be judged, perhaps harshly, on their economic record. If they cannot, their party's candidate will still be judged on that record, but much less harshly. In terms of the psychology of economic voting, this makes good sense. Once-elected presidential candidates ran successfully, in part on an economic platform whose accomplishments can now be—and should be—judged. In contrast, their never-elected candidate rivals as yet have no national economic medals to their credit.

National Economic Voting, Incumbency, and the Time Horizon

Thus far, we have assumed a strictly retrospective model of economic voting. However, even Fiorina, widely regarded as a leading theoretical advocate for retrospective voting in American national elections, has admitted that it might not be only that. In his seminal book, he observed that "the mix of behavior between retrospective and prospective voting is an important question to address" (Fiorina 1981, 15). The question remains important, and much debated, in the economic voting literature. Do voters assess past economic performance, then reward or punish the incumbent accordingly? Or do they form expectations about the economy's future, and on that basis cast their ballots? Initial aggregate investigations invariably posited a retrospective model, following a line first laid down by Kramer (1971). But prospective arguments in the aggregate work have steadily gathered steam, especially since Chappell and Keech (1985). The exchange between Clarke and Stewart (1994), and MacKuen, Erikson, and Stimson (1992a), over the impact of retrospective and prospective economic evaluations on presidential popularity, illustrated continuing controversy over the issue. Most recently, prospective predictor variables have actually been incorporated into some time series models of presidential election outcomes (Lewis-Beck and Tien 1996; Wlezien and Erikson 1996). In a tough current debate over time series evidence, MacKuen, Erikson, and Stimson (1996) contend that the electorate is exclusively forward-looking in their political economic evaluations, while Norpoth (1996b) takes the opposing view that they are exclusively backward-looking. The more moderate position, arguing that these political economic evaluations are both backward and forward, characterizes the earlier work of Clarke and Stewart (1994).

With regard to the relevant individual-level, survey research in particular, the retrospective economic model of presidential choice has been dominant, thanks to the trailblazing studies of Fiorina (1981) and Kiewiet (1983). For example, in their careful examination of the 1992 race, Alvarez and Nagler (1995, 728) find "a very strong effect of the voter's assessment . . . of the *national* economy over the past year." However, some individual-level elections research has stressed the relevance of prospective voting. (See, for instance, Miller and Wattenberg 1985, to which we return below.) In his survey analysis of vote choice in the 1984 presidential election, Lewis-Beck (1988, 133) concludes that "prospective collective economic evaluations are as important as retrospective collective economic evaluations." More recently, Lockerbie (1992) offered a full exploration of prospective voting in U.S. presidential election surveys.

In sum, it seems that national economic voting for president obviously has a retrospective dimension captured, we believe, by the coefficient of the National Business Index. But it also seems necessary to test whether there exists, as well, a prospective dimension. The Economic Future Index (EFI) we propose applies the measurement logic of the NBI to another Michigan Consumer Survey item:

> "Now turning to business conditions as a whole—do you think that during the next 12 months we'll have good times financially, or bad times financially?"

This item on future business conditions possess the same time horizon—one year—as our retrospective variable. Evidence for the special value of aggregating such a prospective item comes from MacKuen, Erikson, and Stimson (1992a, 599): "Judgments whether the economy will improve or falter, for example, may be too noisy for worthwhile analysis at the individual level. But their noise cancels out in the aggregate, to provide the powerful measure of collective judgments of the economic future."

From responses to this item, the EFI is calculated in the same manner as the NBI. The mean EFI = 30.8, which shows that voters typically are, on net, optimistic about the economic future. [This finding receives support from the time series work of Haller and Norpoth (1994, 646), who report that "in looking ahead, people enjoy a certain degree of freedom to follow their wishes. At heart, the U.S. electorate is profoundly optimistic about the economy. There is little willingness to entertain a gloomy outlook for long."] The standard deviation = 25.8 is equivalent to that of NBI, suggesting that neither index is a victim of greater variability from measurement error. If EFI is truly capturing a future economic dimension, then it should be relatively independent of past macroeconomic indicators. This is in fact the case, for when EFI is regressed on the change in real disposable personal income per capita (RDI), the adjusted R^2 = .39. (Recall this is about half the fit generated when NBI, a retrospective measure, was regressed on RDI, also a retrospective measure.) Finally, it is not simply a rationalization, or projection, of NBI. When EFI is regressed on NBI, the adjusted R^2 = .43, indicating that less than half the future collective economic assessment can be accounted for by past collective economic assessment.

The national economic voting model is respecified, with the addition of the EFI variable (Table 11-4, column 1). The coefficients of the political variables continue virtually unchanged from the basic economic voting model (see Table 11-2, column 5). The economic effect from NBI remains highly significant, but is diminished in magnitude. The new economic effect, from EFI, is also highly significant. Further, it is only slightly smaller in magnitude. The economic expectations of voters figure heavily in support of the incumbent, quite independent of their evaluation of the economic past. In fact, the two variables have coefficients that are roughly equivalent in size (.0014 vs. .0011). Generally speaking, both

Table 11-4 National Economic Voting, Incumbency, and the Time Horizon

Variable	OLS		Logit	
	(1)	(2)	(1a)	(2a)
NBI	.0014**	.0018**	.011**	.014**
	(.000)	(.000)	(.001)	(.002)
EFI	.0011**	.0007**	.009**	.005**
	(.000)	(.000)	(.001)	(.002)
No Incumbent Running		−.092**		−.784**
		(.015)		(.126)
No Incumbent Running × NBI		−.0011**		−.009**
		(.000)		(.003)
No Incumbent Running × EFI		.0017**		.016**
		(.000)		(.033)
Incumbent Party	−.063**	−.065**	−.463**	−.500**
	(.004)	(.005)	(.030)	(.041)
Party ID × Incumbent Party	.139**	.139**	.787**	.796**
	(.001)	(.001)	(.013)	(.013)
Race × Incumbent Party	.172**	.172**	1.64**	1.66**
	(.010)	(.010)	(.104)	(.100)
Constant	.486**	.511**	−.153**	.057
	(.006)	(.006)	(.044)	(.050)
Adj. R^2	.49	.49		
Percent predicted			83.0	83.1
N	12,991	12,991	12,991	12,991

Data and Measures: Measures are the same as in Table 11-3, plus EFI = the Economic Future Index, constructed in the same manner as NBI, but using the Michigan Suvey of Consumer Attitudes item on the economic future over the next 12 months; No Incumbent Running × EFI = an interaction term, with the prospective economic variable EFI multiplied by the No Incumbent Running Variable. ** = statistically significant at .001 or better. OLS = ordinary least squares.

past and future economic conditions appear important, and about equally so, for presidential vote choice.

Given the clarity of these results on the time horizon of voting, one may wonder why there has been so much controversy in the literature. How can study X show overwhelming support for a retrospective model, while study Z shows overwhelming support for a prospective model? We believe that such apparently contradictory results stem from certain of our electoral institutions. The constitutional constraints on presidential service and succession already described frequently produce presidential races where no elected incumbent is running. In such a circumstance, we argue that economic voting is more likely to be prospective. Absent a candidate who has already passed the tests of presidential election and office-holding, voters will tend to focus on the incumbent party candidate's economic promises. In contrast, when a popularly elected president is seeking renewal of his or her mandate, voters will tend to be retrospective, focusing on actual economic accomplishments. Hence, depending on incumbency candidate type, economic voting should be either largely retrospective or largely prospective. If this proposition is sound, then the contradictory results on retrospective and prospective economic voting can be reconciled.

These expectations are tested through respecification of the retrospective-prospective model (Table 11-4, column 1) to include two interaction terms: the retrospective variable multiplied by the elected incumbent candidate variable (No Incumbent Running × NBI) and the prospective variable multiplied by the elected incumbent candidate variable (No Incumbent Running × EFI). Results appear in Table 11-4, column 2. The institutional argument receives strong support. The negative sign for the significant retrospective interaction term ($-.0011$), indicates that when an elected incumbent is not running, economic voters are less retrospective. The positive sign for the significant prospective interaction term (.0017) indicates that, under the same conditions, they are more prospective. Thus, the balance of economic voting changes from one type of election to another. When an elected incumbent is running, retrospections clearly dominate (i.e., overall NBI = .0018, overall EFI = .0007). It is almost exactly the opposite when no elected incumbent is running, for prospections dominate (i.e., overall NBI = .0018 $-$ .0011 = .0007; overall EFI = .0007 + .0017 = .0024). Voters seem to follow a V.O. Key model in incumbent elections, punishing or rewarding the president on his or her past economic record. However, in nonincumbent elections, they seem to follow a model from Anthony Downs, focusing on the economic future the candidate outlines. In an informational sense, this is perhaps unsurprising. A voter knows a good deal about the economic performance of a president running for reelection. However, for a candidate who is not president, even a candidate of the presidential party, the voter can really only know the candidate's economic promises.

These findings dovetail nicely with the general work on testing of voting theories by Miller and Wattenberg (1985, 370): "Key's emphasis on retrospective performance applies best to public assessments of incumbents running for reelection. The Downsian model, in contrast, seems best to fit the challengers, who are often evaluated on the basis of their proposed future policies. Finally, Fiorina's concentration on prospective performance provides the best description of candidates running in no incumbent races." These results find confirmation here. We arrive at an important clarification of an enduring controversy in the literature.

Table 11-5   Prediction of Presidential Election Outcomes (Two-Party Vote Share)

Year	Observed (%)	Predicted (%)	Error
1956	57.4	59.6	2.2
1960	49.5	50.8	1.3
1964	61.5	63.6	2.1
1968	49.6	53.3	3.7
1972	60.7	58.9	−1.8
1976	48.0	47.3	−0.7
1980	44.7	41.2	−3.5
1984	59.1	62.9	3.8
1988	53.4	51.7	−1.7
1992	46.8	45.1	−1.7
1996	55.1	56.6	1.5
Average Absolute Error (1956–1996)			2.2

The time horizon of economic voting depends on whether a popularly elected president is standing for reelection: if "yes," then it will be largely retrospective; if "no," then it will be largely prospective.

Last is the question of model performance. Assume that this final equation specification (Table 11-4, column 2), which incorporates incumbency and time horizon effects on the economic vote, is preferred over earlier specifications. How well does it predict overall election outcomes? By plugging in the mean values for each independent variable, the incumbent percentage of the two-party vote for each election, 1956–1996, can be predicted. The results appear in Table 11-5. The model predicts well, with a mean absolute error of only 2.2 percentage points.

Model performance is further noteworthy at the individual level, given the absence of independent variables explicitly measuring campaign dynamics, noneconomic issues such as war or scandal, candidate traits, or administration shifts. This is not to say that these omitted variables are unimportant, for they undoubtedly enhance the theoretical understanding of presidential vote choice. But even without their presence, the rather simple structure that is posited manages an impressive empirical performance, the logistic version (Table 11-4, column 2a) correctly predicting 83.1 percent of the individual votes.

Conclusion

In U.S. presidential elections, American voters routinely take into account national economic conditions. But which conditions? And how to measure them? We argue that voters evaluate multiple macroeconomic indicators, and form their own unique judgments about their performance. These individual assessments, when aggregated, form a national collective perception of the condition of the economy. We formulate a basic evaluative variable, the National Business Index

(NBI), based on survey measures of consumer attitudes. NBI is a summary ret-rospective measure on national economic performance. Analysis suggests that studies utilizing other macro-measures have misestimated the impact of the national economy on presidential elections.

Assuming a classic retrospective economic voting model, the NBI exhibits strong effects. When placed in a model alongside Real Disposable Income Per Capita (RDI), the significant impact of NBI persists but the impact of RDI is washed out. Further, according to the basic equation (Table 11-2, column 5), a one standard deviation drop in the NBI leads to the expectation that the incum-bent will lose 5.5 percent of the two-party popular vote. This is an effect larger than the estimated loss from a comparable drop in the RDI, when that variable is allowed to stand alone. The robustness of the NBI coefficient suggests the crit-ical importance of good economic performance for the reelection prospects of the in-party, as Key might have predicted. The effect from NBI seems real, rather than a product of bias. Various tests demonstrate the exogenous status of the NBI variable. Moreover, they show that NBI is, in fact, an amalgam of voter evalua-tion of different macroeconomic indicators.

While national economic assessments generally move presidential voters, strength of impact sometimes varies with the institutional context of the contest. Divided government itself apparently makes no difference. The presidential office is viewed as the command post of the economy, irrespective of whether the president actually has sufficient control of Congress to implement his or her eco-nomic plan. The president is simply regarded as the chief executive officer of the public economy. However, if the president, because of the constitutional con-straints on service and succession, is unable to run again, then the psychology of the economic vote is rather different. Voters find it easy to praise (or blame) a candidate who is currently president and completing the economic mandate of his or her first term. They look at the record. In contrast, voters find it hard to judge the economic program of a new candidate for the incumbent party. Noth-ing has been delivered, since he has never held the White House. In this case, classic economic voting is much weaker.

If one introduces the assumption of prospective, as well as retrospective, vot-ing, economic effects appear more extensive, redistributing themselves institu-tionally. Overall, these nuances testify to the underappreciated strength of the economic vote in U.S. presidential elections. A classic retrospective model of eco-nomic voting, the Real Disposable Income equation of Table 11-2 (column 1), leaves a prediction error of 3.3 percentage points.[11] In contrast, our incumbency conditioned, retrospective-prospective model of economic voting gives an error of only 2.2 percentage points, as reported in Table 11-5. Such precision is com-parable to the final Gallup Preelection Poll, conducted just days before the pres-idential race, with an average forecasting error of just over 2.0 percentage points. As economic forces, subjective and objective, work through the electorate in mul-tiple and subtle ways, their impact is magnified, and this model specification appears to go far in taking that into account.

Theoretically, the economic voter for the American presidency appears rather sophisticated. When a popularly elected president is able to lead the campaign, economic voting becomes almost exclusively retrospective. He is judged essentially on perceived national economic performance over the past year. But when the incumbent campaign is headed up by a new standard bearer, economic voting becomes almost exclusively prospective. Because the candidate has no track record, he is evaluated on the basis of his or her promised economic program. This shift of time frame for the economic evaluation shows a reasoning voter. In the former case, of the elected incumbent candidate, the voter's primary economic information source comes from the past. In the latter case, of the nonelected, nonincumbent candidate, the voter's primary economic information source comes from promises for the future. Generally speaking, we conclude economic voters are Keysian when a president is running for reelection, but Downsian otherwise. Thus, as institutional requirements change the character of the incumbent candidacy, from an elected president to an untried first-timer, economic voting changes in emphasis from retrospective to prospective.

Is there a general theory of economic voting in presidential elections? Yes, in the sense that there is the same strong reward-punishment response across elections of the same type. The confusion that has arisen in the past is over the type, as defined by the institutional conditions, and over identification of the proper economic indicators. The contextual modeling of the U.S. presidential vote, using the new measures of NBI and EFI, should help reduce this confusion.

Notes

1. These data are available from the Inter-university Consortium for Political and Social Research, University of Michigan, Ann Arbor. They are in no way responsible for the interpretation offered here.
2. Some critics may reject NBI, as they reject all "subjective" measures of the economy. But actually, the measure can be thought of in ways which make it much less subjective in the traditional sense. Imagine that NBI adds together several objective macroeconomic indicators (including RDI), and allows these several objective indicators to be weighted differently (because individuals may apply a different weight to the same objective measures). For example, Sally values a low unemployment rate half as much as Bill does. If the weighting scheme Sally or Bill uses is rational, in an acceptable cost-benefit sense, then the combinations forming NBI are not "subjective," that is, not emotional, arbitrary, idiosyncratic or poetic.
3. The Markus (1988) methodology, a pool of surveys incorporating macro-indicators, has been an important innovation in economic voting research. While highly regarded by many, it is not without its detractors. The core objection comes out of the aggregate character of the economic variable. According to this view, the sample size is more like $N = 11$ (observations on Real Disposable Income for the eleven election years) than $N = 13,000$ (the respondents in the eleven surveys). One consequence of assuming $N = 13,000$ is that statistical significance becomes far too easy to achieve. Another consequence is that year effects (unique to each survey) are liable to attribute strong significance to RDI, when in fact random numbers assigned to the years would produce the same pattern. Below, we attempt to answer both of these criticisms.

An $N = 11$ would mean we have a strictly aggregate (national) level of analysis, on all variables. But this is not the design. We have a pool of surveyed individuals who are scored on many variables, some *individual* and some *contextual*. One of the contextual variables is RDI, and each respondent has one of eleven possible scores on that variable. Another contextual variable is region, and each respondent could be scored North, South, East, or West. Another contextual variable might be community type, perhaps scored urban or rural. And so on. To illustrate, take the hypothetical example of a national election survey ($N = 2,000$) from a single year, Z. Suppose the dependent variable is Vote Turnout (V) and we believe that V is determined by Individual Income (I) and Unemployment Rate in the respondent's state (U). Because there are fifty states, that does not mean that now $N = 50$. Rather, there are a maximum of fifty different "treatments," if you will, on this independent variable, U. Overall $N = 2,000$. To continue the analogy, in our pooled analysis à la Markus of eleven election years, respondents are subjected to eleven different economic treatments, and the overall $N = 13,000$.

Certainly, achieving statistical significance with a sample of 13,000 should not be overinterpreted, but failing to do so might be seen differently. The fact that RDI failed to reach a conventional level of statistical significance when entered into the equations with our National Business Index, NBI (Table 11-2, column 3) could be viewed as very good confirmation of superiority of NBI over RDI.

Finally, the statistical significance of the aggregate economic indicator is not spurious, a mere artifact of a large sample coupled with year effects and randomness. We ran a series of simulations, assigning eleven random dummy counter variables to the different election years. The simulations were based on two types of random variables: (a) combinations of eleven numbers assigned to the different years (1 = 1976, 2 = 1992, 3 = 1960, etc.); and, (b) random assignment of actual values of the National Business Index and the Economic Future Index to various elections. Four tests were actually run: (1) ten random variables were added separately to the vote model (excluding the regular economic variables); (2) ten random variables were merged randomly into five pairs of variables and added to the model; (3) the ten random NBI were added separately to the model; and (4) the ten random NBI and EFI were jointly added to the model.

The test results, in order, were as follows: 1. one coefficient not significant, five negative significant coefficients, four positive significant coefficients, average b = .04 ; 2. one pair of negative significant coefficients, one pair of positive and significant coefficients, three pairs with one positive and one negative coefficient (not all significant); 3. seven negative significant coefficients, three positive significant coefficients, average b = .04 ; 4. four pairs negative coefficients (significant), three pairs mixed coefficients (significant), two pairs with one coefficient significant and one not, one pair with two positive coefficients (significant). In summary, random variables produce unstable, nonsensical, and weak coefficients (two to three times weaker than NBI and EFI). Given the results of these experiments, the probability of getting the type of positive results reported in Tables 11-2 through 11-4 by chance alone is extremely low, to say the least.

4. To check the robustness of our findings, we also added in preliminary analyses a whole set of variables tapping the socioeconomic group components of the presidential vote (see Erikson, Lancaster, and Romero 1989). The inclusion of these variables (age, income, education, union membership, gender, religion), leaves the coefficients of Tables 11-2 through 11-5 nearly identical.

5. Markus (1988, 144) uses an instrumental variables approach to obtain a surrogate measure of the original Personal Finances variable. We did not pursue this refinement, since we are not wrestling with the pocketbook voter hypothesis. Rather, our

focus is on improved measurement of national economic conditions. As the results in Table 11-2 make clear, the coefficients on the Markus national measure, RDI, remain stable, regardless of how Personal Finances are measured.

6. On the basis of various statistical tests, NBI appears to have a greater effect on presidential vote than RDI. RDI fails to register statistical significance, despite the large sample size, when both are included in the specification. But NBI is statistically significant and its inclusion to the model (compare columns 2 and 3, Table 11-2) provides a statistically significant boost to the R^2, according to an F-test on the two different equations (F = 162.16). Moreover, when their effects are examined in rival specifications, where first one is excluded then the other, NBI registers a higher level of significance than RDI, according to the t-ratios (respectively 15.8 to 13.8).

   A more elaborate test of predictive superiority, suggested by the work of DeHoog et al. (1990), makes the dominance of NBI still clearer. First, we regressed the vote on party identification, race, and a series of dummy variables for each presidential year (with 1996 as the missing category). Then, we treated the ten dummy variable coefficients as a dependent variable, and predicted it in separate regressions, one with RDI independent and another with NBI independent. NBI accounted for substantially more variance than RDI, R^2 = .33 versus R^2 = .27. Moreover, the NBI coefficient remained the same as in Table 11-2 (.0020) and was statistically significant at .05, whereas the RDI coefficient was not.

   In sum, by these various tests, the possible empirical effects of NBI are shown superior to RDI, sometimes considerably so.

7. The regression equation used to create the instrumental variable, NBI-hat, is as follows:

$$NBI = -51.9 + 10.2 \text{ Earnings} - 7.3 \text{ Unemployment} - 1.7 \text{ Inflation} + 2.6 \text{ GDP} + 7.1 \text{ RDI}$$
$$R^2 = .88, \text{Adjusted } R^2 = .76$$
$$N = 11 \text{ (presidential election years, 1956–1996)}$$

   The annual rates for unemployment, the inflation (from the CPI), GDP, and the RDI are from the *Economic Report of the President*; earnings refers to average hourly earnings in constant dollars, and is taken from Bureau of Labor Statistics.

   When the basic economic voting equation (Table 11-2, column 5) was reestimated substituting this NBI-hat for NBI, the coefficient = .0020, identical to the original NBI coefficient. Further, the quality of the instrumental variable, NBI-hat, does not depend exclusively on having these five exogenous variables in the prediction equation. If for example the Earnings variable is excluded, the equation reestimated, and a new instrument constructed, the resulting coefficient for this alternative NBI-hat is still .0020, exactly as with the original model. Moreover, the quality of the instrumental variable appears good across the time series of different survey units in the pool, suggesting that no autoregressive conditional heteroskedasticity (ARCH) underlies the results. In particular, the observed and predicted NBI are generally close for all years. The average absolute prediction error is just 6.95, much less than the standard deviation of NBI = 27.3. Also, before the middle year of 1976, only one prediction exceeds this average error, and from 1976 on only two exceed this average.

   A related argument is that the bias in NBI is specifically a partisan bias. To explore this threat, we again used an instrumental variables approach to "purge" NBI of partisan bias, then re-ran the basic model. For each year, we calculated the aggregate partisan balance (APB)—incumbent party identifiers−opposition party identifiers. Then, NBI was regressed on APB and the residuals used to create a proxy variable, RNBI, free of partisan bias. When this proxy variable is substituted in the basic economic voting equation (Table 11-2, column 5), the coefficients remain essentially unchanged, at .0020, suggesting the absence of partisan bias.

8. Of course, an elected president may decide not to run again, even though he is facing no explicit constitutional constraint. This is a rather rare event, however. In the elections under study, this happened only once, with Lyndon Johnson in 1968. Given this circumstance, the implications for economic voting are the same: when no elected president is running, economic voting is expected to be much weaker.

9. Four other measures of divided government were tried, distinguishing between the houses, the lengths of time, and the extent of presidential party control. They are as follows. 1. U2, where 1 = control of both houses for the entire mandate (1964, 68, 80), .5 = control over House or Senate during the entire mandate (84), 0 = otherwise. 2. U3 = proportion of houses controlled by the president during the two two-year periods; maximum = 1 for 1964, 1968, 1980, meaning control over House and Senate for 1961/1962 and 1963/1964, 1965/1966, and 1967/1968, 1977/1978, and 1979/1980—2 (houses) × 2 (two two-year periods) = 4/4 = 1; .5 = 1956, control over House and Senate in 1953/1954 (2 × 1 = 2/4 = .5); .5 = 1984 , control over Senate for the entire mandate (1 × 2 = 2/4 = .5); .5 = 1996, control over House and Senate in 1993/1994 (2 × 1 = 2/4 = .5); .25 = 1988, control of the Senate for 1985/1986 (1 × 1 = 1/4 = .25); 0 = otherwise (i.e., totally divided government, with no control over either of the houses during the two subperiods). 3. U4 = average proportion of seats in the House and the Senate controlled by the party of the president during the four years ((proportion of seats in the House controlled by the party of the president during the four years + proportion of seats in the Senate controlled by the party of the president during the four years) /2). 4. U5 = average proportion of seats in the House and the Senate controlled by the party of the president during the last two years of the mandate ((proportion of seats in the House controlled by the party of the president over the last two years + proportion of the seats in the Senate controlled by the party of the president during the last two years) /2). None of these measures, when included in the model in the same manner as the measure of Table 11-3, managed to demonstrate the hypothesized effect. Our conclusion is that divided government does not influence economic voting.

10. One suggestion is that this finding is due to the fact that economic fluctuations could be more pronounced during the "incumbent" elections. Of the six incumbent election years, economic fluctuation was most extreme in 1980 (where NBI = −48 and RDI actually fell, registering −1.1). Thus, to test the stability of our results, we reran the analysis excluding 1980. After exclusion of this outlier, the coefficients for our key variables remain exactly the same, .0024 for NBI and −.0014 for NBI × NOINC, indicating the robustness of the overall model.

11. In the original Markus (1988, 150) paper, his model generated an absolute average error of 3.0. In the paper updating that work (Markus 1992, 833), his model gave an average prediction error of 2.8, for the elections 1956−1988. When the 1992 and 1996 elections are added to his formulation, as we did, the average error rises to 3.3.

12. Multiple-Stage Explanation of Political F

Warren E. Miller and J. Merrill Shanks

Our strategy for explaining individual differences in vote choice involves a comprehensive set of explanatory ideas or hypotheses that have been suggested by a wide variety of theories and approaches. Our approach to this theoretical and conceptual diversity has been to classify all potential explanations into a small number of general "themes," each of which may include several specific factors that share the same kind of content and may influence the vote through similar processes or mechanisms. Our strategy has been inclusive in two senses. Most of our explanatory themes incorporate a variety of potential explanatory variables of the same general type (for example, current preferences concerning policy direction in many different substantive areas), and our definitions of the various alternative themes are designed to cover the range of explanatory hypotheses that have been suggested by the scholarly literature on electoral behavior. Our conclusions concerning the role of particular explanatory factors or variables in a given election may diverge from those advanced by other analysts because we have used different measurement or statistical procedures, or because of the other explanatory variables involved in our analyses. Our collection of general explanatory themes, however, should incorporate most, if not all, of the suggestions that have been discussed by other scholars concerning the explanation of individual electoral decisions.

Explanatory Themes and Causal Stages

We have classified potential explanations of the vote (and their associated survey-based variables) into one of eight general themes, depending on whether the voter attributes involved are primarily defined in terms of: (1) stable social and economic characteristics, (2) long-term partisan identifications, (3) policy-related predispositions, (4) preferences concerning current policy issues, (5) perceptions of current conditions, national or personal, (6) retrospective evaluations of the current president concerning governmental "results," (7) evaluations of the

Source: Reprinted by permission of the publisher from *The New American Voter,* by Warren E. Miller and J. Merrill Shanks, Cambridge, Mass.: Harvard University Press, Copyright © 1996 by the President and Fellows of Harvard College.

Editors' Note: This chapter includes material from chapters 8, 11, 12, and 17 of *The New American Voter* in order to provide illustrations of the different types of analysis as well as some of the major conclusions presented in that book.

personal qualities of the candidates, or (8) prospective evaluations of the potential future effectiveness of the two parties and their candidates. As emphasized below, two of these explanatory themes are defined in terms of policy-related conflicts within the society (including general policy-related predispositions and current policy preferences), and two themes are defined in terms of consensual criteria for political evaluations (concerning current conditions and personal qualities of the candidates). Within each of these pairs of general explanatory themes, all specific variables share the same kind of analytic content and are assumed to influence vote choice through the same types of causal processes. Because of those similarities, we will eventually be able to assess the combined relevance of all the variables within each explanatory theme as well as the role of each variable. For example, we will be particularly interested in the combined explanatory power of all policy-related preferences, including both predispositions and policy preferences. That combination or aggregation will be mentioned briefly in discussions of specific policy-related variables. We will defer explicit assessments of the overall power or "importance" of each of our eight explanatory themes until after we have examined the apparent effects of individual variables in each of those themes.

In addition to the substantive distinctions among different explanatory themes, our analytic conclusions also rest on crucial assumptions concerning temporal sequence, based on a causal order of six stages in which we believe voters acquire their positions on different types of variables. Within this structure, all of the variables in a given *stage* may have been influenced by variables in earlier stages (as well as by other variables within the given stage), and may have had some influence on one or more variables in later stages, as well as having some direct or unmediated impact on the vote. All of the variables in each explanatory theme have been assigned to the same causal position (or stage), on the basis of our assumptions about the similar kinds of processes involved in their development. It should be noted that we have assigned some explanatory themes to the same causal stage (for example, partisan identification and policy-related predispositions to one stage—the second—and current policy preferences and perceptions of current conditions to another stage—the third). We have made these assignments because of the similarity of the themes in each pair with regard to temporal sequence and because of our conviction that questions about causal relationships between them cannot be resolved. These assumptions about temporal sequence, including the assignment of each explanatory theme to one of six causal stages before the vote, can be seen in Figure 12-1. This aspect of our approach to electoral explanation deserves special emphasis, for these assumptions represent the foundation for our interpretation of all the statistical results to follow.

We have assumed that a variety of stable social and economic characteristics (which constitute the first stage of our model) have played some role in shaping voters' continuing predispositions toward many policy-related conflicts within the society, as well as in shaping their long-term partisan identifications—both

Figure 12-1 Explanatory Themes and Causal Stages

Stage   Substantive Content of Themes Assigned to Each Stage

1 | (1) Stable Social and Economic Characteristics |

2 | (2) Partisan Identification | and | (3) Policy-related Predispositions |

3 | (4) Current Policy Preferences | and | (5) Perceptions of Current Conditions |

4 | (6) Retrospective Evaluations of the President Concerning Governmental "Results" |

5 | (7) Impressions of the Candidates' Personal Qualities |

6 | (8) Prospective Evaluations of the Candidates and the Parties |

        | Vote Choice |

of which have been assigned to the second major stage in our model. On the basis of a variety of evidence, we have concluded that all of the other attitudes that had some impact on voters' choices for president should be assigned to later or subsequent stages in our model. All of those other attitudes may have been influenced by policy-related predispositions or partisan identifications, or by social or economic characteristics—and they may subsequently mediate the relationships between variables in our first two stages and the vote. Such attitudes, however, are not likely to have "caused" the characteristics grouped together in the first two stages. In effect, both types of predispositions, as well as social and economic characteristics, are treated as "givens" for the current election—on the assumption that they were already "in place" before the current campaign began and were generally not changed by short-term forces based on campaign issues or candidate personality (which are the basis for our other explanatory variables).[1]

The third major stage in our model (following partisan and policy-related predispositions) also includes two distinct explanatory themes, neither of which involves any explicit connection with the candidates or parties that are competing in the campaign being analyzed. These two themes are defined in terms of voters' opinions concerning the two different types of "issues" that were emphasized during the current campaign. These two types of opinions are defined in terms of voters' own preferences concerning current conflicts over policy direction and their perceptions of current conditions concerning consensual objectives. None of these opinions and perceptions are expressed in terms of evaluations of the parties or the candidates. As with the partisan and policy-related predispositions in our second stage, the explanatory variables in the third stage (concerning current policy conflicts and conditions) may have had some influence on each other. As in our second stage, we have deliberately not attempted to unravel such relationships and have simply included both types of variables in the same causal stage.

Following voters' preferences concerning current policy issues and their perceptions of current conditions, all of the remaining explanatory themes (and all of the remaining stages in our model) are expressly defined in terms of explicitly partisan *evaluations*. Specifically, the variables in our fourth stage involve retrospective evaluations of the current president concerning the "results" of his administration. Unlike subsequent stages, these evaluations are asymmetric in their focus on only one side of the partisan contest in the current election, on the grounds that most evaluations of the President have been established before the other candidate becomes well known; and, in any event, a challenger has no record for which he can be held accountable in a manner comparable to the incumbent.

Our fifth stage, then, introduces comparative evaluations of the two major candidates with respect to exclusively personal qualities of the leaders, qualities that are not defined in terms of partisanship, policy, conditions, or governmental results. Finally, the variables in our sixth stage, which we assume to be the most proximate to the vote, represent prospective evaluations concerning potential governmental "results," based on hypothetical questions that ask which candidate or party would do "a better job" in handling specific problem areas.

In our model, each successive stage is thus temporally located closer and closer to the vote decision. For that reason, the values of each (successive) set of variables are more and more vulnerable to influence from early choices by the voter. Despite that possibility, however, we shall argue with some care that it nevertheless makes sense to do the best one can with available evidence to consider an independent role for the factors in stages 5 and 6 rather than conclude that "feedback" from an early preference for one candidate overwhelms any attempt to separate cause and effect concerning our most proximate variables and the vote. . . .

Party Identification: Long-Term versus Short-Term Forces

. . . As emphasized in *The American Voter* and many other studies of the American electorate, we believe that long-term partisanship exerts an indirect influence on vote choice by shaping voters' attitudes toward many of the short-term forces in a given campaign, as well as by exerting some direct or unmediated influence of its own on the vote decision.

At this point, however, we should restate our conviction that, given the available data and our repertoire of analytic procedures, the causal relationships between partisan identification and policy-related predispositions must remain both conceptually and statistically indeterminate. Most voters in 1992 had acquired their current partisan identifications *and* their own predispositions toward continuing policy-related conflicts well before that campaign had begun. We assume that the statistical relationships between party identification and our policy-related predispositions are based on a complex and thus far unknown combination of processes that include childhood socialization, exposure to prior events with substantial political consequences, and the persuasive efforts of party leaders—as well as the cumulative influence of policy-related preferences on partisan identifications. Causal interpretation of those statistical relationships lies outside the scope of this [analysis], and our recognition of the complexities involved represents a notable departure from our previous work.[2]

Instead of presenting a single set of estimates which would imply a resolution of this causal ambiguity, Table 12-1 documents the strength of the statistical connections between party identification and the vote, both before and after we take account of different combinations of other explanatory predispositions. Our discussion is based on the same analytic procedures that were used in the [Miller and Shanks 1996] discussion of social and economic characteristics. Thus, Rows 1 and 2 of Table 12-1 present the vote divisions or average votes (scored +1 for Clinton and −1 for Bush) among voters who described themselves as Democrats (rounded to +.81) and Republicans (−.77), and Row 3 presents the simple difference (1.58) between those averages. Row 4 then presents the bivariate (unstandardized) regression coefficient, .78, from an analysis that includes only the trichotomous measure of party identification (based on the initial National Election Studies [NES] question on that topic). The scoring for party identification includes only two "units" (from −1 for Republicans to 0 for Independents, and from 0 to +1 for Democrats), so that the bivariate regression coefficient for party identification, .78, is very close to half of the simple difference between Democrats and Republicans in their average score on the vote (1.58). Rows 5, 7, and 8 present the corresponding regression coefficients for party identification from multivariate analyses which include progressively more explanatory variables, beginning with the social and economic characteristics discussed in the previous chapter [of Miller and Shanks 1996], .70, followed by the specific policy-related predispositions discussed in this chapter, .53, and finally general liberal versus conservative self-designation, .48.[3]

From the modest reduction in coefficients between Rows 4 and 5 (from .78 to .70) it would appear that the electoral effects of partisan identifications are only slightly biased or confounded by the impact of (usually prior) social or economic characteristics on both party identification and the vote. In contrast, the substantial reduction between Rows 5 and 8 (from .70 to .48) suggests that the impact of long-term partisanship may indeed be confounded with that of ideological and other policy-related predispositions—that is, with variables in the other explanatory themes that we have assigned to the same causal stage in our model.

Unfortunately, because all of our predispositions have been assigned to the same causal stage, we are unable to assess the indirect effects of party identification *or* policy-related predispositions on the vote that operate "through" their impact on the other type of predisposition. Such indirect effects seem particularly likely, given the cumulative influence of party leaders on voters' policy-related predispositions and the impact of basic values on adult partisan orientations.

Table 12-1 Alternative Perspectives on the Impact of Party Identification

1. Average Vote (-1 or $+1$) Among Those Who Generally Think of Themselves as a Democrat ($N = 489$)	.81[a]
2. Average Vote (-1 or $+1$) Among Those Who Generally Think of Themselves as a Republican ($N = 323$)	$-.77$[a]
3. Difference in Average Vote: Democrats Minus Republicans	1.58
4. Bivariate Unstandardized Regression Coefficient (Party Identification Scored -1, 0, or $+1$)	.78
5. Coefficient from Multiple Regression with Social and Economic Characteristics Held Constant	.70
6. (Not Relevant for This Table Concerning Party Identification)	—
7. With All Specific Policy-Related Predispositions Also Held Constant	.53
8. With Liberal vs. Conservative Self-Designation Also Held Constant	.48[b]
9. (Not Relevant for This Table Concerning Party Identification)	—
10. With Preferences on All Current policy Issues Also Held Constant	.46
11. With Perceptions of Current Personal and National Conditions Also Held Constant	.44
12. With Retrospective Evaluations of the Current President's Performance Also Held Constant	.25
13. With Evaluations of the Candidates' Personal Qualities Also Held Constant	.22
14. With Prospective Evaluations of Candidates' and Parties' Future Performance Also Held Constant	.16

Note: Coefficients appear in parentheses if the estimated p value is > .1.

[a]The number of cases associated with extreme positions on these and similar measures simply indicate the base on which extreme scores were calculated. Note that the number of cases is unweighted; all other results are weighted.

[b]Indicates estimate of the "apparent total effect" discussed in the text.

Because of this ambiguity, we have selected a "preferred" estimate for the apparent total effect of each predisposition from explanations of equations that include both types of predispositions, as well as social and economic characteristics. Given these uncertainties, the coefficient in Row 8 of Table 12-1 (.48) must be interpreted as a conservative estimate of the "apparent total effect" of party identification on the vote, because it neglects any indirect effects of partisanship through our other (policy-related) predispositions.

The progressive reduction in the remaining coefficients (following the apparent total effect) in Table 12-1 suggests the extent to which the total impact of long-term partisanship on the vote is mediated, or transmitted, by the other intervening variables in our model. In particular, the potential indirect effects of partisanship can be seen in the degree to which the remaining apparent effect of party identification is reduced when we also account for retrospective evaluations of presidential performance (Row 12), comparative evaluations of the two candidates' personal qualities (Row 13), and evaluations of the future performance of the parties and candidates (Row 14). in this sequence of coefficients, the largest single decline in the remaining (or unmediated) impact of party identification can be seen in the difference between .44 (in Row 11, from an analysis which includes current policy preferences and perceptions of current conditions as well as all prior variables) and .25 (in Row 12, from the analysis which also includes explicit evaluations of the current president's performance in office).

Party identification also represents the only type of general attitude or predisposition that is nearly guaranteed to have a continuing "long-term" influence on national elections, for it is always activated (albeit in slightly varying degrees) in elections that call for voters to choose between the two major parties. Finally, it should be noted that party identification retains some apparent "direct effect" on the vote, .16, after we have controlled for *all* of the other explanatory variables in our model. This remaining or uninterpreted effect estimate represents an unknown combination of intervening variables that have been omitted or badly measured in our multivariate analysis. It also includes any direct impact of partisan identification per se—especially when it acts as a "tie breaker" because the effects of other political attitudes are balanced, or as the only influence for individuals who do not have any other basis for choice. . . .

Electoral Effects of Specific Policy Issues

Governmental Assistance to the Disadvantaged

Since 1980, NES surveys have included a battery of questions concerning voters' preferences for the level of federal spending in a wide variety of areas. Each of those questions asks the respondent whether spending should be increased, kept the same, or reduced for specific governmental programs or objectives, several of which are defined in terms of assistance to persons with some kind of economic disadvantage. In the Clinton-Bush contest, as in each of the presidential elections in the 1980s, this topic was very visible in the campaign, and answers to questions about "spending" in particular problem areas were all strongly related to the vote. Respondents who preferred an increase in federal spending to assist poor or disadvantaged citizens were *much* more likely to vote for Bill Clinton—or against George Bush—than were those who preferred a reduction in those areas. This bivariate tendency was evident for all of the eight relevant NES questions in which respondents were asked if they would prefer more, the same, or less federal spending on programs that were at least implicitly defined in terms of assistance to persons with some kind of economic disadvantage.[4]

In 1992, on the basis of multivariate analyses that also included economic conditions, respondents' preferences concerning other current issues, general policy-related predispositions, partisan identification, and social or economic characteristics, the two NES questions which asked about spending on "food stamps" and "the poor" captured most of the statistical connection between spending preferences and the vote. No other question about governmental assistance that could be interpreted in terms of economic disadvantage exhibited a similarly significant relationship with the vote (for Clinton or Bush) when our policy-related variables in other areas, as well as the above two items concerning the disadvantaged, were held constant.

Furthermore . . . that negative result, in which questions about government spending were *not* independently related to the vote choice, includes *all* of eight additional questions about the preferred level of federal spending, as well as the three traditional NES issue questions concerning (1) the government's responsibility for health insurance, (2) the current level of "services and spending," and (3) the familiar question on maintaining a "good job and standard of living." There is, therefore, a surprisingly long list of conflicts related to social welfare policies that, when considered one by one, did not pass even our relatively lenient standard of probable statistical significance (requiring $p < .1$ for distinguishing between Bush and Clinton voters). The list not only includes many topics that had been part of past NES surveys, but also some that NES has considered part of the "core" questions in that series.

For these many reasons, our 1992 analysis of social welfare issues, long a staple of liberal Democratic/conservative Republican disagreements, is based on the simple average of two trichotomous variables concerning government expenditures for food stamps and aid to the poor, labeled as a summary index of policy preferences concerning federal assistance to the disadvantaged.

Table 12-2 presents our standard sequence of descriptive statistics for the relationship between this summary measure and vote choice. In light of the 1994 Republican "contract with America" it is interesting to note that among voters with the clearest sentiments for and against aid to the disadvantaged, those favoring aid outnumbered those opposing aid by a margin of 3 to 1. As with the other explanatory variables discussed in previous chapters [of Miller and Shanks 1996], Row 4 of Table 12-2, with an effect coefficient of .72, provides a convenient way of summarizing the overall strength of this variable's bivariate relationship with the vote. Analysts may disagree, however, concerning the most appropriate set of variables to include or control for in assessing the impact of policy preferences.

At the outset, the original bivariate coefficient linking attitudes toward aid to the disadvantaged and the vote is reduced to .53 (from .72 in Row 4 of Table 12-2) by the inclusion of controls for social or economic characteristics (in Row 5). That coefficient, in turn, is reduced even more, to .31 (in Row 6), when we take account of party identification. The strength of the effect coefficient is further reduced to only .14 after the introduction of additional controls for all of our policy-related predispositions (in Row 9), and to .12 with controls on other policy preferences and conditions (Row 11). Thus, most of the original bivariate coefficient, .60/.72, appears to be confounded in the sense that the policy preferences we are analyzing share a variety of common social, partisan, and policy-related predispositional antecedents with the vote.

The sharp reduction in the apparent effect of policy preferences on aid to the disadvantaged when we control for these three sets of long-term variables is more generally noteworthy. The size of that reduction is similar to the results for

Table 12-2   Policy Preferences Concerning the Disadvantaged

1. Average Vote for Most Liberal Preference (More Spending on Both Questions, $N = 176$)	.74[a]
2. Average Vote for Most Conservative Preferences (Less Spending on Both Questions, $N = 57$)	−.50
3. Difference in Average Vote: Most Liberal Minus Most Conservative	1.24
4. Bivariate Unstandardized Regression Coefficient (Policy Preference Index Scored from −1 to +1)	.72
5. Coefficient from Multiple Regression with Social and Economic Characteristics Held Constant	.53
6. With Party Identification (Party ID) also Held Constant	.31
7. With Specific Policy-Related Predispositions (But NOT Party ID) Also Held Constant	.22
8. With Liberal vs. Conservative Self-Designation Also Held Constant	.19
9. With Party ID AND All Policy-Related Predispositions Also Held Constant	.14
10. With Preferences on All Other Policy Issues Also Held Constant	.13
11. With Perceptions of Current Personal and National Conditions Also Held Constant	.12[b]
12. With Retrospective Evaluations of the Current President Also Held Constant	(.05)
13. With Evaluations of the Candidates' Personal Qualities Also Held Constant	(.06)
14. With Prospective Evaluations of Candidates and Parties Also Held Constant	(.04)

Note: Coefficients appear in parentheses if the estimated p value is > .1.

[a]The number of cases associated with extreme positions on these and similar measures simply indicate the base on which extreme scores were calculated. Note that the number of cases is unweighted; all other results are weighted.

[b]Indicates estimate of the "apparent total effect" discussed in the text.

other explanatory variables defined by policy conflicts. The explanatory variables which represent long-term influences predating the election campaign consistently account for a very large portion of the simple bivariate relationship between each set of current policy preferences and the vote.

Next we should note that it is also generally true that adding the control for preferences pertaining to *other* policy conflicts has little impact on the apparent effect estimates for any of the policy areas that have a significant apparent total effect, that is, for the five topics named earlier. This is not the case for many of the policies that do not meet our threshold of a statistically significant independent effect on the vote. Many of the campaign topics that fall below our rather low threshold for inclusion in our topic-by-topic analysis fail to reflect statistically significant independent effects with the vote because they are placed in competition with other variables that are defined in terms of current policy conflicts. Such variables may in some sense be important when considered apart from other policies in that their relationship to the vote cannot be accounted for by long-term factors. However, it turns out that they are so interrelated with each other, as well as with other policy questions, that controlling for the others eliminates the coefficient that would represent statistical independence for the "failed" items. This pattern not only limits the size of the apparent effect on the vote for specific policy variables, but it compounds the problem of anticipating the extent to which an entire set of policy-related variables may influence the vote. . . .

A final note before proceeding with our analyses of other specific policy conflicts in 1992: In the early stages of the analysis we had come to believe that the causal relationships between current policy preferences and perceptions of "current conditions" were ambiguous or indeterminate. Prior to completing our analysis we had no way of knowing how much current policy preferences were shaped by perceptions of current conditions—or vice versa. For that reason, the perceptions of current conditions are included in the same causal stage in our model as current policy preferences. Row 11 of Table 12-2 presents the apparent impact of policy preferences concerning the disadvantaged, .12, after we control for those conditions, as well as other policy preferences and all prior variables. This is the coefficient that we have designated as the "apparent total effect" of policy preferences in this area. A by-product of our alternative routes to explaining or understanding is the discovery that "perceptions of conditions" and "policy preferences" do not appear to be strongly intercorrelated and, therefore, the question of their causal location relative to each other is not one with major empirical consequences.

Furthermore, most of the apparent effect of policy preferences concerning the disadvantaged noted in Table 12-2 appears to have been mediated by evaluations of George Bush as president, rather than by any impressions of Bill Clinton. The apparent effect of this policy conflict over government aid to the disadvantaged is reduced to an insignificant value (.05) in Row 12 of the table when we also control for evaluations of the president—and it remains insignificant when we also control for other evaluations of the candidates and parties. It would appear that the primary mechanism by which policy preferences in this area influenced the 1992 vote involved their impact on voters' overall assessments of President Bush, rather than their comparison of alternatives offered by Clinton and Bush. . . .

Homosexuals in the Military

During the 1992 campaign, Bill Clinton and the Republican Party adopted visible and contrasting positions concerning the role of homosexuals in American society. The Republican convention and platform emphasized the importance of the "traditional" family in a fashion which suggested clear opposition to homosexual life-styles as well as heterosexual promiscuity. In contrast, the Democratic ticket was visibly supported by organizations that advocated gay and lesbian rights, and candidate Clinton took a clear position against the continuing ban on military service by homosexuals.

Table 12-3   Policy Preferences Concerning Homosexuals in the Military

1. Average Vote for Strongly in Favor ($N = 387$)	.61[a]
2. Average Vote for Strongly Opposed ($N = 366$)	$-.28$
3. Difference in Average Vote: Liberal Minus Conservative	.89
4. Bivariate Unstandardized Regression Coefficient (Policy Preference Index Scored from -1 to $+1$)	.42
5. Coefficient from Multiple Regression with Social and Economic Characteristics Held Constant	.36
6. With Party Identification (Party ID) also Held Constant	.25
7. With Specific Policy-Related Predispositions (But NOT Party ID) Also Held Constant	.15
8. With Liberal vs. Conservative Self-Designation Also Held Constant	.15
9. With Party ID AND All Policy-Related Predispositions Also Held Constant	.13
10. With Preferences on All Other Policy Issues Also Held Constant	.12
11. With Perceptions of Current Personal and National Conditions Also Held Constant	.12[b]
12. With Retrospective Evaluations of the Current President Also Held Constant	(.08)
13. With Evaluations of the Candidates' Personal Qualities Also Held Constant	(.08)
14. With Prospective Evaluations of Candidates and Parties Also Held Constant	(.05)

Note: Coefficients appear in parentheses if the estimated p value is > .1.

[a]The number of cases associated with extreme positions on these and similar measures simply indicate the base on which extreme scores were calculated. Note that the number of cases is unweighted; all other results are weighted.

[b]Indicates estimate of the "apparent total effect" discussed in the text.

Issues related to sexual orientation had clearly been developing for several years; NES Pilot Surveys have explored a variety of alternative policy-related questions concerning homosexuals. The 1992 NES interview schedule included three policy-related questions concerning laws against anti-gay discrimination, military service by homosexuals, and adoption of children by homosexual couples. Responses to each of these questions exhibited some relationship to voters' choices between Clinton and Bush.[5]

As in the preceding analyses of policy-related preferences . . . we examined the relationships between each of these questions about homosexuals and the vote in order to identify specific policy conflicts which exhibited an independent relevance for the vote after we controlled for other policy preferences and all of the variables from earlier stages in our model. Of those three items, *only* the question about support of or opposition to military service by homosexuals exhibited a clear and significant independent relationship to the vote, as shown in Table 12-3. Neither of the other two questions provided any significant explanatory power once other variables in the same causal stage or preceding stages were taken into account.

We should add, however, that our sequence of analyses suggests that the electoral relevance of potential policies toward homosexuals in 1992 may have been based on the repeated (and more general) Republican emphasis on the "traditional family" rather than Bill Clinton's specific advocacy of "gays in the military.". . .

The Logic of Non-Significant Policy-Related Effects: The Case of Abortion

. . . Table 12-4 presents our standard sequence of descriptive statistics for the relationship between voters' policy preferences concerning abortion and their choice between Bush and Clinton. Because of the considerable emphasis on that topic during the 1992 campaign, we present the entire sequence of estimates for abortion, even though the apparent total effect for that variable ultimately turns out to be nonsignificant. We do so because that sequence may clarify the more general statistical competition among other potential explanatory variables. The ongoing conflict over federal policy concerning abortion did not exert an independent impact on the vote in the same sense that policy issues on other topics did, but it may be helpful to emphasize the *rationale* for its omission from the final set of issues with apparent significant effects on the vote.

Rows 1 and 2 of Table 12-4 document the extent to which voters who thought that abortion should "always" be permitted made quite different choices between Clinton and Bush than those who thought it should "never" be permitted. The much more numerous set of voters with the most liberal position concerning abortion were more loyal to Bill Clinton, with a vote division of $+.47$, than the much smaller group against abortion in all circumstances were in their support of George Bush, with a vote division of $-.15$. As indicated in Row 4, the bivariate regression coefficient is quite strong (.40) for the relationship between vote choice and a trichotomous measure of abortion-related preferences, in which all "other" responses are grouped into the middle category. That coefficient is only moderately reduced by controlling for religion and all other social or economic characteristics (to .34 in Row 5). Most of the electoral "connection" is nevertheless removed when we control for voters' other policy-related preferences, including their general views concerning morality and homosexuality (down to .06 in Row 10; see Welch et al. 1995). Furthermore, given the statistical relationships among our full set of policy-related preferences, the coefficient is close to failing to meet our threshold for statistical significance at that point. As a consequence, the introduction of fairly innocuous additional controls for "current conditions" drops the coefficient to a nonsignificant value (.04) in Row 11.

In this sense, policy preferences concerning abortion came quite close to being included in our final explanatory model for 1992 even though the independent influence of those preferences would have been fairly small. As in other domains or explanatory themes in our analysis, the electoral role of variables with fairly small effects may be particularly difficult to distinguish from those of

Table 12-4 Policy Preferences Concerning Abortion

1. Average Vote for Those Who Prefer "Always Permitted" ($N = 558$)	.47[a]
2. Average Vote for Those Who Prefer "Never Permitted" ($N = 107$)	−.15
3. Difference in Average Vote: Always Minus Never	.62
4. Bivariate Unstandardized Regression Coefficient (Policy Preference Index Scored from −1 to +1)	.40
5. Coefficient from Multiple Regression with Social and Economic Characteristics Held Constant	.34
6. With Party Identification (Party ID) also Held Constant	.21
7. With Specific Policy-Related Predispositions (But NOT Party ID) Also Held Constant	.13
8. With Liberal vs. Conservative Self-Designation Also Held Constant	.08
9. With Party ID AND All Policy-Related Predispositions Also Held Constant	.07
10. With Preferences on All Other Policy Issues Also Held Constant	.06
11. With Perceptions of Current Personal and National Conditions Also Held Constant	(.04)[b]
12. With Retrospective Evaluations of the Current President Also Held Constant	(.01)
13. With Evaluations of the Candidates' Personal Qualities Also Held Constant	(.00)
14. With Prospective Evaluations of Candidates and Parties Also Held Constant	(−.01)

Note: Coefficients appear in parentheses if the estimated p value is > .1.

[a]The number of cases associated with extreme positions on these and similar measures simply indicate the base on which extreme scores were calculated. Note that the number of cases is unweighted; all other results are weighted.

[b]Indicates estimate of the "apparent total effect" discussed in the text.

closely related topics. In this case, it is difficult to ignore the strong connection between policy preferences concerning abortion per se and other attitudes toward sexuality and morality, but we do believe that the latter take causal precedence over the differences in policy preferences on abortion per se. . . .

The Importance of Specific Variables and General Themes in 1988 and 1992: Individual Differences and Aggregate Results

To this point, our statistical analyses of electoral decisions have focused on the estimation and interpretation of "apparent effects," based on the relationships between specific explanatory variables and vote choice. Our discussions of those results have occasionally referred to the relative "importance" of different types of explanations for the 1992 election, but all such statements have referred to the size of total effect coefficients for specific explanatory variables. We now shift both the rationale and the logic for evaluating and comparing the importance of different electoral explanations. . . . We begin by distinguishing between two contrasting ways in which some of our individual variables may have played a more important role than others in a given election context. The first is based on their contribution to the *aggregate results* of that election; the second is based on their role in producing *individual differences* in voters' choices in the same election. After presenting both sets of results for specific explanatory variables, we will apply the same criteria to evaluate the importance of the eight general themes that we have used to classify all of the explanatory variables in our model.[6] . . .

The Importance of Explanatory Themes in Producing the Aggregate Results

. . . [W]e can produce combined estimates for the contributions by all the variables in the same explanatory theme by simply summing their signed individual contributions. Table 12-5 presents the simple sums of the apparent (positive or negative) contributions to Bill Clinton's plurality for all of the specific variables in each of our explanatory themes. Some conclusions from this table were already evident in our previous discussion of contributions for specific variables, but we offer the following highlights concerning the attitudinal sources or origins for Bill Clinton's victory in 1992.

As in all other presidential elections since World War II, more 1992 voters reported a continuing identification with the Democratic Party than with the Republicans. That Democratic advantage made a substantial contribution, .07, to Bill Clinton's margin of victory, +.17, based on predispositions that were well in place before the 1992 campaign began. Given changes in the composition of the electorate, as well as occasional changes in party identification by individual voters, the size of that contribution can vary between elections. In 1964, for example, it was doubtless considerably larger than in 1992. This estimate for 1992, however, is similar to that for several recent elections.

Policy-related predispositions provided a substantial net advantage for George Bush, or a negative contribution to the Bill Clinton plurality, of −.05. This contribution offset much of Clinton's advantage in long-term partisan identification. That continued contribution represents a sum of offsetting positive and negative combinations for specific predispositions, . . . each of which presumably was already in place before the election and, when activated by the 1992 campaign, appears to have produced little visible net advantage for one candidate or the other. In these respects, the preelection playing field was close to level or even.

Similarly, voters' preferences on current policy issues appear to have provided no net advantage for either Clinton or Bush. The aggregate consequences for issues where liberal preferences outnumbered conservative views . . . were almost exactly offset by the influences of preferences in policy areas where the distributions of those preferences provided some advantage for Bush. Some aspects of these results, of course, may be an accidental consequence of the NES selection of policy questions. In our view, however, no other issue or set of issues

Table 12-5   Apparent Importance of General Explanatory Themes in 1992 Based on Contributions to the Aggregate Results

(Aggregate Results = Average Vote = + .174)

Name of Explanatory Theme	Transmission: Sum of Contributions Based on All of Each Variable	Source or Origin: Sum of Contributions Based on Unique Parts of Variables
Partisan Identification	.07	.07
Policy-Related Predispositions	−.05	−.05
Current Policy Preferences	.00	.01
Perceptions of Current Conditions	.11	.10
Retrospective Performance Evaluations	.08	−.04
Evaluations of Personal Qualities	.03	.01
Prospective Performance Evaluations	.16	.03

that might have decisively tipped the balance to favor one side or the other comes to mind. All of the most likely possibilities for such an influence have been examined and either failed to meet our modest threshold for statistical significance or have already been included in arriving at the above conclusion.

. . . Voters' perceptions of the economy appear to have made a decisive contribution, .10 in the second column of Table 17.2 [of Miller and Shanks], to Bill Clinton's margin of victory in 1992. That contribution was supplemented by extremely small pro-Democratic contributions associated with other conditions, so that the combined (rounded) contribution of all the "current conditions" in the 1992 NES questionnaire was still .10. That substantial contribution, and the negligible contribution of preferences on current policy issues, were not appreciably modified by removing those portions of policy preferences and perceptions of conditions that can be attributed to partisan and policy-related predispositions.

As shown in the first column in Table 12-5, retrospective evaluations of George Bush's performance as president also appear to have made a substantial contribution to Bill Clinton's victory, +.08. As noted in our discussion of specific variables, however, *all* of that pro-Democratic contribution disappears when we remove the impact of prior variables from the averages for these variables. Indeed, the net contribution of voters' evaluations in this area, −.04, clearly suggests a Bush advantage when we focus on the components of those evaluations that cannot be attributed to the state of the economy and other variables that we have assigned to prior stages in our model. In areas other than the economy, such as foreign affairs and the deficit, voters' evaluations of George Bush as president were more positive than we would have predicted given their partisan identifications, policy-related preferences, and perceptions of current conditions.

Evaluations of the personal qualities of the candidates appear to have made only a modest net contribution to Clinton's plurality, +.03. This result is based on pro-Clinton assessments concerning empathy and effectiveness that were partially offset by negative contributions concerning his integrity. When we remove contributions that may have been transmitted by these evaluations but have already been attributed to prior variables, however, the remaining contribution that should apparently be attributed to the unique content of these personal qualities is close to invisible, +.01. In our view, the personal qualities of the candidates did "make a difference" in the 1992 campaign, but their net contributions were not large, and they involved offsetting evaluations. When discussing the impact of candidates' personal qualities on the outcome of the election . . . cautionary notes should be kept in mind, including the observation that personal appearances and other occasions that may influence impressions of candidates' personal qualities are also occasions for activating other sentiments concerning partisan and policy-related preferences.

Finally, voters' prospective evaluations of the candidates' and parties' future performance appeared to *transmit* major contributions to Clinton's victory, +.16. However, most of that apparent contribution is based on the influence of prior variables whose impact on the vote was merely transmitted through prospective evaluations of the candidates and parties. The only substantial contribution that remains after we remove the contributions we have already attributed to prior variables concerns health care. We are not surprised at this particular remaining contribution associated with prospective performance, for health care is not "covered" by any of our explanatory variables in earlier stages concerning policy-related preferences, current conditions, *or* presidential performance. We are not sure that this aggregate contribution of health care is correctly allotted to the parties instead of the candidates, or to prospective instead of retrospective evaluations, but we are confident that voters' opinions on that topic made some net contribution to Clinton's 1992 plurality.

The Importance of General Themes in Explaining Individual Differences

In mild contrast to the substantial differences among our explanatory themes in their contributions to the aggregate results, each of our general explanatory themes appears to have played a visible role in "producing" the differences between individual voters in their choice for president in 1992. Table 12-6 presents standardized regression coefficients for composite variables for each of our explanatory themes related to individual vote choice. Each of these variables was created as a partial predicted score from the same regression analyses reported in Table 17.5 [of Miller and Shanks], so that each variable represents the combined effects of all of the variables in that explanatory theme. Column 1 presents the standardized regression coefficient for the combined effects of all of those variables, while Column 2 presents the standardized coefficient for the

Table 12-6 Apparent Importance of General Explanatory Themes in 1992 for the Explanation of Individual Differences in Vote Choice

Name of Explanatory Theme	Transmission: Standardized Coefficient for Composite Variable Based on All of Each Variable	Source or Origin: Standardized Coefficient for Composite Variable Based on Unique Parts of Each Variable
Partisan Identification	.40	.40
Policy-Related Predispositions	.41	.41
Current Policy Preferences	.20	.14
Perceptions of Current Conditions	.12	.11
Retrospective Performance Evaluations	.47	.30
Evaluations of Personal Qualities	.19	.11
Prospective Performance Evaluations	.41	.20

combination of residual portions of those variables—after we have removed the influence of variables in prior stages.

As Table 12-6 illustrates, it appears that voters' policy-related predispositions, .41, were just as important as partisan identifications, .40, in producing individual differences in vote choice. We have anticipated this possibility in several previous chapters [of Miller and Shanks 1996], and we believe it is an important characteristic of the 1992 election—as well as other recent elections. Voters' policy preferences on current issues provided some additional explanatory power, .20, as did perceptions of current conditions, .12, and those estimates are only moderately reduced to .14 and .11 when we remove the variability in those variables that can be attributed to factors in prior stages.

Even though our model places perceptions of current conditions before presidential performance evaluations, thereby giving the former "credit" for what may be a joint influence on the vote, evaluations of Bush's performance as president loomed much larger than current conditions as a unique source of differences between voters in their choices for president. In terms of transmitting influence, evaluation of the president's performance, .47, clearly surpassed our other explanatory themes. As a *unique* source of individual decisions, such evaluations were still one of the most important themes. This seems appropriate to an election in which an incumbent president is running for reelection against an opponent who was previously largely an unknown quantity in national politics. Finally, the combined significance of prospective performance evaluations is, not surprisingly, cut in half once we remove the variability in those variables that can be attributed to prior stages.

The relatively limited apparent importance of the candidates' personal qualities calls for some additional comment. In an election in which the personal character of one candidate was given so much attention by the media, it seems surprising that the personal qualities of the candidates ranked at the bottom of our list of explanatory themes in terms of this criterion for electoral relevance. This result, of course, is partially due to our allocation of so much explanatory credit to variables that we have assigned to prior stages.

Furthermore, the focus on personal qualities in our analysis is more narrow than the range of content involved in Republican attacks on Clinton's personal characteristics. Nevertheless, despite NES efforts to provide a comprehensive assessment of the relevant personal traits of presidential candidates, differences between voters in their 1992 choices for president did not appear to be heavily based on personal qualities of the candidates.

In our view, the entries in the second column of Table 12-6 . . . describe the 1992 election in terms of what was really contested, or what was at stake in the minds of the voters. The explanatory variables or themes with the largest values identify those topics which provided the sources of *differences between voters* in their choices for president. These estimates for the relative importance of specific policy-related conflicts clarify the kinds of disagreements that appear to have been activated in shaping voters' choices. Similarly, our estimates concerning this kind of importance for current conditions and performance identify those areas where voters' choices appear to have been shaped by their differential perceptions of governmental results.

If our estimates concerning the importance of specific factors with respect to individual differences identify the political topics that constituted the *content* of a given election, our assessments concerning contributions to the winner's plurality clarify the factors that had the biggest impact on the aggregate *outcome* of the election. Social scientists are intensely interested in understanding the sources of inter-individual variability in electoral choice. Politicians, journalists, and historians, on the other hand, may be somewhat curious about the sources of that variability, but they are usually much more interested in identifying factors which helped or hurt the two candidates — and which "added up" to produce the winning candidate's margin of victory. Answers to the first of those questions (concerning individual differences) must *not* be confused with answers to the second (concerning the aggregate result). . . .

Notes

1. As emphasized repeatedly in this chapter, in assigning both partisan and policy-related predispositions to the same (second) stage in our model, we make no assumption about the degree to which policy-related predispositions may have played some role in the evolution of voters' partisan identifications nor the impact of partisan identifications on policy-related predispositions.
2. See Shanks and Miller (1991) for estimates of apparent effects of policy-related predispositions on the vote that include the indirect effects of such predispositions "through" voters' partisan identifications, based on the provisional (or hypothetical)

assumption that such predispositions are causally prior. See Shanks and Miller (1990) for an analysis that explores the consequences of designating ideological positions as causally prior to partisan identification.

3. Rows 6 and 9 of Table 12-1 are not relevant in assessing the impact of party identification, but are maintained to simplify comparisons across the many tables that are presented in this format.

4. This battery of questions was introduced in the following fashion: "If you had your say in making up the federal budget this year, for which of the following programs would you like to see spending *increased* and for which would you like to see spending *decreased*?" The eight items that concerned general assistance to the disadvantaged were "food stamps," "welfare programs," "financial aid to college students," "solving the problems of the homeless," "child care," "governmental assistance to the unemployed," "poor people," and "aid to big cities."

5. The item used in this area was the following. H8: "Do you think homosexuals should be allowed to serve in the United States armed forces or don't you think so?" A following question then asked if the respondent felt "strongly" or "not strongly" about that preference.

6. For earlier discussions of this fundamental distinction see Achen (1982, 68–77) and Shanks and Miller (1990).

13. The Responsive Voter: Campaign Information and the Dynamics of Candidate Evaluation

Milton Lodge and Marco R. Steenbergen, with Shawn Brau

How much of what kinds of campaign information citizens can recollect about parties, candidates, and issues at the time a decision is called for is the keystone of virtually all contemporary models of individual political behavior and the cornerstone as well for our assessment of the competence of the democratic citizen. The underlying assumption throughout the literature of individual polit-ical behavior is that citizens have a storehouse of political information they can draw on to inform their political behavior, whether in reply to survey questions, in political conversations, or in the voting booth.

In the study of electoral behavior, for example, our very best models of issue voting treat candidate evaluations as a function of the respondent's recall of self and candidate proximities on the issue scales (Enelow and Hinich 1984), while our discipline's most predictive model (arguably, Kelley and Mirer's [1974] "sim-ple act of voting") shows a strong correlation of candidate evaluation with the voter's net recollection of likes and dislikes. Our models of political behavior out-side the polling booth are often memory-based, too (see Price and Zaller 1993), as are our normative expectations about the scope and depth of political knowl-edge that the democratic citizen can and should bring to mind to act purpose-fully (see Barber 1973; Berelson 1952; Berelson, Lazarsfeld, and McPhee 1954; Kessel 1988; Neuman 1986; E. Smith 1989; Weissberg 1974; also see Hanson and Marcus 1993).

All well and good were it not for a most troublesome incongruity—to wit, citizens do not measure up to model specifications. Fifty years of survey data por-tray a rather bleak picture of the American citizen as one who is not nearly as aware as our models suppose and less informed than normative theories proscribe (see Hanson and Marcus 1993; Kinder and Sears 1985). More often than not, when voters are asked on election day about parties, candidates, and issues they are found to be ill informed—the majority of respondents unable, for example, to cite more than two or three likes or dislikes to the National Election Studies (NES) open-ended questions and probes (see E. Smith 1989). And for many of these "good" citizens their responses are, to put it kindly, "diffuse" (Gant and Davis 1984).

That citizens often cannot remember many details of election campaigns is not being contested here, as the evidence is overwhelming. However, we chal-lenge the longstanding assumption that the citizen's failure to recall campaign

Source: American Political Science Review 89, 2 (June 1995): 309–326.

events is necessarily or even primarily a function of political inattentiveness, political ignorance, or (worse yet) irrationality. In contrast to conventional wisdom, we do not interpret the failure of J.Q. Public to recollect basic political facts (Delli Carpini and Keeter 1991; Erskine 1963), or recognize ideological language (Converse 1964), or recall a candidate's characteristics (Abramowitz 1975), or even remember candidate names (Neuman 1986) as a sure sign of an uninformed citizenry acting "in the dark." Rather, we propose here and will test empirically a "bounded rationality" model of candidate evaluation and vote choice that turns the memory-based assumption on its head in arguing that citizens can be (and in fact typically are) responsive to campaign information—their overall evaluations reflecting their assessment of all the information they are exposed to—but are unable, for good reasons, to recollect accurately the considerations that entered into their evaluations.

Recall and the Enigma of the Informed Voter

We propose and find empirical support for a solution to two paradoxes that plague contemporary studies of electoral behavior: (1) the paradox of the informed voter, whereby voters (in the aggregate) oftentimes appear to be choosing the "right" candidate and supporting the "correct" issue stands but apparently without the conceptual or factual wherewithal to make such informed judgments (Page and Shapiro 1992), and (2) the paradoxical discrepancy between survey and experimental research findings, where we typically find in survey research a strong, positive correlation between the mix of pros and cons in memory and the direction and strength of evaluation (Kelley 1983) but can rarely find a direct memory-to-judgment link under experimental conditions (Lodge, McGraw, and Stroh 1989).

Consider two studies that we think point us in the right direction. The first, an experiment by Watts and McGuire (1964), looked at people's recollection of the arguments of a persuasive message over a six-week period. Watts and McGuire found (as do most replications; see Anderson and Hubert 1963; Hastie and Park 1986) *no* systematic effect of recall on the persistence of induced opinion change. Apparently, messages do not lose their effect on people's opinions once the content of the messages is forgotten. Thus it is that voters may be strongly affected by campaign information without such responsiveness being captured in their recollections. This finding is commonplace under laboratory conditions where exposure to the content of messages is known and the researcher can directly compare what information subjects are actually exposed to and what they can later recall (Hastie and Pennington 1989; Lichtenstein and Srull 1987).

Consider next Graber's conclusion to her longitudinal study of the 1976 presidential campaign that "the fact that so little specific information can be recalled from a [news] story does not mean that no learning has taken place. The information base from which conclusions are drawn may be forgotten, while the conclusions are still retained. This seems to happen routinely. Voting choices, for instance, often match approval of a candidate's positions even when voters cannot recall the candidate's positions or the specifics of the policy. In such cases, media facts apparently have been converted into politically significant feelings and attitudes and the facts themselves forgotten" (Graber 1984, 73). Again, campaign messages and events can exert an influence on voters' attitudes independently of their recall of the considerations that entered into their judgments, apparently long after the triggering campaign events have been forgotten.

The issue, then, is not how many campaign events or candidate positions voters can recall accurately at the time they are called on to express a belief or preference but, instead, how *responsive* the citizens' overall evaluation and vote choice are to the political information they considered throughout the campaign. More specifically, how much of what kinds of campaign information do citizens integrate into their summary assessments of candidates and how well does their overall assessment of the candidates reflect their evaluation of all the campaign information they attended to?

As every standard text in cognitive psychology points out (Eysenck and Keane 1990; Lachman, Lachman, and Butterfield 1979), a basic limitation of human information processing is the fallibility of memory: people forget . . . a lot. Memory fades over time and while this process may be faster for some people than others and for some types of information than for others, the inevitable outcome is that people's recollections decrease in number and get fuzzier over time. Thus it may well be that the citizen's inability to recall basic political facts reflects limitations of the human mind rather than unsophistication of the democratic citizen. Our criticism, then, is not just directed against memory-based models of the vote choice but, more broadly, challenges the memory-based assumption underlying contemporary analyses of political behavior in general and, still more broadly, the negative normative conclusions routinely drawn from the citizenry's failure to recall campaign events.

How can information exert an enduring influence on people's opinions despite their inability to retrieve these considerations from memory? One suggestion is that the message-judgment relationship is mediated by a mechanism other than recall. Indeed, Graber (1984) hints at some such process when she claims that voters draw conclusions from campaign information while forgetting its contents. In essence, what she describes is what has come to be called "the on-line model of information processing," which traces its origins to social psychology (Anderson 1991; Hastie and Park 1986; Hastie and Pennington 1989) and has recently been extended to the domain of political impression formation (Lodge, McGraw, and Stroh 1989; Mackie and Anuncion 1990).

A Model of Voter Responsiveness

A schematic depiction of our expectations for an on-line (OL) model of the responsive voter is presented in Figure 13-1. According to this model (see Lodge

Figure 13-1 On-Line Candidate Evaluation Model

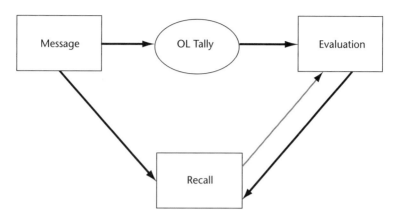

and Stroh 1993), when one's goal is to form an overall impression of some person, place, or thing, most people most of the time appear to act as bounded rationalists in simplifying the judgmental process by drawing politically relevant conclusions from the information at the very moment they encounter it and then and there, when the message is before their eyes, so to speak, spontaneously culling the affective value from each specific candidate message, and immediately integrating these assessments into a "running tally" that holds the individual's summary evaluation of the candidate (as depicted by the solid arrow in Figure 13-1 from Candidate Message to OL Tally). This OL tally, sometimes called an "affect-integrator," is then immediately stored in long-term memory and the considerations that contributed to the evaluation are quickly forgotten (hence the weak—grey—path from Recall to Evaluation). Then, later, when called on to make a judgment—to a pollster or in the voting booth—it is this summary impression, not recollections of the original campaign information, that comes to mind to guide the decision (as anticipated in Figure 13-1 by the strong, direct connection from OL Tally to Evaluation). From this OL perspective, "responsive voters" will decrease their general evaluation of a candidate when confronted with negative information and increase their candidate evaluations when made aware of information that they judge to be positive.[1]

Essentially, then, the OL model posits a strong indirect effect of attention to campaign messages on judgment, mediated by the OL Tally. Moreover, there is not necessarily a strong relationship between the pros and cons that actually enter into the evaluation at the time of exposure and one's recollections of these considerations. The forgetting of the facts—long the bane of memory-based models—is of little consequence to the OL model, since the affective value of campaign messages has already been integrated into the evaluation and vote decision. Thus it is that voters can oftentimes tell you how much they like one candidate or another but not be able to tell you many of their reasons why. Or else (this being the reason, we think, for the strong correlation between recall and evaluation in most surveys like the NES), having forgotten many of the considerations that entered into their overall evaluation, when called on to report the *whys* and *wherefores* for their evaluation, respondents are prone to search memory for supporting "evidence" and dredge up commonsensical rationalizations for their preferences (as suggested by the solid arrow from Evaluation to Recall in Figure 13-1; see Brody and Page 1972; Kunda 1990; Lau 1982; Nisbett and Ross 1980; Rahn, Krosnick, and Breuning 1994; Wilson and Schooler 1991). From this perspective, what citizens are likely to recall about the candidates is their global affective assessment of them, not the specific considerations that actually entered into the evaluation. At best, the citizen's recollections will represent a biased sampling of the actual causal determinants of the candidate evaluation (Anderson and Hubert 1963). At worst (this, we think, being a plausible explanation for marked differences between survey and experimental findings), the correlation between memory and judgment is the result of reversed causality, the causal arrow often going from evaluation to memory.

If the OL model is correct, citizens can be attentive and still not recall much if any campaign information. This model of political information processing has serious implications for how we view the connection between campaign events and political judgment. Inherent in the logic of on-line information processing is a radically different notion of what an informed citizenry means. Rather than measuring the citizen by what he or she can recall from the campaign, as memory-based models tend to do (see Kessel 1988), we ask the normatively more interesting question whether citizens actually incorporate campaign information in political judgment and choice. If, on attending to campaign stimuli, citizens were to first establish and thereafter update their OL tally in response to new information and finally bring this summary evaluation to bear on political judgments, we would claim that the citizens are responsive to and informed by campaign information.[2] On the other hand (this being the alternative hypothesis to be tested in this study), if the citizen's political judgments were found to be but tangentially related to the campaign information he or she was exposed to, then we too would be forced to say that citizens are uninformed.

Experimental Design and Procedure

This study was designed to provide direct comparisons of the OL versus memory-based models of candidate evaluation *over time,* so that a *dynamic* picture of the candidate evaluation process may be obtained. The study addresses two critical questions: (1) Does the relationship typically go from *message to recall memory to evaluation* (as memory-based models suggest), or is the candidate evaluation process more aptly represented by the path from *message (to OL tally) to evaluation?* and (2) How strongly are message and evaluation related, that is, *how responsive are citizens to campaign information?*

Any attempt to disentangle the impact of memory on political judgment must necessarily measure the actual content of candidate messages and look at recall over the more realistic time spans of electoral campaigns. In our view, past research, both experimental and survey, has generally succeeded in satisfying one of these requirements but not both. The strength of the experimental approach is that it allows us to isolate memory effects by controlling the content of messages to which subjects are exposed, thereby getting a direct test of the message-judgment relationship. Unfortunately, an all-too-typical shortcoming of this approach—ours among them (Lodge, McGraw, and Stroh 1989)—has been to look at the relationship between message and recall after only short, single-session time intervals on the order of five or ten minutes, rather than the more relevant day-, week-, and month-long time spans of campaigns. Conversely, in survey research longer time delays are more common (with most NES data based on postelection interviews), but here there is no way to determine what information citizens were actually exposed to (Price and Zaller 1990). This forces researchers to rely on one or another self-reported measure of attention to campaign messages and leaves us with no measure of the order, timing, content, or complexity of the messages. As a result, it is impossible to obtain an accurate estimate of the impact of memory on political judgment.

In the present study we combine the strict control over exposure to campaign messages available to experimenters with the realistic time spans found in surveys by introducing time delays of 1 to 31 days in a $t_1 \times t_2$ design to test the memory-judgment relationship over time. In addition, we obtained a finer-grained analysis of the message-judgment and memory-judgment relationships by considering two factors that are known to influence their size. First, we manipulated the partisan consistency of the candidate profiles that we presented to our subjects, so as to examine our "responsive voter" model when a candidate is somewhat at odds with one's partisan expectations. Second, for half the subjects, we set up a condition in which we tested the OL model against an idealized memory-based model by encouraging subjects to think more deeply about the candidates and their policy positions, hereby mimicking a basic condition of rational voter models.

Sample

A nonrandom sample of 356 nonstudent adults from Long Island, New York, was interviewed by trained college students in the spring of 1991. Fifty percent of the subjects were male, 92 percent white, and 71 percent were college graduates or had had some college. The sample-wide median income was $25,000. More pertinent for our analyses, the sample was about equally split in terms of their partisan affiliation, with 27 percent of the subjects reporting identification with the Republican Party, 33 percent with the Democratic Party, and the remainder calling themselves Independents or reporting no party affiliation.

Experimental Stages

The experiment consisted of three core stages. First, subjects completed a self-administered questionnaire under supervision of our interviewers. The questionnaire asked subjects to evaluate information that would show up in the candidate messages that the subjects read later in this stage of the experiment. Second, a variable $t_1 \times t_2$ delay of 1 to 31 days followed exposure to the campaign information. Finally, a telephone interview took place in which recall data and candidate evaluations were obtained. Of the 356 individuals who completed the t_1 questionnaire, 211 were successfully contacted for the t_2 call-back portion of the experiment, making for a panel attrition rate of 40 percent. More specifically, the experiment consisted of the following parts.

Stage 1(a): Political Beliefs and Preferences. The subjects were recruited to participate in a study that had the ostensible aim of evaluating two competing candidates running for the U.S. Congress. In part (a), subjects read a randomized series of 66 information items that described various policy statements (e.g., "A candidate who supports the death penalty for drug-related murder") or candidate characteristics (e.g., "A candidate who served in the U.S. Navy (1963–1967)"). Subjects were asked to evaluate each policy statement and candidate characteristic on a five-point scale, ranging from "very positive" to "very negative." For each policy statement, subjects were also asked to indicate whether Democrats or Republicans would be likely to support it, this to tap partisan stereotypes in our subjects. This information was later used to assess the prototypicality of the candidates to which we exposed our subjects.

Stage 1(b): Attitude Survey. After evaluating the candidate characteristics and policy statements, subjects were asked for basic demographic information, as well as their party identification, ideological persuasion, political interest and efficacy, and knowledge of contemporary political figures (measured by the recognition of each politico's party affiliation). This section of the survey concluded with a series of questions concerning the importance of the general policy domains (e.g., abortion, crime, the federal deficit) on which the candidates would later make specific policy recommendations. Note that, in addition to providing data on basic subject characteristics, this step also served as a distractor task between the earlier assessment of information and the upcoming exposure to the campaign messages.

Stage 1(c): Information Exposure (Campaign Fact Sheet). After completing the attitude survey, subjects read a one-page facsimile of a campaign fact sheet (reproduced in Appendix A) which presented the party affiliation, seven-issue positions, and nine personal attributes of two congressional candidates (Dave Wagner (R) and Tom Messinger (D), both hypothetical). The format of the fact sheet was modeled on the way candidates are summarily compared on election eve in the local area newspaper, *Newsday.*

The fact sheet included a within-subject manipulation of the candidate profiles. Whereas the Republican candidate adopted consistently Republican stands on the issues (as established in pretests), two of the seven policy stands of the Democrat were somewhat atypical of Democratic candidates. For instance, unlike the prototypical Democrat (but like Tsongas in the 1991–92 primaries) our candidate sought to cut programs to balance the federal budget and (like Clinton) supported the death penalty. As such, he "issue-trespassed" (Norpoth and Buchanan 1992), adopting positions along Republican lines. Thus the candidates were not mirror images of one another: the Democratic candidate deviated on two of seven issues from New Yorkers' stereotypic image of a Democrat. A manipulation check, based on the typicality ratings of the issues for each party in part (a), confirmed the slightly skewed portrait of the Democratic candidate and the prototypicality of the Republican. Our hypothesis is that the somewhat incongruent profile of the Democrat makes him a more complex (and, we think, more realistic) candidate. As a result, the evaluative process should be more difficult for the Democrat than for the Republican candidate, since subjects are denied a simple stereotypic assessment and can less easily rationalize a set of partisan-rooted recollections.

Stage 1(d): Processing-Depth Manipulation. At this point, after having read the candidate fact sheet, half of the subjects (selected randomly) were thanked and dismissed. The remaining 178 subjects received a series of 50+ questions designed to prod them into thinking more about the candidates and their issue stands. These subjects were asked to evaluate the two candidates on a five-point scale that ranged from "very positive" to "very negative," to list their likes and dislikes of each candidate, render 24 trait inferences (Kinder 1986), and make a vote choice. Depending on the number of arguments each subject gave for supporting or opposing a candidate, anywhere from 50 to 62 supplemental questions were being answered.

In having these subjects mull over the campaign information and reconsider its implications, we should expect a deeper level of information processing, which should in turn bolster the memory traces for the campaign message. As a consequence, there should be less forgetting (Craik and Lockhart 1972) and, if memory-based processing works as advertised, a stronger recall-judgment relationship. Conversely, the OL model would predict *minimal differences* between the simple and depth-processing conditions and a message-evaluation effect stronger than the recall-evaluation effect in *both* conditions, as we posit that when forming general impressions of people, places, and things, people quickly forget the considerations that entered into an evaluation once the affective value has been culled from the message.

While the depth-processing manipulation provides a strong test of the OL model, it was also intended to parallel two different types of citizenship that have been described in the literature. When asked explicitly to think about the campaign information and mull over their reasons for supporting one candidate over the other, we suppose subjects took on the role of the citizen that normative theorists have sketched—an individual who processes campaign information in depth to arrive at an informed decision reflecting serious consideration of the pros and cons of a candidate's issues stands. Such in-depth processing is the most elementary requirement for rational citizenship (Barber 1973). In contrast, subjects who were not prodded by the 50+ questions probably did not engage in in-depth processing. Consequently, their behavior should correspond more closely to what is typically described in empirical analyses of citizenship as a citizenry that pays only cursory attention to politics (Berelson 1952; Berelson, Lazarsfeld and McPhee 1954; Lippmann 1991; also see Kinder and Sears 1985) and relies on factors outside of the campaign to forge candidate evaluations (Berelson, Lazarsfeld, and McPhee 1954; Campbell et al. 1960).

Stage 2: Delay. Upon completion of the stage 1 questionnaire all subjects were randomly assigned to one of the 31 $t_1 - t_2$ delays. All subjects were told they would be reinterviewed and left their number for a call-back. When the set time had expired, subjects were contacted by a new interviewer. If contact could not be established, the subject was rotated to the next day and another subject was contacted in lieu. One consequence of this procedure is that the number of call-backs for the different delays is not uniform, as it turned out to be easier to contact people on weekdays than weekends. Nonetheless, we were able to obtain t_2 observations for all possible delays.

Stage 3: Subject Recall and Candidate Evaluation. In the call-back telephone interview, subjects were asked to give their evaluations of the two candidates on a five-point scale, ranging from "very positive" to "very negative." For the subjects who had not been asked the 50+ questions in stage 1(d) this was the first time they offered an evaluation of the candidates. After voicing an evaluation of each candidate, all subjects were asked if there was anything positive or negative they could remember about each candidate, with each query followed by an "Anything else?" probe. The format of the recall questions was essentially that used in the NES, except that we gave our subjects the names of the candidates if they were unable to recall which candidate was the Democrat and which one the Republican.

Stimuli: Campaign Fact Sheet

The campaign information that our subjects received was rather rich in content and tried to mimic real-life campaign stimuli. When presenting their issue positions political candidates (and newspaper summaries) often make a general policy statement, which is then embellished with specific recommendations that moderate the policy statement or elaborate on it. For instance, a political candidate might argue that he "is opposed to abortion" but then qualify his stand by adding "except in the case of rape and incest." Or a politician might say that she is "tough on crime" and then elaborate her policy statement with a call for mandatory jail sentences for, say, drug king-pins.

We call the core policy statements *gists* and the details *specifiers*. All 14 issue positions in the two-candidate fact sheet were *complex statements* combining a gist with one or more specifiers. For instance, the position of the Democratic candidate on the issue of crime and drugs reads as follows (the gist always presented as the first sentence or phrase of the policy statement, with one or more programmatic specifiers following): "Tom Messinger supports federal laws which crackdown on drugs and crime. He favors the death penalty for murderers, mandatory sentences for drug king-pins, and a mandatory waiting period and background check to purchase a firearm. Tom also supports treatment programs for drug addicts."

An important question to be resolved in the upcoming analyses is whether candidate evaluations are responsive just to the issue gists or whether evaluations reflect subjects' assessment of the candidates' complex statements—the gist and specifiers. Recall that in stage 1(a) we had all subjects rate the gists *and* complex policy statements separately so that we could analyze the impact on evaluations of the full message as well as the impact of the gists only. Our OL model posits that the OL tally is responsive to the gists *and* specifiers of campaign messages but that, over time, first the specifiers and then the gists will be forgotten. If so, the OL model would portray the voter as responsive, while a memory-based model would picture the very same voters as unaware and ignorant.

Results

What do the experimental data tell us about memory for campaign facts and their role in the candidate evaluation process? And what do the data tell us about the direct impact of the campaign message on candidate evaluation, that is, the impact that is not mediated by campaign recollections? To determine the effects of campaign messages and recall of these messages, we propose to look first at memory decay—how much of what kinds of information is forgotten over time and how quickly?—then analyze the predictive power of message and recall on candidate evaluation, and conclude with a causal analysis of the candidate evaluation process that is patterned after Figure 13-1.

The Nonpersistence of Memory

When we look at how much our subjects could recall from the campaign messages that they had received, our results are entirely consistent with the dominant finding in studies of individual political behavior (Delli Carpini and Keeter 1991; Erskine 1963; Neuman 1986; E. Smith 1989): *citizens forget . . . a lot,* with about 54 percent of the subjects unable to recollect a single issue that either of the candidates had addressed.[3] The modal number of recalls for the issue gists was zero, with 60.7 percent of the subjects unable to recall a gist—correct or

Figure 13-2 Retrieval in Two-Candidate Elections

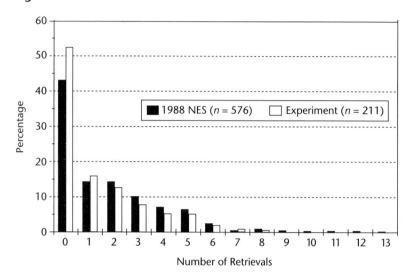

incorrect[4]—for the Republican candidate and 62.1 percent unable to produce gist recollections for the Democrat. Recall for the specifiers was worse still, with close to 80 percent of the subjects not able to recollect even one specifier (again, correctly or incorrectly) for either of the candidates.[5]

This dismal level of recall of campaign information by our subjects is *not* different from what researchers typically find in surveys about real-life candidates. For instance, when we contrast the recalls in our experiment with those for congressional candidates in the 1988 NES, we find a striking congruence. As Figure 13-2 demonstrates, in both samples the modal number of recalls is zero, with very few people providing more than two recollections of the campaign. Indeed, the recall patterns are so similar that there is no statistical difference between them ($\chi^2 = 12.497$, d.f. $= 12$, *ns*).

Voters, then, appear to forget much of the campaign information to which they were exposed. This, however, is not to say that the level of forgetting is constant: some voters under certain conditions will forget more than others. Among the factors that seem to be most instrumental in determining the level of memory decay are political sophistication (Fiske, Kinder, and Larter 1983; McGraw and Pinney 1990) and the depth of information processing (Craik and Lockhart 1972).

We tested these effects using the between-subjects depth-of-processing manipulation of stage 1 of the experiment, as well as a median split of the Subjects in terms of their political knowledge—a standard measure of political sophistication (Zaller 1990).[6] Because recall is also influenced by the time delay after exposure, delay was introduced in the analysis as a covariate. We also included age as a covariate, because past research has shown (and as the senior author can attest) that recall performance deteriorates with age. Separate analyses were performed for the complex statements and for the gists alone.

Repeated-measures ANCOVAs show that the covariates had the strongest impact on the combined[7] gist recalls for both candidates (F[2, 205] = 11.64, p = .000). The strongest effect came from delay (b = −.031, β = −.289, p = .000), with age exerting a somewhat smaller influence (b = −.011, β = −.194, p = .005). The effect of the covariates on recalls of the complex statements for both candidates was somewhat weaker (F[2, 205] = 4.57, p = .011), in large part because the impact of delay was much smaller. Its effect (b = −.012, β = −.159, p = .023) was rivaled by the effect of age (b = −.012, β = −.165, p = .021).

For the gists, there was also a significant main effect for the depth-of-processing manipulation (F[1, 205] = 4.23, p = .041), with subjects exposed to the 50+ follow-up questions to the campaign fact sheet able, as predicted, to recall more than other subjects (the respective means being 1.06 and .74 information items, respectively). No significant effect of the depth-of-processing manipulation was found for the complex statements. Apparently, recall of campaign specifics is not enhanced much by asking people to think about and elaborate on the campaign information.

A more systematic effect on recall was exerted by the structural differences between subjects in their knowledge structures. For the complex statements, one's level of general political knowledge exerted a highly significant effect (F[1, 205] = 5.87, p = .016), with subjects high (above the median) in knowledge showing twice the number of recalls of subjects low in knowledge (the respective means are .57 versus .29 recalls for the two candidates). Political knowledge also had an effect on gist recall. Although this effect was only marginally significant (F[1, 205] = 2.93, p = .088), its size was similar to that found for the depth-of-processing manipulation.

While these results are informative about the factors that affect recall, their real significance is that memory for campaign information was universally weak. Conceivably, subjects could recall up to 14 issue gists but not even the extensive battery of questions and probes that made up the depth-of-processing manipulation brought recall anywhere near this upper limit. Similarly, while political sophisticates recalled twice the number of issues of nonsophisticates, their average recall was still well below a single information item. In conclusion, the recall of campaign information appears dismal even under the best of circumstances, that is, when the information is processed by knowledgeable citizens or is processed in depth.

With recall being so low, an important question becomes what it is that is being recalled. If citizens fall short of possessing a storehouse of campaign information, does what is being recalled at least provide an adequate basis for sound political judgment? Our data, like that of the NES, are not very reassuring of the quality of voters' recollections. First, issues were not recalled because of their salience to our subjects: the null hypothesis that the message is, on average, as important as the recalled information or more important could not be rejected.[8]

Thus, recall appears to be a fairly indiscriminate process, which may easily result in the recollection of issues that are not of great importance to the voter. Second, while the evaluation of the message and the recalled information were positively correlated, the association was rather weak: $r = .268$ for the Republican and $r = .274$ for the Democrat. Hence, what voters recall is, in terms of issue evaluations, not necessarily a fair sample of the full message.

In the light of this evidence, a vote choice that is informed by the campaign issues seems to be out of the question *if* we assume that candidate evaluation is memory-based. Fully 71 percent of our subjects would not be able to make an informed choice, either because they could not recall anything about the two candidates or because they could only provide recalls for a single candidate and could hence not make issue-based candidate comparisons. For the subjects who could recall something (anything, right or wrong) about both candidates ($n = 61$)— and could conceivably thereupon make comparisons — voting would be based on no more than two issues about half of the time.

The memorial wherewithal of voters can be questioned even further if we consider the dynamics of memory, that is, how recollections change over time. In the ANCOVAs we postulated recall to be a linear function of delay. As a first approximation this is not a bad assumption, but better recall models are available. A model that has received particularly strong support in the psychological literature is the *power decay model*, which assumes recalls to decline over time through a power function, such that recollections of campaign messages fade quickly after short time delays and more slowly after longer delays (see Appendix B).

As shown in Figure 13-3, application of the power decay model shows a precipitous decay in subjects' recalls of the issue gists for both candidates, with most of the forgetting occurring within one week after exposure to the campaign fact sheet. For example, considering only those subjects who were randomly assigned to the 50+ questions in the depth-of-processing manipulation (and thus have slightly better recollections), the power decay model predicts that within two days after exposure 25 percent of these subjects would be unable to recall any gists and after six days, the number of recalls would have dropped to zero for half of the subjects (see Appendix B). For the complex statements, recall declined even more steeply, with most of the forgetting occurring within one day after exposure. Moreover, when the recalls of all subjects were considered, still steeper forgetting curves were obtained (results not reported). The conclusion to be drawn from these analyses is clear: *memory for campaign messages not only fades but fades quickly,* the half-life of the message typically being less than a week.

The evidence so far clearly casts doubt on the viability of memory-based assumptions in models of electoral behavior. An obvious question, however, is whether an on-line processing assumption fares any better. To shed light on this issue we would have to look (albeit indirectly) at the decay of the OL tally in memory—"indirectly" because the OL tally is a latent variable and, as such, unobservable. It is possible, however, to gauge memory for candidate evaluations, which may serve as proxies for the OL tally.

Figure 13-3 Forgetting Curves (Democrat)

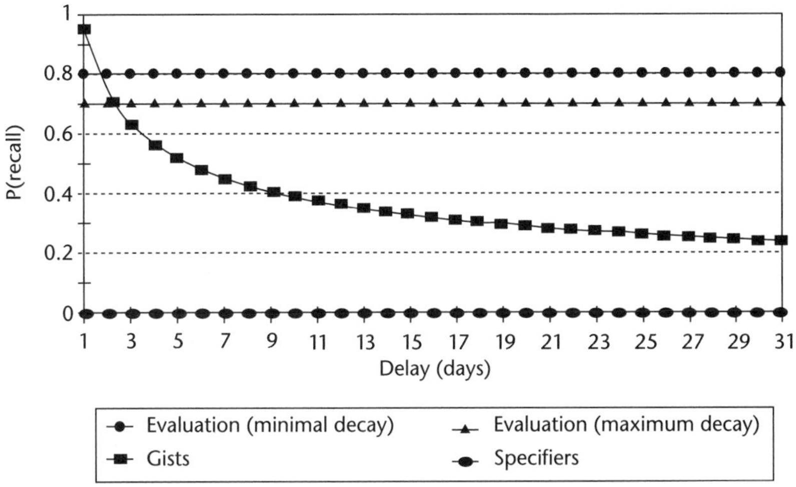

Note: P(recall) is the probability of retrieving at least one item from memory (see Appendix B).

In determining memory for candidate evaluations we make the assumption that, with some degree of error, changes in candidate evaluation reflect an imperfect memory for the OL tally.[9] One possibility is to claim that subjects have forgotten the OL tally if they were capable of providing a candidate evaluation at t_1 (the time of exposure) but not at t_2. A second option is to attribute any change in candidate evaluation to decay of the OL tally. While the first criterion probably underestimates the amount of decay in the OL tally, the second criterion probably overestimates it because opinion change may take place for reasons other than forgetting.[10] The two criteria, then, provide a lower and upper bound on the decay of the OL tally. When we use these two bounds, the top two forgetting curves in Figure 13-3 result. These curves tell a very clear story: a majority of the subjects who provided both t_1 and t_2 candidate evaluations did indeed recall which of the two candidates they liked or disliked. Thus, while memory for the campaign issues declined steadily to low levels, memory for the overall evaluation of the candidates was remarkably robust and stable over time.

In sum, these analyses demonstrate that memory for campaign messages is weak: citizens forget a lot of campaign information rather quickly. By all normative standards—*were we to rely on recall*—the citizen would appear to be rather unaware of what goes on in political campaigns. At best, he or she may remember a thing or two about the candidates and their issue stands but it is clear (from the forgetting curves) that by the time a vote has to be cast much of the information that was attended to has faded from memory.

New Evidence on the Democratic Citizen: Voter Responsiveness

The evidence we have presented so far in essence replicates and expands received wisdom about the American voter. Voters, it would appear, lack the ability to recall essential campaign facts, even (as we have shown here) after short periods of time. And in keeping with received wisdom, one could easily infer from our evidence that voters, unable to recall the most basic issue positions of the candidates, are not politically sophisticated and (so the logic goes) that campaigns are inconsequential because little if any campaign information sticks in voters' minds. However, we counsel caution in drawing such a negative conclusion about the democratic citizen, for we hope to show that it is not the citizen who is at fault but, rather, the memory-based assumption.

We begin our reconsideration of the qualities of the democratic citizen by challenging the implicit assumption in memory-based models that recall is a critical mediator between campaign stimuli and candidate evaluations (see Price and Zaller 1993). We contend that campaigns can have an effect that is quite independent from recall. Instead of being mediated by citizens' recollections of the campaign specifics, this effect is mediated by the OL tally, which integrates the affective evaluation of all the campaign information the citizen is attentive to.

Although we do not have a direct measure of the OL tally itself, we do know what campaign information our subjects were exposed to and their prior evaluations of this information. We can thus correlate subjects' candidate evaluations with their affective responses to the issue positions that the candidates expressed in the campaign fact sheet, which we now label the *candidate message*. To the extent that candidate evaluations are strongly related to candidate messages, we would say that our subjects are responsive to the information in the campaign, *regardless of whether they can actually recall the campaign contents*. On the other hand, should it be shown that message exerts a substantively small effect on candidate evaluation, we would have to conclude that voters are unresponsive to the campaign and would join the ranks of those who question the quality of electoral decision making of democratic citizens. In the ensuing analyses we will move from simple through more rigorous tests of alternative on-line and memory-based models of the responsive voter.

The Role of Message in Candidate Evaluations. A first impression of the impact of message on candidate evaluations can be obtained by considering the zero-order correlations between these variables. Table 13-1 presents these correlations, with message operationalized as the average of a subject's evaluation of *all* the policy stands (gists and specifiers) taken by each candidate in the fact sheet. The message-evaluation correlations, while not overwhelmingly strong, are significant and in the right direction.[11]

If the size of the message-evaluation correlations seems unimpressive, we should keep in mind that the recall-evaluation correlations are weaker still. Recall was operationalized here in a manner similar to message, namely as the

Table 13-1 Message, Recall, and Candidate Evaluation (Pearson Zero-Order Correlations)

| Relationship | All Subjects | Depth-of-Processing Manipulation | |
		Absent	Present
Democrat	($n = 158$)	($n = 84$)	($n = 74$)
Message-evaluation	.2846***	.1891*	.3700**
Recall-evaluation	.2377***	.1691	.2620**
Republican	($n = 160$)	($n = 85$)	($n = 97$)
Message-evaluation	.3796***	.3623***	.3958***
Recall-evaluation	.1932**	.1391	.2622**

*$p < .10$.

**$p < .05$.

***$p < .01$.

average of the evaluations of all gists and specifiers that a subject retrieved from memory for a candidate.[12] If subjects could not retrieve any issue for a candidate the recall score was set to the neutral point.[13] Doing so, we find a rather weak recall-evaluation correlation for the Republican and a somewhat stronger correlation for the Democrat. In both cases, however, the correlation falls short of that observed between message and evaluation.

One circumstance under which one might expect the recall-evaluation correlation to exceed the correlation between message and evaluation would be when voters are stimulated to think hard about the campaign information, as did our subjects in the in-depth-processing condition. As Table 13-1 columns 2–3, indicate, the recall-evaluation correlation does indeed improve when in-depth processing is encouraged. However, even under these most favorable conditions for memory-based processing, the correlation between recall and candidate evaluation does not surpass the correlation between message and candidate evaluation. Thus, even under circumstances that are most congenial to the preservation of campaign information in voters' minds, candidate messages are more strongly correlated with the subjects' overall candidate evaluations than is the affective value of their recollections of campaign events.

Although the correlations are suggestive of the importance of message in the candidate evaluation process, stronger evidence can be obtained by considering recall and message simultaneously in a regression analysis. This analysis also includes party identification (PID) as a predictor of candidate evaluation, as partisanship captures important influences on the vote that are relatively independent of the campaign and its issues. Table 13-2 reports the regression results, with all variables scaled to a 0–1 range to make their regression coefficients directly comparable.

Table 13-2   Message, Recall, Party Identification, and Candidate Evaluation
(OLS Regression)

	Candidate Evaluation	
	Democrat	Republican
Predictor	B	B
Message	.384***	.299***
	(.130)	(.105)
Recall	.149*	.055
	(.082)	(.069)
Party Identification	−.330***	.407***
	(.053)	(.057)
Intercept	.472***	.131**
	(.093)	(.059)
Adjusted R^2	.291	.378
Standard Error of Regression	.190	.190
n	145	147

Note: All variables are scaled in the 0–1 range. Estimated standard errors appear in parentheses.

* $p < .10$.

** $p < .05$.

** $p < .01$.

   The results in Table 13-2 confirm the importance of message in the candidate evaluation process. Not only is message a significant predictor of candidate evaluation, but its impact is substantial, rivaling the effect of PID for the Democratic candidate. Because this candidate's policy stands were somewhat at odds with our subjects' stereotypical image of a Democrat, they added substantially to whatever information the partisan label revealed. Apparently, our subjects were responsive to the somewhat discrepant nature of the Democratic candidate and did not rely solely on their partisan feelings to guide their candidate evaluation.

   Another striking result of the regression analyses in Table 13-2 is that recall does not play much of a role at all. Once we control for the impact of message, recall either becomes statistically insignificant or has a much diminished effect on candidate evaluation.[14] The importance of message for candidate evaluations is illustrated by the fact that the fit of the model deteriorates significantly when message is eliminated as a predictor. Comparisons of the three-variable regression analyses reported in Table 13-2 and the more common regression of recall and PID on evaluation show how critical message is: $F[1, 141] = 8.674, p < .01$, for the Democratic candidate; and $F[1, 143] = 8.177, p < .01$, for the Republican. In contrast, eliminating recall from the regressions in Table 13-2 does not greatly affect the model fit: $F[1, 141] = 3.287, p < .10$, for the Democrat; and $F[1, 143] = .608$, *ns,* for the Republican.

Two important conclusions may be drawn from the regression results. First, in contrast to what political scientists often assume (Kelley 1983; Price and Zaller 1993), recall is not a necessary condition for political information to be influential on the judgments and decisions that democratic citizens make. On the contrary, once the impact of message is considered the effect of recall is greatly reduced. We emphasize this point because it helps account for why experiments and surveys produce different results about the impact of recall on evaluation. Surveys cannot control for message; consequently, much of its effect is absorbed by recall. By taking message explicitly into account, as we did in our experiment, recall plays a lesser role. Thus, the strong showing of recall in surveys may well be a statistical artifact, that is, a product of researchers not specifying the logically prior effect of message on the judgmental process.

Of greater importance than the methodological implication of considering message are the substantive implications for democratic theory. In contrast to the thrust of much empirical work in electoral behavior, we trumpet V. O. Key's dictum: "Voters are not fools." From the on-line perspective, voters are seen as actively bringing their evaluation of the campaign issues to bear on their political evaluations and choices, this being especially apparent when a candidate deviates a bit from partisan expectations. In our view, the regression analyses in Table 13-2 can be readily interpreted in a straightforward way: voters are responsive to political campaigns. No matter how little voters may recall from the campaign, our evidence suggests that *if* attentive to campaign issues and events, they use this information to inform their candidate evaluations.

Caveats. Although we view our results as convincing evidence for voter responsiveness, several questions might be raised. First, it could be argued that the limited effect of recall is a methodological artifact of how we coded missing data to the neutral midpoint of the evaluation scale. By assigning the numerous subjects without retrievals to a neutral point we may have greatly reduced the variance of our recall measures for both candidates (see Little and Rubin 1987), thereby stacking the deck against finding significant recall effects. This does not prove to be a problem, as the variances of the recall measures exceeded those of message. Nonetheless, we reestimated the candidate evaluation models for the subgroup of subjects who had at least one retrieval for a given candidate. Doing so hardly affects the results reported in Table 13-2. Indeed, the results (unreported) for the Republican candidate are almost unchanged. The results for the Democrat show a weakening of the effect of message but *not* to the advantage of recall. In fact, the recall effect becomes somewhat weaker when we consider only those subjects who could recollect at least one pro or con for the Democrat, and it is overshadowed by the effect of message. We consider this evidence that our results concerning the limited role of recall are not a statistical artifact.

A second concern that could be raised is that our findings are an artifact of the way we constructed message and recall. This is a substantively more interesting issue, because it directly pertains to the way we believe information is integrated. So far, we have postulated a simple additive rule, whereby the evaluations of all information items are equally weighted and then summed. However, this is only one of many possible information integration rules, albeit one that is rather prevalent in political science. Hence it is legitimate to ask whether our results would look different if we were to use a different integration rule.

Although this is not the place to discuss the many ways in which voters can combine campaign information (see Taber and Steenbergen 1994), we did replicate our analyses employing an information integration rule that is most favorable toward recall, namely Kelley and Mirer's (1974) "simple act of voting," which (as noted earlier) is a straightforward memory-based model. This rule postulates that voters classify the issues that they recall into likes and dislikes. For each candidate, the voter subtracts the dislikes from the likes to arrive at net liking scores. The candidate with the largest number of net likes is the preferred candidate, with PID acting as a tie-breaker in the case where two candidates receive the same net liking score

Table 13-3 reports the results for the Kelley-Mirer information integration rule, as applied first to recall and then (by extension) to message, operationalizing this as the between-candidate difference in net liking scores for all the statements in the candidate fact sheet. Since recall and message are on different scales we report both unstandardized and standardized regression coefficients. The dependent variable in the analysis is the difference in evaluation between the Democratic and Republican candidates.

The results for a recall-only model, which are reported in the first two columns, are congruent with what Kelley and Mirer (1974) find, namely, significant recall effects and critical effects from PID as a tie-breaker.[15] In addition, there is a strong effect from recall tie. If recall and PID are set to 0, so that the recall tie dummy is 1, our subjects favored the Democratic candidate (intercept is 2.086 + .443). If recall is not 0, so that there is no recall tie, the baseline evaluation of the candidates was about neutral (intercept is .443).

The role of recall dwindles, however, when we include the difference in net liking scores for candidate messages. As Table 13-3, columns 3–4 demonstrate, the results for the Kelley-Mirer information integration rule mimic the results in Table 13-2, showing a significant and substantively sizable effect from message and an insignificant effect from recall ($p < .15$). Note also that the standardized regression coefficient for message is considerably higher than for recall. This finding not only illustrates the robustness of the message effect across different information integration rules but also offers an interesting commentary on Kelley and Mirer's (1974) model. The strong memory-based effects that their model suggests do not appear to be very robust: as soon as message is entered as a control variable, the importance of recall as a determinant of candidate evaluation fades.

While the critical role of message in candidate evaluation appears to be robust, skeptics might question our assumption that the voters are responsive to the entire message rather than parts of it. Specifically, the question is whether voters only use their gist evaluations to judge political candidates or whether they

Table 13-3 Message, Recall, Party Identification, and Candidate Evaluation: Kelley-Mirer Model (OLS Regression)

Predictors	Recall Only		Recall and Message	
	B	β	B	β
Message [Net Likes(Dem) − Net Likes(Rep)]	—	—	0.76*** (.017)	.339
Recall [Net Likes(Dem) − Net Likes(Rep)]	.296*** (.079)	.283	.125 (.083)	.120
Recall Tie	2.086*** (.482)	.643	1.420*** (.484)	.438
Message Tie	—	—	1.380 (2.395)	.119
PID * Recall Tie	−.806*** (.137)	−.857	−.616*** (.138)	−.655
PID * Message Tie	—	—	−.503 (.620)	−.168
Intercept	.443** (.179)	—	.082 (.191)	—
Adjusted R^2	.269		.348	
Standard Error of Regression	1.385		1.308	
n	152		152	

Note: Dependent variable is difference in candidate evaluations between the Democrat and Republican. Estimated standard errors appear in parentheses.

** $p < .05$.

*** $p < .01$.

also bring the candidates' elaborations and qualifications into play. The answer to this question is important for determining exactly how responsive voters are to political campaigns.

We assessed the extent of voter responsiveness through a model comparison test. In a first model we predicted the evaluation of each candidate by the average evaluation of that candidate's complex statement (both gists and specifiers). The second model eliminated the specifiers, that is, the average evaluation of all specifiers to an issue gist, allowing us to compare the fit of this gist-only model with the full model. In both models, PID was entered as a control variable. Eliminating the specifiers decreases the model fit significantly: $F[7, 110] = 2.113, p < .05$, for the Democrat; and $F[7, 123] = 1.855, p < .10$, for the Republican. It appears, then, that our subjects took the entire message into account in their candidate evaluations and not just the general themes.

The Candidate Evaluation Process: A Causal Model

The results up to this point provide strong evidence for our theoretical claims. First, voters do seem to incorporate campaign information in their candidate

Figure 13-4 Causal Candidate Evaluation Model

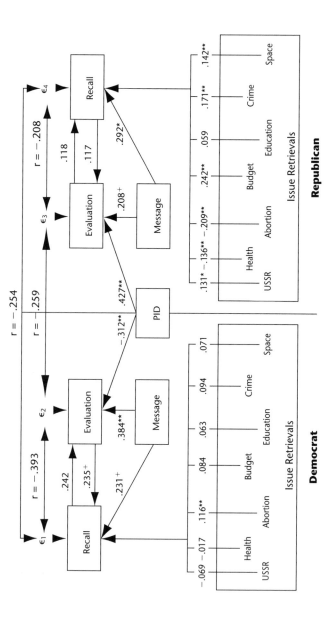

Note: n = 144. Model fit: Normal theory χ² = 57.847, df = 46, p = .113; Robust χ² = 62.469, df = 46, p = .053; Comparative Fit Index (CFI) = .998. All variables scaled in 0-1 range. ** p < .01, *p < .05, + p < .10.

evaluations; that is, they are responsive. Second, recollections of the campaign play at best a modest role in the candidate evaluation process and are clearly subsidiary to the impact of message. So far, however, our analyses have fallen short of considering the model proposed in Figure 13-1. That is, we have so far given recall and message the same causal status, although we know that message is logically prior to recall. Moreover, we have so far assumed that recall causes candidate evaluation, while our theory suggests that voters' recollections may actually be the product of these evaluations. This implicit acceptance of a basic premise of memory-based candidate evaluation models may have resulted in the overestimation of recall effects.

Figure 13-4 displays a model that more closely corresponds to the theoretical notions set forth in Figure 13-1, adding the distinctive feature that it considers both candidates simultaneously. The candidate evaluation portion of this model is similar to the regression analysis in Table 13-2: candidate evaluation is modeled as a function of recall, message, and PID.

The recall portion of our model reflects three possible mechanisms that can generate the affective value of voter recollections. First, recall can be driven by whatever issues a voter happens to retrieve from memory for a given candidate. This mechanism does not assume a particular evaluative direction in the retrieval of issues. No assumption is made, for example, that retrievals are more likely for issues that were evaluated consistently with subjects' candidate evaluations. Indeed, the correlation between the issue retrieval dummies (0 = no retrieval, 1 = retrieval) and candidate evaluations tends to be low and is, except for one out of 14 cases, statistically insignificant. (The average polychoric correlation between candidate evaluation and issue retrieval is .143 for the Democrat and $-.090$ for the Republican).

The two other mechanisms that may drive recall are directional in nature. One of these mechanisms postulates that recall is a function of candidate message. Specifically, recall is assumed to absorb the evaluative implications of the campaign, such that retrievals are a fair sample of the campaign items to which voters were exposed. Alternatively, we postulate a rationalization effect whereby recall is driven by candidate evaluation. If existent, we expect this effect to be positive, meaning that retrieval is biased in favor of items that are affectively consistent with one's overall evaluation of the candidate.[16] Notice that this biased retrieval effect competes with the first recall effect that we described.

Three further comments are in order for the model depicted in Figure 13-4. First, no effect from PID on recall was specified, since both variables are hardly correlated ($r = -.061$, ns, for the Democrat; $r = .119$, $p < .10$, for the Republican). Second, the model contains correlated errors ($\epsilon_1, \ldots, \epsilon_4$) between the recalls and evaluations of each candidate, between the recalls for both candidates, and between the evaluations of both candidates. Finally, all variables in Figure 13-4 are scaled in the 0–1 range, so that unstandardized parameter estimates are directly comparable.[17]

The model in Figure 13-4 fits the data adequately (as indicated, in particular, by the Comparative Fit Index) and reinforces the main findings of our previous analyses. That is, we find a sizable and statistically significant effect of message on candidate evaluation, while the effect of recall is substantively small and not significant. Figure 13-4, however, also shows that it can be quite misleading to assume that recall is causally prior to candidate evaluation. Although only marginally significant, Democratic candidate evaluation has a sizable and positive effect on the recall for this candidate, indicating the presence of a biased retrieval mechanism. Note that this effect is similar in magnitude to the effect of message on recall, suggesting that retrieval may be as much the product of voters' judgments of a candidate as it is the product of their processing of campaign messages. As a consequence, recall may be a very poor proxy for measuring how voters respond to campaign information.

It should be noted that we only find an effect of candidate evaluation on recall for the Democratic candidate. Note that unlike the Republican candidate, who espoused a consistent party line, the Democrat "trespassed" on Republican turf on two of his seven issue positions. Consequently, this candidate was not only liked by subjects who identified themselves as Democrats but also by about 36 percent of the Republican identifiers, who favored these Republican policies (sometimes more so than the Democrats). The latter group, in particular, may have felt a need to rationalize their positive evaluations of a Democrat, hence recalling issues that were consistent with their candidate evaluation. No such similar need existed for Democratic identifiers with respect to the Republican candidate, since only 10 percent of the Democrats liked this candidate. This may account for the insignificance of biased recall for the Republican and the stronger showing of the first recall mechanism that we postulated, namely, recall based on whatever issues voters retrieve from memory. Of course, it only reinforces our main conclusion if our subjects were so sensitive to the stereotypicality of candidates: voters are responsive to the features of a campaign.

Conclusions

Our results point in two directions. First, voters appear to be responsive to the campaign information that they receive, even in the low-stimulus election that we presented to our subjects. Second, this responsiveness is not reflected in voter recollections of the campaign. Even after a short delay voters are unable to recall many of the campaign facts and this includes circumstances in which the number of facts is small and the conditions for memory-based processing favorable. These results have important methodological, substantive, and normative consequences.

Methodological Implications. Methodologically, our findings suggest that it is easy to overstate the role of memory in political judgment when all that is available are survey data. Models of the vote choice typically find strong effects of recall on candidate evaluations in survey data. Surveys, however, can neither measure directly nor control for what information voters are actually exposed to during the campaign. Consequently, they are unable to determine the direct impact of campaign events on political judgment and choice.

Our findings suggest that proper control for campaign exposure will dramatically reduce the effect from recall to the point that it is unclear that the recollection of campaign events matters much at all. The required controls, however, can practically only be obtained in an experimental setting where the researcher has the ability to systematically influence the amount, type, and timing of the information that subjects receive. Hence, we believe that statistical inferences about the role of recall in political judgment are better made with experimental than with survey data.

Substantive Implications. Substantively, our results provide commentary on three topics central to the study of electoral behavior: (1) our understanding of the bases of voting behavior, (2) our understanding of campaigns, and (3) our understanding of political information processing.

In terms of the bases of electoral behavior, our results give further credence to earlier criticisms of memory-based models of candidate evaluation (Lodge, McGraw, and Stroh 1989; Lodge and Stroh 1993). Here, in looking at recall over more realistic time intervals and under circumstances ideally suited to memory-based information processing, recall played at best a modest role in the candidate evaluation process, after message had been controlled for. We view this as evidence that we should integrate message-based models of vote choice into the analysis of electoral behavior.

An emphasis on the content and structure of candidate messages (see Rahn, Aldrich, and Borgida 1994) might well lead to a more positive appreciation of the role of campaigns and media effects. If recall were the only mechanism through which campaign information could affect political judgment and choice, then our data suggest that campaigns are inconsequential for most voters. However, we find that campaign messages have a substantial impact on evaluations independent of recall. The way in which this influence was brought about in our experiment mimics Lazarsfeld, Berelson, and Gaudet's (1948) understanding of campaign effects. That is, we measured prior attitudes about a range of issues and assumed that these attitudes would be mobilized by the campaign as candidates addressed the issues. Our results indicate that this type of campaign effect can be very strong, adding sustaining evidence to prior work on the importance of campaigns (Bartels 1993; Marcus and MacKuen 1993).

Finally, our results suggest a very different model of information processing than is oftentimes assumed in political science. Our discipline relies too heavily on—and often draws the wrong conclusions from—the assumption that political information can only exert an effect on political judgment if citizens remember it. To cite Price and Zaller, "For many—and quite possibly most—survey research purposes, news stories that are encountered but not comprehended and *retained* have little importance because they have few detectable consequences for the person's store of information, attitudes, opinions, or behaviors" (1993, 135; emphasis ours).

In contrast to Price and Zaller (and many other scholars) we believe there are many circumstances (political campaigns being a case in point) under which memory does not play a critical mediating role. We have demonstrated that campaign facts can exert an influence over political judgment even for subjects who could recall few if any of these facts. The mechanism that we propose for these campaign effects is a version of the on-line model of information processing: the campaign raises issues that mobilize issue opinions that voters subsequently integrate along with other factors like PID, into a running affective tally for each candidate. In this process recollections do not play a decisive role, short of the requisite that the OL tally be recalled.

Normative Implications. In our view, the most important conclusion to be drawn from this research lies in the normative domain. Much has been said about the failure of citizens to live up to democratic standards (see Hanson and Marcus 1993). Often these standards have been stated in terms of how much political information citizens can recollect in reply to knowledge questions or open-ended questions about their likes and dislikes of candidates, parties, and issues. Our findings run counter to this outlook: we suggest that information holding is but one standard of good citizenship and not necessarily an appropriate or important one (see Graber 1984). Rather than judge the citizen as we would a student taking an exam, we think it far more valid to judge the citizenry in terms of how much impact this information has on their judgments. What is important is not so much whether citizens can recall a little or a lot of information but that their political judgments and choices reflect their evaluation of the information. Because recall is, as we have seen, not a critical mediator of campaign information, the question about the impact of information is quite independent from the question of recall.

This being the case, some recasting of research questions is called for. If the issue is not how much information people can recollect about the candidates but how much of what kinds of information they actually entertain over the course of the campaign, then we need to focus on what campaign information is available and the conditions under which citizens will make the cognitive effort to mull over this information and expend scarce attentional resources to integrate the affective value of messages into an overall impression of candidates and issues. From this bounded rationalist perspective, a critical question for democratic theory focuses on the information integration rules people use to increase or decrease their OL tallies. Only when this question is answered can we then ask whether responsive voters are also reasonable people.

Appendix A

In stage 1c, subjects read the campaign fact sheet presented in Table 13A-1.

Table 13A-1 Candidate Fact Sheet

	Dave Wagner, Republican	Tom Messinger, Democrat
Background	Born: February 11, 1944. Hometown: Erie, Pennsylvania. Education: A.B., University of Pennsylvania; LL.B, Washington University. Career Highlights: U.S. Navy (1963–1967), City Councilman (1972–1974), Assistant Director of State Budgeting (1982–1986), and State Senator (1986–present). Married to Ruth, two children—Betty and Mary.	Born: March 4, 1943. Hometown: Greensburg, Pennsylvania. Education: B.A., M.B.A. Slippery Rock School of Business. Career Highlights: U.S. Air Force (1962–1965), County Commissioner (1968–1974), State Assemblyman (1976–1984) and State Secretary of Commerce (1986–present). Married to Gladys, three children—Frank, Beth and Peter.
Soviet Union	America should provide technical assistance to the newly independent Soviet republics in order to improve the internal distribution of food and establish an economy based on private-ownership. Dave also favors granting most-favored-nation trading status to the newly formed governments.	The United States ought to help the Soviet Union continue its democratic and economic reforms. This includes food shipments, low-interest loan guarantees, and diplomatic recognition of the independent republics.
Health care	Dave believes the government is not the solution to the nation's health care crisis. He opposes programs that force businesses to provide health care to their workers. Instead, Dave advocates limits on damage awards in medical lawsuits, more competition among medical professionals, and responsible health habits.	Tom supports the establishment of a federal health insurance program by requiring businesses to insure their workers or contribute to a government health-insurance fund. The program would include prenatal and infant check-ups, screening for common cancers, and regular physical examinations.
Abortion	Dave Wagner wants to prohibit abortions in all cases, except those threatening the mother's life. He also advocates the counseling of pregnant women about adoption, education programs that emphasize sexual responsibility and abstinence, and overturning the Supreme Court's *Roe v. Wade* decision.	Tom supports the abortion rights of women. He also supports the prevention of unwanted pregnancies, counseling pregnant women on their medical options, including abortion, and rules allowing Medicaid to pay for abortions for poor women who are victims of rape and incest.

table continues

Table 13A-1 *continued*

	Dave Wagner, Republican	Tom Messinger, Democrat
Budget deficit	Raising taxes is an anti-growth policy, and gives our economic competitors an unfair advantage. Instead, the government should cut unnecessary programs and improve efficiency in order to comply with the Deficit Reduction Act.	To meet the deficit-reduction targets, the government should improve its efficiency and eliminate non-essential programs. Under no circumstances should the government raise taxes to balance the budget.
Education	Dave supports the reform of our nation's education system. He advocates merit-based salary increases for teachers, nation-wide standards in basic school subjects, and school voucher-systems, which give parents the right to choose the best school for their children.	Tom favors an expansion of federal education programs. This includes the establishment of nation-wide testing for high-school student competency, giving parents the right to choose the best school for their children, and the creation of federally financed "magnet-schools."
Crime and drugs	Dave favors an aggressive war against crime and drugs in our neighborhoods. This includes the interdiction of drugs before they cross our borders and police crack-downs on casual drug-use. Furthermore, he supports the confiscation of drug-offender possessions and the death penalty for drug-related murder.	Tom supports federal laws which crack-down on drugs and crime. He favors the death penalty for murderers, mandatory sentences for drug king-pins, and a mandatory waiting period and background check to purchase a firearm. Tom also supports treatment programs for drug addicts.
Space program	The United States should expand NASA's space program. This includes the construction of new space shuttles and the eventual establishment of a permanent base on the Moon.	Tom favors the re-ordering of our priorities in outer space. He wants to cut the space station budget, and use unmanned rockets to lift satellites into orbit.

Appendix B: The Statistical Analysis of Memory Decay

Cognitive and experimental psychology have had a long tradition of describing the functional form of forgetting over time. Researchers have adhered traditionally to Ebbinghaus' (1964) seminal work on forgetting curves, which relied on logarithmic functions. However, recent evidence, based on a wide variety of experimental conditions and response modalities, suggests that a power decay function provides a better and more general description of memory decay (Wixted and Ebbesen 1991; see also Wickelgren 1974). This decay function is commonly formulated as $y = \alpha t^\beta + \epsilon$ over the domain $t \in <0, \infty>$. Here y is a recall performance measure (e.g., the number of items from a list that can be recalled), ϵ is a disturbance term, t is the delay between exposure to information and its recall, and $\beta \leq 0$ is a decay parameter that determines the decay rate $[dy/dt = \beta(y/t)]$. Given the form of the decay rate, it is clear that the power decay model implies that memory decay slows down as the delay increases or as the amount of information in memory decreases.

The final parameter of the power decay model is $\alpha \geq 0$. This is a scaling parameter that ensures that y is not automatically 1 when t equals 1. This would be undesirable, because y can be measured on many different scales, depending on what recall performance measure is used and how much information subjects were exposed to. A substantive interpretation of α is that it gives the recall performance after a time delay of one unit (e.g., a day).

The power decay model is usually applied to recall performance measures that assess how much information is retained in memory. Information-based performance, however, may be problematic to analyze statistically when only one information item was attended to. In that case y is a dichotomous variable (subjects either recalled or did not recall the information item), and all the standard problems with analyzing dichotomous variables (e.g., heteroscedasticity) will enter the analysis. Solutions for these problems are readily available for linear models that are estimated through ordinary least squares, but equivalent solutions for nonlinear models are less straightforward.

To overcome the statistical problems involved in analyzing the power decay model for dichotomous recall-performance measures, we constructed an alternative measure that is both intuitive and easy to handle in statistical analysis. We define recall performance as the *proportion* of subjects who were exposed to some information set of one or more items and who could recollect one or at least one item after t units of delay. This definition permits the estimation of forgetting curves in cases where only one item is subject to memory decay, as in the case of candidate evaluations.

Given the generality of the power decay model, we believe that a definition of y in terms of proportions of subjects is appropriate. This definition causes no special problems statistically. The power decay model for proportions can be estimated through standard nonlinear regression algorithms, subject to a specific loss function. We employed a sequential quadratic programming algorithm that

Table 13A-2   Memory Decay Models (Nonlinear Regressions)

Model (Subjects with in-depth processing)	Estimated α	Estimated β
Recall Democratic candidate		
Evaluation (upper bound on memory decay)	.714*	−.015
Evaluation (lower bound on memory decay)	.811*	.000
Gists (≥1 gist)	.953*	−.382*
Specifiers (≥1 specifier)	.247	−.219
Recall Republican candidate		
Evaluation (upper bound on memory decay)	.730*	−.127
Evaluation (lower bound on memory decay)	.839*	−.016
Gists (≥1 gist)	.955*	−.369*
Specifiers (≥1 specifier)	.358	−.233

$^*p < .05$ (based on bootstrapped standard errors).

minimizes the sum of squared residuals (Thisted 1988). Estimation was subject to the normal constraints—$\alpha \geq 0$, $\beta \leq 0$—as well as the additional constraint, $\alpha \leq 1$, that was imposed to secure that the predicted values of y are in agreement with the probability axiom that proportions cannot exceed 1. The estimates were weighted to accommodate the fact that y is a statistic (i.e., a proportion) that may be based on different sample sizes for each t.

Notes

1. Whether the rules for integrating information into a summary judgment are normatively correct or not is a different question. See Taber and Steenbergen (1994) for a description and analysis of various decision rules for integrating information into vote choice.
2. The notion of voter responsiveness was introduced earlier by Pomper (1975) to distinguish voting behavior that is attentive to the issues of the day from behavior that is driven only by long-term or stable factors such as race and party identification. Our usage of the term is essentially in line with this definition, although our approach is quite different from that by Pomper.
3. When both issues and candidate characteristics were considered the percentage of recalls increased somewhat, although not by very much. In keeping with most voting models, we will consider only issue recalls in the remainder of this paper. However, had we included recalls of candidate characteristics as well, our results would have essentially been the same.
4. Memory-based models of candidate evaluation are generally oblivious about whether recalls are factually correct or not. For this reason we analyzed the recall data without regard for their validity.
5. Specifier recalls were only counted when a subject also recalled the corresponding gist, that is, when a subject recalled the complex issue position. This restriction was imposed because specifiers only make sense in the light of an associated gist.

6. The political knowledge scale consisted of six items concerning the party affiliation of national political figures. Each item was scaled from -1 (incorrect response) to 1 (correct response), with 0 indicating *don't know*. The items form a moderately strong stochastic cumulative scale under Mokken's scale model (H = .54), with a decent reliability of .754 (Sijtsma, Debets, and Molenaar 1990). Although the political knowledge items are themselves memory-based, we are confident in using them as independent variables, because the memory task involved is rather distinct: the knowledge questions rely on recognition, whereas recollections of the campaign information were obtained through cued recall.

7. The combined recall for both candidates was one type of dependent variable that was analyzed in the repeated-measures ANCOVAs. The other dependent variable was the difference in recalls between the two candidates, which permits an analysis of the within-subjects manipulation of partisan consistency. Since no significant effect of this manipulation was found, we will only report the results for the combined candidate recalls.

8. Considering Average Importance of Message (Sum of Importances for All Issues ÷ Number of Issues) − Average Importance of Recalls (Sum of the Importances for All Recalls ÷ Number of Recalls), we obtained the following test results: t(76) = 1.567, $p = .94$ for the Republican; t(66) = 1.006, $p = .84$ for the Democrat.

9. This assumption is reasonable for two reasons. First, the campaign fact sheet was the only information that we disseminated to our subjects, so that changes in candidate evaluation cannot be attributed to the intake of new information about the candidates. Second, because the race between the candidates was low-stimulus (many of our subjects admitted to have little interest in the race) it is questionable that our subjects spent much time in rethinking the candidates' issue positions. Hence, cognitive responses to the information are an implausible mechanism for producing changes in attitudes toward the candidates.

10. One reason for opinion change, of course, is measurement error. To reduce this problem we assessed change in candidate evaluation in terms of collapsed versions of the candidate evaluation scales, distinguishing only between negative, neutral, and positive feelings toward a candidate. Opinion change was defined as the movement from one affective category to another.

11. *Candidate evaluation* always refers to the judgments of the candidates that subjects gave in the t_2 portion of our study.

12. Because we now define recall in evaluative terms, we will no longer use it to describe the act of retrieving information from memory. This is now referred to as *retrieval*.

13. This procedure implies that subjects without recalls are equated with subjects who recall items that they feel neutral about or subjects who recall a mix of items that neutralize each other. We view this as imminently reasonable, since a lack of recalls should have the same effect as neutral recalls, namely that voters cannot decide which candidate they like best on the basis of their issue recollections.

14. Analyses with recall and PID as the sole predictors of candidate evaluation show a significant recall effect for the Democratic candidate ($b = .221, p = .007$). A similar analysis for the Republican candidate reveals an insignificant effect of recall, but its effect size is almost twice as large as that in the analysis reported in Table 13-2.

15. In this analysis we adopted the methodologically unconventional method of specifying an interaction with PID without including PID itself in the regression. Although this specification preserves the tenets of the Kelley-Mirer information integration rule, we did reestimate the model including PID as a main effect. Doing so, we find that the interaction of PID and recall ties becomes statistically insignificant, while the main effect of PID is highly significant. However with respect to the relative impact of message and recall, nothing substantial changes in the patterns reported in Table 13-3.

16. A positive effect of candidate evaluation on recall can imply one of two things. First, there may be biased retrieval. Second, voters may have unbiased retrieval but change the affect for retrieved items so as to be consistent with their candidate evaluation. We have precluded this latter mechanism by using the affective values for gists and specifiers that were measured before our subjects were exposed to the candidates.

17. The model was estimated through EQS version 4.0 using generalized least squares. Because of a lack of normality of the endogenous variables conditional on the exogenous variables, normal standard errors and test statistics are incorrect. Therefore, robust standard errors were obtained, while the Bentler-Satorra scaling correction was applied to obtain a correct model test (see Bentler 1992).

PART IV
DIVIDED GOVERNMENT

14. Do Voters Prefer Divided Government?

The early empirical and theoretical work on voting behavior analyzed presidential elections. It implicitly assumed that voting for all offices is based on similar principles, a position that misses many important differences inherent in other offices, particularly legislative seats. Furthermore, voting for one office may not be independent of voting for other offices. That is, people may have preferences for the overall direction of the government—the executive and the legislative branches combined—and therefore vote for the legislative branch on the basis of which party controls the executive. Thus looking at voting for president by itself may be misleading. Minimally, these two points—the possibility of other factors being involved in voting for legislators and the possibility of interdependence in voting for executives and legislators—make it important to look at voting beyond the presidential level.

There are a large number of topics that can be studied involving voting beyond the presidential level. The determinants of voting for these other offices have been extensively examined, sometimes just applying the same models used for presidential voting and sometimes modifying those models to better accommodate the specifics of those offices. For example, as might be expected (given our discussion in Chapter 10), particular attention has been given to the importance of economic-based voting. More generally, there has been debate as to the relative importance of national factors versus local factors, even in voting for U.S. congressional and state offices (Niemi and Weisberg 1993a, chap. 15; 1993b, chap. 13). There has also been controversy as to whether these races should be primarily understood as referenda on incumbents or as contests by challengers (Weisberg, Heberlig, and Campoli 1999, chap. 8). Among the many topics that have been dissected are the incumbency advantage, the quality of the candidates, split-ticket voting, and the effects of campaign finance. Each of these topics is important and will be discussed in this chapter.

The main focus of this chapter will be on a specific topic that has implications of considerable significance for the U.S. political system: divided government—the control of the executive and legislative branches by different political parties. Divided government is not new in the United States, but it became so common in the last half of the twentieth century that researchers began to focus for the first time on its causal basis. There is now lively dispute over the topic. One provocative side is that divided government results from intentional party balancing on the part of voters. The opposite view is that divided government is just an accidental result of split-ticket voting. That line of controversy is followed in this chapter, and several other aspects of subpresidential voting are introduced along the way.

Voting Beyond the Presidency

Appreciation of the debate over the electoral sources of divided government requires understanding the broader literature on the determinants of voting beyond the presidency. The early literature assumed the importance of the standard three factors—party identification, attitudes on issues, and orientation toward the candidates—but recognized that their relative role would vary by office. One major difference across offices was the voter's likely amount of information about the candidates. Congressional elections, for example, were considered to be low information contests in comparison to presidential elections, and the implication was that there would probably be even less information about most state and local races. With voters likely to have less information for lower offices, the early literature assumed that party identification would become the major determinant of the vote for those offices, since the candidates' party ties are usually on the ballot.

The Michigan researchers conducted their first congressional election survey in 1958, and the results of that study bolstered the image just presented. For example, they found that people could not even recall the name of their member of Congress, issues were of minor importance in voting, and knowledge of which party controlled Congress was barely over the level expected if people were just guessing (Stokes and Miller 1962; Miller and Stokes 1963). If candidates and issues were not important, then partisanship had to be the main factor affecting these elections.

This led to the Michigan researchers' "surge and decline" theory of the dynamics of congressional elections (A. Campbell 1960). Independents—who might not otherwise vote—join the electorate in presidential election years and vote for the presidential candidate who is favored by short-term forces, producing a surge of votes for the congressional candidates of that candidate's party. When those short-term forces diminish in midterm elections, there is a decline in turnout and a return to a partisan electorate, resulting in the familiar pattern of seat losses for the president's party at the midterm. Empirical evidence eventually accumulated against the original argument (Wolfinger, Rosenstone, and McIntosh 1981). James Campbell (1987, 1997) found empirical support for a revised theory of surge and decline: short-term factors affect the vote direction of independents, but not their turnout, while those same short-term forces affect the turnout of partisans but not their vote choice. This argument, of course, maintains the original emphasis on the role of partisanship in congressional elections.

By the 1970s researchers felt that the image of congressional voting as exclusively partisan did not square with their emerging view of Congress. It did not account sufficiently for the importance of incumbency, and asking voters to recall the name of their member of Congress did not correspond to the structure of the ballot (Mann 1978). These congressional researchers developed several new questions for the 1978 National Election Studies (NES) survey, and the results confirmed their expectations. Most voters could recognize (although not spontaneously recall) the name of their member of Congress, and they had a reasonable level of contact with and knowledge about that incumbent (Mann and Wolfinger 1980). The candidate factor was more important than the original research suggested, particularly in regard to incumbency.

At the same time, a different group of researchers began to argue that the state of the economy was an important part of congressional elections, especially for explaining midterm election results. Tufte (1975) demonstrated that the extent of seat loss in Congress by the president's party was a function of the president's popularity and the state of the economy (which also affects the president's popularity). Erikson's (1990a) updating through 1986 found that the economy was not significant, although Jacobson (1990a) defended its significance.[1] More recently, the virtually unprecedented gain in House seats by the president's party at a midterm election in 1998, when the economy was very strong, seems to vindicate Tufte's argument. The relationship between the economy and voting for Congress is less evident in survey data (for example, Fiorina 1978), although Kramer (1983) showed how shifts in the economy that lead to changes in the vote between elections need not be picked up by individual-level, cross-sectional surveys. In any case, there is now considerable research on economic voting for Congress, which brings issue voting back into the equation in voting for legislators.

Voting for the U.S. Senate is also understood to involve more than just partisanship. Senate elections are considered different from House elections in that the challenger is likely to be much better known. Yet Westlye (1991) found that Senate races vary considerably in their intensity, with some hard-fought races and others in which the challenger is virtually unnoticed. The NES conducted its first extensive surveys on Senate races in the 1988–1990–1992 cycle. This Senate Election Study led to research on how the determinants of voting differ according to the intensity of the race. Kahn and Kenney's (1997) analysis, for example, finds that policy, ideology, partisanship, and retrospective evaluations of the president and the economy matter more in high-intensity races. Looking at the same data, Koch (1998) only finds presidential approval to be more important in those races while ideology is less important. Atkeson and Partin (1995) find that the vote for senators was tied to approval of presidential performance, but economic evaluations were not relevant, fitting with a "federalist" view of subpresidential elections that voters react to the different roles of different branches and levels of government (Stein 1990, Carsey and Wright 1998).

As this review shows, our view of voting for legislators is now considerably more complex than that originally inherited from the presidential voting studies. Yet this direct focus on voting for legislators still misses one of the most important political developments of recent decades: the preponderance of divided government at both the national and state levels. Simply expanding our view from presidential voting to voting for legislators is insufficient to explain why voters frequently choose different parties to control the executive and legislative branches.

Divided Government Results from Intentional Electing of Different Parties

There have been long periods of divided government at the national level in U.S. history, but the concept received little attention until fairly recently. Divided government occurred more often than unified government during the 1840–1860 and 1874–1896 periods, but it occurred only after four of the twenty-six elections from 1900 through 1950 (Fiorina 1996, 7). The pattern for the first half of the twentieth century was reversed in the second half, as is evident in Table 14-1. *The American Voter* was written on the basis of the elections of the 1950s, which led to a Republican president and a Democratic Congress from 1955 through 1960, but the authors did not discuss divided government and its causes. The Democrats controlled both branches from 1961 through 1968 and again from 1977 through 1980, but Republican presidents Richard Nixon, Gerald Ford, Ronald Reagan, and George Bush all faced a Democratic House and generally a Democratic Senate. By the time that Bush was elected to face a Democratic Congress, the political science literature began to conceptualize the notion of divided government and seek explanations. Several explanations were offered, although as we shall see, some did not fit a few years later when Bill Clinton was surprised by Republican victories in the 1994 congressional elections that led to divided government from 1995 through 2000. All in all, divided government resulted from sixteen of the twenty-four elections from 1952 through 1998, making it the norm rather than the exception. Divided government also became more prevalent at the state level: unified government held for 85 percent of the states after the 1946 election, compared to less than 45 percent by the late 1980s (Fiorina 1996, 25).

A simplistic view of the dynamic underlying divided government is that voters change one branch of government after a long period of unified control to register their distress with deteriorating conditions, as in 1994 when the public turned against forty years of Democratic control of the House of Representatives. This explanation, however, does not account for the persistence of divided government over a lengthy period of time (Fiorina 1996, 72). One could add in incumbency—reasoning that once divided government is created, the tendency of incumbents to be reelected would help maintain divided government—but that creates a compound explanation that is deficient because it cannot be disconfirmed. Finding a continuation of divided government would be used as evidence in favor of incumbency, while finding a change to unified government would be used as evidence of voter dissatisfaction with divided control.

Table 14-1 Periods of Unified and Divided Government, 1901–2002

Period	Divided/ Unified	President	Senate	House
1901–1910	Unified	Republican	Republican	Republican
1911–1912	Divided	Republican	Republican	Democrat
1913–1918	Unified	Democrat	Democrat	Democrat
1919–1920	Divided	Democrat	Republican	Republican
1921–1930	Unified	Republican	Republican	Republican
1931–1932	Divided	Republican	Republican	Democrat
1933–1946	Unified	Democrat	Democrat	Democrat
1947–1948	Divided	Democrat	Republican	Republican
1949–1952	Unified	Democrat	Democrat	Democrat
1953–1954	Unified	Republican	Republican	Republican
1955–1960	Divided	Republican	Democrat	Democrat
1961–1968	Unified	Democrat	Democrat	Democrat
1969–1976	Divided	Republican	Democrat	Democrat
1977–1980	Unified	Democrat	Democrat	Democrat
1981–1986	Divided	Republican	Republican	Democrat
1987–1992	Divided	Republican	Democrat	Democrat
1993–1994	Unified	Democrat	Democrat	Democrat
1995–2000	Divided	Democrat	Republican	Republican
2001–2002	Unified	Republican	Republican	Republican
1901–1952	Divided 15% (4/26 times)			
1953–2000	Divided 67% (16/24 times)			

The more intriguing argument that some researchers have made is that voters are intentionally electing different parties. There are actually two separate, systematic explanations that are purposive in character. The most provocative explanation claims that the public chooses one party to control one branch because the other party controls the other branch. By contrast, the weaker version just asserts that the public has different reasons in mind in choosing to have the Democrats control one branch and the Republicans the other. We start with this second version.

It is reasonable to suggest that voters use different considerations in voting for different offices. Voters might see the parties as having different strengths and choose for an office the party whose strengths best fit that office. This theory was developed just before the 1994 election, by which time the country had elected a Democratic House for forty years while choosing Republican presidents for twenty-six of those years. Jacobson (1990c) first advanced the argument that the public was choosing Republican candidates for president because they were seen as better at producing diffuse collective benefits (such as handling inflation and national defense) while electing Democratic Congresses because the Democrats were more associated with distributing benefits to congressional districts. Jacobson (1991) shows that in 1988 the Republicans were considered better able to handle such matters as the budget deficit, which was seen as an important national problem but not an important issue in the House campaign. Conversely, the Democrats were seen as best able to handle the environment and domestic policy, which were viewed as more important at the district level than at the national level. Alvarez and Schousen (1993) also found that national issues affected presidential voting in 1988 but not congressional voting, in line with Jacobson's hypothesis.

A variant of this explanation was offered by Petrocik (1991, also Petrocik and Doherty 1996). Petrocik presented an "issue ownership" theory that each party is seen as better able to handle particular issues. Republicans have been successful at turning presidential elections into referenda on issues such as national defense and taxes, on which they have an advantage. Survey respondents who recall Democratic issues are more likely to vote Democratic for Congress, and similarly those who recall Republican issues are more likely to vote Republican for Congress, although issues are more marginal for congressional elections, which advantages incumbents. Petrocik also showed that the incumbency bonus vanished when the voters' issue agenda was in conflict with the incumbent's party (such as when voters represented by a Democrat mentioned issues on which the Republicans have "ownership"), but 71 percent of respondents did not cite any issue as a factor in their district.

The idea underlying the Jacobson and Petrocik arguments makes perfect sense. Voters may use different considerations in voting for different offices, and each party may have an advantage on different types of issues, so one party may have an advantage for the presidency and the other for Congress. However, it has not been demonstrated that the people with those combinations of views were the ones splitting their tickets and thereby creating divided government.

Another problem with these arguments is that divided government took a different shape with the 1994 election. The original Jacobson and Petrocik arguments were advanced in 1990–1991, when the phenomenon being explained was why Republican presidents were facing Democratic Congresses. Starting in 1994, however, a Democratic president was facing a Republican Congress. The logic that Jacobson and Petrocik used no longer fit—people were not electing a Democratic Congress to distribute benefits to their districts nor to protect social welfare benefits. Still, it is possible to modify these arguments to make them work better. Perhaps the public no longer needed to elect Republican presidents because of defense after the Cold War ended. Similarly, perhaps the public was more concerned with reducing government spending in the 1990s, which meant having to elect a Republican Congress given that the president was a Democrat. Yet this form of argument makes these explanations seem ad hoc. It should be possible to state the conditions leading to divided government without first analyzing the shape of public opinion when it occurs.

In the end, the Jacobson and Petrocik explanations are interesting in that they provide rational justifications for ballot splitting. Each merits more examination with more detailed survey data over varied conditions. Both argue that the public intentionally chooses different parties to control the two branches. However, neither argues that the public is choosing one party to control one branch because the other party controls the other branch, which is the claim that we turn to next.[2]

The most influential explanation of divided government as intentional is that voters purposely create divided government through policy balancing. Moderate voters might regard unified Democratic control of government as too liberal and unified Republican control as too conservative. Voters preferring moderate policies might therefore prefer a divided government in which Congress moderates the president's policies, and they may be voting so as to create such a government. This argument has become important in the literature, so the remainder of this section will be devoted to it.

Morris Fiorina (1988, 1992, 1996) developed and formalized the policy-balancing argument (which is also referred to as party balancing). He hypothesized a unidimensional system in which unified Democratic control would lead to the most liberal policies, whereas a Democratic executive with a Republican legislature would have moderate liberal policies. A Republican executive with a Democratic legislature would have moderate conservative policies, while unified Republican control would lead to the most conservative policies. Voters in the center would prefer one of the divided government scenarios to unified government because they are policy balancing. Fiorina's argument is reprinted in Chapter 15.

Other authors have also contributed to the development of this explanation. Erikson (1988) and Alesina and Rosenthal (1989) hypothesized that voters intentionally have the parties check each other, as a partisan analogue to the checks and balances built into our constitutional system. Alesina and Rosenthal (1995, 44) put it most directly: "Divided government does not happen by accident. . . . Divided government occurs because moderate voters like it, and they take advantage of 'checks and balances' to achieve moderation. In dividing government, the voters force the parties to compromise: divided government is a remedy to political polarization." Their logic works perfectly in explaining a movement to divided government at the midterm election, when the identity of the president is known so that it can be balanced by voting for the other party for Congress. This logic also holds for presidential election years if voters know who is likely to win the presidency; if the pivotal voter does not know which party will win the presidency, they argue that he or she would vote a split ticket so as to avoid the possibility of an overly polarized government.[3] At an even broader level, Ingberman and Villani (1993) developed a game theoretic model in which the parties are motivated solely to win elections, with an equilibrium position in which the parties adopt widely separated positions and divided government and split-ticket voting occur with high probability.

This policy-balancing model assumes a fairly sophisticated electorate, one that is more sophisticated than the findings reviewed in Chapter 6 suggest, which has made the approach controversial. Is the electorate sophisticated enough to balance party policies by dividing partisan control of government? Voters need not, of course, go through a mathematical averaging of the party positions to policy balance, but the question becomes whether they can do such comparisons of policies at a more intuitive level. It has also been pointed out that in a closely balanced party system, divided government could result even if a small proportion of voters engage in such policy balancing.

While the idea of intentional party balancing is creative, it has been hard to verify. Actually asking people whether they prefer unified or divided government would give only a rough test, as that question is hypothetical so answers may not correspond their behavior when confronting real decisions. Scholars have employed several indirect tests of the party-balancing hypothesis, with mixed results (see Chapter 15). Early studies seemed to refute the hypothesis, but later studies have devised new survey questions and more refined analytical approaches that have tended to support it.

Some of the early null results were based on the following NES question: "Do you think it is better when one party controls both the presidency and Congress, better when control is split between Democrats and Republicans, or doesn't it matter?" Multivariate analysis found that people who favored divided government were no more likely to split their ballots than were those who favored unified government, either in 1992 (Sigelman, Wahlbeck, and Buell 1997) or 1994 (Lacy 1998). In one of the few empirical studies of ticket splitting at the subpresidential level, Beck, Baum, Clausen, and Smith (1992) report that views on the desirability of divided government do not relate significantly to split-ticket voting. Yet this evidence is limited by the fact that the standard survey question does not correspond to the actual choices faced by voters.

Dean Lacy (1994) has rephrased policy balancing in terms of whether people have "nonseparable preferences." People's preferences over control of the executive and the legislature are nonseparable if which party they want to have control one branch depends on which controls the other branch, whereas their preferences are separable if preferences for one branch do not depend on control of the other. A 1994 statewide survey in Ohio included the question, "If the president is a Democrat, would you prefer that the Democrats or the Republicans control Congress?" with a similar question asking preferences if the president is a Republican. More than one-third of voters had nonseparable preferences (Lacy 1998, 90). Part of this group (18 percent of the sample) wanted divided government (a Democratic Congress if the president is Republican and a Republican Congress if the president is Democrat), and another part (19 percent) wanted unified government (a Democratic Congress if the president is Democrat and a Republican Congress if the president is a Republican).

One testable implication of the policy-balancing argument is that the level of split-ticket voting would depend on how different the policy positions of the two parties are. If the policies were fairly close, then few people would be between them and straight ticket voting might prevail. But if the parties then polarize, the distance between them would increase, and more voters would prefer split outcomes than unified ones.

Some early tests of Fiorina's theory approached the problem from this spatial perspective. NES questions have long asked voters to locate themselves and candidates on a liberal-conservative scale. Analyzing 1972–1988 NES data, Alvarez and Schousen (1993) did not find moderate voters more likely to vote a split ticket; Born (1994) also did not obtain significant results. In 1996 Lacy and Paolino (1998) changed the task slightly by having respondents place on the scale the policies they thought the federal government would enact if each major-party candidate won the presidential election. Majorities of respondents saw the personal positions of each candidate as different from what would be the government's policies if that candidate were elected, and most saw the candidates as more extreme than the government policies would be if they were elected. Their results confirmed their expectations of policy balancing: distances from expected government positions, rather than from candidates, were significant in predicting the vote in their multivariate model. This article is one of the first pieces to find strong empirical evidence for the Fiorina policy-balancing argument.

More specification of where policy balancing should be expected also leads to some significant results. Garand and Lichtl (2000) found support for policy balancing when two propositions are tested in the same equation: ticket splitting should be greater for voters located between their perceptions of the two party's ideological positions and for those who see more interparty distance between the parties. Born (2000a) shows that this effect disappears in the 1972–1992 studies when the confounding effects of relative party closeness are controlled. He does, however, find support for that proposition in 1996, with greater split-ticket voting for those voters located between the parties who saw more distance between them. Mattei and Howes (2000) obtain some balancing behavior among knowledgeable voters anticipating a presidential victory for their favored candidate in 1996, but they report that they cannot duplicate that result for previous years.

The importance of theoretical clarity is also the message of Smith, Brown, Bruce, and Overby (1999). They argue that it is essential to separate from the outset the citizens who always have separable and nonseparable preferences. They asked a 1996 national sample: "If (Bob Dole/Bill Clinton) were to be elected president which would you prefer: a (Republican/Democratic) Congress to help him pass his agenda, or a (Democratic/Republican) Congress to serve as a check on his agenda?" Most respondents (59 percent) gave consistent partisan responses (wanting their party to control Congress regardless of which party controlled the White House), but 27 percent preferred divided government. Only 6 percent favored unified government in any case (a Democratic Congress if Clinton was elected and a Republican Congress if Dole was elected). Partisan preference by itself explains much more of the variance for those with separable rather than nonseparable preferences, which means that studies that look at all respondents together violate some of the standard statistical assumptions regarding the distribution of error variance. When Smith et al. predict the House vote on the basis of regular party preference and also a conditional measure that shows preferences for people with nonseparable preferences, both terms are significant.

That shows that the type of policy balancing that Fiorina hypothesized has important effects in a model that properly matches the theoretical complexity of the topic.

Fiorina's policy balancing is an important theoretical argument. Early empirical studies found little support for it, but the Lacy-Paolino and the Smith et al. pieces show that policy-balancing effects can be found through a combination of careful theorizing and development of new survey questions that fit with that conceptualization. It need not take a lot of intentional policy-balancing voting to create divided government when the parties are of fairly equal strength. However, before fully accepting the view that divided government is intentional, it is necessary to consider the arguments that have been made that divided government occurs by accident.

Divided Government Is an Unintentional Consequence of Candidate Voting

Rather than accepting divided government as a purposive outcome, the alternative position is that it is an unintentional result of voting on the basis of the candidate factor. As will also be discussed in Chapter 21, political parties have declined in importance and there is evidence (albeit disputed) of a decline in voting on the basis of partisanship. At the high point of partisan strength in this country, party machines made the government work (especially the patronage machines of urban parties that dispensed jobs to loyal voters), the parties turned out their loyalists at elections, and those voters cast straight-party ballots. Those days have ended, with a shift to candidate-centered politics. Candidates use the modern media to make their own appeals to voters without emphasizing their party, and many voters pick and choose between candidates of each party by casting split-ticket ballots.[4]

Divided government can thus be seen as part of party-system disintegration (Jacobson 1990c). The proportion of independents has increased (from less than 25 percent of the population to about 35 percent, if all self-identified independents are included; see Table 17-1), while voting a straight party ticket has decreased (from 12 percent of voters in 1952 to a high of 30 percent in 1972 according to NES data, although the figure fell back to 17 percent in 1996).[5] In focusing on the candidate factor in voting, it is possible to emphasize the candidate pools for different offices, the importance of incumbency, and the quality of challengers. Each of these arguments appears in the literature.[6]

The candidate pools argument is that the two branches will often be controlled by different parties in an era of candidate-centered politics if one party is consistently able to recruit stronger candidates for one branch of government but not for the other. Different versions of this argument have been advanced for the state and national levels.

The state level has been marked by a pattern of Republican chief executives and Democratic legislatures (Fiorina 1994). The Republicans controlled many state legislatures after World War II, at a time when being a legislator was only a part-time job. Legislatures then became more professionalized, the job became full-time in many states, and the pay increased correspondingly. The claim is that when legislative service became a full-time job, Republican business people were less willing to give up their careers to run for the legislature. By contrast, Democrats were likely to see legislative pay as higher than they could earn in the private sector and therefore were more willing to run. Fiorina (1996) argues that this dynamic led to better qualified Democratic than Republican candidates and therefore to more Democrats being elected. A related recruitment argument is that Republicans have less interest in running for office since they do not believe in government intervention (Ehrenhalt 1991). Either way, divided government often results since the Democrats tend to win the legislature regardless of which party wins the governorship. This argument also indirectly affects the national level since the greater number of Democratic state legislators provides a larger pool of potential Democratic candidates for Congress.

The candidate pool argument has also been used to explain divided government at the national level from the 1950s through the early 1990s. Democratic domination of Congress resulted, according to this explanation, from Republicans, favoring a minimalist conception of government, being less likely to desire a political career (Jacobson 1990c, 20). Jacobson (1990c, 62–64) speaks directly about the weakness of Republican congressional challengers in the 1984–1988 period as contributing to divided government during those years. At the presidential level, the Democratic primary electorate nominated candidates who were seen as very liberal (such as McGovern, Mondale, and Dukakis), while the Republican Party was able to bridge its ideological differences and nominate candidates who had a broader appeal in the general election (Wattenberg 1991a). Thus divided government resulted because the Republicans were advantaged for the presidency while the Democrats were advantaged for Congress.

This explanation fails to account for divided government in the mid-1990s, when a Republican Congress was elected to accompany a Democratic president. Apparently Republican Party leaders recognized their problem in attracting congressional candidates and aggressively recruited stronger candidates, which is sometimes given as an explanation of how they were able to win control of Congress in 1994 and return the nation to divided government (Jacobson 1996). However, even this point does not explain the continuation of divided government throughout the decade.

A second, more complete explanation that views divided government as accidental has to do with the incumbency advantage combined with the nature of challengers. The usual form of this argument is that incumbent legislators tend to get reelected regardless of their party affiliation, which can lead to one party controlling the legislature for a long period of time even though contests for the executive branch are more competitive. Campaign finance matters also tend to get wrapped into this explanation, in that incumbency confers an advantage in securing campaign funds.

This view of divided government emerges from the analysis of split-ticket voting by Burden and Kimball in Chapter 16. Using newly developed estimates of split-ticket voting,[7] Burden and Kimball analyze the factors that lead to more ticket splitting in some districts than in others. They confirm that having an incumbent member of Congress increases ticket splitting in favor of that incumbent (that is, many people vote for the incumbent for Congress even if they vote for the other party for president). More important, they can place that result in the context of other factors that affect split-ticket voting. In particular, they emphasize the importance of campaign spending for split-ticket voting. The more lopsided the campaign spending, the more the "poor" candidate's message is drowned out and the greater the vote for the advantaged candidate, regardless of party. Campaign spending is a measure of the competitiveness of the race and, as we shall see below, of the quality of the challenger, so this result again emphasizes the importance of candidate factors for divided government.

Burden and Kimball are also able to test Fiorina's prediction that intentional ticket splitting is most likely when the candidates are far apart on policies. Using data from the NES Senate Election Study, they find that the perceived ideological distance between President Bush and a state's Democratic Senate candidate was not significantly related to the vote, nor was the distance between Dukakis and the Republican candidate. Indeed, they find House voters seeking ideological consistency, more likely to vote for Bush and the House Democratic candidate the more conservative the Democratic incumbent's voting record.[8] This result is confirmed in Burden and Kimball's (forthcoming) more extensive analysis of ticket splitting in the 1972–1996 period.

The policy consistency finding fits with some other research results suggesting that people who vote for candidates from different parties are just voting a consistent ideological position. Frymer (1994) and Frymer, Kim, and Bimes (1997) show that Democratic members of the House who came from districts that gave the Republican presidential candidate a majority in the 1980s were relatively conservative. People in those districts who voted for both a Republican president and a Democratic representative were thus voting a consistent policy preference.[9] Fiorina (1996, 154–155) criticized the Frymer evidence, noting that without knowing the position of the Republican congressional candidate in those districts it was possible that many of the split-ticket voters in those districts had policy positions that should have led them to vote a straight Republican ticket. Burden and Kimball do not encounter this problem since the data they use include perceptions of both candidates' positions.

Burden and Kimball also show that ticket splitting and divided outcomes in a district (the district votes for one party for president while electing a representative from the other party) are not the same. They demonstrate a high relationship between split-ticket voting among Bush voters in 1988 and election of a Democrat to Congress. However, they also find that ticket splitting was high both among Bush voters in districts that elected Democrats to Congress and among Dukakis voters in districts that elected Republicans to Congress, regardless of which presidential candidate won those districts, showing again the importance of local factors in ticket splitting.

This picture of split-ticket voting and divided government again suggests the importance of candidate factors—incumbency and candidate spending.[10] Born (2000b) shows that the rise of split-ticket voting from 1856–1868 to 1972–1992 is directly associated with incumbency, more so than with the decline in the partisan strength of the electorate. The importance of incumbency in congressional elections is of long standing, but it has received more attention as legislative races are seen as local (Niemi and Weisberg 1993b, chap. 13). This allows legislative contests to be decided with less regard to national or state trends, allowing for different outcomes for different levels of office. At least for a time, the increased localization of congressional politics led to a phenomenon known as "vanishing marginals" (Mayhew 1974): fewer members of Congress have marginal seats, making them electorally secure. Incumbents, by focusing on constituency service to increase their reelection margins, were relatively immune to national partisan trends, thus contributing to divided government (Ansolabehere, Brady, and Fiorina 1992). Yet studies often find that both local and national forces are significant in congressional elections. For example, Patterson and Monson (1999) find that evaluations of Republican incumbents affected voting for the House in 1996, but so did evaluations of the Republican 104th Congress (see also Campbell 1997 on national forces that affect voting for state legislatures). The localization of congressional and state politics is not sufficient to account for divided government, although it may be an ingredient.[11]

Ironically, the incumbency advantage has led to a focus in the literature on the challenger. Since the incumbent has an advantage, defeating that incumbent requires a strong challenger—one with name recognition and with enough money to wage a high-intensity campaign. This inevitably leads to the questions of when strong challengers emerge and what makes for a quality challenger.

Political forces can affect whether strong challengers are nominated. Strategic politicians are most likely to challenge incumbent members when their party is favored in the election (Jacobson and Kernell 1983), which, in part, involves the popularity of the president and the state of the economy. For example, during a Democratic presidency, a well-known Republican politician might take on a Democratic member of Congress if the economy is weak and the president is unpopular, but that same individual might wait to run if the economy is strong and the president is popular. Politicians have to decide early whether to run, so what matters is the state of the economy and the president's popularity a year or more prior to the election. As Box-Steffensmeier (1996) shows, high-quality challengers can also be deterred by the campaign war chests that incumbents amass.

Candidate quality also matters in Senate elections. Lublin (1994) finds that challengers with previous electoral experience (U.S. representative, former senator, governor, and lesser statewide official) receive 5–7 percent more of the vote against incumbent senators than do challengers without prior office experience (see also Squire 1989, 1992). A large election margin and large war chest also make it less likely that such strong challengers run (Squire 1991). A strong challenger is more likely to run when the president is of the opposite party and especially when the president of the opposite party has low approval ratings. National economic conditions have a greater impact on whether there is a strong challenger than state conditions, but state conditions still have a significant impact.[12]

One advantage that a quality challenger has is that he or she is more likely to be able to raise large amounts of campaign funds. Challengers who cannot raise much money cannot run an effective campaign and typically lose by a large margin, while challengers who can raise large amounts of money are more likely to be competitive. Further, Canon (1993) differentiates between two types of "amateur" challengers: "ambitious amateurs," who are serious about winning (as indicated by being a celebrity, having received a substantial vote in a previous congressional election, or entering after another candidate is already running), and "experience-seeking amateurs," who have little chance of winning. Ambitious amateurs are more likely to run against vulnerable incumbents, whereas experience-seeking amateurs run even when the incumbent is reasonably safe. Ansolabehere, Snyder, and Stewart (2000) find, however, that much of the incumbency advantage is due to the incumbent's personal vote—the vote that results from how legislators serve their constituents through casework—rather than to challenger quality considerations.

While the main emphasis in the literature is on challenger quality, Mondak (1995) and his colleagues (McCurley and Mondak 1995; Mondak, McCurley, and Millman 1999) have shown that the quality of the incumbent is also relevant. Incumbents have reputations in terms of their level of competence and their integrity, and these studies show those factors also affect their vote. However, Adams and Squire (1997) showed the vulnerability of Senate incumbents did not affect the emergence of experienced challengers in 1992, which suggests the limit of this argument.

A related issue has been the role of campaign spending in congressional elections, and especially whether it is solely a means for challengers to counter the incumbency advantage or whether incumbent spending also has a direct pay-off in terms of votes. The early result (Jacobson 1978) was that incumbents received fewer votes as they spent more money. The simple explanation of this counterintuitive result is that incumbents spend large amounts of money on campaigns only if they feel they will be in a difficult campaign, so that the incumbent's campaign spending is actually endogenous in that it is affected by how close the race is. By contrast, spending by challengers has consistently been found to be significant in affecting vote totals because they need to spend large amounts of money on their campaigns to equalize the playing field (Jacobson 1978). Later studies have found incumbent spending to be significant as well, once it could be modeled properly by handling problems such as reciprocal causation, for both the Senate (Gerber 1998) and House (Green and Krasno 1988; cf. Jacobson 1990b) and especially for House incumbents without much seniority (Erikson and Palfrey 1998).

The interrelated factors discussed in the several preceding paragraphs — the incumbency advantage, candidate quality, and campaign spending — all emphasize the importance of candidates in congressional elections. The argument is that divided government results from voters being affected by these factors in their voting for Congress in a candidate-centered era in which people no longer automatically vote a straight ticket.

Conclusion

The search for the causes of divided government was a growth industry in the 1990s, and there is no sign of abatement of that trend. The debate between policy balancing and party decline as explanations of divided government is likely to continue for some time. The notion of nonseparable preferences is attractive to rational choice theorists, while the study of incumbency effects fits well with current directions in research on legislatures, so we expect to see articles on each side of this debate in the next few years.

Still, we are uncomfortable about one aspect of the divided government topic that has received little attention: Why did we have unified government for so long? We now have several explanations for the prevalence of divided government in the second half of the twentieth century, but do any of these also account for the prevalence of unified government in the first half of that century? If divided government resulted from voters intentionally choosing different parties to handle different issues or because of voters' preference for policy voting, then why did that happen more after 1952 than earlier in the century? One answer is that party voting was more important than candidate voting in that period. However, we would expect researchers who believe that divided government has been intentional on the part of voters to instead answer that one party was near enough the median voter in that earlier period that party balancing was not necessary. We would like to see studies of divided government that examine both its presence and its absence.

It is important to look back and see how far we have come in our understanding of legislative elections as a broader arena of electoral behavior. Research on legislative elections is no longer confined to the paradigm set by research on presidential voting. These elections are not just seen as low-information contests in which people fail to recognize who they are voting for or even which party controls the body; the recent debate assumes that voters have some information and asks whether voters consciously choose divided government or pick and choose between their preferred candidates, both legislative and executive, regardless of party labels.

In focusing on divided government in this chapter, we implicitly assume that it matters whether the control of the government is unified or divided. That too, though, is the subject of controversy. Schattschneider (1942) maintained that at least the volume of legislation would not be affected by divided control, although some controversial bills are obstructed in that situation. Nevertheless, the contrary view (popular in the press) is that divided government leads to gridlock, such as in Cox and Kernell's (1991) emphasis on its negative effects with regard to budget priorities. The debate was sharpened by Mayhew's (1991) systematic study showing that significant enactments occurred as often with divided government as with unified government. Krehbiel (1998) also argues that gridlock is not confined to divided government, and that the supermajoritarian procedures of our system can lead to gridlock regardless of partisan control patterns. Still, Kelly (1993) found unified government produced more legislation that was seen as important *both* when it was enacted and afterward (whereas Mayhew had looked at legislation that was seen as important *either* when it was enacted or afterward). Looking at bills that are not enacted, Edwards, Barrett, and Peake (1997) showed that divided government prevented important legislation from passing in the years they studied (1947–1992). Coleman (1999) also found that unified government produced more significant laws and is more responsive to the public mood. In particular, his analysis revealed greater production of important laws under unified government when the mood of the public was liberal and when the ruling party had enough votes to stop a Senate filibuster.

The debate over the consequences of divided government goes beyond the amount of legislation produced. Rohde and Simon (1985) show that presidential vetoes occur more often with divided government. Fiorina (1996, 107) concludes that divided governments are not necessarily less active than unified and that budgetary difficulties do not happen exclusively with divided governments. He asks if it is necessarily bad that divided government leads to more scrutiny of presidential appointments and treaties. At the state level, Alt and Lowry (1994) find that unified government leads to faster reactions to budgetary shocks by adjusting taxes. Suffice it to say that there is as little scholarly consensus on the consequences of divided government as on its causes.

It is hard to predict whether divided government will continue to remain prevalent, just as it would have been difficult in 1990 to predict the course of congressional elections in the following decade. It had become common among congressional scholars by 1990 to use the term *majority party* synonymously with the Democratic Party, as if that party had a lock on the House of Representatives, but the congressional elections of the 1990s contained surprises. The 2000 election further emphasized that the difference between unified and divided government can be very small, even as small as a few hundred disputed ballots in one state.

The importance of the debate in this chapter does not depend on whether divided government continues. Even though divided government ended in 2000 (since the Republican vice president can break the fifty-fifty tie in the Senate), it is important to remember that the last time it ended (after the 1992 election) it returned unexpectedly in just two years. There may be characteristics of the current political situation that make divided government likely—whether because voters consciously prefer policy balancing or because of the increased importance of candidates instead of parties. In any case, the lesson that is most important to retain is that we should no longer look at voting for executives and legislatures in isolation. The interdependencies must be examined directly.

Notes

1. Splitting the difference, Campbell (1997, 225) found that the effect of the economy was significant but not very strong.
2. The Jacobson and Petrocik arguments are often treated in the literature (for example, Mattei and Howes, 2000) as alternatives to Fiorina's policy-balancing argument, which is presented next. Some authors have explicitly referred to those arguments as seeing divided government as unintentional on the part of voters, which is in a sense correct. Our treatment follows Fiorina (1996), who includes Jacobson in his chapter 5 on voters choosing divided government rather than in his chapter 4 on unintentional consequences (also Burden and Kimball forthcoming include Jacobson as part of the intentional argument). Our feeling is that Jacobson and Petrocik see voters as explicitly choosing different parties to control the different branches because of their different policies, whereas the unintentional arguments view divided government as coming more from voting based on the candidate factor. Thus we include Jacobson and Petrocik as a less stringent form of the Fiorina argument, recognizing that there are also real differences between these explanations.
3. This logic for presidential election years seems to imply that the party of presidential candidates who win in landslides should fare worse in congressional voting than the party of presidential candidates who win by narrow margins, but Campbell (1996, 240–241) shows there is instead a strong positive correlation between presidential and congressional votes.
4. A close balance between the number of supporters of each party makes divided government more likely, since the shift of a few votes here or there can divide the government. We would not see this as an explanation of divided government as much as a condition that makes its occurrence more possible. Divided government occurred through most of the Eisenhower administration and all of the Nixon-Ford years, even though party competition was still limited in the South.
5. These are percentages voting for the same party for the president and House. Burden and Kimball (forthcoming) obtain estimates slightly higher for contested-seat districts and 10 points higher when uncontested seats are included.
6. We do not view the unintentional arguments as saying that split-ticket voting is a direct cause of divided government. As Fiorina has argued, split-ticket voting may be a necessary condition for divided government, but it is not an explanation inasmuch as unified government frequently occurs even when split-ticket voting is prevalent. Instead we view the unintentional arguments as saying that divided government results from voting on the basis of the candidates rather than the parties. Voters are not intentionally choosing to balance parties or policies or get particular combinations of parties across branches of government; rather, divided government can occur unintentionally if voters are choosing the most acceptable, most visible, or best-funded candidates who happen to be from different parties. There can then be systematic correlates of divided government to the extent that there are explainable determinants of candidate acceptability, visibility, and funding, including determinants that may correlate with specific offices.
7. While it is clear that divided government is intimately connected with split-ticket voting, it has been difficult to assess the exact level of split-ticket voting. Surveys do not include enough respondents in a district to measure split-ticket voting in each district, and NES surveys have been inaccurate in reconstructing the congressional vote because of some combination of memory issues and question wording problems (Wright 1993). Aggregate election returns by district show the number of votes cast for each candidate, but just subtracting the number of votes cast for a party's presidential and congressional candidates is not an accurate measure of split-ticket voting. First, that measure would miss the countervailing results that occur when some

people vote Republican for president and Democratic for Congress, while other voters split their ticket in the opposite direction. Also, that measure would miss the effect of abstention: the presidential and congressional vote totals for candidates of the same party differ if fewer people vote for Congress than for president—known as the roll-off problem. More generally, the problem is one of ecological inference: estimating individual-level behavior from aggregate-level data. Burden and Kimball use King's (1997) solution to the ecological inference problem to measure ticket splitting by district. Note that this approach rests on a number of statistical assumptions that can be challenged (see Cho and Gaines 2001 and the rebuttal by Burden and Kimball in the 2001 *American Political Science Review*), so we would not be surprised if later work leads to some modifications.

8. Kimball (1997) also does not find evidence in NES data of moderate voters who might have split their tickets to balance policy.

9. Similarly Grofman, Koetzle, McDonald, and Brunell (2000) show that for congressional districts that elect Democrats to the House, districts with members who voted more conservative in Congress were more likely to give the Republican presidential candidate a majority, and conversely for districts that elect Republicans to the House.

10. Institutional factors also matter, particularly straight-ticket options on the ballot (such as the party lever in some states) as Campbell and Miller (1957) demonstrated with individual data.

11. Incumbents clearly have an advantage in House elections, but it has been difficult to measure that advantage. A basic decision is whether to measure the effect of incumbency on the vote or on the election outcome. One of the best regarded vote-denominated measures is Gelman and King's (1990), which corrects for the underestimate of the incumbency advantage in measures based on the vote share of the winning candidate. They use the incumbent party's vote differential over successive elections to measure how much greater a share of the two-party vote is associated with incumbency. The value of incumbency has increased over time according to this measure, making incumbents less vulnerable to party tides (Ansolabehere, Brady, and Fiorina 1992) but still susceptible to local factors. Incumbents, however, can win with higher margins without their being more likely to win the next time (Jacobson 1987, 128–130), which suggests the utility of outcome-denominated measures of the incumbency advantage. Carey, Niemi, and Powell (2000) and Berry, Berkman, and Schneiderman (2000) analyze the incumbency advantage at the state level using such a measure. Carey et al. estimate that advantage by state and then examine its determinants, finding that the incumbency advantage is greatest for chambers with single-member districts, two-year terms, and high professionalization as indicated by high salaries, long sessions, and considerable money for staffs and other support. Incumbents would be hardest to dislodge in such chambers, increasing the chances for divided government, depending on the outcome of the race for governor.

12. It is notable that Burden and Kimball do not find challenger experience to have significant direct effect on split-ticket voting, but, as they recognize, experienced challengers are able to obtain more campaign funding, which is important in their results.

Further Readings

Understanding Legislative Elections
Campbell, James E., *The Presidential Pulse of Congressional Elections*, 2d ed. (Lexington: University Press of Kentucky, 1997). Theory of and evidence for surge and decline in legislative elections at federal and state levels.

Fowler, Linda L., *Candidates, Congress, and the American Democracy* (Ann Arbor: University of Michigan Press, 1993). The importance of studying candidacies to understand congressional election outcomes.

Weisberg, Herbert, Eric Heberlig, and Lisa Campoli, "How Do Candidacies Affect Elections?" In *Classics in Congressional Politics,* ed. Weisberg, Herberlig, and Campoli (New York: Longman, 1999). Review of the literature on the role of incumbency and challengers in congressional elections.

State Legislative Elections

Atkeson, Lonna Rae, and Randall W. Partin, "Economic and Referendum Voting: A Comparison of Gubernatorial and Senatorial Elections," *American Political Science Review* 89 (1995): 99–107. Governors are held accountable for state economic conditions, while senators are not.

Carey, John M., Richard G. Niemi, and Lynda W. Powell, "Incumbency and the Probability of Reelection in State Legislative Elections," *Journal of Politics* 62 (2000): 671–700. Incumbency advantage is related to institutional characteristics; incumbents in single-member districts, with four-year terms and high salaries, have a greater advantage.

Carsey, Thomas M., and Gerald C. Wright, "State and National Factors in Gubernatorial and Senatorial Elections," *American Journal of Political Science* 42 (1998): 994–1002. Voting in gubernatorial elections responds to the state economy, while voting in senate elections responds to the national economy.

Senate Elections

Adams, Greg D., and Peverill Squire, "Incumbent Vulnerability and Challenger Emergence in Senate Elections," *Political Behavior* 19 (1997): 97–111. Senate challenger quality increases with the size of the pool of potential high-quality challengers.

Kahn, Kim Fridkin, and Patrick J. Kenney, *The Spectacle of U.S. Senate Elections* (Princeton: Princeton University Press, 1999). When competition between Senate candidates is strong, the media and voters respond to campaign themes and issues.

Lublin, David Ian, "Quality, Not Quantity: Strategic Politicians in U.S. Senate Elections, 1952–1990," *Journal of Politics* 56 (1994): 228–241. Potential Senate challengers take local and national political and economic factors into account in making their candidacy decisions.

Westlye, Mark C., *Senate Elections and Campaign Intensity* (Baltimore: Johns Hopkins University Press, 1991). The personal attributes of Senate candidates attract media attention and elite support, determining how competitive the races will be.

The Causes of Divided Government

Fiorina, Morris P., *Divided Government,* 2d ed. (Boston: Allyn & Bacon, 1996). The causes and consequences of divided government at the national and state levels, with an emphasis on intentional policy balancing.

Jacobson, Gary C., *The Electoral Origins of Divided Government* (Boulder, Colo.: Westview, 1990). Examination of structural and political explanations of divided government before the 1990s.

Petrocik, John R., "Divided Government: Is It All in the Campaigns?" In *The Politics of Divided Government,* ed. Gary W. Cox and Samuel Kernell (Boulder, Colo.: Westview, 1991). Presents a theory of issue ownership by the parties.

Split-Ticket Voting

Born, Richard, "Policy-Balancing Models and the Split-Ticket Voter, 1972–1996," *American Politics Quarterly* 28 (2000): 131–162. Policy balancing can explain split-ticket voting only in 1996.

Frymer, Paul, Thomas P. Kim, and Terri L. Bimes, "Party Elites, Ideological Voters, and Divided Party Government," *Legislative Studies Quarterly* 22 (1997): 195–216. Voters split their tickets to achieve ideological consistency.

Grofman, Bernard, William Koetzle, Michael McDonald, and Thomas L. Brunell, "A New Look at Split-Ticket Outcomes for House and President: The Comparative Midpoints Model," *Journal of Politics* 62 (2000): 34–50. A comparative midpoints model is developed to test the ideological consistency of split-ticket voting.

Lacy, Dean, and Philip Paolino, "Downsian Voting and the Separation of Power," *American Journal of Political Science* 42 (1998): 1180–1199. Support for policy balancing is found by looking at voters' distances from expected government positions.

Smith, Jr., Charles E., Robert D. Brown, John M. Bruce, and L. Marvin Overby, "Party Balancing and Voting for Congress in the 1996 National Election," *American Journal of Political Science* 43 (1999): 737–764. Support for policy balancing is found by looking at voters with separable and nonseparable preferences.

Consequences of Divided Government

Coleman, John J., "Unified Government, Divided Government, and Party Responsiveness," *American Political Science Review* 93 (1999): 821–835. Congress passes more significant legislation during periods of unified government.

Mayhew, David R., *Divided We Govern: Party Control, Lawmaking, and Investigations, 1946–1990* (New Haven: Yale University Press, 1991). Divided government does not detract from congressional actions.

Websites

Almanac of American Politics: http://www.freedomchannel.com/almanac/almanac_of_amer_pol.cfm. Detailed information about each congressional district and current member of Congress.

House of Representatives: http://clerkweb.house.gov/elections/elections.htm. Historical election returns back to 1920.

National Conference of State Legislatures: http://www.ncsl.org. Information about legislators and legislatures along with links to states' legislative websites.

15. Balancing Explanations of Divided Government

Morris Fiorina

Until recently analyses of elections for different public offices proceeded in isolation from one another. Presidential elections analyses employed one set of major concepts—parties, issues, ideology, and candidate traits. Congressional elections analyses employed a different set—incumbency, campaign spending, the quality of challengers. The major point of contact between the two areas of work was the notion of presidential coattails: the popularity of presidential candidates and the performance of the incumbent president have some impact on the fortunes of congressional candidates. Numerous studies suggested, however, that this impact had been declining (Edwards 1980, 70–78). While this large body of work did not explicitly address the subject of divided government, the explanation implied by it would simply be that voters vote *differently* for different offices. Research would have offered no specific explanation for opposite patterns in different states, it would only have said that the candidates and what they embodied must have differed in ways sufficient to produce the opposing patterns.

Very recently a number of analysts have proposed what I will term "balancing" explanations of divided government. These explanations presume that some citizens have a general appreciation of the institutional structure of American government and that such institutional considerations enter into their voting decisions. . . . [B]alancing arguments have an element of purpose or intention in them. To forestall misunderstanding, let me be very clear about this point.

To suggest that some voters make choices that have the consequence of dividing government is not to claim that there are millions of voters walking around saying "I voted for George Bush because I felt he was better than Mike Dukakis, but I voted for a Democratic representative because I wanted to attach a ball and chain to Bush's ankle." It is unlikely that many such voters exist. But voters may be doing something less conscious. Having made a decision to support Bush and feeling less than enthusiastic about it, they may be predisposed to listen to Democratic appeals for other offices. Having tentatively decided to support Richard Nixon or Ronald Reagan and having been nervous about their decision, voters might have been susceptible to the appeals of other Democratic candidates. While not consciously choosing a divided government, people may have a vague appreciation of the overall picture that plays some role in how they vote.

Source: Excerpts from pp. 63–65, 72–81, 151–153 from *Divided Government,* 2nd edition, by Morris Fiorina. Copyright © 1995 by Allyn & Bacon. Reprinted by permission of Addison-Wesley Educational Publishers.

People could be voting as if they are making conscious choices to divide government even if their individual decisions are well below the conscious level.

A number of polls have shown that Americans approve of divided government. In an NBC News/*Wall Street Journal* (*WSJ*) survey taken before the 1988 elections, 54 percent of likely voters preferred that different parties control the presidency and Congress while only 32 percent preferred unified government (Perry 1988). In an October 1990 NBC/*WSJ* survey (*Public Perspective* 1991), the margin of divided government supporters was about 3:1 (67:23 percent). While such sentiments certainly do not imply that so many voters consciously choose divided control, they do indicate that the idea of divided government is sufficiently meaningful that voters do not hesitate to offer an evaluation of one, an evaluation coincidentally consistent with what they collectively choose.[1] That is the notion underlying balance models: the overall pattern of election outcomes is consistent with the notion of an electorate behaving *as if* it were consciously choosing or rejecting divided government. . . .

In Search of Moderation

In an earlier article (Fiorina 1988) that addressed divided control during the Reagan administration, I proposed a model of policy or ideological balancing. While this model provides explanations for a [wide] range of developments . . . it makes assumptions about voters that are unlikely to be literally satisfied in large numbers. Thus, I emphasize the *as if* character of the model: the electorate in the large seems to behave as if it were balancing the policies or ideologies of the opposing parties by placing them in control of different institutions.

The model is a spatial model; voters and parties are arrayed along a policy or ideological dimension that runs from left to right (Figure 15-1). Such models have been developed by researchers as a way of representing common political discourse. Consider the frequency of spatial metaphors in political discussion—"parties of the left and right," "move to the center," "extreme left," "ultraright," "being outflanked," and so forth.[2] Voters are assumed to have most preferred positions, called "ideal points," and to become progressively less favorable to policies as the policies depart from their ideal in either direction. Parties, in turn, adopt positions in order to appeal to voters and win elections. In Figure 15-1 we array four voters, denoted V_1, V_2, V_3, V_4, from the far left to the far right, and place party D on the left, and party R on the right. The vertical line between V_2 and V_3 is a *cutting line* that separates all voters who are closer to D from those closer to R. If more voters lie to the left of the cutting line than to the right, D wins.

Now, to breathe some life into this abstract representation, imagine that Figure 15-1 represents a hypothetical political system, a system that somewhat resembles—*in greatly simplified form*—the United States circa 1984. This hypothetical system has two parties: the San Francisco Democrats (D) and the Reagan Republicans (R). Neither party is a microcosm of the electorate. When voters look at party D, they see disproportionate numbers of minorities, gay rights

Figure 15-1 Electoral Choice in a Unitary System

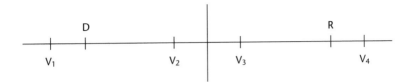

activists, radical feminists, and peaceniks; when voters look at party R, they see disproportionate numbers of fundamentalists, bigots, pro-life activists, and chicken-hawks (again, I emphasize that this is a hypothetical situation constructed to allow a clear argument). When the voters compare the policy positions of the two parties, they see distinct differences. On economic policy, the D party favors higher income taxes and more spending on human services on the grounds that most citizens are rich and can easily afford it. On the other hand, the R party favors tax breaks for the rich and reduced human services spending on the grounds that the poor are mostly lazy and undeserving. On foreign policy, the D party says true democracy is found only in certain Third World workers' paradises. In contrast the R party says nuclear war is really nothing to worry about so long as you have three feet of dirt and a shovel. I could go on in this vein, but I trust the point is clear.

For voter V_1, a liberal activist, party D stands for all that is good and true. Voter V_4, a conservative activist, feels a similar affection toward party R. But voters V_2 and V_3, moderate middle-of-the-road citizens, are much less enthusiastic about their choices. They are tolerant of minority groups and points of view but remain wedded to traditional values. They want low taxes but also a cushion for economic losers. They want an adequate defense but prefer negotiation to confrontation. In a parliamentary system such as that of Great Britain, such moderate voters must like it or lump it; their choices are limited to casting an unenthusiastic vote for the closer party or abstaining.[3] If everyone votes, V_2 votes for D and V_3 for R.

But suppose that our hypothetical political system has a presidential form of government, like the United States, with independent elections for executive and legislative offices. For purposes of simplifying the argument, assume that the legislature is unicameral. Then, the voters in the hypothetical system have the option of voting for unified control of legislative and executive institutions, or of voting for divided control. This means that they can choose among four "platforms" rather than two:

DD: unified D
DR: divided—D executive/R legislature
RD: divided—R executive/D legislature
RR: unified R

Figure 15-2 Electoral Choice in a Separation-of-Powers System

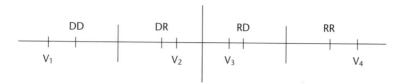

Voters understand, of course, that the executive and the legislature together determine public policy, so that when control of the two institutions is divided, any adopted policies must be compromises between the two party's platforms. A common algebraic way of representing such a compromise is by a weighted average:

Policy = q(executive policy) + $(1 - q)$(legislative policy)
$(0 < q < 1)$

The weight, q, represents the power of the executive, and the complementary weight $(1 - q)$ the power of the legislature. If $q = .5$, the executive and legislature are equally powerful, and public policy is a 50:50 mixture of what the two institutions favor. If voters believe that the executive is twice as influential as the legislature in determining policy, then q would be $\frac{2}{3}$ and $(1 - q)$ would be $\frac{1}{3}$. If the latter situation is the case, then voters in this hypothetical society would face the choices depicted in Figure 15-2 rather than Figure 15-1. DR is the position determined by the equation ($\frac{2}{3}$D + $\frac{1}{3}$R), and RD is the position determined by ($\frac{2}{3}$R + $\frac{1}{3}$D).

There are now three cutting lines. As before, the middle cutting line separates those voters closer to position DD, a unified Democratic government, from those closer to position RR, a unified Republican government. But two other cutting lines now separate split-ticket voters from straight-ticket voters. Voters between the left and center cutting-lines are closest to the DR position (divided government with a Democratic executive and Republican legislature) and will split their tickets accordingly, while voters between the center and right cutting lines are closer to the RD position (divided government with a Republican executive and Democratic legislature) and will split their tickets the opposite way. Given the option of splitting their tickets, V_2 and V_3 are now much happier with their choices.

Depending on voter preferences, divided government can easily result. Figure 15-3 depicts a situation in which 25 percent of the electorate lies in the DD interval (everyone left of the left cutting line). Such voters are closest to DD and cast a straight D ticket. Similarly, 20 percent of the electorate lies in the DR interval, 35 percent in the RD interval, and 20 percent in the RR interval. This electorate casts 55 percent of its vote for the Republican executive candidate (everyone in RD and RR) and 60 percent of its vote for Democratic legislative candidates (everyone in DD and RD).

Figure 15-3 Example of Divided Government

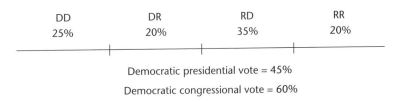

Democratic presidential vote = 45%

Democratic congressional vote = 60%

   In this simple policy-balancing model, ticket-splitters come from the central, moderate range of the ideological spectrum. More extreme voters cast straight tickets, while moderate voters are more likely to split their tickets. Not surprisingly, this happens to be true in recent American elections. In 1984 and 1988, for example, there is a significant relationship between ticket-splitting and placing oneself in the middle ranges of a liberal-conservative scale.[4]
   Additional insight can be obtained by examining some dynamics of this simple model. Suppose that at one time competitive pressures have brought the parties very close together, so that many feel there's not a dime's worth of difference between them. Under such conditions, split-ticket voting is minimized, as the left and right cutting lines move very close to the center (Figure 15-4, top). Most voters will fall into either the DD or the RR intervals, where straight-ticket voting is their choice (not that it makes a lot of difference). Now, suppose that factors *other than a shift in voter preferences* lead the parties to polarize. Perhaps dissatisfied activists in the R party come to believe that there is a large conservative population that does not vote out of disgust with the lack of choice the parties offer, so the R party moves right to offer the electorate "a choice, not an echo." Perhaps intense disagreement with party policies and the emergence of new social movements lead the D party to move left. In this changed situation there is a significant increase in ticket splitting as the left and right cutting lines move apart (Figure 15-4, bottom).
   Is the resemblance of this simple model to recent American electoral history purely coincidental? In 1964 the Goldwater movement captured the Republican party, and in 1968 the Democrats split into new politics and traditionalist wings. During that interval of time, ticket-splitting in presidential-House races jumped 10 percent. If polarization of the two parties in fact contributed to the rise in ticket-splitting, as the model suggests, it identifies a striking irony in the efforts of contemporary ideologues. Demanding a choice, not an echo, they pulled their candidates toward more extreme positions. But preferring the echo to the choice, an increasing number of voters split their tickets. Activists tried to impose principled programmatic government; voters responded with divided government.
   Can the pattern of split-ticket voting be explained by such a model? Yes, it emerges as a simple function of the weight, q. When $q > .5$ (the executive is

Figure 15-4 Effect of Party Polarization

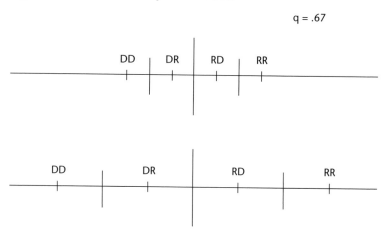

relatively more influential than the legislature in determining policy), voters will support the executive candidate of the party closer to them on the issues. Certainly, on the national level most analysts have viewed the presidency as stronger than the Congress at least since the time of FDR; thus, ticket splitting would be composed primarily of Republican president/Democratic congressional voters when the Republicans are closer to the median voter on the issues than are the Democrats. On first hearing this might seem to contradict the available evidence since there was much discussion of Mondale's being closer to the electorate than Reagan was in 1984. But the Republican *party* was clearly perceived as closer to the median than the Democrats (Table 15-1), and issues on which Mondale was closer, such as the ERA and Central America, were simply not of major concern to voters who were not already Democratic loyalists. There is little doubt that on core issues involving race, taxes, and traditional values, Reagan was closer than Mondale (Table 15-2). More recently, using extensive evidence from the 1988 NES Senate study, Erikson (1990b) shows that the Republican party and George Bush were closer to the average voter than the Democratic party and Michael Dukakis, and, more generally, Republican House and Senate candidates on average were perceived as closer to the average voter than their Democratic opponents.

Not only does a policy balancing model explain the national pattern of Republican presidents/Democratic Congresses, but it can explain the unusual state patterns as well. Within the model, Democratic-headed divided government can occur in two ways. The first is if the Democrats are closer to the electorate on the issues. In that event the national pattern would be reversed. Thinking of the states in which Democratic-headed divided government occurs—North Dakota, Idaho—this possibility seems somewhat unlikely. The second explanation of Democratic-headed divided government lies in the influ-

Table 15-1 Voter Policy Positions Compared with Perceptions of Party Positions (Averages on Seven-Point Scales)

	Democratic position	Citizen position	Republican position
Liberal-conservative ideology[a]	3.1	4.3	5.1
Government provision of public services[a]	5.3	3.8	2.9
Aid to minorities[a]	3.0	4.2	4.6
U.S. involvement in Central America	4.5	4.5	3.0
Defense spending	3.2	4.0	5.4
Aid to women[a]	3.1	3.9	4.6
Cooperation with Soviet Union[a]	3.2	4.1	4.9
Government responsibility for jobs and living standards[a]	3.1	4.4	4.9

[a]Republican Party closer to mean voter position.

Source: 1984 NES.

ence parameter, q. If the executive is perceived as *less* influential than the legislature ($q < .5$), contrary to our assumption about the president vis-à-vis Congress, then ticket-splitters vote for the legislative candidate of the closer party and the executive candidate of the farther one. Thus, states with governors who are institutionally weak would produce patterns of ticket-splitting opposite those found in national elections.

In sum, a model of policy balancing has considerable explanatory power when applied to contemporary American electoral history. It can explain differential patterns of ticket-splitting (and divided government) and changes over time in the incidence of ticket-splitting. Though many analysts will view the assumed calculations as beyond the capacity of real-world voters, it would not be the first time that the collective wisdom of the electorate surprised the experts. For too long political scientists have focused on the failings and flaws of the individual citizen. Only recently have we begun to realize that *collectivities* of citizens display an impressive measure of what would be considered rational, responsible behavior. Converse (1990), for example, has observed that, collectively, the citizenry is far more intellectually organized than the *individuals* he studied earlier, a point given theoretical underpinning by Feld and Grofman (1988). And far more extensively, Page and Shapiro (1992) show how public opinion—as distinct from the opinions of individual citizens—is coherent and responsive. Perhaps Ladd's (1990) reference to divided government as "cognitive Madisonianism" is more than a fanciful metaphor.

Probably the most important point to take away from the preceding discussion is the crucial importance of party polarization. When the parties are relatively close, near the center of gravity of the electorate, ticket-splitting declines. When the parties move away from each other, following their own internal dynamics toward the extremes of the voter distribution, they open up a

Table 15-2   Voter Policy Positions Compared with Perceptions of Reagan and Mondale Positions, 1984 (Averages on Seven-Point Scales)

Issue	Reagan position	Citizen position	Mondale position
Fewer services or increased spending?	2.74	3.86	5.11
Government should aid minorities, or they should help themselves	4.66	4.08	3.04
Government should guarantee jobs and standard of living, or individual responsibility	5.15	4.34	3.16

Source: 1984 NES.

large policy range in which ticket-splitting is the voter response. Small, well-organized cadres of unrepresentative political activists can determine the party positions, but large, unorganized electorates can prevent such positions from being implemented. . . .*

Research on Purposive Explanations

[The previous section] discussed a number of purposive explanations for the split-ticket voting that underlies contemporary patterns of divided control. These have in common the idea that some voters, perhaps unconsciously, are engaging in some kind of balancing act when they vote, leaning toward one party when voting for the executive but countering that vote with a different one when voting for legislators. Voters could be balancing off Democratic competence in domestic policy against Republican competence in foreign and macroeconomic policy as suggested by Gary Jacobson, or balancing off conservative Republicans with liberal Democrats as I had suggested earlier, or even voting for gridlock when both parties seemed corrupt and untrustworthy. The policy or ideological balancing model, in particular, has stimulated a lively controversy.

In [the previous section] I observed that *ceteris paribus* balancing models predict that ticket-splitting would be most common among people between the two parties—moderates, relatively speaking—and noted that the evidence was consistent with that prediction (note 4). I did not make much of the finding since it seemed so obvious. Moreover, other logics would also suggest that people between the parties are more likely to split. For example, people between the parties might view them as equally good or bad and consequently would be indifferent between them. It would not be surprising if such "indifferents" scattered their votes among candidates of both parties.

Editors' Note: The preceding sections were taken from the original 1992 edition of Fiorina's book. He added the following section to the 1996 edition in order to evaluate research written in the intervening years.

Somewhat surprisingly, Alvarez and Schousen (1993) find that this prediction is not upheld when looking at voter and candidate placements in the 1972–1988 American National Election Studies. Born (1994), who is otherwise critical of balancing models, reports more positive findings, although they are not statistically significant. Garand and Lichtl (2000) report stronger positive findings for the 1992 national elections. They also find that people who express an abstract preference for divided over unified government are more likely to split their ticket, although this effect is contingent on voters' having a certain level of political knowledge.

Only Born has attempted to assess the other predictions generated by the policy balancing model. He finds that the "pattern prediction" that specifies *how* the voter will split her vote between president and House is clearly supported by the data both at the individual and aggregate levels (Born 1994, 107–108). He also attempts to test the dynamic predictions of the model—for example, that increasing polarization will lead to increasing ticket-splitting, *ceteris paribus*. He views the results as generally negative, while I view them as generally positive, but, since the tests are based on variation across only five election studies (1972–1988) all of which come *after* the sharp rise in national ticket splitting, the findings are inconclusive (Fiorina 1994).

Along somewhat different lines, Borrelli (1995) reports mixed results for ideological balancing models in explaining state divided government. Alesina and Rosenthal (1989) find temporal balancing models (on-year to off-term) useful in explaining the results of mid-term national elections. Finally, Schmidt, Kenny, and Morton (1996) report clear support for balancing in Senate elections. Other things being equal, Senators running for reelection between 1962 and 1990 did from 5–17 percent better when the sitting Senator not up for reelection was a member of the other party.

All in all, the empirical support for the kind of policy balancing model sketched in [the previous section] is mixed. I would agree with Borrelli's (1995) assessment that such models remain "in the ring." Many colleagues believe that such models make too severe informational demands on the voter. But I never advanced such a model as an explanation of *all* ticket-splitting. About 25 percent of the voters split their tickets between presidential and House decisions. About one-third of them fall into the high information category where Garand and Lichtl (2000) find evidence for purposive ticket-splitting. That means about 8 percent of the voters could be engaging in intentional behavior. A net shift of about that size turned American politics on its head in 1994. . . .

Notes

1. A generation ago political analysts made much of the fact that fewer than half the voters knew which party controlled the House before Eisenhower's reelection in 1956. When Nixon was reelected in 1972, fully three-fourths of the voters knew that the Democrats controlled the House. In the interim some learning evidently occurred.

2. The seminal work is Downs (1957, chap. 7). For a comprehensive survey of the spatial modeling literature see Enelow and Hinich (1984).

3. Unless a third party enters the arena, as in fact happened in 1979 when Labour leaders dissatisfied with the drift of their party joined with the Liberals to form the Alliance.

4. Split-ticket voting is significantly associated with moderate ideological positioning and weak partisanship:

$$1988 \text{ Ticsplit} = -1.28 + .13 \text{ ideology} + .20 \text{ party ID}$$
$$(7.50) \quad (2.39) \qquad\quad (3.82)$$

$$1984 \text{ Ticsplit} = -1.61 + .14 \text{ ideology} + .24 \text{ party ID}$$
$$(8.63) \quad (2.54) \qquad\quad (5.82)$$

(probit estimates, t-statistics in parentheses). The seven-point ideology and party identification scales are "folded" so that they run from 1 to 4 (extremist to moderate, strong partisan to pure independent, respectively).

16. A New Approach to the Study of Ticket Splitting

Barry C. Burden and David C. Kimball

The 1990s have witnessed a flurry of research on split-ticket voting and divided government in the United States (Alesina and Rosenthal 1995; Alvarez and Schousen 1993; Beck et al. 1992; Born 1994; Cox and Kernell 1991; Fiorina 1996; Frymer, Kim, and Bimes 1997; Galderisi 1996; Jacobson 1990c). Both are more common features of the political landscape today than in previous periods of American history and thus warrant this scholarly attention. Fifteen of the last 22 national elections have produced divided government, and surveys show that split-ticket voting rates are higher than in previous decades. There is little consensus on what causes ticket splitting. Some researchers argue that it is done intentionally in an attempt to produce the proper mix of policies or keep the political parties in check (Alesina and Rosenthal 1995; Fiorina 1996; Ingberman and Villani 1993). Others believe it is the unintentional by-product of other factors, such as the competitiveness of congressional elections (Jacobson 1997; Kimball 1997), the blurring of ideological boundaries between the parties (Born 1994; Kimball 1997; Soss and Canon 1995), and ballot mechanisms (Beck 1997; Campbell and Miller 1957). Whatever the eventual answer, it is clear that scholars need to rethink voting behavior to produce a theory that explains ticket splitting (Sundquist 1988). Indeed, Fiorina (1996, 129) claims in his definitive *Divided Government* that "ticket-splitting and other aspects of the relationships between voting for different offices should become a central focus of research."

We take up Fiorina's charge by using a new statistical method (King 1997) to produce more accurate estimates of the direction and magnitude of split-ticket voting in each state and congressional district in 1988. We apply the method to presidential and congressional voting behavior by estimating president/House and president/Senate ticket splitting. The estimates are then used in a series of analyses to compare our ecological estimates to other estimates and to explain why ticket splitting is so common in some places and nonexistent in others. The 1988 elections are an ideal context in which to study split-ticket voting. Unlike earlier periods in American electoral history, which produced divided government during midterm elections, the 1980s witnessed split outcomes in presidential years as well. In fact, it was the simultaneous election of George Bush with the maintenance of the Democratic status quo in Congress in 1988 that interested many researchers in split-ticket voting (Fiorina 1996; Jacobson 1990c).

Source: American Political Science Review 92, 3 (September 1998): 533–544.

Though this case is theoretically appropriate, inferences about the direction and magnitude of ticket splitting have been hindered because of data limitations. Aggregate measures have been used in the literature for several decades but are flawed by the well-known "ecological fallacy," which refers to the hazards of making individual-level inferences from aggregate data. Survey data also have been used, but national samples are not large enough to make inferences about voting behavior in particular districts. We employ King's technique to produce more accurate estimates of split-ticket voting within districts and states. Unlike earlier studies based on just a few data points (indexed by time), our data set contains hundreds of observations (indexed by district), making it easier to generalize. We demonstrate the validity of these estimates and then combine them with other data to determine what causes American voters to split tickets. We find strong evidence for the contention that candidates — not voters — are primarily responsible for producing divided government. Most variation in the extent of ticket splitting across districts and states is not due to policy balancing on the part of voters.

It is worth studying ticket splitting at the district and state level because election outcomes are determined within these electoral units (Wright 1989). Voters within these geographical boundaries, not the national population, determine the composition of Congress and the Electoral College. Our approach allows us to link ticket splitting directly with divided government because we can compare levels of ticket splitting to the election outcome in each state or district.

Using Ecological Inference to Study Ticket Splitting

Given the ubiquity of divided government in American national politics, it is important to understand how many voters split their ballots and why. Accurate estimates will help us understand the extent to which divided government is the will of the voters. Why voters split tickets is a continuing research question in studies of electoral behavior. Unfortunately, the data used to answer the question have not been up to the task. Here, we consider the two traditional approaches — using individual survey and aggregate election data — and demonstrate why the new method is an improvement.

In addition to King's method, several other techniques developed in political science, sociology, statistics, and other fields may be helpful in drawing individual inferences from aggregate data. Perhaps the earliest is the "method of bounds" (Duncan and Davis 1953), which uses a deterministic relationship between aggregate quantities to narrow the range of possible values of the individual-level parameters of interest. Some have applied that method while adding external assumptions or substantive knowledge to narrow even more the logical bounds around the individual-level parameters (Achen and Shively 1995; Shively 1991; Sigelman 1991). The most commonly used ecological inference method is probably Goodman's (1959) regression technique. Though Goodman warned against its use, one may estimate individual-level parameters through simple linear regression, assuming that the parameters do not vary across districts (or vary randomly across districts around their global values).

Approaches to the ecological inference problem have become remarkably complex since that time. Achen and Shively (1995) survey the latest techniques, many of which allow for some relaxation of Goodman's constancy assumption or incorporate other substantive assumptions about the individual-level parameters and their relationships with aggregate-level variables. Most of these techniques estimate only one global set of individual-level parameters, however, not a pair for each electoral district, which is essential for our purposes. King's method provides district-level estimates of the quantities of interest and the uncertainty associated with them without making unreasonable assumptions about the constancy of the parameters we are estimating. It also permits us to work *between* the individual and aggregate levels of analysis, which helps us link ticket splitting, to split-party election outcomes. In addition, while others have noted a connection between the method of bounds and Goodman's regression (Achen and Shively 1995), King's approach may be the first to combine the insights of both earlier methods.

Individual Data

As with other voting studies, analyses of ticket splitting rely primarily on survey data. The National Election Studies (NES), for instance, routinely asks a sample of Americans how they voted in the most recent elections. These data have been informative for examining the national trend in ticket splitting over the last 45 years and some of its determinants. A serious problem is that one cannot decompose national survey samples into smaller units of aggregation, such as states or voting districts, because of the number of cases required for such an analysis (Voss, Gelman, and King 1995). The NES interviews about 2,000 people each election year; so relatively few respondents come from each state and even fewer are drawn from any given House district. This makes estimates inefficient, if they are possible at all. Furthermore, a representative national sample usually is not representative of voters from each state or congressional district (Westlye 1991).[1]

Compounding the problem is the potential for inaccurate reports of voting behavior in surveys (Abramson and Claggett 1991; Campbell et al. 1960; Silver, Anderson, and Abramson 1986; Wright 1993). Proportions based on survey data are only unbiased if respondents report their voting behavior accurately.[2] For example, researchers have pointed out that the NES overstates support for the winning (Wright 1990) and incumbent (Eubank and Gow 1983; Gow and Eubank 1984) congressional candidates.[3] This is due either to forgetfulness over time, social desirability pressures, or a question wording artifact (Box-Steffensmeier and Jacobson 1995; Jacobson and Rivers 1993; Wright 1990). Others argue that surveys tend to overstate voter turnout (Abramson and Claggett 1991; Campbell et al. 1960; Silver, Anderson, and Abramson 1986). Thus, a study of voting data at an aggregated level is a worthwhile supplement to self-reported voting patterns derived from surveys.

Aggregate Data

Aggregate election data also have been used to examine split-ticket voting. Burnham's (1965, 1970) comprehensive analysis of American political realignments cites ticket splitting as a sign of large-scale political change. His operationalization of split-ticket voting is the simple difference between the highest and lowest Democratic percentage of the two-party vote among races within each state. Burnham admits that his indicator is "measured rather crudely," although it was one of the best available at the time. As is well known, the problem with such a measure is that making individual inferences from aggregate data may lead to false conclusions. Furthermore, Burnham's method can only estimate total ticket splitting, not its direction; the method cannot distinguish those who select a Republican president and a Democratic congressional candidate from those who choose a Democratic president and a Republican for Congress.

Rusk (1970) uses the same aggregate measure while pointing out two of its flaws. First, "it would not detect mutual crossovers between the two parties" (1224); second, differences in the type of election being held in the states the same year threaten interstate comparisons, a problem Rusk calls the "race composition factor." The latter is a concern, but consider the more immediate ramifications of mutual crossover. Even if two states have the same contests on the ballot, Burnham's measure understates ticket splitting, since ballots split in opposite directions cancel out one another. For instance, a value of zero may mean that no split-ticket voting occurred (as Burnham and Rusk assume) or that every voter is casting a split ticket. The truth is likely to lie somewhere in between. Much may be happening at the individual level, but aggregate data cannot reveal it, a consequence of the ecological fallacy that has plagued social science for decades (King 1997; Robinson 1950).

Another aggregate technique relies on the two-office split result, which assumes that a difference in party outcomes for two offices in the same district is evidence of widespread ticket splitting. The increasing proportion of congressional districts with split results in presidential and House contests is used to infer that ticket splitting has increased over time (Cummings 1966; Fiorina 1996). But Feigert (1979) shows that this technique can produce inaccurate estimates and instead finds a high correlation between split districts and ballot roll-off.[4] Below, we show that once the direction of ticket splitting is properly estimated, there is a conditional relationship between split-ticket voting and split outcomes.

With the development of a solution to the ecological inference problem, we can produce district- and state-level estimates of the proportion of voters casting split ballots that avoid the problems described above. Since we use aggregate data, survey misreporting is not a concern; only collective (and anonymous) votes

Table 16-1   Voting in Maryland's Sixth Congressional District, 1988

Presidential Voting Decision	House Voting Decision			Total
	Byron (D)	Halsey (R)	Abstain	
Dukakis (D)		*Dukakis splitters*		82,781
Bush (R)	*Bush splitters*			158,808
Total	166,753	54,528	20,308	241,589

are needed. In addition, King's method allows us to account for both types of ticket splitting, thus avoiding the crossover problem in previous aggregate measures. Before turning to the estimation itself, we briefly describe the ecological inference problem.

The Problem as a 2 × 3 Contingency Table

The general ecological inference problem may be conceptualized as a standard contingency table with missing data. The marginals of the table are known, since they are based on aggregate data, but the cell percentages are unknown (King 1997; Markus 1974). Table 16-1 lays out the ecological inference problem in estimating ticket splitting, using 1988 congressional election results from Maryland's Sixth District as an example. We choose this district for illustration because it produced a split-party result that matched the national pattern: a Republican (George Bush) at the presidential level and a Democrat (Beverly Byron) at the congressional level. Since the presidential contest usually appears at the top of the ballot and is the more visible race, we assume that voters make their presidential choice first. Voters then have three options in the congressional races that appear farther down the ballot: (1) vote Democratic, (2) vote Republican, or (3) abstain.[5] From election returns we know how many voters in Maryland's Sixth District chose Bush in the presidential contest (158,808), and we know how many voters selected Byron, the Democratic candidate for the House (166,753), but we do not know how many of the Bush voters split their ballot by also selecting Byron. Presumably, this was common, since each candidate carried the district by a hefty margin. We do know that the number of Bush voters who split their ballot ("Bush splitters") is between 83,972 (the Byron total minus the Dukakis total, or .528 of all Bush voters in the district) and 158,808 (all Bush voters), a wide interval. Similarly, we have reason to believe that slightly more than 20,000 presidential voters "rolled off" by not casting a vote in the House race, but we do not know whether abstention in the House contest was more prevalent among Bush or Dukakis voters.

Our estimation of ticket splitting is a two-stage process that divides Table 16-1 into two 2 × 2 tables that are analyzed sequentially for every district. First, we estimate the fraction of Dukakis and Bush voters who also cast a vote in the

House contest (or the proportions that do not fall in the "Abstain" column). Those estimates are then combined with the other known aggregate information to estimate ticket splitting ("Bush splitters" and "Dukakis splitters").[6] It is important to control first for ballot roll-off in the congressional contest, because voters who abstain from that race cannot split their ballot. In addition, if there are partisan differences in roll-off, then aggregate measures of ticket splitting that fail to account for roll-off are biased.[7]

When discussing our estimates of split-ticket voting, we will use a two-letter abbreviation to indicate the four possible voting patterns; the first letter is the party of the presidential candidate chosen, and the second letter is the party of the congressional candidate chosen. For instance, an RD voter is one who voted for Bush and the Democratic congressional candidate.

Data and Method

The main data set consists of only the number of votes received by the presidential, House, and Senate candidates in each congressional district or state (from Barone and Ujifusa 1989) to provide the known quantities in Table 16-1.[8] Voters in 1988 could have split their ballot in one of two ways: Bush and a congressional Democrat, or Dukakis and a congressional Republican. "Bush splitters" denotes the former, and "Dukakis splitters" denotes the latter. Ultimately, we are more interested in Bush splitters because of the divided government pattern of the 1980s.[9]

The first run included only presidential and House data, with 74 uncontested House races excluded from the procedure. In the uncontested districts, voters only had one choice for the House; the exclusions do not affect the estimates for the other districts. In addition, a South dummy variable was used as a covariate to account for possible aggregation bias and to improve the estimates. Because the degree of split-level partisanship in the South is unique, we suspect that aggregating votes may conceal more ticket splitting in the South than elsewhere. The second run produced estimates of president/Senate ticket splitting within states. Since there were only 33 Senate races in 1988, estimates based on so few observations would be inefficient. Thus, the House data were included to improve the Senate estimates.

Our estimates reveal that ticket splitting varies substantially across districts and states, even within the same election year. After removing the uncontested House races, the proportion of Bush splitters in a district ranges from .03 to .90, with a standard deviation of .19. The proportion of Bush splitters was under .1 in 23 percent of the districts, but it exceeded .5 in 27.3 percent of the districts. There was less variation in the district-level fraction of Dukakis splitters, which ranges from .02 to .72, with a standard deviation of .14. The proportion of Dukakis splitters was under .1 in 42.1 percent of the districts and above .3 in 29.6 percent of the districts. The relationship between the two types of ticket splitting is negative and strong ($r = .94$); in districts with many Bush splitters, there were

Table 16-2   Mean President/House Ticket Splitting by District Outcome, 1988

Ticket-Splitting Type	District Outcome			
	RR	RD	DR	DD
Bush splitters	.11	.57	.09	.59
	(.08)	(.24)	(.05)	(.24)
Dukakis splitters	.41	.09	.43	.07
	(.22)	(.06)	(.13)	(.05)
Number of districts	163	135	12	125

Note: Standard deviations of the point estimates are in parentheses.

few Dukakis splitters. Nevertheless, some form of ticket splitting was quite common in many congressional districts in 1988.

Because these are maximum likelihood estimates, King's method also produces standard errors for the two ticket-splitting parameters for each congressional district. In this case it yields fairly precise estimates of ticket splitting. The mean standard error of our district-level estimates for Bush splitters is .04, while for Dukakis splitters it is .05. Thus, traditional 95 percent confidence intervals drawn around our estimates would cover a range of about 15–20 percentage points.

The Validity of Our Estimates

The Relationship between Split-Ticket Voting and Divided Outcomes

Does ticket splitting matter if only a minority of voters are involved? Can a small proportion of voters who split their ballot produce divided government? Are higher levels of ticket splitting associated with split outcomes when votes are aggregated at the district level? Table 16-2 provides the mean level of each type of president/House ticket splitting in different types of districts in 1988. Ticket splitting by Bush voters is quite high (.57) in districts that chose Bush and a Democrat but low (.11) in RR districts. Nevertheless, ticket splitting and divided outcomes are not entirely synonymous, though they are sometimes treated as such. Substantial numbers of voters split their ticket even in districts where candidates of the same party are elected. For example, .59 of Bush voters (on average) split their ticket in DD districts. Notice that Dukakis splitters are most common in DR and RR districts, and Bush splitters are most frequent in RD and DD districts. In accord with the argument we make below, this suggests that the primary determinant of ticket splitting is the local congressional race, not a national mandate for split control.

Consider that Bush can be expected to defeat Dukakis in more conservative districts. When a Democratic congressional candidate wins in such a district, it is likely due to a high rate of ticket splitting among Bush voters. If divided outcomes

Table 16-3   Logit Equation Predicting Divided Outcomes (RD versus RR
                 Districts) by Split-Ticket Voting

Variable	b
Bush splitters	63.84***
	(16.29)
Constant	−18.71***
	(4.77)
n	298
Correctly predicted	98.3%
Log-likelihood	−11.82

Note: Standard errors are in parentheses. ***$p < .001$, two-tailed t test.

and split-ticket voting were unrelated, then one would expect no connection
between the fraction of Bush splitters in a district and an RD election result.

To test this connection, we examine the relationship between the level of
ticket splitting among Bush voters and the probability of districts having a unified Republican electoral outcome (RR) or a divided outcome (RD). The estimation is a logit model in which the dependent variable is the probability of
selecting a Democratic congressional candidate, conditional on the selection of a
Republican for president. The results, found in Table 16-3, show that the relationship between ticket splitting among Bush voters and the election of a Democrat to the House is remarkably strong. The classification rate of the one-vari-
able model improves upon the naive baseline significantly, mispredicting less
than 2 percent of districts based only on our knowledge of ticket splitting among
Bush voters. The logit equation predicts that if more than .29 of the Bush voters
split their ballot, then there is a better than 50 percent chance that the district
will elect a Democrat to the House. Thus, both the direction and frequency of
ticket splitting determine divided outcomes. This strong association between
divided outcomes and our estimates of ticket splitting further validates the use of
King's method in this case.

Comparisons with Individual Estimates

It is useful to compare our ecological-based estimates with those from a
more traditional individual-level source. Table 16-4 presents both for a quick
comparison, along with estimates using Goodman's regression to show how
much we improve on previous ecological inference methods. Using the 1988
NES, the estimated proportion of Bush voters who also chose a Democrat for the
House (Bush splitters) is .341, as compared to our estimate of .331. The corresponding proportion of Dukakis splitters is a little less than half that, at .151, as
compared to our ecological estimate of .198. At the national level our ecological
estimates of ticket splitting are close to those produced by the NES, with smaller
standard errors to boot. The NES estimates have standard errors of about .025,

Table 16-4 Three Estimates of President/House Ticket Splitting, 1988

	Proportion Splitting Ballots		
Source	Bush Voters	Dukakis Voters	All Voters
Ecological estimate	.331 (.006)	.198 (.007)	.271
NES estimate	.341 (.021)	.151 (.016)	.254
Goodman estimate	.033 (.032)	−.108 (.037)	.018

Note: Standard errors are in parentheses.

or 2.5 percent, so the 95 percent confidence interval around the national point estimates includes our estimates, making them statistically indistinguishable.

For the 33 Senate races in 1988, split-ticket voting was about as common as in the House contests. Roughly one in three Bush voters chose a Democratic Senate candidate, and about one in five Dukakis voters chose a Republican for the Senate. To compare the ecological estimates with individual data, we estimated split-ticket voting from the 1988 Senate Election Study (SES), which drew representative samples of about 75 people from each state with a Senate race that year. As Table 16-5 indicates, the ecological estimates of president/Senate ticket splitting are a bit lower than those produced by the SES, but we did not weight the SES data by state population, which may explain why those estimates are higher. Also, small states (where ticket splitting was more common in 1988) are overrepresented in the SES. Finally, while the Goodman estimates are close to the other two in this case, the large standard errors indicate a high level of uncertainty in the Goodman estimates.

Explaining Variation in Ticket Splitting across Districts and States

In the previous section we found tremendous variation in ticket splitting across congressional districts and states. In this section we attempt to explain why split-ticket voting is more common in some electoral units than in others. We present results of multivariate analyses using our district and state point estimates of split-ticket voting as dependent variables. Our analysis provides a direct comparison of competing theories of split-ballot voting.

On the one hand, intentional theories are based on the notion that some voters prefer divided government and pursue it. Ideological moderates purposely vote for presidential and congressional candidates of different parties so that the separate branches of government will check each other (Alesina and Rosenthal 1995; Erikson 1988; Fiorina 1996; Jacobson 1990c). Thus, split-ticket voting is consciously used to produce divided government. Some survey respondents claim that they prefer divided to unified control of government (Fiorina 1996). Ticket splitting may be a viable strategy for balancing the extreme positions of

Table 16-5   Three Estimates of President/Senate Ticket Splitting, 1988

	Proportion Splitting Ballots		
Source	Bush Voters	Dukakis Voters	All Voters
Ecological estimate	.285 (.017)	.187 (.020)	.237
Senate Election Study estimate	.333 (.020)	.255 (.022)	.298
Goodman estimate	.359 (.190)	.262 (.226)	.313

Note: Standard errors are in parentheses.

opposite party candidates, thereby producing moderate policies favorable to the median voter.

On the other hand, unintentional theories posit that split‑ticket voting is a by‑product of other forces, such as weak partisan attachments (Petrocik and Doherty 1996), ballot mechanisms (Beck 1997; Campbell et al. 1960; Campbell and Miller 1957), and the level of competition in congressional contests (Jacobson 1990c). The lack of intention is attributed only to voters; candidates play an important role in producing split‑ticket voting. For example, Bush voters in a district with an unchallenged Democratic candidate for Congress in 1988 have little choice but to vote for the Democrat or abstain. Furthermore, as party attachments in the electorate have weakened, campaigns have become more candidate centered (Wattenberg 1991b), making it more likely that voters will choose candidates from different parties, even if not motivated by the specific goal of divided government. Jacobson (e.g., 1997) demonstrates that well‑funded candidates with previous political experience are most adept at attracting voters from the opposite party. Voters simply may select the most visible or most appealing candidate for each office; given the low level of competition in many congressional contests, this decision rule often leads to ticket splitting.

Since the direction of ticket splitting is important in determining the election outcome, we treat the two types of ballot splitting (RD versus DR) separately. We estimated two linear regression equations to determine the factors that influence the fraction of Bush voters who select a Democrat for Congress and the fraction of Dukakis voters who select a Republican for Congress, using states or districts as our units of analysis. We focused most of our attention on RD splitting, since the 1988 election produced a Republican president and a Democratic Congress. We included two explanatory variables to account for the nature of the congressional campaign. One is a dummy variable for the party of the incumbent, who often develops a personal bond with constituents that crosses party lines (Fenno 1978). We expect that RD ticket splitting will be higher in contests with a Democratic incumbent and that DR splitting will be more common when the incumbent is Republican. The other variable is a measure of the Democratic candidate's spending as a fraction of total spending in the congressional contest. Campaigns are contests of competing messages crafted to attract voters, and the spending variable measures the extent to which the Democrat's campaign message is dominating that of the Republican. In addition, the spending measure allows us to control for the fact that campaign costs vary from one district to another. We expect that campaign spending will be positively associated with RD ticket splitting and negatively associated with DR splitting.

We also included a dummy variable for districts or states in the South. Since World War II, the South has supported Republican presidential candidates and Democratic congressional candidates more often than the rest of the country. Frymer (1994) and Frymer, Kim, and Bimes (1997) argue that RD ticket splitting has been more common in the South because Democratic candidates for Congress have been able to position themselves toward the conservative end of the ideological spectrum, thus capturing the support of many Republican presidential voters. It is argued that moderate to conservative voters use simple proximity decisions to select congressional Democrats and presidential Republicans. We likewise expect RD ticket splitting to be more common in the South.

It has been suggested that ticket splitting is less common in states with a straight-party option on the ballot (Beck 1997; Campbell and Miller 1957; Rusk 1970). As Campbell et al. (1960, 275) note, "any attempt to explain why the voter marks a straight or split ballot must take account of the physical characteristics of the election ballot." They found that split-ticket voting was about 8 percent higher in states without a straight-party option in the 1950s. In 1988, 20 states had a ballot that allowed voters to pull one lever or check one box to vote a straight ticket (Brace 1993). Thus, we included a dummy variable for states with a straight-party option, and we expect it to be negatively associated with both types of ticket splitting.

The intentional theories offer few hard predictions, but Fiorina (1996) presents a clear hypothesis. Based on a simple spatial voting model in which moderate voters are located between an extremely conservative Republican Party and an extremely liberal Democratic Party, he finds that classic proximity voting may no longer be rational when candidates are far from a voter's ideal point. Instead, candidates from opposite parties are chosen for different offices so that they will be required to compromise and produce moderate policies after taking office. A key tenet of this argument, which Fiorina says is "probably the most important point," is the following prediction: "When the parties are relatively close, near the center of gravity of the electorate, ticket-splitting declines. When the parties move away from each other . . . they open up a large policy range in which ticket-splitting is the voter response" (Fiorina 1996, 81).[10]

We have a unique opportunity to test this hypothesis with available Senate data. The SES asked voters in states with Senate races to place the presidential and senatorial candidates on a seven-point ideological scale.[11] Taking the mean placements of the four candidates in each state, we computed the mean distance between Bush and the Democratic Senate candidate. Based on the prediction from Fiorina's balancing perspective, we should find a positive relationship between this distance and RD voting. In other words, RD ticket splitting should increase as the distance between Bush and the Democratic Senate candidate increases.

Table 16-6   Regressions for RD Ticket Splitting

Variable	President/House			President/Senate		
	OLS *b*	WLS *b*	OLS β	OLS *b*	WLS *b*	OLS β
Ideological distance	—	—	—	−.029	−.042	−.088
				(.039)	(.049)	
Democratic	.107***	.095***	.279	.096*	.077	.297
incumbent	(.015)	(.023)		(.044)	(.055)	
Spending ratio	.350***	.443***	.664	.290**	.379**	.511
	(.021)	(.031)		(.084)	(.105)	
Ballot format	−.032***	−.074***	−.083	−.067	−.071	−.197
	(.008)	(.011)		(.037)	(.045)	
South	.052***	.116***	.116	.037	.017	.090
	(.009)	(.012)		(.046)	(.053)	
Constant	.065***	.049***		.138	.132	
	(.008)	(.011)		(.082)	(.098)	
Standard error	.073	.101		.093	.108	
n	361	361		32	32	
Adjusted R^2	.855	.845		.678	.686	

Notes: Uncontested races are excluded. Cell entries are regression coefficients with standard errors in parentheses. *p < .05, **p < .01, ***p < .001, two-tailed *t* test. OLS = ordinary least squares, WLS = weighted least squares.

Table 16-6 presents regression results using RD ticket splitting as the dependent variable. The first column reports traditional ordinary least squares (OLS) estimates and the second column presents weighted least squares (WLS) estimates to account for the differing standard errors associated with our point estimates of ticket splitting.[12] In the WLS analysis, observations are weighted by the inverse of these standard errors, thus giving greater weight to observations with more precise estimates of ticket splitting. Because OLS and WLS produced similar results, we retained the OLS estimates because of their intuitive interpretations. The final column reports standardized OLS coefficients to assess the relative effects of the explanatory variables. Just a few independent variables do an impressive job of explaining variation in ticket splitting. Though parsimonious, the OLS model explains 86 percent of the variation in the president/House results and 68 percent of the variance in the president/Senate results.[13] This amount of explained variance is high in comparison to other voting behavior models but is especially surprising given that the dependent variable is merely a point estimate based on ecological data.[14]

The House and Senate equations differ only in that the Senate includes a measure of ideological distance between Bush and the Democratic senatorial candidate. Note that its coefficient is negative and statistically insignificant. The lack of significance is likely due to the small number of cases (*n* = 32) and corresponding degrees of freedom since the zero-order correlation between RD ticket splitting and the ideological difference between the candidates is −.370 ($p < .05$). Contrary to the balancing hypothesis, this means that RD ticket splitting does not increase as the parties polarize and that it may actually decrease. Split ballots are most common when Bush and the Democratic candidate are nearest each other, blurring their ideological differences enough to make partisan considerations in voting behavior less important (Frymer 1994; Kimball 1997). This finding fits with the Downs (1957) expectation that, in an attempt to win votes, party platforms will be ambiguous and overlapping.

In the House equation, RD voting is more common in the South. According to the OLS results, about 5 percent more Bush voters chose the Democratic House candidate in the South than elsewhere. Assuming for the moment that Democratic candidates are relatively conservative in the South, the distance between their position and that of Bush should be relatively small (Frymer, Kim, and Bimes 1997). Despite this, ticket splitting is higher, not lower. Again, intentional theories that attribute ideological balancing motives to split-ticket behavior are not supported.

The other variables in the equation are all significant and have the expected signs. The presence of a Democratic incumbent boosts RD ticket splitting by roughly ten percentage points in both House and Senate contests, holding other variables constant. Furthermore, a straight-party ballot mechanism decreases RD splitting about three percentage points in the House races and almost seven percentage points in the Senate contests. The greatest influence by far, however, is campaign spending. Recall that this variable is operationalized as the Democratic proportion of all congressional campaign spending. The OLS coefficient of .35 indicates that a Democratic House candidate who matches the Republican opponent dollar for dollar can increase RD ticket splitting by a whopping 17.5 percentage points over a Democrat who spends no money on the campaign. The parameter estimate of .29 in the Senate equation indicates that a Democratic senatorial candidate who matches the Republican opponent in spending will increase RD voting by nearly 15 percentage points over a Democrat who spends no money on the campaign. Furthermore, the relative effect of spending is overwhelming, as the standardized regression coefficient is roughly twice as large as that of the next most important variable.[15] Before exploring this finding, let us consider a similar regression, shown in Table 16-7, in which the dependent variable is the fraction of Dukakis voters who chose a Republican congressional candidate. The independent variables remain the same except that ideological distance is now measured between Dukakis and the Republican senatorial candidate, and the incumbency dummy now denotes a Republican. The analysis again points to the importance of the candidates in the congressional contest. For example, a Republican incumbent increases DR voting in House contests by about nine percentage points, other things being equal. In addition, spending remains the most critical factor, whether judged by the standardized coefficient or substantively, by interpreting the unstandardized coefficient. As a Republican candidate's share of total

Table 16-7   Regressions for DR Ticket Splitting

Variable	President/House			President/Senate		
	OLS b	WLS b	OLS β	OLS b	WLS b	OLS β
Ideological distance	—	—	—	.002	−.0004	−.007
				(.036)	(.044)	
Republican	.085***	.101***	.300	.044	.008	.200
incumbent	(.011)	(.014)		(.036)	(.043)	
Spending ratio	−.252***	−.265***	−.659	−.225***	−.315***	−.610
	(.015)	(.018)		(.059)	(.068)	
Ballot format	.003	.005	.011	.034	.032	.153
	(.006)	(.006)		(.028)	(.033)	
South	.007	.005	.023	−.001	−.004	−.005
	(.006)	(.008)		(.032)	(.039)	
Constant	.309***	.313***	—	.277***	.353***	—
	(.013)	(.016)		(.070)	(.084)	
Standard error	.052	.059		.069	.078	
n	361	361		32	32	
Adjusted R^2	.863	.852		.585	.602	

Note: Uncontested races are excluded. Cell entries are regression coefficients with standard errors in parentheses. ***$p < .001$, two-tailed t test. OLS = ordinary least squares, WLS = weighted least squares.

congressional campaign spending goes from zero to 100 percent, DR ticket splitting increases by about 25 percentage points in the House contest and about 23 percentage points in the Senate race. That is, the percentage of Dukakis splitters may jump by more than 20 points based on congressional spending patterns alone. Certainly, campaign spending is a proxy for other factors, such as the relative quality and experience of the candidates, but it also is critical to ticket splitting. Candidates spend most of their funds on advertising to increase their visibility and emphasize positive, familiar images in the minds of voters (Herrnson 1997; Jacobson 1997). To the extent that a congressional candidate can dominate advertising and frame the campaign, he or she will attract more votes from the opposite party.

With regard to the Senate, as in Table 16-6, the results for ideological distance in Table 16-7 reveal that this is not a statistically significant influence on DR ticket splitting. In our model, increased distance between Dukakis and the Republican senatorial candidate does not produce more ticket splitting, contrary to predictions of the balancing perspective. Furthermore, DR voting is no more common in the South than in other regions of the country. The South in the 1980s was unique for one type of ticket splitting: a Republican for president and a Democrat for Congress. Finally, while a straight-party ballot option reduced RD ticket splitting in both Senate and House races, it did not have a noticeable effect on DR outcomes in 1988.

A more interesting setting may be the House elections. After all, government was divided along president/House lines throughout the 1980s, while both Senate and White House were controlled by Republicans for six years. It is more difficult for voters to split government control using their Senate vote, because there are only 33 races in a given election year. Our test of ideological balancing in presidential and senatorial elections did not support intentional theories, but comparable survey data were not available for the House. Instead, we used ideological scores for Democratic incumbents, since Democrats were a large majority in 1988, although this necessarily limits our test to RD splitting.[16] Our measure is the Poole and Rosenthal (1997) NOMINATE score, which is based on statistical analyses of roll-call voting.[17] In contrast to the SES data, based on citizen surveys, NOMINATE is more clearly exogenous to the vote decision. We used first-dimension point estimates from the 100th House to measure the ideological position of incumbent candidates. Values range from −1 (most liberal) to +1 (most conservative). If voters are more likely to split their ballot when the parties are polarized, then the ideological position coefficient ought to be negative. In other words, if motivated to balance extreme positions, then Bush voters would be more likely to split their ticket for a liberal than a conservative Democratic House candidate.

We included this ideology measure in a regression equation similar to the ones in Tables 16-6 and 16-7, except that the incumbent dummy was removed by necessity. We also added a dummy indicating the presence of an "experienced" Republican challenger in the House contest (one who previously had held elective office or had run for a House seat). Table 16-8 reports the results. Though spending remains the most important influence on RD voting, the extremism of the Democratic incumbent plays a part as well. The coefficient is positive and significant, indicating that the proportion of RD voters increases in accord with Democratic conservatism. Assuming that Bush adopts a right-of-center position, RD voting is more likely if the House Democratic candidate is closer to Bush, which means that voters seek ideological consistency rather than balance. This is consistent with arguments made by Frymer (1994) and Petrocik and Doherty (1996).

Substantively, the coefficient on the ideological variable means that the RD proportion increases by 13 percentage points when the Democrat moves one unit in the conservative direction on the [−1,1] NOMINATE interval. This is not a small effect and, in standardized terms, ranks only behind ballot format and the influence of money. Furthermore, the ideological variable reduces the magnitude of the coefficient for the South variable. This suggests that RD ticket splitting is higher in the South at least partly because the Democratic candidates position themselves closer to the conservative end of the spectrum.

The most robust finding from Table 16-8 and the other regression analyses is that congressional campaign spending has a dramatic influence on the percentage of voters who split their ballot. As the Democratic candidate's share of spending rises, so does the proportion of Bush voters who vote for that candidate. This relationship remains the strongest force in ticket splitting, even when

Table 16-8 Factors Influencing RD Splitting in Districts with a Democratic
               Incumbent

Variable	OLS *b*	WLS *b*	OLS β
Conservatism of Democratic incumbent	.132**	.255***	.22
	(.039)	(.053)	
Spending ratio	.327***	.508***	.47
	(.041)	(.056)	
Experienced Republican challenger	−.014	−.031	−.07
	(.013)	(.018)	
Ballot format	−.065***	−.122***	−.31
	(.012)	(.016)	
South	.041**	.092***	.17
	(.016)	(.020)	
Constant	.250***	.170**	—
	(.039)	(.055)	
Standard error	.083	.106	
N	190	190	
Adjusted R^2	.369	.655	

Note: Analysis only includes districts with a challenged Democrat. Cell entries are regression coefficients with standard errors in parentheses. **$p < .01$, ***$p < .001$, two-tailed *t* test. OLS = ordinary least squares, WLS = weighted least squares.

controlling for such related and theoretically important variables as challenger quality. In fact, the challenger quality coefficient, while having the expected negative sign, is not statistically significant. That effect is clearly captured in the spending variable, as experienced challengers are most adept at cutting into an incumbent's spending advantage (Jacobson 1997). As we elaborate below, it is not the inherent quality of candidates that matters but their ability to represent a credible alternative to the incumbent.

To illustrate the critical role of spending, Figure 16-1 presents a simple scatterplot showing the share of Democratic spending and the proportion of Bush splitters in contested House districts. The least-squares regression line is superimposed. The relationship is clearly linear, positive, and strong considering the crudeness of the data ($r = .91, p < .001$). Though money has been shown to be an important variable in congressional campaigns (Jacobson 1997), its power to induce ticket splitting has been largely unexplored (cf. Kimball 1997).

We suggest that campaign spending increases voter defection from the opposite party by drowning out the opponent's message. As the spending proportion of the Democrat nears 100 percent, the Republican's self-promotion is scarcely noticed by voters. Lopsided spending patterns—near both ends of Figure 16-1—indicate one-sided messages in a campaign. As Zaller (1992) has shown, a campaign or other media message can have a substantial effect on public opinion when countervailing messages are absent. The dominant campaign's repeated advertising raises the number of favorable "considerations" associated

Figure 16-1 Split-Ticket Voting by House Campaign Spending

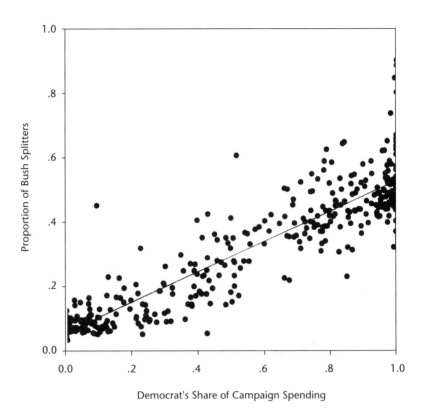

Democrat's Share of Campaign Spending

with that candidate in the minds of potential voters. In the voting booth, they have little incentive to vote for the unknown candidate.

This examination of the causes of split-ticket voting at the district and state level finds that most of the influences are outside the voter's control, which supports the unintentional theories of divided government. This does not mean that divided control is an accident. Voters appear to be rationally choosing the candidates who seem the most competent, defined by the cues of incumbency and campaign spending, the two largest influences on split-ticket voting. Though ideological position is a factor when congressional incumbents are on the ballot, voters do not intentionally balance a conservative presidential candidate with a liberal congressional candidate to achieve moderate policy outcomes. Our evidence indicates that split-ticket voting actually decreases as candidates move farther apart. Voters choose sincerely in presidential and congressional campaigns but must resort to the best—sometimes the only—congressional candidate when intercandidate quality differences are large.

Conclusion

Amid the flurry of research on divided government and split-ticket voting, this article makes two contributions. First, it uses a new ecological inference technique to produce more accurate and efficient estimates of the direction and magnitude of ticket splitting in different states and congressional districts. Previous research had to depend on aggregate data—thereby inducing the ecological inference problem—or individual-level survey data that could not be used to estimate district-level parameters. These new estimates alone are valuable, for they demonstrate considerable variation in the direction and magnitude of ticket splitting from one electoral unit to the next. Though our application was to 1988, we believe that our conclusions apply to most modern presidential elections.

The second contribution lies in explaining the newly revealed split-ticket voting patterns. Accounting for some intentional and unintentional forces that affect voting behavior, we find that the latter exert a tremendous influence. Though voters act reasonably considering the array of candidates offered to them, they apparently do not consciously choose divided government in the face of feasible alternatives. Elite decisions, including the decision of particular candidates to run for Congress, coupled with the financial advantages that most incumbents possess drive voters toward split ballots.

APPENDIX: King's Method

King's ecological inference technique involves a combination of procedures. It begins by treating the problem as a $2 \times C$ table in which the marginals are known from aggregate data but the cells are not. Notation for the known and unknown quantities can be found in Table 16A-1. First, the *method of bounds* is employed to restrict estimates of β_i^w and β_i^b, the cell quantities of interest, to a narrower region than the [0,1] interval (Duncan and Davis 1953). In our application, β_i^w is the proportion of Bush voters who split their tickets, and $1 - \beta_i^b$ is the proportion of Dukakis voters who split their tickets. Knowing these deterministic bounds increases the amount of information that can be used in a statistical model. King's method posits a probabilistic distribution of the quantities of interest that assumes that β_i^w and β_i^b, are distributed truncated bivariate normal (TBN), conditional on X_i.

Using the TBN distributional assumption, one can create a tomography plot (β_i^w by β_i^b), in which each line represents a district. The true values of β_i^w and β_i^b must fall somewhere on the line. The normality assumption helps detect a mode on the tomography plot where most of the lines cross and improves estimates by "borrowing strength" from other districts. Intuitively, the most likely values for β_i^w and β_i^b are nearest the mode, which is the peak of the three-dimensional normal bell shape.

After adding a couple of modest assumptions, five intermediate parameters that define the TBN distribution are estimated via a maximum likelihood func-

Table 16A-1 Ecological Inference Notation for District i

Presidential Voting Decision	House Voting Decision				Fraction of All Voters
	Democrat	Republican	Vote (Subtotal)	Abstain	
Democrat (Dukakis)	β_i^b	$1 - \beta_i^b$	λ_i^b	$1 - \lambda_i^b$	X_i
Republican (Bush)	β_i^w	$1 - \beta_i^w$	λ_i^w	$1 - \lambda_i^w$	$1 - X_i$
Fraction of voters	T_i	$1 - T_l$	V_i	$1 - V_i$	1

tion (i.e., two means, two standard deviations, and a correlation that make up the vector ψ). The parameters are then transformed and rescaled. Values of these parameters are drawn from the posterior distributions using importance sampling. The means of the distributions of β_i^w and β_i^b are used as point estimates, and standard errors (and confidence intervals) are based upon the variation in the simulated values. This is a real benefit, as earlier methods suffered from an inability to report accurate levels of uncertainty associated with point estimates (King, Keohane, and Verba 1994). This is the intuition; see section III of King (1997) for a complete description of the method.

Notes

1. Some may advocate the use of exit polls to estimate ticket splitting within each state and district, but these usually do not include data to parcel respondents into congressional districts and until recently many exit polls did not ask people to report their House vote. In any event, the representativeness of respondents in exit polls is frequently in question (Asher 2001).
2. Technically, estimates may be unbiased if reporting errors are random. Systematic misreporting in a particular direction induces bias.
3. To the extent that incumbency contributes to ticket splitting (Alvarez and Schousen 1993; Born 1994), a pro-incumbency bias means that the NES may overestimate the extent of split-ticket voting in national elections in the 1980s (Wright 1990).
4. Feigert (1979) actually recommended the use of ecological inference techniques in further study of ticket splitting but lamented that valid methods did not exist at the time. While ecological inference techniques have been used to examine the extent to which voters switch parties from one election to the next (Achen and Shively 1995; Gosnell 1937), to our knowledge no one has used these techniques to study ticket splitting.
5. We ignore votes for third-party candidates. Few voters chose such candidates in 1988.
6. With King's *EzI* program (version 1.21), we used the EI command to make the first-stage estimates and the EI2 command to make the second-stage estimates. See King (1997, chapter 15) and the Appendix for a more detailed description of this method.
7. According to our estimates, Democrats were somewhat more likely than Republicans to abstain from the House contest. In addition, ballot roll-off was quite high in some

congressional districts, especially if an incumbent ran unopposed or faced token opposition. As it turns out, our ticket-splitting estimates did not change substantially when we did not control for ballot roll-off. For an example that controls for roll-off in studying racially polarized voting, see Palmquist and Voss (1996).

8. Eleven districts (from Arkansas, Florida, Louisiana, and Oklahoma) that featured uncontested House races were excluded from our analysis because election totals were not available. The state either did not put the House contest on the ballot (as in Louisiana when a candidate won a majority of the vote in the open primary) or did not tabulate the House vote in these districts. Survey respondents from these districts (61 total) were dropped from the 1988 NES sample for the comparisons of ticket-splitting estimates presented here. The Appendix offers a brief description of King's ecological inference method.

9. The RD pattern of national government common in the 1970s and 1980s is remarkable. Indeed, according to Fiorina (1989, 140), "the emergence of a two-tier system in which Republican presidential majorities coexist with Democratic congressional majorities is the single most important feature of contemporary politics."

10. Fiorina models voter behavior as if it were conscious. Our test appropriately examines voter behavior without peering inside the "black box" to check the assumptions about process.

11. "Unless we have data on both the Democratic incumbent and her Republican challenger, and unless we can put the presidential candidates and the voters on the same scale, we cannot differentiate among such different situations and hence decide whether ticket-splitting is consistent with an ideological consistency or ideological balancing model" (Fiorina 1996, 155). The SES data satisfy these criteria.

12. The substantive results are unchanged if two-sided tobit models are estimated to account for a dependent variable censored at zero and 1.0.

13. The Senate analysis is based on 32 states because the 1988 SES did not obtain candidate placement information from Nevada respondents.

14. One may argue that our ideological distance measure will not work properly if both Senate candidates fell on the same side of the median voter in a particular state. Using the SES, however, in almost every state the mean ideological placement for respondents fell in between the mean placements of the two Senate candidates (Erikson 1990b).

15. One may object that we have not accounted for the effect of the presidential candidates on ticket splitting. It is possible that some voters defect from their identified party in the presidential contest. To control for the presidential contribution, we included Bush's fraction of the vote in the regression models presented here. This did not improve the fit of the models and did not alter the effects of the other variables. In addition, it produced substantively weak and inconsistently signed regression coefficients. For example, the Bush variable had a positive coefficient ($p = .03$) in the first House model in Table 16-6, but a negative coefficient ($p = .24$) in the first House model in Table 16-8. The effect in Table 16-6 (although substantively small) suggests that Bush contributed to ticket splitting by attracting some Democratic votes.

16. RD splitting was the more common form in 1988 and corresponded to the election of Bush and a Democratic House. When we examined DR splitting, the results were similar to those presented in Table 16-8: Ticket splitting by Dukakis voters was more frequent in districts with a Republican incumbent toward the liberal end of the spectrum.

17. NOMINATE is a maximum likelihood technique that uses roll-call data ("yeas" and "nays") to estimate the ideal points of legislators. It is based on a multidimensional spatial model in which legislators take roll-call positions that are nearest their ideal

point with some error, thus making it probabilistic (Burden 1997). As is common practice, we use first-dimension NOMINATE scores, which explain more than 80 percent of the variance in roll-call voting patterns. Furthermore, we use a particular dynamic variant, D-NOMINATE. Substantive results are no different if other forms of NOMINATE are used; they correlate with one another at well above .95. See Poole and Rosenthal (1997) for a comprehensive review.

PART V
PARTY IDENTIFICATION

17. How Much Does Politics Affect Party Identification?

Ever since V. O. Key (1959) wrote of voters' "standing decisions," it has been recognized that many citizens develop long-standing psychological attachments to political parties. University of Michigan researchers of the 1950s called this "party identification" or "partisanship" and conceptualized it as a long-term factor in voting. The assumption underlying this conceptualization is that party identification is highly stable throughout people's lives. Because of this individual-level stability, partisanship is also relatively stable at an aggregate level. Early work seemed to show that this was the case. Party identification was thought to originate from one's childhood socialization into politics, primarily via the family; changes in partisanship occurred mainly as a result of infrequent party realignments. Even when there were challenges to this view of extreme stability, as when the number of Independents increased in the mid-1960s, the source seemed to be generational differences since the increase was disproportionately among the young. Thus, for many years, party identification was seen as highly stable, with the implication that partisanship was relatively unaffected by ordinary political events.

Research over the past decade has called the claimed stability of partisanship into question, and the debate over its stability has become increasingly heated in recent years. If individual partisanship is not necessarily stable, then it might be much more responsive to happenings in the political world. Thus the debate over the extent of stability of partisanship leads to the question of how responsive partisanship is to political forces. This is not just an academic debate, as it would affect practical politics—whether political campaign managers can hope to change party identification as they try to influence campaign outcomes. When one looks at the debate carefully, even those researchers who view partisanship as changeable still recognize that it is relatively stable, but they argue that it varies systematically with other political and economic variables.[1]

The Party Identification Concept and Scale

It is useful to set the controversy over the responsiveness of party identification in the more general context of theoretical perspectives underlying the concept. The original development of the party identification concept in *The American Voter* (Campbell, Converse, Miller, and Stokes 1960) was based on social psychology. The authors dealt with partisanship as an attitude, using reference group theory to suggest that people identify with groups such as parties just as they identify with religions or social classes. An alternative theoretical perspective was later developed out of rational choice work, in particular Fiorina's (1981, reprinted as Chapter 14 in *Classics in Voting Behavior*) view of party identification as a "running tally" of retrospective evaluations based on reactions to current political happenings. These remain the two most important theoretical perspectives on party identification, though we shall see that both have been updated since their original formulation.

While there have been different interpretations of the concept, the National Election Studies (NES) has used a standard set of three survey questions to measure party identification since 1952. These questions (see Table 17-1) lead to a seven-point classification: strong Democrats, weak Democrats, Independents who lean toward the Democrats, pure Independents, Independents who lean toward the Republicans, weak Republicans, and strong Republicans.

Two major measurement concerns have arisen regarding the seven-point scale. The first has to do with its "intransitivity." As Petrocik (1974, reprinted as Chapter 26 in *Classics in Voting Behavior*) showed, its relationship to several other variables is not monotonic, with leaners often behaving in a more partisan manner than weak partisans. Many explanations of this intransitivity have been offered as well as several remedies. The intransitivity also raises the more general question of what to make of the leaners. Keith et al. (1992) demonstrate that leaners behave like weak partisans in many respects and conclude that the two should be combined. According to that approach, the apparent increase in the proportion of Independents since the 1950s is artifactual since the pure Independent category has grown very little, with only about one-tenth of the electorate being Independents. Warren Miller (1991a), among others, instead contends that what matters is only the answer to the first party identification question—whether the person is a Republican, Democrat, or Independent—because that question elicits long-term identification with a party rather than just political preference. Furthermore, he argues that leaners behave like Independents rather than partisans with respect to partisan activities. That argument implies that leaners should be treated as Independents rather than as partisans.

The other measurement concern involves the dimensionality of the seven-point scale. As Weisberg (1980, reprinted as Chapter 27 in *Classics in Voting Behavior*) has argued, there could be multiple dimensions underlying party identification, such as independence being a separate dimension from the Republican-Democrat divide. In that case, strength of partisanship should not be measured with the same scale as we measure degree of independence. Evidence has been provided for (Alvarez 1990) and against (McDonald and Howell 1982; Green 1988) this multidimensional perspective, but the usual view is that the seven-point scale does reasonably well in measuring partisanship in the current era regardless of this possibility while recognizing that it might be useful to study political independence separately from partisan strength.

Table 17-1 Party Identification in the United States, 1952–1996

Party Identification	1952	1956	1960	1964	1968	1972	1976	1980	1984	1988	1992	1996
Strong Democrat	22%	21%	20%	27%	20%	15%	15%	18%	17%	17%	18%	18%
Weak Democrat	25	23	25	25	25	26	25	23	20	18	18	19
Independent Democrat	10	6	6	9	10	11	12	11	11	12	14	13
Pure Independent	6	9	10	8	11	13	15	13	11	11	12	8
Independent Republican	7	8	7	6	9	10	10	10	12	13	12	11
Weak Republican	14	14	14	14	15	13	14	14	15	14	14	16
Strong Republican	14	15	16	11	10	10	9	9	12	14	11	13
Democratic presidential vote	44%	42%	50%	61%	43%	38%	50%	42%	41%	46%	43%	49%
Republican presidential vote	55	57	50	38	43	61	48	52	59	54	38	41

Note: This classification is based on the following question series: "Generally speaking, do you usually think of yourself as a Republican, a Democrat, an Independent, or what? (If partisan:) "Would you call yourself a strong (Republican/Democrat) or a not very strong (Republican/Democrat)?" (If not partisan:) "Do you think of yourself as closer to the Republican or Democratic Party?" Column percentages do not add up to 100 because apoliticals (respondents who do not have a partisanship and are not interested in politics) are not included in this table.

Source: Weisberg (1999, 685, Table 12-2), based on the 1952–1996 National Election Studies surveys.

Trends in the distribution of partisanship on the seven-point scale are shown in Table 17-1. These aggregate results show some change. Along with the increase in Independents in the late 1960s and beyond, the Democrats saw their considerable advantage in the 1950s through the 1970s considerably diminished in the 1980s and 1990s.[2] Still, the overall pattern is highly stable, rather than fluctuating wildly over these decades. Yet this does not by itself answer the question of how stable partisanship has been over the period. Aggregate stability can conceal considerable change at the individual level, as would happen if the movement of some groups in a Republican direction was compensated by the shift of other groups in a Democratic direction. Also, the measurements in this table are far enough apart that there could have been back-and-forth change between shorter time intervals that is not evident in these values.

Partisanship Is Routinely Affected by Politics

There was some early evidence that party identification was changeable in the 1956–1958–1960 NES panel study (Dreyer 1973), but that finding was discounted at the time because it did not fit with the long-term status accorded to partisanship in the Michigan model of voting. Most of the change found in these early studies was into and out of political independence (e.g., Converse 1966) rather than change between the two parties. This result was soon followed by a sharp critique of that long-term status from abroad. Thomassen (1976) found that partisanship was actually less stable than individual voting in the Netherlands. He concluded that party identification was affected by the vote in that country rather than being causally prior to it, so it could not be viewed as a long-term factor. Researchers duplicated Thomassen's results for other countries (Holmberg 1981; LeDuc 1981), suggesting that the long-term status of partisanship in the United States was the exception rather than the rule. However, even that claim soon came under attack.

Theoretical work began to question the view that partisanship was an "unmoved mover" that could affect other political attitudes without being affected by political events. Party identification had been treated as "exogenous" in early models — affecting attitudes toward candidates and issues and the vote decision but not affected by those variables. Then Jackson (1975), Page and Jones (1979), Markus and Converse (1979) (reprinted as Chapters 13 and 14 in *Classics in Voting Behavior*), and Franklin and Jackson (1983) developed models that treated party identification as "endogenous," with issue positions and previous votes affecting partisanship. Especially important was Fiorina's (1981) interpretation of partisanship as a "running tally" of evaluations of current political happenings. There was still a high degree of continuity in party evaluations, according to Fiorina, but partisanship is constantly being tested with information about current politics. According to this theory, partisanship is directly affected by politics, although party identification is still "sticky" in that past partisanship retards the tendency of new events to produce change. The running tally notion does not imply that people will necessarily change their partisanship because of new information; in part this is because interpretations of new political information are themselves affected by the person's current partisanship, so the effect of new information will generally be to reinforce existing party identification.

Some later work has further elaborated this theory. One way of operationalizing the running tally notion mathematically is by way of a "Bayesian" updating approach (named for Bayes's probability theorem) in which people have a partisanship value that gets continually updated based on current experiences. Fiorina's model actually permitted differential weights on past partisanship and current happenings, while the Bayesian approach weights each on the basis of how much informational content it has. Achen (1992) has most explicitly developed this Bayesian model of a "current party identification" (see also Smith 1993) and has derived several important nonintuitive conclusions. One is that demographic variables should not be included as predictors in theoretical equations explaining partisanship or the vote, since the latter are based on beliefs about the future; at most demographics can be used as proxies for more theoretically meaningful quantities. Another is that party identification cannot be modeled through linear equations, since the impact of recent events depends on the respondent's age: recent events will most affect the partisanship of the young, whose partisanship is based on fewer historical events.[3]

Several studies using more extensive over-time data have also found that partisanship is responsive to political events and more changeable than previously assumed. Allsop and Weisberg (1988) showed that partisanship was responsive to campaign events when it varied systematically in nightly tracking polls taken during the 1984 presidential election campaign. Brody and Rothenberg (1988) demonstrated that short-term factors could account for changes in partisanship in the 1980 NES panel study. Lockerbie (1989) also found systematic change in the 1980 panel study, as well as in the earlier NES 1956–1958–1960 and 1972–1974–1976 panels, showing responsiveness to prospective economic evaluations. Using a multiwave "socialization study" in which a national sample of high school seniors and their parents were interviewed in 1965, with reinterviews in 1973 and 1982, Niemi and Jennings (1991) found a decrease in similarity in partisanship in later waves. Furthermore, the partisan shifts in adulthood were associated with issue positions, dispelling the early view that party identification was inherited from parents with little impact of subsequent issues (see also Luskin, McIver, and Carmines 1989). Rapoport (1997) found that changes in party identification at the individual level across waves of the socialization panel study can be accounted for partially by attitudes toward presidential candidates. Elsewhere, analyzing five panel studies, Stewart and Clarke (1998) found that issue and leader evaluations affect party identification in Canada (see also the study of Australian partisanship by Marks 1993).

The key work in this stream of research is the 1989 article by MacKuen, Erikson, and Stimson (referred to as MES, for short) on "macropartisanship." The authors find systematic changes in aggregate party identification as measured by the Gallup poll over a long time period. Identification as a Democrat varied from slightly more than half of major party identifiers in the late 1940s to nearly 70 percent by the mid-1970s and back to slightly more than half by the 1984 election. Most important, macropartisanship varied in response to changes in presidential popularity and in response to trends in views about the health of the national economy. This is strong evidence that partisanship is affected by politics.[4]

Further research using different polls also found that partisanship is affected by political variables. Weisberg and Smith (1991) constructed a monthly composite measure of party identification in the early 1980s and found that it varied with changes in presidential approval and objective economic indicators (inflation and unemployment rates). Weisberg and Kimball (1995) obtained similar results for the 1989–1992 period with CBS News/*New York Times* Poll data.

A core problem here is whether these changes in macropartisanship are as transitory as yesterday's news or if they have a lasting impact. Box-Steffensmeier and Smith (1996) have subsequently shown that the MES Gallup series is "fractionally integrated," meaning that the persistence of partisanship over time is not complete and there is heterogeneity of individual behavior (with respect to persistence). Whereas MES concluded that partisan changes are permanent on a scale of just months, Box-Steffensmeier and Smith show that such changes are permanent more on the scale of years, which is still much less than the traditional view that they are permanent on the scale of decades. Similar results of high persistence that is not permanent have now been found in a study of the popularity of twenty-six parties in eight other countries (Byers, Davidson, and Peel 2000).

One potential problem with the recent research has to do with the unit of measurement—whether the data are individual or aggregate. As suggested by the title "Macropartisanship," MacKuen, Erikson, and Stimson's argument is based on aggregate data. Finding change at the aggregate level suggests that there must be change at the individual level, but there is less evidence at that level except for a few panel studies (Dreyer 1973; Fiorina 1981; Brody and Rothenberg 1988), and, as noted, partisanship is characterized by relatively high levels of individual persistence.[5]

The apparent incongruity of arguing that there is aggregate instability when partisanship is thought to be relatively stable at the individual level has led to several attempts to reconcile the two, but none has been totally convincing. One possibility is that relative positions on the partisanship continuum may be stable while the continuum is shifting toward one party (Green and Palmquist 1994). The heterogeneity of the electorate and the persistence of exogenous factors that affect individual partisanship have also been advanced as explanations (Box-Steffensmeier and Smith 1996). Or it may be that small changes in individual partisanship are enough to produce large changes at the macro level (Erikson, MacKuen, and Stimson 1996). Finally, the difference may be that more change is found with the frequent (often quarterly) measurements used in macropartisanship studies than with panel studies of individual partisanship, which are usually based on waves a few years apart (Weisberg 1998a).

The studies reviewed in this section focus on Democratic versus Republican identification and ignore independence, but there is some similar evidence of change in independence due to political factors. Clarke and Suzuki (1993) model independence, using 1953–1988 Gallup data—the same data as used by MES but scored so that the focus is on Independents versus partisans rather than Democrats versus others. Their predictors are inflation, unemployment, scandals, Vietnam, rally events, and elections. They use a switching regression analysis model to find an optimal point for distinguishing between "regimes," and they find this to be mid-1967. Before that, economic factors did not affect independence, although Vietnam and rally events did; after that, economic and political factors both became more important.

Haynes and Jacobs (1994) include independence in an analysis of 1953–1990 Gallup polls by using multinomial logit analysis on a three-category party identification variable: Republicans versus Democrats versus Independents. They argue that MES and others make a fundamental mistake in not treating Independents separately (and their logic would imply that Clarke and Suzuki should not have combined Republican and Democratic partisans in their analysis). As predictor variables, they include the unemployment rate, inflation rate, and popularity level of the president, with separate predictors for each of these three for Republican and Democratic presidents. By separating out Independents, they are able to show that a bad economy can lead to greater independence rather than to switches from one party to the other, as MES implicitly assume. By looking at Republican and Democratic presidencies separately, they are able to show that both inflation and unemployment during a Republican presidency lead to reductions in identification with that party, but that does not happen when those conditions occur under Democratic presidents. At the same time, putting in separate economy and approval variables for Republican and Democratic presidents may be a case of using too many predictors. The articles by Clarke and Suzuki and by Haynes and Jacobs may not be definitive, but together they make an important case that the determinants of changes in political independence should be examined more systematically alongside changes in partisanship per se.

Partisanship Is Fairly Immune to Politics

As we turn to the counterargument, it is useful to go back to the original source. *The American Voter* originally maintained that party identification was fairly immune to politics except under unusual circumstances (best exemplified by severe economic depression). The authors admitted that "it is even possible that the flow of events may place [the citizen's] party in such an unfavorable position as to bring an actual change in his identification. But this is unusual; more typically party identification is not only sustained but strengthened by the passing show of political acts and actors" (165). Thus, not even *The American Voter* claimed that party identification was completely immune to politics—it could change during realignments, and there was some influence of politics even in normal times. Yet the predominant view of party identification that emerges from the early work is that it is "a durable attachment, not readily disturbed by passing events and personalities" (151).

The American Voter used reference group theory of the 1950s as the basis for its approach, but that theory is not used much in social psychology today (Weisberg and Greene forthcoming). It has been supplanted by "social identity theory" (Tajfel et al. 1971) and variants thereof, which provide more theoretical explanations of why people identify with groups than reference group theory did. Social identity theory is based on the "minimal group paradigm" that bias in favor of an in-group can be created out of a need to identify with a group even without overt competition between groups. Social identity then is the part of a person's identity resulting from groups. This theory is spurring new research on the bases of party identification in Britain (Kelly 1988, 1989) and the United States (Greene 1999), as well as work on the strength of identification (Weisberg and Hasecke 1999).

The dynamics that Campbell et al. posit in *The American Voter* for party identification are that it typically develops as part of childhood socialization, with children tending to learn their partisanship from their parents; it then becomes stronger and correspondingly less likely to change as people age.[6] This dynamic has an important implication at the macro-level. The basic argument (Converse 1969) is that partisanship in a nation will also increase with the length of time for which it is held, up to an equilibrium value that Converse estimated at the time as around 72 percent of the citizenry having partisan attachments. However, Inglehart and Hochstein (1972) add that there can be major crises that modify the rate of development. Leithner (1997) analyzes partisanship trends from this perspective and finds that partisanship increased faster in Australia and New Zealand than the Converse model predicts; the occurrence of crises was at least as important as the lapse of time in explaining the development of partisanship. The important implication of this result is that new democracies cannot expect a smooth road to a stable political system just because the passage of time will increase partisanship; crises can accelerate or erode the development of partisanship and thus possibly make the electoral system unsteady.[7]

There is an important body of recent research that bolsters the original claims in *The American Voter* that party identification is highly stable and usually immune to politics, challenging the evidence summarized in the previous section. These arguments tend to be methodologically difficult and are sometimes quite arcane, but the measurement argument by Miller (1991) is easy to grasp. Miller contends that all that matters is the respondent's answer to the first party identification question—"Generally speaking, do you usually think of yourself as a Republican, a Democrat, an Independent, or what?"—and that these answers have been highly stable when some realignment is put aside. In particular, answers to the first question were stable for northern white voters from 1952 to 1980. There was realignment for white male southerners during that period and significant changes for blacks, but the real issue to Miller is whether party identification is stable under normal conditions, and he views the evidence of stability for northern white voters to be definitive. In a similar vein, Miller and Shanks (1996) argue that partisanship is a very stable political attitude, and if partisanship is that stable, it is minimally affected by politics.

The article by Miller (1992) reprinted here as Chapter 18 carries his analysis further by adding a generational perspective. One potential dynamic for aggregate change in partisanship is generational replacement, with a new generation attaining voting age with a different partisan distribution than the oldest generation that is leaving the electorate. This chapter provides analysis of the party identification of the pre-New Deal generation, the New Deal generation, and a post-New Deal generation. Miller strongly argues that the generational approach illuminates more than the running tally notion. Indeed, he terms the running tally view "mischievous" because it does not take into sufficient account either the persistence of partisanship or the lack of a previous tally for young nonidentifiers who are mobilized to identify with a party.[8]

The more technical argument involving the stability of party identification is that the apparent change in aggregate partisanship that MES and others claim to have found is instead due to random measurement error, which is inevitable in any measurement. This work is based on a technical distinction between two concepts: reliability and stability. The reliability of a measure takes into account random measurement error, while the stability of a measure has to do with the extent of true change in its value over time. Simply looking at change in people's partisanship at two points in time confounds instability with unreliability since some apparent change is just the effect of randomness.

Applying this framework, several studies have now found a very high level of stability for partisanship but a somewhat lower level of reliability, meaning that the changes observed in party identification are due more to random measurement error than to real change.[9] For example, Weisberg (1983, fn. 5) used a procedure by Heise (1971) that assumes constant reliability and found that the average corrected stability across four waves of the 1980 NES panel study was .98, with a reliability of .89. Both values are near their maximal values of 1.0, but the stability level is nearly perfect while the reliability value indicates the presence of some measurement error. Green and Palmquist (1994) applied the Wiley and Wiley (1970) method that permits varying reliabilities to nine U.S. panel studies with at least three waves of party identification measures. For waves less than two years apart, the stability values, corrected for unreliability, have a median value of .98; for those two years apart the median stability value is .94; for those eight years or more apart it is .84. This declining stability over longer time spans is what should be expected. The median reliability is .88, again showing that the party identification scale is affected more by random measurement error than by real change. Schickler and Green (1997) obtain similar findings for partisanship in multiwave panel studies of Britain, Germany, and Canada—partisanship is highly stable once random error is taken into account, except that partisanship became more changeable in the mid-1980s in Canada with the growth of regional parties in Quebec and western Canada.

Not only does measurement error detract from usual estimates of the stability of party identification, according to this argument, but it also distorts estimates of the extent to which other variables affect partisanship. More specifically, Green and Palmquist (1990) show how it can result in exaggeration of the influence of short-term forces on partisanship. They reanalyze several datasets, showing how purported short-term influences on partisanship diminish when measurement error is taken into account.

The type of estimation performed in these studies requires panel data, which is not always available. In an attempt to estimate the reliability of the party identification scale without panel data, Green and Schickler (1993) analyzed a National Opinion Research Center study that included the standard party identification scale and a seven-point partisanship self-placement scale (where respondents locate themselves on a labeled 1–7 scale). This leads to an estimate of .87 for the reliability of the party identification scale, confirming the results summarized above.

Yet, a problem with measurement error arguments is that the Heise, Wiley and Wiley, and related correction methods all rest on technical assumptions regarding error properties and interrelations that can themselves be challenged. For example, modeling party identification as a combination of long- and short-term influences or as having different degrees of stability for different types of citizens (such as its being more stable for strong partisans) could give different results.

Moving past the methodological arguments that partisanship is more stable than it may seem, there is also research that contradicts the finding that party identification behaves in an endogenous manner. In particular, two studies that use continuous monitoring of attitudes across an election campaign find that changes in partisanship are not due to other relevant forces. In the 1988 Canadian general election, Johnston (1992) finds that party identification was not moved by campaign forces that had large effects on vote intention. Similarly, Whiteley (1988) did not find partisanship in the United States to vary with changing views of issues, candidates, or vote intentions during the 1984 campaign. While these are important studies, it is difficult to reconcile them with studies that find such endogenous effects, other than the possibility that such effects occur in some elections but not others or the possibility that differences in study design and size are somehow responsible for the contradictory results.

The finding that macropartisanship varies with the economy can also be challenged. There are many aggregate economic series, from subjective consumer confidence measures to more objective indicators such as inflation and unemployment statistics, change in the gross domestic product, and change in the stock market. Finding that one of these series is significantly related to public attitudes in one of many possible statistical formulations may not in itself be definitive. Unless the relationship that is found turns out to have predictive value, the result may just hold for a limited time period, such as a single presidential administration. That would mean that economic conditions affect party identification only under limited conditions—conditions that we have not yet been able to specify fully.

The Debate Continues

The ongoing nature of this controversy is best testified to by the fact that the December 1998 issue of the *American Political Science Review* contains another Green, Palmquist, and Schickler (GPS) article and a response by Erikson, MacKuen, and Stimson (1998). This debate is a direct confrontation over the evidence as to the stability of partisanship and the responsiveness of party identification to political forces. Since these articles are too technical to reprint, we asked each set of authors to provide a summary of their current positions, which are included in this book as chapters 19 and 20.

Green, Palmquist, and Schickler (1998) attempt to replicate the original work by MacKuen, Erikson, and Stimson (1989), but their results differ markedly. They conclude that "partisanship is strongly determined by its past and responds to political or economic fortunes in a limited and gradual fashion" (892). For one thing, the MES set of Gallup surveys was incomplete, and consumer sentiment and presidential approval have less influence in the complete set. For another, MES use specific dummy variables to represent separate administrations, which GPS feel is an instance of overfitting the data in a manner that distorts the resulting equations. They further attempt to replicate the MES (1992) analysis of CBS News/*New York Times* poll data, finding weaker effects when the time series is extended from 1981 to 1996 instead of just focusing on the Reagan years.

GPS develop their own model, an "error correction model" in which changes in one time series are dependent not only on recent changes in the explanatory variable, but also on how far the partisanship value in the previous time period was from its predicted equilibrium value. Error correction models are based on a tendency for the value of the dependent variable in one time period to compensate for its being too far from the predicted equilibrium the previous time. Using this approach, they estimate that the MES estimates overstate the endogenous nature of partisanship by a factor of two to three. To produce a ten-point shift in macropartisanship, they find that consumer sentiment must fall for four years, not the five quarters that MES report. In the end, they feel that partisanship adapts to changing circumstances at such a sluggish pace that "only dramatic and *sustained* [emphasis in the original] shifts in the political fortunes of a party precipitate sizable changes in the macropartisan balance" (896).

Erikson, MacKuen, and Stimson's (1998) response insists on the importance of using separate dummy variables for each administration rather than mingling different presidents of the same party. They feel that these dummy variables recognize that partisanship is a function of the political and economic history of the time. As an illustration, they compare the first administrations of Bill Clinton and Jimmy Carter. Within each, higher approval and more positive consumer sentiment is related to higher Democratic partisanship. Clinton had better approval statistics and the economy was better in his term, but macropartisanship was less Democratic in the Clinton term than in Carter's. They claim that this difference is due to differences in the political history before Clinton (Republican gains in the Reagan years) and before Carter (Republican losses from the Watergate scandal). They also use an error correction model in this piece, finding again that the equilibrium value of macropartisanship is a dynamic function of political and economic forces, but with a faster response to political news than to economic change. In this model the most useful prediction for the next quarter is from the current predicted equilibrium macropartisanship (based on the cumulative innovations in presidential approval and consumer sentiment) rather than from the current macropartisanship value, which, barring further disruptions, will tend to revert to its current predicted equilibrium. The authors conclude that macropartisanship is indeed "largely shaped by presidential approval and consumer sentiment" (901).

The brief essays in this book by these two sets of authors summarize their current positions, with the figures displaying their main contentions. Erikson, MacKuen, and Stimson, in Chapter 20, use graphs to show that, within presidential administrations, macropartisanship clearly varies with the economy and presidential approval. They argue that macropartisanship is a series with a long memory, with cumulative changes in the economy and presidential approval having long-lasting impacts. By contrast, Green, Schickler, and Palmquist, in Chapter 19, present a figure showing that forecasts of macropartisanship into the 1990s based on equations derived from the 1952–1988 period that MES employ sharply overestimate the Democratic advantage. The implication that they derive from this finding is that the link between macropartisanship and political conditions is weak, in their words "more muted than originally thought." They conclude that party identification is stable and not affected much by day-to-day politics.

While both sides make strong points in these essays, we would expect the debate to continue. MES would likely counter that GPS should be making allowances for differences between presidential administrations.[10] If GPS show that forecasting into the future does not work with the MES model, does that mean that the modeling enterprise is wrong or that a better model is required with more predictor variables (rather than fewer, as GPS argue)? Or might it simply suggest that the dynamics of partisanship changed in the 1990s? GPS would probably in turn complain that MES have changed the terms of the debate by extending their series into the 1990s and by providing yet a different model, making it hard to pin down the specifics of their differences. They would argue that if the basic model they use in Chapter 19 does not forecast reasonably, then no other model is likely to work. The deep divide between these positions suggests conflicting viewpoints well into the future.

Conclusion

The debate as to the properties of party identification is likely to continue unabated into the future. There is some agreement, but much disagreement remains. Should partisanship be seen as stable? Or is it unstable, either at the individual or the aggregate level? Does it vary with other political variables and with public satisfaction with the economy? Or is it like approval of presidents and prime ministers, which varies with the economy in some circumstances but not others? The answers to these questions rest partially on technical matters that only a specialist in the methodology of time series could hope to disentangle, but there are important underlying substantive issues (such as the role of changing generations) that should be addressed by voting behavior researchers more generally.

Some approaches have been suggested that try to bridge the two sides of this debate. One is to admit that the party identification scale itself could have both long- and short-term aspects and attempt to estimate them separately. Applying such logic, Smith, Harding, and Crone (1990) found that the long-term elements predominate, but the short-term element may be enough to permit some degree of instability and hence responsiveness to political forces. Another reasonable middle-ground is the Box-Steffensmeier and Smith (1996) result mentioned above: that partisan changes are more permanent than MacKuen, Erikson, and Stimson find but still much less permanent than the traditional view of glacial change.

In any case, there are some clear results from this line of research on the properties of party identification. For one, answers to the party identification question change over time. Call this instability or unreliability, but the responses are not constant over time. Also, there is some apparent pattern to these changes. Whether this is systematic or artifactual, party identification does vary with some other factors. Maybe all apparent political influences on partisanship disappear with a complicated enough model, but does that mean that party identification cannot be affected by political factors? For example, if a simple plot shows that the proportion of people identifying with the incumbent's party fluctuates regularly with monthly unemployment rates, that still provides meaningful information even if the relationship vanishes after controlling on a dozen other variables. What is less clear is the degree of persistence of changes in party identification— whether they are just temporary "blips" or have lasting effects.

Another point to emphasize is the limited range of change in party identification. Regardless of whether one believes party identification to be an unmoved mover, no one would argue that it changes sharply. MacKuen, Erikson, and Stimson (1989) may demonstrate some change at the aggregate level, but it is change in a restricted interval. At the same time, regardless of whether one believes party identification to be sticky, no one would argue that it does not change at all, either at the individual or the aggregate level. Even Miller admits in Chapter 18 that there is change to partisanship. The question becomes whether the amount of change that occurs is better characterized as large enough to be meaningful or small enough to be ignored under normal circumstances, and this is where analysts differ in their interpretations.

Consider next how this debate looks to the political parties themselves. Should the parties accept the current party identification division as immutable? Not necessarily. The disadvantaged party can try to move the distribution in its direction, while the advantaged party can try to build on its advantage (possibly to win unified control of government). Maybe the resultant changes will not be permanent, but there is no reason for a party to feel that it cannot move the distribution a few points in its favor over the course of the campaign. A party that is advantaged in terms of presidential approval and the economy can benefit from that advantage. Using these factors to improve the party's identification level might benefit not only the presidential candidate but also the party's congressional campaign and its future prospects.

Finally, how should this debate look to a student of politics? Can partisanship be fairly immune to politics, or is it inevitably affected by politics? To ask this somewhat differently, is the party identification distribution today really the same as it was five years ago, or ten years ago, or when it was first measured, or have there been important changes due to political factors? Is politics today the same as a half-century ago, or has it changed in crucial ways? And, most fundamentally, would party identification be meaningful if it were apolitical to its core?

Notes

1. An important distinction to raise early is between individual and aggregate stability. These are separate, though interrelated, questions: how stable is party identification for individuals and how stable are aggregated levels of partisanship? The early work viewed both as highly stable. Studies that view partisanship as more changeable usually deal with aggregated time series (in part because repeated cross-section surveys are now abundant while over-time data about individuals are still relatively rare), although we shall see that some panel studies also have demonstrated the existence of individual change. Reliance on aggregated time series leads to the question of how attitudes can change at that level while being stable at the individual level.

2. See also the discussion in Bartels (2000) of the changing importance of partisanship.

3. Gerber and Green (1998) have challenged Achen's Bayesian model, claiming that it still implies more change in partisanship among older voters than empirical studies find.

4. Abramson and Ostrom (1991) criticized the MES work on the grounds that the Gallup poll wording of the party identification question ("In politics, as of today, do you consider yourself a Republican, a Democrat, or an Independent?") was more short-term than the NES wording. MES (1992) responded by showing that their results in "Macropartisanship" could also be obtained using data from the CBS News/*New York Times* poll, which uses wording ("Generally speaking, do you usually think of yourself as a. . . ") virtually identical to that in the NES surveys. Abramson and Ostrom also point out that the Gallup measure does not probe the partisanship of leaners, so that the MES analysis does not test their volatility, but it is not clear that this would make a large difference as Abramson and Ostrom find a .97 correlation between NES macropartisanship series with and without leaners treated as partisans.

5. Flanigan, Rahn, and Zingale (1989) found high partisan instability in a year of repeated interviewing, but there were only about two dozen people in one community in that study.

6. Work in the field of political socialization tended to support this view. See, among others, Greenstein (1965), Jennings and Niemi (1968, 1981), and Niemi and Jennings (1991).

7. At the micro level, an implication of Converse's model is that in new electorates partisanship will be stronger among the young. Niemi, Powell, Stanley, and Evans (1985) found that this was not true in each of several cases, with middle-aged or older respondents often having stronger identifications. They suggest several possible explanations, one of which is that the life cycle itself has something to do with the development of partisanship.

8. A generational perspective implies some disjuncture in intergenerational transmission but not necessarily a great deal. To change aggregate partisanship, the generation entering the electorate has to be different from the one leaving it, which is akin to saying that youths have to differ from their grandparents. Given the passage of time involved, either the parents or the out-going generation (grandparents) may have been affected by a realignment, disrupting intergenerational agreement.
9. A full discussion of research on the measurement properties of the party identification scale and alternative measures of partisanship is provided in Weisberg (1999).
10. Erikson, MacKuen, and Stimson make allowances for separate administrations in their error correction model in Chapter 20 in their "political innovations" term, which starts at zero for each administration.

Further Readings

The Partisanship Concept
Achen, Christopher, "Social Psychology, Demographic Variables, and Linear Regression," *Political Behavior* 14 (1992): 195–211. Bayesian updating model of partisanship with important methodological implications.
Fiorina, Morris, *Retrospective Voting in American National Elections* (New Haven: Yale University Press, 1981). Partisanship as a running tally of political evaluations.
Weisberg, Herbert, and Steven Greene, "The Political Psychology of Party Identification." In *Electoral Democracy*, ed. Michael MacKuen and George Rabinowitz (Ann Arbor: University of Michigan Press, forthcoming). Reexamination of the theoretical basis of party identification on the basis of modern political psychology.

Aggregate Stability and Change
Box-Steffensmeier, Janet M., and Renée Smith, "The Dynamics of Aggregate Partisanship," *American Political Science Review* 90 (1996): 567–580. Shocks to aggregate partisanship have lasting, but not permanent, effects.
Erikson, Robert, Michael MacKuen, and James Stimson, "What Moves Macropartisanship?" *American Political Science Review* 92 (1998): 901–912. An error correction model indicating that macropartisanship changes significantly in response to the macroeconomy.
Green, Donald, Bradley Palmquist, and Eric Schickler, "Macropartisanship: A Replication and Critique," *American Political Science Review* 92 (1998): 883–899. Macropartisanship adjusts to short-term shocks in a limited and gradual fashion.
MacKuen, Michael B., Robert S. Erikson, and James A. Stimson, "Macropartisanship," *American Political Science Review* 83 (1989): 1125–1142. Original argument that macropartisanship changes in response to presidential popularity and the macroeconomy.

Individual Stability and Change
Green, Donald, and Eric Schickler, "Multiple-Measure Assessment of Party Identification," *Public Opinion Quarterly* 57 (1993): 503–535. Partisanship is stable in panel studies, after correcting for reliability.

Miller, Warren, and J. Merrill Shanks, *The New American Voter* (Cambridge: Harvard University Press, 1996). Defense of original view of party identification, showing it to be stable over time and still important in affecting the vote decision.

Intergenerational Transmission of Partisanship
Niemi, Richard G., and M. Kent Jennings, "Issues and Inheritance in the Formation of Party Identification," *American Journal of Political Science* 35 (1991): 970–988. The family of origin plays an important role in the partisan development of offspring, even into adulthood.

Cross-National Perspectives on Partisanship
LeDuc, Lawrence, "The Dynamic Properties of Party Identification: A Four Nation Comparison," *European Journal of Political Research* 9 (1981): 257–268. Party identification changes with the vote in some European nations.

Schickler, Eric, and Donald Green, "The Stability of Party Identification in Western Democracies," *Comparative Political Studies* 30 (1997): 450–483. Panel studies show that partisanship is highly stable across several countries.

Measurement of Partisanship
Weisberg, Herbert F., "Political Partisanship." In *Measures of Political Attitudes,* ed. John P. Robinson, Phillip R. Shaver, and Lawrence S. Wrightsman (San Diego: Academic Press, 1999). Summary discussion of measurement issues related to several measures of partisan direction, strength, and independence.

Political Independence
Clarke, Harold, and Motoshi Suzuki, "Partisan Dealignment and the Dynamics of Independence in the American Electorate," *British Journal of Political Science* 24 (1993): 57–77. The responsiveness of trends in independence to political and economic factors.

Haynes, Stephen, and David Jacobs, "Macroeconomics, Economic Stratification, and Partisanship," *American Journal of Sociology* 99 (1994): 70–103. Simultaneous analysis of macro-level determinants of macropartisanship and independence.

Keith, Bruce E., et al., *The Myth of the Independent Voter* (Berkeley: University of California Press, 1992). The number of Independents has increased very little, contrary to common beliefs, since leaners are really partisans.

18. Generational Changes and Party Identification

Warren E. Miller

The discussion of the nature of party identification—its origins and its consequences—has been informed by an assortment of contributions. Some have been predominantly conceptual or theoretical (Beck 1974; Converse and Pierce 1985); most have combined analytic modeling with reconceptualization or conceptual elaboration (Converse 1976; Page and Jones 1979; Converse and Markus 1979; Weisberg 1980; Fiorina 1981; Franklin and Jackson 1983; Miller 1992b); still other contributions have relied heavily on innovations in measurement (Carmines, McIver, and Stimson 1987; Green and Palmquist 1990; Mattei and Niemi 1991) or on the exploitation of unique data sources (Jennings and Niemi 1968, 1981; Jennings and Markus 1984; Beck and Jennings 1991; Teixeira 1987; Abramson 1989).[1]

The continuation of the discussion is important because the most radical of the revisionist perspectives—those that treat party identification as a relatively volatile phenomenon, one readily susceptible to change in response to short-term influences, a running tally of contemporary as well as more historic influences and therefore endogenous to short-term analyses of individual electoral behavior— challenge the widely accepted theoretical paradigm of decision making by voters that was presented in *The American Voter*. That analytic model, most recently elaborated by Shanks and Miller (1991), presumes—among other things—a causal structure of voter decision making in which temporal continuity is provided in the form of stable, long-term predispositions (including, but not limited to, party identification) that shape responses to election-specific, short-term influences.

The evolving discussion of party identification, its measurement and meaning, is, in particular, also a case study in the problem of providing an operational definition of a concept that then permits the delineation of circumstances that test the meaningfulness of the concept as measured. This chapter adds to the discussion of party identification by identifying a set of circumstances under which the basic measure of party identification, applied to a significant body of voters, has produced results fully in line with the original concept of an enduring predisposition largely impervious to changing election-specific events. In addition, we consider briefly the massive and apparently enduring realignment of party identifications in the South that took place between 1960 and 1988. Finally, the discussion identifies two different sets of circumstances surrounding the national realignment of party cleavages that occurred between 1980 and 1988.

Source: *Political Behavior* 14, 3 (1992): 333–360.

Our argument is quite straightforward. The period stretching from the early 1960s to the mid-1980s has been a period of turmoil in American national politics. Turbulent events and dramatic failures of national leadership have raised serious questions about many of our political institutions. We believe this era has shaped the basic party predispositions of the young cohorts of voters who have come of age since 1968, while not affecting the older generations in a similar way. It is a period that has produced generation effects that have altered the basic parameters of American national politics.

The growth of the National Election Studies (NES) into a time series covering almost four decades greatly facilitates inquiry into the impact of historic public events on the body politic. In this chapter we shall examine the possibility that the past three decades were filled with events that made the political involvement of the younger generation of voters distinctively different from that of their elders. We believe the relevant events began with the urban riots and civil rights violence of the late 1960s and extended through the assassinations of the Kennedys and Reverend King. The events that molded the first post–New Deal generation included the evolution of political protest into a national counterculture movement; they extended into the triumphant protest and the tragic end of the Vietnam War and the disillusioning fate of the Nixon presidency.

It is a bit too early to know whether the Carter, Reagan, and Bush administrations restored a stability akin to that which followed World War II. We shall note indicators that suggest such a return to a kind of normalcy, but we may also see the continuing aftermath of such extended experiences as an impotent Carter presidency, the Iran-Contra fiasco under Reagan, and the domestic social and economic crises of the turn of the decade.

The national experiences of the decades bounded by the mid-1960s and the late 1980s were certainly not all bad. Nevertheless, the cohorts who have come of age during that epoch would appear to bear scars from a socializing environment that has influenced the development of their identities as partisans and apparently has retarded their mobilization as voters. The distinctiveness of the first post–New Deal generation is the general topic of this chapter; we are primarily concerned with the distinctive contribution of this generation to the national contours of party identification.

In a closely related earlier article we commented at length on some of the technical limitations encountered in using the NES studies as vehicles for cohort or generational analysis. In particular, we noted the obstacles to documenting the extent to which apparent generational distinctiveness was or was not simply a passing phase of the life cycle of a new generation. We also presented an analytic scheme appropriate for examining generational differences in voter turnout while variously taking into account party identification, educational, and other differences that separate the generations from each other (Miller 1992b).

In order to maintain continuity with the results of that analysis of voter turnout, we use the same analytic scheme in this discussion. The basic point is to compare citizens who differ primarily in the nature of the political epochs that influenced their initial awareness of the world of politics, epochs that shaped their identifications, perceptions, values, and preferences on matters political. Because of the extraordinary differences in educational background associated with different political generations, particular attention is given to the effects associated with education.

One of the more recent and most illuminating articles in a long series of cohort analyses is Abramson's thoughtful discussion of "Generations and Political Change in the United States" (Abramson 1989). That article, as well as the immediate predecessor to this discussion (Miller 1992b), is as much interested in using cohort analysis to understand aggregate change in national parameters as to understand the theoretical dimensions of party identification itself. In the Abramson mode, the present discussion is also manifestly devoted to extending our understanding of the dramatic changes in the national distributions of party identification that have taken place in the past 30 years. In doing so, however, we inevitably will consider implications for our view of the nature of party identification.

Political Generations and Electoral Epochs

The present discussion, as the Abramson analysis before it, rests on an initial inspection of some 17 four-year cohorts in each of the 10 elections covered by the Michigan/NES presidential studies. The cohorts are defined by the election years in which individuals were first eligible to vote for president. The cohorts have been examined in the South and non-South separately, for black citizens and nonblack, and for voters, nonvoters, and the total electorate. Again, the presentation has been simplified by restricting the analysis to nonblack voters, by combining the 17 cohorts to form 3 generations, and by collapsing the 10 elections into 3 electoral epochs. Both the operational definition of the generations and the bounding of the epochs were prompted by a blend of observed empirical regularities and a desire to fit a priori notions (pre–New Deal, post–New Deal) that could be easily communicated.

The oldest of the generations, the *pre–New Deal generation,* consists of citizens whose first votes, and therefore whose presumed periods of early adult or preadult politicization, preceded the first Roosevelt election in 1932. The next generation was socialized predominantly under Democratic presidential leadership. It consists of those whose first years of voting eligibility may have embraced the first Roosevelt election in 1932 or any of the subsequent elections up through 1964. Thus, the periods of the New Deal, the Fair Deal, the New Frontier, and the Great Society define an electoral epoch eventually dominated by the *New Deal generation.* The third generation in our analysis consists of the still-growing set of citizens whose early adult experiences included the turmoil of the late 1960s, the Vietnam War, the counterculture, and the Watergate scandals of the Nixon Administration. This *post–New Deal generation* is defined as open-ended and still growing; it therefore includes, as well, those socialized by the political dramas associated with the presidencies of Carter, Reagan, and

Bush. Indeed, one of the signal features of this analysis consists of evidence suggesting that voters who came of age in 1980, 1984, and 1988 have much in common with the cohorts of 1968, 1972, and 1976, including the attributes that distinguish them from the older cohorts of the New Deal generation (Miller 1992b).[2]

The electoral epochs defined for the analysis are dictated, in part, by the sheer availability of data from elections engaging these three generations. The first time period includes the elections of 1952, 1956, and 1960. (It would have been extraordinarily helpful if the period had started with studies in the 1930s, or at least the 1940s. The endpoint, 1960, was selected because it marked the high point of postwar voter turnout.) The elections of the 1950s were dominated by the pre–New Deal and New Deal generations. The next or middle time period, 1964–1976, includes two Democratic and two Republican electoral victories. It encompasses the emergence of the post–New Deal generation and the rapid decline of the pre–New Deal generation. The third time period begins with the Reagan election of 1980 and embraces an epoch in which the post–New Deal generation increasingly defines the electorate (Miller 1992b), and in which voter turnout reaches a low point following 1960.

Both our earlier (1992) discussion of the role of party identification in affecting the decline of turnout and the present discussion are intended to address conceptual or theoretical questions concerning the basic nature and role of party identification. But neither discussion gives more than passing attention to changes in the party identification of the black citizenry. This is because the impact of political events associated with the civil rights movement and national partisan competition for the black vote are so intrusive as to complicate the analysis of the changing nature and role of party identification among black citizens. There is obviously more to be learned about party identification through an analysis of differences in racial experiences, but that exploration must come later. A second constraint on the generality of our conclusions is imposed by our decision to look only at voters. This decision reflects earlier findings that the party identifications of nonvoters apparently account for much of the confusion that has accompanied attempts to establish the origins, enduring nature, and consequences of party identification (Miller 1991a).

Generational Differences in
Party Identification and Voter Turnout

Our analysis of the decline in turnout over the past 30 years concluded that the puzzle of declining turnout (in the face of increased education of the citizenry and the relaxation of legal constraints on voting) is transformed, but not resolved, through the application of a cohort/generational analysis (Miller 1992b). We observed that from the 1950s through the 1980s there was no decline in the rates of turnout across the nine election-year cohorts of the broadly defined New Deal generation; and their steady rate of election-day participation casts doubt on some of the explanations of decline based on the presumption of *individual citizen withdrawal* from political involvement. Rather than explanations of disengagement rooted in citizens' declining feelings of trust, increased sense of alienation, loss of confidence in their efficacy as participants, or in the deterioration of a shared sense of civic obligation, the argument is that declining aggregate rates of turnout through 1988 were the direct result of the continually increasing size of an extraordinarily nonparticipant post–New Deal generation as a component of the electorate.

In the search for the explanation of generational differences in voter turnout, it was noted that the post–New Deal generation differed from the older generation both in the incidence of party identification and in turnout differences between identifiers and nonidentifiers. The aggregate decline in the proportion of party identifiers among nonblack citizens over the years from the late 1950s to the late 1970s (heavily treated in the literature as evidence of dealignment reflecting massive rejection of the traditional party system) was almost entirely a function of the low incidence of party identification, or high incidence of Independents, in the rapidly growing post–New Deal generation. Given the persistent pattern that finds nonidentifiers voting less than identifiers, the increased incidence of Independents meant an overall decrease in turnout rates.

Although this might be seen as a rather straightforward consequence of post–New Deal electors growing up in an antiparty era, a second feature is less readily explicable. Independents in the post–New Deal generation have a turnout record even lower (in comparison to the turnout record of post–New Deal party identifiers) than do the Independents of the older New Deal generation (when compared to their partisan peers). As a consequence, of course, even though there are intergenerational differences in turnout among party identifiers, generational turnout differences are much larger among nonidentifiers.

The analysis results are congruent with expectations that because party identification involves citizens in politics and political participation the absence of party identification is associated with less involvement and less participation. The reduced incidence of party identification in the post–New Deal generation is consonant with Beck's argument that periods of aggregate dealignment or realignment are made possible by a lessening of intrafamilial ties and an increased propensity of young adults to chart their own course as they are influenced by political events that dominate their own time of coming of age (Beck 1974, 1977). We are left, however, with a new conundrum as to why the behavior of identifiers as well as nonidentifiers should vary across generations. It makes theoretical sense to observe that generational differences would be minimized among people who have in common an identification with a political party. But apart from a possible partial explanation rooted in life-cycle effects (which was evaluated and rejected in the article on turnout, see Miller 1992b), there is no obvious and theoretically satisfying explanation for either set of generational differences, and particularly not for the extraordinarily low relative turnout rate among post–New Deal Independents.

Generational Differences in the
Partisan Balance of Party Identification

As a first step in extending this inquiry, it is useful to return to the analysis of the changing incidence of party identifiers and Independents through a parallel examination of southern and nonsouthern nonblack voters. At this point our interest in accounting for changes in national parameters shifts from declining turnout to the partisan realignment of the late 1980s. The regional comparison of changes over the past 30 years makes explicable some otherwise conflicting evidence of the nature of change in party identification.

To look first at citizens living outside the 13 states of the South, we find confirmation of an earlier generalization arguing the relative stability of party identification across much of the time period preceding the election of 1984 (Miller 1991a).[3] As Table 18-1 reveals, in the North there are striking *generational* differences within both of the first two time periods of our analytic scheme, but there are no significant *period* or *life cycle* effects altering the party balance in the transition between the 1950s and the late 1960s/early 1970s. Within both generations and all three educational subsets, presented in Table 18-1, the net balance of Republican and Democratic identifications among nonblack voters outside the South was essentially unchanging.[4] This is not too surprising given other evidence of aggregate stability among nonsouthern voters (Miller 1991a). We now see that further disaggregation, by education and generation combined, still does not uncover evidence of significant shifts in party identification over the full quarter century covered by the analysis.

It is equally clear, however, that the Reagan/Bush era of the 1980s did produce a marked diminution of earlier Democratic majorities and, among the better-educated voters, a distinctive increase in Republican pluralities. Although there is some unevenness across educational comparisons and within generational comparisons, in general there was an overall pro-Republican shift of some 10 to 15 points between the time of the first Reagan election and the first Bush victory (Shanks and Miller 1991).[5]

There are at least four notable features about the contribution of the post–New Deal generation to the changing contours of party identification among northern voters: First it is clear that the entry of the post–New Deal generation into the electorate benefited the Democratic Party, at least in relative terms, at the turn of the decade of the 1970s. Among voters with at least some college education, for example, the Democratic plurality of 6 points within the post–New Deal generation in the period 1964–1976 contrasted with a 15-point Republican plurality among comparably educated voters of the older New Deal generation in the same time period. The 21-point generational difference declined to 13 points in the later Reagan-Bush years; nonetheless, the fact that Republican strength in the 1980s was greatest in the New Deal segment of the electorate, a segment that will decline both in relative and absolute numbers in the years immediately ahead, complicates any projection of future party fortunes.

Table 18-1 The Incidence of Party Identifications, by Period, Education, and Political Generation: Northern White Voters

Education	Generation	Democratic			Independent			Republican		
		1952–1960	1964–1976	1980–1988	1952–1960	1964–1976	1980–1988	1952–1960	1964–1976	1980–1988
0–8 years	Pre-New Deal	41	53	*	23	18	*	36	29	*
	New Deal	55	58	48	23	17	24	22	25	28
	Post-New Deal	—	*	*	—	*	*	—	*	*
9–12 years	Pre-New Deal	33	32	*	22	20	*	47	48	*
	New Deal	46	43	37	27	29	30	27	28	33
	Post-New Deal	—	33	30	—	54	42	—	13	28
13 years or more	Pre-New Deal	17	19	*	14	12	*	69	69	*
	New Deal	23	24	25	32	37	29	44	39	45
	Post-New Deal	—	27	27	—	51	39	—	21	34

Note: The three entries for a given time period on each row add up to 100 percent of the row.

*Too few cases for reliable estimates.

A second noteworthy aspect of generational contributions to changes in party balance is provided by the indication that, after the 1970s, the post–New Deal generation led the absolute growth of Republican strength and the relative decline in Democratic ranks in the 1980s. Republican identifications increased in every education/generation category, but most sharply in those involving the post–New Deal generation.

Less evident, but of perhaps greater theoretical significance, are the specific origins of the post–1976 shift in partisan balance within the post–New Deal ranks. First, the numbers of Democratic identifiers did not decline appreciably either among the high school or the college groups. Second, the proportions of Republicans did increase—by 13 points among the college educated and by 15 points in the high school group. Both things could be true, of course, only because Republican growth came at the expense of a commensurate decline in numbers of nonidentifiers. And the supply of nonidentifiers, in turn, had been produced by their extraordinary prominence among the post–New Deal cohorts as they were mobilized to vote in the elections of 1968, 1972, and 1976. At both education levels, fewer than one in two of all post–New Deal generation voters went to the polls as party identifiers in those elections. In the next electoral period, the Reagan-Bush electoral epoch, the proportions of Independents dropped to magnitudes similar to those of the New Deal generation in the preceding time period.

In the South, the story was dramatically different. As has been noted elsewhere (Black and Black 1987; Miller 1991a), a realignment of southern voters had begun with the Kennedy election in 1960. Although the realignment did not markedly influence the least well educated (those with less than nine years of formal education), the erosion of Democratic strength and the growth in Republican numbers in the South commenced immediately after that election, and, as Table 18-2 documents, the rate of change was a direct function of education. Among the members of the pre–New Deal generation, for example, the Democratic pluralities of the 1950s, going from low to high education, ranged from 33 points among the less well educated to 58 points among the college educated. Thirty years later, in the 1980s, the comparable figures for the New Deal generation were a 55-point margin for the Democrats among the grade-school population, 28 points for high school, and 2 points among the college-educated voters.

The realignment begun in the 1960s continued in the Reagan-Bush years, but the largest shift had come with the time of political trauma in the late 1960s and early 1970s, with most change occurring among the best educated southern voters. Between the 1970s and the 1980s, the trends were in the same direction as in the North, but change took place at a somewhat slower pace than in the preceding decades. Nevertheless, the picture across our three time periods is one of continuing realignment that by 1988 had produced a virtual total erosion of the one-time Democratic dominance within the southern states.

In the North, the growth of Republican strength was fueled by the astoundingly large contingent of voters professing no party identification in the ranks of

Table 18-2 The Incidence of Party Identifications, by Period, Education, and Political Generation: Southern White Voters

Education	Generation	Democratic			Independent			Republican		
		1952–1960	1964–1976	1980–1988	1952–1960	1964–1976	1980–1988	1952–1960	1964–1976	1980–1988
0–8 years	Pre–New Deal	64	63	*	5	12	*	31	25	*
	New Deal	70	63	67	11	18	20	19	19	12
	Post–New Deal	—	*	*	—	*	*	—	*	*
9–12 years	Pre–New Deal	53	57	*	20	16	*	27	27	*
	New Deal	78	55	47	13	26	34	9	18	19
	Post–New Deal	—	43	40	—	27	32	—	30	28
13 years or more	Pre–New Deal	68	43	*	22	19	*	10	38	*
	New Deal	59	46	35	19	30	32	22	24	33
	Post–New Deal	—	33	33	—	45	31	—	22	36

Note: The three entries for a given time period on each row add up to 100 percent of the row.

*Too few cases for reliable estimates.

Table 18-3 Correlation of Partisan Direction of Party Identification (Democrat, Independent, or Republican) with Years of Education: Northern White Voters*

Political Generation	1952–1960	1964–1976	1980–1988
Pre-New Deal	.24*	.24	—
New Deal	.18	.16	.13
Post-New Deal	—	.10	.05

*Entries are tau$_c$.

the post–New Deal generation. In the South, the same post–New Deal generation made a much smaller contribution of voters with no party identification. True, among the college educated in the South the New Deal figure of 30 percent nonidentified was clearly exceeded by the 45 percent Independents among the post–New Deal electors; but in the North, the 29 percent not identified within the college-educated New Deal group were overwhelmed by the Independents who constituted 54 percent of the more numerous post–New Deal cohorts. Within the high school group in the South, the New Deal/post–New Deal proportions of 26 and 27 percent nonidentifiers compared to 29 and 54 percent in the North. In the South, the Republican surge largely predated Reagan and Bush, and in the Reagan-Bush years it did not come at the expense of declining numbers of Independents but seemed to come quite directly from Democratic ranks (Black and Black 1987). In the North, the shift in party balance came only subsequent to the mobilization of nonpartisans in the 1970s and seems to have been drawn largely from their ranks.

In both regions, the shifts in party numbers were accompanied by, if not caused by, a realignment of social groups. We have already noted in the South that the educational correlates of party identification were completely inverted. There the college-educated voters underwent a massive realignment as Democratic pluralities of 60 percent (80 Democrats to every 20 Republicans) were replaced by parity or even a small Republican advantage in the post–New Deal generation. Among the least well educated, however, there was simply no discernable decrease in the preponderance of Democrats. The net result was to associate Democratic preferences with the least well-educated voters and Republican preferences with college education.

In the North, the social composition of partisan groupings also changed, but in a somewhat different manner. Our understanding of the shifts in party identification in the North is complicated by the generational differences in the social correlates of partisan preferences. As Table 18-3 suggests, in both the early and middle periods, members of the pre–New Deal generation exhibited a strong traditional correlation of better-educated Republicans and less well-educated Democrats. In all three time periods, the education/party preference correlation within the New Deal generation was still substantial, although apparently in

Table 18-4 Party Voting, 1980–1988

Education	Political Generation	Democrat	Republican	Tau$_c$	N
Grade School	Pre-New Deal	(100)*	—	.86	39
	New Deal	82**	94	.58	204
	Post-New Deal	—	—	.69	22
High School	Pre-New Deal	(87)	(91)	.74	74
	New Deal	78	92	.64	859
	Post-New Deal	77	80	.59	567
College	Pre-New Deal	(94)	(100)	.58	43
	New Deal	74	95	.57	627
	Post-New Deal	79	97	.68	923

Note: Entries based on pooled data from 1980, 1984, and 1988 National Election Studies.

*( ) = less than 30 cases.

**Entries are proportions voting for voter's party's candidate.

decline in the 1980s. Within the post–New Deal groups, however, there is little question but that by the 1980s party identification was only a limited function of formal education and all the social and economic advantages that education represents. While the social composition of party groups in the South underwent a revolutionary inversion, the comparable relevance of educational attainment among voters in the North has simply gone into eclipse.

If the educational correlates of party identification were dramatically different in the 1980s, some of the political correlates of party identification in the post–New Deal generations were perhaps surprisingly familiar. For example, although a very large proportion of the Republicans in the youngest generation were newcomers to the party, their votes in the elections of the 1980s were every bit a match for the partisanship of Republicans in the older generations. As Table 18-4 indicates, party voting of the post–New Deal generation was not diluted on either side of the aisle.[6]

Party and Policy

Moreover, on a number of questions of public policy preference, the party differences within the post–New Deal cohorts were even sharper than within the older cohorts. This was particularly true of attitudes toward such contemporary issues as defense spending, governmental aid for minorities, popular support for civil rights leaders, and abortion. On each of these topics the addition of the young post–New Deal cohorts to the electorate heightened the issue polarization of partisan voters. In every instance, younger Democratic Party identifiers were distinctly more liberal than were older Democrats of the New Deal generation. On the question of governmental aid to minorities, young Republicans expressed even greater opposition than did older Republicans of the New Deal generation;

the same was true of young Republicans in the high school group where abortion and defense spending were concerned. Elsewhere the young Republicans were more passive contributors to increased party polarization by virtue of simply being less far to the left of their older partisan cohorts than the young Democrats were to the left of their older cohorts. The configuration reflecting a heightened issue polarization contributed by the still growing post–New Deal generation is typified in Table 18-5.

A quite different pattern of generational differences characterized another set of issues including such diverse and longstanding topics as détente, the expansion of government service and domestic spending, an active role for the federal government in maintaining jobs and a high standard of living, and gender equality. On each of these topics party differences within the post–New Deal generation simply paralleled party differences within the older New Deal cohorts, but in every instance the attitudes of the younger voters, Republicans, Independents, and Democrats alike, were distinctly to the left of those of the New Deal generation. And, generally, younger Republican party identifiers were every bit as much to the left of their elders as the younger Democrats were to the left of their older cohorts. This was as true of the domestic issues on which the parties are traditionally and sharply divided (domestic services and spending, jobs and standard of living) as of the more recent and less partisan questions, such as involved in supporting gender equality. This pattern of generational differences is captured by Table 18-6.

Implications for the Future

Commensurate with the results of our inquiry into generation-induced compositional changes in the party identifications of voters, indicators of generational differences on policy preferences challenge our anticipation of the future as they give us new insights into the consequence of the changing generational composition of the electorate.

To return to Table 18-1 for a moment in order to accentuate this point, the Republican entries in Table 18-1 stand at least some expectations on their heads. It has long been the better part of conventional wisdom to think that the electorate became more "Democratic" as the pre–New Deal generation disappeared and was replaced by the cohorts of the New Deal-Great Society epoch. With a realignment of party control favoring the Republicans, the New Deal cohorts, in turn, were presumably to be replaced by a new generation that would be another clearly pro-Republican (or at least less Democratic) generation. It is now evident, however, that the growth component of the electorate, the predominantly college-educated post–New Deal generation, is *less* Republican (and equally Democratic) when compared to the aging New Deal cohorts.

In a politically static scenario, controlled entirely by demographic mortality rates, the inexorable generational exchange within the high school group would have minimal net impact on the balance between the parties, but the dying out

Table 18-5 Net Policy Preference, 1980–1988: Governmental Aid to Minorities

Education	Political Generation	Party Identification			Party Polarization	
		Democrat	Independent	Republican	Difference of Party Means	Rank Order Correlation*
Grade School	New Deal	-7**	-20**	32**	25	.09
	Post–New Deal	—	—	—	—	—
High School	New Deal	-7	-35	-41	34	.16
	Post–New Deal	+2	-31	-49	51	.22
	Generational Differences	+9	+4	-8	+17	+.06
College	New Deal	+4	-18	-33	37	.16
	Post–New Deal	+15	-1	-42	57	.24
	Generational Differences	+11	+17	-9	+20	+.08

Note: Entries based on pooled data from 1980, 1984, and 1988 National Election Studies.

*Entry is tau$_c$ correlation for Party Identification by uncollapsed issue preferences.

**Entries are means based on proportions favoring aid minus proportions opposed to aid.

Table 18-6 Net Policy Preference, 1980–1988: Increase Government Services and Domestic Spending

Education	Political Generation	Party Identification			Party Polarization	
		Democrat	Independent	Republican	Difference of Party Means	Rank Order Correlation*
Grade School	New Deal	+46**	0	−26	72	.29
	Post-New Deal	—	—	—	—	—
High School	New Deal	+29	−20	−41	70	.32
	Post-New Deal	+34	+10	−16	50	.21
	Generational Differences	+5	+30	+25	−20	−.11
College	New Deal	+18	−20	−44	62	.28
	Post-New Deal	+44	+4	−38	82	.33
	Generational Differences	+26	+24	+6	+20	+.05

Note: Entries based on pooled data from 1980, 1984, and 1988 National Election Studies.

*Entry is tau$_c$ correlation for Party Identification by uncollapsed issue preferences.

**Entries are proportions yes minus proportions no.

of the college-educated New Dealers would reduce, not increase, the Republican margin. Just as our three generations are sharply different in their modal rates of voter turnout, with each successive generation turning out at rates below that of the next older generation, so each succeeding generation has been less Republican and relatively more Democratic than its immediate predecessor.[7] These differences come as something of a surprise, obscured by the overall national shift favoring the Republicans in the mid- and late 1980s. And now, to top off these complexities, the disappearing cohorts, predominantly conservative Republican identifiers, will apparently be succeeded by visibly more liberal contingents from the post–New Deal generation.

Implications for Party Identification

At the aggregate level where national parameters are found, generational analysis is a helpful diagnostic tool. We have learned, for example, that the post–New Deal generation not only contributed massively to a passing phase of diminished partisanship in the electorate but it contributed to the 30-year national decline in turnout. The post–New Deal generation is making a continuing contribution to a realignment of the social foundations of Democratic and Republican politics, and it is leading the shift away from Democratic dominance and toward parity between the two parties. At the same time, it is complicating extrapolations into the future because in the 1980s it contained fewer college-educated Republicans than did the older cohorts of the New Deal generation, and on both sides of the aisle it promised more support for liberal governmental policies than has been forthcoming from the New Deal generation.

The analysis in this discussion also carries implications for a number of theories about the nature of party identification. First, we now have three large pieces of temporal evidence pertaining to stability and change. In the wake of numerous analyses emphasizing short-term change in party identification — most of them based on the total eligible electorate, South as well as North, black as well as nonblack, and nonvoters as well as voters voting in a limited number of elections — the historical record for nonblack northern voters is one of remarkable resistance to change over almost a 30-year period, 1952 to 1980. And, while net aggregate distributions often conceal gross microlevel variation, it is difficult to imagine such net stability over time being the product of an extended alternation of compensating shifts favoring first one party and then the other, either on an aggregated or individual voter level.

On the other hand, for an equally long interval between 1960 and 1988, the voters of the South reflect a continuing realignment of support for the Democratic and Republican parties. Both the erosion of Democratic dominance and the shift in the social cleavages differentiating the parties are most evident in the younger, post–New Deal generation in the South. More generally, however, the southern model for describing change seems to involve a direct exchange of partisan loyalties — Republican numbers increase as the number of

Democrats decreases. It is, of course, quite possible that the pattern of unidirectional aggregate net change could rest on a transformation matrix populated by Democrats first becoming nonpartisans and then evolving into Republicans. This would be consistent with Beck's thesis that a relaxation of the bonds of intrafamilial transmission would precede realignment (Beck 1974, 1977). The treatment of this realignment by Earl and Merle Black is, however, quite reasonable as a regional version of policy-driven conversion in party identifications (Black and Black 1987).

In the North the latter-day realignment from 1980 to 1988 suggests mobilization models in which nonpartisans move asymmetrically into one party. Two phases capture the transformation of the Reagan years: The first phase was a positive response by the less politicized younger citizens to Reagan's Republican leadership. The second phase engaged the older, more politicized voters who were moved to adopt Republican Party identifications as they began to identify themselves as conservatives (Shanks and Miller 1991). Now it appears that the first set of changes may have a unique source in the nonpartisanship of the post–New Deal generation that fueled the realignment in the North.

The three configurations of stability and change suggest that unitary generalizations such as "party identification is a running tally of . . . (performance evaluations, issue preferences, leadership traits)" are more mischievous than helpful. The major connotation of "running tally" is susceptibility to change, characterized by a malleability that can be shaped by vacillating short-term forces. The data reviewed in this discussion are consonant with the manifold evidence that factors influencing the formation and the change of party identification are often far removed from the socializing influences of a family tradition. Persuasive evidence from the Jennings panel argues that issue preferences first replace and then supplement family influence in the formation of the party identifications of young adults. However, neither our data nor the Jennings data seem well suited to the "running tally" characterization.

In conjunction with other analyses (Miller 1991a) the evidence from older generations of nonsouthern, nonblack voters in the present discussion suggests great persistence and stability of party identifications, even in the presence of events that have a large impact on younger voters. Moreover, the change in the identifications of the younger white voters in the North in turn has been inferentially less a matter of a "new tally" for those already identified with a party and more a matter of a "new tally" that mobilizes young nonidentifiers and turns them into partisan young adults.

Data from nonblack voters in the South suggest long-term unidirectional change (from 1960 to 1988), which has been something other than an ephemeral response to short-term influences. In short, the rhetorical variants on "running tally" as a characterization of party identification are convenient figures of speech that profoundly underestimate the sometime stability of party identification and gloss over the variety of specific circumstances that may be conducive to lasting change. With the sorting out of generational effects, we may begin to reorder our understanding of both the origins of party identification and the subsequent sources of change.

One of the larger remaining challenges is to understand better the roles of partisan leadership and policy preferences in the shaping of new party identifications. The present analysis does little more than affirm the importance of learning more. Why should post–New Deal partisans accentuate established party differences on questions of public policy? Because they have come to their party identifications as a result of their policy preferences? Or because leadership preferences based on presidential performance evaluations have led to the party positions taken by the leaders? Or to mention the other remarkable set of evidence, how does one account for the relative liberal proclivities of an entire new generation? The leftward march of post–New Deal Democrats might be seen as a reaction to the conservatism of the Reagan and Bush administrations. But if the ranks of Republican Party identifiers have been swelled by recent converts or the newly mobilized who have faithfully voted Republican for president, why should they be so much to the left of their partisan elders on such symbolic party stands as opposition to an activist role for the federal government in domestic issues?

The present analysis has reemphasized the policy correlates of party identification, particularly among the post–New Deal cohorts. However, neither it nor any other contemporary analysis has directly confronted the role of partisan leadership in articulating party norms for the party faithful. I have argued elsewhere (by force of theory and logic, not with direct empirical evidence) that assertive partisan leadership must often be the first step in partisan conversion and the acceptance of partisan orthodoxy on matters of policy (Miller and Levitin 1976; Miller 1990).

Although it is tempting simply to assert the importance of politicizing events that make political generations something more than demographic artifacts, the implications for our understanding of the substantive correlates of party identification cannot be ignored. The examination of generational differences in political involvement and partisan preferences has illuminated the nature of many changes in the parameters of American national electoral behavior. In some instances, it has clarified the processes of change; in others, it has largely substituted one set of explanations for another. Even in the latter case, however, it has often ruled out some classes of explanation that otherwise would have contended for our attention. In no instance has cohort/generational analysis provided a definitive resolution of problems confronting our understanding of political change. It has, however, returned out attention to the political origins of change.

At this stage in the study of electoral behavior, and given the rich array of implications flowing from our generational analyses, it seems clear that the true "independent variables" in the study of electoral behavior lie with the external world of politics. It was the experiences of a generation socialized by an epoch, somehow communicated and transmitted across age peers, that created the post–New Deal generation. With ingenuity we may yet further specify the details of the origins of the politics of that generation. The key must lie in the impact of the series of political events, experiences, and interpretations on a subsequent set of identifications, values, perceptions, and behaviors that, in fact, will constitute the electoral politics of the 1990s.

Notes

1. The sustained work of M. Kent Jennings and his colleagues Paul A. Beck and Richard G. Niemi on various problems related to the origins and attributes of party identification has not been thoroughly appreciated by most scholars writing on the topic. In particular, scholars of electoral behavior have paid too little attention to that evidence derived from the three-wave, 17-year panel study of political socialization that has peen developed and maintained by Jennings. See Beck (1977, 1982, 1984, 1989); Beck and Jennings (1975, 1979, 1991); Jennings and Markus (1984); Jennings and Niemi (1968, 1974, 1975, 1978, 1981); Niemi et al. (1980); and Niemi and Jennings (1991).

2. Moreover, it is also the case that there is a striking and reassuring parallelism and complementarity in our characterizations of generational differences and the reports of Jennings et al. on their comparisons of a single two-year filial cohort with their parental generation. The findings from our series of independent cross-sections and their three-wave panel study are consonant in every respect and on every dimension where direct comparison from published literature is possible.

3. Following the argument made in "Back to the Basics," only the three categories generated by the first question eliciting party identification are used. The strong/weak distinction among identifiers is ignored; "leaning" nonidentifiers are categorized as Independents.

4. This is not the case for the low education in the pre–New Deal generation; however, the 1964–1976 entries are based on small samples. Moreover, a temporal disaggregation of the two time periods does not reveal any other substantial year-by-year variability beyond that associated with sampling error.

5. Elsewhere, we report a drop in the Democratic plurality among all voters from 14 percentage points in 1980 to 3 points in 1988 in our analysis of the 1988 election. Note that the change in party balance occurred *after* the Reagan election of 1980, not before. In the previous *Political Behavior* article on turnout (Miller 1992b), we elaborate on the importance of the changing sizes of our analytic categories. In brief, the New Deal generation is dying out—the youngest were 50 in 1990—and the post–New Deal generation—the baby boomers—is growing rapidly, particularly so for those with some college education.

6. For a more detailed discussion of the stability of party voting through time, see Miller (1990, 1991a, and 1992b).

7. Concerning generational differences in turnout, see Miller (1992b).

19. Partisan Stability: Evidence from Aggregate Data

Donald P. Green, Bradley L. Palmquist, and Eric Schickler

Partisanship is arguably *the* central explanatory concept in the field of electoral studies. Not only do partisan attachments strongly predict how individuals vote, the distribution of these attachments in the electorate provides powerful clues as to how elections will be decided for years to come. Party identification supplies ballast to the political system, preventing electoral outcomes from swinging beyond certain bounds (Campbell et al. 1960). The intense scholarly interest in what MacKuen, Erikson, and Stimson (1989) have termed *macropartisanship* reflects the ongoing concern with the nature of this ballast. How stable is the partisan balance and to what extent does macropartisanship itself change in the wake of economic downturns or political scandal?

It is important to call attention at the outset to what aggregate data—summary statistics on the overall proportions of Democrats and Republicans—can and cannot tell us about the nature of party identification. Unlike surveys that reinterview a certain group of people over time, aggregate studies look at a series of surveys, each of which interviews different people. Thus aggregate data cannot tell us whether individuals have changed their minds or whether the composition of the population has changed due to immigration and generational replacement. Moreover, aggregate changes may mean that all voters have changed their opinions slightly or that just a few voters have changed dramatically. Given the uncertainties of interpretation, the study of macropartisanship is best characterized as the study of how the electorate changes over time. As we will see, sometimes factors that shape the partisan complexion of the electorate seem to have little effect on the partisan attachments of particular individuals.

The statistical analysis of macropartisanship tends to focus on two interrelated questions. The first concerns the stability of the ratio of Democrats and Republicans. Analysts seek to describe how the partisan division within a society has changed over time, perhaps by comparison to other types of political opinions, such as presidential approval. A second question concerns the sources of change. MacKuen et al. (1989, 1992) focus attention on two factors: consumer optimism and evaluations of presidential performance. They hypothesize that favorable economic conditions foster attachments to the president's party, which is implicitly credited for prosperity. By the same token, presidential popularity (which is to a large extent a reflection of economic conditions) brings new adherents to the president's party. In sum, identification with the incumbent's party is said to rise or recede depending on the economic and political climate.

Although this literature is often technical and arcane, the basic research strategy is straightforward. Analysts track swings in economic performance or presidential popularity and examine whether partisanship changes concomitantly. Macropartisanship is measured using quarterly data from the Gallup polls,[1] and consumer sentiment is gauged using the University of Michigan's Index of Consumer Sentiment, which ranges from 0 to 200. The fact that both of these measures are drawn from different surveys bolsters the analysis. The same cannot be said of analyses that examine how macropartisanship changes with presidential approval; the measure of the latter is also derived from Gallup polls, and there is some indication that this fact may itself contribute to the correlation between the two measures (Green, Palmquist, and Schickler 1998). All three measures are graphed in Figure 19-1 for the period covering the first quarter of 1953 (1953: 1) through the fourth quarter of 1999 (1999: 4).

Macropartisanship, as operationalized by MacKuen et al. (1989), is the percentage of Democrats divided by the percentage of Democrats and Republicans. Because it is the ratio of two percentages, it is somewhat more volatile than if it were simply the percentage of Democrats. Nevertheless, the series is remarkably placid, particularly when compared to the percentage of the public that approves of the president's performance in office. Presidential approval has a standard deviation of 11.6 and occasionally swings by more than 30 percentage points in the span of a year. By contrast, macropartisanship has a standard deviation of 4.6, and two-thirds of the observations during the past half-century have fallen within the range of 55 to 65 percent. Given this sluggish pattern of change over time, it would be surprising if economic and political conditions were found to have strong effects.

Clearly, some of the public's political assessments are strongly influenced by the economy. As Figure 19-1 makes apparent, presidential approval surges and falls in response to economic cycles. Thus it is natural to ask whether economic cycles themselves lead to partisan change, perhaps as the result of changes in presidential popularity. To test this proposition, we start with a simple time series regression model:

$$Macropartisanship_t = a + b(Macropartisanship_{t-1}) + c(Consumer\ Sentiment_t) + u_t$$

In this equation, time is indexed by the subscript t. Notice that when $c = 0$, macropartisanship is simply a function of its past values, plus a disturbance (u_t). When c is not zero, the model implies that macropartisanship changes in response to short-term shifts in economic conditions. Any change to macropartisanship at one point in time affects future values of macropartisanship, so a one-unit shift in economic conditions changes macropartisanship by cb during the quarter after the shift occurred. The values of the parameters a, b, and c can be estimated using regression analysis.

Table 19-1 reports the results of this and other regression models to illustrate how the results change as new predictors are introduced.[2] When we assume

Figure 19-1 Macropartisanship, Presidential Approval, and Consumer Sentiment, 1953–1999

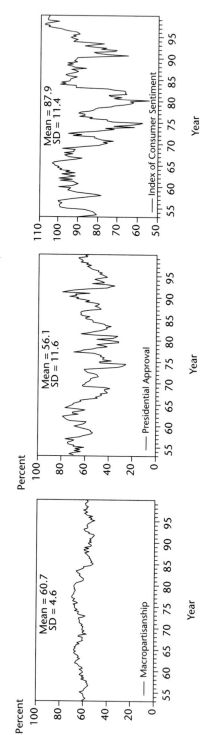

Table 19-1 Results from Alternative Time-Series Models of Macropartisan Change, 1953:1–1999:4

	Model 1	Model 2	Model 3	Model 4	Model 5	Model 6
Macropartisanship, lagged on quarter	.92 (.03)	.95 (.03)	.92 (.03)	.96 (.02)	.87 (.03)	.92 (.03)
Party (−1 = GOP, 1 = Dem)			−2.36 (1.08)	−2.27 (.84)	−2.41 (1.06)	−2.28 (.80)
Michigan Index of Consumer Sentiment × Party			.027 (.012)	.026 (.009)	−.003 (.015)	.001 (.012)
Presidential approval × party					.049 (.015)	.040 (.012)
Constant	4.88 (1.77)	2.99 (1.53)	4.94 (1.83)	2.60 (1.50)	7.66 (1.96)	4.75 (1.58)
One period moving average		.20 (.08)		.24 (.08)		.25 (.08)
Adjusted R^2	.84	.85	.84	.85	.85	.86
Q-statistic (16 lags)	26.5, p = .05	21.8, p = .11	27.6, p = .04	19.5, p = .19	30.4, p = .02	19.4, p = .20

Notes: $N = 188$. Entries are coefficients, with standard errors in parentheses.

c to be zero (Model 1), we estimate b to be .92. This estimate climbs to .95 in Model 2 when we make allowances for the fact that macropartisanship measures contain sampling error (see Green et al. 1998).[3] Evidently, anything that perturbs the distribution of partisanship (e.g., new people entering the electorate) leaves a long-lasting imprint. When consumer sentiment is added to the equation (Models 3–4), c is estimated to be approximately .026. This estimate is statistically significant but small. A two standard deviation swing in consumer sentiment (22.8 index points) produces a change of just three-fifths of a percentage point in macropartisanship during that quarter. Evidently only very large economic shocks sustained over long stretches of time are sufficient to alter the partisan balance.

When presidential approval is added to the regression equation (Models 5–6), the effects of economic conditions vanish. Economic conditions matter because they influence presidential popularity; they have no direct effect of their own. Presidential approval's effects are again statistically significant but small. Taking sampling error into account (Model 6), we find its coefficient to be .04, which implies that a two standard deviation change in approval (23.2 percentage points) translates into slightly less than a one percentage-point change in macropartisanship. Again, it is apparent that appreciable movement in macropartisanship requires the political climate to change dramatically over long stretches of time.

The regression models presented in Table 19-1 are by no means the only ones that could be applied to these data. Elsewhere (Green et al. 1998) we review and critique a wide array of modeling approaches. It turns out, however, that unless the analyst imposes extreme assumptions on these models, the results come out more or less as described in Table 19-1. Macropartisanship responds in a limited and gradual fashion to changes in political and economic conditions.

In some sense, however, models such as those presented in Table 19-1 *overstate* the influence of economic and political conditions. The reason goes beyond issues of question wording, sampling artifacts, and the choice of regression estimators, important though they may be. Since MacKuen et al. (1989) brought these trends to the attention of the discipline, scholars have returned to them again and again, continually reanalyzing the same period. This is a common problem in the statistical analysis of time-series and often causes analysts to overfit the idiosyncrasies of a particular set of data—that is, they develop measures and regression models that follow the twists and turns observed over a stretch of time, forgetting that the purpose of time-series regression is to estimate the parameters a, b, and c. The most common symptom of overfitting is that models developed to analyze a particular time period perform badly when applied to new data points. Put somewhat differently, there is little surprise in finding a statistically significant correlation between economic conditions and macropartisanship in data covering the period 1953–1999; after all, 140 of the 188 quarterly observations inspired the initial MacKuen et al. report, and 176 of 188 were analyzed by Erikson, MacKuen, and Stimson (1998) and Green et al.

Figure 19-2 Observed, Fitted, and Forecasted Macropartisanship, Using Consumer Sentiment as a Predictor

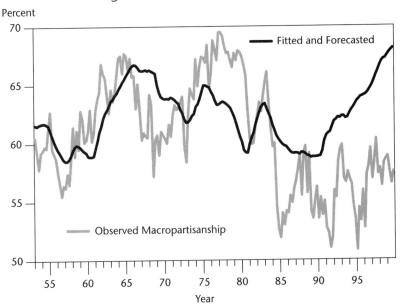

Percent

Note: Fitted values (through the fourth quarter of 1988) were generated based on Model 4; later values were forecasted based on that model. The fitted and forecasted values use consumer sentiment at time *t*, but not macropartisanship at time *t*-1, to predict macropartisanship at time *t*.

(1998). To gauge the validity of these models, we must examine how well they forecast observations that come in after the ink has dried.

The period after 1989 makes for a telling test of the hypothesis that partisanship is shaped by "fundamental" economic and political conditions (Erikson et al. 1998). President George H. Bush's popularity soared and plummeted, and the economy went in and out of recession. For the first time in decades, a Democratic president presided over a period of economic growth. According to Models 3–6 in Table 19-1, Democratic partisanship should have soared to levels reminiscent of the 1960s. As Figure 19-2 illustrates, forecasts generated by Model 4 using data for the period 1953:1–1988:4 suggest that in 1999:4 macropartisanship should be at 68.1. Economic fundamentals were as good as they have ever been. From Figure 19-3 we see that forecasts based on Model 6, which includes presidential popularity as a predictor, also anticipate sharp movement in the Democratic direction. By 1999:4 macropartisanship is predicted to reach 66.6. Neither forecast is at all close to the actual value of 57.5, which is scarcely different from the 56.9 recorded at the beginning of President Bill Clinton's second term. Contrary to the model's predictions, Democratic partisanship has failed to rise with

Figure 19-3 Observed, Fitted, and Forecasted Macropartisanship, Using Presidential Approval as a Predictor

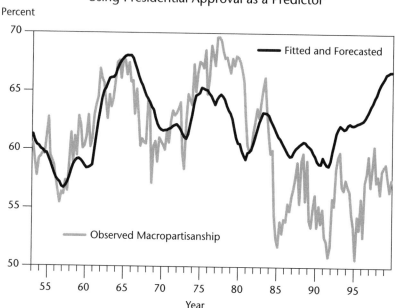

Note: Fitted values (through the fourth quarter of 1988) were generated based on Model 6; later values were forecasted based on that model. The fitted and forecasted values use presidential approval at time t, but not macropartisanship at time t-1, to predict macropartisanship at time t.

strong economic growth and a long string of solid presidential approval scores. The farther one strays from the data that first inspired the macropartisanship literature, the more inaccurate the out-of-sample forecasts become.

Flawed out-of-sample forecasts suggest that the link between macropartisanship and political conditions is more muted than originally thought. While it is no doubt true that it is easier to attract adherents to the Democratic Party when it presides over good times, what is remarkable is the limited extent to which party identification responds to the political environment. As Gerber and Green (1998) point out in their analysis of both individual-level survey data and aggregate trends, party identification has remained more or less constant even amid sharp swings in the public's perception of which party is better able to manage economic and foreign affairs. It is not that people fail to notice political events or to change their minds about the parties. It is simply that party identification is different from a simple evaluation of which party is best. Party identification is at root a form of social identity: one thinks of oneself as a Democrat or Republican. Even when a party's fortunes are down, one may nonetheless think of oneself as part of a social group called Democrats or Republicans.

The study of aggregate time-series has come a long way in recent years. Formerly scholars limited their attention to the biennial surveys conducted by the National Election Studies; now it is possible to track partisan movements on a quarterly or even monthly basis, linking them to short-term changes in economic conditions or presidential popularity. This new line of research, we believe, complements the study of individual level panel data. Both literatures attest to the stability of partisan attachments over time. Looking at a wide variety of panel studies conducted in the United States and other countries, Green and Palmquist (1990, 1994) and Schickler and Green (1997) find that individuals tend to retain their partisan affiliations over time, even amid political and economic turmoil. Revisiting the work of some previous scholars (Fiorina 1981; Franklin and Jackson 1983), Green and Palmquist (1990) and Schickler and Green (1995) find that partisan identities are unaffected by individuals' retrospective assessments of presidential performance or their ideological proximity to the presidential candidates. The "unmoved mover" conception of party identification has weathered decades of criticism from scholars attempting to show that these identities are merely stand-ins for other sorts of political evaluations. In the end, the accumulated scholarship shows that stability is indeed the outstanding feature of party identities.

Notes

1. A long-simmering debate surrounds the way that partisanship is measured in Gallup surveys. Gallup asks respondents whether "in politics, as of today" they consider themselves Democrats, Independents, or Republicans. National Election Studies surveys introduce the question with the phrase "in general" and omit the phrase "as of today," which is believed to focus too much attention on short-term evaluations of parties and candidates.
2. The regression models in Table 19-1 control for the party of the incumbent. Consumer sentiment and approval are multiplied by the party variable to take into account the fact that economic growth and presidential popularity increase Democratic partisanship only when a Democrat is in office. For more discussion of these measures, see Green et al. (1998).
3. The one-period moving average (MA) term in the even-numbered models corrects for the fact that macropartisanship is measured with sampling error. When sampling error is accounted for in this way, the estimates of b tend to increase while the estimates of c tend to decrease. For more discussion of MA(1) errors, see Green et al. (1998).

20. Macropartisanship:
The Permanent Memory of Partisan Evaluation

Robert S. Erikson, Michael B. MacKuen, and James A. Stimson

In a 1989 article we presented a measure of "macropartisanship" as the time series of the Democratic percent of Republican and Democratic Party identifiers in Gallup surveys going back to the 1940s (MacKuen et al. 1989). The article showed that macropartisanship not only moves over time, but does so in part as a reflection of consumer sentiment and presidential approval. When consumers are optimistic and people approve the president, identification with the presidential party increases.

No complicated statistical arguments are required to appreciate these relationships. Figure 20-1 overlays the time series of macropartisanship, presidential approval, and consumer sentiment by presidential administration, Dwight Eisenhower through Bill Clinton (first term). For each president, approval tracks consumer sentiment and macropartisanship tracks both consumer sentiment and approval.

This evidence challenges the once dominant orthodoxy that party identification is essentially a constant rather than a variable. How, one might ask, could partisanship be so stable at the individual level yet so movable in the aggregate? If partisanship is largely frozen in place by early adulthood as often thought, how could it be so responsive to the routine currents of economic and political fortune represented by consumer sentiment and presidential approval?

These are serious questions that deserve serious answers. We start with the facts of micro-level stability and macro-level variability and ask: By what theoretical argument could they both be correct? According to the traditional theory of partisanship, as handed down by *The American Voter* (Campbell et al. 1960), people are imprinted with fixed party identifications learned from their parents and modified by early political experiences around the time of the first vote. If adults trace their partisanship to their youth, there must be an element of stability. But if adult partisanship responds to economic and political inputs, we must also allow for occasional change. Thus we need a micro- and macro-level model whereby individuals are influenced by their parents and the economic and political climate of their formative years, as well as by economic and political inputs across the span of their adulthood. This model must allow people to change their partisanship as a function of new information but with no forgetting of the past.

To fit this set of requirements, partisanship must contain the element of an integrated series, representing the permanent transmission of partisanship from one's parents and early environment *plus* the accumulation of permanent shocks

Figure 20-1 Macropartisanship, Presidential Approval, and Consumer Sentiment, 1953–1996, by Presidency

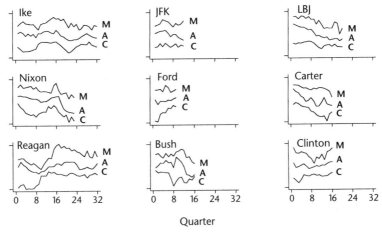

Note: M = macropartisanship; A = presidential approval; C = consumer sentiment.

across one's adult lifetime. Whereas some influences on partisanship are transient, the inputs into the integrated series are permanent. For individuals, these permanent inputs can be idiosyncratic. In the aggregate, the idiosyncratic inputs cancel out, leaving as a residue the systematic influences of shared economic and political events. These shared influences are small when measured in the context of individual partisan differences yet appear large in the aggregate. For instance, consider a shock that causes 1 percent of partisans to switch their identifications from Democratic to Republican. This change would be microscopic when measured in the context of individual-level survey analysis. This same shock would constitute a visible percentage point movement when graphed as part of the aggregate-level time series analysis.

We claim that macropartisanship contains a permanent memory of political and economic inputs. As we will see, this argument is consistent with the data as well as theory. The evidence shows macropartisanship to behave as an integrated series with permanent inputs. Moreover, these inputs can be identified as the same economic and political shocks that cause changes in consumer sentiment and presidential approval.

The Statistical Model

Macropartisanship contains both a permanent and a transient component:

$$M_t = M_t^* + u_t$$

where M_t = the observed partisan division in surveys, M_t^* = the permanent (equilibrium) component, and u_t = the autoregressive short-term component, or the "error." M_t^* is the electorate's collective memory of party performance; u_t, the error, is the transient response to politics of the moment, such as the short-term forces of a presidential campaign. It is the permanent component that attracts our interest. Its permanence means that even small changes have lasting consequences.

$$M_t^* = M_0^* + \sum_{i=1}^{t} v_i$$

$$= M_0^* + w_1 \sum_{i=1}^{t} e_i + w_2 \sum_{i=1}^{t} p_i$$

where M_t^* is a random walk generated by cumulative random shocks, v_t, which in turn are the (weighted) sum of cumulative economic shocks (e_t) and cumulative political shocks (p_t) and M_0^* is an arbitrary base starting point (1953:1 in our series). Because the e_t and p_t shocks can be estimated from the presidential approval and consumer sentiment series (see below), M_t^* can be estimated directly.

   Equilibrium partisanship (M_t^*) represents the long memory of political and economic shocks. When the political or economic times cast favor on the presidential party, the presidential party gains. When the times cast disfavor on the presidential party, the presidential party loses. These gains and losses accumulate without decay so that each new shock leaves a permanent trace on the partisan record. Their accumulation represents the running tally of party performance.

   Unlike macropartisanship, the *Index of Consumer Sentiment* (*ICS*) and presidential approval each behave as AR1 stationary time series, as if observations form a cyclical series oscillating around a constant equilibrium value. Regressing *ICS* on its lagged values:

$$ICS_t = 8.99 + 0.90 ICS_{t-1} + e_t$$
$$\quad\quad (2.98) \quad (0.03)$$

where ICS_t = the *Index of Consumer Sentiment* in quarter t and e_t = the disturbance. Adjusted R^2 = .80; N = 175; standard errors are in parentheses. With an autoregressive coefficient of 0.90, the net impact of each quarterly shock to ICS decays by 10 percent per quarter. Over the long run of even a few years, ICS reverts toward its constant equilibrium of about 88 points on a 0–200 scale. This behavior as a stationary series makes sense because when consumers evaluate economic conditions they weigh current economic indicators the heaviest and discount the past. Meanwhile, the estimated disturbance for this series — the "e_t"s — add up to comprise the economic component of macropartisanship.

Table 20-1 Regressing Macropartisanship on Cumulative Economic and Political Shocks

	Gallup, 1953–1996 ($N = 176$)	Gallup, 1976–1996 ($N = 84$)	CBS News/ New York Times, 1976–1996 ($N = 84$)
Constant	64.24	66.73	65.92
	(0.48)	(1.07)	(1.05)
Cumulative economic shocks	0.15	0.17	0.15
	(0.01)	(0.02)	(0.02)
Cumulative political shocks	0.12	0.17	0.17
	(0.01)	(0.01)	(0.01)
Adjusted R^2	.595	.772	.766

Notes: Standard errors in parenthesis. Predicted values from these equations comprise estimates of equilibrium macropartisanship (M_t^*).

Regressing presidential approval on its lagged values:

$$Approval_t = 3.79 + 0.92 Approval_{t-1} + a_t$$
$$(1.95)\quad (0.03)$$

where $Approval_t$ = approval in quarter t and a_t = the disturbance. Adjusted R^2 = .920; $N = 169$; standard errors are in parentheses. With an autoregressive coefficient of .92, the net impact of each quarterly shock to approval declines by 8 percent per quarter. Over the long run of even a few years, approval reverts toward its constant equilibrium value of a bit under 50 percent approval. This behavior as a stationary series makes sense because when citizens evaluate the president they weigh current performance the heaviest and discount the past.

Approval shocks are partly due to economic perceptions. We wish to purge approval shocks of their economic component, to obtain a measure of strictly political shocks. Regressing approval shocks on economic shocks, we get:

$$a_t = -0.45 + 0.43 e_t + 0.16 e_{t-1} + p_t$$
$$(0.35)\quad (0.07)\quad (0.07)$$

where p_t = the disturbance. Adjusted R^2 = .18; $N = 168$; standard errors are in parentheses. Now we have the economic shocks, the "e_t"s, and the political shocks, the "p_t"s. We sum each set of shocks to form two cumulative series, after first reversing their signs when a Republican is president.

We next account for macropartisanship in terms of cumulative economic shocks and cumulative political shocks. The simplest way of doing this is via

Figure 20-2 Quarterly Partisanship and its Equilibrium Value, Gallup and CBS/*New York Times*, 1976–1996

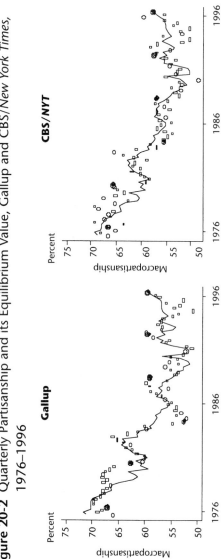

Note: Presidential election quarters are highlighted. The graph line equals equilibrium partisanship.

Table 20-2   Predicting Future Macropartisanship from Current Observed Values (M_t) plus Current Equilibrium Values ($M_t{}^*$), 1976–1996

Dependent Variable	Gallup		CBS/*NYT*	
	M_t	$M_t{}^*$	M_t	$M_t{}^*$
M_{t+1}	0.70	0.35	0.49	0.50
($N = 83$)	(0.07)	(0.10)	(0.10)	(0.11)
M_{t+2}	0.55	0.50	0.31	0.67
($N = 82$)	(0.09)	(0.12)	(0.10)	(0.12)
M_{t+3}	0.38	0.65	0.23	0.74
($N = 81$)	(0.11)	(0.15)	(0.07)	(0.12)
M_{t+4}	0.24	0.78	0.26	0.67
($N = 80$)	(0.12)	(0.16)	(0.11)	(0.12)
M_{t+5}	0.04	0.96	0.19	0.71
($N = 79$)	(0.13)	(0.17)	(0.12)	(0.14)
M_{t+6}	−0.12	1.01	0.09	0.77
($N = 78$)	(0.20)	(0.19)	(0.13)	(0.14)

Note: Entries are regression coefficients, with standard errors in parenthesis, predicting future macropartisanship (M_{t+s}) from (M_t) and ($M_t{}^*$)

ordinary least squares (OLS), as shown in Table 20-1.[1] Table 20-1 estimates $M_t{}^*$ as the predicted values from regression equations explaining macropartisanship from economic and political shocks. Equations are shown measuring macropartisanship from Gallup data from 1953 to 1996 and from both Gallup and CBS News/*New York Times* data from 1976 to 1996. The equations are remarkably similar; for 1976–1996, cumulative economic and political shocks account for 77 percent of the variance in macropartisanship. Figure 20-2 graphs the Gallup and the CBS News/*NYT* versions of M_t and M_t^* for 1976–1996.

The driving force of macropartisanship (M_t) is M_t^*, the equilibrium partisanship based on cumulated political and economic shocks. The proof is in the ability of estimated equilibrium partisanship to predict the partisan future. Let us set the task of predicting macropartisanship in future quarters, say one to six quarters ahead. We ask: Which better predicts the partisan future: current macropartisanship (M_t^c) or current equilibrium partisanship (M_t^{c*})?

Using OLS, Table 20-2 predicts future macropartisanship at various leads from current values of M_t and M_t^*, 1976–1996. To predict future Gallup readings four or more quarters ahead, the current equilibrium value provides more information than current macropartisanship. For the CBS/*NYT* series, the predictive dominance of the equilibrium values is even stronger. For predicting one quarter ahead, M_t^c and M_t^{c*} perform about equally. For longer leads (even a mere two quarters), M_t^{c*} predicts better than M_t^c.

To know the fundamentals represented by cumulative changes in consumer senti-ment and approval is more important than knowing the current value of macroparti-sanship. The equilibrium value represents the fundamentals; any current deviation from this value will be short-lived. Moreover, the fundamentals provide stability, correlating at 0.97 with its lagged values.

Discussion

The fundamentals of macropartisanship are comprised of the permanent political and economic shocks from the past and present. The key to under-standing the macropartisanship series is its long memory. The response of macropartisanship to new economic and political inputs may be imperceptibly small at the time of occurrence, but it will be long-lasting. Consider the exam-ple of Watergate. President Richard Nixon's declining popularity was far more noticeable than the small decline in Republican Party identification. Yet, as Nixon left the scene, the pro-Democratic Watergate shocks persisted to provide an otherwise inexplicable level of Democratic identification during the Gerald Ford and Jimmy Carter presidencies. Similarly, the more visible long-term Republican gain of the 1980s provided a new base of Republican strength that limited the Democratic recovery in macropartisanship starting late in the George Bush administration.

Today's partisanship is shaped by the good economic times of the Clinton years, the successful Gulf War, Reagan's recession and recovery, Carter's failures, and Watergate, to name a few events. It is also a function of Vietnam, the JFK legacy, the 1950s, World War II, the New Deal, and much more. Just as these events impact presidential popularity in the short term, they leave a smaller but permanent imprint on partisanship for the long term.

Note

1. The interested reader is encouraged to consult Erikson et al. (1998) for our full-blown error correction modeling. In ECMs, one method for estimating equilibrium values is via OLS. The estimates of Table 20-1 are virtually identical to the estimates from the more complicated "one-step" methodology employed in our 1998 article.

PART VI
PARTY SYSTEM CHANGE

21. Is the Party System Changing?

By its nature, politics is ever changing. Much of that change is ephemeral, lasting not much longer than yesterday's headlines. Yet some changes last longer and therefore command more attention. In the field of voting and elections, this description is certainly true. There are inevitably changes in vote totals and winning candidates from one election to the next, and yet there is continuity as well, as incumbent candidates often win and parties themselves change only rarely. In this unending ebb and flow, the important changes are the ones that have ramifications for future elections.

Of particular importance are changes in the party system itself, as occurred around 1816 when the Federalists disappeared from the scene and in the 1850s when the Republican Party replaced the Whigs. For the past 150 years, the identities of our two major parties have been the same, and even third-party challenges have been short-lived. Still, there have been important changes in the relative strength and bases of support of the parties. These are commonly referred to as party realignments, and they form the basis for demarcating "party systems" that are sometimes used to divide American electoral history into meaningful periods (Burnham 1991). But realignment is only one kind of change. Another possibility is party "dealignment"—when the overall importance of partisanship declines, as marked by such trends as less identification with parties or a weaker relationship between partisanship and voting. Or the reverse can happen: partisanship can be reinvigorated and party ties can become more important.

Detecting party realignment and dealignment is easiest when done in historical perspective. Thus, for example, there is general agreement that there was party realignment in a Republican direction in 1896, followed by the New Deal realignment in a Democratic direction around 1932, with the resulting New Deal alignment generally thought to have lasted *at least* through 1960. There is less agreement, however, as to the nature of political change "recently"—where recently now extends back to the 1960s. There is evidence of significant realignment of some social groups in the 1980s, although less indication of major change in the overall balance between the parties (even though it is clear that the balance favored the Democrats less in the 1990s than it did in the 1950s). There is considerable evidence that there was a dealignment that affected voters and elections in the 1970s, leading to a period of candidate-centered politics, which perhaps is still in effect today. Yet there is also an indication that partisanship again became more important by the end of the twentieth century. This is a vital debate, as it directly has to do with how we should be interpreting contemporary politics.

A Post-New Deal Realignment Has Occurred

The concept of party realignment is used in several related ways. The most basic definition involves political change of the sort that happened in the 1850s and 1930s.[1] Political pundits sometimes restrict the definition to switches in which party is in the majority, but political scientists have more often applied it to any durable movement in levels of party support. If there has been realignment since the New Deal years, it has obviously not been a replacement of a major party or a change in which is the majority party. That makes it important to keep in mind three other ways in which durable change can occur. First, there can be long-lasting changes in the policy direction of the government (Clubb, Flanigan, and Zingale 1980). Second, there can be lasting changes in the issue basis of the party system (Sundquist 1983). Finally, there can be enduring changes in the alignment of social groups with the parties, including compensating changes that occur when groups of equal size switch parties in opposite directions without changing the overall partisan balance. All these kinds of durable change have at one time or another been referred to as realignments.

In looking for realignments, it is also important to recognize that they need not be abrupt. V. O. Key Jr. (1955) originally applied the term *realignment* to sharp changes in the party system[2] associated with a "critical election," but later he generalized it to include more gradual "secular realignments" (Key 1959). Indeed, one can speak of realigning periods, recognizing that realignments often take a few years, sometimes because they affect different states or regions in different elections. Carmines and Stimson (1989) have written of "issue evolutions" instead of realignments, with the term *evolution* further emphasizing that electoral change need not be abrupt.

With this background we can turn to the question of whether there has been realignment since the New Deal realignment in the 1930s. Experts do not agree. Certainly there has not been an abrupt realignment of that scale, although some statistical analyses have found break points in electoral series that suggest realignments around 1960 and 1972. If there has been realignment, it is of a different type than the 1896 and 1932 varieties. There is also evidence of issue evolutions during this period and changes in the social group bases of the parties.

Two recent analyses of historical voting patterns are of particular importance, although they arrive at different conclusions. Using county and city data, Nardulli (1995) examined voting change between 1828 and 1984, looking for shifts in voting in 215 homogeneous electoral regions in the nation. He found realignment around the elections of 1836 (a Whig realignment), 1856 (antebellum Republican), 1896 (a pro-Democratic populist realignment quickly followed by a pro-Republican industrial realignment), and between 1876 and 1904 in the South (which he labels a Jim Crow realignment). In the twentieth century Nardulli found realignments around the elections of 1932 (New Deal Democratic), 1948 (post-World War II Republican), and 1960 (a New Frontier realignment of major urban areas).

Bartels (1998a) applied a different methodology to look at electoral change after 1868. He calculated the long-term impact of each presidential election, taking into account estimates of the national and subnational forces (at the state level) in an election as well as their persistence over the next seven elections. The 1932 election stands out as a critical election with this methodology, with 1880 coming in second, that being the election in which the South reverted to Democratic voting after the end of Reconstruction. The 1896 election was not seen as a critical election using this methodology since its electoral impact did not persist beyond 1900. Bartels's method shows that 1972 might also be a critical election, ranking behind only 1932, 1880, and 1920, but Bartels could not test post-1972 elections since his method requires seven elections afterwards to determine that lasting change has occurred. However, he shows that there was less volatility in the electoral outcomes of the presidential elections of the 1980s and 1990s compared to the 1960s and 1970s, as measured by the vote swings from election to election.

Turning to government policy shifts, there have been some swings since the New Deal days, but most are not at the level of realignment. While the 1950s were not marked by an extension of New Deal programs, the Eisenhower administration did not roll back them back either. John Kennedy's New Frontier and Lyndon Johnson's Great Society programs intensified the New Deal programs, but they can still be seen as continuations. The subsequent Nixon, Ford, and Carter administrations presented only minor variations on these themes. The first significant change was a shift to the right during what is sometimes called the "Reagan Revolution" of the 1980s, with attempts to cut back the role of the federal government. One could reasonably view this change as being confirmed by the Republican takeover of the House of Representatives in 1994 and President Bill Clinton's subsequent admission that "the era of big government is over." These policy shifts occurred after the periods studied by Nardulli and Bartels, so their work is not necessarily in conflict with this analysis.

Rather than relying on aggregate election returns or analysis of policy directions, it is possible to look at realignment in the post-1950 period through survey data. Table 17-1 showed us that the Democratic lead in party identification has diminished since the 1950s, though most surveys still find more Democratic identifiers than Republicans. This is suggestive of realignment, but the real power of the survey evidence is in looking for realignment at the issue and social group levels.

Carmines and Stimson (1989) found issue evolution in the 1960s in how race came to influence the division between the parties. They showed how changes in the position of the parties in Congress on the race issue preceded party polarization on the issue in the mass electorate. Republicans in Congress had been more liberal on race than Democrats through the 1950s, but that situation was transformed when the Democratic Congress passed the 1964 Civil Rights Act and the Republican presidential candidate, Barry Goldwater, cast a vote against its enactment. Soon afterward Democratic identifiers among the mass public became more pro-civil rights than Republican identifiers, through shifts of partisanship by blacks and southern whites, which will be discussed further below. More recently, Adams (1997) has shown that issue evolution occurred in the 1980s on the abortion issue, although it is not of the scope of the shift that Carmines and Stimson described.

Post-1950 realignment is most visible with survey data in the analysis of social groups. Different groups have shifted in each direction, making the net change in partisanship less than the total amount of change. But it is clear that group voting patterns have been altered in recent decades. Some might object to viewing all these group changes as realignment, but they are important from the realignment point of view when they are part of an overall change in the groups from which the parties draw their support.

In Chapter 22 Stanley and Niemi trace the changes in the group basis of party identification over the National Election Studies (NES) surveys from 1952 through 1996. Their analysis of Democratic and Republican identification is multivariate, assessing the effects of each demographic variable with the other demographic variables controlled. Change is indeed visible. The trend that stands out most dramatically with respect to the incremental support from group membership for Democratic identification is the declining distinctiveness of native white southerners, a group that was notably Democratic in the 1950s but was barely distinguishable from the rest of the country by the 1990s. The voting changes of this group also played a prominent role in Chapter 18, by Warren Miller, which discusses realignment during the Reagan administration, with conservative Democrats, particularly in the South, moving to the Republican Party.

This basic argument is supported by Abramowitz and Saunders's (1998) demonstration of an ideological realignment of the electorate during the Reagan and post-Reagan years. Not only did the Democratic majority of the 1970s decline by the 1990s, especially among white males and southern whites, but ideology and partisanship became much more correlated among people who are aware of differences between the political parties. Abramowitz and Saunders's results end with the 1994 election, which instituted a Republican majority in the House of Representatives for the first time in forty years. While the 1994 election may be atypical in ways that skew their results, one of their important conclusions remains true: "The increasing ideological polarization of the Democratic and Republican Parties in the Reagan and post-Reagan eras made it easier for voters to recognize the differences between the parties' policy stands," (649) and that has led to some voters moving to the party whose policy stands they like. Levine, Carmines, and Huckfeldt (1997) also show that over the period from 1972 through 1992 ideology played an increasing role in shaping partisanship, even with controls for group membership and other demographic factors.

Stanley and Niemi's analysis of gender, race, and ethnicity groups merits further attention. Considerable attention has been given to the gender gap that developed in the 1980 election, with women being more likely to vote Democratic than men. Stanley and Niemi show that the marginal impact of being female not only remained in the Democratic direction in the 1990s but once again hit its highest value in 1996. Yet they argue that, even if the gender gap were to grow in the next few elections, gender is unlikely to be the basis for party realignment because both parties must appeal to both genders and cannot afford to write off half of the electorate.[3]

The contributions of women and men to the gender gap have been studied by Norrander. Her analysis shows that the gender gap was created by men moving away from the Democratic Party faster than women did (1999b; see also Wirls 1986). She finds that the gender gap increased in the 1996 election due to "compassion issues." The movement away from the Democratic Party by men was originally greater in the South, but by 1996 it was also apparent among northerners, although at a slower rate (Norrander 1999a). There also has been an "independence gap," with women being on average 6 percent less likely than men to be Independent, visible in all Michigan election studies back through 1952 (Norrander 1997). More precisely, men were more likely to be Independent leaners while women were more likely to be weak partisans. Most accounts of the gender gap in the media are based on the core partisanship question, without asking Independents if they are closer to a party, which has the effect of emphasizing women's greater concentration among Democrats. Including leaners as partisan would show that the gap is also due to men being more Republican. Kaufmann and Petrocik (1999) agree that the gender gap was produced by the changing partisanship of men, but they identify the cause more with social welfare issues.

In their decomposition of the vote, Miller and Shanks (1996) found that the gender gap in voting in 1992 appears at first to be due to a Democratic advantage in partisanship among women. However, partisanship and policy predispositions should have combined to yield a stronger Democratic vote among women than actually occurred, counteracted apparently by women being more favorable than men to George Bush. Several other factors have been examined in searching for the causal basis of the gender gap, including gender differences on attitudes toward the use of military force, the welfare state, the economy, and feminist issues. Manza and Brooks (1998) locate the origins of the gender gap in women's increased labor force participation, whereas by 1992 feminist consciousness also became a significant causal factor. Additionally, their modeling demonstrates the importance of differing views on social service spending, with working women being more liberal on social services and this being a proximate cause of the gender gap.

The black vote became predominately Democratic during the New Deal days—to the extent that blacks were able to vote—but the Stanley and Niemi analysis shows that it became even more Democratic starting with the 1964 election. Miller and Shanks (1996) find the black vote to be especially distinctive, and it remained distinctive after they controlled for partisanship, ideology, policies, presidential performance, and candidate evaluations, meaning that conventional explanations could not fully account for the high Democratic vote among blacks in 1992.

Stanley and Niemi also focus on Hispanics, an ethnic group whose partisan trends are of recent interest. Non-Cuban Hispanics were an increased fraction of the Democratic coalition in 1996, after the Republican Party became associated with a series of anti-immigrant actions nationally and especially in California. The Republican Party position on these issues moderated in the 2000 election, although exit polls show that most Hispanics still voted for Gore over Bush. This is an unusually difficult group to mobilize on behalf of one party because there are political differences among the nationality groups that comprise the Hispanic community, as evidenced by the large Bush vote among Cuban-Americans in Florida in 2000.

In addition to these social variables, there has been attention to marriage differences in voting. Starting with the 1972 presidential contest between Richard Nixon and George McGovern, married people have been voting more Republican than nonmarried, where the latter includes divorced, separated, widowed, never-married, and people living together as partners (Weisberg 1987). This marriage gap can partly be explained in terms of race and income, especially since unmarried people tend to have lower incomes, which correlates with voting more Democratic. Miller and Shanks (1996) locate the 1992 voting gap between the married and never-married in other social and economic characteristics and in policy-related predispositions, particularly ideology and moral tolerance. In 1992 a further voting difference emerged, with parents of young children voting more Democratic than those without young children (Arnold and Weisberg 1996). The marriage gap remains larger than the gender gap, and it has led to politicians appealing to voters on the basis of family issues (Weisberg and Kelly 1997).

When looking at group realignment, there is a large number of potential groups to examine as well as multiple ways to define groups. Definitions often affect results. The early work on religion, for example, distinguished mainly between Protestants, Catholics, and Jews, with Protestants voting more Republican than the other religious groups in the 1950s. There has been renewed attention to religion and the vote since 1980, but this research has also demarcated religions differently and defined concepts more carefully. Much of the focus has been on differentiating types of Protestants, especially Evangelicals, as well as better measuring religious commitment. Thus Layman (1997) shows that evangelical Protestants are the group that moved over to the Republican Party the most between 1980 and 1994, with people who are very committed to their religion becoming more likely to vote Republican.

Miller and Shanks (1996) also give considerable attention to the changed role of religion in voting from 1980 through 1992. The general trend across the electorate in that period was toward a greater proportion of the two-party vote being Democratic, but committed Evangelicals shifted in a pro-Republican direction. Miller and Shanks compare that result with the equal increase in the size of secular, nonreligious voters, with a large swing of that group in the Democratic direction. The party identification of committed Evangelicals also moved strongly in the Republican direction, whereas other groups were more stable (except for the small group of people in minor religious traditions included in the "other" category that moved strongly in the Democratic direction). Along with changes in partisanship, Miller and Shanks also show that committed adherents were more conservative on issues such as moral traditionalism, evaluations of homosexuals, and ideology than were their nominal co-religionists, and that is true for mainline Protestants, Catholics, and Evangelicals. However, the committed Evangelicals were the most conservative, underlining the importance of that group to understanding trends in American politics during this period. Overall, the growing importance of religion, the shift of committed Evangelical Protestants, and the countervailing shifts of voters preferring a minor religion or no religion at all are among the largest sociodemographic trends found in the Miller and Shanks analysis of the 1980–1992 period.

Layman and Carmines (1997) have placed the research on religious groups in broader perspective in their examination of the argument that American politics is becoming more value-based. They find that cultural orientations have indeed become important, but in only one of two possible senses. They do not find much support for the differences between materialists (whose primary goals are financial well-being) and postmaterialists (whose primary goals are noneconomic), as suggested by Inglehart (1977; Abramson and Inglehart 1986). However, they do find that religion is important in the sense of cultural differences between religious traditionalists and those rejecting religious traditionalism. While one can argue that affluence has led to more emphasis on noneconomic concerns over economic goals, Layman and Carmines' multivariate analysis found that religious traditionalism generally had a greater effect than postmaterialism on party identification and ideology in most of the presidential elections between 1980 and 1992. Religious traditionalism also was significantly related to major-party voting in 1984, 1988, and 1992, while postmaterialism was not.

Finally, there have been subtle changes in the class basis of voting in the United States. Unskilled workers' support for Democratic candidates declined due to the Democrats' declining support for the welfare state (Brooks and Manza 1977a). Professionals have shifted away from supporting Republican presidential candidates because of their own more liberal attitudes toward social issues, while managers have maintained their Republican voting record (Brooks and Manza 1977b).

While the research reviewed above looks at changes in voting of particular social groups, sociologists Clem Brooks and Jeff Manza (1997c) have traced changes in the overall importance of the social group basis of voting. They find that social group cleavages in the NES data actually increased from 1960 through 1992, but the increase was totally associated with increased race cleavage. Beyond that, the gender cleavage increased, the religious cleavage (when divided as Catholic, Jewish, no religion, and liberal, moderate, and conservative Protestant) diminished, and the class cleavage (based on occupational categories) remained constant.

One common aspect to the research reviewed in this section is that it is national in scope, which means that it implicitly assumes that social-demographic factors have the same influence everywhere. Research by Jackson and Carsey (1999) finds to the contrary. They use 1988 and 1992 exit polls for the eleven largest states, examining major-party votes to compare the relative importance of social-demographic variables. For example, they find evidence of a gender gap in most states, but not in Michigan or Ohio in either year nor in Pennsylvania in 1988. Overall, their pattern of results suggests that the New Deal Democratic coalition still exists in Michigan, Ohio, and Pennsylvania, while there is more evidence of postmaterialist social divisions in California, New York, Massachusetts, and North Carolina. Social group influence need not be uniform.

The evidence reviewed in this section shows that there has been some realignment in the United States since the New Deal Realignment of the 1930s, including ideological realignment and long-term movement by several social groups. In an earlier work, Stanley and Niemi (1995) have written of the demise of the Democratic Party's New Deal coalition. Yet their analysis in Chapter 22 of this book concludes that, at least through 1996, the Republicans had not found a set of group attachments that would give them long-term majority status. If this is realignment, it is realignment that weakened a majority party without resulting in a new, durable majority party coalition.

While these studies give evidence of realignment, particularly of social groups, many observers would not view that as the main party change in American politics in recent decades. There has been change between parties, but there also has been change away from parties. As a result, many analysts would argue that the real change that has occurred is party dealignment rather than realignment.

Shift to Candidate-Centered Politics

Have American politics realigned or dealigned? While there are some signs of realignment, there are even more signs of dealignment. The decline of political parties actually started in the first half of the twentieth century. The cities of the nation were once run by urban party machines, which provided employment and services to many people. With civil service reforms on the one hand and the development of nonpartisan city services on the other hand, these secondary roles of the parties declined. Most urban political machines had lost their legendary powers by 1950.

Political parties also declined in power at the national level as the nature of winning party nominations changed. Party bosses had traditionally controlled nominations, but that began to change in the early 1900s when many states instituted primary elections. Yet even as late as 1968 primaries were of secondary importance in winning the presidential nomination. After President Lyndon Johnson made a late unexpected decision not to seek reelection, Vice President Hubert Humphrey won the Democratic nomination without contesting a single primary. The Democratic Party convention then decided to adopt new rules for the selection of delegates to future national nominating conventions. These reforms had the effect of making presidential primaries the main means of choosing convention delegates. Since 1972 primaries have been of critical importance for both parties, allowing unknown contenders to win nomination without the backing of old-time party bosses. Candidate-centered politics had arrived at the elite level.

Voting specialists point to evidence of a decline in mass-level partisanship at about the same time. In the 1960s and 1970s several political developments led to lower levels of identification with the major parties and greater self-identification as political Independents (see Table 17-1). The civil rights revolution had the side-effect of moving many southern Democrats toward Independent status. The Vietnam War resulted in more young people thinking of themselves as Independents. Reaction against urban unrest, the crime problem, campus unrest, and antiwar protests led to some northern Democrats moving toward independence. As was seen in the previous section, some Democrats became Republicans during this period, but many people who left the Democratic Party instead became Independents.

The increase in the proportion of Independents was only one of several trends that point to dealignment and the growth of candidate-centered politics after the 1950s. Split-ticket voting also increased. Fewer people saw important differences between the parties. Feeling thermometer ratings of both parties declined. Indeed, Wattenberg (1998) shows that more people became neutral toward both major parties, while fewer were positive toward one party and negative toward the other.

As Aldrich and Niemi show in Chapter 23, these were just a few of several trends in public opinion and voting that came together during this period. While details differ somewhat for each indicator, the authors show that the overall trend (using the sum of deviations from mean levels for each indicator) was toward candidate-centered politics. In particular, Figure 23-10 shows that the 1960s were a critical period, with politics shifting from one equilibrium to a different one. Party-centered politics had been transformed into candidate-centered politics.

Voting for third-party and Independent candidates is another ingredient of a political dealignment. As Rosenstone, Behr, and Lazarus (1996, 181) state, "major party failure is the primary force motivating third party voting in America." There were indeed three important minor-party presidential candidates between 1950 and 1998: George Wallace running on the American Independent Party label in 1968, John Anderson running as an Independent in 1980, and H. Ross Perot running on the Reform Party ticket in the 1990s.[4] In each case, Independents and those with weak partisanship were most likely to vote for the non-major-party candidate, as were young people and those who evaluated the major parties and their nominees negatively (Rosenstone, Behr, and Lazarus 1996, Table 9.1). Unfortunately the NES surveys include few specific questions about these candidates, making it difficult to assess the basis of their support as completely as would be desired.

The large vote Perot obtained in 1992—nearly 20 percent of the total—makes it particularly important to understand how the determinants of that vote relate to dealignment themes. Asher (1995) found that few variables significantly affected evaluations of Perot. Age was the most important predictor, with the young supporting him more because they are less partisan. More knowledgeable citizens were less favorable to him, while those more interested in politics were more favorable. Alvarez and Nagler's (1995) analysis of the vote choice between Bush, Clinton, and Perot in 1992 shows that Perot's support was related to the deficit issue. Still, their analysis and that of Asher (1995) find little systematic basis for Perot support, at least to the extent that the NES questions allow for an examination of that support. The lack of systematic basis leads Asher to infer that Perot's appeals to reform government are what led to his support, but Alvarez and Nagler find he did not draw support from the voters most desiring change in Washington. Alvarez and Nagler conclude that Perot took more votes from Bush, but when Lacy and Burden (1999) include nonvoting in the analysis they instead find that Perot hurt Clinton more. There is more agreement that Perot's candidacy was at least partly responsible for the increased turnout in the 1992 election (Nichols and Beck 1995; Lacy and Burden 1999).

The conclusions by Rosenstone, Behr, and Lazarus (1996) about the 1992 Perot success emphasize the importance of candidate-centered politics to his vote totals. Their general model of third-party voting predicted a third-party candidate in 1992, but it predicted only a 6 percent vote for that candidate. They discount conventional explanations of Perot's success and argue instead that the key was his breaking the constraints that usually impede third-party candidates. In particular, his ability to fund his own campaign to the tune of more than $70 million led to television ads, ballot access, media coverage, and participation in the debates, all of which produced a level of credibility that distinguished him from the usual third-party candidate. Perot's unusually high third-party vote serves to emphasize that the United States has moved into an era of candidate-centered politics.

Intriguingly, there is evidence that dealignment was part of a trend that extended beyond the United States. Long-established voting patterns have weakened in many countries, with greater volatility of the vote. As one important example, Särlvik and Crewe (1983) wrote of the 1970s as a "decade of dealignment" in Great Britain. In several nations this dealignment has involved the growth of new parties, including environmental Green parties as well as some right-wing parties. Indeed Dalton, Flanagan, and Beck (1984, 451) argued that "electoral alignments are weakening, and party systems are experiencing increased fragmentation and volatility. . . . Virtually everywhere among the industrial democracies, the old order is crumbling." Dalton (1984) tied this dealignment to cognitive mobilization in advanced industrial societies resulting in more sophisticated individuals who lack partisan ties, people whom Dalton terms "apartisans." A more recent study by Dalton (2001) finds that the percentage of party identifiers decreased in seventeen of nineteen advanced industrial democracies. Dalton and Wattenberg (2001) conclude that there is a trend toward dealignment in party attachments and political behavior in most countries.

This crossnational pattern could be due, in part, to a decline of class divisions in Western societies. With greater affluence among all classes, there has been less need for class-based divisions. Inglehart (1977, 1990) has gone further to argue that there has been a shift from materialist to postmaterialist politics, with the success of environmental parties being one of several indicators of this shift. The evidence on the effect of postmaterialism on American politics is mixed. As mentioned in the previous section, Layman and Carmines (1997) do not find evidence of postmaterialism affecting partisanship or presidential vote, although Jackson and Carsey (1999) interpret the patterns of social group change in voting in some states as evidence of the politics of postmaterialism.

An important side-effect of the dealignment and the shift to candidate-centered politics is the prevalence of divided government in the United States, as discussed in Part IV of this book. The increase in independence has led to an increase in split-ticket voting, which has in turn resulted in divided government. Fiorina (1996, 44–45) refers to party decline as a precondition for divided government, rather than an explanation, but regardless of how it is viewed, dealignment has permitted long periods of divided government.

The inevitable question is whether dealignment will lead to the "end of parties." Burnham (1970) spoke of long-term electoral disaggregation and party decomposition, beginning in the late 1890s and interrupted only temporarily by the increase in party feelings during the New Deal period. Even without looking at the pre-1950 antecedents of party decline, many observers of the popular culture wonder whether the ability of candidates nowadays to communicate directly to voters through the television and the Internet has not made political parties into anachronisms.

One counterargument is that dealignment might be part of a recurring pattern in U.S. politics, as in Paul Beck's (1974) discussion of normal politics-realignment-dealignment cycles. The traditional account (see Chambers and Burnham 1975) is that realignments occurred around the elections of 1828, 1860, 1896, and 1932[5] (which is the counting that explains why Aldrich and Niemi in Chapter 23 describe the changes in the 1970s as marking the sixth American party system), leading to the view that realignments usually occur every twenty-eight to thirty-six years (Sellers 1965). Beck supplied a theoretical basis to this cycling, using generational and political socialization themes. He describes a dynamic in which a "realignment generation" experiences the realigning crisis directly as they reach political maturity and move to support a party. The next generation—the "children of realignment"—hear about the realignment crisis from their parents and accept their parents' partisanship, but they lack the intensity of their parents' identification. The following generation—"the children of normal politics"—picks up little about the long-past realignment crisis, so they are more likely to be political Independents while being "ripe for realignment" if a new crisis occurs. According to this perspective, a realignment should have occurred in the 1960s, but the lack of a crisis sufficient to cause realignment resulted in the children of normal politics remaining independent, thereby creating long-term dealignment.[6] Yet the thrust of Beck's theory is that the dealignment is temporary; realignment will occur again as soon as there is a sufficient crisis that the party system cannot handle.

Both the end-of-parties and the cyclical dealignment arguments are interesting, but one should not go too far with either. While we have seen that there is considerable support for the view that politics has become more candidate-centered, there also is evidence to the contrary. Indeed, some observers would argue that parties became more important in voting in the 1990s than they were thirty years earlier.

Partisanship Is Reinvigorated

How real is party dealignment in this country? At one level, it seems obvious that the system is less partisan than it once was. Yet there is important evidence in the opposite direction. The first arguments claiming that partisanship had been reinvigorated were made at the organizational level. Two studies are of particular importance in this regard. Cotter, Gibson, Bibby, and Huckshorn (1984) documented the growth of campaign-centered operations of the political parties, with large paid staffs, sizable budgets, and substantial financial support for selected candidates. Herrnson (1988, 1994) determined that congressional campaign committees were very active in supporting candidates and providing services for their campaigns. Additionally, the national and state parties are now raising large amounts of "soft money" and channeling that money into the most competitive races, making candidates more dependent on party organizations for funding. Party organizations are stronger than they were thought to be, albeit below the legendary levels ascribed to the urban machines of earlier generations.

In examining the possible increase in partisanship, it is also important to emphasize the increased polarization of politics in Congress and in national political discourse. While there is always partisanship in Congress, there was also considerable bipartisanship in the 1950s through 1970s. Party relations in Congress began to fray in the 1980s as a result of partisan battles, especially the confirmation fights in the Senate over President Bush's nominations of former senator John Tower to be his secretary of defense and of Clarence Thomas to be an associate justice of the Supreme Court. Partisanship in Congress became even more extreme during the Clinton administration, culminating in President Clinton's impeachment by the House of Representatives and the Senate vote on his removal. The voting cohesion of the parties in Congress has increased, while there are more votes in which the majorities of the two parties vote in opposite directions. As the level of partisanship increased in Congress, it would not be surprising if there was a similar increase among the public.

While it is conventional to point to the increase in political independence as a sign of partisan deterioration, not all evidence is in that direction. As explained in Chapter 17, Keith et al. (1992) argue that independence did not really increase as much as usually is claimed. The claim that independence has increased is based on answers to the first party-identification question—"Generally speaking, do you usually think of yourself as a Republican, a Democrat, an Independent, or what?" The proportion of people saying they are Independents according to that item is quite large, sometimes even larger than the proportion claiming to consider themselves part of the larger major party. Yet most of those Independents are more than willing to say which party they are closer to on the second question—"Do you think of yourself as closer to the Republican or Democratic Party?" Keith and colleagues show that Independent leaners (those who answer "Independent" on the first question but admit to being closer to a party on the follow-up probe) behave like weak partisans on many dependent variables. As a result, their book is entitled *The Myth of the Independent Voter*, emphasizing the extent to which they feel that the growth of Independents has been overstated.

The growth in independence, even on the first party-identification question, seems to have come to a halt long ago. There was an increase in independence in the late 1960s and early 1970s, but there is not much sign of continued growth. Indeed, Weisberg (1998b) called attention to decline in 1996 in the proportion of Independents according to both NES and CBS News/*New York Times* poll data. The level of independence may still be greater than in the 1950s, but it has at least stabilized and may be diminishing.

Bartels's (2000) argument is that partisanship has also been reinvigorated at the level of the mass public. The proportion of party identifiers among voters in the NES 1996 sample is back to the level of the 1950s, although there has been a decline in partisan loyalties among nonvoters. His analysis also shows that party identification is once again a strong predictor of the presidential vote. Partisan voting is weaker in congressional elections than it was in the 1950s, but Bartels shows that it too has increased since 1978. According to this perspective, David Broder's (1971) proclamation in his book title *The Party's Over* may have been premature; Larry Sabato (1988) may have been closer to the mark with his book title, *The Party's Just Begun*.

This partisan resurgence view is stated in a different way by James Campbell (1997, 221–230), who argues that the increase in partisanship is due to realignment. He calls this a "staggered realignment," with dealignment during 1968–1980 as a preliminary phase followed by realignment since 1984. The proportion of strong identifiers fell 9 percent in the dealignment period (as compared to 1952–1964), with little change in the Democrat-Republican balance, but went back up 5 percent in the realignment phase (1984–1996) with a 6.5 percent shift in the Republican direction.

The evidence of party realignment along ideological lines discussed earlier in this chapter, especially Abramowitz and Saunders (1998), can also be taken as a reinforcement of the role of party in voting. When there was a greater discrepancy between party and ideology, there was more reason for strong liberals and conservatives to vote against their party. Similarly, the sorting out of the parties on such social issues as race, abortion, and gun control leads to greater consistency between party and issues, especially for single-issue voters. With the party alignment now more ideological in character (Knight and Erikson 1997), fewer citizens encounter a discrepancy between their ideology and their party when they vote. Voting can be more partisan because it is more ideological and issue-based.

Aldrich and Niemi (in Craig 1995) ended with speculation as to whether the Republicans winning control of Congress in 1994 signaled party realignment and the start of a seventh party system. Aldrich (1999) has since contended that 1992–1994–1996 may be the beginnings of another critical era. He highlights three types of changes that occurred in those years: changes in Congress (including Republican control of southern delegations), changes in public attitudes (including an increase in strong partisans and a decrease in Independents among whites), and changes in voting (a fall in split-ticket voting and a decline in the value of incumbency). The Aldrich and Niemi chapter shows changes through 1992, but the changes since then may signal that the shift to candidate-centered politics is over. Partisan polarization may have led to a resurgence of partisanship. Aldrich states this very strongly: "The conclusion seems inescapable. The 1990s to this point have seen a reversal of the patterns of voting that typified the candidate-centered era, especially in congressional voting" (26).

The difficulty with this conclusion is that it is too early a judgment. Changes invariably occur from election to election. Party system change is something that can be seen best from historical perspective. Thus the pattern that Aldrich and Niemi present in Figure 23-10 shows important change because the 1970s and 1980s were so different from the 1950s. Had the apparent trend line been reversed in the 1970s and 1980s, they would not have made the claim that the country had moved to a sixth party system. Extending that logic, whether the country has moved to a seventh party system depends on whether the changes that Aldrich finds in the 1990s remain into the early 2000s. If they are reversed, then the judgment would be that the era of candidate-centered politics had been volatile in the 1990s, not that we had entered a new party system. Similarly Bartels's evidence of partisan resurgence must also await the test of time.

Conclusion

The question of party realignment versus dealignment has been with us for several decades now. On the one hand, there always seem to be scholars anxious to proclaim that the long-awaited realignment has finally arrived. On the other hand, there always seem to be researchers who think the greater change is the increased volatility of the electorate due to dealignment. What is new in the debate this time is the argument that partisanship may be reinvigorated.

If there is any agreement about change in the U.S. party system, it is that there has been meaningful change. The politics of the first decade of the 2000s are not those of the 1930s. We are past the New Deal realignment, but it is harder to say where we are now. The party system is more aligned with ideology than a few decades ago, and some social groups have shifted with that change. The era of Democratic dominance may be over, but it has not been replaced by an era of Republican dominance. Politics is less party-centered and more candidate-centered, while there is also evidence of a resurgence of party as a factor in voting.

This debate turns out to be one of the most difficult to resolve, at least in the short run, because it depends on long-term developments. A single presidential election cannot suffice to show a trend. Even the results of two or three elections might just be due to short-term candidate or issue factors rather than more permanent shifts in the party system. It is difficult for political scientists to wait upon the verdict of history, but this is one controversy on which history gets the final word.

Notes

1. There remains controversy over the mechanisms underlying even the realignments that are most agreed upon; see Niemi and Weisberg (1993a, chap. 28). Also, Ladd (1991) argues that the realignment concept itself is of limited value and that the discipline's concentration on realignments is an instance of overgeneralizing from one or two unique historical events.
2. The treatment of realignments as abrupt suggests the applicability of catastrophe theory to studying realignments, as reviewed in Weisberg (1998a).
3. The gender gap is not often thought of in realignment terms, but it would be realignment if the Democrats could count on the support of a majority of women and adopted issue positions that appeal disproportionately to women.
4. Support for third parties may also reflect realignment. George Wallace's 1968 candidacy was part of the realignment of southern white conservatives out of the Democratic Party and into the Republican Party, but the disarray of the Reform Party in the 2000 presidential election suggests that Perot's 1992 and 1996 candidacy will not become part of a true realignment.
5. As we have seen in the above discussion of realignment, neither Nardulli nor Bartels would fully agree with that listing of realigning elections.
6. However, we have already seen that there are claims of realignment at that point, including the Bartels (1998) statistical analysis, which detects one in 1972; the Carmines and Stimson (1989) discussion of issue evolution in the 1960s around the race issue; and the discussion of change among southern whites by Miller (Chapter 18) and by Stanley and Niemi (Chapter 22).

Further Readings

Partisan and Ideological Realignment

Abramowitz, Alan I., and Kyle L. Saunders, "Ideological Realignment in the U.S. Electorate," *Journal of Politics* 60 (1998): 634–652. An ideological realignment occurred after 1980.

Bartels, Larry, "Electoral Continuity and Change, 1868–1996," *Electoral Studies* 17 (1998): 301–326. Historical analysis of realignments using state data since 1868.

Levine, Jeffrey, Edward Carmines, and Robert Huckfeldt, "The Rise of Ideology in the Post-New Deal Party System," *American Politics Quarterly* 25 (1997): 19–34. Ideology has become more important in determining partisanship since 1972.

Nardulli, Peter, "The Concept of a Critical Realignment, Electoral Behavior, and Political Change," *American Political Science Review* 89 (1995): 10–22. Historical analysis of realignments using county and city data from 1828 through 1984.

Social Groups Change

Layman, Geoffrey, "Religion and Political Behavior in the United States," *Public Opinion Quarterly* 61 (1997): 288–316. Changing voting of evangelical Protestants.

Miller, Warren, and J. Merrill Shanks, *The New American Voter* (Cambridge: Harvard University Press, 1996). Examination of religion and other sociodemographic variables to see which remain significant in affecting the vote with multivariate controls.

Norrander, Barbara, "Is the Gender Gap Growing?" In *Reelection 1996*, ed. Herbert Weisberg and Janet Box-Steffensmeier (New York: Chatham House, 1999). The gender gap in voting is due to changes by men rather than women.

Partisan Dealignment

Wattenberg, Martin, *The Rise of Candidate-Centered Politics: Presidential Elections of the 1980s* (Cambridge: Harvard University Press, 1991). Analysis of presidential elections of the 1980s, emphasizing the consequences of weak parties.

Wattenberg, Martin, *The Decline of American Political Parties: 1952–1996* (Cambridge: Harvard University Press, 1998). The public has become neutral toward the parties.

Partisan Resurgence

Bartels, Larry, "Partisanship and Voting Behavior, 1952–1996," *American Journal of Political Science* 44 (2000): 35–50. The impact of partisanship on the vote has been invigorated.

22. Party Coalitions in Transition:
Partisanship and Group Support, 1952–1996

Harold W. Stanley and Richard G. Niemi

Group support for the political parties is of perennial concern to politicians and political scientists alike. Indeed, we often define parties and their ideological positions in terms of the groups of individuals that are said to support the party or to benefit from its positions on major issues. Thus, for example, we say in shorthand form that the Democrats are the party of the poor or that the Republicans are better for business interests, that the Democrats (for nearly a century after the Civil War) were strongest in the South, and that Cuban Americans are highly supportive of the Republicans.

In recent years, there has been a weakening of long-time patterns of party support to the point that one can speak of a breakdown of the old system. The so-called New Deal coalition, which took shape in the 1930s, involved broad support of the Democrats by native white southerners, labor union and working-class households, African Americans, Jews, and, to a lesser extent, Catholics. During the 1950s, breaks in this coalition began to appear, as native southern whites supported Republican candidates for the presidency; yet the coalition remained largely intact, as even these southern whites continued to think of themselves as Democratic partisans. Further weakening occurred in the ensuing years, so much so that we wrote after the 1992 election that "it is time to declare the New Deal [Democratic] coalition dead" (Stanley and Niemi 1995, 237).

The obituary for the New Deal coalition can be found in the 1994 and 1996 elections, in which the Republicans captured majority control of the House and Senate for the first time since 1952. Yet no sooner is one coalition gone than we want to know the shape of that to follow. Is there a pattern of group support in 1994 and 1996 that outlines what is to come?

More specifically, do changing patterns of party support suggest the beginning of a new, long-lasting form of coalitional behavior that will support continued Republican domination, or do they at least indicate competitive elections in which the majority in a series of elections shifts back and forth between the parties? Was President Bill Clinton able to win reelection by reinvigorating a coalitional base that had existed in 1992?

Source: Harold W. Stanley and Richard G. Niemi, "Party Coalitions in Transition: Partisanship and Group Support, 1952–1996," in *Reelection 1996: How Americans Voted,* ed. Herbert F. Weisberg and Janet M. Box-Steffensmeier, pp. 162–180. Copyright © 1999 by Chatham House Publishers.

We approach these questions by examining expressed loyalty to the political parties — that is, self-reported partisanship — over time, which essentially updates our earlier analyses of group support. We are concerned with continuity from past to present, but we are especially interested in the potential for a new system of group support that may signal the start of yet another fundamental change in voters' relations with the parties — the rise of another new party system. Thus, while presenting group partisanship figures for all presidential elections since the 1950s, we concentrate our analysis on the changing patterns found in the late 1980s and in the first half of the 1990s.

Analyzing Group Support

Group support can mean a number of different, though related, things. In the past, we have looked primarily at what is called party identification — that is, which party people say they "generally support" (Stanley and Niemi 1995). Political scientists and pollsters use self-reports of this sort in an effort to assess "enduring" or long-term support for the parties, in contrast to the more short-term support gathered by specific candidates.[1] It is now well known that self-reports of party support are not entirely free of which way the political winds are blowing in response to particular campaigns, partisan scandals, and so on (see, for example, MacKuen, Erikson, and Stimson 1989; Weisberg and Smith 1991). Nevertheless, party identification, or partisanship, is less transient than individuals' voting behavior. This is especially true when one thinks of presidential voting; the presidential election is so visible that all but the most isolated individuals (who are not likely to vote in any event) have heard or read about and probably exchanged thoughts about both candidates. Hence, presidential preferences fluctuate to a degree that partisanship does not. Therefore, it is useful to consider party support in this "generic" sense.

There remains the question of how, statistically, we should assess the support of each group for a party or candidate. We could simply show the partisanship of each group — that is, how many native southern whites, urban residents, blacks, white Protestant fundamentalists, and so on, say they generally support Democrats versus Republicans. For some purposes, this approach is exactly what one wants. A problem is that such simple accounts are misleading because the groups are overlapping. For example, blacks tend to reside in urban areas. Thus, if one finds that blacks and urban residents tend to support Democrats, one is talking largely about the same people. Do both characteristics tend to make people Democratic? Trying to answer such questions raises several problems, but one is certainly aided by the use of multivariate statistical procedures (that is, procedures that incorporate multiple variables "all at once" rather than one at a time). In this chapter we use multivariate logit analysis.[2] While this technique is complicated, a careful reading of our tables and the explanations we provide for them should make the results understandable.

The Models

We begin by describing the multivariate models that form the basis of our analysis. In this presentation, we draw on National Election Studies (NES) data from presidential elections since 1952. We define three models of party support that collectively cover the 1952–1996 period.[3] For comparisons over the entire period, it is important to consider all three models, and we have previously done so (Stanley and Niemi 1991). For the present analysis, we emphasize the latest model, which can be estimated virtually without change since 1980. That model incorporates the New Deal elements, gender, church attendance, income, white Protestant fundamentalists, Hispanic origin, 1943–1958 birth cohort (baby boomers), and 1959–1978 birth cohort (so-called Generation X).[4] The primary dependent variables to be explained are Democratic identification and Republican identification.[5]

For several reasons, we use separate models for Democratic and Republican identification. First, to the extent that the New Deal coalition has broken up— a thesis we developed four years ago (Stanley and Niemi 1995)—we want to be certain of that judgment, and a model of Democratic identification is most appropriate for that test. More significantly, we want to see the extent to which formerly Democratic groups have moved over to supporting the Republican Party (as opposed to becoming Independent), so a model for each party is necessary. Finally, for newer groups, we want to see whether hypothesized connections to the Republicans have taken hold. As noted earlier, our focus here is on the continuing nature of the changes as reflected in the late 1980s and in the 1990s.

Results

The groups of interest are of two kinds. First are the core groups of the so-called New Deal coalition—blacks, Jews, Catholics, members of union households, and native white southerners. These are groups that gave strong support to the Democratic Party and Democratic candidates in the 1930s and for decades thereafter. Second are "newer" groups that have become more visible in the past decade or so and, in addition to the traditional groups, are the sets of individuals for whose support the parties are vying. The newer groups include women, Hispanics, churchgoers in general and Christian fundamentalists in particular, and groups defined by age or "generation."

We look at support for each party separately; while support that does not go to one party most often goes to the other, voters are more independent than they were before the 1960s, so one sometimes finds that neither party receives a boost from a particular group. The top half of Table 22-1 presents the mean predicted probability (based on the results from the logit analysis) that a group member claims Democratic identification in each presidential election year since 1952 and the two most recent congressional elections. Essentially, these numbers are the proportions of Democrats in each group before imposing any controls for

Table 22-1 Mean and Incremental Probabilities of Democratic Identification for Members of Each Group

	1952	1956	1960	1964	1968	1972	1976	1980	1984	1988	1990	1992	1994	1996
Mean probabilities[a]														
Black	.53	.51	.45	.74	.85	.67	.74	.74	.62	.65	.64	.64	.62	.65
Catholic	.56	.52	.64	.59	.53	.50	.50	.43	.43	.37	.45	.41	.38	.43
Jewish	.73	.62	.52	.57	.50	.52	.58	.81	.60	.36	.62	.63	.48	.63
Female	.48	.42	.49	.53	.48	.43	.42	.44	.40	.40	.43	.39	.35	.44
Native southern white	.77	.71	.72	.72	.53	.52	.52	.49	.41	.40	.38	.33	.31	.36
Union household member	.54	.51	.57	.64	.50	.46	.47	.47	.47	.42	.51	.47	.41	.43
Regular churchgoer	.50	.46	.49	.53	.47	.44	.43	.40	.37	.39	.43	.36	.35	.36
Income: top third	.43	.40	.43	.42	.39	.34	.32	.35	.32	.28	.35	.29	.19	.30
White Protestant fundamentalist	—	—	—	—	—	.46	.43	.56	.41	.37	.34	.31	.23	.34
Hispanic, non–Cuban	—	—	—	—	—	—	—	.55	.48	.52	.51	.44	.43	.52
Born 1959–1970	—	—	—	—	—	—	—	.33	.31	.27	.30	.29	.31	.36
Born 1943–1958	—	—	—	—	—	—	—	.39	.34	.34	.43	.37	.26	.38
Incremental probabilities[b]														
Black	.17	.20	.11	.31	.50	.37	.45	.47	.34	.40	.31	.38	.37	.32
Catholic	.21	.20	.31	.18	.18	.20	.22	.14	.13	.09	.12	.15	.14	.11
Jewish	.39	.32	.18	.20	.19	.27	.36	.55	.34	.17	.33	.39	.27	.31
Female	.01	−.05	.05	.01	.04	.05	.03	.08	.05	.08	.03	.05	.04	.08
Native southern white	.45	.42	.41	.33	.20	.18	.22	.13	.07	.11	.04	.06	.05	.01
Union household member	.14	.12	.15	.18	.07	.09	.11	.11	.13	.11	.15	.15	.09	.07
Regular churchgoer	.00	−.02	−.03	−.02	−.01	.03	.03	−.04	−.04	−.02	.01	−.03	.04	−.07
Income: top third	.07	−.04	−.07	−.15	−.07	−.07	−.11	−.07	−.07	−.07	−.09	−.10	−.17	−.08

White Protestant											
fundamentalist	—	—	—	.08	.05	.25	.10	.07	.01	.04	−.04	.03
Hispanic, non−Cuban	—	—	—	—	—	.18	.07	.16	.13	.08	.06	.11
Born 1959−1970	—	—	—	—	—	−.16	−.16	−.19	−.19	−.15	−.11	−.07
Born 1943−1958	—	—	—	—	—	−.09	−.11	−.09	−.05	−.05	−.09	−.02

Notes: The three models containing the different variables were evaluated through 1996. However, presentation is greatly simplified by showing only the following: 1952–1968 values are based on the model with eight variables; 1972–1976 values are based on the model with nine variables; 1980–1996 entries are based on the model with twelve variables. Values that can be estimated with more than one model seldom differ by more than .01 from one model to another.

[a] Cells are the mean of the predicted probabilities of Democratic identification for all group members in each year.

[b] Cells are the average of the difference, for each group member, between the individual's predicted probability of Democratic identification (based on all of the other characteristics in the multivariate model) and what the individual's probability would have been without the effect of the group membership.

Sources: 1952–1996 National Election Studies.

other group memberships. Note that Democratic partisanship declined for every group in 1994 except for those born between 1959 and 1970. The changes are often small; but recall that partisanship is generally quite stable in the face of temporary partisan tides. Thus, the force of the Republican tide in 1994 is demonstrated by the fact that virtually all groups were affected. In the case of many of the New Deal groups, this represented the continuation of a change that had been taking place for many years. Note, for example, the continued slide of native white southerners, Catholics, and members of union households. The same was true of support from Christian fundamentalists. In other instances, however, the decline in 1994 represented a reversal of recent patterns of support; note, especially, Hispanics, where support dropped in both 1992 and 1994, and baby boomers (born between 1943 and 1958), where support dropped precipitously in 1994.

That the uniform and sometimes sudden move toward the Republicans in 1994 was temporary is demonstrated by the equally uniform shift in group support back to the Democrats in 1996. Though the Democrats failed to win control of Congress, they won back virtually all their losses in partisanship in 1994. This helped make it possible for President Clinton to win reelection despite the midterm losses to his party. Perhaps even more important from a long-run perspective, the notion of a new partisan era launched by Newt Gingrich and the Contract with America in 1994 appears to be undermined by the fact that professed support for the Democrats returned to its pre-Contract level among all groups. If there is to be a new (continuous) Republican majority it is not clear in these figures where it will find its base.[6]

Although the number of Democratic supporters declined in each group in 1994, the incremental impact of membership in a particular group, shown in the bottom half of Table 22-1, gives us a different view of group effects. These numbers show how much more likely an individual is to be a Democratic identifier because of membership in a specific group; that is, the numbers consider all the other group ties of each individual and how likely those ties are to make the person Democratic. Their movements sometimes diverge considerably from the overall support levels in the top half of the table. Notably, they show that *incremental* support for the Democratic Party barely slipped at all for a number of groups in 1994, thus reinforcing the interpretation of that year as a temporary departure from longer-term movements. The long-term trends are still evident. The one that stands out especially vividly involves native white southerners; in the 1950s such individuals were at least 40 percent more likely to support the Democratic Party, taking into account their other characteristics. That figure declined steadily until finally, as of 1996, it stood virtually at ground zero, and native white southerners were no more likely to be Democrats than anyone else with the same characteristics.

Among the newer groups, one of the most significant results is that the gender gap appears to be alive and well as of the mid-1990s.[7] Even though other characteristics pushed them in a Republican direction, so that overall fewer

Table 22-2 Mean and Incremental Probabilities of Republican Identification for Members of Each Group

	1952	1956	1960	1964	1968	1972	1976	1980	1984	1988	1990	1992	1994	1996
Mean probabilities[a]														
Black	.13	.19	.17	.07	.02	.08	.05	.04	.04	.06	.05	.04	.03	.03
Catholic	.18	.21	.15	.17	.15	.14	.16	.19	.20	.27	.23	.19	.25	.24
Jewish	.00	.11	.08	.06	.05	.09	.08	.00	.10	.12	.10	.05	.13	.03
Female	.29	.32	.31	.25	.23	.24	.27	.23	.27	.28	.23	.24	.30	.23
Native southern white	.09	.12	.11	.09	.09	.15	.16	.18	.22	.21	.20	.26	.40	.29
Union household member	.22	.21	.17	.14	.20	.16	.14	.13	.20	.21	.20	.15	.24	.17
Regular churchgoer	.28	.29	.30	.26	.24	.26	.28	.28	.32	.32	.28	.31	.36	.36
Income, top third	.31	.34	.31	.32	.28	.30	.30	.30	.35	.35	.33	.34	.43	.35
White Protestant fundamentalist	—	—	—	—	—	.21	.21	.16	.22	.26	.28	.32	.42	.34
Hispanic, non-Cuban	—	—	—	—	—	—	—	.13	.09	.05	.12	.15	.19	.11
Born 1959–1970	—	—	—	—	—	—	—	.14	.25	.28	.27	.23	.31	.26
Born 1943–1958	—	—	—	—	—	—	—	.21	.28	.27	.24	.27	.36	.29
Incremental probabilities[b]														
Black	-.27	-.21	-.27	-.28	-.35	-.25	-.27	-.26	-.35	-.34	-.29	-.30	-.37	-.30
Catholic	-.24	-.20	-.29	-.22	-.23	-.19	-.18	-.12	-.16	-.08	-.11	-.17	-.17	-.09
Jewish	-.41	-.30	-.32	-.33	-.33	-.29	-.28	-.33	-.33	-.31	-.26	-.34	-.28	-.27
Female	.03	.07	.02	.00	-.02	.01	.05	-.02	.00	-.00	-.04	-.10	-.05	-.03
Native southern white	-.35	-.32	-.35	-.31	-.30	-.17	-.16	-.09	-.08	-.14	-.14	-.10	.02	-.03
Union household member	-.09	-.12	-.17	-.16	-.08	-.12	-.14	-.14	-.11	-.13	-.11	-.15	-.08	-.14
Regular churchgoer	.05	.05	.06	.05	.04	.05	.06	.08	.08	.06	.06	.09	.05	.15

table continues

Table 22-2 *continued*

	1952	1956	1960	1964	1968	1972	1976	1980	1984	1988	1990	1992	1994	1996
Income: top third	.05	.06	.02	.10	.03	.08	.08	.09	.09	.06	.09	.11	.14	.07
White Protestant fundamentalist	—	—	—	—	—	-.06	-.06	-.12	-.14	-.06	-.01	-.02	.00	-.01
Hispanic, non-Cuban	—	—	—	—	—	—	—	-.05	-.12	-.21	-.11	-.06	-.11	-.15
Born 1959–1970	—	—	—	—	—	—	—	-.06	.02	.02	.04	.00	.06	.01
Born 1943–1958	—	—	—	—	—	—	—	-.01	.03	-.02	-.02	.00	.04	.00

[a]Cells are the mean of the predicted probabilities of Republican identification for all group members in each year.

[b]Cells are the average of the difference, for each group member, between the individual's predicted probability of Republican identification (based on all of the other characteristics in the multivariate model) and what the individual's probability would have been without the effect of the group membership.

Sources: 1952–1996 National Election Studies.

women in 1994 said they supported the Democrats, the marginal impact of being female remained in the Democratic direction in 1994 and then tied for its highest value ever in 1996, helping Clinton win reelection and stemming the tide that occurred in 1994. Among another new group, regular churchgoers, the incremental impact of group membership was actually more pro-Democratic in 1994 than it had been two years earlier.

What does all this mean for the Republican Party? With respect to the older groups, the Republicans can be heartened by the fact that they were able to attract higher proportions of all the groups except blacks in 1994 (see Table 22-2). But they were able to retain that level of support only among frequent churchgoers. Moreover, the incremental probabilities (see Table 22-2, bottom half) suggest that things were far from rosy even in 1994, and they left a very mixed picture in 1996. Republicans were able to retain control of Congress, but support in terms of underlying partisanship enabled a popular president to win reelection quite handily and congressional Democrats to hold their own.

Groups that were moving away from the Democrats were not wildly embracing the Republicans. Jews, who leaned less toward the Democrats in 1994 than in 1992, leaned even farther away from the Republicans in the same year (see Table 22-2, bottom half).[8] Native southern whites are increasingly Republican supporters (Table 22-2, top half), and someday there may be a "multiplicative" effect that propels additional white southerners toward the Republican Party because many around them are Republican.[9] At present, however, the tendency among native southern whites toward the Republican Party is due largely to their other attributes; when these are taken into account, the latest reading shows them with no incremental likelihood of being Republican (Table 22-2, lower half). Over the years, Catholics and members of union households have become less pro-Democratic, but the marginal push from these characteristics is still away from the Republicans; among Catholics, the (negative) incremental probability was as large in 1994 as it had been at any time in the past twenty years; among union households, it was as large as most other years since 1952. What sympathy the Democrats have lost among a number of their former supporting groups has gone toward identification as an Independent, not to the Republicans.

The news is marginally better for the Republicans when we consider the newer groups, where there is a vague outline of a coalition that could provide the Republicans with the hope of continued majorities in Congress. After receiving the support of between 24 and 30 percent of regular churchgoers for several decades, that proportion jumped to an estimated 36 percent in both 1994 and 1996 (Table 22-2, top half). The overlapping group of white Protestant fundamentalists also increased their support of the Republicans, as did baby boomers, Generation X, and those in the top third of the income distribution.

The Republican hold on these groups is somewhat tenuous, however, because they have not developed specific group appeals that bind any of these groups to the Republican Party. Regular churchgoers perhaps provide the most likely target. Republicans have consistently had an advantage among this group, and that advantage was greater in 1992 and 1996 than in most of the preceding years. Those in the top third of the income distribution provide another likely target, as they have also been marginally more supportive of Republicans since at least 1972, with this support, too, reaching new heights in two of the last three election years. Yet just how tough the task is for Republicans comes from observing their incremental appeal to white Protestant fundamentalists. In the 1970s and well into the 1980s, the tendency of this group was away from the Republicans and toward the Democrats. Probably as a result of strong support for moral and so-called family values by Presidents Reagan and Bush, this tendency has been neutralized. But note that it has been *neutralized,* not reversed.

The prospects of a generational appeal—either to boomers or to the subsequent generation—do not find much support here either. As we noted in an earlier analysis, the incremental push of being young (or now, middle-aged, as the boomers move through the life cycle) is better described as an anti-Democratic force than as a pro-Republican force. Both of the age groups in Tables 22-1 and 22-2 have consistently high increments in favor of independence (not shown), a reflection of the dealigning forces that have characterized American politics since the mid-1960s.

Finally, Republicans appear not to be making any headway in appealing to the growing bloc of Hispanics. Of all the changes in party support between 1994 and 1996, this is perhaps the least surprising and the most obviously connected to recent party ideology and behavior. Throughout 1995 and 1996, including just months before the election, Republicans in Congress supported anti-immigrant legislation while Democrats opposed it. In the House, for example, a majority of Democrats voted against (76–117) while Republicans were nearly unanimous in voting for (229–5)[10] a bill that would have denied illegal immigrants certain welfare benefits and would have made it harder for the government to prove job discrimination against Hispanics. In the Senate, Democrats were almost unanimous in support (41–5) and Republicans were almost unanimous in opposition (5–47) to a bill that would allow certain legal immigrants to continue to receive welfare benefits.[11] If this pattern of voting continues (as it did during 1997), it should not be surprising if Hispanics turn even more sharply away from the Republicans and toward the Democrats.

Changes in group support, if viewed over the entire period for which we have data—now stretching to more than four decades—have been dramatic enough for us four years ago to write of the demise of the New Deal coalition. But if one's interest is in the past few years, looking to interpret the 1996 Clinton reelection as well as to see whether 1994 was the start of a new period of Republican parity or dominance, the changes are far less certain. The Republicans were clearly able to draw temporary support virtually across the board in 1994. Republicans might have been especially encouraged by the fact that this support was apparent in self-identified partisan leanings, as shown here, not in the vote alone. But the 1994 and 1996 figures show how fragile that support was.

The Republicans have still not been able to find a set of group attachments that seem capable of propelling them into long-term majority status. The future, viewed in terms of group support, appears to have potential for fluidity and possibly even major realignments (inasmuch as group ties are generally weaker than decades ago), but it is not yet clear that group attachments will swing heavily in one direction or the other, except possibly in one election at a time. And if the Republicans do maintain their majority in Congress, it is not yet clear that one or two groups alone will provide the foundation of the support coalition.

Group Support and the Party Coalitions

Now our attention turns to the party coalitions. In the first two sections of Tables 22-3 and 22-4 we show the mean predicted probability of Democratic or Republican identification in the United States and, below that, the percentage of each coalition with a given group characteristic. This breakdown of the coalitions is in terms of overlapping groups. The percentages describing the party coalitions thus add to more than 100, as, for example, a black female churchgoer is counted in each of three categories.

Several changes are notable, and their impact on the party system is now becoming more apparent. Perhaps the most striking change is the declining proportion of women in the Republican coalition.[12] In the 1980s, "gender gap" was used to describe the greater support of women, compared with men, for the Democrats. That meant, coincidentally, that a greater proportion of the Democratic coalition was female—from 3 to 6 percentage points more than in the Republican coalition (Tables 22-3 and 22-4).[13] Beginning in 1988 the gap widened, first because of a jump in the proportion of women among Democrats and then because of a substantial drop in the proportion of women among Republicans. In 1992, for the first time since at least 1952, men outnumbered women in one of the party coalitions. Despite a temporary reversal in 1994, the dominance of men in the Republican Party increased to a still higher level in the 1996 presidential election. At the same time, women have become three-fifths or even more of the Democratic coalition. In short, at the time of the second Clinton election, the two parties differed to a greater extent than ever in their relative proportions of female supporters.

Another change began quietly and, for a time, appeared to affect the two parties in the same way. Beginning with a rise in the mid-1980s among Democrats, and then with more steady increases in both parties in the early 1990s, the proportion of Hispanics began to take on some significance. While always a higher proportion of Democratic supporters, the percentages were small and therefore the partisan difference was not great. By 1996, however, it appeared that Hispanics would remain a very small proportion of the Republican coalition while becoming a more substantial force among Democrats. While still "only" about 12 percent of the Democratic coalition, Hispanics had become as large a percentage of party supporters as blacks were prior to 1964. The contrast with

Table 22-3 Size and Composition of the Democratic Coalition

	1952	1956	1960	1964	1968	1972	1976	1980	1984	1988	1990	1992	1994	1996
Democratic identification in the United States[a]— predicted probability	48	44	47	52	45	41	40	42	38	36	41	36	33	39
Percentage of Democratic coalition with a given group characteristic[b]														
Black	10	10	8	14	18	16	18	20	18	25	23	25	23	21
Catholic	27	25	30	26	26	31	33	27	32	27	32	30	32	28
Jewish	5	5	4	3	3	3	4	6	4	2	3	4	3	3
Female	55	53	59	57	59	60	61	62	60	65	58	58	60	64
Native southern white	26	27	28	21	20	21	21	22	20	23	18	17	19	17
Union household member	32	32	33	30	28	30	28	29	27	24	23	23	23	20
Regular churchgoer	42	45	51	45	41	42	44	38	38	42	44	42	47	36
Income: top third	37	28	39	29	27	27	29	25	27	26	30	29	17	26
White Protestant fundamentalist	—	—	—	—	—	17	15	20	16	20	16	15	14	14
Hispanic, non–Cuban	—	—	—	—	—	—	—	4	7	8	7	9	11	12
Born 1959–1970	—	—	—	—	—	—	—	5	13	16	22	24	27	25
Born 1943–1958	—	—	—	—	—	—	—	34	34	35	34	34	25	31
Percentage of Democratic identifiers in group continuing to claim Democratic identification after removing Democratic tendency of defining group characteristic[c]														
Black	68	61	76	59	41	45	39	36	45	38	51	41	41	51
Catholic	62	61	52	69	66	61	57	67	68	75	72	64	63	75
Jewish	46	48	65	65	62	47	38	32	43	54	47	37	44	50
Female	102	111	91	98	92	89	94	81	87	79	94	86	89	83
Native southern white	42	41	43	54	62	64	57	74	82	72	88	83	84	98
Union household member	75	77	74	72	85	81	76	76	72	74	71	69	77	85
Regular churchgoer	100	104	106	103	101	93	93	110	111	96	97	109	89	120
Income: top third	17	110	116	136	117	122	134	119	121	123	125	136	188	127

White Protestant fundamentalist	—	—	—	—	—	82	88	55	75	80	97	87	119	91
Hispanic, non-Cuban	—	—	—	—	—	—	—	68	86	70	74	81	87	79
Born 1959–1970	—	—	—	—	—	—	—	148	150	170	163	150	134	120
Born 1943–1958	—	—	—	—	—	—	—	122	132	127	112	114	136	106

Relative size (in percentages) of Democratic coalition after removing group characteristic

Black	97	96	98	94	89	91	89	87	90	85	89	85	86	90
Catholic	90	90	86	92	91	88	86	91	90	93	91	89	88	93
Jewish	97	98	99	99	98	98	98	96	98	99	98	98	98	98
Female	101	106	94	99	95	93	96	89	92	86	97	92	94	89
Native southern white	85	84	84	90	93	92	91	94	96	94	98	97	97	100
Union household member	92	93	91	92	96	94	93	93	92	94	93	93	95	97
Regular churchgoer	100	102	103	101	101	97	97	104	104	98	98	104	95	107
Income: top third	106	103	106	110	105	106	110	105	106	106	107	110	115	107
White Protestant fundamentalist	—	—	—	—	—	97	98	91	96	96	100	98	103	99
Hispanic, non-Cuban	—	—	—	—	—	—	—	99	99	98	98	98	98	98
Born 1959–1970	—	—	—	—	—	—	—	102	106	111	114	112	109	105
Born 1943–1958	—	—	—	—	—	—	—	108	111	109	104	105	109	102

[a]These estimates, derived from the model, are virtually identical to the actual percentage of Democratic identifiers.

[b]Figures derived from taking the mean predicted probability of Democratic identification for a group in a particular year (Table 22–1) multiplied by that group's number of respondents, and dividing this product by the number of Democratic identifiers.

[c]Figures derived by recalculating the probabilities of Democratic identification without the effect of, say, white Protestant fundamentalist identification, then taking the mean of these probabilities for all respondents who were white Protestant fundamentalists. The ratio of this revised mean probability to the mean probability that includes the effect of white Protestant fundamentalism gives the ratio of the hypothetical size to the actual one.

Source: 1952–1996 National Election Studies.

Table 22-4 Size and Composition of the Republican Coalition

	1952	1956	1960	1964	1968	1972	1976	1980	1984	1988	1990	1992	1994	1996
Republican identification in the United States[a]—predicted probability	27	29	29	25	24	24	24	23	28	29	25	26	32	27
Percentage of Republican coalition with a given group characteristic[b]														
Black	5	6	4	3	1	3	2	2	1	3	3	2	1	1
Catholic	15	15	10	16	14	15	18	21	21	24	26	20	22	22
Jewish	0	1	1	1	1	1	1	0	1	1	1	0	1	0
Female	57	61	56	56	54	57	65	57	56	58	51	49	53	46
Native southern white	5	7	7	5	6	10	10	15	15	15	15	19	25	19
Union household member	22	20	15	14	20	17	14	15	16	14	14	10	14	10
Regular churchgoer	40	43	47	47	39	42	47	49	45	43	47	51	50	49
Income: top third	47	36	42	47	37	40	46	40	40	39	44	48	39	42
White Protestant fundamentalist	—	—	—	—	—	13	12	11	12	17	21	21	27	19
Hispanic, non–Cuban	—	—	—	—	—	—	—	2	2	1	3	4	5	3
Born 1959–1970	—	—	—	—	—	—	—	3	14	20	31	27	28	24
Born 1943–1958	—	—	—	—	—	—	—	33	38	34	30	35	35	33

[a]These estimates, derived from the model, are virtually identical to the actual percentage of Republican identifiers.

[b]Figures derived from taking the mean predicted probability of Republican identification for a group in a particular year (Table 22-2) multiplied by that group's number of respondents, and dividing this product by the number of Republican identifiers.

Source: 1952–1996 National Election Studies.

African Americans is telling in another way as well. From 1984 through 1992, the proportion of blacks among Democratic supporters was from two-and-a-half to more than three times that of Hispanics. In 1994 and 1996, that proportion fell substantially. Even if it fluctuates over the next several election cycles, it appears that Hispanics are becoming a more dominant force within the party at the expense of African Americans. Also on the Democratic side, the proportion of identifiers in union households continued a downward slide from about a third of the coalition in 1960 to a fifth in 1996.[14]

On the Republican side, native southern whites have become a substantial part of the Republican coalition by virtue of their increasing tilt toward that party. As late as 1990, this group was a larger fraction of the Democratic than of the Republican coalition. In the past three elections, however, this has been reversed, in a very small way at first but by a large margin in 1994. Figures for 1996 suggest that this reversal may be here to stay. Along with the large fraction of fundamentalists in the party, we may be seeing the outlines of a new and more durable Republican coalition, heavily weighted in the South and with a minority but substantial contingent of fundamentalist white Protestants.

What would happen to the coalitions if they were to lose the partisan tendency due to each group characteristic? Here we show results only for the Democratic coalition (Table 22-3, second panel).[15] These results show just how resilient the Democratic coalition is. In the early 1990s, it appeared that increasing numbers of black, Jewish, and union supporters would desert the Democrats if the party did not appeal specifically to their groups. But by 1996, support from most groups turned upward again. Republicans have not been able to make a sustained appeal to these groups; were Democrats to reduce their group-specific appeals, most would still continue to support the party.

This point is made more dramatically in the final panel in Table 22-3. It shows the effect on the size of the Democratic coalition of removing each group characteristic. Right up through 1996, the party benefits from a combination of overlapping characteristics. Only blacks (and women in 1996) dip as low as 90 percent, suggesting that the party would remain close to its current size even if it lost its specific appeal to any one group. This may be partly a result of President Clinton's studied effort to appeal to a broad range of groups and to avoid being "captured" by any one. Ironically, a broad-based appeal may have made the Democrats simultaneously more appealing to members of each specific group.

Conclusion

From the perspective of President Clinton's reelection, 1996 can be viewed is a year in which partisan support rebounded from what proved to be a temporary movement toward the Republicans in 1994. (That rebound may ultimately prove temporary as well.) The rebound did not occur in all groups, but it was apparent in both what we have called old and new groups. Especially noteworthy is the fact that among two groups, one large (women) and one small but growing (Hispanics), support for Democrats actually surpassed its 1992 level.

With a longer time frame in mind, the early 1990s can also be viewed as a continuation of processes that have been under way for several decades. The movement away from the Democratic Party by native southern whites, for example, began in the 1960s, and members of union households began to move in the 1970s. The Hispanic population, and hence its contribution to the party coalitions, has been on the rise for at least fifteen years. Yet several watershed changes have occurred very recently. First, native southern whites, perhaps for the first time ever, had an incremental push (very slightly) favorable to the Republicans, and in the past two elections they were estimated to be a greater fraction of Republican than of Democratic identifiers. Second, members of union households sank to just one-fifth of all Democratic supporters in 1996. Third, Hispanics, while not increasing their marginal support for the Democrats, are now a much more substantial fraction of the coalition, while African Americans have stabilized in size or are possibly declining as a fraction of all Democrats.

A significant threshold was also passed when, in 1986 and in all but one subsequent year, white Protestant fundamentalists became a larger fraction of Republican than of Democratic identifiers. Despite overt Republican appeals since the early 1980s, the incremental push from being a fundamentalist was toward the Democrats until it evened out, or reversed, in the 1990s. Now Republicans are basically even in their appeal, and more of their identifiers claim to be a part of this group.

What of the future? Three developments highlighted by our analysis are especially worthy of note. The most visible is the changing gender composition of the parties. The gender gap has now existed for a decade and has reached the point where 60 percent or more of Democrats are women while a majority of Republicans are men. Yet, despite its size and salience, we think that this division is unlikely to continue for long, and it will certainly not be the basis on which either party attempts to build its coalition. Neither party can afford to ignore half the population; each, therefore, will attempt to build its support among both men and women. Republicans currently seem to be doing little to develop their appeal to women, and the gap among party identifiers may continue to grow for a few more elections. Yet it will not be the basis of a partisan realignment.

The second major development concerns the partisan support shown by Hispanics. If the anti-immigrant stance of the Republican Party continues unabated, we are likely to see a clear shift in favor of Democratic support in the electorate. Thus far, Republicans seem to have calculated that they can gain overall support by their position; that may be, but among Hispanics themselves, a continuation of recent party actions will clearly push them in a Democratic direction.

The third major development is related to the second, and it largely affects the Democratic Party. We were inclined a few years ago to ask whether the Democrats would become the party of minorities, as blacks continued their high level of support and Hispanics began to be a more meaningful presence. In part, that has happened; these two groups now constitute about a third of the coalition, rising quickly from about 20 percent in the early 1980s. At least as important, however, is that the Democratic Party is rapidly changing into a party with two sizable minority groups. As Hispanics increase in number, it may be increasingly difficult to satisfy both groups. It is difficult even to guess how the party system will change if future developments cause a major rift within the Democratic Party. Yet, however it turns out, this recent change in the pattern of group support may be the most significant new development to occur in the wake of the demise of the New Deal coalition.

Notes

1. Party identification, or partisanship, has been measured regularly since 1952 by both commercial pollsters and academic researchers. There is a long history of research on the meaning and measure of partisanship, both in the United States and abroad. See, for example, Niemi and Weisberg (1993a). For the distribution of partisanship over time, see Table 17-1 in this volume.
2. Logistic regression is an appropriate method to use when the dependent variable is dichotomous. As we explain later, we have two dependent variables: whether a respondent is Democratic or not, and whether a respondent is Republican or not. In this circumstance, logit analysis is more appropriate than so-called ordinary least squares regression.
3. We might ideally have a single equation, one that assesses the contribution of every relevant group over the entire period under study. In fact, we need several models. This is primarily because the groups considered relevant change over time. Hispanics, for example, were simply not a large enough group to be considered politically significant before the 1980s. Religious fundamentalists were a large enough group, but they were not considered a coherent political force until the mid-1970s. As a result, survey questions needed to identify the appropriate groups have not been asked over the entire period. There was no reason to think about measuring religious fundamentalism in the 1950s and 1960s. In addition, how to measure this concept has been debated widely (see, for example, Rothenberg and Newport 1984). And, obviously, certain groups defined by birth dates—such as those born after 1958—could not be relevant until recently.
4. The results reported here differ slightly from those in our earlier articles. In earlier analyses we included working class among the groups. That variable was not included in the 1996 NES data set; we opted to exclude it from all earlier years rather than begin yet another new model. Examination of the models for all prior years with and without the class variable reveals very small differences for the coefficients of all other variables.
5. For our analysis, we used respondents' answers to the first NES partisanship question—on the direction of their partisanship—ignoring the follow-up response about intensity. (Regarding the handling of the "leaners," see Niemi and Weisberg 1993b, 278–279.)
6. That Republicans were able to maintain their majority in Congress despite the temporary nature of the shift in partisanship can be explained on the basis of the advantage of incumbency in congressional voting and to other, more temporary factors. See Patterson and Monson (1999).
7. See Norrander (1999) for a full discussion of the gender gap.

8. One should not overinterpret fluctuations for relatively small groups, such as the Jewish population. Figures may change sharply simply because they are based on a small number of cases.

9. This kind of effect, in which people are influenced in their partisanship or voting behavior by what kinds of people are around them, was identified as long ago as 1954 in Berelson, Lazarsfeld, and McPhee's (1954) study of the largely Republican community of Elmira, New York. Taking a term from horse racing, they referred to this as the "breakage effect."

10. Vote on HR-2202 September 1996 (*Congressional Quarterly Almanac*, 1997, H–142).

11. Vote on S-1956, 23 July 1996 (*Congressional Quarterly Almanac*, 1997, S–39). In addition, Republican governor Pete Wilson continued to take a strong anti-immigrant stance in California.

12. Another striking change in the party coalitions, the greater proportion of the young, is politically significant but demographically inevitable as the older generations are replaced by the younger.

13. Historically, a greater proportion of men than women have been Independents (Miller, Miller, and Schneider 1980, 88), so females constituted a majority of both parties.

14. This is a function, in part, of declining membership in unions.

15. Comparable results for Republicans would be convenient, but those results have a distorting mirror-image aspect. Given the general Democratic tendencies of the group ties, removing the group ties means that the groups' share of Republican identifiers, perhaps tiny to begin with, often swells to greater than 100 percent of its former size.

23. The Sixth American Party System: Electoral Change, 1952–1992

John H. Aldrich and Richard G. Niemi

Over the more than 200 years of U.S. history, there have been dramatic changes in the patterns of electoral politics. During most of the nineteenth century, for example, voters went to the polls in much higher proportions than at any time during the twentieth century; attachments to political parties were much stronger than they are today; and voters rarely split their tickets, partly because of their strong party feelings but also because—prior to 1890—the parties themselves controlled voting procedures and made it difficult if not impossible to cast votes for candidates from more than one party.

In order to make sense of the changes that have occurred, historians and political scientists often speak of "party systems," referring to periods of a generation or more in which electoral politics differ distinctly from the periods before and after. A standard interpretation (e.g., Chambers and Burnham 1975) is that there have been five American party systems, the first beginning around 1796 with the emergence of two-party competition between the Federalists and Jeffersonian Republicans, and the last starting in the early 1930s with the rise to majority status of New Deal Democrats.[1] We demonstrate in this chapter that, in fact, a new party system—the sixth party system—emerged in the 1960s and has now existed for a quarter-century. We justify our conclusions by documenting a wide variety of changes that took place as the fifth party system ended and the sixth one began.

The "critical era" between the fifth and sixth systems is unique in that it is the first transition period for which we have public opinion survey data to help us understand how attitudes and behaviors were altered.[2] For earlier cases, including the 1930s, we must rely on so-called aggregate data such as how various states, cities, or wards voted, or on the recollections of people interviewed long after the fact. Both of these techniques are useful and have given us some insight into the kinds of transformations that occurred during the New Deal realignment of the 1930s (Andersen 1979; Gamm 1989). They obviously cannot, however, provide information about the full range of changes that are presumed to have characterized the era.

Source: From *Broken Contract,* by Stephen Craig. Copyright © 1995 by Westview Press, a member of the Perseus Books Group. Reprinted by permission of Westview Press, a member of Perseus Books, L.L.C.

For the analysis that follows, we begin by reviewing a number of election-related attitudinal and behavioral changes that took place during the 1960s.[3] These are called *micropatterns* because we are looking at one "indicator" (or measure) at a time. We then collect all of these individual changes into a *macropattern*—capturing in one figure a summary of the changes discussed earlier. The latter allows us to make generalizations about changes during transitions between party systems, that is, to draw conclusions that might apply to earlier as well as to future transitions. Finally, because we are talking about changes in *party* systems, we discuss the role of political parties in the candidate-centered era that emerged from the turmoil of the 1960s critical period.

From the Fifth to the Sixth Party Systems: Micropatterns

What distinguishes a critical era between party systems is a set of rapid changes in a broad range of crucial political variables, where these changes, once made, endure. That is, we begin with a system, here a party system, at equilibrium. The critical era is a period—a relatively short period—of disequilibrium. After this short period, the system settles into a new equilibrium state for some period of time, historically for between thirty and forty years. We take these two characteristics—the equilibrium-disequilibrium-new equilibrium cycle and the short but intense duration of the disequilibrium relative to both preceding and proceeding equilibrium periods—as the central defining characteristics of party systems and the critical eras between them.

Changes during the 1960s can be seen in a broad range of party- and election-related variables; collectively, the patterns outlined in this chapter confirm that massive alterations did indeed characterize the American political universe throughout the decade. Many of our measures are drawn from the National Election Studies (NES) surveys and therefore are available only since 1952. This gives us three presidential elections (1952–1960) held prior to the critical era, plus five (1976–1992) that lie beyond the critical period. The 1964 and 1968 elections are the ones most clearly within the critical period. The most central of these critical years is 1968, with 1964 sometimes setting patterns in motion and sometimes marking the end of the old. In most observations, the 1972 election falls into the new equilibrium period and is treated as such in our later summarization.

Party Identification

Partisanship of Blacks. There were two remarkable changes in partisanship among African Americans during the 1960s. From 1952 to 1962 the proportion of blacks considered as "apolitical" was quite high (a steady 15–18 percent).[4] In 1964, this percentage dropped to approximately the same low level as among whites and has hovered in that range ever since (Figure 23-1). This is a good example of a shift in equilibrium levels occurring all at once. It can be attributed

Figure 23-1 Partisanship Among Blacks, 1952–1992

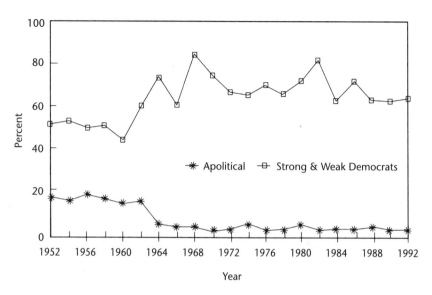

Source: American National Election Studies.

to the same events that made civil rights prominent on the list of what citizens regarded as the nation's most important problems (see further on).

A second change is the dramatic increase in the proportion of blacks who, beginning in 1964, identified with the Democratic Party. The pattern here is a bit more complicated, with percentages rising and falling at least partly in response to specific political events. The surge in 1968, for example, is due to a decline in the proportion of Independents—probably reflecting former Alabama governor George Wallace's use of that term in his bid for the presidency under the American Independent Party label. At any rate, Figure 23-1 reveals considerable volatility throughout the realigning period and a reasonably steady state thereafter.

Partisanship of Whites. White partisanship also changed markedly in the mid-1960s (Figure 23-2). The proportion of "pure" Independents (i.e., those claiming not to lean toward either party) was at 9 percent or less through 1964; this was followed, however, by a substantial increase between 1964 and 1972 into what could be seen—despite the dip in 1982—as an essentially steady state since then. The proportion of *all* Independents (including "leaners") also jumped in 1966, then showed a more gradual increase through 1972, a smaller and less consistent increase through 1978, and finally a sharp decline and subsequent rebound in recent years. All Independents constituted about the same

Figure 23-2 Partisanship Among Whites, 1952–1992

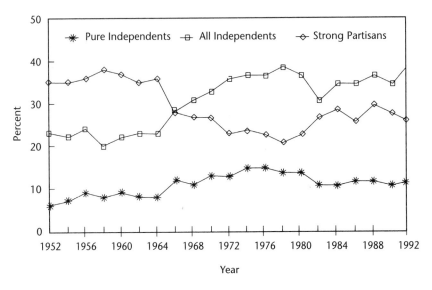

Source: American National Election Studies.

share of the electorate in the late 1980s and early 1990s as in the early- to mid-1970s; in every measurement, they registered well above levels observed in the 1950s. Thus, once again, a major increase over the 1964–1972 period appears to have given way to a more or less steady (and higher) rate of independence as time passed.

We should take special note of the 1966 election because it represents both the first and largest rise in independence during the critical era and the point at which total Independents initially outnumbered strong partisans—a "crossing" that endured through 1992. As shown in Figure 23-2, the proportion of strong partisans (Republicans and Democrats combined) varied little from 1952 through 1964. It declined sharply, though, in 1966—the largest change in any two-year period under examination—and then continued to sag through 1978, before climbing back to about where it was in 1966 (still well below the 1950s level).[5]

Party Support Coalitions. The biggest shift in this area is the declining support of southern whites for the Democratic Party, beginning in earnest around 1962 or 1964. A useful long-term perspective can be obtained by calculating "incremental probabilities" that show, on average, how much more likely it is that a person will be a Democrat (rather than a Republican) because he or she happens to be a native southern white; they can be thought of as comparing

Figure 23-3 Party Images, 1952–1992

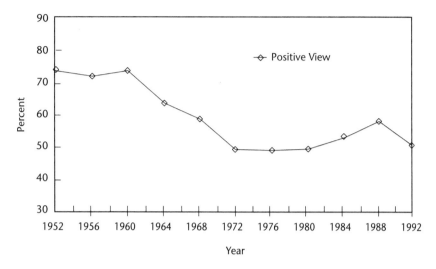

Source: Wattenberg (1987 and personal communication).

Note: Shown is the percentage who view at least one party positively.

persons with an identical set of other characteristics — e.g., religion, union membership, or social class — and then determining the relative likelihood that the native southern white will be Democratic. These probabilities hovered close to 0.42 from 1952 through 1960, then dropped precipitously to about 0.20 in 1968. Thereafter, they never reached more than half their early value before declining to an all-time low of 0.05 in 1990 and 1992 (Stanley and Niemi 1995).

Another important change has to do with the percentage of the Democratic coalition claiming to be working class. Through 1960, the working class made up between 65 and 70 percent of all Democratic identifiers; following declines that occurred throughout the 1960s, this proportion has hovered around 55 percent through 1992 (see Stanley and Niemi 1995).

Party Images. Coincidental with the weakening of partisanship was a sharp change in affect toward the political parties (Figure 23-3). In response to open-ended questions concerning what they liked and disliked about the Democratic and Republican parties, nearly three-quarters of NES respondents through 1960 viewed at least one party favorably.[6] That percentage dropped 10 points by 1964 and another 15 points by 1972. It remained at roughly the same level for several elections before rising somewhat in the 1980s and then dropping back again in 1992.

Figure 23-4 Most Important Problem, 1952–1992

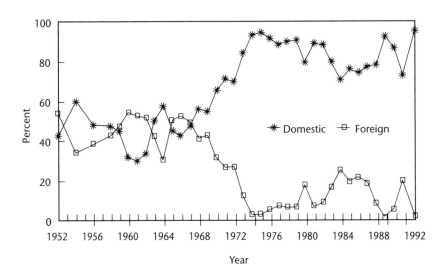

Source: Stanley and Niemi (1994, 164).

Note: Shown is the percentage citing foreign versus domestic, polls averaged November–October, Gallup data.

Issues

Most Important Problems. One indicator of the issues that parties and politicians face is provided by individuals' assessments of the most important problem facing the nation. The specific problems cited are highly variable, but most can be categorized as referring to either domestic or foreign policy. Figure 23-4 provides the distribution of domestic versus foreign problems between 1952 and 1992. It shows a major change beginning just before 1968 and continuing through 1974, with short spikes thereafter. The pattern is one of a reasonable balance between domestic and foreign concerns from 1952 to 1967, but a predominantly domestic agenda after 1974. If one "subtracts out" Vietnam—an issue described as "intermestic" by some observers (e.g., Hess and Nelson 1985) because it combined domestic impact with foreign policy—the change took place at the height of the critical period, about 1965 or 1966.

The Basis of Issue Conflict. Carmines and Stimson (1989) have developed impressive evidence of changes in the direction of racial attitudes during the 1960s (Figure 23-5). With respect to the electorate, they showed, first, that the clarity of party stands on racial issues—as measured by the degree to which cit-

Figure 23-5 Clarity of Party Racial Issue Stands and Public Affect
Toward Parties, 1956–1980

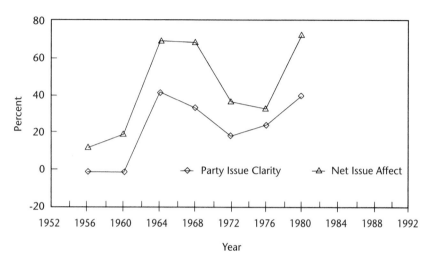

Source: Carmines and Stimson (1980, 165).

izens perceived the Democrats as more liberal than the GOP with regard to
desegregation—increased dramatically between 1960 and 1964. Despite some
fluctuations, clarity remained well above 1950s levels thereafter;[7] the Carmines-
Stimson series ended in 1980 at almost the exact point reached in 1964. They
also showed something called "net public affect"—in other words, the extent to
which racial liberals and conservatives had different overall evaluations of the
parties. Here, too, there was a sharp increase between 1960 and 1964: In the
1950s, racial liberals and conservatives liked the two parties about equally well;
beginning in the early 1960s, however, affect toward the parties quickly became
related to issue positions (conservatives being more favorable toward the Republicans, liberals toward the Democrats). Fluctuations after that remained at a level
clearly above that of the earlier decade.

Issue-Party and Candidate Linkages. There has been considerable change
over time in the extent to which issues are linked to parties versus candidates.
In response to "likes" and "dislikes" questions about parties and candidates,
some respondents link issues to both of these actors and some link issues to
only one. Figure 23-6 reports the percentages of those mentioning domestic
policies *only* in evaluating the political parties or *only* in evaluating the candidates (the remainder mentioned both). What is remarkable is the high incidence of linking issues to parties but not candidates before 1964—and the

Figure 23-6 Party-Candidate Linkages on Domestic Issues, 1952–1992

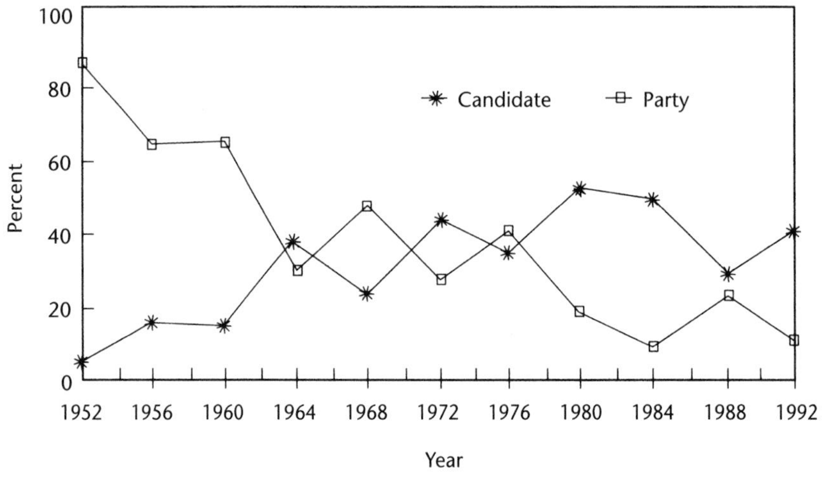

Source: Wattenberg (1980, 84–85, and personal communication).

abrupt change in 1964 to an even mixture of the two. After 1964 there were fluctuations, but always with a more even balance between issue-party and issue-candidate connections. Parties were the linkage between issues and voter choices before 1964; over the next thirty years, presidential elections became much more candidate centered.

Geer (1992, 52, and personal communication) reported an analogous measure of issue- and party-candidate linkages but focused just on New Deal issues (e.g., employment, social welfare programs, agricultural and labor policy, housing, education, and the like). Use of New Deal themes in evaluating the *parties* declined sharply from 1952 to 1956, remained about the same through 1968, then dropped again in 1972 and remained steady through 1992. Use of New Deal policies in evaluating presidential *candidates* climbed steadily from 1952 to 1972, except for a sharp drop in 1968; if we set aside a large increase that took place in 1984, use of such policies remained at about the same level through 1992. The pattern is not exactly as one might expect. Yet it is notable that New Deal issues were used primarily when referring to parties prior to 1972—and about equally for parties and candidates since then.

Interest and Involvement

When thinking about critical electoral eras, we need to consider political interest and participation. Indeed, V. O. Key (1955) claimed that increased interest and involvement are hallmarks of critical elections but that signs of heightened popular engagement should decline to more normal levels once the critical period has passed. Only two of the three measures examined in this section follow Key's prediction; the one that does not nevertheless reflects an important feature of mass politics in the sixth party system.

Interest in the Presidential Campaign. The public's level of interest jumped sharply in the no-incumbent presidential race of 1960 from what it had been during the two Eisenhower elections. It stayed high in 1964 despite the presence of an incumbent and a one-sided contest, then rose again in 1968. After that, there was a decline to 1950s levels — except for 1976, when higher interest may have been an aftereffect of the Watergate scandal. Notwithstanding the influence of incumbency and of election-specific events, a pattern of greater interest at the height of the critical era emerges.

Protest Behavior. Questions about signing petitions, participating in marches and demonstrations, and so on, were not asked in national surveys until the 1970s. Yet surely in the 1960s the level of "unconventional" behavior was greater than at any time since perhaps the 1930s and at any time since. Large-scale participation in the civil rights movement began with the Freedom Riders in 1961, escalated with the March on Washington in 1963, and continued with numerous smaller demonstrations and marches that took place throughout the remainder of the decade. Protests over the Vietnam War were greatest in connection with the presidential election of 1968, though they began a year or two earlier and did not stop until the United States withdrew the last of its troops in January 1973. Active, visible participation was therefore at its height during the entire critical era.

Voting Turnout. Voting is yet another form of participation, and if it were taken as simply a measure of involvement, we would expect an increase during the critical period and then decline once the period ended. But there are many factors that affect turnout (e.g., strength of partisanship in the electorate, feelings of political efficacy or inefficacy,[8] legal requirements for voting, etc.)—plus one, the structure of political parties, that is central to our account of the critical period and its aftermath (see further on). As a result, the pattern here is expected to be more consistent with the other micropatterns analyzed than was true for either general interest or protest.

Figure 23-7 shows that turnout rates in presidential elections were at a postwar high in 1960, at which point a long-term slide began. The biggest part of the decline was completed by 1972, though there was a further notable decline in 1988 followed by a rebound in 1992 (see Horn and Conway 1996). Turnout in off-year congressional elections increased moderately during the early 1960s before dropping to a new level after 1970. Hence, most of the decline in both presidential and congressional voting had occurred by 1974.

Figure 23-7 Turnout in Presidential and Congressional Elections, 1952–1992

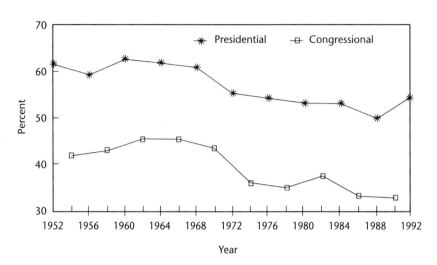

Source: Ornstein, Mann, and Malbin (1992, 48), updated by authors.

Voting and Election Outcomes

Split-Ticket Voting. Split-ticket voting increased greatly over the period observed. A steady state existed from 1952–1960 in state and local races, with ticket-splitting at 26–31 percent (Figure 23-8). This figure jumped to over 60 percent by 1974 and, though it fell after that, it remained far above 1950s levels. Two other measures of split-ticket voting also were very nearly constant from 1952 to 1960 with (1) about 15 percent supporting different parties for president and the House and (2) roughly 10 percent doing the same in House and Senate races. In 1964, Senate-House ticket-splitting nearly doubled to 18 percent; it again increased sharply in 1978, then fell back to about the level of 1974. The president-House measure did not change much until after 1964, a big jump occurred between 1968 and 1972, and in later years it stayed fairly steady at about 25 percent.

Party-Line Voting. Besides looking at split-ticket voting, one can assess the relevance of partisanship by examining directly its relationship to the vote (i.e., the extent to which citizens support the candidate of their preferred party in an election). For presidential voting, this relationship declined sharply during the 1960s and then rose back to its original level after 1972. In 1956 and 1960, the simple two-party correlation between partisanship and presidential vote choice was strong (Pearson's $r = 0.68$ and 0.70, respectively). In 1964 and again in 1968

Figure 23-8 Split-Ticket Voting, 1952–1992

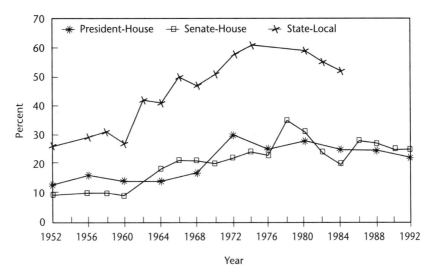

Source: Stanley and Niemi (1994, 446).

it weakened noticeably (0.62 and 0.50), and remained at the same low level (0.51) in 1972 (Nie, Verba, and Petrocik 1979, 165). It quickly bounced back, however, climbing to 0.63, 0.66, 0.70, 0.71, and 0.74 between 1976 and 1992. Although not truly representing a *new* steady-state value, the pattern here is consistent with an out-of-equilibrium relationship in the critical period leading to a lower-than-usual relationship between partisanship and the vote; this was followed by a redefined basis of partisanship and, hence, a reequilibration between party identification and the vote during the new steady-state period.

For House and Senate voting, the patterns are somewhat volatile, but there was clearly a rise in party defections during the 1960s (Stanley and Niemi 1994, 142). On the House side, there was another smaller and temporary increase in 1978. It is helpful to our argument that in both houses, the defection rate in 1992 was almost exactly that of 1968.

Presidential Coattails. Another sign of the disjuncture between presidential and House voting has to do with the erosion of presidential coattails, i.e., the ability of a popular candidate for president to attract votes for other candidates running on the party's ticket. Looking just at House races, the coattails of both Republican and Democratic standard-bearers weakened initially and then became stronger over the period from 1956 to 1964. Between 1968 and 1980 they fluctuated somewhat—but, except for the Reagan landslide in 1980, at a clearly reduced level compared with earlier years (Calvert and Ferejohn 1983,

416). This particular analysis has not been extended beyond 1980, though most election experts concluded that presidential coattails also were relatively "short" in 1984, 1988, and 1992.

A related measure is the percentage of split-district outcomes, referring to the number of congressional districts that vote one way for president and the other way in House or Senate contests. These figures lend less support to our argument than others, with a fairly steady increase in split-district outcomes being evident from 1952 to 1972 (Stanley and Niemi 1994, 147). Still, over the entire span from 1964 to 1992, only twice has the proportion dipped as low as 30 percent — its highest point in the earlier period.

House Incumbent Security. The collective safety of House incumbents can be measured by the proportion with "landslide" victories (where landslide victories are defined as those in which the winner receives at least 60 percent of the two-party vote). The number of such races was fairly substantial by 1964, but it nonetheless increased further in the years that followed (Figure 23-9). The first big jump came between 1964 and 1972 as the proportion of safe seats went from about 60 percent to 80 percent. This percentage fluctuated from 1972 through 1984, then rose to new heights in 1986–1988 before dropping back again. On the Senate side, there seems to be little pattern that might be traceable to the critical era.

One can also examine the extent to which high return rates for incumbents are due to personal factors (reflecting positive voter evaluations of the representative himself or herself) versus party or presidential fortunes (over which the individual representative usually has little or no control). Alford and Brady (1989a) developed measures of "retirement slump" and "sophomore surge,"[9] and using these components, they apportioned the safety of incumbents seeking reelection to party and personal bases. Historically, party has been a positive factor for incumbents because most of them come from districts in which a majority of voters identify with their party. Alford and Brady show that from 1848 to 1986, party ebbed and flowed with no obvious change in terms of its overall importance over time. In contrast, the personal status of the incumbent was a negligible factor through 1958 — but it became a positive value in 1960, increased steadily through 1970, and then fluctuated; after 1970, party and incumbency were close to equal in their respective values.[10] It is unfortunate that for our purposes, the Alford-Brady measures are not defined for two out of five election years in any decade, making them unsuitable for our later analysis.

Confidence in Government

. . . [T]he origins of today's climate of popular discontent can be traced back to the 1960s. Specifically, a collection of items thought to measure trust or confidence in government revealed a dramatic loss of trust after 1964 (see Craig 1996); in light of the Watergate scandal, it is not surprising that these measures

Figure 23-9 Percentage of Incumbents Gaining Sixty Percent of the Vote or More, 1960–1992

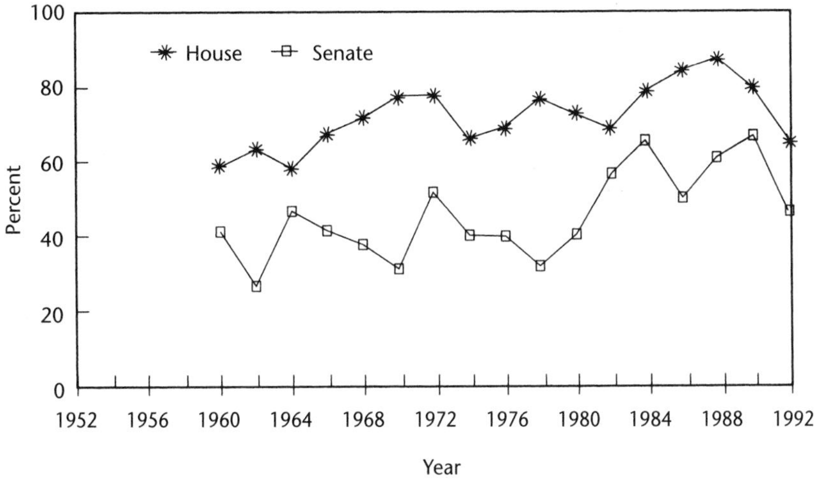

Source: Stanley and Niemi (1994, 128–129).

continued to slide throughout the next decade as well. Although confidence was partially restored during the early 1980s, this short-term gain was reversed between 1984 and 1992. At no time did any of the indicators return to anything close to 1950s levels.

From the Fifth to the Sixth Party Systems: The Macropattern

Central to our argument is that the patterns discussed thus far in a variable-by-variable fashion are consistent across a wide variety of measures. In particular, we contend that (1) there was an equilibrium in the fifth party system, (2) this equilibrium was disrupted during the 1960s, and (3) a new equilibrium had emerged by 1972. The final stage of our analysis provides an overview of this process, combining most of the indicators used in the previous section into a single model.

Our data are presidential-year values for twenty-seven of the measures previously shown; each of the twenty-seven has values for all or most of the election years from 1952 to 1992.[11] These variables are measured on very different scales and with widely varying ranges, so in order to combine them for an assessment of the overall pattern, we first standardized them such that each had a mean of 0 and a variance of 1 across the eleven elections.[12] We next set the "polarity" (i.e., multiplied the standardized measure by −1 where appropriate) so that low (negative) standardized values were expected before 1964 and high

Figure 23-10 Macropattern, 1952–1992

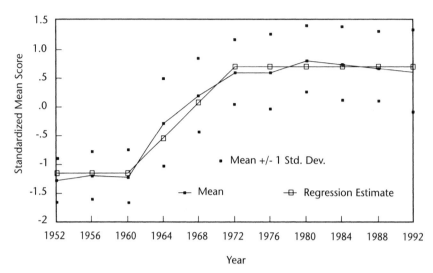

Source: Calculated by the authors.

Note: Shown are mean and +/-1 standard deviation of 27 standardized variables.

(positive) values were expected from 1972 to 1992. Finally, the standardized measures were combined into a single variable with 268 observations (297 minus missing data).

Figure 23-10 charts the mean score of this combined, standardized set of measures for each election year. It is quite evident that the annual means are low and comparable in the pre-1960s elections and that they increased dramatically and almost linearly in 1964, 1968, and 1972. After 1972, there were only small changes in the election-year averages. The pattern of means in the sixth party system (1972–1992) is, like that in the fifth (1952–1960), nearly flat. The difference between the average on our measure before 1964 (−1.24 in standardized units) and at the new equilibrium, beginning in 1972 (0.66), is quite large and obviously statistically significant.

Another way to look at the standardized measure is shown in Table 23-1, where we report for each presidential election year the number of instances in which the measure is positive and negative. Prior to 1964, all 73 observations are negative; there is, in other words, not a single instance for the entire period in which the value for any of the variables is at or above the mean. Beginning in 1972, 88 percent of the cases are positive (only 17 of 141 falling below the mean level). For the two realigning elections, however, we find exactly the same number of cases above and below average: 26 percent (7 of 27) above average in 1964, 74 percent (20 of 27) in 1968.[13]

Table 23-1 Number of Times the Standardized Summary Variable Is Above or Below the Mean, by Year

	1952	1956	1960	1964	1968	1972	1976	1980	1984	1988	1992
At or above mean	0	0	0	7	20	24	22	25	19	17	17
Below average	21	25	27	20	7	3	4	2	2	3	3

Note: This table is based on the 27 measures used to construct Figure 23-10. See text for further discussion.

Source: American National Election Studies, 1952–1992.

In sum, the data support our contention that there was major and systematic change in a wide range of variables over the period in question. Moreover, this change is almost exactly the kind we would expect if the equilibrium account is correct: Substantial stability is followed, during the realignment, by massive change—which is in turn followed by substantial stability in the postcritical era.

Institutionalization of the Candidate-Centered Party System

Our empirical analysis provides strong evidence of the cycle of equilibrium-disequilibrium-new equilibrium that is at the heart of changes in party systems. The many series of micropatterns, along with the macropattern displayed in Figure 23-10, vividly demonstrate the rapid, fundamental change in the political order that took place in the 1960s. Just as striking is the portrayal of a new equilibrium in the 1970s and 1980s. Instead of continuing instability, which some believe to be characteristic of this period, we see a degree of stability quite similar to the supposedly quiescent 1950s. It is our view that the current equilibrium era represents a distinct sixth party system—one that we call the "candidate-centered party system." This section proceeds with three claims, two made rather briefly. We begin by pointing to the rise of candidate-centered elections in the 1960s, note several aspects of a policy basis to that critical era, and then argue in more detail about the institutionalization of the new party system in the 1970s and 1980s.

Many analysts agree that elections have been more candidate than party centered since the 1960s. Shively (1992), for example, studied presidential elections since the 1840s and found that until 1960, change in the vote from one election to another was primarily due to differential *mobilization.* This is precisely what one would expect in party-centered elections, whereby the attractiveness of one candidate over the other is revealed by the favored party's greater success in turning out its loyalists. Beginning in 1960, though, Shively found that *conversion* had become the principal force in generating interelection vote shifts. Such a pattern is consistent with candidate-centered elections in which the stronger candidate woos supporters to his or her side from the opposition. Similarly, Alford and Brady (1989a), using the series cited previously, argued that the strength of incumbency in congressional elections changed in 1960 from exclusively party factors to an equal impact of party and individual factors. These two accounts mesh smoothly with Wattenberg's (1987, 1990; see Figures 23-3 and 23-6) findings that in the 1960s and thereafter, fewer citizens expressed *any* likes *or* dislikes of the parties on standard NES open-ended questions; this was interpreted by Wattenberg as an indication of the increasing irrelevance of parties to voters' assessments of candidates, issues, or contemporary politics in general.

Studies such as these conclusively document the candidate-centered nature of elections today, a pattern that first became evident in the critical era of the 1960s. It also appears that a "policy realignment" occurred at about the same time. On the domestic side, Carmines and Stimson (1989), Edsall (1991), and others have described dramatic changes in the parties' stands on civil rights, racial, and other domestic issues during the 1960s; they also have noted the extent to which this new alignment was perceived clearly by the electorate. In foreign affairs, the 1960s witnessed a breakup of the bipartisan consensus over the Cold War and relations with the Soviet Union (see Destler, Gelb, and Lake 1984)—a breakup due to the Vietnam War, which led to a new partisan cleavage over foreign and defense policies at both the elite level and that of the mass public.

But although mass (and elite) opinions and behavior fit closely with the equilibrium-disequilibrium-new equilibrium cycle, and significant policy realignment can also be found in the 1960s, we differ from those who saw largely instability and dealignment (e.g., Jensen 1981; Silbey 1991) in our belief that what has happened since the critical era involves a new *form* of political parties: the "candidate-centered" parties. Moreover, this new form has become sufficiently institutionalized since the early 1970s to conclude that this period saw the emergence of a new, and quite different, party *system*.

Let us consider, then, the form of party that this new party system replaced. Created in the 1830s, the earlier party was a *mass-based* party centered mainly on winning elections—i.e., on mobilizing voters to get to the polls and support the party's candidates on election day. Accounts from the "golden age" of parties in the late nineteenth century use such terms as "armies" and "religious movements" to describe the intense feelings that surrounded partisan election campaigns. In particular, candidates relied on the parties to carry their message (see Herrnson, Patterson, and Pitney 1996); it was not until the turn of the century, for example, that presidential nominees actually campaigned in person. With the secret ballot not adopted in most places until at least the late 1880s, parties distributed their own "party strip" ballots—which meant that incumbents' reelection fortunes usually depended as much on the overall success of the party as on their own personal strengths. As a result, the freedom to maneuver after being elected was constrained by the knowledge that they would have to depend on help from the party if they wanted to win another term (see Burnham 1970).

Although U.S. parties became progressively weaker throughout the twentieth century, their basic form (mass organizations designed to get out the vote), remained that set down in the Jacksonian era. In contrast, the current party is configured very differently: Elections center on the individual candidates, and the "party-in-the-electorate" has greatly deteriorated as an unnecessary and often irrelevant loyalty. The critical era of the 1960s was, therefore, critical for the party as well as the polity as a whole. Both parties reformed their institutions and practices after (and even during) this critical era.

The most visible action on the Democratic side began with the adoption of rules changes proposed by the McGovern-Fraser Commission in 1972; numerous other reforms followed, primarily affecting the selection and instruction of delegates to the national nominating convention (see Crotty and Jackson 1985). Some critics (e.g., Polsby 1983) have argued that these reforms undermined the party by wresting control over presidential nominations from party elites and moving it to voters, candidates, and the media. Yet Reiter (1985) has convincingly demonstrated that the supposed ill effects of the new rules largely predated their adoption. Thus, it is better to see Democratic reforms of the 1970s as adjusting the party to the new realities of candidate-centered elections—or, at most, as pushing it further along that path. Perhaps more consequential was a different aspect of these and related changes, i.e., the fact that they imposed national rules over those developed by the state parties and, at times, over laws passed by state legislatures. That is, the reforms were an important step in the process of *nationalizing* political parties.

The GOP generally followed, if often far more weakly than the Democrats, a similar path toward procedural reform. However, Republicans took the lead in making changes that served to further nationalization in other ways (while at the same time strengthening state and local party organizations)—and this time, it was the Democrats who played catch-up. What we are referring to are efforts in both camps to professionalize, institutionalize, and build up the resource base of "parties-as-organizations" (Herrnson 1988; Kayden and Mahe 1985). To a greater degree than ever before, party organizations no longer ran campaigns; doing so became the responsibility of individual candidates. But they did begin to provide critical *services* and technological *expertise* to candidates, from recruiting and training them to providing assistance in polling, media operations, direct mail, fundraising, assistance with legal requirements, and the like. In addition, under campaign finance legislation enacted by Congress in the 1970s, parties were able to contribute at least limited direct funding (as well as additional "soft money") to assist campaigns; they also created such devices as "bundling" gifts from political action committees and channeling this money to candidates.[14] In fact, evidence gathered over the years indicates that party organizations have indeed become stronger, more professionalized, better financed, and more fully institutionalized at the national, state, and local levels (Cotter et al. 1984; Gibson et al. 1983; Herrnson 1988).

A third component of the political party is the "party-in-government." With the Democratic majority in Congress deeply divided during the 1960s and 1970s over civil rights, Vietnam, and other issues, typical measures of the "strength" of parties as legislative voting blocs declined and the so-called conservative coalition (where a majority of Republicans and southern Democrats are pitted against a majority of northern Democrats) came to rival party as the principal basis of congressional voting. At about the same time, reform efforts within Congress began to gain increasing support from members. According to David Rohde (1991), changes enacted in the mid-1970s provided the institutional basis for "conditional party government" by, among other things, strengthening the role of the Democratic caucus (the name given to meetings of all Democrats in the chamber) and of the House and majority party leadership.[15] By "conditional," Rohde meant that an American version of party government was made more feasible through these reforms, provided that a key condition was met. The condition was simply that party members must have sufficient interests in common to desire acting collectively to achieve common policy goals. In the late 1970s and 1980s, this condition began to be satisfied more fully—with the result that the voting strength of party increased dramatically and, by some measures, reached highs unsurpassed since early in the century.

Growing satisfaction of the conditions necessary to sustain conditional party government (i.e., greater intraparty agreement and more pronounced interparty divisions on policy goals) was an indirect consequence of the critical era of the 1960s. For example, one of the great achievements made possible by the parties' policy shift on civil rights was passage of the Voting Rights Act in 1965. This legislation effectively enfranchised blacks and dramatically increased their proportion of the voting public, especially in the South. And as we saw earlier, blacks realigned to become overwhelmingly Democratic in their party affiliations during the 1960s while significant numbers of native white southerners moved to the GOP. The result was that, particularly in presidential and congressional elections, Republican candidates found themselves able to compete with mounting success in southern politics.

For many southern Democratic politicians, the inclusion of blacks and the defection of large numbers of conservative whites led to electoral and reelectoral coalitions that were more liberal than in the past. Accordingly, as Rohde shows, there were some instances in which formerly conservative southern Democrats in Congress began voting much like their northern counterparts. Especially in districts where public opinion leaned to the right, Democrats were often replaced by conservative Republicans; in other districts, moderate and even liberal Democrats succeeded their conservative predecessors. By the late 1970s and 1980s, the southern Democratic congressional delegation had started to look more like northern Democrats. Because these two groups tended to have numerous policy views in common, the conditions of conditional party government were more fully satisfied. Thus, the party-in-government eventually strengthened as a result of the critical era of the 1960s and internal reforms in Congress.

Denise Baer (1993, 2), in trying to "codify and define an emerging consensus among a variety of party scholars concerning the institutionalization of party," has suggested that the contemporary "institutionalized parties are characterized by an integrative party community, the development of stable factions, increased organizational interdependence, and an increased organizational vitality" (28). We may fairly conclude that today's political party is institutionalized as the representational vehicle for the sixth party system, but the new party is far different from its predecessor, which for all intents and purposes collapsed in the critical era of the 1960s. The old party was designed to control elections and therefore to control access to office, and to use that access for securing the spoils needed to maintain a well-oiled and effective machine. The quintessential example of this form of party was the local machine, led by someone who might or might not hold office himself but who sought to control the fates of those who did. The new form of party is not such a machine. It is, instead, an organization designed to serve the interests of its central actors—its candidates and officeholders. Although well-financed and professionalized, the organization no longer dominates campaigns; candidates do. The party stands in service to its candidates, and it is the candidates whom the voters see and evaluate.

We might say that, in effect, the decaying "party-in-the-electorate" has been replaced by a vital "party-in-elections." Whether in elections or in government, the modern party organization serves its officeseekers and officeholders—thereby making the candidate-centered election system viable and facilitating the exercise of a version of party government, provided the necessary conditions are met. As noted, the key condition for party-in-government to be effective is that its officeholders find common policy ground among themselves. In office, as in elections, this is a defining characteristic of the politician-centered party. And the critical era of the 1960s, in partisan terms, is marked above all by a fundamental transformation to just this sort of party system.

Conclusion

It is time to declare the existence of a sixth American party system. The United States experienced a critical-election era in the 1960s, as is amply demonstrated by the collection of changes we have reviewed. It was a change unlike previous realignments, but all such periods are in some ways unique. As anticipated, there is a new equilibrium in the same indicators that were so stable in the 1950s and changed so dramatically in the 1960s. It has taken a series of elections for this to become clear, but it is now amply apparent.

The last major analysis of an entire spectrum of descriptors of the American electorate was in *The Changing American Voter* (Nie, Verba, and Petrocik 1979; originally published in 1976). Covering as it did the previous equilibrium, the realignment period, and the first of the postrealignment elections—and being written in reaction to the masterful description of the 1950s in *The American Voter* (Campbell et al. 1960)—it is not at all surprising that what the authors emphasized was the change that racked the electorate as well as our theoretical understanding of public opinion and voting. With the decline in partisanship, which had been regarded as the bedrock of the electorate's understanding and evaluation of parties and candidates, it is small wonder that dealignment and volatility became the new catchwords.

Just as *The Changing American Voter* heralded a revised view of voters and elections based on the data then available, it is time for a reassessment based on the entire period from 1952 to the present. What such a review indicates is (1) an equilibrium period for 1952–1960 as was described in *The American Voter;* (2) a period of turmoil documented in *The Changing American Voter* that can now be properly interpreted as a realignment of numerous features of the electorate; and (3) a not previously recognized equilibrium period since 1972. The new equilibrium is unlike the old—the curve in Figure 23-10 shows no hint of a return to the previous level—but that is not surprising. Reestablishment of the old order is not a characteristic of any of the previous critical eras.

There seems to be consensus on the appropriate name for the sixth party system. What most clearly characterizes the period since the 1960s is the decline of parties in the electorate and the rise of candidate-centered parties. When partisanship gave way as the underpinning of electoral decisions, candidates came to the fore. Parties did not merely stand aside, however, and preside over their own decay. They changed their representative character and the ways in which they related to candidates and emerged as still viable institutions in the American electoral world.

The sixth American party system—the candidate-centered party system—has been with us since 1972. Changes that occurred during the 1960s were so great and so pervasive that they cry out to be called a critical-election period. The new system of candidate-centered parties is so distinct and so portentous that one can no longer deny its existence or its character. With this recognition, we have come full cycle in our study of the American electorate. We began in an equilibrium period; lived through, documented, and observed a critical realignment; and can now, with the perspective of time, recognize the new stability.

When the periodicity of American electoral history first became apparent to scholars, we might have thought that this completed our understanding of voting behavior. What we realize instead is that each new critical era establishes patterns that are unlike the old and that need analysis and interpretation of their own. So our study of voting behavior is not complete. Still, we have reaffirmed the view that voters, parties, and their interaction—including macropatterns of electoral history—can be understood using many of the concepts that have been developed over the decades since the Columbia and Michigan groups first began the empirical study of electoral behavior and since V. O. Key Jr. (1955, 1964) wrote his brilliant studies of political parties and introduced critical elections as a central concept for understanding American political history.

Notes

1. The first party system began with the creation of the earliest U.S. political parties—Federalists and Jeffersonian Republicans—in the 1790s; it was in disarray by the 1820s. The second party system emerged with the rise to power of Jacksonian democracy and the mass-based parties of the 1820s and 1830s, and it lasted into the 1850s. The third party system was fully in place by 1860 with the election of the first Republican president, Abraham Lincoln; it was characterized by close competition between Republicans and Democrats. The fourth party system was formed in 1894–1896 as the GOP achieved a level of dominance that remained largely unbroken until the Great Depression. The fifth party system was forged in the 1930s as Democrats became the dominant party. For additional details, see Sundquist (1983), Clubb, Flanigan, and Zingale (1980), Brady (1988), Reichley (1992), Aldrich (1995).

2. The election(s) that usher in a new party system may constitute a "realignment," in which the minority party at the time becomes a majority (winning most of the votes cast and capturing most elective offices at all levels); this happened most clearly in the 1930s. But changes in party systems also may be realized as fundamental shifts in partisan institutional arrangements, e.g., when an altogether new party comes onto the scene (like the Republicans in the nineteenth century). For this reason, we prefer the more general term "critical election" or "critical era." See Aldrich (1995) for a more thorough discussion of the earlier party systems and the critical eras between them.

3. Our analysis does not exhaust all possible measures, but we believe that it does tap each of the major components proposed by "realignment" theorists as they apply to the mass electorate. Moreover, we have not selected only the best-fitting measures; indeed, a few are discussed that do not fit very well at all (e.g., salience of New Deal issues, presidential and House split-district outcomes), although these are included in the macroanalysis even after establishing their lack of fit.

4. The NES classifies as "apolitical" those individuals who express neither a partisan preference nor an attachment to independence; as their name implies, apoliticals tend to be uninterested, uninvolved, ill informed, and generally unconnected to the world of politics and government.

5. The decline in numbers of strong partisans (and parallel increase in Independents) that occurred in 1992 was, we suspect, a short-term response to events—especially Ross Perot's presidential bid.

6. Favorable evaluations are indicated when the number of likes exceeds the number of dislikes for a particular party.

7. Changed popular perceptions were, in fact, rooted in reality: In Congress, a racial liberalism index based on members' roll-call votes shows Republicans in both houses to have been more liberal than Democrats from 1945 through 1964. But a dramatic reversal occurred in the mid-1960s, followed by a further increase in party differences during the 1970s (Carmines and Stimson 1989, 163).

8. On the concept of political efficacy and its relation to voter turnout, see Craig, Niemi, and Silver (1990), Craig (1996), and Horn and Conway (1996).

9. Retirement slump reflects the tendency for the in-party's candidate to fare less well in an open-seat contest immediately following the retirement of an incumbent. Sophomore surge refers to the tendency for incumbent congressmen to do better in their first bid for reelection than they did when they won initially.

10. A similar trend is evident in the Senate, but these conclusions apply most clearly to House races (where smaller, more homogeneous constituencies give representatives a greater opportunity to interact and communicate with potential voters).

11. Excluded are interest in campaigns (because it is theoretically expected to have a different pattern) and Alford and Brady's measure of retirement slump and sophomore surge (because of its unmeasurability in 40 percent of the cases). Of the various NES

items that tap citizen feelings of trust and external efficacy, only "public officials don't care" was included because it was the only one asked in presidential surveys prior to 1964. To avoid redundancy, we used the percentage of all Independents for whites (but not pure Independents), the racial liberalism of House and Senate Democrats (but not Republicans), and the item in Figure 23-6 (but not the numbers from Geer).

12. This is a common form of standardization, used to make items comparable when they are measured on different scales. It uses the formula $Z_i = (x_i - \bar{x})/s_x$ where x_i stands for each of the values across the eleven elections. . . . The values (i.e., the x's) are thus measured in terms of standard deviations above or below the mean of that variable across time.

13. We can also summarize the progression of the twenty-seven individual measures over time via a simple regression. The standardized measure is regressed on a realignment variable that is 0 for the fifth-party-system years, 0.333 for 1964 and 0.667 for 1968 (in order to capture the apparently linear change over the course of the realignment), and 1 for the sixth-party-system years. The result is as follows:

Standardized summary variable = $-1.169 + 1.870(X)$,
                                          (.063)   (.083)
where X = 0 for 1952–1960, 0.333 for 1964, 0.667 for 1968, 1 for 1972–1992. (Standard errors in parentheses.)
Adj. R^2 = 0.656; N = 268

The predicted difference between the fifth and sixth party systems is a very substantial 1.9 standardized units.

The fit of this model is superior to one that assumes a linear increase (adjusted $R^2 = 0.58$), and it is nearly as good as one that allows each year to assume its actual mean value on the standardized measures. The latter had an adjusted R^2 of 0.69, which is the maximum possible obtainable from any combination of election-year values. We also estimated models with a linear "drift" within a given party system, but the estimate of change was not significant in either system.

14. For further information on campaign financing (including such practices as "soft money" and "bundling"), see Sorauf (1988), Alexander (1992), and Magleby and Nelson (1990).

15. These reforms were adopted primarily (but not exclusively) by Democrats in the House of Representatives. They included giving the Democratic caucus more say in choosing committee chairs and the Speaker greater control over assigning bills to committees and scheduling legislation, among numerous others.

References

Abramowitz, Alan I. 1975. "Name Familiarity, Reputation, and the Incumbency Effect in a Congressional Election." *Western Political Quarterly* 28: 668–684.

_____. 1988. "An Improved Model for Predicting Presidential Outcomes." *PS: Political Science and Politics* 21: 843–847.

_____. 1995. "It's Abortion, Stupid: Policy Voting in the 1992 Presidential Election." *Journal of Politics* 57: 176–186.

_____. 1996. "Bill and Al's Excellent Adventure: Forecasting the 1996 Presidential Election." *American Politics Quarterly* 24: 434–442.

Abramowitz, Alan I., and Kyle L. Saunders. 1998. "Ideological Realignment in the U.S. Electorate." *Journal of Politics* 60: 634–652.

Abramson, Paul R. 1989. "Generations and Political Change in the United States." *Research in Political Sociology* 4: 235–280.

Abramson, Paul R., and John H. Aldrich. 1982. "The Decline of Participation in America." *American Political Science Review* 76: 502–521.

Abramson, Paul R., John H. Aldrich, Phil Paolino, and David Rohde. 1992. " 'Sophisticated' Voting in the 1988 Presidential Primaries." *American Political Science Review* 86: 55–69.

Abramson, Paul R., and William Claggett. 1991. "Racial Differences in Self-Reported and Validated Turnout in the 1988 Presidential Election." *Journal of Politics* 53: 186–197.

Abramson, Paul R., and Ronald Inglehart. 1995. *Value Change in Global Perspective.* Ann Arbor: University of Michigan Press.

Abramson, Paul R., and Charles W. Ostrom Jr. 1986. "Generation Replacement and Value Change in Six Western European Societies." *American Journal of Political Science* 30: 1–25.

_____. 1991. "Macropartisanship: An Empirical Reassessment." *American Political Science Review* 85: 181–192.

Achen, Christopher. 1975. "Mass Political Attitudes and the Survey Response." *American Political Science Review* 69: 1218–1231.

_____. 1982. *Interpreting and Using Regression.* Beverly Hills, Calif.: Sage.

_____. 1992. "Social Psychology, Demographic Variables, and Linear Regression: Breaking the Iron Triangle in Voting Research." *Political Behavior* 14: 195–211.

Achen, Christopher H., and W. Phillips Shively. 1995. *Cross-Level Inference.* Chicago: University of Chicago Press.

Adams, Greg D. 1997. "Abortion: Evidence of an Issue Evolution." *American Journal of Political Science* 41: 718–737.

Adams, Greg D., and Peverill Squire. 1997. "Incumbent Vulnerability and Challenger Emergence in Senate Elections." *Political Behavior* 19: 97–111.

Aldrich, John H. 1995. *Why Parties? The Origin and Transformation of Party Politics in America.* Chicago: University of Chicago Press.

_____. 1999. "Political Parties in a Critical Era." *American Politics Quarterly* 27: 9–32.

Aldrich, John, and Forrest Nelson. 1984. *Linear Probability, Logit, and Probit Models.* Beverly Hills, Calif.: Sage.

Aldrich, John H., and Richard G. Niemi. 1996. "The Sixth American Party System: Electoral Change, 1952–1992." In *Broken Contract?* ed. Stephen C. Craig. Boulder, Colo.: Westview.

Aldrich, John H., John L. Sullivan, and Eugene Borgida. 1989. "Foreign Policy and Issue Voting: Do Presidential Candidates 'Waltz before a Blind Audience?' " *American Political Science Review* 83: 123–141.

Alesina, Alberto, John Londregan, and Howard Rosenthal. 1993. "A Model of the Political Economy of the United States." *American Political Science Review* 87: 12–33.

Alesina, Alberto, and Howard Rosenthal. 1989. "Partisan Cycles in Congressional Elections and the Macroeconomy." *American Political Science Review* 83: 373–398.

_____. 1995. *Partisan Politics, Divided Government, and the Economy.* New York: Cambridge University Press.

Alexander, Herbert E. 1975. *Financing the 1972 Election.* Lexington, Mass.: Lexington Books.

_____. 1979. *Financing the 1976 Election.* Washington, D.C.: CQ Press.

_____. 1983. *Financing the 1980 Election.* Lexington, Mass.: Lexington Books.

_____. 1992. *Financing Politics: Money Elections, and Political Reform,* 4th ed. Washington, D.C.: CQ Press.

Alexander, Herbert E., and Monica Bauer. 1991. *Financing the 1988 Election.* Boulder, Colo.: Westview Press.

Alexander, Herbert E., and Brian A. Haggerty. 1987. *Financing the 1984 Election.* Lexington, Mass.: Lexington Books.

Alford, John R., and David W. Brady. 1989. "Personal and Partisan Advantage in U.S. Congressional Elections, 1846–1986." In *Congress Reconsidered,* 4th ed., ed. Lawrence C. Dodd and Bruce I. Oppenheimer. Washington, D.C.: CQ Press.

Allsop, Dee, and Herbert Weisberg. 1988. "Measuring Change in Party Identification in an Election Campaign." *American Journal of Political Science* 32: 996–1017.

Almond, Gabriel A. 1960 [1950]. *The American People and Foreign Policy.* New York: Praeger.

Alt, James E. 1985. "Political Parties, World Demand, and Unemployment: Domestic and International Sources of Economic Activity." *American Political Science Review* 79: 1016–1040.

Alt, James E., and Robert C. Lowry. 1994. "Divided Government, Fiscal Institutions, and Budget Deficits: Evidence from the States." *American Political Science Review* 88: 811–828.

Althaus, Scott L. 1995. "Can Collective Opinion Redeem an Ill-Informed Public?" Paper presented at the annual meeting of the American Association of Public Opinion Research, Ft. Lauderdale, Fla.

_____. 1996a. "Opinion Polls, Information Effects, and Political Equality: Exploring Ideological Biases in Collective Opinion." *Political Communication* 13: 3–21.

_____. 1996b. "Who Speaks for the People? Political Knowledge, Representation, and the Use of Opinion Surveys in Democratic Politics." Ph.D. diss., Northwestern University.

_____. 1998. "Information Effects in Collective Preferences." *American Political Science Review* 92: 545–558.

Alvarez, R. Michael. 1990. "The Puzzle of Party Identification." *American Politics Quarterly* 18: 476–491.

_____. 1992. "Issues and Information in Presidential Elections." Ph.D. diss. Duke University.

Alvarez, R. Michael, and Charles H. Franklin. 1994. "Uncertainty and Political Perceptions." *Journal of Politics* 56: 671–688.

Alvarez, R. Michael, and Jonathan Nagler. 1995. "Economics, Issues, and the Perot Candidacy: Voter Choice in the 1992 Presidential Election." *American Journal of Political Science* 39: 714–744.

_____. 1998. "Economics, Entitlements, and Social Issues: Voter Choice in the 1996 Presidential Election." *American Journal of Political Science* 42: 1349–1363.

Alvarez, R. Michael, and Matthew M. Schousen. 1993. "Policy Moderation or Conflicting Expectations? Testing the Intentional Models of Split-Ticket Voting." *American Politics Quarterly* 21: 410–438.

Andersen, Kristi. 1979. *The Creation of a Democratic Majority, 1928–1936.* Chicago: University of Chicago Press.

Anderson, Christopher. 1995. *Blaming the Government: Citizens and the Economy in Five European Democracies.* Armonk, New York: M. E. Sharpe.

_____. 2000. "Economic Voting and Political Context: A Comparative Perspective." *Electoral Studies* 19: 151–170.

Anderson, Norman H. 1991. "Functional Memory in Person Cognition." In *Information Integration Theory*, vol. 1: *Cognition*, ed. Norman H. Anderson. Hillsdale, N.J.: Erlbaum.

Anderson, Norman H., and Stephen Hubert. 1963. "Effects of Concomitant Recall on Order Effects in Personality Impression Formation." *Journal of Verbal Learning and Verbal Behavior* 2: 379–391.

Ansolabehere, Stephen, David W. Brady, and Morris P. Fiorina. 1992. "The Vanishing Marginals and Electoral Responsiveness." *British Journal of Political Science* 22: 21–38.

Ansolabehere, Stephen, and Shanto Iyengar. 1995. *Going Negative: How Political Advertising Shrinks and Polarizes the Electorate.* New York: Free Press.

_____. 1996. "The Craft of Political Advertising: A Progress Report." In *Political Persuasion and Attitude Change,* ed. Diana C. Mutz, Paul M. Sniderman, and Richard A. Brody. Ann Arbor: University of Michigan Press.

Ansolabehere, Stephen, Shanto Iyengar, Adam Simon, and Nicholas Valentino. 1994. "Does Attack Advertising Demobilize the Electorate?" *American Political Science Review* 88: 829–838.

Ansolabehere, Stephen, James M. Snyder Jr., and Charles Stewart III. 2000. "Old Voters, New Voters, and the Personal Vote: Using Redistricting to Measure the Incumbency Advantage." *American Journal of Political Science* 44: 17–34.

Arnold, Laura, and Herbert F. Weisberg. 1996. "Parenthood, Family Values, and the 1992 Presidential Election." *American Politics Quarterly,* 24: 194–220.

Asher, Herbert. 1995. "The Perot Campaign." In *Democracy's Feast: Elections in America,* ed. Herbert F. Weisberg. Chatham, N.J.: Chatham House.

_____. 2001. *Polling and the Public,* 5th ed. Washington, D.C.: CQ Press.

Astin, Alexander W., Sarah A. Parrott, William S. Korn, and Linda J. Sax. 1997. *The American Freshman: Thirty Year Trends.* Los Angeles: Higher Education Research Institute, UCLA.

Atkeson, Lonna Rae, and Randall W. Partin. 1995. "Economic and Referendum Voting: A Comparison of Gubernatorial and Senate Elections." *American Political Science Review* 89: 99–107.

Austen-Smith, David, and Jeffrey S. Banks. 1996. "Information Aggregation, Rationality, and the Condorcet Jury Theorem." *American Political Science Review* 90: 34–45.

Ayres, B. Drummond, Jr. 1995. "Easier Voter Registration Doesn't Raise Participation." *New York Times,* December 3.

Baer, Denise L. 1993. "Who Has the Body? Party Institutionalization and Theories of Party Organization." *American Review of Politics* 14: 1–38.

Baker, Keith M., ed. 1976. *Condorcet: Selected Writings.* Indianapolis: Bobbs-Merrill.

Barber, James David. 1973. *Citizen Politics.* Chicago: Markham.

Barnes, Samuel H. 1990. "Partisanship and Electoral Behavior." In *Continuities in Political Action: A Longitudinal Study of Political Orientations in Three Western Democracies,* ed. M. Kent Jennings and Jan W. van Deth. Berlin: Walter de Gruyter.

Barnes, Samuel, Max Kaase, et al. 1979. *Political Action: Mass Participation in Five Western Democracies.* Beverly Hills, Calif.: Sage.

Barone, Michael, and Grant Ujifusa. 1989. *The Almanac of American Politics, 1990.* Washington, D.C.: National Journal.

Bartels, Larry M. 1986. "Issue Voting under Uncertainty: An Empirical Test." *American Journal of Political Science* 30: 709–728.

_____. 1988. *Presidential Primaries and the Dynamics of Public Choice.* Princeton: Princeton University Press.

_____. 1990. "Public Opinion and Political Interests." Paper presented at the annual meeting of the Midwest Political Science Association, Chicago.

_____. 1991. "Constituency Opinion and Congressional Policy-Making: The Reagan Defense Buildup." *American Political Science Review* 85: 457–474.

_____. 1992. "The Impact of Electioneering in the United States." In *Electioneering: A Comparative Study of Continuity and Change,* ed. David Butler and Austin Ranney. Oxford: Clarendon Press.

_____. 1993. "Messages Received: The Political Impact of Media Exposure." *American Political Science Review* 87: 267–285.

_____. 1996. "Uniformed Votes: Information Effects in Presidential Elections." *American Journal of Political Science* 40: 194–230.

_____. 1998a. "Electoral Continuity and Change, 1868–1996." *Electoral Studies* 17: 301–326.

_____. 1998b. "Where the Ducks Are: Voting Power in a Party System." In *Politicians and Party Politics,* ed. John G. Geer. Baltimore: Johns Hopkins University Press.

_____. 2000. "Partisanship and Voting Behavior, 1952–1996." *American Journal of Political Science* 44: 35–50.

Bauer, Monica, and John R. Hibbing. 1989. "Which Incumbents Lose in House Elections: A Response to Jacobson's 'The Marginals Never Vanished.'" *American Journal of Political Science* 33: 262–271.

Bay, Christian. 1968. "Needs, Wants and Political Legitimacy." *Canadian Journal of Political Science* 1: 241–260.

Beck, Paul Allen. 1974. "A Socialization Theory of Partisan Realignment." In *The Politics of Future Citizens: New Dimensions in the Political Socialization of Children,* Richard G. Niemi and associates. San Franciso: Jossey-Bass.

_____. 1977. "Partisan Development in the Postwar South." *American Political Science Review* 71: 477–496.

_____. 1982. "Realignment Begins: The Republican Surge in Florida." *American Politics Quarterly* 10: 421–438.

_____. 1984. "The Dealignment Era in America." In *Electoral Change in Advanced Industrial Democracies,* ed. Russell J. Dalton, Scott C. Flanagan, and Paul Allen Beck. Princeton: Princeton University Press.

_____. 1986. "Model Choice in Political Science: The Case of Voting Behavior Research, 1946–1975." In *Political Science: The Science of Politics,* ed. Herbert F. Weisberg. New York: Agathon.

_____. 1989. "Incomplete Realignment: The Reagan Legacy for Parties and Elections." In *The Reagan Legacy: Promise and Performance,* ed. Charles O. Jones. Chatham, N.J.: Chatham House.

_____. 1997. *Party Politics in America,* 8th ed. New York: Longman.

Beck, Paul Allen, Lawrence Baum, Aage R. Clausen, and Charles Smith Jr. 1992. "Patterns and Sources of Ticket Splitting in Subpresidential Voting." *American Political Science Review* 86: 916–928.

Beck, Paul A., and M. Kent Jennings. 1975. "Parents as 'Middle-Persons' in Political Socialization." *Journal of Politics* 37: 83–107.

_____. 1979. "Political Periods and Political Participation." *American Political Science Review* 73: 737–750.

_____. 1991. "Family Traditions, Political Periods, and the Development of Partisan Orientations." *Journal of Politics* 53: 742–763.

Belknap, George, and Angus Campbell. 1951. "Political Party Identification and Attitudes toward Foreign Policy." *Public Opinion Quarterly* 15: 601–623.

Bennett, Stephen Earl. 1988. " 'Know-Nothings' Revisited: The Meaning of Political Ignorance Today." *Social Science Quarterly* 69: 476–490.

_____. 1995. "Americans' Knowledge of Ideology, 1980–1992." *American Politics Quarterly* 23: 259–78.

Bennett, Stephen Earl, and Eric W. Rademacher. 1997. "The 'Age of Indifference' Revisited: Patterns of Political Interest, Media Exposure and Knowledge about Generation X." In *After the Boom: The Politics of Generation X,* ed. Stephen C. Craig and Stephen Earl Bennett. Lanham, Md.: Rowman and Littlefield.

Bennett, W. Lance. 1988. *News—The Politics of Illusion,* 2nd ed. New York: Longman.

_____. 1992. *The Governing Crisis: Media, Money and Marketing in American Elections.* New York: St. Martin's.

Bentler, Peter M. 1992. *EQS Structural Equations Program Manual.* Los Angeles: BMDP Statistical Software.

Berelson, Bernard R. 1952. "Democratic Theory and Public Opinion." *Public Opinion Quarterly* 16: 313–330.

Berelson, Bernard R., Paul F. Lazarsfeld, and William N. McPhee. 1954. *Voting: A Study of Opinion Formation in a Presidential Campaign.* Chicago: University of Chicago Press.

Berg, Sven. 1993. "Condorcet's Jury Theorem, Dependency among Jurors." *Social Choice and Welfare* 10: 87–95.

Berinsky, Adam. 1999. "The Two Faces of Public Opinion." *American Journal of Political Science* 43: 1209–1230.

Berry, William D., Michael Berkman, and Stuart Schneiderman. 2000. "Legislative Professionalism and the Incumbency Advantage: A Contextual Analysis of State Elections." *Journal of Politics* 62: 671–700.

Bishop, George, Robert Oldendick, and Alfred Tuchfarber. 1983. "Effects of Filter Questions in Public Opinion Surveys." *Public Opinion Quarterly* 47: 528–546.

Black, Earl, and Merle Black. 1987. *Politics and Society in the South.* Cambridge: Harvard University Press.

Black, Joan S. 1983. "General Electric Brings the Polls to Life." *Public Opinion* 6: 27.

Blood, Deborah J., and Peter C. B. Phillips. 1995. "Recession Headline News, Consumer Sentiment, and the State of the Economy." *International Journal of Public Opinion Research* 7: 2–22.

Books, John, and Charles Prysby. 1999. "Contextual Effects on Retrospective Economic Evaluations: The Impact of the State and Local Economy." *Political Behavior* 21: 1–16.

Born, Richard. 1979. "Generational Replacement and the Growth of Incumbent Re-election Margins in the U.S. House." *American Political Science Review* 73: 811–817.

———. 1994. "Split-Ticket Voters, Divided Government, and Fiorina's Policy-Balancing Model." *Legislative Studies Quarterly* 19: 95–115.

———. 2000a. "Policy-Balancing Models and the Split-Ticket Voter, 1972–1996." *American Politics Quarterly* 28: 131–162.

———. 2000b. "Congressional Incumbency and the Rise of Split-Ticket Voting." *Legislative Studies Quarterly* 25: 365–387.

Borrelli, Stephen. 1993. "Party Polarization, Ideological Balancing, and Divided Government in the American States." Paper presented at the annual meeting of the Midwest Political Science Association, Chicago.

Bower, Robert T. 1985. *The Changing Television Audience in America.* New York: Columbia University Press.

Box, George E. P., and Gwilym M. Jenkins. 1976. *Time Series Analysis: Forecasting and Control.* San Francisco: Holden-Day.

Box-Steffensmeier, Janet M. 1996. "A Dynamic Analysis of the Role of War Chests in Campaign Strategy." *American Journal of Political Science* 40: 352–371.

Box-Steffensmeier, Janet M., and Gary Jacobson. 1995. "Question Wording and the House Vote: Some Experimental Evidence." Paper presented at the annual meeting of the Southern Political Science Association, Atlanta, Ga.

Box-Steffensmeier, Janet M., and Renée Smith. 1996. "The Dynamics of Aggregate Partisanship." *American Political Science Review* 90: 567–580.

Boyd, Richard W. 1981. "The Decline of U.S. Voter Turnout: Structural Explanations." *American Politics Quarterly* 9: 133–159.

Brace, Kimball W., ed. 1993. *The Election Data Book: A Statistical Portrait of Voting in America, 1992.* Lanham, Md.: Bernan.

Brady, David W. 1988. *Critical Elections and Congressional Policy Making.* Stanford: Stanford University Press.

Brady, Henry E., and Richard Johnston. 1987. "What's the Primary Message: Horse Race or Issue Journalism?" In *Media and Momentum: The New Hampshire Primary and Nomination Politics,* ed. Gary R. Orren and Nelson W. Polsby. Chatham, N.J.: Chatham House.

Brady, Henry E., and Paul M. Sniderman. 1985. "Attitude Attribution: A Group Basis for Political Reasoning." *American Political Science Review* 79: 1061–1078.

Brady, Henry E., Sidney Verba, and Kay Lehman Schlozman. 1995. "Beyond SES: A Resource Model of Political Participation." *American Political Science Review* 89: 271–294.

Brehm, John, and Wendy Rahn. 1995. "An Audit of the Deficit in Social Capital." Unpublished manuscript, Duke University.

_____. 1997. "Individual-Level Evidence for the Causes and Consequences of Social Capital." *American Journal of Political Science* 41: 999–1023.

Broder, David S. 1971. *The Party's Over: The Failure of Politics in America.* New York: Harper and Row.

Brody, Richard A. 1977. "Stability and Change in Party Identification: Presidential to Off-Years." Paper presented at the annual meeting of the American Political Science Association, Washington, D.C.

_____. 1978. "The Puzzle of Participation in America." In *The New American Political System,* ed. Anthony King. Washington, D.C.: American Enterprise Institute.

_____. 1991. *Assessing the President: The Media, Elite Opinion, and Public Support.* Stanford: Stanford University Press.

Brody, Richard A., and Benjamin I. Page. 1972. "The Assessment of Policy Voting." *American Political Science Review* 66: 450–458.

Brody, Richard A., and Lawrence S. Rothenberg. 1988. "The Instability of Partisanship: An Analysis of the 1980 Presidential Election." *British Journal of Political Science* 18: 445–466.

Brooks, Clem, and Jeff Manza. 1997a. "Class Politics and Political Change in the United States, 1952–1992." *Social Forces* 76: 379–408.

_____. 1997b. "The Social and Ideological Bases of Middle-Class Political Realignment in the United States, 1972 to 1992." *American Sociological Review* 62: 191–208.

_____. 1997c. "Social Cleavages and Political Alignments: U.S. Presidential Elections, 1960 to 1992." *American Sociological Review* 62: 937–946.

Bryce, James. 1893. *The American Commonwealth.* New York: Macmillan.

Burden, Barry C. 1997. "Deterministic and Probablistic Voting Models." *American Journal of Political Science* 41: 1150–1169.

Burden, Barry C., and David C. Kimball. 1998. "A New Approach to the Study of Ticket Splitting." *American Political Science Review* 92: 533–544.

_____. Forthcoming. *Why Americans Split Their Tickets: Campaigns, Competition, and Divided Government.* Ann Arbor: University of Michigan Press.

Burnham, Walter Dean. 1965. "The Changing Shape of the American Political Universe." *American Political Science Review* 59: 7–28.

_____. 1970. *Critical Elections and the Mainsprings of American Politics.* New York: Norton.

_____. 1974. "Theory and Voting Research: Some Reflections on Converse's 'Change in the American Electorate.' " *American Political Science Review* 68: 1002–1023.

_____. 1989. "The Reagan Heritage." In *The Election of 1988: Reports and Interpretations,* ed. Gerald M. Pomper et al. Chatham, N.J.: Chatham House.

_____. 1991. "Critical Realignment: Dead or Alive?" In *The End of Realignment? Interpreting American Electoral Eras,* ed. Byron E. Shafer. Madison: University of Wisconsin Press.

Butler, David, and Donald E. Stokes. 1969. *Political Change in Britain.* New York: St. Martin's.

_____. 1974. *Political Change in Britain: The Evolution of Electoral Choice,* 2nd ed. New York: St. Martin's.

Byers, David, James Davidson, and David Peel. 2000. "The Dynamics of Aggregate Political Popularity: Evidence from Eight Countries." *Electoral Studies* 19: 49–62.

Cain, Bruce, John Ferejohn, and Morris P. Fiorina. 1987. *The Personal Vote: Constituency Service and Electoral Independence.* Cambridge: Harvard University Press.

Calvert, Randall L., and John A. Ferejohn. 1983. "Coattail Voting in Recent Presidential Elections." *American Political Science Review* 77: 407–419.

Calvert, Randall L., and Michael B. MacKuen. 1985. "Bayesian Learning and the Dynamics of Public Opinion." Paper presented at the annual meeting of the Midwest Political Science Association, Chicago.

Cambridge Reports, Inc. 1985. *America Looks Ahead.* Cambridge, Mass.: Author.

Campbell, Angus. 1960. "Surge and Decline: A Study of Electoral Change." *Public Opinion Quarterly* 24: 397–418.

Campbell, Angus, Philip E. Converse, Warren E. Miller, and Donald E. Stokes. 1960. *The American Voter.* New York: Wiley.

Campbell, Angus, and Warren E. Miller. 1957. "The Motivational Basis of Straight and Split Ticket Voting." *American Political Science Review* 51: 293–312.

Campbell, James E. 1987. "The Revised Theory of Surge and Decline." *American Journal of Political Science* 31: 165–183.

_____. 1996. "Polls and Votes: The Trial-Heat Presidential Election Forecasting Model, Certainty, and Political Campaigns." *American Politics Quarterly* 24: 408–433.

_____. 1997. *The Presidential Pulse of Congressional Elections,* 2nd ed. Lexington: University Press of Kentucky.

_____. 2000. *The American Campaign: U.S. Presidential Elections and the National Vote.* College Station: Texas A&M University Press.

Campbell, James E., and James Garand. 2000. *Before the Vote: Forecasting American National Elections.* Thousand Oaks, Calif.: Sage.

Campbell, James E., and Kenneth A. Wink. 1990. "Trial-Heat Forecasts of the Presidential Votes." *American Politics Quarterly* 18: 251–269.

Canon, David T. 1993. "Sacrificial Lambs or Strategic Politicians? Political Amateurs in U.S. House Elections." *American Journal of Political Science Review* 37: 1119–1141.

Cantril, Hadley, with Mildred Strunk. 1951. *Public Opinion, 1935–1946*. Princeton: Princeton University Press.

Caplow, Theodore, Howard M. Bahr, John Modell, and Bruce A. Chadwick. 1991. *Recent Social Trends in the United States: 1960–1990*. Montreal: McGill-Queen's University Press.

Carey, John M., Richard G. Niemi, and Lynda W. Powell. 2000. *Term Limits in the State Legislatures*. Ann Arbor: University of Michigan Press.

_____. 2000. "Incumbency and the Probability of Reelection in State Legislative Elections." *Journal of Politics* 62: 671–700.

Carmines, Edward G., John P. McIver, and James A. Stimson. 1987. "Unrealized Partisanship: A Theory of Dealignment." *Journal of Politics* 49: 376–400.

Carmines, Edward G., and James A. Stimson. 1980. "The Two Faces of Issue Voting." *American Political Science Review* 74: 78–91.

_____. 1989. *Issue Evolution: Race and the Transformation of American Politics*. Princeton: Princeton University Press.

Carnegie Council on Adolescent Development. 1993. *A Matter of Time: Risk and Opportunity in the Nonschool Hours*. New York: Carnegie Corporation of New York.

Carsey, Thomas M., and Gerald C. Wright. 1998. "State and National Factors in Gubernatorial and Senatorial Elections." *American Journal of Political Science* 42: 994–1002.

Caspary, William R. 1970. "The 'Mood Theory': A Study of Public Opinion and Foreign Policy. *American Political Science Review* 64: 536–547.

Cassel, Carol A., and Robert C. Luskin. 1988. "Simple Explanations of Turnout Decline." *American Political Science Review* 82: 502–521.

Ceasar, James, and Andrew Busch. 1993. *Upside Down and Inside Out: The 1992 Elections and American Politics*. Lanham, Md.: Rowman and Littlefield.

Cells, William, III. 1993. "Study Says Half of Adults in U.S. Can't Read or Handle Arithmetic." *New York Times* September 9: A1, A22.

Chaiken, Shelly. 1979. "Heuristic versus Systematic Information Processing and the Use of Source versus Message Cues in Persuasion." *Journal of Personality and Social Psychology* 37: 1387–1397.

Chambers, William Nisbet, and Walter Dean Burnham, eds. 1975. *The American Party Systems*, 2nd ed. New York: Oxford University Press.

Chappell, Henry W., and William R. Keech. 1985. "A New View of Political Accountability for Economic Performance." *American Political Science Review* 79: 10–27.

Chappell, Henry W., and Motoshi Suzuki. 1993. "Aggregate Vote Functions for the U.S. Presidency, Senate, and House." *Journal of Politics* 55: 207–217.

Cho, Wendy K. Tam, and Brian J. Gaines. 2001. "Reassessing the Study of Split-Ticket Voting." *American Political Science Review* 95: forthcoming.

Chubb, John E. 1988. "Institutions, the Economy, and the Dynamics of State Elections." *American Political Science Review* 82: 133–154.

Clarke, Harold D., and Marianne C. Stewart. 1994. "Prospections, Retrospections, and Rationality: The 'Bankers' Model of Presidential Approval Reconsidered." *American Journal of Political Science* 38: 1104–1123.

Clarke, Harold D., and Motoshi Suzuki. 1993. "Partisan Dealignment and the Dynamics of Independence in the American Electorate, 1953–88." *British Journal of Political Science* 24: 57–77.

Clubb, Jerome M., William H. Flanigan, and Nancy H. Zingale. 1980. *Partisan Realignment: Voters, Parties, and Government in American History.* Beverly Hills, Calif.: Sage.

Cohen, Jacob, and Patricia Cohen. 1983. *Applied Multiple Regression/Correlation Analysis for the Behavioral Sciences,* 2nd ed. Hillsdale, N.J.: Lawrence Erlbaum.

Coleman, James. 1990. *Foundations of Social Theory.* Cambridge: Harvard University Press.

Coleman, John J. 1996. *Party Decline in America: Policy, Politics, and the Fiscal State.* Princeton: Princeton University Press.

_____. 1999. "Unified Government, Divided Government, and Party Responsiveness." *American Political Science Review* 93: 821–835.

Comstock, George. 1989. *The Evolution of American Television.* Newbury Park, Calif.: Sage.

Comstock, George, Steven Chaffee, Nathan Katzman, Maxwell McCombs, and Donald Roberts. 1978. *Television and Human Behavior.* New York: Columbia University Press.

Condorcet, Marie-Jean-Antoine-Nicolas Caritat, Marquis de. 1785. *Essai sur l'application de l'analyse a la probabilité des decisions rendues a la pluralite des voix.* New York: Chelsea, 1972. Portions translated by Baker (1976).

Condry, John. 1993. "Thief of Time, Unfaithful Servant: Television and the American Child." *Daedalus* 122: 259–278.

Connolly, William E. 1972. "On 'Interests' in Politics." *Politics and Society* 2: 459–477.

Conover, Pamela Johnston, and Stanley Feldman. 1989. "Candidate Perception in an Ambiguous World: Campaigns, Cues and Inference Processes." *American Journal of Political Science* 33: 912–940.

Converse, Philip E. 1964. "The Nature of Belief Systems in Mass Publics." In *Ideology and Discontent,* ed. David E. Apter. New York: Free Press.

_____. 1966. "On the Possibility of Major Political Realignment in the South." In *The American Voter,* Angus Campbell, Philip E. Converse, Warren E. Miller, and Donald E. Stokes. New York: Wiley.

_____. 1969. "Of Time and Partisan Stability." *Comparative Political Studies* 2: 139–171.

_____. 1970. "Attitudes and Nonattitudes: Continuation of a Dialogue." In *The Quantitative Analysis of Social Problems,* ed. Edward Tufte. Reading, Mass.: Addison-Wesley.

_____. 1974. "Comment on Burnham's 'Theory and Voting Research.'" *American Political Science Review* 68: 1024–1027.

_____. 1976. *The Dynamics of Party Support: Cohort-Analyzing Party Identification.* Beverly Hills, Calif.: Sage.

_____. 1990. "Popular Representation and the Distribution of Information." In *Information and Democratic Processes,* ed. John A. Ferejohn and James H. Kuklinski. Urbana: University of Illinois Press.

Converse, Philip E., and Gregory B. Markus. 1979a. *"Plus ça Change. . . :* The New CPS Election Study Panel." *American Political Science Review* 73: 32–49.

Converse, Philip E., and Roy Pierce. 1985. "Measuring Partisanship." *Political Methodology* 11: 143–166.

_____. 1986. *Political Representation in France.* Cambridge: Harvard University Press.

Cooper, Barry, Allan Kornberg, and William Mishler. 1988. "The Reagan Years: Turning to the Right or Groping Toward the Middle?" In *The Resurgence of Conservatism in Anglo-American Democracies,* ed. Barry Cooper, Allan Kornberg, and William Mishler. Durham, N.C.: Duke University Press.

Cotter, Cornelius P., James L. Gibson, John F. Bibby, and Robert J. Huckshorn. 1984. *Party Organizations in American Politics.* New York: Praeger.

Cox, Gary W. 1999. "Electoral Rules and the Calculus of Mobilization." *Legislative Studies Quarterly* 24: 387–419.

Cox, Gary W., and Jonathan N. Katz. 1996. "Why Did the Incumbency Advantage in U.S. House Elections Grow?" *American Journal of Political Science* 40: 478–497.

Cox, Gary W., and Samuel Kernell, eds. 1991. *The Politics of Divided Government.* Boulder, Colo.: Westview.

Craig, Stephen C. 1996. "The Angry Voter: Politics and Popular Discontent in the 1960s." In *Broken Contract?* ed. Stephen C. Craig. Boulder, Colo.: Westview.

Craig, Stephen C., Richard Niemi, and Glenn E. Silver. 1990. "Political Efficacy and Trust: A Report on the NES Pilot Study Items." *Political Behavior* 12: 289–314.

Craik, Fergus I. M., and Robert S. Lockhart. 1972. "Levels of Processing: A Framework for Memory Research." *Journal of Verbal Learning and Verbal Behavior* 11: 671–684.

Crewe, Ivor. 1981. "Electoral Participation." In *Democracy at the Polls,* ed. David Butler, Howard Penniman, and Austin Ranney. Washington, D.C.: American Enterprise Institute.

Crewe, Ivor, and David Denver, eds. 1985. *Electoral Change in Western Democracies.* London: Croom Helm.

Crewe, Ivor, and Martin Harrop, eds. 1989. *Political Communications: The General Election Campaign of 1987.* Cambridge: Cambridge University Press.

Crotty, William, and John S. Jackson III. 1985. *Presidential Primaries and Nominations.* Washington, D.C.: CQ Press.

Cummings, Milton C., Jr. 1966. *Congressmen and the Electorate.* New York: Free Press.

Current Population Reports. 1995 (and earlier years). Washington, D.C.: U.S. Bureau of the Census.

Cutler, Blaine. 1990. "Where Does the Free Time Go?" *American Demographics* (November): 36–39.

Cutler, Neil E. 1969. "Generation, Maturation, Party Affiliation: A Cohort Analysis." *Public Opinion Quarterly* 33: 583–588.

Dahl, Robert A. 1961. *Who Governs? Democracy and Power in an American City.* New Haven: Yale University Press.

_____. 1989. *Democracy and Its Critics.* New Haven: Yale University Press.

Dalton, Russell J. 1984. "Cognitive Mobilization and Partisan Dealignment in Advanced Industrial Societies." *Journal of Politics* 46: 264–284.

_____. 1996a. *Citizen Politics: Public Opinion and Political Parties in Advanced Industrial Democracies,* 2nd ed. Chatham, N.J.: Chatham House.

_____. 1996b. "Political Cleavages, Issues, and Electoral Change." In *Comparing Democracies: Elections and Voting Behavior in Global Perspective,* ed. Lawrence LeDuc, Richard G. Niemi, and Pippa Norris. Thousand Oaks, Calif.: Sage.

_____. 2001. "The Decline of Party Identification." In *Parties without Partisans: Political Change in Advanced Industrial Democracies,* ed. Russell J. Dalton and Martin P. Wattenberg. Oxford: Oxford University Press.

Dalton, Russell J., Paul A. Beck, and Robert Huckfeldt. 1998. "Partisan Cues and the Media: Information Flows in the 1992 Presidential Election." *American Political Science Review* 92: 111–126.

Dalton, Russell J., Scott C. Flanagan, and Paul Allen Beck. 1984. *Electoral Change in Advanced Industrial Democracies: Realignment or Dealignment?* Princeton: Princeton University Press.

Dalton, Russell J., and Martin P. Wattenberg. 2001. "Partisan Change and the Democratic Process." In *Parties without Partisans: Political Change in Advanced Industrial Democracies,* ed. Russell J. Dalton and Martin P. Wattenberg. Oxford: Oxford University Press.

Davis, James A. 1980. "Conservative Weather in a Liberalizing Climate: Changes in Selected NORC General Social Survey Items, 1972–1978." *Social Forces* 58: 1129–1156.

Davis, James A., and Tom W. Smith. 1990. *General Social Surveys, 1972–90: Cumulative Codebook.* Chicago: National Opinion Research Center.

_____. *General Social Surveys, 1972–1994.* [machine readable data file]. NORC ed. Chicago: National Opinion Research Center, producer, 1994; Storrs, Conn.: The Roper Center for Public Opinion Research, University of Connecticut, distributor.

Dawes, Robyn M. 1988. *Rational Choice in an Uncertain World.* New York: Harcourt Brace Jovanovich.

Declerq, Eugene R., Thomas L. Hurley, and Norman R. Luttbeg. 1975. "Voting in American Presidential Elections: 1956–1972." *American Politics Quarterly* 3: 222–246.

DeHoog, Ruth Hoogland, David Lowery, and William E. Lyons. 1990. "Citizen Satisfaction with Local Governance: A Test of Individual, Jurisdictional, and City-Specific Explanations." *Journal of Politics* 52: 807–837.

Delli Carpini, Michael X., and Scott Keeter. 1991. "Stability and Change in the U.S. Public's Knowledge of Politics." *Public Opinion Quarterly* 55: 583–612.

_____. 1992. "An Analysis of Information Items on the 1990 and 1991 NES Surveys." Report to the Board of Overseers for the National Election Studies.

_____. 1993. "Measuring Political Knowledge: Putting First Things First." *American Journal of Political Science* 37: 1179–1206.

_____. 1995. "Political Knowledge and Enlightened Group Interests." Paper presented at the annual meeting of the American Political Science Association, Chicago.

_____. 1996. *What Americans Know about Politics and Why It Matters.* New Haven: Yale University Press.

Destler, I. M., Leslie H. Gelb, and Arthur Lake. 1984. *Our Own Worst Enemy: The Unmaking of American Foreign Policy.* New York: Simon and Schuster.

de Tocqueville, Alexis. 1945 [1835, 1840]. *Democracy in America.* 2 vols. New York: Vintage Books.

DeVries, Walter, and V. Lance Tarrance. 1972. *The Ticket-Splitter: A New Force in American Politics.* Grand Rapids, Mich.: William B. Eerdmans.

Dimock, Michael A., and Samuel L. Popkin. 1995. "Knowledge, Trust, and International Attitudes." Paper presented at the annual meeting of the American Political Science Association, Chicago.

Dobb, Anthony N., and Glenn F. Macdonald. 1979. "Television Viewing and Fear of Victimization: Is the Relationship Causal?" *Journal of Personality and Social Psychology* 37: 170–179.

Downs, Anthony. 1957. *An Economic Theory of Democracy.* New York: Harper and Row.

Dreyer, Edward C. 1973. "Change and Stability in Party Identification." *American Journal of Political Science* 35: 712–722.

Duncan, Otis Dudley, and Beverly Davis. 1953. "An Alternative to Ecological Correlation." *American Sociological Review* 18: 665–666.

Durr, Robert H. 1993. "What Moves Policy Sentiment?" *American Political Science Review* 87: 158–170.

Ebbinghaus, Hermann. 1964. *Memory: A Contribution to Experimental Psychology.* New York: Dover.

Edsall, Thomas Byrne, with Mary D. Edsall. 1991. *Chain Reaction: The Impact of Race, Rights, and Taxes on American Politics.* New York: Norton.

Edwards, George C., III. 1980. *Presidential Influence in Congress.* San Francisco: Freeman.

Edwards, George C., III, Andrew Barrett, and Jeffrey Peake. 1997. "The Legislative Impact of Divided Government." *American Journal of Political Science* 41: 545–563.

Edwards, Patricia Klobus, John N. Edwards, and Ann DeWitt Watts. 1984. "Women, Work, and Social Participation." *Journal of Voluntary Action Research* 13: 7–22.

Efron, Bradley, and Gail Gong. 1983. "A Leisurely Look at the Bootstrap, the Jackknife and Cross-Validation." *American Statistician* 37: 36–48.

Ehrenhalt, Alan. 1991. *The United States of Ambition: Politicians, Power, and the Pursuit of Office.* New York: Times Books.

Elazar, Daniel J. 1966. *American Federalism: A View from the States.* New York: Crowell.

Enelow, James M., and Melvin J. Hinich. 1984. *The Spatial Theory of Voting: An Introduction.* Cambridge: Cambridge University Press.

Entman, Robert M. 1989. *Democracy without Citizens: Media and the Decay of American Politics.* New York: Oxford University Press.

Erikson, Robert S. 1971. "The Advantage of Incumbency in Congressional Elections." *Polity* 3: 395–405.

———. 1982. "The 'Uncorrelated Errors' Approach to the Problem of Causal Feedback." *Journal of Politics* 44: 863–881.

———. 1988. "The Puzzle of Midterm Loss." *Journal of Politics* 50: 1011–1029.

———. 1989a. "Economic Conditions and the Presidential Vote." *American Political Science Review* 83: 567–573.

———. 1989b. "The Puzzle of Low Voter Turnout in the United States." In *Perspectives on American and Texas Politics,* 2nd ed., ed. Donald Lutz and Kent Tedin, Dubuque, Iowa: Kendal/Hunt.

———. 1990a. "Economic Conditions and the Congressional Vote: A Review of the Macro-Level Evidence." *American Journal of Political Science* 34: 373–399.

———. 1990b. "Roll Calls, Reputations, and Representation in the U.S. Senate." *Legislative Studies Quarterly* 15: 623–640.

———. 1995. "State Turnout and Presidential Voting: A Closer Look." *American Politics Quarterly* 23: 387–396.

Erikson, Robert S., Thomas D. Lancaster, and David W. Romero. 1989. "Group Components of the Presidential Vote, 1952–1984." *Journal of Politics* 51: 337–346.

Erikson, Robert S., and Norman R. Luttbeg. 1973. *American Public Opinion: Its Origins, Content, and Impact.* New York: Wiley.

Erikson, Robert S., Norman R. Luttbeg, and Kent L. Tedin. 1988. *American Public Opinion: Its Origins and Impact,* 3rd ed. New York: Macmillan.

Erikson, Robert S., Michael B. MacKuen, and James A. Stimson. 1996. "Party Identification and Macropartisanship: Resolving the Paradox of Micro-

Level Stability and Macro-Level Dynamics." Paper presented at the annual meeting of the American Political Science Association, San Francisco.

_____. 1998. "What Moves Macropartisanship? A Response to Green, Palmquist, and Schickler." *American Political Science Review* 92: 901–912.

Erikson, Robert S., and Thomas R. Palfrey. 1998. "Campaign Spending and Incumbency: An Alternative Simultaneous Equations Approach." *Journal of Politics* 60: 355–373.

Erskine, Hazel Gaudet. 1963. "The Polls: Textbook Knowledge." *Public Opinion Quarterly* 27: 133–141.

Eubank, Robert B., and David John Gow. 1983. "The Pro-Incumbent Bias in the 1978 and 1980 National Election Studies." *American Journal of Political Science* 27: 122–139.

Eulau, Heinz, and Michael S. Lewis-Beck. 1985. *Economic Conditions and Electoral Outcomes.* New York: Agathon.

Eysenck, Michael W., and Mark T. Keane. 1990. *Cognitive Psychology: A Student's Handbook.* Hillsdale, N.J.: Erlbaum.

Fair, Ray C. 1988. "The Effect of Economic Events on Votes for President: 1984 Update." *Political Behavior* 10: 168–179.

_____. 1996. "The Effect of Economic Events on Votes for President: 1992 Update." *Political Behavior* 18: 119–139.

Feigert, Frank B. 1979. "Illusions of Ticket-Splitting." *American Politics Quarterly* 7: 470–488.

Feld, Scott L., and Bernard Grofman. 1988. "Ideological Consistency as a Collective Phenomenon." *American Political Science Review* 82: 773–788.

Feldman, Stanley. 1988. "Structure and Consistency in Public Opinion: The Role of Core Beliefs and Values." *American Journal of Political Science* 32: 416–438.

_____. 1989. "Measuring Issue Preferences: The Problem of Response Instability." *Political Analysis* 1: 25–60.

Fenno, Richard F., Jr. 1978. *Home Style: House Members in Their Districts.* Boston: Little, Brown.

Ferejohn, John A., and Randall L. Calvert. 1984. "Presidential Coattails in Historical Perspective." *American Journal of Political Science* 28: 127–146.

Ferejohn, John A., and James H. Kuklinski, eds. 1990. *Information and Democratic Processes.* Urbana: University of Illinois Press.

Ferguson, Thomas, and Joel Rogers. 1986. *Right Turn: The Decline of Democrats and the Future of American Politics.* New York: Farrar, Strauss and Giroux.

Finkel, Steven E. 1993. "Reexamining the 'Minimal Effects' Model in Recent Presidential Campaigns." *Journal of Politics* 55: 1–21.

Finkel, Steven E., and John G. Geer. 1998. "A Spot Check: Casting Doubt on the Demobilization Hypothesis." *American Journal of Political Science* 42: 573–595.

Fiorina, Morris P. 1977. "An Outline for a Model of Party Choice." *American Journal of Political Science* 21: 601–626.

_____. 1978. "Economic Retrospective Voting in American National Elections: A Microanalysis." *American Journal of Political Science* 22: 426–443.

_____. 1981. *Retrospective Voting in American National Elections.* New Haven: Yale University Press.

_____. 1988. "The Reagan Years: Turning toward the Right or Groping toward the Middle." In *The Resurgence of Conservatism in Anglo-American Democracies,* ed. Barry Cooper, Allan Kornberg, and William Mishler. Durham, N.C.: Duke University Press.

_____. 1989. *Congress: Keystone of the Washington Establishment,* 2nd ed. New Haven: Yale University Press.

_____. 1994. "Response to Born." *Legislative Studies Quarterly* 19: 117–125.

_____. 1996. *Divided Government,* 2nd ed. Needham Heights, Mass.: Allyn and Bacon.

Fishkin, James S. 1991. *Democracy and Deliberation: New Directions for Democratic Reform.* New Haven: Yale University Press.

_____. 1995. *The Voice of the People: Public Opinion and Democracy.* New Haven: Yale University Press.

Fishman, Mark. 1980. *Manufacturing the News.* Austin: University of Texas Press.

Fiske, Susan T., Donald R. Kinder, and W. Michael Larter. 1983. "The Novice and the Expert: Knowledge-Based Strategies in Political Cognition." *Journal of Experimental Social Psychology* 19: 381–400.

Fiske, Susan T., Richard R. Lau, and Richard A. Smith. 1990. "On the Varieties and Utilities of Political Expertise." *Social Cognition* 8: 31–48.

Fiske, Susan T., and Shelly E. Taylor. 1991. *Social Cognition,* 2nd ed. New York: McGraw-Hill.

Flanigan, William H., Wendy M. Rahn, and Nancy H. Zingale. 1989. "Political Parties as Objects of Identification and Orientation." Paper presented at the annual meeting of the Western Political Science Association. Salt Lake City, Utah.

Franklin, Charles H. 1991. "Eschewing Obfuscation? Campaigns and the Perception of U.S. Senate Incumbents." *American Political Science Review* 85: 1193–1214.

Franklin, Charles H., and John E. Jackson. 1983. "The Dynamics of Party Identification." *American Political Science Review* 77: 957–973.

Franklin, Mark N. 1996. "Electoral Participation." In *Comparing Democracies: Elections and Voting in Global Perspective,* ed. Larry LeDuc, Richard G. Niemi, and Pippa Norris. Thousand Oaks, Calif.: Sage.

Franklin, Mark N., and Wolfgang P. Hirczy de Miño. 1998. "Separated Powers, Divided Government, and Turnout in U.S. Presidential Elections." *American Journal of Political Science* 42: 316–326.

Franklin, Mark, Thomas T. Mackie, Henry Valen, et al. 1992. *Electoral Change: Responses to Evolving Social and Attitudinal Structures in Western Countries.* Cambridge: Cambridge University Press.

Franklin, Mark, Richard G. Niemi, and Guy Whitten. 1994. "Two Faces of Tactical Voting." *British Journal of Political Science* 24: 549–557.

Franklin, Mark, Cees van der Eijk, and Erik Oppenhuis. 1995. "The Motivational Basis of Electoral Participation: European Elections Provide a Critical Test." Paper presented at the European Consortium for Political Research Joint Sessions Workshop, Bordeaux.

Freedman, Paul, and Ken Goldstein. 1999. "Measuring Media Exposure and the Effects of Negative Campaign Ads." *American Journal of Political Science* 43: 1189–1208.

Freeman, John R. 1983. "Granger Causality and the Time Series Analysis of Political Relationships." *American Journal of Political Science* 27: 327–358.

Freeman, John R., Daniel Houser, Paul M. Kellstedt, and John T. Williams. 1998. "Long-Memoried Processes, Unit Roots, and Causal Inference in Political Science." *American Journal of Political Science* 42: 1289–1327.

Frymer, Paul. 1994. "Ideological Consensus within Divided Party Government." *Political Science Quarterly* 109: 287–311.

Frymer, Paul, Thomas P. Kim, and Terri Bimes. 1997. "Party Elites, Ideological Voters, and Divided Party Government." *Legislative Studies Quarterly* 22: 195–216.

Fuchs, Peter, and Hans-Dieter Klingemann. 1995. "Citizens and the State: A Relationship Transformed." In *Citizens and State,* ed. Hans-Dieter Klingemann and Peter Fuchs. Oxford: Oxford University Press.

Fukuyama, Francis. 1995. *Trust: The Social Virtues and the Creation of Prosperity.* New York: Free Press.

Funk, Carolyn. 1996. "Understanding Trait Inferences in Candidate Images." In *Research in Micropolitics,* ed. Michael Delli Carpini, Leonie Huddy, and Robert Shapiro. Greenwich, Conn.: JAI.

Galderisi, Peter F., ed. 1996. *Divided Government: Change, Uncertainty, and the Constitutional Order.* Lanham, Md.: Rowman and Littlefield.

Gamm, Gerald H. 1989. *The Making of New Deal Democrats: Voting Behavior and Realignment in Boston, 1920–1940.* Chicago: University of Chicago Press.

Gans, Curtis B. 1978a. "MacNeil/Lehrer Report." Public Broadcasting Service, November 7.

_____. 1978b. "The Empty Ballot Box: Reflections on Nonvoters in America." *Public Opinion* 1, 4: 54–57.

_____. 1997. "It's Bruce Who Got the Turnout Story Wrong." *Public Perspective* 8: 44–48.

Gans, Herbert. 1979. *Deciding What's News.* New York: Vintage.

Gant, Michael, and Dwight Davis. 1984. "Mental Economy and Voter Rationality: The Informed Citizen Problem in Voting Research." *Journal of Politics* 46: 132–153.

Garand, James. 1991. "Electoral Marginality in State Legislative Elections." *Legislative Studies Quarterly* 16: 7–28.

Garand, James C., and Marci Glaslock Lichtl. 2000. "Explaining Divided Government in the United States: Testing an Intentional Model of Split-Ticket Voting." *British Journal of Political Science* 30: 173–191.

Geer, John G. 1992. "New Deal Issues and the American Electorate, 1952–1988." *Political Behavior* 14: 45–65.

_____. 1998. "Campaigns, Party Competition, and Political Advertising." In *Politicians and Party Politics,* ed. John G. Geer. Baltimore: Johns Hopkins University Press.

Gelman, Andrew, and Gary King. 1990. "Estimating Incumbency Advantage without Bias." *American Journal of Political Science* 34: 1142–1164.

_____. 1993. "Why Are American Election Polls so Variable when Votes Are so Predictable?" *British Journal of Political Science* 23: 409–451.

Gerber, Alan. 1998. "Estimating the Effect of Campaign Spending on Senate Election Outcomes Using Instrumental Variables." *American Political Science Review* 92: 401–411.

Gerber, Alan, and Donald P. Green. 1998. "Rational Learning and Partisan Attitudes." *American Journal of Political Science* 42: 794–818.

Gerber, Elisabeth R., and Arthur Lupia. 1993. "When Do Campaigns Matter? Informed Votes and the Responsiveness of Electoral Outcomes." Unpublished paper, California Institute of Technology and University of California, San Diego.

Gerbner, George, Larry Gross, Michael Morgan, and Nancy Signorielli. 1980. "The 'Mainstreaming' of America: Violence Profile No. 11." *Journal of Communication* 30: 10–29.

Gibson, James L., and Richard D. Bingham. 1985. *Civil Liberties and Nazis: The Skokie Free Speech Controversy.* New York: Praeger.

Gibson, James L., Cornelius P. Cotter, John F. Bibby, and Robert J. Huckshorn. 1983. "Assessing Party Organizational Strength." *American Journal of Political Science* 27: 193–222.

Gibson, John, and Anna Cielecka. 1995. "Economic Influences on the Political Support for Market Reform in Post-Communist Transitions: Some Evidence from the 1993 Polish Parliamentary Elections." *Europe-Asia Studies* 47: 765–785.

Giles, Micheal, and Marilyn Dantico. 1982. "Political Participation and the Neighborhood Social Context." *American Journal of Political Science* 26: 144–150.

Ginzberg, Eli. 1943. *The Unemployed.* New York: Harper and Brothers.

Glenn, Norval D. 1987. "Social Trends in the United States: Evidence from Sample Surveys." *Public Opinion Quarterly* 51: S109–S126.

Glynn, Carroll J., Susan Herbst, Garrett J. O'Keefe, and Robert Y. Shapiro. 1999. *Public Opinion.* Boulder, Colo.: Westview.

Goldberg, Arthur S. 1966. "Discerning a Causal Pattern among Data on Voting Behavior." *American Political Science Review* 60: 913–922.

Goodman, Leo. 1959. "Some Alternatives to Ecological Correlation." *American Journal of Sociology* 64: 610–624.

Gosnell, Harold. 1937. *Machine Politics: Chicago Model.* Chicago: University of Chicago Press.

Gow, David John, and Robert B. Eubank. 1984. "The Pro-Incumbent Bias in the 1982 National Election Study." *American Journal of Political Science* 28: 224–230.

Graber, Doris A. 1984. *Processing the News: How People Tame the Information Tide.* New York: Longman.

_____. 1993. *Mass Media and American Politics.* Washington, D.C.: CQ Press.

Granger, Clive W. J. 1969. "Investigating Causal Relations by Econometric Models and Cross Spectral Methods." *Econometrica* 37: 424–438.

Green, Donald Philip. 1988. "On the Dimensionality of Public Sentiment toward Partisan and Ideological Groups." *American Journal of Political Science* 32: 758–780.

Green, Donald Philip, and Jonathan S. Krasno. 1988. "Salvation for the Spend-thrift Incumbent: Reestimating the Effects of Campaign Spending in House Elections." *American Journal of Political Science* 32: 884–907.

Green, Donald Philip, and Bradley Palmquist. 1990. "Of Artifacts and Partisan Instability." *American Journal of Political Science* 34: 872–902.

_____. 1994. "How Stable Is Party Identification?" *Political Behavior* 16: 437–466.

Green, Donald Philip, Bradley Palmquist, and Eric Schickler. 1998. "Macropartisanship: A Replication and Critique." *American Political Science Review* 92: 883–899.

Green, Donald Philip, and Eric Schickler. 1993. "Multiple-Measure Assessment of Party Identification." *Public Opinion Quarterly* 57: 503–535.

Greenberg, Edward S., and Benjamin I. Page. 1997. *The Struggle for Democracy,* 3rd ed. New York: Longman.

Greene, Steven H. 1999. "Understanding Party Identification: A Social Identity Approach." *Political Psychology* 20: 393–403.

Greenstein, Fred I. 1965. *Children and Politics.* New Haven: Yale University Press.

Grier, Kevin B., and Joseph P. McGarrity. 1998. "The Effect of Macroeconomic Fluctuations on the Electoral Fortunes of House Incumbents." *Journal of Law and Economics* 41: 143–161.

Grofman, Bernard, William Koetzle, Michael McDonald, and Thomas L. Brunell. 2000. "A New Look at Split-Ticket Outcomes for House and President: The Comparative Midpoints Model." *Journal of Politics* 62: 34–50.

Grofman, Bernard, and Guillermo Owen, eds. 1986. *Information Pooling and Group Decision Making.* Greenwich, Conn.: JAI Press.

Haller, Brandon H., and Helmut Norpoth. 1994. "Let the Good Times Roll: The Economic Expectations of U.S. Voters." *American Journal of Political Science* 38: 625–650.

Hamilton, Alexander, James Madison, and John Jay. 1961 [1787–1788]. *The Federalist Papers.* Clinton Rossiter, ed. New York: New American Library.

Hanson, Russell L., and George E. Marcus. 1993. "Introduction: The Practice of Democratic Theory." In *Reconsidering the Democratic Public,* ed. George E. Marcus and Russell L. Hanson. University Park: Pennsylvania State University Press.

Hastie, Reid, and Bernadette Park. 1986. "The Relationship between Memory and Judgments Depends on whether the Task Is Memory-Based or On-Line." *Psychological Review* 93: 258–268.

Hastie, Reid, and Nancy Pennington. 1989. "Notes on the Distinction between Memory-Based versus On-Line Judgments." In *On-Line Cognition in Person Perception,* ed. John N. Bassili. Hillsdale, N.J.: Erlbaum.

Haynes, Stephen, and David Jacobs. 1994. "Macroeconomics, Economic Stratification, and Partisanship: A Longitudinal Analysis of Contingent Shifts in Political Identification." *American Journal of Sociology* 99: 70–103.

Heckelman, Jac C. 2000. "Revisiting the Relationship between Secret Ballots and Turnout: A New Test of Two Legal-Institutional Theories." *American Politics Quarterly* 28: 194–215.

Heise, David R. 1971. "Separating Reliability and Stability in Test-Retest Correlation." In *Causal Models in the Social Sciences,* ed. Hubert M. Blalock. Chicago: Aldine.

Herrnson, Paul S. 1988. *Party Campaigning in the 1980s.* Cambridge: Harvard University Press.

_____. 1994. "The Revitalization of National Party Organizations." In *The Parties Respond: Changes in the American Party System,* 2nd ed., ed. Louis S. Maisel. Boulder, Colo.: Westview.

_____. 1997. *Congressional Elections: Campaigning at Home and in Washington,* 2nd ed. Washington, D.C: CQ Press.

Herrnson, Paul S., Kelly D. Patterson, and John J. Pitney Jr. 1996. "From Ward Heelers to Public Relations Experts: The Parties' Response to Mass Politics." In *Broken Contract?* ed. Stephen C. Craig. Boulder, Colo.: Westview.

Hess, Stephen, and Michael Nelson. 1985. "Foreign Policy: Dominance and Decisiveness in Presidential Elections." In *Elections of 1984,* ed. Michael Nelson. Washington, D.C.: CQ Press.

Hibbing, John R., and Elizabeth Theiss-Morse. 1995. *Congress as Public Enemy: Public Attitudes toward American Political Institutions.* New York: Cambridge University Press.

Hibbs, Douglas A., Jr. 1982. "On the Demand for Economic Outcomes: Macroeconomic Outcomes and Mass Political Support in the United States, Great Britain, and Germany." *Journal of Politics* 44: 426–462.

Hicks, Alexander H., and Duane H. Swank. 1992. "Politics, Institutions, and Welfare Spending in Industrialized Democracies, 1960–1982." *American Political Science Review* 86: 658–674.

Highton, Benjamin, and Raymond E. Wolfinger. 1998. "Estimating the Effects of the National Voter Registration Act of 1993." *Political Behavior* 20: 79–104.

Hill, Stuart. 1992. *Democratic Values and Technological Choices.* Stanford: Stanford University Press.

Hirczy, Wolfgang. 1992. "Electoral Participation." Ph.D. diss., University of Houston.

_____. 1995. "Explaining Near-Universal Turnout: The Case of Malta." *European Journal of Political Research* 27: 255–272.

Hirsch, Paul M. 1980. "The 'Scary World' of the Nonviewer and Other Anomalies: A Reanalysis of Gerbner et al.'s Findings on Cultivation Analysis, Part I." *Communication Research* 7: 403–456.

Hochschild, Jennifer. 1981. *What's Fair? Americans' Attitudes toward Distributive Justice.* Cambridge: Harvard University Press.

Holbrook, Thomas M. 1996a. *Do Campaigns Matter?* Thousand Oaks, Calif.: Sage.

_____. 1996b. "Reading the Political Tea Leaves: A Forecasting Model of Contemporary Presidential Elections." *American Politics Quarterly* 24: 506–519.

Holmberg, Sören. 1981. "Party Identification Compared across the Atlantic." In *Elections at Home and Abroad,* ed. M. Kent Jennings and Thomas E. Mann. Ann Arbor: University of Michigan Press.

Horn, Randolph E., and M. Margaret Conway. 1996. "Public Judgment and Political Engagement in the 1992 Election." In *Broken Contract?* ed. Stephen C. Craig. Boulder, Colo.: Westview.

Huckfeldt, Robert. 1979. "Political Participation and the Neighborhood Social Context." *American Journal of Political Science* 23: 579–592.

_____. 1986. *Politics in Context: Assimilation and Conflict in Urban Neighborhoods.* New York: Agathon.

Huckfeldt, Robert, and John Sprague. 1995. *Citizens, Politics, and Social Communication: Information and Influence in an Election Campaign.* New York: Cambridge University Press.

Hughes, Michael. 1980. "The Fruits of Cultivation Analysis: A Re-examination of the Effects of Television Watching on Fear of Victimization, Alienation, and the Approval of Violence." *Public Opinion Quarterly* 44: 287–303.

Huntington, Samuel P. 1968. *Political Order in Changing Societies.* New Haven: Yale University Press.

Ingberman, Daniel, and John Villani. 1993. "An Institutional Theory of Divided Government and Party Polarization." *American Journal of Political Science* 37: 429–471.

Inglehart, Ronald. 1977. *Silent Revolution: Changing Values and Political Styles among Western Publics.* Princeton: Princeton University Press.

_____. 1990. *Cultural Shift in Advanced Industrial Society.* Princeton: Princeton University Press.

_____. 1997. *Modernization and Postmaterialism: Cultural, Economic, and Political Change in 43 Societies.* Princeton: Princeton University Press.

Inglehart, Ronald, and Avram Hochstein. 1972. "Alignment and Dealignment of the Electorate in France and the United States." *Comparative Political Studies* 5: 343–372.

Iyengar, Shanto. 1991. *Is Anyone Responsible? How Television News Frames Political Issues.* Chicago: University of Chicago Press.

Iyengar, Shanto, and Donald R. Kinder. 1987. *News That Matters: Agenda-Setting and Priming in a Television Age.* Chicago: University of Chicago Press.

Jackman, Robert W. 1987. "Political Institutions and Voter Turnout in the Industrial Democracies." *American Political Science Review* 81: 405–423.

Jackman, Robert W., and Ross A. Miller. 1995. "Voter Turnout in the Industrial Democracies during the 1980s." *Comparative Political Studies* 27: 467–492.

Jackson, John E. 1975. "Issues, Party Choice, and Presidential Votes." *American Journal of Political Science* 19: 161–185.

Jackson, Robert A., and Thomas M. Carsey. 1999. "Group Components of U.S. Presidential Voting across the States." *Political Behavior* 21: 123–151.

Jacobson, Gary C. 1978. "The Effects of Campaign Spending in Congressional Elections." *American Political Science Review* 72: 769–783.

_____. 1987. "The Marginals Never Vanished: Incumbency and Competition in Elections to the U.S. House of Representatives." *American Journal of Political Science* 31: 126–141.

_____. 1990a. "Does the Economy Matter in Midterm Elections?" *American Journal of Political Science* 34: 400–404.

_____. 1990b. "The Effects of Campaign Spending in House Elections: New Evidence for Old Arguments." *American Journal of Political Science* 34: 334–362.

_____. 1990c. *The Electoral Origins of Divided Government.* Boulder, Colo.: Westview.

_____. 1991. "The Persistence of Democratic House Majorities." In *The Politics of Divided Government.* ed. Gary W. Cox and Samuel Kernell. Boulder, Colo.: Westview Press.

_____. 1996. "The 1994 House Elections In Perspective." *Political Science Quarterly* 111: 203–223.

_____. 1997. *The Politics of Congressional Elections,* 4th ed. Boston: Addison-Wesley.

Jacobson, Gary C., and Samuel Kernell. 1983. *Strategy and Change in Congressional Elections.* New Haven: Yale University Press.

Jacobson, Gary C., and Douglas Rivers. 1993. "Explaining the Overreport for the Incumbent in the National Election Studies." Paper presented at the annual meeting of the Western Political Science Association, Pasadena, Calif.

Jahoda, Marie, Paul Lazarsfeld, and Hans Zeisel. 1933. *Marienthal.* Chicago: Aldine-Atherton.

Jennings, M. Kent, and Gregory B. Markus. 1984. "Partisan Orientation over the Long Haul: Results from the Three-Wave Political Socialization Panel Study." *American Political Science Review* 78: 1000–1018.

Jennings, M. Kent, and Richard G. Niemi. 1968. "The Transmission of Political Values between Parent and Child." *American Political Science Review* 62: 169–184.

_____. 1974. *The Political Character of Adolescence.* Princeton: Princeton University Press.

_____. 1975. "Continuity and Change in Political Orientations: A Longitudinal Study of Two Generations." *American Political Science Review* 69: 1316–1335.

_____. 1978. "The Persistence of Political Orientations: An Over-Time Analysis of Two Generations." *British Journal of Political Science* 8: 333–363.

_____. 1981. *Generations and Politics.* Princeton: Princeton University Press.

Jensen, Richard. 1981. "The Last Party System: Decay of Consensus, 1932–1980." In *The Evolution of American Electoral Systems,* ed. Paul Kleppner. Westport, Conn.: Greenwood Press.

Johnston, Richard. 1992a. "Party Identification and Campaign Dynamics." *Political Behavior* 14: 311–331.

_____. 1992b. "Party Identification Measures in the Anglo-American Democracies: A National Survey Experiment." *American Journal of Political Science* 36: 542–559.

Johnston, Ron, Charles Pattie, Daniel Dorling, Iain MacAllister, Helena Tunstall, and David Rossiter. 2000. "Local Context, Retrospective Economic Evaluations, and Voting: The 1997 General Election in England and Wales." *Political Behavior* 22: 121–143.

Jones, Charles O. 1981. "New Directions in U.S. Congressional Research." *Legislative Studies Quarterly* 6: 455–468.

Kahn, Kim Fridkin, and Patrick J. Kenney. 1997. "A Model of Candidate Evaluations in Senate Elections: The Impact of Campaign Intensity." *Journal of Politics* 59: 1173–1205.

_____. 1999. "Do Negative Campaigns Mobilize or Suppress Turnout? Clarifying the Relationship between Negativity and Participation." *American Political Science Review* 93: 877–889.

Kahneman, Daniel, Paul Slovic, and Amos Tversky, eds. 1982. *Judgement under Uncertainty: Heuristics and Biases.* New York: Cambridge.

Karatnycky, Adam. 1995. "Democracies on the Rise: Democracies at Risk." *Freedom Review* 26: 5–10.

Katz, Elihu, and Paul Lazarsfeld. 1955. *Personal Influence.* New York: Free Press.

Katz, Richard. 1997. *Democracy and Elections.* New York: Oxford University Press.

Kaufmann, Karen M., and John R. Petrocik. 1999. "The Changing Politics of American Men: Understanding the Sources of the Gender Gap." *American Journal of Political Science* 43: 864–887.

Kayden, Xandra, and Eddie Mahe Jr. 1985. *The Party Goes On: The Persistence of the Two-Party System in the United States.* New York: Basic Books.

Keech, William R. 1982. "Of Honeymoons and Economic Performance: Comment on Hibbs." *American Political Science Review* 77: 92–111.

Keith, Bruce E., David B. Magleby, Candice J. Nelson, Elizabeth Orr, Mark C. Westlye, and Raymond E. Wolfinger 1977. "The Myth of the Independent Voter." Paper at the annual meeting of the American Political Science Association.

_____. 1992. *The Myth of the Independent Voter.* Berkeley: University of California Press.

Kelley, Stanley, Jr. 1983. *Interpreting Elections.* Princeton: Princeton University Press.

Kelley, Stanley, Jr., and Thad W. Mirer. 1974. "The Simple Act of Voting." *American Political Science Review* 68: 572–591.

Kelly, Caroline. 1988. "Intergroup Differentiation in a Political Context." *British Journal of Social Psychology* 27: 319–332.

_____. 1989. "Political Identity and Perceived Intragroup Homogeneity." *British Journal of Social Psychology* 28: 239–250.

Kelly, Sean Q. 1993. "Divided We Govern: A Reassessment." *Polity* 25: 475–484.

Kenny, Christopher. 1992. "Political Participation and Effects from the Social Environment." *American Journal of Political Science* 36: 259–267.

Kenski, Henry. 1977. "The Impact of Economic Conditions on Presidential Popularity." *Journal of Politics* 39: 764–773.

Kernell, Samuel. 1978. "Explaining Presidential Popularity." *American Political Science Review* 72: 506–522.

Kessel, John H. 1988. *Presidential Campaign Politics.* Homewood, Ill.: Dorsey.

Kessel, John H., and Herbert F. Weisberg. 1999. "Comparing Models of the Vote: The Answers Depend on the Questions." In *Reelection 1996: How Americans Voted,* ed. Herbert F. Weisberg and Janet M. Box-Steffensmeier. New York: Chatham House.

Key, V. O., Jr. 1955. "A Theory of Critical Elections." *Journal of Politics* 17: 3–18.

_____. 1959. "Secular Realignment and the Party System." *Journal of Politics* 21: 198–210.

_____. 1961. *Public Opinion and American Democracy.* New York: Knopf.

_____. 1964. *Politics, Parties, and Pressure Groups,* 5th ed. New York: Crowell.

_____. 1966. *The Responsible Electorate: Rationality in Presidential Voting, 1936–1960.* Cambridge: Harvard University Press.

Key, V. O., Jr., and Frank Munger. 1959. "Social Determinism and Electoral Decision: The Case of Indiana." In *American Voting Behavior,* ed. Eugene Burdick and Arthur Brodbeck. Glencoe, Ill.: Free Press.

Kiewiet, D. Roderick. 1983. *Macroeconomics and Micropolitics: The Electoral Effects of Economic Issues.* Chicago: University of Chicago Press.

Kiewiet, D. Roderick, and Douglas Rivers. 1985. "A Retrospective on Retrospective Voting." In *Economic Conditions and Electoral Outcomes,* ed. Heinz Eulau and Michael S. Lewis-Beck. New York: Agathon.

Kimball, David C. 1997. "The Divided Voter in American Politics." Ph.D. diss., Ohio State University.

Kinder, Donald R. 1986. "Presidential Character Revisited." In *Political Cognitions,* ed. Richard R. Lau and David Sears. Hillsdale, N.J.: Lawrence Erlbaum.

Kinder, Donald R., and D. Roderick Kiewiet. 1981. "Sociotropic Politics: The American Case." *British Journal of Political Science* 11: 129–162.

Kinder, Donald R., and Thomas R. Palfrey. 1993. "On Behalf of an Experimental Political Science." In *Experimental Foundations of Political Science,* ed. Donald Kinder and Thomas Palfrey. Ann Arbor: University of Michigan Press.

Kinder, Donald R., and David O. Sears. 1985. "Public Opinion and Political Action." In *Handbook of Social Psychology,* ed. Gardner Lindzey and Eliot Aronson. New York: Random House.

King, Gary. 1989. *Unifying Political Methodology: The Likelihood Theory of Statistical Inference.* Cambridge: Cambridge University Press.

_____. 1997. *A Solution to the Ecological Inference Problem: Reconstructing Individual Behavior from Aggregate Data.* Princeton: Princeton University Press.

King, Gary, Robert O. Keohane, and Sidney Verba. 1994. *Designing Social Inquiry: Scientific Inference in Qualitative Research.* Princeton: Princeton University Press.

Knight, Kathleen, and Robert S. Erikson. 1997. "Ideology in the 1990s." In *Understanding Public Opinion,* ed. Barbara Norrander and Clyde Wilcox. Washington, D.C.: CQ Press.

Knoke, David, and Michael Hout. 1974. "Social and Demographic Factors in American Political Party Affiliations, 1952–72." *American Sociological Review* 39: 700–713.

Koch, Jeffrey W. 1998. "Electoral Competitiveness and the Voting Decision: Evidence from the Pooled Senate Election Study." *Political Behavior* 20: 295–311.

Kramer, Gerald H. 1971. "Short-Term Fluctuations in U.S. Voting Behavior, 1896–1964." *American Political Science Review* 65: 131–143.

_____. 1983. "The Ecological Fallacy Revisited: Aggregate- versus Individual-Level Findings on Economics and Elections and Sociotropic Voting." *American Political Science Review* 77: 92–111.

Krasno, Jonathan S. 1994. *Challengers, Competition, and Reelection.* New Haven: Yale University Press.

Krehbiel, Keith. 1998. *Pivotal Politics: A Theory of U.S. Lawmaking.* Chicago: University of Chicago Press.

Krosnick, Jon A., and Laura A. Brannon. 1993. "The Impact of the Gulf War on the Ingredients of Presidential Evaluations: Multidimensional Effects of Political Involvement." *American Political Science Review* 87: 963–975.

Krosnick, Jon A., and Donald R. Kinder. 1990. "Altering the Foundation of Support of the President through Priming." *American Political Science Review* 84: 497–512.

Krosnick, Jon A., and Michael Milburn. 1990. "Psychological Determinants of Political Opinionation." *Social Cognition* 8: 49–72.

Kuklinski, James H., and Norman H. Hurley. 1994. "On Hearing and Interpreting Political Messages: A Cautionary Tale of Citizen Cue-Taking." *Journal of Politics* 56: 729–751.

Kunda, Ziva. 1990. "The Case for Motivated Reasoning." *Psychological Bulletin* 108: 480–498.

Lachman, Roy, Janet Lachman, and Earl Butterfield. 1979. *Cognitive Psychology and Information Processing.* Hillsdale, N.J.: Erlbaum.

Lacy, Dean. 1994. "Nonseparable Preferences in Politics." Ph.D. diss., Duke University.

_____. 1998. "Congressional Elections: Progenitors of Divided Government." In *Great Theatre: The American Congress in the 1990s,* ed. Herbert F. Weisberg and Samuel C. Patterson. Cambridge: Cambridge University Press.

Lacy, Dean, and Barry C. Burden. 1999. "The Vote-Stealing and Turnout Effects of Ross Perot in the 1992 U.S. Presidential Election." *American Journal of Political Science* 43: 233–255.

Lacy, Dean, and J. Tobin Grant. 1999. "The Impact of the Economy on the 1996 Election." In *Reelection 1996: How Americans Voted,* ed. Herbert F. Weisberg and Janet M. Box-Steffensmeier. Chatham, N.J.: Chatham House.

Lacy, Dean, and Philip Paolino. 1998. "Downsian Voting and the Separation of Power." *American Journal of Political Science* 42: 1180–1199.

Ladd, Everett Carll. 1983. "Public Opinion: Questions at the Quinquennial." *Public Opinion* 6: 20, 41.

_____. 1990. "Public Opinion and the 'Congress Problem.'" *The Public Interest* 100: 66–67.

_____. 1991. "Like Waiting for Godot: The Uselessness of 'Realignment' for Understanding Change in Contemporary American Politics." In *The End of Realignment? Interpreting American Electoral Eras,* ed. Byron E. Shafer. Madison: University of Wisconsin Press.

_____. 1999. *The Ladd Report.* New York: Free Press.

Ladha, Krishna K. 1992. "The Condorcet Jury Theorem, Free Speech, and Correlated Votes." *American Journal of Political Science* 36: 617–634.

LaPiere, R. T. 1934. "Attitudes vs. Action." *Social Forces* 13: 230–237.

Lau, Richard R. 1982. "Negativity in Political Perceptions." *Political Behavior* 4: 353–377.

_____. 1985. "Changing Perspectives on Political Thinking." Paper presented at the annual meeting of the American Political Science Association, New Orleans.

_____. 1986. "Political Schemata, Candidate Evaluations, and Voting Behavior." In *Political Cognition: The 19th Annual Carnegie Symposium on Cognition,* ed. Richard R. Lau and David O. Sears. Hillsdale, N.J.: Lawrence Erlbaum.

_____. 1989. "Construct Accessibility and Electoral Choice." *Political Behavior* 11: 5–32.

_____. 1992. "Searchable Information during an Election Campaign." Unpublished manuscript. Rutgers University.

_____. 1995. "Information Search during an Election Campaign: Introducing a Process Tracing Methodology for Political Scientists." In *Political Information Processing,* ed. Milton Lodge and Kathleen McGraw. Ann Arbor: University of Michigan Press.

Lau, Richard R., and David P. Redlawsk. 1992. "How Voters Decide: A Process Tracing Study of Decision Making during Political Campaigns." Paper presented at the annual meeting of the American Political Science Association, Chicago.

_____. 1997. "Voting Correctly." *American Political Science Review* 91: 585–598.

_____. 2001. "An Experimental Study of Information Search, Memory, and Decision Making during a Political Campaign." In *Citizens and Politics: Perspectives from Political Psychology,* ed. James Kuklinski. Cambridge: Cambridge University Press.

Lau, Richard R., and David O. Sears, eds. 1986. *Political Cognition: The 19th Annual Carnegie Symposium on Cognition.* Hillsdale, N.J.: Lawrence Erlbaum.

Lau, Richard R., Lee Sigelman, Caroline Heldman, and Paul Babbitt. 1999. "The Effects of Negative Political Advertisements: A Meta-Analytic Assessment." *American Political Science Review* 93: 851–876.

Layman, Geoffrey C. 1997. "Religion and Political Behavior in the United States: The Impact of Beliefs, Affiliations, and Commitment from 1980 to 1994." *Public Opinion Quarterly* 61: 288–316.

Layman, Geoffrey C., and Edward G. Carmines. 1997. "Cultural Conflict in American Politics: Religious Traditionalism, Postmaterialism, and U.S. Political Behavior." *Journal of Politics* 59: 751–777.

Lazarsfeld, Paul, Bernard Berelson, and Hazel Gaudet. 1944, 1948. *The People's Choice: How the Voter Makes Up His Mind in a Presidential Campaign.* New York: Duell, Sloan, and Pearce; Columbia University Press.

LeDuc, Lawrence. 1981. "The Dynamic Properties of Party Identification: A Four-Nation Comparison." *European Journal of Political Research* 9: 257–268.

LeDuc, Lawrence, Richard G. Niemi, and Pippa Norris, eds. 1996. *Comparing Democracies: Elections and Voting in Comparative Perspective.* Thousand Oaks, Calif.: Sage.

Lee, Eun Sul, Ronald N. Forthofer, and Ronald J. Lorimor. 1989. *Analyzing Complex Survey Data.* Newbury Park, Calif.: Sage.

Leege, David C., and Lyman Kellstedt, eds. 1993. *Rediscovering the Religious Factor in American Politics.* Armonk, N.Y.: M. E. Sharpe.

Leighley, Jan. 1990. "Social Interaction and Contextual Influences on Political Participation." *American Politics Quarterly* 18: 459–475.

Leithner, Christian. 1997. "Of Time and Partisan Stability Revisited: Australia and New Zealand 1905–90." *American Journal of Political Science* 41: 1104–1127.

Levine, Jeffrey, Edward G. Carmines, and Robert Huckfeldt. 1997. "The Rise of Ideology in the Post-New Deal Party System, 1972–1992." *American Politics Quarterly* 25: 19–34.

Levitt, Steven D., and Catherine D. Wolfram. 1997. "Decomposing the Sources of Incumbency Advantage in the U.S. House." *Legislative Studies Quarterly* 22: 45–60.

Lewis-Beck, Michael S. 1988. *Economics and Elections: The Major Western Democracies.* Ann Arbor: University of Michigan Press.

———. 1991. "Introduction." In *Economics and Politics: The Calculus of Support,* ed. Helmut Norpoth, Michael S. Lewis-Beck, and Jean-Dominique Lafay. Ann Arbor: University of Michigan Press.

Lewis-Beck, Michael S., and Martin Paldam, eds. 2000. "Economics and Elections." *Electoral Studies* (special issue) 19 (June/September).

Lewis-Beck, Michael S., and Tom Rice. 1992. *Forecasting Elections.* Washington, D.C.: CQ Press.

Lewis-Beck, Michael S., and Andrew Skalaban. 1989. "Citizen Forecasting: Can Voters See into the Future?" *British Journal of Political Science* 19: 146–153.

Lewis-Beck, Michael S., and Charles Tien. 1996. "The Future in Forecasting: Prospective Presidential Models." *American Politics Quarterly* 24: 468–491.

Lichtenstein, Meryl, and Thomas Srull. 1987. "Objectives as Determinants of the Relationship between Recall and Judgment." *Journal of Experimental Social Psychology* 23: 93–118.

Lijphart, Arend. 1997. "Unequal Participation: Democracy's Unresolved Dilemma." *American Political Science Review* 91: 1–14.

Lindblom, Charles E. 1965. *The Intelligence of Democracy.* New York: Free Press.

Lippmann, Walter. 1955. *Essays in the Public Philosophy.* Boston: Little, Brown.

———. 1991 [1922]. *Public Opinion.* New Brunswick: Transaction.

Lipset, Seymour Martin. 1976. "The Wavering Polls." *Public Interest* 43: 70–89.

Little, Roderick J. A., and Donald B. Rubin. 1987. *Statistical Analysis with Missing Data.* New York: Wiley.

Lockerbie, Brad. 1989. "Change in Party Identification: The Role of Prospective Economic Evaluations." *American Politics Quarterly* 17: 291–311.

———. 1991. "The Influence of Levels of Information on the Use of Prospective Evaluations." *Political Behavior* 13: 223–235.

———. 1992. "Prospective Voting in Presidential Elections, 1956–88." *American Politics Quarterly* 20: 308–325.

Lodge, Milton, Kathleen M. McGraw, and Patrick Stroh. 1989. "An Impression-Driven Model of Candidate Evaluation." *American Political Science Review* 83: 399–419.

Lodge, Milton, and Marco R. Steenbergen, with Shawn Brau. 1995. "The Responsive Voter: Campaign Information and the Dynamics of Candidate Evaluation." *American Political Science Review* 89: 309–326.

Lodge, Milton, and Patrick Stroh. 1993. "Inside the Mental Voting Booth: An Impression-Driven Model of Candidate Evaluation." In *Explorations in Political Psychology*, ed. Shanto Iyengar and William J. McGuire. Durham: Duke University Press.

Lublin, David Ian. 1994. "Quality, Not Quantity: Strategic Politicians in U.S. Senate Elections, 1952–1990." *Journal of Politics* 56: 228–241.

Lupia, Arthur. 1994. "Short Cuts versus Encyclopedias: Information and Voting Behavior in California Insurance Reform Elections." *American Political Science Review* 88: 63–76.

Lupia, Arthur, and Mathew D. McCubbins. 1998. *The Democratic Dilemma: Can Citizens Learn What They Need to Know?* New York: Cambridge University Press.

Luskin, Robert C. 1987. "Measuring Political Sophistication." *American Journal of Political Science* 31: 856–899.

Luskin, Robert C., John P. McIver, and Edward G. Carmines. 1989. "Issues and the Transmission of Partisanship." *American Journal of Political Science* 33: 440–458.

Mackie, Diane, and Arlene Anuncion. 1990. "On-Line and Memory-Based Modification of Attitudes: Determinants of Message Recall-Attitude Change Correspondence." *Journal of Personality and Social Psychology* 59: 5–16.

Mackie, Thomas T., and Richard Rose. 1991. *The International Almanac of Electoral History*, 3rd ed. Houndmills: Macmillan. Washington, D.C.: CQ Press.

MacKuen, Michael B. 1984. "Exposure to Information, Belief Integration, and Individual Responsiveness to Agenda Change." *American Political Science Review* 78: 372–391.

MacKuen, Michael B., Robert S. Erikson, and James A. Stimson. 1988. "On the Importance of Economic Experience and Expectations for Political Evaluations." Paper presented at the annual meeting of the American Political Science Association, Washington, D.C.

———. 1989. "Macropartisanship." *American Political Science Review* 83: 1125–1142.

———. 1992a. "Peasants or Bankers? The American Electorate and the U.S. Economy." *American Political Science Review* 86: 597–611.

———. 1992b. "Question Wording and Macropartisanship." *American Political Science Review* 86: 475–486.

_____. 1996. "Comment on [Presidents and the Prospective Voter]." *Journal of Politics* 58: 793–801.

Maggiotto, Michael A., and William Mishler. 1987. "Tracing the Economic Roots of Partisanship: A Time Series Analysis, 1946–1984." Paper presented at the annual meeting of the Midwest Political Science Association, Chicago.

Magleby, David B., and Candice J. Nelson. 1990. *The Money Chase: Congressional Campaign Finance Reform.* Washington, D.C.: Brookings.

Mann, Thomas E. 1978. *Unsafe at Any Margin: Interpreting Congressional Elections.* Washington, D.C.: American Enterprise Institute.

Mann, Thomas E., and Raymond E. Wolfinger. 1980. "Candidates and Parties in Congressional Elections." *American Political Science Review* 74: 617–632.

Mannheim, Karl. 1952. "The Problem of Generations." In *Essays on the Sociology of Knowledge,* ed. Paul Kecskemeti. New York: Oxford University Press.

Mansbridge, Jane J. 1983. *Beyond Adversary Democracy.* Chicago: University of Chicago Press.

Manza, Jeff, and Clem Brooks. 1998. "The Gender Gap in U.S. Presidential Elections: When? Why? Implications?" *American Journal of Sociology* 103: 1235–1266.

_____. 1999. *Social Cleavages and Political Change: Voter Alignments and U.S. Party Coalitions.* New York : Oxford University Press, 1999.

Marcus, George, and Michael MacKuen. 1993. "Anxiety, Enthusiasm, and the Vote: The Emotional Underpinnings of Learning and Involvement during Presidential Campaigns." *American Political Science Review* 87: 672–686.

Marks, G. N. 1993. "Partisanship and the Vote in Australia." *Political Behavior* 15: 137–166.

Markus, Gregory B. 1974. "Electoral Coalitions and Senate Roll Call Behavior: An Ecological Analysis." *American Journal of Political Science* 18: 595–607.

_____. 1982. "Political Attitudes during an Election Year: A Report on 1980 NES Panel Study." *American Political Science Review* 76: 538–560.

_____. 1988. "The Impact of Personal and National Economic Conditions on the Presidential Vote: A Pooled Cross-Sectional Analysis." *American Journal of Political Science* 32: 137–154.

_____. 1992. "The Impact of Personal and National Economic Conditions on Presidential Voting, 1956–1988." *American Journal of Political Science* 36: 829–834.

Markus, Gregory B., and Philip E. Converse. 1979. "A Dynamic Simultaneous Equation Model of Electoral Choice." *American Political Science Review* 73: 1055–1070.

Marsh, David, Hugh Ward, and David Sanders. 1991. "Modeling Government Popularity in Britain, 1979–87." In *British Parties and Elections Yearbook,* ed. Ivor Crewe and Pippa Norris. London: Simon and Schuster.

Mattei, Franco, and John S. Howes. 2000. "Competing Explanations of Split-Ticket Voting in American National Elections." *American Politics Quarterly* 28: 379–407.

Mattei, Franco, and Richard G. Niemi. 1991. "Unrealized Partisans, Realized Independents, and the Intergenerational Transmission of Party Identification." *Journal of Politics* 53: 161–174.

Mayer, William. 1992. "How and Why American Public Opinion Changed between 1960 and 1988." *The Changing American Mind.* Ann Arbor: University of Michigan Press.

Mayhew, David R. 1974. "Congressional Elections: The Case of the Vanishing Marginals." *Polity* 6: 295–317.

_____. 1991. *Divided We Govern: Party Control, Lawmaking, and Investigations, 1946–1990.* New Haven: Yale University Press.

McClosky, Herbert. 1964. "Consensus and Ideology in American Politics." *American Political Science Review* 58: 361–382.

McClosky, Herbert, and Alida Brill. 1983. *Dimensions of Tolerance: What Americans Believe about Civil Liberties.* New York: Russell Sage Foundation.

McClosky, Herbert, and John Zaller. 1984. *The American Ethos: Public Attitudes toward Capitalism and Democracy.* Cambridge: Harvard University Press.

McCurley, Carl, and Jeffery J. Mondak. 1995. "Inspected by #1184063113: The Influence of Incumbents' Competence and Integrity in the U.S. House Elections." *American Journal of Political Science* 39: 864–885.

McDonald, Michael D., and Susan E. Howell. 1982. "Reconsidering the Reconceptualization of Party Identification." *Political Methodology* 8: 73–91.

McDonald, Michael P., and Samuel L. Popkin. 1999. "Measuring Turnout Rates Correctly: Rates Are Not Declining in Recent United States Elections." Unpublished paper, Vanderbilt University.

McGraw, Kathleen M., and Neil Pinney. 1990. "The Effects of General and Domain-Specific Expertise on Political Memory and Judgment." *Social Cognition* 8: 9–30.

McKelvey, Richard D., and Peter C. Ordeshook. 1985. "Sequential Elections with Limited Information." *American Journal of Political Science* 29: 480–512.

_____. 1986. "Information, Electoral Equilibria, and the Democratic Ideal." *Journal of Politics* 48: 909–937.

Meehl, Paul E. 1954. *Clinical versus Statistical Predictions: A Theoretical Analysis and Review of the Literature.* Minneapolis: University of Minnesota Press.

Meyrowitz, Joshua. 1985. *No Sense of Place: The Impact of Electronic Media on Social Behavior.* New York: Oxford University Press.

Michener, James. 1969. *Presidential Lottery: The Reckless Gamble in Our Electoral System.* New York: Random House.

Milbrath, Lester. 1965. *Political Participation.* Chicago: Rand McNally.

Milbrath, Lester, and M. L. Goel. 1977. *Political Participation: How and Why Do People Get Involved in Politics?,* 2nd ed. Chicago: Rand McNally.

Miller, Arthur H., Warren E. Miller, Alden S. Raine, and Thad A. Brown. 1976. "A Majority Party in Disarray: Policy Polarization in the 1972 Election." *American Political Science Review* 70: 753–778.

Miller, Arthur H., and Martin P. Wattenberg. 1981. "Policy and Performance Voting in the 1980 Election." Paper presented at the annual meeting of the American Political Science Association, New York.

_____. 1985. "Throwing the Rascals Out: Policy and Performance Evaluations of Presidential Candidates, 1952–1980." *American Political Science Review* 79: 359–372.

Miller, Arthur H., Martin P. Wattenberg, and Oksana Malanchuk. 1986. "Schematic Assessments of Presidential Candidates." *American Political Science Review* 80: 521–540.

Miller, Joanne M., and Jon A. Krosnick. 1996. "News Media Impact on the Ingredients of Presidential Evaluations: A Program of Research on the Priming Hypothesis." In *Political Persuasion and Attitude Change,* ed. Diana C. Mutz, Paul M. Sniderman, and Richard A. Brody. Ann Arbor: University of Michigan Press.

Miller, Nicholas R. 1986. "Information, Electorates, and Democracy: Some Extensions and Interpretations of the Condorcet Jury Theorem." In *Information Pooling and Group Decision Making,* ed. Bernard Grofman and Guillermo Owen. Greenwich, Conn.: JAI.

Miller, R. G. 1974. "The Jackknife: A Review." *Biometrika* 61: 1–15.

Miller, Warren E. 1986. "Party Identification and Political Belief Systems: Changes in Partisanship in the United States, 1980–84." *Electoral Studies* 5: 101–121.

_____. 1990. "The Electorate's View of the Parties." In *The Parties Respond,* ed. Sandy Maisel. Boulder, Colo.: Westview.

_____. 1991a. "Party Identification, Realignment, and Party Voting: Back to the Basics." *American Political Science Review* 85: 557–568.

_____. 1991b. "Party Identification." In *Encyclopedia of American Political Parties and Elections,* ed. Sandy Maisel. New York: Garland.

_____. 1992a. "Generational Change and Party Identification." *Political Behavior* 14: 333–352.

_____. 1992b. "The Puzzle Transformed: Explaining Declining Turnout." *Political Behavior* 14: 1–43.

Miller, Warren E., and Teresa E. Levitin. 1976. *Leadership and Change.* Cambridge: Winthrop.

Miller, Warren E., Arthur H. Miller, and Edward J. Schneider. 1980. *American National Election Studies Data Sourcebook, 1952–1978.* Cambridge: Harvard University Press.

Miller, Warren E., and J. Merrill Shanks. 1996. *The New American Voter.* Cambridge: Harvard University Press.

Miller, Warren E., and Donald E. Stokes. 1963. "Constituency Influence in Congress." *American Political Science Review* 57: 45–56.

Miller, Warren E., and Santa A. Traugott. 1989. *American National Election Studies Data Sourcebook, 1952–1986*. Cambridge: Harvard University Press.

Mills, C. Wright. 1971. *The Power Elite*. London: Oxford University Press.

Mitchell, Glenn E., and Christopher Wlezien. 1995. "The Impact of Legal Constraints on Voter Registration, Turnout, and the Composition of the American Electorate." *Political Behavior* 17: 179–202.

Mochmann, Ekkehard, Ingvill C. Oedegaard, and Reiner Mauer. 1998. *Inventory of National Election Studies in Europe 1945–1995*. Bergisch: Edwin Ferger Verlag.

Mondak, Jeffery J. 1994. "Question Wording and Mass Policy Preferences: The Comparative Impact of Substantive Information and Peripheral Cues." *Political Communication* 11: 165–183.

_____. 1995. "Competence, Integrity, and the Electoral Success of Congressional Incumbents." *Journal of Politics* 57: 1043–1069.

Mondak, Jeffery, Carl McCurley, and Steven Millman. 1999. "The Impact of the Incumbents' Levels of Competence and Integrity in the 1994 and 1996 U.S. House Elections." In *Reelection 1996: How Americans Voted*, ed. Herbert F. Weisberg and Janet M. Box-Steffensmeier. New York: Chatham House.

Mondak, Jeffery J., Diana C. Mutz, and Robert Huckfeldt. 1996. "Persuasion in Context: The Multilevel Structure of Economic Evaluations." In *Political Persuasion and Attitude Change*, ed. Diana C. Mutz, Paul M. Sniderman, and Richard A. Brody. Ann Arbor: University of Michigan Press.

Monroe, Alan D. 1975. *Public Opinion in America*. New York: Dodd, Mead.

Monroe, Kristen. 1981. "Presidential Popularity: An Almon Distributed Lag Model." *Political Methodology* 7: 43–70.

Mooney, Christopher Z., and Robert D. Duval. 1993. *Bootstrapping: A Nonparametric Approach to Statistical Inference*. Newbury Park, Calif.: Sage.

Mueller, John. 1970. "Presidential Popularity from Truman to Johnson." *American Political Science Review* 64: 18–34.

_____. 1973. *War, Presidents, and Public Opinion*. New York: Wiley.

_____. 1992. "Democracy and Ralph's Pretty Good Grocery: Elections, Equality, and the Minimal Human Being." *American Journal of Political Science* 36: 983–1003.

_____ 1999. *Capitalism, Democracy, and Ralph's Pretty Good Grocery*. Princeton: Princeton University Press.

Nadeau, Richard, and Michael Lewis-Beck. 2001. "National Economic Voting in U.S. Presidential Elections." *Journal of Politics* 63: 159–181.

Nadeau, Richard, and Richard G. Niemi. 1999. "Rating the Chancellors and Their Budgets." *Political Studies* 46: 857–876.

Nadeau, Richard, Richard G. Niemi, and Timothy Amato. 2000. "Elite Economic Forecasts, Economic News, Mass Economic Expectations, and Voting Intentions in Great Britain." *European Journal of Political Research* 38: 135–170.

Nadeau, Richard, Richard G. Niemi, David P. Fan, and Timothy Amato. 1999. "Elite Economic Forecasts, Economic News, Mass Economic Judgments, and Presidential Approval." *Journal of Politics* 61: 109–135.

Nadeau, Richard, Richard G. Niemi, and Antoine Yoshinaka. 2001. "A Cross-National Analysis of Economic Voting: Taking Account of the Political Context across Time and Nations." *Electoral Studies* forthcoming.

Nagel, Jack H., and John E. McNulty. 1996. "Partisan Effects of Voter Turnout in Senatorial and Gubernatorial Elections." *American Political Science Review* 90: 780–793.

Nannestad, Peter, and Martin Paldam. 1997. "From the Pocketbook of the Welfare Man: A Pooled Cross-Section Study of Economic Voting in Denmark, 1986–92." *British Journal of Political Science* 27: 119–135.

Nardulli, Peter F. 1995. "The Concept of a Critical Realignment, Electoral Behavior, and Political Change." *American Political Science Review* 89: 10–22.

National Association of Secretaries of State. 1999. *New Millennium Project, Part I: American Youth Attitudes on Politics, Citizenship, Government and Voting.* Lexington, Ky.: Author.

National Commission on Civic Renewal. 1998. *A Nation of Spectators: How Civic Disengagement Weakens America and What We Can Do about It.* Washington, D.C.: Author.

Nelson, Thomas E., and Donald R. Kinder. 1996. "Issue Framing and Group-Centrism in American Public Opinion." *Journal of Politics* 58: 1055–1078.

Nelson, Thomas E., Zoe Oxley, and Rosalee A. Clawson. 1997. "Toward a Psychology of Framing Effects." *Political Behavior* 19: 221–246.

Neuman, W. Russell. 1986. *The Paradox of Mass Politics: Knowledge and Opinion in the American Electorate.* Cambridge: Harvard University Press.

Nichols, Stephen M., and Paul Allen Beck. 1995. "Reversing the Decline: Voter Turnout in the 1992 Election." In *Democracy's Feast: Elections in America,* ed. Herbert F. Weisberg. Chatham, N.J.: Chatham House.

Nie, Norman H., and Lutz Erbring. 2000. "Internet and Society: A Preliminary Report." Stanford Institute for the Quantitative Study of Society, Stanford University.

Nie, Norman H., Jane Junn, and Kenneth Stehlik-Barry. 1996. *Education and Democratic Citizenship in America.* Chicago: University of Chicago Press.

Nie, Norman H., Sidney Verba, and John Petrocik. 1976, 1979. *The Changing American Voter.* Harvard University Press.

Niemi, Richard G., and M. Kent Jennings. 1991. "Issues and Inheritance in the Formation of Party Identification." *American Journal of Political Science* 35: 970–988.

Niemi, Richard G., and Jane Junn. 1998. *Civic Education: What Makes Students Learn?* New Haven: Yale University Press.

Niemi, Richard G., Richard S. Katz, and David Newman. 1980. "Reconstructing Past Partisanship: The Failure of the Party Identification Recall Questions." *American Journal of Political Science* 24: 633–651.

Niemi, Richard G., John Mueller, and Tom W. Smith. 1989. *Trends in Public Opinion: A Compendium of Survey Data.* New York: Greenwood.

Niemi, Richard G., G. Bingham Powell Jr., Harold W. Stanley, and C. Lawrence Evans. 1985. "Testing the Converse Partisanship Model with New Electorates." *Comparative Political Studies* 18: 300–322.

Niemi, Richard G., and Lynda W. Powell. 2000. "The Effects of Term Limits on Knowing and Contacting State Legislators." Paper presented at the conference, "Coping with Term Limits: Ohio and the Nation," Bliss Institute of Applied Politics, Columbus, Ohio.

Niemi, Richard G., and Julia Smith. 2001. "Enrollments in High School Government Classes: Are We Short-Changing Both Citizenship and Political Science Training?" *PS: Political Science and Politics,* forthcoming.

Niemi, Richard G., Harold W. Stanley, and Ronald J. Vogel. 1995. "State Economies and State Taxes: Do Voters Hold Governors Accountable?" *American Journal of Political Science* 39: 936–957.

Niemi, Richard G., and Herbert F. Weisberg. 1976. "Are Parties Becoming Irrelevant?" In *Controversies in American Voting Behavior,* ed. Richard G. Niemi and Herbert F. Weisberg. San Francisco: W. H. Freeman.

_____, eds. 1984. *Controversies in Voting Behavior,* 2nd ed. Washington, D.C.: CQ Press.

_____, eds. 1993a. *Classics in Voting Behavior.* Washington, D.C.: CQ Press.

_____. eds. 1993b. *Controversies in Voting Behavior,* 3rd ed. Washington, D.C.: CQ Press.

Nieuwbeerta, Paul. 1995. *The Democratic Class Struggle in Twenty Countries, 1945–90.* Amsterdam: Thesis Publishers.

Nisbett, Richard E., and Lee Ross. 1980. *Human Inference: Strategies and Shortcomings of Social Judgment.* Englewood Cliffs, N.J.: Prentice-Hall.

Nisbett, Richard E., and Timothy D. Wilson. 1977. "Telling More Than We Can Know: Verbal Reports on Mental Processes." *Psychological Review* 84: 231–259.

Norpoth, Helmut. 1996a. "It's Bill Clinton, Stupid! Forecasting the 1996 Presidential Election." Paper presented at the annual meeting of the Midwest Political Science Association, Chicago.

_____. 1996b. "Presidents and the Prospective Voter." *Journal of Politics* 58: 776–792.

_____. 1996c. "Rejoinder." *Journal of Politics* 58: 802–806.

_____. 1996d. "The Economy." In *Comparing Democracies: Elections and Voting Behavior in Global Perspective,* ed. Lawrence LeDuc, Richard G. Niemi, and Pippa Norris. Thousand Oaks, Calif.: Sage.

Norpoth, Helmut, and Bruce Buchanan. 1992. "Wanted—The Education President: Issue Trespassing by Political Candidates." *Public Opinion Quarterly* 56: 87–99.

Norpoth, Helmut, Michael S. Lewis-Beck, and Jean-Dominique Lafay, eds. 1991. *Economics and Politics: The Calculus of Support.* Ann Arbor: University of Michigan Press.

Norpoth, Helmut, and Thom Yantek. 1983. "Macro-Economic Conditions and the Fluctuations of Presidential Popularity: The Question of Lagged Effects." *American Journal of Political Science* 27: 785–807.

Norrander, Barbara. 1989a. "Explaining Cross-State Variation in Independent Identification." *American Journal of Political Science* 33: 516–536.

———. 1989b. "Ideological Representativeness of Presidential Primary Voters." *American Journal of Political Science* 33: 570–587.

———. 1990. "The Evolution of the Gender Gap." *Public Opinion Quarterly* 54: 566–576.

———. 1997. "The Independence Gap and the Gender Gap." *Public Opinion Quarterly* 61: 464–476.

———. 1999. "Is the Gender Gap Growing?" In *Reelection 1996: How Americans Voted,* ed. Herbert F. Weisberg and Janet M. Box-Steffensmeier. New York: Chatham House.

Nunn, Clyde A., Harry J. Crockett Jr., and Allen Williams. 1978. *Tolerance for Nonconformity: A National Survey of Changing Commitment to Civil Liberties.* San Francisco: Jossey-Bass.

Oliver, J. Eric, and Raymond E. Wolfinger. 1999. "Jury Aversion and Voter Registration." *American Political Science Review* 93: 147–152.

Oppenhuis, Erik. 1995. "Voting Behavior in the European Community: A Comparative Analysis of Electoral Participation and Party Choice." Ph.D. diss., University of Amsterdam.

Ornstein, Norman J., Thomas E. Mann, and Michael J. Malbin. 1992. *Vital Statistics on Congress.* Washington, D.C. CQ Press.

Ostrom, Charles W., Jr., and Dennis M. Simon. 1985. "Promise and Performance: A Dynamic Model of Presidential Popularity." *American Political Science Review* 79: 334–358.

Pacek, Alexander C. 1994. "Macroeconomic Conditions and Electoral Politics in East Central Europe." *American Journal of Political Science* 38: 723–744.

Pacek, Alexander C., and Benjamin Radcliff. 1995. "The Political Economy of Competitive Elections in the Developing World." *American Journal of Political Science* 39: 745–759.

Page, Benjamin I. 1978. *Choices and Echoes in Presidential Elections.* Chicago: University of Chicago Press.

Page, Benjamin I., and Calvin Jones. 1979. "Reciprocal Effects of Policy Preferences, Party Loyalties and the Vote." *American Political Science Review* 73: 1071–1089.

Page, Benjamin I., and Robert Y. Shapiro. 1983. "Effects of Public Opinion on Policy." *American Political Science Review* 77: 175–190.

_____. 1992. *The Rational Public: Fifty Years of Trends in Americans' Policy Prefer-ences.* Chicago: University of Chicago Press.

Paldam, Martin. 1991. "How Robust Is the Vote Function? A Study of Seven-teen Nations over Four Decades." In *Economics and Politics,* ed. Helmut Nor-poth, Michael S. Lewis-Beck, and Jean-Dominique Lafay. Ann Arbor: University of Michigan Press.

Palfrey, Thomas R., and Keith T. Poole. 1987. "The Relationship between Infor-mation, Ideology, and Voting Behavior." *American Journal of Political Science* 31: 511–530.

Palmer, Harvey D. 1999. "Making Sense of the Noise in Personal Financial Evaluations: Reconsidering the Evidence of Pocketbook Economic Voting." Unpublished paper, University of Mississippi.

Palmquist, Bradley, and D. Stephen Voss. 1996. "Racial Polarization and Turnout in Louisiana: New Insights from Aggregate Data Analysis." Paper presented at the annual meeting of the Midwest Political Science Association, Chicago.

Parry, Geriant, George Moyser, and Niel Day. 1990. *Political Participation and Democracy in Britain.* New York: Cambridge University Press.

Pateman, Carole. 1970. *Participation and Democratic Theory.* Cambridge: Cam-bridge University Press.

Patterson, Samuel C., and Joseph Quin Monson. 1999. "Reelecting the Repub-lican Congress: Two More Years." In *Reelection 1996: How Americans Voted,* ed. Herbert F. Weisberg and Janet M. Box-Steffensmeier. New York: Chatham House.

Patterson, Thomas, and Robert McClure. 1976. *The Unseeing Eye: The Myth of Television Power in National Elections.* New York: Putnam.

Peffley, Mark. 1984. "The Voter as Juror: Attributing Responsibility for Eco-nomic Conditions." *Political Behavior* 6: 275–294.

Perry, James W. 1988. "United We Stand May Be the U.S. Ideal, but Divided We Vote Has Become the Reality." *Wall Street Journal,* November 14, A20.

Petrocik, John R. 1974. "An Analysis of the Intransitivities in the Index of Party Identification." *Political Methodology* 1: 31–47.

_____. 1981. *Party Coalitions: Realignment and the Decline of the New Deal Party System.* Chicago: University of Chicago Press.

_____. 1991. "Divided Government: Is It All in the Campaigns?" In *The Politics of Divided Government,* ed. Gary W. Cox and Samuel Kernell. Boulder, Colo.: Westview Press.

_____. 1996. "Issue Ownership in Presidential Elections, with a 1980 Case Study." *American Journal of Political Science* 40: 825–850.

Petrocik, John R., and Joseph Doherty. 1996. "The Road to Divided Govern-ment: Paved without Intention." In *Divided Government: Change, Uncer-tainty, and the Constitutional Order,* ed. Peter F. Galderisi. Lanham, Md.: Rowman and Littlefield.

Piven, Frances Fox, and Richard A. Cloward. 1977. *Poor People's Movements.* New York: Vintage.

Polsby, Nelson W. 1983. *Consequences of Party Reform.* New York: Oxford University Press.

Pomper, Gerald M. 1972. "From Confusion to Clarity: Issues and American Voters, 1956–1968." *American Political Science Review* 66: 415–428.

_____. 1975. *Voters' Choice: Varieties of American Electoral Behavior.* New York: Harper and Row.

Poole, Keith T., and Howard Rosenthal. 1997. *Congress: A Political-Economic History of Roll Call Voting.* New York: Oxford University Press.

Popkin, Samuel. 1991. *The Reasoning Voter: Communication and Persuasion in Presidential Campaigns.* Chicago: University of Chicago Press.

_____. 1994. *The Reasoning Voter: Communication and Persuasion in Presidential Campaigns,* 2nd ed. Chicago: University of Chicago Press.

Popkin, Samuel L., and Michael A. Dimock. 1995. "Cognitive Engagement and Citizen World Views." Paper presented at the annual meeting of the PEGS Conference on Citizen Competence and the Design of Democratic Institutions, Washington, D.C.

Postman, Neil. 1985. *Amusing Ourselves to Death: Public Discourse in the Age of Show Business.* New York: Viking-Penguin.

Powell, G. Bingham, Jr. 1980. "Voting Turnout in Thirty Democracies: Partisan, Legal and Socio-Economic Influences." In *Electoral Participation: A Comparative Perspective,* ed. Richard Rose. London: Sage.

_____. 1986. "American Voter Turnout in Comparative Perspective." *American Political Science Review* 80: 17–43.

Powell, G. Bingham, Jr., and Guy D. Whitten. 1993. "A Cross-National Analysis of Economic Voting: Taking Account of the Political Context." *American Journal of Political Science* 37: 391–414.

Powers, Denise V., and James H. Cox. 1997. "Echoes from the Past: The Relationship between Satisfaction with Economic Reforms and Voting Behavior in Poland." *American Political Science Review* 91: 617–634.

Price, Vincent, and John Zaller. 1990. "A Study of Everyday Memory: Learning and Forgetting the News." Paper presented at the annual meeting of the Midwest Political Science Association, Chicago.

_____. 1993. "Who Gets the News? Alternative Measures of News Reception and Their Implications for Research." *Public Opinion Quarterly* 57: 133–164.

Prothro, James W., and Charles M. Grigg. 1960. "Fundamental Principles of Democracy: Bases of Agreement and Disagreement." *Journal of Politics* 22: 276–294.

Public Broadcasting Corporation. 1996. "National Issues Convention Deliberative Poll Reveals Significant Change in Delegates' Views on Key Issues." Press release by Public Broadcasting Corporation, January 25.

Public Perspective. 1991. "Public Scrutiny: Divided Government." 2 (Jan./Feb.): 86.

_____. 1995. "People, Opinion, and Polls: American Popular Culture." 6: 37–48.

Putnam, Robert D. 1993. *Making Democracy Work: Civic Traditions in Modern Italy.* Princeton: Princeton University Press.

_____. 1995a. "Bowling Alone." *Journal of Democracy* 9: 65–78.

_____. 1995b. "Bowling Alone, Revisited." *The Responsive Community* (Spring): 18–33.

_____. 1995c. "Tuning In, Tuning Out: The Strange Disappearance of Social Capital in America." *PS: Political Science & Politics* 28: 664–683.

_____. 1996. "Bowling Alone: Democracy in America at the End of the Twentieth Century." In *Democracy's Victory and Crisis: Nobel Symposium No. 93.* ed. Axel Hadenius. New York: Cambridge University Press.

_____. 2000. *Bowling Alone: The Collapse and Revival of American Community.* New York: Simon and Schuster.

Rabinowitz, George, and Stuart Elaine Macdonald. 1989. "A Directional Theory of Issue Voting." *American Political Science Review* 83: 93–121.

Rahn, Wendy. 1993. "The Role of Partisan Stereotypes in Information Processing about Political Candidates." *American Journal of Political Science* 37: 472–496.

Rahn, Wendy M., John H. Aldrich, and Eugene Borgida. 1994. "Individual and Contextual Variations in Political Candidate Appraisal." *American Political Science Review* 88: 193–199.

Rahn, Wendy M., John H. Aldrich, Eugene Borgida, and John L. Sullivan. 1990. "A Social-Cognitive Model of Candidate Appraisal." In *Information and Democratic Processes,* ed. John A. Ferejohn and James H. Kuklinski. Urbana: University of Illinois Press.

Rahn, Wendy M., and Katherine J. Cramer. 1996. "Activation and Application of Political Party Stereotypes: The Role of Television." *Political Communication* 13: 195–212.

Rahn, Wendy M., Jon A. Krosnick, and Marijke Breuning. 1994. "Rationalization and Derivation Processes in Survey Studies of Political Candidate Evaluation." *American Journal of Political Science* 38: 582–600.

Rapoport, Ronald B. 1997. "Partisanship Change in a Candidate-Centered Era." *Journal of Politics* 59: 185–199.

Reichley, A. James. 1992. *The Life of the Parties: A History of American Political Parties.* New York: Free Press.

Reif, Karlheinz. 1985. "Ten Second-Order Elections." In *Ten European Elections,* ed. Karlheinz Reif. Aldershot: Gower.

Reif, Karlheinz, and Hermann Schmitt. 1980. "Nine Second-Order National Elections: A Conceptual Framework for the Analysis of European Election Results." *European Journal of Political Research* 8: 3–44.

Reiter, Howard L. 1985. *Selecting the President.* Philadelphia: University of Pennsylvania Press.

RePass, David E. 1971. "Issue Salience and Party Choice." *American Political Science Review* 65: 389–400.

Richardson, Lilliard E., and Grant W. Neeley. 1996. "The Impact of Early Voting on Turnout: The 1994 Elections in Tennessee." *State and Local Government Review* 28: 173–179.

Riker, William H., and Peter Ordeshook. 1968. "A Theory of the Calculus of Voting." *American Political Science Review* 62: 25–42.

Robertson, David. 1976. "Surrogates for Party Identification in the Rational Choice Framework." In *Party Identification and Beyond: Representations of Voting and Party Competition,* ed. Ian Budge, et al. London: Wiley.

Robinson, John. 1981. "Television and Leisure Time: A New Scenario." *Journal of Communication* 31: 120–130.

_____. 1990a. "The Time Squeeze." *American Demographics* 12 (2): 30–33.

_____. 1990b. "I Love My TV." *American Demographics* 12 (9): 24–27.

Robinson, John, and Geoffrey Godbey. 1995. *Time for Life.* Unpublished manuscript, University of Maryland.

Robinson, William S. 1950. "Ecological Correlations and the Behavior of Individuals." *American Sociological Review* 15: 351–357.

Rohde, David W. 1991. *Parties and Leaders in the Postreform House.* Chicago: University of Chicago Press.

Rohde, David W., and Dennis M. Simon. 1985. "Presidential Vetoes and Congressional Response: A Study of Institutional Choice." *American Journal of Political Science* 29: 399–427.

Rosenstone, Steven J. 1983. *Forecasting Presidential Elections.* New Haven: Yale University Press.

Rosenstone, Steven J., Roy L. Behr, and Edward H. Lazarus. 1996. *Third Parties in America,* 2nd ed. Princeton: Princeton University Press.

Rosenstone, Steven J., and John Mark Hansen. 1993. *Mobilization, Participation, and Democracy in America.* New York: Macmillan.

Rothenberg, Stuart, and Frank Newport. 1984. *The Evangelical Voter.* Washington, D.C.: Free Congress Research and Educational Foundation.

Rusk, Jerrold G. 1970. "The Effect of the Australian Ballot Reform on Split Ticket Voting: 1876–1908." *American Political Science Review* 64: 1220–1238.

_____. 1974. "Comment: The American Electoral Universe: Speculation and Evidence." *American Political Science Review* 68: 1028–1049.

Sabato, Larry J. 1988. *The Party's Just Begun: Shaping Political Parties for America's Future.* Glenview, Ill.: Scott, Foresman.

Salisbury, Robert H. 1985. "Blame Dismal World Conditions on . . . Baseball." *Miami Herald,* May 18, 27A.

Sanders, David. 1991. "Government Popularity and the Next General Election." *Political Quarterly* 62: 235–261.

_____. 1993. "Why the Conservatives Won—Again." In *Britain at the Polls 1992,* ed. Anthony King et al. Chatham, N.J.: Chatham House.

Sanders, David, David Marsh, and Hugh Ward. 1993. "The Electoral Impact of Press Coverage of the British Economy, 1979–87." *British Journal of Political Science* 23: 175–210.

Särlvik, Bo, and Ivor Crewe. 1983. *Decade of Dealignment: The Conservative Victory of 1979 and Electoral Tends in the 1970s.* Cambridge: Cambridge University Press.

Schattschneider, E. E. 1942. *Party Government.* New York: Rinehart.

_____. 1960. *The Semi-Sovereign People: A Realist's View of Democracy in America.* New York: Holt.

Schelling, Thomas C. 1978. *Micromotives and Macrobehavior.* New York: Norton.

Schickler, Eric and Donald Philip Green. 1995. "Issue Preferences and the Dynamics of Party Identification: A Methodological Critique." In *Political Analysis,* vol. 5, ed. John R. Freeman. Ann Arbor: University of Michigan Press.

_____. 1997. "The Stability of Party Identification in Western Democracies: Results from Eight Panel Studies." *Comparative Political Studies.* 30: 450–483.

Schmidt, Amy, Lawrence Kenny, and Rebecca Morton. 1996. "Evidence on Electoral Accountability in the U.S. Senate: Are Unfaithful Agents Really Being Punished?" *Economic Inquiry* 34: 545–567.

Schmitt, Hermann, and Sören Holmberg. 1995. "Political Parties in Decline?" In *Citizens and the State,* ed. Hans-Dieter Klingemann and Dieter Fuchs. Oxford: Oxford University Press.

Schor, Juliet. 1991. *The Overworked American.* New York: Basic Books.

Schulman, Mark A., and Gerald M. Pomper. 1975. "Variability in Electoral Behavior: Longitudinal Perspectives from Causal Modeling." *American Journal of Political Science* 19: 1–18.

Schumpeter, Joseph A. 1950 [1942]. *Capitalism, Socialism, and Democracy.* 3rd ed. New York: Harper and Row.

Sellers, Charles. 1965. "The Equilibrium Cycle in Two Party Politics." *Public Opinion Quarterly* 29: 16–38.

Shaffer, Stephen D. 1981. "A Multivariate Explanation of Decreasing Turnout in Presidential Elections, 1960–1976." *American Journal of Political Science* 25: 68–95.

Shanks, J. Merrill, and Warren E. Miller. 1990. "Policy Direction and Performance Evaluation: Complementary Explanations of the Reagan Elections." *British Journal of Political Science* 20: 143–235.

_____. 1991. "Partisanship, Policy and Performance: The Reagan Legacy in the 1988 Election." *British Journal of Political Science* 21: 129–197.

Shapiro, Robert Y., and Glenn R. Dempsey. 1982. "Polling the Pollsters: The Less Famous National Opinion Surveys." Unpublished paper, NORC, Chicago.

Sharkansky, Ira. 1969. "The Utility of Elazar's Political Culture." *Polity* 2: 66–83.

Shaw, Daron R. 1999a. "The Effect of TV Ads and Candidate Appearances on Statewide Presidential Votes, 1988–96." *American Political Science Review* 93: 345–362.

_____. 1999b. "A Study of Presidential Campaign Event Effects from 1952 to 1992." *Journal of Politics* 61: 387–422.

Shively, W. Phillips. 1980. "The Nature of Party Identification: A Review of Recent Developments." In *The Electorate Reconsidered,* ed. John C. Pierce and John L. Sullivan. Beverly Hills, Calif.: Sage.

_____. 1991. "A General Extension of the Method of Bounds, with Special Application to Studies of Electoral Transition." *Historical Methods* 24: 81–94.

_____. 1992. "From Differential Abstention to Conversion: A Change in Electoral Change, 1864–1988." *American Journal of Political Science* 36: 309–330.

Sigelman, Lee. 1991. "Turning Cross Sections into a Panel: A Simple Procedure for Ecological Inference." *Social Science Research* 20: 150–170.

Sigelman, Lee, Paul R. Wahlbeck, and Emmett H. Buell Jr. 1997. "Vote Choice and the Preference for Divided Government: Lessons of 1992." *American Journal of Political Science* 41: 879–894.

Sigelman, Lee, and Ernest Yanarella. 1986. "Public Information on Public Issues: A Multivariate Analysis." *Social Science Quarterly* 67: 402–410.

Sijtsma, Kees, Pierre Debets, and Ivo W. Molenaar. 1990. "Mokken Scale Analysis for Polychotomous Items: Theory, a Computer Program, and an Empirical Application." *Quality and Quantity* 24: 173–188.

Silbey, Joel H. 1991. "Beyond Realignment and Realignment Theory: American Political Eras, 1789–1989." In *The End of Realignment? Interpreting American Electoral Eras,* ed. Byron E. Schafer. Madison: University of Wisconsin Press.

Silver, Brian D., Barbara A. Anderson, and Paul R. Abramson. 1986. "Who Overreports Voting?" *American Political Science Review* 80: 613–624.

Simon, Herbert A. 1979. "Information Processing Models of Cognition." *Annual Review of Psychology* 30: 363–396.

Simon, Rita James. 1974. *Public Opinion in America: 1936–1970.* Chicago: Rand McNally.

Sims, Christopher R. 1977. "Exogeneity and Causal Ordering in Macroeconomic Models." In *New Methods of Business Cycle Research,* ed. Christopher R. Sims. Minneapolis: Federal Reserve Bank.

Smith, Charles E., Jr. 1993. "An Information-Processing Theory of Party Identification." Ph.D. diss., Ohio State University.

Smith, Charles E., Jr., Robert D. Brown, John M. Bruce, and L. Marvin Overby. 1999. "Party Balancing and Voting for Congress in the 1996 National Election." *American Journal of Political Science* 43: 737–764.

Smith, Charles E., Jr., David R. Harding, and Martha Crone. 1990. "Estimating the Separate Effects of Party Identification and Short-Term Partisan Forces on the Vote." Paper presented at the annual meeting of the Southern Political Science Association, Tampa, Fla.

Smith, Charles E., Jr., Peter M. Radcliffe, and John H. Kessel. 1999. "The Partisan Choice: Bill Clinton or Bob Dole?" In *Reelection 1996: How Americans Voted,* ed. Herbert F. Weisberg and Janet M. Box-Steffensmeier. New York: Chatham House.

Smith, Eric R. A. N. 1989. *The Unchanging American Voter.* Berkeley: University of California Press.

Smith, Eric, and Peverill Squire. 1990. "The Effects of Prestige Names in Question Wording." *Public Opinion Quarterly* 54: 97–116.

Smith, Hedrick. 1988. *The Power Game: How Washington Works.* New York: Random House.

Smith, Tom W. 1982. "General Liberalism and Social Change in the Post World War II America: A Summary of Trends." *Social Indicators Research* 10: 1–28.

_____. 1989. "Liberal and Conservatism Trends in the United States since World War II." GSS Social Change Report no. 29. Chicago: National Opinion Research Center.

Smith, Tom W., with Guy J. Rich. 1980. *A Compendium of Trends on General Social Survey Questions.* NORC Report no. 29. Chicago: National Opinion Research Center.

Sniderman, Paul M. 1993. "The New Look in Public Opinion Research." In *Political Science: The State of the Discipline II,* ed. Ada W. Finifter. Washington, D.C.: American Political Science Association.

Sniderman, Paul M., Richard A. Brody, and Philip E. Tetlock. 1991. *Reasoning and Choice: Explorations in Political Psychology.* New York: Cambridge University Press.

"The Solitary Bowler." 1995. *The Economist* 334 (February 18): 21–22.

Sorauf, Frank J. 1988. *Money in American Elections.* Glenview, Ill.: Scott, Foresman.

Soss, Joe, and David T. Canon. 1995. "Partisan Divisions and Voting Decisions: U.S. Senators, Governors, and the Rise of a Divided Federal Government." *Political Research Quarterly* 48: 253–274.

Southwell, Patricia L., and Justin I. Burchett. 2000. "The Effect of All-Mail Elections on Voter Turnout." *American Politics Quarterly* 28: 72–79.

Squire, Peverill. 1989. "Challengers in U.S. Senate Elections." *Legislative Studies Quarterly* 14: 531–547.

_____. 1991. "Preemptive Fundraising and Challenger Profile in Senate Elections." *Journal of Politics* 53: 1150–1164.

_____. 1992. "Challenger Quality and Voting Behavior in U.S. Senate Elections." *Legislative Studies Quarterly* 17: 247–263.

Stanley, Harold W., and Richard G. Niemi. 1991. "Partisanship and Group Support, 1952–1988." *American Politics Quarterly* 19: 189–210.

_____. 1994. *Vital Statistics on American Politics,* 4th ed. Washington, D.C.: CQ Press.

_____. 1995. "The Demise of the New Deal Coalition: Partisanship and Group Support, 1952–1992." In *Democracy's Feast: Elections in America,* ed. Herbert F. Weisberg. Chatham, N.J.: Chatham House.

_____. 1998. *Vital Statistics on American Politics, 1997–1998.* Washington, D.C.: CQ Press.

_____. 1999. "Party Coalitions in Transition: Partisanship and Group Support, 1952–96." In *Reelection 1996: How Americans Voted,* ed. Herbert F. Weisberg and Janet M. Box-Steffensmeier. New York: Chatham House.

_____. 2000. *Vital Statistics on American Politics, 1999–2000.* Washington, D.C.: CQ Press.

Stein, Robert M. 1998. "Early Voting." *Public Opinion Quarterly* 62: 57–69.

_____. 1990. "Economic Voting for Governor and U.S. Senator: The Electoral Consequences of Federalism." *Journal of Politics* 52: 29–53.

Stein, Robert M., and Patricia A. Garcia-Moner. 1997. "Voting Early but Not Often." *Social Science Quarterly* 78: 657–671.

Stewart, Marianne C., and Harold D. Clarke. 1998. "The Dynamics of Party Identification in Federal Systems: The Canadian Case." *American Journal of Political Science* 42: 97–116.

Stimson, James A. 1975. "Belief Systems: Constraint, Complexity, and the 1972 Election." *American Journal of Political Science* 19: 393–417.

_____. 1991. *Public Opinion in America.* Boulder, Colo.: Westview.

Stokes, Donald E., and Warren E. Miller. 1962. "Party Government and the Saliency of Congress." *Public Opinion Quarterly* 26: 531–546.

Stouffer, Samuel. 1954. *Communism, Conformity, and Civil Liberties.* Garden City, N.Y.: Doubleday.

Sullivan, John L., James E. Piereson, and George E. Marcus. 1982. *Political Tolerance and American Democracy.* Chicago: University of Chicago Press.

Sundquist, James L. 1983. *Dynamics of the Party System: Alignment and Realignment of Political Parties in the United States,* rev. ed. Washington, D.C.: Brookings.

_____. 1988. "Needed: A Political Theory for the New Era of Coalition Government in the United States." *Political Science Quarterly* 103: 613–635.

Sussman, Barry. 1988. *What Americans Really Think and Why Our Politicians Pay No Attention.* New York: Pantheon.

Taber, Charles S., and Marco Steenbergen. 1994. "Computational Experiments in Electoral Behavior." In *Political Judgment,* ed. Milton Lodge and Kathleen M. McGraw. Ann Arbor: University of Michigan Press.

Tajfel, Henri, C. Flament, M. G. Billig, and R. F. Bundy. 1971. "Social Categorization: An Intergroup Phenomenon." *European Journal of Social Psychology* 1: 149–177.

"Task Force on Civic Education." 1997. *PS: Political Science and Politics* 30: 744–745.

Tate, Katherine. 1994. *From Protest to Politics: The New Black Voters in American Elections.* Cambridge: Harvard University Press.

Taylor, D. Garth. 1980. "Procedures for Evaluating Trends in Public Opinion." *Public Opinion Quarterly* 44: 86–100.

Teixeira, Ruy A. 1987. *Why Americans Don't Vote: Turnout Decline in the United States, 1960–1984.* New York: Greenwood.

———. 1992. *The Disappearing American Voter.* Washington, D.C.: Brookings.

Thisted, Ronald A. 1988. *Elements of Statistical Computing: Numerical Computation.* New York: Chapman and Hall.

Thomas, Sue, and Clyde Wilcox. 1998. *Women and Elective Office: Past, Present, and Future.* New York: Oxford University Press.

Thomassen, Jacques. 1976. "Party Identification as a Cross-National Concept." In *Party Identification and Beyond,* ed. Ian Budge, Ivor Crewe, and Dennis Farlie. London: Wiley.

Timmer, S. G., J. Eccles, and I. O'Brien. 1985. "How Children Use Time." In *Time, Goods, and Well-Being,* ed. F. T. Juster and F. B. Stafford. Ann Arbor: University of Michigan, Institute for Social Research.

Timpone, Richard J. 1998. "Structure, Behavior, and Voter Turnout in the United States." *American Political Science Review* 92: 145–158.

Tingsten, Herbert. 1937. *Political Behavior.* London: King.

Topf, Richard. 1995. "Electoral Participation." In *Citizens and the State,* ed. Hans-Dieter Klingemann and Dieter Fuchs. Oxford: Oxford University Press.

Tufte, Edward. 1975. "Determinants of the Outcomes of Midterm Congressional Elections." *American Political Science Review* 69: 812–826.

———. 1978. *Political Control of the Economy.* Princeton: Princeton University Press.

Tullock, Gordon. 1967. *Toward a Mathematics of Politics.* Ann Arbor: University of Michigan Press.

Tversky, Amos, and Daniel Kahneman. 1974. "Judgment under Uncertainty: Heuristics and Biases." *Science* 185: 1124–1131.

Uslaner, Eric M. 1995. "Faith, Hope, and Charity: Social Capital, Trust, and Collective Action." Unpublished manuscript, University of Maryland.

van der Eijk, Cees, Mark Franklin, and Michael Marsh. 1996. "What Voters Teach Us about Europe-Wide Elections: What Europe-Wide Elections Teach Us about Voters." *Electoral Studies* 15: 149–166.

van der Eijk, Cees, Mark Franklin, et al. 1996. *Choosing Europe? The European Electorate and National Politics in the Face of the Union.* Ann Arbor: University of Michigan Press.

Verba, Sidney, and Norman H. Nie. 1972. *Participation in America: Political Democracy and Social Equality.* New York: Harper and Row.

Verba, Sidney, Norman H. Nie, and Jae-on Kim. 1978. *Participation and Political Equality*. Cambridge: Cambridge University Press.

Verba, Sidney, Kay Lehman Schlozman, and Henry E. Brady. 1995. *Voice and Equality: Civic Voluntarism in American Politics*. Cambridge: Harvard University Press.

Voss, D. Stephen, Andrew Gelman, and Gary King. 1995. "Preelection Survey Methodology: Details from Eight Polling Organizations, 1988 and 1992." *Public Opinion Quarterly* 59: 98–132.

Wattenberg, Martin P. 1987. "The Hollow Realignment: Partisan Change in a Candidate-Centered Era." *Public Opinion Quarterly* 51: 58–74.

_____. 1990. *The Decline of American Political Parties, 1952–1988*. Cambridge: Harvard University Press.

_____. 1991a. "The Republican Presidential Advantage in the Age of Party Disunity." In *The Politics of Divided Government*, ed. Gary W. Cox and Samuel Kernell. Boulder, Colo.: Westview.

_____. 1991b. *The Rise of Candidate-Centered Politics: Presidential Elections of the 1980s*. Cambridge: Harvard University Press.

_____. 1997. "The Crisis of Electoral Politics." *The Atlantic Monthly* 282 (4): 42–46.

_____. 1998a. *The Decline of American Political Parties: 1952–1996*. Cambridge: Harvard University Press.

_____. 1998b. "Turnout Decline in the U.S. and Other Advanced Industrial Democracies." Unpublished paper, University of California, Irvine.

Watts, William A., and William J. McGuire. 1964. "Persistence of Induced Opinion Change and Retention of the Inducing Message Contents." *Journal of Abnormal and Social Psychology* 68: 233–241.

Weisberg, Herbert F. 1980. "A Multidimensional Conceptualization of Party Identification." *Political Behavior* 2: 33–60.

_____. 1983. "A New Scale of Partisanship." *Political Behavior* 5: 363–376.

_____. 1987. "The Demographics of a New Voting Gap: Marital Differences in American Voting." *Public Opinion Quarterly* 51: 335–343.

_____. 1998a. "Nonlinear Models of Electoral Change: The Implications of Political Time and Chaos Theory for the Study of Mass Political Behavior." *Electoral Studies* 17: 369–382.

_____. 1998b. "The 1996 Election: Independents on the Decline." *Votes and Opinions* (March/April): 14–15.

_____. 1999. "Political Partisanship." In *Measures of Political Attitudes*, ed. John P. Robinson, Phillip R. Shaver, and Lawrence S. Wrightsman. San Diego: Academic Press.

Weisberg, Herbert F., and Steven H. Greene. Forthcoming. "The Political Psychology of Party Identification." In *Electoral Democracy*, ed. Michael MacKuen and George Rabinowitz. Ann Arbor: University of Michigan Press.

Weisberg, Herbert F. and Edward B. Hasecke. 1999. "What Is Partisan Strength? A Social Identity Theory Approach." Paper presented at the annual meeting of the American Political Science Association, Atlanta.

Weisberg, Herbert F., Eric S. Heberlig, and Lisa M. Campoli, eds. 1999. *Classics in Congressional Politics.* New York: Longman.

Weisberg, Herbert F., and April Kelly. 1997. "Families First in the 1996 Presidential Election? Soccer Moms and the Married as Target Groups." Paper presented at the annual meeting of the Southern Political Science Association, Norfolk, Va.

Weisberg, Herbert F., and David C. Kimball. 1995. "Attitudinal Correlates of the 1992 Presidential Vote: Party Identification and Beyond." In *Democracy's Feast: Elections in America,* ed. Herbert F. Weisberg. Chatham, N.J.: Chatham House.

Weisberg, Herbert F., Jon A. Krosnick, and Bruce Bowen. 1996. *An Introduction to Survey Research, Polling, and Data Analysis,* 3rd ed. Thousand Oaks, Calif.: Sage.

Weisberg, Herbert F., and Stephen T. Mockabee. 1999. "Attitudinal Correlates of the 1996 Presidential Vote: The People Reelect a President." In *Reelection 1996: How Americans Voted,* ed. Herbert F. Weisberg and Janet M. Box-Steffensmeier. New York: Chatham House.

Weisberg, Herbert F., and Charles E. Smith Jr. 1991. "The Influence of the Economy on Party Identification in the Reagan Years." *Journal of Politics* 53: 1077–1092.

Weissberg, Robert. 1974. *Political Learning, Political Choice, and Democratic Citizenship.* Englewood Cliffs, N.J.: Prentice-Hall.

———. 1998. *Political Tolerance: Balancing Community and Diversity.* Thousand Oaks, Calif.: Sage.

Welch, Michael R., David C. Leege, and James C. Cavendish. 1995. "Attitudes toward Abortion among U.S. Catholics." *Social Science Quarterly* 76: 142–157.

Westlye, Mark C. 1991. *Senate Elections and Campaign Intensity.* Baltimore: Johns Hopkins University Press.

Whiteley, Paul F. 1988. "The Causal Relationships between Issues, Candidate Evaluations, Party Identification, and Vote Choice." *Journal of Politics* 50: 961–984.

Whitten, Guy D., and Harvey D. Palmer. 1999. "Cross-National Analyses of Economic Voting." *Electoral Studies* 18: 49–67.

Wickelgren, Wayne A. 1974. "Single-Trace Fragility Theory of Memory Dynamics." *Memory and Cognition* 2: 775–780.

Wilcock, Richard, and Walter H. Franke. 1963. *Unwanted Workers.* New York: Free Press.

Wiley, David E., and James A. Wiley. 1970. "The Estimation of Measurement Error in Panel Data." *American Sociological Review* 35: 112–117.

Williams, Tannis Macbeth, ed. 1986. *The Impact of Television: A Natural Experiment in Three Communities.* New York: Academic Press.

Wilson, James Q., and John J. Dilulio Jr. 1995. *American Government,* 6th ed. Lexington, Mass.: D.C. Heath.

Wilson, Timothy D., and Jonathan W. Schooler. 1991. "Thinking Too Much: Introspection Can Reduce the Quality of Preferences and Decisions." *Journal of Personality and Social Psychology* 60: 181–192.

Wirls, Daniel. 1986. "Reinterpreting the Gender Gap." *Public Opinion Quarterly* 50: 316–330.

Wittman, Donald A. 1989. "Why Democracies Produce Efficient Results." *Journal of Political Economy* 97: 1395–1424.

_____. 1995. *The Myth of Democratic Failure: Why Political Institutions Are Efficient.* Chicago: University of Chicago Press.

Wixted, John T., and Ebbe B. Ebbesen. 1991. "On the Form of Forgetting." *Psychological Science* 2: 409–415.

Wlezien, Christopher, and Robert S. Erikson. 1996. "Temporal Horizons and Presidential Election Forecasts." *American Politics Quarterly* 24: 492–505.

_____. 2000. "The Timeline of Election Campaigns." Paper presented at the annual meeting of the Midwest Political Science Association, Chicago.

Wolfinger, Raymond E., and Steven J. Rosenstone. 1980. *Who Votes?* New Haven: Yale University Press.

Wolfinger, Raymond E., Steven J. Rosenstone, and Richard A. McIntosh. 1981. "Presidential and Congressional Voters Compared." *American Politics Quarterly* 9: 245–256.

Wright, Gerald C. 1989. "Level-of-Analysis Effects on Explanations of Voting: The Case of the 1982 U.S. Senate Elections." *British Journal of Political Science* 19: 381–398.

_____. 1990. "Misreports of Vote Choice in the 1988 NES Senate Election Study." *Legislative Studies Quarterly* 15: 543–563.

_____. 1993. "Errors in Measuring Vote Choice in the National Election Studies, 1952–88." *American Journal of Political Science* 37: 291–316.

Wright, Gerald C., Robert S. Erikson, and John P. McIver. 1985. "Measuring State Partisanship and Idealogy with Survey Data." *Journal of Politics* 47: 479–489.

Yankelovich, Daniel. 1991. *Coming to Public Judgment: Making Democracy Work in a Complex World.* Syracuse: Syracuse University Press.

Zaller, John R. 1985. "Pre-Testing Information Items on the 1986 NES Pilot Survey." Report to the National Election Study Board of Overseers.

_____. 1990. "Political Awareness, Elite Opinion Leadership, and the Mass Survey Response." *Social Cognition* 8: 125–153.

_____. 1992. *The Nature and Origins of Mass Opinion.* Cambridge: Cambridge University Press.

_____. 1996. "The Myth of Massive Media Impact Revisited: New Support for a Discredited Idea." In *Political Persuasion and Attitude Change,* ed. Diana C.

Mutz, Paul M. Sniderman, and Richard A. Brody. Ann Arbor: University of
    Michigan Press.
Zaller, John R., and Stanley Feldman. 1992. "A Simple Theory of the Survey
    Response: Answering Questions versus Revealing Preferences:" *American
    Journal of Political Science* 36: 579–616.
Zaller, John R., and Mark Hunt. 1995. "The Rise and Fall of Candidate Perot:
    The Outsider vs. the System." *Political Communication* 12: 97–123.
Zechman, Martin J. 1979. "Dynamic Models of the Voter's Decision Calculus."
    Public Choice 34: 297–315.

Name Index

✧ ✧ ✧

Abramowitz, Alan I., 189, 200–201, 241, 374, 384, 386

Abramson, Paul R, 6, 9–10, 20, 72, 81*n*–82*n*, 163*n*, 303, 335*n*, 338, 377

Achen, Christopher, 239*n*, 302–303, 319*n*, 325, 335*n*, 336

Adams, Greg D, 284, 289

Aldrich, John H., 9–12, 20, 72, 81*n*–82*n*, 137*n*, 163*n*, 181, 263, 379, 381, 384, 425*n*

Alesina, Alberto, 194*n*, 277, 299, 301, 309

Alexander, Herbert E., 163*n*, 426*n*

Alford, John R., 416, 420, 425*n*

Allsop, Dee, 12

Almond, Gabriel A., 115

Alt, James E., 286

Althaus, Scott L., 103, 110*n*, 114, 116–117, 129

Alvarez, Michael, 185–186, 189–190, 211, 276, 278–279, 299, 301*n*, 319*n*, 323, 380

Amato, Timothy, 7, 111*n*, 196–197

Andersen, Kristi, 405

Anderson, Barbara, 6, 303

Anderson, Christopher, 20, 189, 194*n*, 197

Anderson, John, 160, 163*n*, 379

Anderson, Norman H., 241–242, 244

Ansolabehere, Stephen, 5, 30, 183, 191, 198, 283, 288*n*

Anuncion, Arlene, 242

Arafat, Yasser, 131

Arnold, Laura, 376

Asher, Herbert, 319*n*, 380

Astin, Alexander W., 105

Atkeson, Lonna Rae, 184, 273, 289

Austen-Smith, David, 116

Ayres, B. Drummond, Jr., 98*n*

Babbitt, Paul, 30, 36, 187, 199

Baer, Denise L., 423

Bahr, Howard M., 50

Banks, Jeffrey, 116

Barber, James David, 240, 248

Barnes, Samuel, 84, 94, 97*n*, 99*n*

Barone, Michael, 306

Barrett, Andrew, 286

Bartels, Larry M., 2, 9, 102–103, 107, 110*n*, 112, 114, 116, 118–120, 122, 127, 137*n*–138*n*, 141, 153–154, 163*n*, 182, 187, 191, 196*n*, 197, 263, 335*n*, 373, 383–386

Bartolini, Stefano, 20

Bauer, Monica, 183

Baum, Lawrence, 11, 278

Beck, Paul Allen, 6, 11, 15, 20, 187, 195*n*–196*n*, 197, 278, 301, 310–311, 338, 340, 342, 353, 355*n*, 380–382

Behr, Roy L., 379–380

Bennett, Lance W., 116

Bennett, Stephen Earl, 105, 114–115, 139

Bentham, Jeremy, 118

Bentler, Peter M., 270

Berelson, Bernard R., 8, 108, 115, 139–140, 182, 190, 240, 248, 263, 404

Berinsky, Adam, 6

Berkman, Michael, 183, 288*n*

Berry, William D., 183, 288*n*

Bibby, John F., 382, 421

Billig, M. G., 328

Bimes, Terri L., 282, 290, 301, 311

Bingham, Richard D., 104

Bishop, George, 12, 129

Black, Earl, 345, 347, 353

Black, Joan S., 169

Black, Merle, 345, 347, 353

Blair, Tony, 3

Blood, Deborah J., 111*n*

Books, John, 184

Borgida, Eugene, 11–12, 181, 263

Born, Richard, 279, 283, 290, 299, 301, 319*n*

Borrelli, Stephen, 299

Bowen, Bruce, 4

Bower, Robert T., 63, 68*n*
Box-Steffensmeier, Janet M., 10, 20, 283, 303, 327, 334, 336
Boyd, Richard W., 98*n*
Brace, Kimball W., 311
Brady, Henry E., 12, 25–27, 35, 66*n*–67*n*, 95, 111*n*
Brady, David W., 85, 104, 183, 283, 416, 420, 425*n*
Brau, Shawn, 5, 6, 16, 116, 146, 192
Brehm, John, 29, 39
Breuning, Marijke, 244
Brill, Alida, 104
Broder, David S., 383
Brody, Richard A., 12, 20, 22, 69, 81*n*, 100, 105–106, 110*n*, 113–115, 119, 198, 244, 326–327
Brooks, Clem, 183, 188, 375, 377
Brown, Robert D., 9, 12, 279, 280, 290
Brown, Thad, 9
Bruce, John M., 279–280, 290
Bruening, Marijke, 5
Brunell, Thomas L., 288*n*, 290
Buchanan, Bruce, 247
Buell Emmett H., Jr., 278
Bundy, R. F., 328
Burchett, Justin I., 32
Burden, Barry, 6, 13, 186, 189, 190, 282, 287*n*, 288, 321*n*, 380
Burke, Edmund, 118
Burnham, Walter Dean, 99*n*, 139, 304, 371, 381, 405, 420
Burns, Nancy, 36
Bush, George, 2–3, 70, 72, 131–132, 138*n*, 154, 160, 190, 202, 208, 225, 227–228, 230–232, 234, 237, 274, 282, 291, 296, 301, 305–310, 312, 315, 318–319, 320*n*, 339, 341, 343, 345, 347, 354, 361, 370, 375, 380, 382, 396
Bush, George W., 5, 376
Butler, David, 13, 55
Butterfield, Earl, 242
Byers, David, 327

Calhoun-Brown, Allison, 36
Callaghan, James, 3
Calvert, Randall L., 415
Campbell, Angus, 8, 15, 24, 120, 139, 180, 248, 272, 288*n*, 301, 303, 310–311, 322, 329, 356, 364, 423

Campbell, James E., 19, 181, 192–193, 194*n*, 196*n*, 198, 200–201, 272, 283, 287*n*, 288, 383
Campoli, Lisa M., 271, 289
Canon, David T., 284, 301
Cantril, Hadley, 168, 169
Caplow, Theodore, 50
Carey, John M., 19*n*, 183, 288*n*, 289
Carmines, Edward G., 326, 338, 372–374, 377, 381, 385, 410–411, 420
Carsey, Thomas M., 273, 289, 378, 381
Carter, Jimmy, 70, 72, 77, 138*n*, 163*n*, 207, 332, 340, 370, 373
Caspary, William R., 174
Cassel, Carol A., 34*n*, 81
Cavendish, James C., 232
Chadwick, Bruce A., 50
Chaffee, Steven, 68
Chaiken, Shelly, 111*n*
Chambers, William Nisbet, 381, 405
Chappell, Henry W., 194*n*, 211
Cho, Wendy Tam, 288*n*
Churchill, Winston, 1
Cielecka, Anna, 184
Claggett, William, 303
Clarke, Harold D., 189, 196, 211, 326–328, 337
Clausen, Aage R., 9, 11, 278
Clawson, Rosalee A., 6,
Clinton, William, 2–3, 58, 132, 138*n*, 154, 160, 189–190, 202, 207, 225, 227–228, 230–232, 234–236, 238, 247, 274, 279, 332, 361, 364, 370, 373, 380, 382, 387, 392, 395–397, 401
Cloward, Richard A., 90
Clubb, Jerome M., 372, 425*n*
Cohen, Jacob, 97*n*
Cohen, Patricia, 97*n*
Coleman, James, 65*n*
Coleman, John J., 38, 286, 290
Comstock, George, 61, 63–64, 68*n*
Condorcet, Marquis de, 116
Condry, John, 65
Connolly, William E., 118, 141
Conover, Pamela Johnston, 107
Converse, Philip E., 8–9, 13, 15, 24, 55, 67*n*, 99*n*, 102, 114–115, 117, 139, 146, 180–181, 241, 297, 303, 310–311, 322, 325, 329, 335*n*, 338, 356, 364, 423
Conway, M. Margaret, 413, 425*n*
Cooper, H., 8
Cooper, Joseph, 6

Cotter, Cornelius P., 382, 421
Cox, Gary W., 35n, 194n, 285, 290, 301
Cox, James H., 184
Craig, Stephen C., 405, 416, 425n
Craik, Fergus, 247
Cramer, Katherine J., 120
Crewe, Ivor, 19, 87, 90, 187, 380
Crockett, Harry J., Jr., 104
Crone, Martha, 334
Crotty, William, 421
Cummings, Milton C., Jr., 304
Cutler, Blaine, 66n

Dahl, Robert A., 118, 140–141
Dalton, Russell J., 6, 21, 29, 183, 187,
   188, 195n, 197, 380–381
Dantico, Marilyn, 97n
Davidson, Chandler, 19n
Davidson, James, 327
Davis, Beverly, 302, 315, 318
Davis, Dwight, 240
Davis, James A., 65n, 168–169
Dawes, Robyn M., 163n
Day, Neil, 97n
Debets, Pierre, 269n
DeHoog, Ruth Hoogland, 219n
de la Garza, Rudolph, 13
Delli Carpini, Michael X., 103–104, 109,
   112, 114–121, 129, 131, 137n, 139, 141,
   153–154, 241, 249
Dempsey, Glenn R., 169
Denver, David, 187
de Sola Pool, Ithiel, 59, 65
Destler, I. M., 420
de Tocqueville, Alexis, 168
Dimock, Michael A., 120, 129
Dobb, Anthony N., 64
Doherty, Joseph, 276, 310, 315
Dole, Robert, 190, 279
Dorling, Daniel, 184
Downs, Anthony, 64, 117, 141, 164, 214,
   300n, 313
Dreyer, Edward C., 325, 327
Dukakis, Michael, 2, 70, 72, 131, 208,
   281–282, 291, 296, 305–310, 313–314,
   318, 320n
Duke, David, 87
Duncan, Otis Dudley, 302, 315, 318
Durr, Robert H., 194n

Ebbesen, Ebbe B., 267
Ebbinghaus, Hermann, 267

Eccles, J., 64
Edsall, Mary D., 420
Edwards, George C., III, 286, 291
Edwards, John N., 48
Edwards, Patricia Klobus, 48
Ehrenhalt, Alan, 281
Eisenhower, Dwight, 287n, 299n, 364,
   373, 413
Elazar, Daniel J., 67
Enelow, James M., 240, 300n
Entman, Robert M., 165
Erbring, Lutz, 29
Erikson, Robert S., 11, 33, 110n, 168,
   184–185, 189, 191–192, 194, 196, 200,
   202, 207, 211–212, 218n, 273, 277, 284,
   296, 309, 320n, 326–327, 331–334,
   336n, 336, 356–357, 360–361, 364, 370,
   384, 388
Erskine, Hazel Gaudet, 241, 249
Eubank, Robert B., 303
Eulau, Heinz, 200
Evans, C. Lawrence, 335
Evans, Geoffrey, 20
Eysenck, Michael W., 242

Fair, Ray C., 200–201
Fan, David, 7, 111n, 196
Feigert, Frank B., 304, 319n
Feld, Scott L., 297
Feldman, Stanley, 102, 107, 115, 165–166
Fenno, Richard F., Jr., 310
Ferejohn, John A., 115, 415
Ferguson, Thomas, 175
Finkel, Steven E., 7, 186
Fiorina, Morris P., 16, 36, 140, 146, 183,
   185, 200, 211, 214, 273–274, 277,
   279–283, 286, 287n–288n, 289,
   291–292, 298–299, 301, 304, 309, 311,
   320n, 323, 325, 327, 336, 338, 363, 381
Fishkin, James S., 118
Fishman, Mark, 139
Fiske, Susan T., 118, 140, 250
Flament, C., 328
Flanagan, Scott C., 21, 187, 380
Flanigan, William H., 20, 335n, 372, 425n
Ford, Gerald, 208, 274, 287n, 370, 373
Fowler, Linda, 289
Franke, Walter H., 47
Franklin, Charles H., 325, 338, 353, 363
Franklin, Mark N., 21, 31, 35n, 88–89,
   92, 93–94, 97n–99n
Frankovic, Kathleen, 12

Freedman, Paul, 7
Freeman, John, 194*n*
Frymer, Paul, 282, 290, 301, 311, 313, 315
Fuchs, Peter, 84, 97*n*
Fukuyama, Francis, 51
Funk, Carolyn, 181, 190, 198

Gaines, Brian J., 288*n*
Galderisi, Peter F., 301
Gamm, Gerald H., 68*n*
Gans, Curtis B., 82*n*
Gans, Herbert, 139
Gant, Michael, 240
Garand, James C., 181, 183, 279, 299
Garcia-Moner, Patricia A., 32
Gaudet, Hazel, 8, 181, 263
Gay, C., 13
Geer, John G., 7, 412, 426
Gelb, Leslie H., 420
Gelman, Andrew, 183, 187, 288*n*, 303
Gerber, Alan, 284, 335*n*, 362
Gerbner, George, 64
Gibson, James L., 104, 382, 421
Gibson, John, 184
Giles, Michael, 97*n*
Gingrich, Newt, 392
Ginzberg, Eli, 47
Glaser, William, 8
Glenn, Norval D., 66*n*
Glynn, Carroll J., 2
Godbey, Geoffrey, 46, 49, 53, 61, 63,
    66*n*-67*n*
Goel, M. L., 97*n*
Goldstein, Ken, 7
Goldwater, Barry, 2, 72, 75, 374
Goodman, Leo, 302-303, 308-309
Gorbachev, Michail, 131
Gore, Albert, 5, 376
Gosnell, Harold, 319
Gow, David John, 303
Graber, Doris A., 68*n*, 241, 242, 264
Grant, J. Tobin, 185
Green, Donald Philip, 284, 323, 327,
    330-333, 335*n*, 336-338, 357, 360,
    362-363
Greene, Steven H., 328-329, 336
Greenstein, Fred I., 335*n*
Grier, Kevin B., 194*n*
Grigg, Charles M., 104, 140
Grocer, Ralph, 113
Grofman, Bernard, 19, 116, 288*n*, 290,
    297

Gross, Larry, 64
Gurin, Gerald, 8

Haggerty, Brian A., 163*n*
Haller, Brandon H., 212
Hamilton, Alexander, 167, 177
Hansen, John Mark, 24, 26-28, 30,
    34*n*-35*n*, 40, 69, 70, 81, 85, 87, 97*n*, 104
Hanson, Russell L., 240, 264
Harding, David R., 334
Harris, Louis, 169
Harrop, Martin, 19,
Hasecke, Edward B., 329
Hastie, Reid, 241-242
Hatchett, S., 12
Haynes, Stephen, 328, 337
Heberlig, Eric S., 271, 289
Heckelman, Jac C., 35*n*
Heise, David R., 330-331
Heldman, Caroline, 30, 36, 187, 199
Herbst, Susan, 2
Herrnson, Paul S., 314, 382, 420-421
Hess, Stephen, 410
Hibbing, John R., 111*n*, 112, 183
Hibbs, Douglas A., 200, 202
Hicks, Alexander M., 2, 19
Highton, Benjamin, 31-33, 36
Hinich, Melvin J., 240, 300*n*
Hirczy, Wolfgang, 35*n*, 88, 90, 97*n*-98*n*
Hirsch, Paul M., 64
Hochschild, Jennifer, 166
Hochstein, Avram, 329
Holbrook, Thomas M., 7, 192, 193, 198,
    200
Holmberg, Sören, 187, 325
Horn, Randolph C., 413, 425*n*
Houser, Daniel, 194*n*
Howell, Susan E., 323
Howes, John S., 279, 287*n*
Hubert, Stephen, 241, 244
Huckfeldt, Robert, 6, 97*n*, 119, 184,
    195*n*-196*n*, 197, 374
Huckshorn, Robert J., 382, 421
Hughes, Michael, 64,
Humphrey, Hubert, 70, 72, 75
Huntington, Samuel P., 140
Hurley, Norman H., 104, 112

Ingberman, Daniel, 277, 301
Inglehart, Ronald, 21, 29-30, 37, 329,
    377, 381
Iyengar, Shanto, 5, 165, 191, 198

Jackman, Robert W., 35*n*, 36, 87
Jackson, Jesse, 77
Jackson, John E.,12, 325, 338, 363
Jackson, John S. III, 421
Jackson, Robert A., 378, 381
Jacobs, David, 328, 337
Jacobson, Gary C., 183, 185, 194*n*, 273,
   275–276, 280–281, 283–284,
   287*n*–288*n*, 289, 298, 301, 303,
   309–310, 314, 316
Jahoda, Marie, 47
Jarit, Jennifer, 113
Jay, John, 167
Jefferson, Thomas, 167
Jennings, M. Kent, 326, 335*n*, 337–338,
   353, 355*n*
Jensen, Richard, 420
Johnson, Lyndon, 2, 72, 75, 208, 220*n*,
   373, 379
Johnston, Richard, 331
Johnston, Ron, 184
Jones, Calvin, 181, 325, 338
Jones, Charles O., 183, 207
Junn, Jane, 24, 25*n*, 27, 36, 94, 100, 104,
   109, 110*n*

Kaase, Max, 94
Kahn, Kim Fridkin, 8, 30, 273, 289
Kahneman, Daniel, 111*n*, 141
Katz, Richard S., 84, 91, 355
Katzman, Nathan, 68
Kaufmann, Karen M., 375
Kayden, Xandra, 421
Keane, Mark T., 242
Keech, William R., 211
Keeter, Scott, 102–104, 109, 112,
   114–121, 129, 131, 137*n*, 139, 141,
   153–154, 249
Keith, Bruce E., 383
Kelley, Stanley, Jr., 146, 240–241,
   257–259, 269*n*
Kellstedt, Lyman, 184*n*
Kellstedt, Paul M., 183
Kelly, April, 376
Kelly, Caroline, 329
Kelly, Sean Q., 286
Kennedy, John F., 58, 72–73, 208, 339,
   345, 370, 373
Kennedy, Ted, 131
Kenney, Patrick J., 30, 273, 289
Kenny, Christopher, 97
Kenny, Lawrence, 299, 301

Keohane, Robert O., 319
Kernell, Samuel, 185, 194*n*, 283, 285, 290,
   301
Kessel, John H., 5, 189–190, 240, 244
Key, V. O., Jr., 17, 105, 129, 168, 180, 185,
   208, 214, 257, 322, 372, 413, 424
Kiewiet, D. Roderick, 194*n*, 200, 202, 211
Kim, Jae-on, 84, 94–95, 97*n*, 99*n*
Kim, Thomas P., 282, 290, 311
Kimball, David C., 6, 282, 287*n*–288*n*,
   301, 313, 316, 326
Kinder, Donald R., 6, 165, 181, 190–191,
   194*n*, 240, 248, 250
King, Gary, 137*n*, 183, 187, 288*n*,
   301–305, 307, 318–319, 320*n*
King, Martin Luther, Jr., 339
Klingemann, Hans-Dieter, 84, 97*n*
Knight, Kathleen, 384
Koch, Jeffrey W., 273
Koetzle, William, 288*n*, 290
Kohei, Shinsaku, 21
Korn, William S., 105
Kovenock, David, 12,
Kramer, Gerald H., 184–185, 202, 211,
   273
Krasno, Jonathan S., 194*n*, 284
Krehbiel, Keith, 191, 194*n*, 196, 207,
   211–212, 263, 286
Krosnick, Jon A., 4–5, 101, 114,
   117–119, 165, 195*n*, 244
Kuklinski, James H., 103–104, 112–113,
   115
Kunda, Ziva, 244

Lachman, Janet, 242
Lachman, Roy, 242
Lacy, Dean, 13, 185–186, 189–190, 278,
   279–280, 380
Ladd, Everett Carll, 34*n*, 168, 297, 290,
   385
Ladha, Krishna, 116
Lafay, Jean-Dominique, 194*n*, 200
Lake, Arthur, 420
Lancaster, Thomas D., 218*n*
LaPiere, R.T., 112*n*
Larter, W. Michael, 250
Lau, Richard R, 30, 36, 107, 118, 140,
   142, 146, 153, 162*n*, 187, 191, 199, 244
Layman, Geoffrey C., 183, 376–377, 381,
   386
Lazarsfeld, Paul F., 8, 47, 108, 115,
   139–140, 181, 190, 240, 248, 263, 404

Lazarus, Edward H., 380
LeDuc, Lawrence, 21, 83n, 84, 98n, 325, 337
Leege, David C., 183, 232
Leighley, Jan, 97n
Leithner, Christian, 329
Levine, Jeffrey, 374, 386
Levitin, Teresa E., 354
Levitt, Steven D., 194n
Lewis-Beck, Michael S., 184–185, 189, 194n–195n, 197, 200–201, 207, 211
Lichtenstein, Meryl, 241
Lichtl, Marci Glaslock, 279, 299
Lijphart, Arend, 29
Lincoln, Abraham, 425
Lindblom, Charles E., 140
Lippmann, Walter, 118, 141, 164, 168, 248
Little, Roderick J. A., 257
Lockerbie, Brad, 114, 117, 211, 326
Lockhart, Robert S., 247
Lodge, Milton, 5–6, 16, 19, 116, 146, 192, 196n, 198, 241–242, 245, 263
Londregan, John, 194n
Lowery, David, 219n
Lowry, Robert C., 286
Lublin, David Ian, 283, 289
Lupia, Arthur, 5, 100, 106, 111n, 112–113, 115
Luskin, Robert C., 34n, 81, 137, 326
Luttbeg, Norman R., 168
Lyons, William E., 219n

Macdonald, Glenn F., 160
Macdonald, Stuart Elaine, 156, 158, 160
Mackie, Diane, 242
Mackie, Thomas T., 21, 84, 90–91
MacKuen, Michael B., 110n, 184, 189, 326–327, 331–334, 336, 356–357, 360–361, 364, 370, 388
Madison, James, 167, 177
Magleby, David B., 323, 337, 383, 426n
Mahe, Eddie, Jr., 421
Mair, Peter, 20
Maisel, L. Sandy, 9
Malanchuk, Oksana, 190
Malbin, Michael, 414
Mann, Thomas E., 195n, 273
Mannheim, Karl, 55
Mansbridge, Jane J., 118, 141
Manza, Jeff, 183, 188, 375, 377

Marcus, George E., 104, 146, 240, 263–264
Marks, G.N., 326
Markus, Gregory B., 102, 181, 184, 187, 194n, 196, 202–203, 205, 217n, 218n, 220n, 305, 338, 355n
Marsh, David, 111n
Marsh, Michael, 87
Marx, Karl, 117
Mattei, Franco, 279, 287n
Matthews, Donald, 12
Mauer, Reiner, 14, 21
Mayer, William, 169
Mayhew, David R., 283, 286, 290
McAllister, Ian, 21, 184
McClosky, Herbert, 104, 140
McClure, Robert, 12, 190
McCombs, Maxwell, 68
McCubbins, Mathew D., 5, 100, 106, 111–112
McCurley, Carl, 284
McDonald, Michael P., 26, 64, 146, 288n, 290, 323
McGarrity, Joseph P., 194n
McGovern, George, 160–161, 281, 376, 421
McGraw, Kathleen M., 5, 116, 119, 146, 192, 198, 241–242, 245, 250, 263
McGuire, William J., 241
McIver, John P., 11, 326, 338
McKelvey, Richard D., 5
McNulty, John E., 33
McPhee, William N., 8, 108, 115, 139–140, 181, 190, 240, 248, 404
Meehl, Paul E., 163n
Meyrowitz, Joshua, 64
Michener, James, 110n
Milbrath, Lester, 24, 97n
Milburn, Michael, 101, 114, 117, 119
Mill, John Stuart, 118
Miller, Arthur H., 3, 9, 168, 404
Miller, Joanne M. 195n
Miller, Nicholas, 116
Miller, Ross A., 36, 87
Miller, Warren E., 8–10, 15, 20, 22, 24, 27–29, 55, 58, 67n, 139, 168, 197, 288n, 301, 303, 310–311, 322–323, 329–330, 334, 336, 338–343, 345, 353–354, 355n, 356, 364, 374–377, 385n, 386, 404n, 423
Millman., Steven, 284
Mills, Charles W., 139
Mirer, Thad W., 146, 240, 258–259, 269n

Mitchell, Glenn E., 31, 33, 36, 98n
Mochmann, Ekkehard, 14, 21
Mockabee, Stephen T., 185, 190
Modell, John, 50, 184
Moiser, George, 97n
Molenaar, Ivo W., 269n
Mondak, Jeffrey J., 7, 115, 198, 284
Mondale, Walter, 72, 281, 296
Monroe, Alan D., 168
Monson, Joseph Quin, 283, 403n
Morgan, Michael, 64, 219n
Morton, Rebecca, 299
Mueller, John, 108–109, 113, 140, 168
Mutz, Diana C., 184, 198

Nadeau, Richard, 7, 111n, 184–185, 189, 191
Nagel, Jack H., 33, 185–186, 190, 196–197
Nagler, Jonathan, 189, 211, 380
Nannestad, Peter, 206
Nardulli, Peter F., 372–373, 385–386
Neeley, Grant W., 32,
Nelson, Candice J., 323, 337, 383, 426n
Nelson, Forrest, 137
Nelson, Michael, 410
Nelson, Thomas E., 6
Neuman, W. Russell, 111n, 116, 129, 240–241, 249
Newman, David, 355
Newport, Frank, 403n
Nichols, Stephen M., 380
Nie, Norman H., 12, 24–25, 27, 29, 36, 84, 86, 94–95, 97n, 99n, 180, 187
Niemi, Richard G., 7, 19n, 20–21, 23, 25, 35n, 83n, 84, 93, 98n, 100, 109, 110n–111n, 168, 180, 183–184, 187–189, 191, 194n–196n, 197, 271, 283, 288n, 289, 326, 335n, 337, 338, 355n, 374–376, 378–379, 381, 384–385, 387–389, 403n, 409–410, 415–417, 425n
Nieuwbeerta, Paul, 183
Nisbett, Richard E., 5, 141, 244
Nixon, Richard, 58, 70, 72, 75, 138n, 160–161, 173, 176, 178, 208, 247, 287n, 288n, 291, 299n, 370, 373, 376
Norpoth, Helmut, 185, 189, 194n, 197, 200–201, 211–212, 247
Norrander, Barbara, 11, 375, 386, 403n
Norris, 20–21, 83n, 84, 98n
Nunn, Clyde A., 104

O'Brien, I., 64
Oedegaard, Ingvill C., 14, 21
O'Keefe, Garrett J., 2
Oldendick, Robert, 129
Oliver, J. Eric, 32
Oppenhuis, Erik, 89, 97n
Ordeshook, Peter C., 5, 23
Ornstein, Norman, 414
Orr, Elizabeth, 323, 337, 383
Ostrom, Charles W., Jr., 335n
Overby, L. Marvin, 279–280, 290
Owen, Guillermo, 116
Oxley, Zoe, 6

Pacek, Alexander C., 184
Page, Benjamin I., 12, 19, 104, 107–108, 112, 114–115, 120, 139, 176, 178, 181, 241, 244, 297, 325, 338
Paldam, Martin, 189, 194n, 197, 206
Palfrey, Thomas R., 284
Palmer, Harvey D., 189, 194n, 197
Palmquist, Bradley, 320n, 327, 330–333, 336, 338, 357, 360, 363
Paolino, Philip, 9, 163n, 279, 280, 290
Park, Bernadette, 241–242
Parrott, Sarah A., 105
Parry, Geraint, 97n
Partin, Randall W., 184, 273, 289
Patterson, Kelly D., 420
Patterson, Samuel C., 283, 403n
Patterson, Thomas, 12, 190
Pattie, Charles, 184
Peake, Jeffrey, 286
Peel, David, 327
Peffley, Mark, 207
Pennington, Nancy, 241–242
Perot, Ross, 3, 13, 26, 160, 163n, 190, 379–380, 385, 425n
Perry, James W., 292
Petrocik, John R., 180, 187, 192, 196n, 198, 276, 287n, 290, 310, 315, 323, 375, 423
Philips, Peter C. B., 111n
Pierce, Roy, 13, 338
Piereson, James E., 104
Pinney, Neil, 119, 250
Pitney, John J., Jr., 420
Piven, Frances Fox, 90
Polsby, Nelson W., 421
Pomper, Gerald M., 180, 268
Poole, Keith T., 315, 321n

Popkin, Samuel L., 26, 106, 111*n*, 112–113, 115, 120, 129
Postman, Neil, 64,
Powell, G. Bingham, 36
Powell, Lynda W., 19*n*, 31, 86, 87, 97*n*, 183, 189, 288*n*, 289, 335*n*
Powers, Denise V., 184
Price, Vincent, 240, 245, 254, 257, 263–264
Prothro, James W., 12, 104, 140
Prysby, Charles, 184
Putnam, Robert D., 28–30, 34*n*–35*n*, 36, 38, 40, 42, 47, 105

Quayle, Dan, 132
Quirk, Paul, 112–113

Rabinowitz, George, 146, 156, 158, 160
Radcliff, Benjamin, 184
Radcliffe, Peter M., 189–190
Rademacher, Eric W., 105
Rahn, Wendy M., 5, 11–12, 29, 39, 120, 244, 263, 335*n*
Raine, Alden S., 9
Rapoport, Ronald B., 326
Reagan, Ronald, 2–3, 70, 72, 138*n*, 152, 163*n*, 175, 208, 274, 291, 296, 332, 339–341, 343, 345, 347, 353–354, 355*n*, 370, 373–374, 396, 415
Redlawsk, David P., 107, 142
Rehnquist, William, 131–132
Reichley, A. James, 425*n*
Reif, Karlheinz, 21, 93
Reiter, Howard L., 421
RePass, David E., 180
Rice, Tom, 200–201
Rich, Guy J., 168–169
Rich, Robert, 113
Richardson, Bradley, 21
Richardson, Lilliard E., 32
Riker, William H., 23
Rivers, Douglas, 202, 303
Roberts, Donald, 68
Robinson, John, 46, 49, 53, 61, 63, 66*n*–67*n*, 337
Robinson, William S., 304
Rogers, Joel, 175
Rohde, David W., 9–10, 20, 163*n*, 286, 422
Romero, David W., 218*n*
Roosevelt, Franklin, 14, 340
Rose, Richard, 21, 84, 90–91

Rosenstone, Steven J., 24, 26–28, 30–31, 33, 34*n*–35*n*, 40, 69, 70, 81, 85, 87, 90, 97*n*, 104, 202, 272, 379–380
Rosenthal, Howard, 194*n*, 277, 299, 301, 309, 315, 321
Ross, Lee, 141, 244
Rossiter, David, 148
Rothenberg, Lawrence S., 326–327
Rothenberg, Stuart, 403*n*
Rousseau, Jean-Jacques, 139
Rubin, Donald B., 257
Rusk, Jerrold G., 9, 82*n*, 99*n*, 304

Sabato, Larry J., 311, 383
Salisbury, Robert H., 68*n*
Sanders, David, 111*n*, 189, 191
Särlvik, Bo, 380
Saunders, Kyle L., 374, 384, 386
Sax, Linda J., 105
Schattschneider, E. E., 140, 285
Schelling, Thomas C., 167
Schickler, Eric, 330–333, 336–337, 357, 360, 363, 363*n*
Schlozman, Kay Lehman, 12, 25–27, 35–36, 66*n*–67*n*, 85, 95, 104
Schmidt, Amy, 299
Schmitt, Hermann, 93, 187
Schneider, Edward J., 168, 404
Schneiderman, Stuart, 183, 288*n*
Schooler, Jonathan W., 244
Schor, Juliet, 46
Schousen, Matthew M., 276, 279, 301, 319
Schultz, George, 131
Schwieder, David, 113
Sears, David O., 140, 240, 248
Sellers, Charles, 381
Shaffer, Stephen D., 81
Shanks, J. Merrill, 9–10, 20, 27–29, 55, 58, 67*n*, 183, 185–186, 189, 195*n*–196*n*, 197, 221*n*, 225, 228, 235–237, 238*n*–239*n*, 329, 336, 338, 343, 353, 375–377, 385–386
Shapiro, Robert Y., 2, 19, 104, 107–108, 112, 114–115, 139, 164, 169, 176, 178, 241, 297
Sharkansky, Ira, 67
Shaver, Philip R., 337
Shaw, Daron R., 6–7, 192, 198
Shively, W. Phillips, 302–303, 319*n*, 419
Sigleman, Lee, 30, 36, 116, 187, 199, 278, 302

Signorielli, Nancy, 64
Sijtsma, Kees, 269*n*
Silbey, Joel H., 420
Silver, Brian D., 6, 303
Silver, Glenn E., 425*n*
Simon, Adam, 5
Simon, Dennis M., 286
Simon, Rita James, 169
Skalaban, Andrew, 207
Skocpol, Theda, 36
Slovic, Paul, 141
Smith, Charles E., 11, 189–190,
   278–280, 290, 325–326, 334, 388
Smith, Eric R. A. N., 100, 115, 240, 249
Smith, Julia, 109
Smith, Renée, 327, 334, 336
Smith, Richard A., 118
Smith, Tom W., 65*n*, 168–169
Sniderman, Paul M., 20, 100, 104, 106,
   110*n*–111*n*, 113–115, 119, 198
Snyder, James M., Jr., 183, 284
Sorauf, Frank J., 426*n*
Soss, Joe, 301
Southwell, Patricia L., 32
Sprague, John, 119
Squire, Peverill, 115, 283–284, 289
Srull, Thomas, 241
Stanley, Harold, 23*n*, 251, 83, 184,
   187–188, 196*n*, 335*n*, 374–376, 378,
   387–389, 409–410, 415–417
Steenbergen, Marco R., 5–6, 16, 116,
   146, 192, 258, 268
Stehlik-Barry, Kenneth, 24–25, 27, 36,
   104
Stein, Robert M., 32, 184, 273
Stewart, Charles III, 284
Stewart, Marianne C., 196–197, 326
Stimson, James A., 2, 19, 102, 110*n*, 114,
   117, 184, 189, 191, 194*n*, 196, 207,
   211–212, 326–327, 331–334, 336, 338,
   356–357, 360–361, 364, 370, 372–374,
   385, 388, 411, 420
Stokes, Donald E., 8, 13, 15, 24, 55, 139,
   180, 272, 303, 310–311, 322, 329, 356,
   364, 410, 423
Stouffer, Samuel, 104
Stroh, Patrick, 5, 116, 146, 192, 198,
   241–243, 245, 263
Strunk, Mildred, 168
Sullivan, John L., 11–12, 104, 181
Sundquist, James L., 301, 372, 425*n*
Sussman, Barry, 168

Suzuki, Motoshi, 194*n*, 327–328, 337
Swank, Duane H., 2, 19

Taber, Charles S., 258, 268
Tajfel, Henri, 328
Tate, Katherine, 12–13, 183
Taylor, Shelly E., 140
Tedin, Kent L., 168
Teixeira, Ruy A., 24, 27, 33, 35, 81, 338
Tetlock, Philip E., 20, 100, 105–106,
   110*n*, 113–115, 119
Thatcher, Margaret, 2, 3, 131
Theiss-Morse, Elizabeth, 111*n*, 112
Thisted, Ronald A., 268
Thomas, Clarence, 382
Thomas, Sue, 19*n*
Thomassen, Jacques, 325
Tien, Charles, 200–201, 211
Tilly, Charles, 57
Timmer, S. G., 64,
Timpone, Richard J., 13, 26, 35
Tingsten, Herbert, 87
Topf, Richard, 97*n*
Tower, John, 382
Traugott, Santa A., 168
Tsongas, Paul, 247
Tuchfarber, Alfred, 129
Tufte, Edward, 194*n*, 200, 273
Tullock, Gordon, 23
Tunstall, Helena, 184
Tversky, Amos, 111*n*, 141

Ujifusa, Grant, 7, 306
Uslaner, Eric M., 65*n*

Valen, Henry, 21, 188
Valentino, Nicholas, 5
van der Eijk, Cees, 87–89, 92–94, 97*n*,
   99*n*
Ventura, Jesse, 3, 33
Verba, Sidney, 12, 25, 27, 35–36,
   66*n*–67*n*, 84–87, 94–95, 97*n*–99*n*, 104,
   180, 187, 319, 423
Villani, John, 277, 301
Vogel, Ronald J., 184
Voss, D. Stephen, 303, 320*n*

Wahlbeck, Paul R., 278
Walker, Jack, 112*n*
Wallace, George, 72, 75, 379, 385, 407
Ward, Hugh, 111*n*, 189, 191
Watanuki, Joji, 21

Wattenberg, Martin, 3, 29, 32, 187,
  189–190, 211, 214, 281, 310, 379, 381,
  386, 409, 412, 420
Watts, Ann DeWitt, 48
Watts, William A., 241
Weisberg, Herbert F., 4–5, 10, 12, 20,
  35n, 110n , 180, 183, 185, 190,
  194n–195n, 271, 283, 289, 323–330,
  336–337, 338, 376, 383, 385, 388, 403n
Weissberg, Robert, 108, 240
Welch, Michael R., 232
Westlye, Mark C., 273, 289, 303, 323, 337
White, Stephen, 21
Whiteley, Paul F., 197, 331
Whitten, Guy D., 93, 189, 197
Wickelgren, Wayne A., 267
Wilcock, Richard, 47,
Wilcox, Clyde, 19n
Wiley, David E., 330–331
Wiley, James A., 330–331
Williams, Allen, 104
Williams, John T., 184n
Williams, Tannis Macbeth, 63
Wilson, Pete, 404
Wilson, Timothy D., 5

Wink, Kenneth A., 200
Wirls, Daniel, 375
Wittman, Donald A., 114
Wixted, John T., 267
Wlezien, Christopher, 31, 33, 36, 98n,
  192, 200, 202, 211
Wolfinger, Raymond E., 24, 31–33, 36,
  72, 90, 97n, 272–273, 323, 337, 383
Wolfram, Catherine D., 194
Wright, Gerald C., 6, 11, 273, 287n, 289,
  302–303, 319n
Wright, Jim, 131
Wrightsman, Lawrence S., 337

Yankelovich, Daniel, 169
Yanarella, Ernest, 116
Yeltsin, Boris, 132
Yoshinaka, Antoine, 189, 197

Zaller, John R., 5, 101–102, 104, 110n,
  112, 114–115, 117, 137n, 166, 191–192,
  196n, 198, 240, 245, 250, 254, 257,
  263–264, 316
Zeisel, Hans, 47
Zingale, Nancy H., 20, 335n, 372, 425n

Subject Index

✧ ✧ ✧

Abortion, 122–125, 126–127, 135–136, 173, 176, 189, 232–233, 374
ABC News/*Washington Post* Poll, 169
Abstention. *See* Voting turnout
Affirmative action, 128, 135
African Americans. *See also* Civil rights; Race; Realignment, and race
  and issues, 123
  and party identification, 341, 375–376, 387, 390–391, 393–394, 395, 398–400, 401, 402, 403, 406–407
  and voting turnout, 12, 24–25, 74–78
Age. *See also* Party identification, and the life cycle; Voting turnout, and age
  and issues, 123
  and political information, 105, 114
Aggregate versus individual analysis, 6
  of economic voting, 211
  of party identification, 327, 335n, 356, 363, 365
  and public opinion, 297
American Independent Party, 379, 407
Antidemocratic views, 104, 108
Apartisans, 381
Apoliticals, 324n, 406–407, 425n
Australia, 84, 326, 329
Austria, 84

Bandwagon effects. *See* Primary elections
Bayesian updating, 325, 335n
Belgium, 84
Bulgaria, 84
Brazil, 84
Breakage effect, 404n

Campaign spending, 380, 382, 425n. *See also* Congressional elections, and campaign expenditures
California, 378
Campaigns. *See also* On-line information processing

effects of, 7, 181–182, 186–187, 189–190, 192–193, 196n, 198, 249–259, 260–262, 263–264
Canada, 13, 384, 26, 330, 331
Candidate-centered politics. *See* Political parties, decline of
Candidates. *See also* Congressional elections, importance of candidates; Voting choice, determinants of
  evaluations, 189–190, 198
  evaluation process, 198, 254–259, 260–262
  issue stands, 146, 160
  pool, 280–281
  and voting choice, 3–4, 15, 17, 101, 185, 224, 226, 235–236, 237–238, 240
Catastrophe theory, 385n
Catholics, 376–377, 387, 390–391, 392, 393–394, 395, 398–400
CBS/*New York Times* Poll, 11, 13, 169, 326, 332, 335n, 368–369, 383
China, 177
Civic education, 109
Civil rights, 374, 422. *See also* Realignment, and race
Civil Rights Act of 1964, 75–77, 81, 374
Civil service, 378
Cleavages, and voting choice, 188
Coattail effects, 291, 415–416. *See also* Surge and decline
Cohort analysis, 339–340
Columbia voting studies, 8, 14
Comparative National Elections Project, 14
Comparative Study of Electoral Systems, 14
Conditional party government, 422
Congressional elections. *See also* Candidates; Senate elections
  and campaign expenditures, 281, 282, 283, 284, 310–311, 312–314, 315–317, 382

challenger quality, 282, 283, 284, 288*n*,
    315–316
divided outcomes, 282–283
and the economy, 273, 287*n*
incumbency, 273, 274, 281, 282, 283,
    284, 288*n*, 310, 312–313, 314, 403*n*,
    416–417, 420
information level, 272–273
local factors, 18, 283
midterm elections, 272, 273, 299
national factors, 17, 283
and party identification, 17, 272, 415
Conservative coalition, 422
Content analysis, 6–7, 193
Continuous monitoring studies, 10–11,
    326
Controversies, 16–19
Costa Rica, 84
Costs of voting, 15, 23, 90–91
Critical elections. *See* Realignment
Cuban Americans, 376, 387
Cynicism. *See* Political trust/cynicism
Czech Republic, 84

Dealignment, 18, 371, 378–382,
    383–384, 386, 420. *See also* Party identi-
    fication, distribution of
    outside the United States, 380–381
Death penalty, 134, 176
Defense spending, 128
Deficit reduction, 128, 235
Deliberative opinion polls, 118, 129
Democratic Party rules, 379, 421
Democratic theory, 1, 108, 112*n*,
    139–140, 264
Democrats. *See* Party identification; Politi-
    cal parties; names of individual leaders in
    Name Index
Denmark, 29, 84
Divided government, 271–321. *See also*
Split-ticket voting
    consequences of, 285–286, 290
    and dealignment, 381
    and economic voting, 207–209, 216,
        220*n*
    historically, 274–275, 285, 301
    intentional, 274–280, 287*n*, 301,
        309–310, 311
    and issues, 275–276
    and policy balancing, 277–280,
        291–300
    in states, 274, 280–281, 296–297

unintentional, 280–285, 287*n*, 301,
    310, 317
and voting turnout, 35

Ecological inference, 6, 288*n*, 302–305,
    318–319, 319*n*
Economy. *See also* Congressional elections,
    and the economy; Divided government,
    and economic voting; Party identifica-
    tion, and the economy; Senate elections,
    and the economy; State legislative elec-
    tions, effects of economy on
    comparative studies of, 196–197
    measures of, 200, 201–202, 204–205,
        215–216, 217*n*
    personal vs. national factors, 200
    retrospective vs. prospective views, 185,
        189, 200, 211–214, 216–217
    and voting/government popularity,
        184–185, 189, 194*n*–195*n*, 202–217,
        235
Education
    and civic engagement, 25–26, 43–45
    and issues, 123
    and participation, 104
    and party identification, 343–352
    relative, and participation, 25
Elections. *See also* Congressional elections;
Realignment
    of 1940, 14
    of 1960, 73
    of 1964, 2, 295
    of 1968, 73, 295
    of 1972, 152
    of 1976, 152, 181
    of 1980, 2, 3, 73, 152
    of 1984, 152, 295
    of 1988, 73, 152, 305–317
    of 1992, 189, 190, 224–238, 380
    of 1994, 274, 275, 281, 387, 392, 396,
        401
    of 1996, 189, 190, 392, 396, 401
    of 2000, 286
    forecasting, 181, 194*n*
    functions of, 1–4, 19
    and public policy, 2–3, 19
Environmental parties. *See* Green Party
Error-correction models, 322, 370*n*
Estonia, 84
Evangelicals, 376–377
Events data, 7, 192–193
Exit polls, 11, 13, 319*n*

Experiments. *See* Methodology, experimental methods
Europe, 85, 93–94, 101. *See* Liberal/conservatism dimension, in Europe. *See also* individual country listings
   Eastern, 85, 114

Family issues, 376
Federalist Party, 371, 405, 425*n*
Finland, 84, 92
Florida, 194*n*
Foreign policy. *See also* Korean War; Vietnam; World War II
   attitudes on, 126–128, 132–133, 171–174, 177–178
Framing, in experiments and surveys, 6
France, 84
Fundamentalists, 390–391, 392, 393–394, 395, 396, 398–400, 401, 402, 403*n*
Funnel of causality, 15

Gallup Poll, 7, 11, 40, 169–170, 216, 326, 327, 328, 332, 335*n*, 357, 363*n*, 364, 368–369
Gay issues, 134, 136, 189, 230–232, 239*n*
Gender. *See also* Women
   and issues, 123–125, 375
   and party identification, 339–341, 375, 378, 385*n*, 390–391, 392, 393–394, 395, 397, 398–400, 401, 402, 403*n*, 404*n*
   and turnout, 339, 341–342, 355*n*
General Social Survey, 11, 40, 46, 49, 53–54, 56, 58, 65*n*–68*n*, 169, 175, 177
Generations, political, 349
   and issue attitudes, 348–351, 354
   and party identification, 329–330, 336*n*, 343–348, 352, 390–391, 392, 393–394, 395, 396, 398–400
   and political information, 299*n*
   and realignment, 381–382
   and social capital, 28–29, 35, 52–60
   and voting turnout, 27–28, 341–342
Germany, 14, 92, 99*n*, 177, 330
Great Britain, 2, 3, 13, 14, 19*n*, 84, 86, 92, 97*n*, 99*n*
Great Society, 76, 373
Greece, 84
Green Party, 380, 381
Gulf War, 3, 370
Gun control, 173

Heuristics. *See* Information, use of heuristics
Hispanics, and party identification, 376, 390–391, 392, 393–394, 396, 397, 398–400, 401, 402, 403, 403*n*
House of Representatives, reforms, 422, 425n. *See also* Congressional elections
Hungary, 84

Iceland, 84
Ideology, 18. *See also* Information, political
   and partisanship, 238*n*–239*n*, 374, 384, 386
   and split-ticket voting, 277, 279, 282, 288*n*, 292–296, 297, 299, 300*n*, 312–317, 320*n*
Immigration, 67*n*, 396, 402, 404*n*
Impeachment, 382–383
Income. *See* Socioeconomic status
Incumbents. *See also* Congressional elections, incumbency
   advantage in voting, 183, 188, 288*n*
   and economic voting, 202–204, 208–214, 220*n*
Independents. *See* Party identification, dimensionality of; Independents, measurement of
Index of Consumer Sentiment, 357, 366
India, 84, 86, 92, 98*n*, 99*n*
Information, political. *See also* Congressional elections, information level; Ideology; Realignment, and ideology; On-line information processing; Region, and ideology; Sophistication of voters
   aggregation effects, 107–108, 112, 115–116, 164–167
   and congressional elections, 272–273, 285, 299
   experts, 106, 110, 191
   and group interests, 109, 154
   level of, 17, 18, 100, 101, 110*n*, 139, 164, 240–241
   limited, effects of, 100–105, 112
   measurement of, 120, 131–132, 137*n*, 269*n*
   and participation, 104
   and political generations, 299
   use of heuristics, 106–107, 111*n*, 113, 115, 120, 129, 141, 155
Institutional factors, 288*n*, 311, 312–313, 314, 316
Internet, 6, 7, 19–20, 37, 290

Interest. *See* Political interest
Ireland, 84
Israel, 84
Issue evolution. *See* Realignment
Issues. *See also* Abortion; Campaign,
   effects of; Civil rights; Death penalty;
   Defense spending; Deficit reduction;
   Economy; Environment; Foreign policy;
   Gay issues; Party identification, and
   issues; Postmaterialism; School prayer;
   Vietnam; Voting choice, determinants of
   ownership, 192, 276
   and parties, 411–412
   and voting choice, 15, 17, 221–224,
      226–227, 227–234, 234–238,
      259–262
Issue publics, 180
Issue trespassing, 247
Italy, 84

Japan, 14, 84, 99n
Jews, 387, 390–391, 393–394, 395,
   398–400, 401, 404n

Korean War, 177, 178
Knowledge. *See* Information, political

Latino National Political Survey, 11–12
Latvia, 84
Legislative professionalism, 281
Life cycle effects, 54. *See also* Generations,
   political; Party identification, and the life
   cycle; Voting turnout, and age
Lithuania, 84
Low information rationality, 106–107,
   115, 140
Luxembourg, 84

Macropartisanship. *See* Party identification
Madisonianism, 297
Malta, 84, 88
Marriage
   and participation, 50, 60
   and voting choice, 183, 188, 376
Mass media, 12
   and election campaigns, 17
   and public opinion, 165, 190–192,
      195n–196n, 197–198, 241–242
   and social capital, 61–64
Massachusetts, 378
Memory. *See also* On-line information
   processing

of campaigns, 249–253, 264
   decay model, 252–253, 267–268
   effects of, 254–259, 262–264
Methodology
   bloc-recursive models, 186,
      194n–195n, 222–224
   experimental methods, 5–6, 19n,
      118–119, 142–146, 241, 245–249
   selection bias, and voting turnout, 26
   for studying campaigns, 262–263
   survey methods, 4–5
Michigan, 378
Michigan surveys, 7–11, 13, 14–15, 16,
   272–273
Midterm elections. *See* Congressional
   elections, midterm elections
Mobilization. *See* Voting turnout, and
   mobilization
Most important problem, 168, 410
Motor Voter. *See* National Voter Registration Act

National Black Election Study, 11–13
National Opinion Research Center sur-
   veys, 11, 12, 331. *See also* General Social
   Survey
NBC News/*Wall Street Journal* Poll, 292
National Election Studies
   accuracy, 5–6, 287n, 303, 319n
   limitations of, 303
National Voter Registration Act, 32, 33
Negative campaigning, 36, 30, 187, 191,
   198–199
Netherlands, 84, 95, 99n, 325
New Deal, 373. *See also* Realignment, of
   the 1930s
   coalition, 183, 378, 387, 389
   issues, 412
New Economy, 3
New Frontier, 373
New York, 378
New Zealand, 84, 329
Nigeria, 99n
NOMINATE scores, 315, 320n–321n
Nonseparable preferences, 278, 279
Nonvoting. *See* Voting turnout
North Carolina, 378
Norway, 92

Ohio, 278, 378

On-line information processing, 111*n*, 129, 140, 192, 198, 241–244, 247–248, 252–253, 254–262, 263–264

Opinions, stability of, 101

Panel studies, 7–10, 325, 326, 327, 330, 353, 355*n*, 363

Parenthood, 376

Participation, political. *See also* Voting turnout
  and education, 104
  and gender, 36
  levels of, 40, 78–79, 94–95
  and religion, 36
  unconventional, 30

Party-as-organization, 421

Party balancing. *See* Policy balancing

Party identification, 322–370, 388. *See also* Congressional elections, and party identification; Voting choice; determinants of
  dimensionality of, 323
  distribution of, 324, 358, 365, 383, 405, 407–408
  and the economy, 206–207, 326, 327–328, 331, 332–333, 356–362, 364, 365, 366–367, 369–370
  endogeneity of, 222, 224–225, 238*n*, 325, 363
  equilibrium level, 329, 406, 417, 423–424
  and generations, 329–330, 336*n*, 339–341, 343–348, 349, 352
  Independents, 11, 280, 322, 323, 324, 327–328, 335*n*, 337, 342, 345, 347, 375, 379, 383, 407, 408, 425*n*
  intransitivity of, 323
  and the life cycle, 329, 335*n*, 380
  measurement of, 322–323, 324, 329, 335*n*, 336*n*, 337, 355*n*, 363*n*, 383, 403*n*
  outside the United States, 325, 326, 329, 330, 331, 337, 363
  and political forces, 18, 322, 325–333
  and presidential popularity, 326, 328, 332–333, 356–363, 364–365, 366
  reliability of, 330, 331, 352
  as running tally, 323, 325, 330, 338, 353
  and social groups, 374–378, 387–404
  stability of, 18, 322, 324, 326, 327, 330, 334, 335*n*, 336–337, 355*n*, 357–363, 364–370, 388

by state, 11
  transmission between generations, 322, 326, 335*n*, 337, 342, 353, 355*n*, 364
  and voting choice, 15, 182, 186, 187–188, 224–227, 237, 335*n*, 383, 414–415
  and voting turnout, 73–74, 88–89, 342, 383

Party images, 409

Party-in-government, 422

Party-in-the-electorate, 421

Party resurgence, 18, 371, 382–385, 386

Party systems, 18, 371, 381, 384, 405–406, 417–424

Pennsylvania, 378

Period effects, 54–55

Pocketbook voting. *See* Economy, personal versus national factors

Poland, 84

Policy balancing, 277–280

Political efficacy, and turnout, 425*n*

Political interest, 413

Political knowledge. *See* Information, political

Political parties. *See also* Party identification
  and candidates, 420–421
  decline of, 280, 310, 378–379, 405, 419–424
  party organization, 421
  polarization of, 277, 295, 297–298, 374, 382–383

Political psychology. *See* Social psychology

Political socialization, 110*n*, 225. *See also* Generations, political; Party identification, transmission between generations

Political tolerance. *See* Tolerance, political

Political trust/cynicism, 105, 111*n*, 416–417

Polls. *See* ABC News/*Washington Post* Poll; CBS News/*New York Times* Poll; NBC News/*Wall Street Journal* Poll, Gallup Poll; General Social Survey

Portugal, 84

Postmaterialism, 30, 377, 381

Prediction models of elections, 181, 194*n*, 200

Presidential popularity. *See* Congressional elections, and presidential popularity; Party identification, and presidential popularity

Primary elections, 9, 378–379

Protestants, 376–377

Protest behavior, 413

Psychological approach. *See* Social psychology

Public opinion
  manipulation of, 103–104, 108
  and policy, 2–3, 19–20
  stability of, 107–108, 167–168, 171–179

Question-wording effects, 5, 190

Race. *See also* African Americans; Civil Rights; Realignment, and race
  and social capital, 51–52
  and vote choice, 183, 203–204, 210

Racial issues, 410–411

Rational choice, 15–16, 17, 323

Rational voter model. *See* Issues, and voting choice; Spatial model; Voting choice, determinants of, rationality of

Reagan revolution, 323

Realignment, 371–378, 386. *See also* Dealignment; Party identification, distribution of
  contemporary, 18, 371–372, 378, 385
  definition of, 372, 385*n*
  frequency of, 381, 405
  and ideology, 374
  and issues, 372, 373–374, 420
  and party identification, 373, 424
  and policy change, 372, 373
  process of, 372, 385, 419
  and race, 329, 373–374, 385*n*, 425*n*
  and region, 329
  and social groups, 374–378, 386
  in the 1820s, 381
  in the 1830s, 372
  in the 1850s, 372, 381, 425*n*
  in the 1880s, 373
  in the 1890s, 371, 372–373, 381, 425*n*
  in the 1930s, 371, 372, 373, 381, 405, 425*n*
  in the 1940s, 373
  in the 1960s, 371, 373, 382, 385*n*, 405, 406
  in the 1970s, 373, 385*n*
  in the 1980s, 343–348, 352, 353, 371, 373, 374, 383–384
  in the 1990s, 384

Recognition and understanding. *See* Information, political

Reference group theory, 323, 328

Reform Party, 379, 380, 385*n*

Region
  and ideology, 311
  and party identification, 343–348, 352–353, 374, 376–377, 387, 390–391, 392, 393–394, 395, 398–400, 401, 402, 409–410, 422
  and split-ticket voting, 311, 312, 313, 314, 316

Registration. *See* Voting turnout, and registration laws

Reliability, 330

Religion. *See also* names of specific religions
  and party identification, 376–377, 390–391, 392, 393–394, 395, 396, 398–400, 401, 402
  and voting choice, 14, 15, 183, 188

Republicans. *See* Party identification; Political parties; names of individual leaders in Name Index

Republican Party, 371, 372, 425*n*

Retirement slump, 416, 425*n*

Retrospective voting, 185, 189, 211–217, 323

Right-left. *See* Liberal-conservative dimension

Roll-call voting, 315

Roll-off, 304, 305, 306, 319*n*–320*n*

Romania, 96*n*

Russia, 84

Salience. *See* Issues, salience of

Senate elections, 273, 289, 299, 425*n*
  challenger quality, 283–284
  and the economy, 284
  incumbency, 416–417
  and party identification, 415
  and split-ticket voting, 309–310, 312–313, 314–315

Senate Election Study, 10, 11, 273, 309–315, 320*n*

Sex. *See* Gender

Single-issue voters, 384

Social capital
  decline of, 40–41
  definition of, 38–39, 65*n*
  explanations for decline, 41–55

Social groups. *See* Party identification, and social groups; Realignment, and social groups

Social identity theory, 328–329, 362
Social psychology, 5, 14–15, 16–17, 20, 106–107, 116, 118, 140–141, 241–244, 322–323, 328–329
Social security, 133
Social trust, 44–45, 47–48, 50–52, 54–58, 59, 62, 68n
Socialization. *See* Political socialization
Socioeconomic status. *See also* Education
  and party identification, 387, 390–391, 393–394, 395, 396, 398–400, 403n, 409
  and voting choice, 14, 15, 377–378
Sociotropic voting. *See* Economy, personal versus national factors
Sophistication of voters, 17, 277–278, 297
Sophomore surge, 416, 425n
South. *See* Region
Soviet Union, 177, 420
Spain, 14, 84
Spatial model, 292, 300n
Split-ticket voting, 11, 278, 280, 282–283, 287n, 290, 294, 295, 299, 300n, 301–321. *See also* Divided government; Region, and split-ticket voting; Senate elections, and split ticket voting
  and House races, 306–307
  and institutional factors, 288n, 311, 312–313, 314, 316
  causes of, 301
  measuring, 287n–288n, 301–306, 308–309
  and presidential candidates, 320n
  rate of, 280, 287n, 379, 405, 414
  and Senate races, 309–310
  and divided-outcomes, 282–283, 304, 307–308, 416
State legislative elections, 6, 11, 19n, 289
  and divided government, 274, 280–281, 296–297, 299
  incumbency, 288n
  and national forces, 283
Strategic politicians hypothesis, 283
Strategic voting, 13, 19n, 163n
Surge and decline, 272, 287n, 288
Sweden, 29, 84
Switzerland, 35n, 84, 86–87, 90–94, 95, 98n, 99n

Taxes, 128, 161
Telephone interviews, 11
Television. *See* Mass media

Term limits, 134
Thermometer scores, 379
Third parties, 300n, 319n, 379–380, 385n
Time series analysis, 326–327, 332–333, 357, 359–363, 363n, 364–370, 425n
Tolerance, political, 108, 176
Tomography, 318
Tracking polls. *See* Continuous monitoring studies
Trust. *See* Political trust/cynicism; Social trust
Turnout. *See* Voting turnout

Unions, and party identification, 387, 390–391, 392, 393–394, 395, 398–400, 401, 402, 404n
United Kingdom. *See* Great Britain

Vanishing marginals. *See* Congressional elections, incumbency
Venezuela, 84
Vietnam War, 177, 178, 340, 379, 413, 420, 422
Voter News Service, 11, 13
Voting choice. *See also* Economy, and voting/government popularity; Issues, and voting choice; On-line information processing; Party identification and voting choice; Prediction models of elections
  accuracy in surveys, 303
  determinants of, 17, 180–182, 187–190, 193–194, 221–238
  group attachments and, 182
  models of, 11, 13, 14–16, 146, 147, 157–159, 185–186, 194n–195n, 221–224, 225–227, 233–238, 240, 259–262
  rationality of, 141–142
Voting turnout. *See also* names of individual countries; Participation; Party identification, and voting turnout
  accuracy in surveys, 303
  and age, 54–56, 71–72, 76–79, 89
  comparative, 37, 84
  decline in, 16–17, 22–33, 69–81, 97, 342
  and individual factors, 22–30, 34n, 69–72, 74, 75–79, 80–81, 85–86, 88–89, 98n
  and legal/institutional factors, 30–33, 36, 71, 74–77, 85–88, 90–93, 96, 98n, 99n

and mobilization, 24, 35n, 70–71,
  73–74, 75–80, 87–88, 97n
and party identification, 383
rates of, 18, 23, 26, 29, 83–84, 404,
  413–414
rationality of, 15, 23
and registration laws, 31–33, 35n,
  74–77, 81, 82n, 90, 92, 98n
and salience of the election, 87–88,
  93–94, 96, 99n
and social factors, 27–30, 34n, 36

Watergate, 173, 176, 177, 178, 332, 340,
  370, 413
Websites. *See* Internet
Whig Party, 371, 372
Women
  and declining social capital, 48–50
  rights of, 161
World War II, 177, 178

Yugoslavia, 99